BIOTECHNIQUES

THEORY & PRACTICE

A TEXT-BOOK FOR UNIVERSITY STUDENTS

DR. S. V. S. RANA
PROFESSOR OF ZOOLOGY
C.C.S MEERUT UNIVERSITY
MEERUT

RASTOGI
PUBLICATIONS
'GANGOTRI' SHIVAJI ROAD, MEERUT-250002

BIOTECHNIQUES

THEORY & PRACTICE

A TEXT-BOOK FOR UNIVERSITY STUDENTS

NEW DELHI OFFICE :
9, RANI JHANSI ROAD
(MOTIA KHAN)
NEW DELHI - 110055

BIOTECHNIQUES
THEORY & PRACTICE

ISBN : 978-81-7133-993-8

TITLE CODE NO. : **BC–43**

THIRD EDITION (SECOND REPRINT) : **2021**

PRICE : ₹ **385.00**

PUBLISHED BY RAKESH KUMAR RASTOGI FOR RASTOGI PUBLICATIONS, 'GANGOTRI' SHIVAJI ROAD, MEERUT - 250002
website: www.rastogipublications.com email: info@rastogipublications.com
PRINTED AT NATIONAL OFFSET PRINTERS, MEERUT. INDIA.
PHONES: (0121)2516080, 2515142 (JMD/04012/ 3 Ed.)

Preface to the Third Edition

In the last five years since I revised the second edition of this book, it is surprising to note that significant advances in the understanding and development of analytical techniques have been made. I was satisfied by adding new information on topics viz., organ culture, culture media, practical fixation solutions, biological stains and spectrophotometry. A new chapter on mas spectrophotometry was also included in that edition. However, now I realize that it again needs revision again. As several Indian Universities revised / updated their syllabi of Microbiology, Biotechnology, Chemistry, Biochemistry, Bio Sciences, Life Sciences, Molecular Biology, Pharmacy etc., there was a need to revise the book. Most of these courses necessarily contain one or two papers dealing with bio-instrumentation and techniques. Therefore, it became mandatory to update the reader of this book on these recent developments.

I am sure the reader will appreciate that two chapters i.e. spectrophotometry and microscopy have been throughly revised in the present edition. Raman spectroscopy with its application in biology have been described in details. Similarly chapter on microscopy deals with the recent development in confocal microscopy, atomic force microscopy, FTIR and other recent techniques. In addition, widely used tests viz. Ames Text, Comet assay etc. have also been included at appropriate places. Methods of environmental analysis have also been revised and updated.

Overall, I have made an effort to expand the scope of the book whilst retaining the essential contents of its first and second editions. Whilst no human effort is without error and this book is no exception, it is expected that this edition will further facilitate the understanding on laboratory methods in applied biological sciences. I hope the students and teachers will enjoy learning and practicing the techniques described in this book.

I must thank my publisher, Rastogi Publications, Meerut for their keen interest in this book. Suggestions / comments from its readers are always welcome.

Department of Zoology
C.C.S. Meerut University
Meerut

—Prof. S.V.S. Rana

Preface to the First Edition

Biology is like a vast continent. It joins with neighbouring areas of chemistry, physics, medicine, technology and even with mathematics. The promise of applied biology to change the quality of life has been dramatically realized over the course of this century. The explosive growth of cell and molecular biology and biotechnology and their myriad applications in agriculture and medicine have propelled biology to the forefront of science. All these developments are the result of sophistication in biological methods and techniques that made biological studies more precise, quick, quantitative and reproducible. It has joined hands with nanotechnology too.

As an experimental biologist I had the opportunity to deal with different techniques. I started with histopathology and histochemistry in 1968 and in 2000 worked with HPLC and NMR spectroscopy. During this period, I experienced enormous difficulties in understanding the basic principles of various analytical techniques. To my dismay, I found that these methods were either too exhaustively described or too little information was available in the text books. The initial stimulus for writing this book arose out from these difficulties experienced in recommending a single text book to biology students that may teach them different techniques of qualitative and quantitative biology. The objective of this book is to bring together in one book ail those sub-disciplines of biology that brought it to new millennium.

The topics covered in this book are taught either at a College or University level in biology, botany, zoology, biochemistry, molecular biology, microbiology, biotechnology, pharmacy, medicine, agriculture, ecology and environmental science as well as chemistry. Each chapter introduces the reader the principle of the technique. This introduction is followed by a discussion on the method. While it is not intended that it should be a book of recipes, technique details and many of the methods are briefly described. It might help those readers who have no practical experience. They can appreciate the steps involved in the analysis. The book is expected to provide sufficient information to enable the students to select a technique or series of techniques that would be appropriate for a particular analysis would help to develop a valid and reliable analytical method.

The revised edition of the book contains twenty nine chapters. It starts with a simple introduction of bioassay and ends with the preparation of routine laboratory reagents. A student can find details of several methods viz. bioassay, cell and tissue culture, basic requirements in a biological laboratory, fixation, histological techniques, microscopy, centrifugation, spectrophotometry, electron spin resonance spectroscopy and nuclear magnetic resonance spectroscopy, x-ray diffraction, chromatography, electrophoresis, PCR, immunodiagnostic methods, radioisotope techniques, and electrochemical methods. Methods of environmental analysis have also been discussed in this book. There are separate chapters on air pollution analysis, monitoring of ambient air pollution, water pollution analysis, soil pollution and pesticide analysis and noise pollution measurement. Application of computer in modern biological analysis has also been described. Detailed chapters on management of laboratory animals, surgical techniques and biostatistics further increase the scope of the book.

I hope that students and teachers will enjoy reading this book as an important tool in practicing biological sciences.

Valuable suggestions and comments for the improvement of the book shall be highly appreciated.

—S.V.S. Rana

Department of Zoology
C.C.S. Meerut University
Meerut

Contents

1. Assay Methods 1–7

Selection of a Valid Method; Bioassay; Reliability of Data; UNITS, CONVERSION AND ABBREVIATIONS Metric and English Units.

2. Cell and Tissue Culturc 8–29

Microbial Cell Culture; Culture Media; Plant Cell and Tissue Culture; Animal Cell Culture; Organ Culture; Synthetic Medium; Growth Media for Mammalian Cell Culture; Most Commonly Used Media and Solutions for Bacteria; Ames Test; Principle and Tester Strains; Specific Techniques; Metabolizing System: Rat Liver S9 Mix; Future Prospects; Flow Cytometry ; Advantages of Flow Cytometry; Stains; FCM in Microbiology.

3. Basic Requirements in a Biological Laboratory 30–40

Instruments and Appliances; Tools; Glassware; Miscellaneous.

4. Fixation 41–55

Coagulants; Non-Coagulants; Chemistry of Fixation; Chemical Actions of Vapour Fixatives; Practical Fixative Solutions; Freeze-Drying; Cryopreservation.

5. Histological Methods 56–71

Fixation; Dehydration; Clearing; Embedding; Microtomy; Staining; Stains; Uses of Stains; Classification of Stains; Mechanism of Staining; Cytochemical Stains; Chemistry of Staining; Interpreting Sections ; Helpful Hints; Artifacts.

6. Microscopy 72–96

Light Microscopy; Phase Contrast Interference Microscopy; Interference Microscopy; Ultra-Microscopy; Polarization Microscopy; Fluorescence Microscopy; Electron Microscopy; Confocal Microscopy ; Atomic Force Microscopy; Cryoelectron Microscopy; Image Analysis and Video Microscopy; Telemicroscopy; Optical Characterization and Imaging of Biological Tissues; Advantages and Disadvantages of Three Types of Microscopy; Sample Preparation; Freeze-fracture Electron Microscopy.

7. Centrifugation 97–105

Principle of Centrifugation; Types of Centrifuges; Applications of Analytical Centrifugation; Precautions.

8. Spectrophotometry 106–140

Beer-Lambert Relationship; Instrumentation; Applications of Spectrophotometry; Atomic Spectroscopy; Flame Emission Photometry; Atomic Absorption Spectrophotometry; Spectrofluorimetry; Luminometry; Infrared Spectroscopy; Qualitative Uses and Interpretation of Spectra; Instrument Considerations; Fourier Transform IR Spectrometers; Applications of Infrared Spectroscopy; Analysis of Stroke-Induced Changes by Near-Infrared Spectroscopy; Applications in Toxicological Studies; Specialized Instrumentation; Raman Spectroscopy; Surface Plasmon Resonance (SPR) Spectroscopy.

9. Mass Spectrometry 141–147

Simplified Schematic of a Mass Spectrometer; Matrix Assisted Laser Desorption Ionization (MALDI); Simplified Schematic of MALDI-TOF Mass Spectrometry (Linear Mode) (TofSpec); Positive or Negative Ionization; Detection and Recording of Sample Ions; Tandem Mass Spectrometry; Uses of Mass Spectrometry.

10. Electron Spin Resonance and Nuclear Magnetic Resonance Spectroscopy 148–159

Electron Spin Resonance and Spin-trapping ; Instrumentation; Applications; Nuclear Magnetic Resonance Spectroscopy; Instrumentation; Applications.

11. X-Ray Diffraction 160–166

Fiber Diffraction; Crystal Diffraction; Instrument; Applications.

12. Chromatography 167–180

Liquid Solid Chromatography (Adsorption Chromatography); Liquid-liquid Chromatography; Paper Chromatography; High Performance Liquid Chromatography (HPLC); Gas-Liquid Chromatography (GLC); Chromatofocusing; Affinity Chromatography.

13. Electrophoresis 181–190

Instrumentation.

14. Polymerase Chain Reaction (PCR) 191–198

Principle and Working Mechanism; Constraints in PCR; Practical Modifications of the PCR Technique; Recent Developments in PCR Techniques; Applications.

15. Immunodiagnostic Methods 199–218

Antibodies; Immunoassay; Immunoprecipitation; Radioimmunoassay (RIA); Homogeneous Assay (EMIT); Immunofluorescence Techniques; Immunocytochemistry.

16. Radio-isotopes Techniques 219–231

Nature of Radioactivity; Types of Radioactivity; Methods for Detection and Measurement of Radioactivity; Autoradiography and its Applications; IP Autoradiography System (IPAS).

17. Electrochemical Techniques & Biosensors 232–244

Principles of Electrochemical Techniques; Classification of Electrochemical Techniques; Potentiometry; Ion-selective Electrodes; Conductimetry; Coulometric Analysis; Biosensors.

18. Methods of Environmental Analysis 245–253

Methods for Quantitative Analysis; Gravimetric Method; Volumetric Methods; Ultraviolet and Visible Spectrophotometry; Infrared and Raman Spectroscopy; Light Scattering Techniques; Molecular Luminescence Methods; Atomic Absorption Spectroscopy (AAS); Atomic Emission Spectroscopy; Radio Analytical Methods; Electro Analytical Techniques; Ring-oven Technique; Separation Methods.

19. Air Pollution Analysis 254–266

Introduction; Sampling of Gaseous Pollutants; Analysis of Aerosols; Analysis of Gaseous Pollutants; Sulphur dioxide Analysis; H_2S Analysis; NO-NOx Analysis; CO-CO_2 Analysis; Ozone Analysis; NH_3-Analysis; Organic Gases and Vapour Analysis.

20. Monitoring of Ambient Air Pollution 267–274

Air Pollution Monitoring Instruments; Meteorological Instruments; Monitoring of Sulphur Dioxide; Monitoring of NO-NOx; Monitoring of CO, CO_2; Monitoring of Hydrocarbons (HC) and Ozone; Monitoring of Suspended Particulate Matter.

21. Water Pollution Analysis 275–285

Physical Examination of Water; Chemical Characterisation of Water; Biological Investigation of Water; Biological Water Quality Assessment, Importance, Objectives and Scope; Biological Water Quality Criteria (BWQC); Benthic Macro-Invertebrates Taxa; Steps Involved for Bio-Monitoring of Surface Water Bodies in Problem Areas in the Country.

22. Soil Pollution and Pesticide Analysis 286–291

Role of Micronutrients in Soil; Analysis of Micronutrients in Soil; Trace Elements Analysis in Soil; Pesticides and Pollution; Pesticide Analysis; Chromatographic Characterisation of Pesticides; Polarographic Analysis of Pesticides; Spectroscopic Analysis of Pesticides.

23. Noise Pollution Measurement 292–294

What is Noise ?; Noise Measurement; Noise Mapping; Anechoic Chamber; Environment and Noise Measurements.

24. Applications of Computer in Modern Biology 295–306

Bioinformatics; Genomics; Genome Mapping; Gene Cloning; Gene Sequencing with Dideoxynucleotides; Proteomics.

25. Perfusion, Organ Ablations / Surgical Techniques 307–318

Perfusion Techniques; Overiectomy in Rodent; Orchidectomy in Rodent; Adrenalectomy in Rodent ; Thyroidectomy in Rat; Parathyroidectomy in Pigeon; Parabiosis in Rat.

26. Management of Laboratory Animals 319–330

Laboratory Animal; Animal Procurement; Quarantine, Stabilization and Separation; Surveillance, Diagnosis, Treatment; and Control of Disease; Animal Care and Technical Personnel; Personal Hygiene; Animal Experimentation Involving Hazardous Agents; Duration of Experiments; Physical Plan; Environment; Animal Husbandry; Personnal and Training; Laboratory Animal Ethics.

27. Biostatistics 331–342

Sampling and Sampling Methods; Sampling and Sampling Designs; Selection of Appropriate Method of Sampling; Measures of Central Tendency; Median; Median for Group Data; Mode; Measures of Dispersion or Spread; Range; Mean Deviation; Standard Deviation; Variance; Standard Error of the Mean (SEM); Coefficient of Variation; Tests of Significance.

28. Preparation of Reagents, Stains and Buffers 343–351

Molar Solution; Normal Solution; Chemical Fixatives; Stains; Other Useful Reagents; Mounting Media; Preparation of Buffers; Andre's Mounting Medium; Gary's Magic Mountant; Gelatin/Glycerol Mountant; Mayer's Albumin; Methacrylate; Mollenhauer's Mixture No. 2 ; Mountants, Nonaqueous.

29. Hazardous Laboratory Materials/Chemicals 352–359

❑ **Suggested Further Readings** 361–364

1 Assay Methods

Different areas of biological sciences use a variety of laboratory methods to determine the physical, and chemical composition of biological samples. The information gained from an analysis is presented as a laboratory report. Two types of reports may be prepared. A qualitative report simply indicates the presence or absence of a substance or a group of substances in a biological sample whereas a quantitative report describes the amount of a particular substance present in the sample. When a result is compared with a reference sample showing the increase or decrease in the amount of substance, such report is called semi-quantitative. Quantity of a substance is measured in a suitable unit. These are called as units of measurement. It is always desirable to test the reliability of quantitative results. The reliability is assessed by suitable statistical methods.

Selection of a Valid Method

In order to select a suitable method, it is essential to know the physical and chemical properties of the test substance (table 1). Some methods are used only for the detection of a substance (**qualitative methods**) while other may form the basis of valid **quantitative methods**. Most analytical methods involve several preparative steps before the final measurements can be made. All steps may not be necessary in an analysis and sometimes it is possible to combine two or more preparative methods. Table 1. describes a general scheme of analysis.

Proteins are the major components by bulk in many biological samples and hence the weighing of a dried sample would give an

Table 1. **Physical basis of Analytical Methods.**

Physical properties which can be measured with some degree of precision	Examples of properties used in the quantitation of Protein	Lead	Oxygen
Extensive			
Mass	+	+	+
Volume			
Mechanical			
Specific gravity	+		
Viscosity	+		
Surface tension	+		
Spectral			
Absorption	+		
Emission			
Fluorescence			
Turbidity	+	+	
Rotation			
Electrical			
Conductivity			
Current/voltage			+
Half-cell potential			+
Nuclear			
Radioactivity			

estimate of the amount of protein present. Similarly solutions which contain protein show values for specific gravity and surface tension which are in some way related to protein content. Measurements of the turbidity resulting from the precipitation of protein and the absorption of radiation at specific wavelengths have all been used quantitatively.

The lead content of biological samples is usually very small rendering gravimetric methods impracticable and methods have often relied upon the formation of coloured complexes with a variety of dyes. More recently, the development of absorption spectroscopy (see chapter–8) using vaporized samples has provided a sensitive quantitative method. Oxygen measurements using specific electrodes (see chapter-15) offer a level of sensitivity which is unobtainable using volumetric gas analysis.

Bioassay

A bioassay involves the measurement of a response of an organism or a target organ to the test compound and may be conducted *in vivo* using live animals or *in vitro* using isolated organs or tissue preparations.

In vivo models

In vivo techniques are applied to multicellular organisms. The whole organism or a specific organ can be isolated and perfused with nutrients. Alternatively whole plants or parts of plants suspended in a physiological solution can be used.

1. Animal studies. A variety of laboratory animals are used in biochemical/physiological studies. Fundamental research viz: medical and clinical research, veterinary and agricultural research, manufacture of vaccines, antibodies and hormones, testing drugs or other biological products and toxicological investigations are carried out on laboratory animals. Experiments on animals and the extrapolation of the results to humans is a pre-requisite to clinical trials. Mice, rats, guinea pigs, rabbits and golden hamster are most commonly used because they are easy to maintain under laboratory conditions, they can be handled easily and sufficient background information is available. In addition, dogs, cats and primates are also used. In most of the countries, the use of laboratory animals is strictly controlled by federal departments that issue licenses for work involving live vertebrates. Biological strain, age, sex, nutritional status, circadian rhythms and

Table 2. **Generalized method of analysis.**

The major manipulative steps in a generalized method of analysis	Examples of specific methods	
	Determination of pH using a glass electrode	**Determination of glucose using a fully automated analysis system**
Purification of the test substance ↓		Dialysis
Development of a physical characteristic by the formation of a derivative ↓		Production of a colour using a specific reagent ↓
Detection of an inherent or induced physical characteristic ↓	Potential difference between two electrodes	Photoelectric detector ↓
Signal amplification ↓	↓	Electronic ↓
Signal measurement ↓	Voltmeter ↓	Galvanometer ↓
Computation ↓	Calibrated scale on meter ↓	Electronic calculator ↓
Presentation of result	Visual	Print-out

stress state of the animals, all have to be closely regulated to minimize variability in results. In metabolic studies, results obtained are compared with a control group that has received a placebo (a completely inert substance such as lactose). In man or laboratory animals, the concentrations of metabolites are measured in blood, urine, faeces, bile, expired air, sweat or saliva. Since many excretion products in urine and faeces are conjugated (i.e. linked to polar molecules such as glucuronic acid, sulphate and glycine), it is essential that samples are hydrolysed enzymically or chemically before the free metabolites are extracted and identified by established analytical techniques.

The fate of a compound in a living laboratory animal may also be studied through vascular perfusion of attached organs such as liver and kidney (see chapter-16). This procedure involves infusing the compound through a fine hollow needle inserted into the artery carrying blood to the organ and performing subsequent analysis on the blood being transported from the organ by the corresponding vein.

Recently, several ethical issues addressing whole animal experimentation have led to the development of suitable alternative methods as well as reducing the number of animals used for essential experimentation.

2. Plant studies. Fundamental pathways such as photosynthesis, respiration, photorespiration nitrogen assimilation etc. which are aspects of primary metabolism related to ATP and pyridine nucleotide turnover have been studied using higher plants. Plants are now increasingly been used in applied research in fields such as plant pathology, plant breeding, food research, environmental pollution, xenobiotic testing and in the research for so called secondary products such as pharmaceuticals, pigments, perfumes and natural agrochemicals. Modern plant biochemistry is now associated with molecular biological techniques to gene cloning.

Methods available in plant studies depend on objectives. Whole plants may be grown outside in field pots or in greenhouses or environmental chambers where factors such as temperature, light, relative humidity and gaseous environment can be controlled within specified limits. Any test compound may be added to compost or to sand/rock wood mixtures when plants are grown hydroponically in chemically defined nutrient solutions. Essential micronutrients such as Mn^{2+},B^{2+}, Zn^{2+}, Cu^{2+} and Mo^{2+} can also be added. Test compounds may be injected in roots, included in the rhizosphere or applied to the foliage by painting or spraying. Dilute organic solvents or mild detergents promote uptake through the waxy cuticle. Gases are taken up through stomata. The subsequent distribution occurs through plasmodesmata or through vascular system. Subsequent techniques may also be applied for metabolic investigations. Since metabolic rate of plants is lower than animals, they do not contain higher concentration of enzymes.

In vitro models

The term *in vitro* literally means in glass. It is applicable to all those applications when studies on a biological material are made in artificial physical and/or chemical environments. Intact micro-organisms, isolated organelles, excised parts of animals and plants and enzyme preparations are maintained through cell and tissue culture methods. Recently developed methods have found applications in biological sciences.

Cell culture techniques allow the developmental potential (**totipotency**) of cells to be studied in artificial environment. Details of cell/tissue/organ culture techniques are described in chapter-2.

Reliability of Data

All numerical/experimental data are subject to error for a variety of reasons. Therefore, it is essential to quantify the error in a suitable way, simple statistical methods help in making decisions based on analytical data. Some of the fundamental concepts are discussed below.

Random error

In any experiment, all the measurements made are not identical. These variations between replicate observations may be due to a number of reasons. For example these might be frictional effects on a balance, parallax effects on the reading of a pipette etc. Although random error can not be avoided, it can be reduced by careful technique.

Mean

Simplest way of avoiding these variations is to find out a mean. An average of all measurements is known as mean ($\overline{X}$).

Systematic error

The errors that generally occur during a method or procedure are known as systematic errors. They are constant in character and can not be treated statistically. This error may further be classified into three types.

1. Errors of method. Different analytical methods are available to make an observation. Each method faces some interference which, if overlooked results into the introduction of an error. A method is standardized or validated under certain set of conditions that becomes less valid when conditions are changed. For example the potentiometric measurement of pH is temperature dependent and the use of reference and test solutions at different temperatures without any compensation will result into error in the measurement.

2. Instrumental factors. Each instrument has many components, each one shows some degree of instability. Therefore, these chances of random error always exist. On prolonged use, these components develop fatigue that causes drift in readings. The incidence of these errors is inversely proportional to the cost of the instrument, but this is not always the case and analytical instruments should be chosen and used carefully.

3. Error of operation. Sometimes, relatively consistent errors can be introduced by carelessness or ignorance. The measure of equipment will cause an increase in differences in replicate results. While designing and using a particular instrument, it is desirable to keep number of manipulations at minimum and all necessary operations are undertaken carefully.

Assessment of analysis

Analytical methods should be precise, accurate, sensitive, and specific but due to reasons outlined above, all methods do not fully meet these criteria. Therefore, it is important to these know about terms.

1. Precision. Precision simply means reproducibility. It is defined as closeness of replicate measurements which can be associated with random error of the method. Assessment of precision involves mean ($\overline{X}$) and standard deviation (*S*).

Coefficient of variation is a way of indicating the variation which may occur about any mean value and is calculated by expressing the standard deviation as a percentage of the mean value.

$$\text{Coefficient of variation } (V) = \frac{S}{\text{mean}} \times 100$$

2. Accuracy. Accuracy is defined as the closeness of the mean of replicate analyses to the

Table 3. **The gradually increasing Cusum plot up to day eleven does not indicate that the method was out of control but that the accepted mean value of 100 mg-l was *too* low, However, the sudden change in direction on day twelve is indicative of a significant change in the batch mean. In many cases the change in direction may not be so dramatic and hence not so obvious until several points have been plotted.**

Day	Mean	Difference from accepted	Cumulative sum
1	104	+ 4	+ 4
2	99	− 1	+ 3
3	104	+ 4	+ 7
4	100	0	+ 7
5	103	+ 3	+ 10
6	99	− 1	+ 9
7	103	+ 3	+ 12
8	102	+ 2	+ 14
9	99	− 1	+ 13
10	103	+ 3	+ 16
11	100	0	+ 16
12	96	− 4	+ 12
13	97	− 3	+ 9
14	99	− 1	+ 8

true value of the sample. Accuracy can be calculated by comparing the means of replicate analyses by using 't' test.

3. Sensitivity. The sensitivity of a method is defined as ability to detect small amount of test substance. It can be assessed by quoting amount of substance that can be detected or any specified amount of test substance detected. Values of sensitivity may vary depending upon the concentration of test substance.

4. Specificity. Specificity is defined as the ability to detect the test substance. Specificity is often linked with sensitivity. It is possible to reduce the sensitivity of a method with the result that interference effects become less significant and the method is specific although less sensitive to the test substance.

5. Quality assurance. In order to produce reliable results, all analytical methods should be carefully designed and their precision and accuracy must be determined. The attitude of staff is of vital importance and they must be motivated to produce reliable data.

6. Control samples. In addition to the organizational approach to the problem, it is always desirable to devise a system that can give a warning when unforesan factors cause a loss in precision or accuracy. Therefore, control samples are always analyzed with test samples at intervals depending upon the number of test samples. The basis of a quality assurance programme is the assumption that if the control result falls within these defined limits, the test results produced at the same time are acceptable.

Presentation of data

To draw specific conclusions from any biological analysis, the data is to be interpreted in terms of certain units. To denote one observation, several units are available that often pose problems. Therefore, in 1960, **Le Systems International** d' Units (SI, Units) was introduced. This system aimed to produce a universal system of units in which only one unit was used for any physical quantity.

For example, the table (4) given below describes seven base units which are independent of each other but which can be combined in various ways to provide a range of derived units (table 5). Each unit is capable of describing a physical quantity. Coherence in these derived units can be maintained because no conversion factors are involved at this stage but in order to provide units of convenient size for different applications a series of standard obtained with coherent units to determine alternate size but only one prefix should be used at one time.

The system (**SI units**) defines seven base units (table 4.) which are independent of each other but which can be combined in various ways to provide a range of derived units (table 5.) each one capable of describing a physical quantity. Coherence is

Table 4. **SI base units.**

Physical quantity	SI base unit	Symbol
Length	Metre	M
Mass	Kilogram	kg
Time	Second	s
Electric current	Ampere	A
Thermodynamic temperature	Kelvin	K
Luminous intensity	Candela	cd
Amount of substance	Mole	mol

Table 5. **Derived units.**

Physical quantity	Derived unit	Symbol name
Area	Square metre	m^2
Volume	Cubic metre	m^3
Velocity	Metre per second	$m\ s^{-1}$
Density	Kilogram per cubic metre	$kg\ m^{-3}$
Force	Kilogram per square metre per second	$kg\ m\ s^{-2}$ Newton
Pressure	Newton per square metre	Nm^{-2} Pascal
Substance concentration	Mole per cubic metre	$mol\ m^{-3}$

maintained in these derived units because no conversion factors are involved at this stage but in order to provide units of convenient size for different applications a series of standard prefixes may be used. These are multiplies used with coherent.

Certain difficulties arise when attempts are made to use only coherent derived units. In the case of the measurement of mass, for which the name of the base unit is the kilogram, it is unacceptable to use additional standard prefixes, for example millikilogram, etc. It is therefore accepted that in order to prevent confusion, all multiples of mass should be quoted in terms of the gram and not the kilogram while still retaining the kilogram as the base unit for mass. A similar problem occurs in the measurement of volume. Here the unit for volume is cubic metre (m^3) which is derived from the base unit.

The more commonly used litre is a more convenient volume and is the same as a cubic decimetre (dm^3) which, although it is an acceptable derived unit, is not coherent due to the use of the prefix 'deci-'. For convenience, the term litre and its symbol (l) are accepted but it should be noted that whatever name and symbol are used, consistency in their use is important.

The SI unit of enzyme activity is the katal and is defined as the amount of enzyme which will catalyse the conversion of 1 mole convenient for routine use. Despite the fact that the International

Table 6. **Multiples and sub-multiples of units.**

Factor	Prefix		Prefix		Symbol
	Name	Symbol	Name	Name	
10^1	deca-	da	10^{-1}	deci-	d
10^2	hecto-	h	10^{-2}	centi-	c
10^3	kilo-	k	10^{-3}	milli-	m
10^6	mega-	M	10^{-6}	micro-	µ
10^9	giga-	G	10^{-9}	nano-	n
10^{12}	tera-	T	10^{-12}	pico-	p
			10^{-15}	femto-	f
			10^{-18}	atto-	a

Unit of enzyme activity (1 micromoles per minute) is not an acceptable SI unit it is still frequently used. The relationship between these two units is as follows :

1 nanokatal = 0.06 IU

UNITS, CONVERSION AND ABBREVIATIONS

Metric and English Units

1 liter (L) = 1000 milliliter (mL)
1 gallon (gal) = 3.784 L
1 L = 0.264 gal
1 quart (qt) = 0.9464 L = 946.4 mL
1 L = 1.057 qt
1 fluid ounce = 29.6 mL
1 mL = 1000 microliters (μL)
1 kg = 1000 grams (g)
1 g = 1000 milligrams (mg)
1 mg = 1000 micrograms (μg)
1 μg = 1000 nanograms (ng)
1 ng = 1000 picrogram (pg)
1 kg = 2.205 pounds (lb)
1 lb = 453.6 g
1 ounce (oz) = 28.35 g
1 cubic meter (m3) = 1,000,000 cubic centimeters (cc) or cm3 lcc=lmL
1 m3 = 1000 L

Conversions

⇒ Concentration of a solution as weight percent (w/w)

$$\frac{\text{Mas of solute (g)} \times 100\%}{\text{100g solution}}$$

⇒ Concentration of a solution as volume percent (v/v)

$$\frac{\text{mL substrance} \times 100\%}{\text{100 mL solution}}$$

⇒ Concentration of a solution as weight per volume percent (w/v)

$$\frac{\text{Mass of substrance (g)} \times 100\%}{\text{100 mL solution}}$$

⇒ Concentration, as part per million (ppm) = mg substance/L solution; that is, ppm = mg/L or μg/mL or ng/μL; part per billion (ppb) = ng/L or ng/mL.

⇒ 1 Atmosphere (atm) = 760 torr
= 760 mm mercury
= 14.6 pounds per square inch (psi)
= 101.306 kPa

⇒ °F = (1.8 x °C) + 32

⇒ $°C \; \frac{°F - 32}{1.8}$

⇒ K (Kelvin) = °C + 273

⇒ $\text{Density} = \frac{\text{mass}}{\text{volume}}$

(The units commonly used for density are g/mL for liquids, volume g/cm^3 for solids, and g/L for gases.)

⇒ 1 mole (mol) = molecular or formula weight in grams (Le., 1 mol NaOH = 40 NaOH)

⇒ $\text{Molarity (M)} = \frac{\text{mol of substance}}{\text{liter solution}}$

⇒ Normality

$$\text{(N)} = \frac{\text{Gram equivalent weight of substance}}{\text{liter solution}}$$

or milligram equivalent/mL solution

⇒ STP = Standard Temperature and Pressure, which is O°C and 1 atm

⇒ NTP = Normal Temperature and Pressure, which is 25°C and 1 atm

(At STP volume of 1 mol of any gas = 22.4 L, while at NTP 1 mol of any gas would occupy 24.45 L.)

⇒ Ideal gas equation: $PV = nRT$

where P = pressure,
V = volume,
T = temperature (K),
R = 0.082 L.atmlmol.K
(when pressure and volumc arc expressed in atm and L, respectively.)

⇒ Vapor pressure is the pressure of a vapor in equilibrium with its liquid or solid form. It is temperature dependent, and expressed in mm Hg or torr. It is a characteristic of the volatility of a substance. The higher the vapor pressure of a substance, the more volatile it is. Vapor pressure data in this text are presented at the temperature 20°e.

⇒ Density of a gas at STP

$$= \frac{\text{gram molecular weight (mole)}}{\text{22.4L}}$$

⇒ Density of a gas at NTP

$$= \frac{\text{gram molecular weight (mole)}}{\text{22.45L}}$$

Important Questions

1. How will you select a valid method for biological analysis? Discuss the concept of bioassay in the analysis of samples of plant or animal origin.
2. Define bioassay. How will you perform a bioassay using an *in vitro* model?
3. Enumerate different statistical methods that can be used to test the reliability of data.
4. Describe briefly the following :
   (i) Presentation of data, (ii) Quality assurance, (iii) Precision & accuracy.

2 Cell and Tissue Culture

In modern context, tissue culture usually refers to the long-term culture of dispersed animal cells, plant cells and microorganisms viz: bacteria, fungi, actinomycetes, yeasts, unicellular and filamentous algae and protozoa. As such its history goes back to the beginning of Biology. However, it was only at the end of the 19th century that **Roux** demonstrated the viability of cells outside the body in physiological saline and not until 1907 when **Harrison** showed the outgrowth of neurons from explanted tissue. These explant cultures were grown in a lymph clot, a technique replaced by the plasma clot and perfected by **Carrel**. **Carrel** and **Burrows** showed the growth promoting activities of a chick embryo extract, using rigid control of sterility. They could maintain a strain of cells for over 34 years. However, it was only towards the end of the 1940s when manipulatable cell lines were established and the tissue culture as we know it, might have started.

Microbial Cell Culture

Many biochemical and physiological studies directed towards understanding fundamental life processes are conducted using model bacteria e.g. *Escherichia coli, Bacillus subtilis,* yeast e.g. *Saccharomyces cerevisae, Candida albicans,* and model algae e.g. *Chlorella vulgaris* and *Chlamydomonas dysosmos.*

Microbial cultures have widespread industrial uses e.g. for large scale production of alcohols, amino acids, coenzymes, growth regulators, organic acids, polysaccharides, solvents, sterols, surfactants,

Table 1. **Properties of some commonly used media for growing various microorganisms.**

Medium	Type	Special ingredient	Use for organisms
1. Ashbey's Medium	Chemically Defined	N-free, containing glucose	Heterotrophic, free-living N-fixing bacteria, *Azotobacter*
2. Brain heart Infusion agar	Non-chemically Defined	Glucose	Streptococci and Pneumococci
3. Czapek-Dox Medium	Chemically defined	Sucrose	Moulds, especially Aspergilii and Penicillia
4. Malt extract Medium	Non-chemically defined	Vitamins	Yeasts and *Acetobacter*
5. Nutrient medium	Non-chemically defined	Peptone	Many non-fastidious bacteria, including *E. coli*, *B. cereus*, *S. aureus* and *P. aeruginosa*
6. George's Medium	Mineral salt medium	Peptone	Algae
7. Waksman's sulphur medium	Chemically defined organic medium	Sulphur energy source bacteria	Autotrophic, Sulphur-oxidizing bacteria, *Thiobacillus*
8. Winogradsky's Medium	Enriched and differential	NH_4^+ as energy source	Autotrophic, nitrifying bacteria, *Nitrosomonas* and *Nitrobacter*
9. Blood agar		Blood	Many fast growing bacteria including Streptococci and *Neisseria gonorrhoeae* Gives evidence of hemolysis
10. Chocolate agar	Enriched	Blood agar is heated to disrupt the blood cells	Neisseria
11. Filde's medium	Nutrient medium	Contains enzymic digest of blood	*Haemophilus* and *Clostridium tetani*
12. Eosin (EMB) agar	Selective and Differential	Eosin and methyleneblue	For differentiating *E. coli* and *Aerobacter aerogenes*
13. MacConkey's agar medium	Selective and differential	Bile salts, crystal-violet and neutral red	For determining the number of coliforms in water and faeces.
14. Mannitol salt agar medium	Selective and differential	Sodium chloride, phenol red	For the isolation of *Salmonella* and *Shigella* Staphylococcl
15. Selenite broth	Enrichment	Sodium selenite	*Salmonella*
16. Thayer-Martin agar	Selective	Antibiotics	*Neisseria*
17. Chopped meat glucose broth	Selective	Cysteine	Anaerobes
18. Sabouraud agar	Selective	Glucose	Pathogenic fungi

vitamins etc. Microbial degradation of waste products particularly those from agricultural and food industries is another important industrial application of microbial cells in culture especially in the degradation of toxic wastes or **bioconversion** of waste in useful products. Biomass production as single cell from different protein substrates is another examples of microbial culture applications. Studies on bacterial genetics in particular have led to the development of genetic engineering techniques. **Recombinant DNA techniques** have emerged as ever-expanding science that involve gene manipulations.

Culture Media

The food material on which microorganisms are grown in the laboratory is known as culture medium (pl. media) and the growth itself is called as culture. Culture media vary in form and composition depending upon the species to be cultivated. They can be nutritionally classified as **chemolithotroph**, **chemoorganotroph**, **photolithotroph**, cell line. Typically, a minimal medium for the growth of a fully biosynthetically competent chemoautotroph would contain salts of Na^+, K^+, Ca^+, Mg^+, NH_4^+ or NO_3^-, Cl^-, HPO_4^2, SO_4^{2-} and a simple carbon source such as glucose. Media have further been classified using different criteria viz: chemical composition, physical and utility purpose. There are three main types of culture media.

(1) natural or empirical cultural media
(2) semi-synthetic media
(3) synthetic or chemically defined culture media

Several media are available commercially offering some advantage for the isolation, maintenance, characterization or growth of certain groups of organisms. The following table describes certain properties of the commercially used media.

Plant Cell and Tissue Culture

This technique refers to the long term *in vitro* incubation parts of mosses, liverworts and vascular plants (ferns, gymnosperms and angiosperms) in or on a suitable medium under defined environmental conditions. Essentially the methodology of tissue culture consists of separating cells, tissues, organs of a plant called explants, and growing them aseptically on a nutrient medium under controlled conditions of temperature and light. Many types of explants contain meristematic tissue capable of cell division. The explants give rise to an unorganized proliferative mass of differentiated cells known as callus. Callus is often used as the starting material for suspension culture in which a mixture of both a liquid medium that is aerated artificially to prevent cells from becoming waterlogged. Undifferentiated cells comprise cells with a small amount of cytoplasm but large vacuoles. Such tissue develops localized growth centres called meristemoids, from which caulogenesis (shoot induction), rhizogenesis (root initiation) or both may ensure. The ability of callus to undergo such organogenesis is genetically controlled but may be manipulated by changing cytokinin to auxin ratio in the medium.

Plant cell and tissue culture techniques can be divided into five classes based on the type of the material used.

1. Callus culture. The culture of callus (cell masses) on agar media produced from one explant of seedling or other plant source.

2. Cell culture. The culture of cells in liquid media usually aerated by agitation.

3. Organ culture. The aseptic culture of embryos, anthers (spores), ovaries, roots, shoots or other organs on nutrient media.

4. Meristem culture. The aseptic culture of shoot meristems or other explant tissue on nutrient media to get complete plants.

5. Protoplast culture. The aseptic isolation and culture of plant protoplasts from cultured cells or plant tissue.

A wide range of different types of medium is now available commercially in powder form. Tissue culture medium is to be either autoclaved or filter sterilized before use. Common examples of media are—**Murashige and Skoog medium** (MS), Gamborg B5, Nitsche, Shenck and Hildebrandt and McCown's **Woody Plant Medium** (WPM). In addition to a balanced mixture of macro and micronutrients, which provide correct water potential in the medium, most of the osmotically active solute is also provided as soluble carbon source.

Animal Cell Culture

Animal cells are derived from tissue explants or from disaggregated embryos. Many of the cell lines originally isolated in the late 1940s and early 1950s are still in use today, illustrating their long term culturability. These include the L-cell line that Earle showed could be dispersed and planted as single cells to grow up as clones. Similarly He La cells were derived from a human cervical tumor and Chinese hamster ovary (CHO) cells from a disaggregated ovary. A key parallel event was the development of defined culture media. These were originally developed from physiological salt solutions defined by Earle and Ham, although it was Eagle who developed the complex media with over 25 ingredients. Other media developed for short term work include Tyrode's medium, Young's medium, Locke's medium, Meng's medium and Da Jalon's medium derived from Ringer's solution which was first to be formulated. Typically salt solutions contain different combinations of the major salts viz: NaCl, KCl, $MgSO_4$, $CaCl_2$, $NaHCO_3$, and KH_2PO_4 in various concentrations. Other inclusions are vitamins, carbon sources, amino acids and proteins. Proteins usually comprise either plasma or serum proteins. Serum contain important growth factors such as **insulin like growth factors** (IGF), epidermal growth factor (EGF) or platelet derived **growth factor** (PDGF) which are essential for long term growth of more highly differentiated excised tissues.

Other factors such as gaseous exchange, pH and temperature are critically important for long term maintenance of cells in culture. Medium buffered with 30mM bicarbonate has to be maintained in air containing 5% CO_2 to keep the pH between 7·3 and 7·5. Antibiotics active against a range of contaminating microorganisms may be incorporated, filter sterilized at concentrations from 2·5 to 10 μg cm^{-3} and are claimed to be effective for 5 days at 37°C.

Cells in culture include **macrophages**, T and B lymphocytes and polymorphonuclear leukocytes. Pioneering studies established that varying degrees of growth of tissues was possible *in vitro* in sterile medium containing salts, carbohydrates, vitamins and amino acids, and serum supplements. Animal cells may be subdivided broadly into those that remain viable only when attached to a solid substrate (e.g. primary cultures or diploid fibroblast cells) and those that will proliferate as suspensions e.g. human tumor cells, He La cells and hybridomas. Newly isolated or primary cell cultures of non-tumor cells typically show anchorage dependence by growing *in vitro* only when attached to a surface, which may be either other cells (as *in vivo)* or plastic, gelatin or collagen, but rarely glass. Primary cell lines spread over the surface as mono layers but will not overlayer show confiuence, which severely limits cell density in culture. This problem can be overcome by using cell support systems (microbeads or hollow fibres), which are considered below.

In general terms, highly differentiated excised tissue is more difficult to establish *in vitro* as primary cell lines either because the cells tend to differentiate immediately or because they will not subculture in medium devoid of growth factors or steroid hormone supplements typically found in serum, e.g. IGF, EGF, PDGF or oestrogen.

Organ Culture

Organ cultures are not as widely used as cell cultures. They require considerably more effort to initiate and can not subsequently be propagated. In general, organ culture can be maintained for up to three weeks and at least some of the histological structure of the tissue with same phenotypic characteristics can be studied. Tissue or whole organ from the embryo survives better and may show some net growth in culture. Under normal conditions (20% oxygen at atmospheric pressure), the radius of an organ culture is limited to a maximum of 500 μg. The inward diffusion of oxygen and the outward diffusion of carbon dioxide are optimized by growing the tissue at the air-liquid interface. Nutrition is provided through a semipermeable porous membrane or a stainless steel mesh grid. Organ culture have been found particularly useful in cultivation of skin, faetal bone and various embryonic organs during organogenesis.

Culture of mature organs in a synthetic medium

Organ culture originated in the Strangeways Laboratory in 1930s. Initially the method has been chiefly used for the culture of embryonic organ rudiments (Trowell, 1959). Such cultures not only maintain their histological organization but grow in size and differentiate in a more or less normal manner until they become too large to survive *in vitro*. The reasons why the method was largely restricted to embryonic organs appear to be (i) whole organs from embryos are so small that they can be cultured entire, (ii) embryonic tissues, in contrast to mature tissues, are remarkably resistant to the rather anoxic conditions prevailing in this type of culture, and (iii) interest was chiefly centered on the study of morphogenesis *in vitro*.

After several modifications and improvements in the original methods, it could be possible to keep fully differentiated organs (or parts thereof) alive *in vitro* without either growth or dedifferentiation. It would have been applied for many experimental studies on organ physiology, metabolism and pathology. The basic method and the synthetic medium were developed originally for the culture

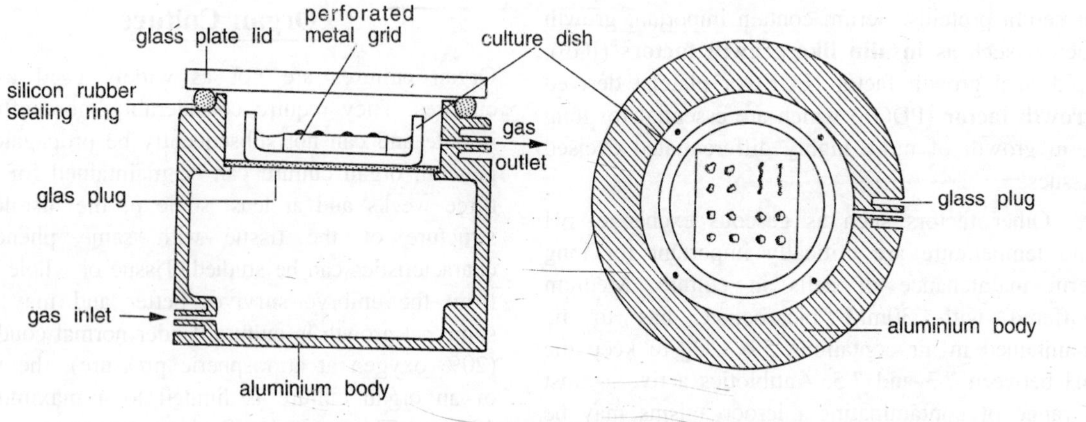

Fig. 1. Diagrammatic representation of a culture chamber as seen in horizontal sector and from above.

of lymph nodes. Since then, the apparatus has been improved and the medium simplified.

Apparatus

The standard culture chamber is shown in figure. 1. It houses up to 20 cultures, each about 2 mm diameter, in 5-6 ml of fluid culture medium. This chamber, which is made mostly of aluminium and has a built-in gas reservoir.

The culture medium is contained in a shallow dish (D) made of hard glass or of fuzed silica (vitreosil). These dishes are made from ordinary capsules (crystallizing dishes) 48 mm outside diameter, by grinding them down to an outside height of 10 mm. In the dish stands a square metal grid (G) which is made by bending over the two ends of a flat piece of perforated metal to make short legs. The top of the grid is 25 × 25 mm and the legs are 4 mm high. The material used is stainless steel "expanded metal", 1.5 mm mesh, 0.005 inch thick. In earlier work the grids were made from tantalum wire gauze; these grids, though satisfactory in use, were costly and rather difficult to fabricate owing to the soft nature of the material (the top of the grid must be absolutely flat). The expanded metal grids are very easy to make and altogether more robust.

On top of the grid is placed a 27 × 27 mm piece of lens paper (Green's C105). Sufficient medium is present just to reach and wet the lens paper and the cultures are planted on the wet paper. During the course of cultivation certain organs may adhere to the paper and entangled fibres of paper may cause difficulty in the subsequent histological section cutting. If necessary, the difficulty can be avoided by using a sheet of 2% agar, 1 mm thick, in place of the lens paper. This is made by pouring a predetermined volume of molten 2% agar (Davis) in 0·7% NaCl into a stainless steel tray of known area. When set, squares of agar are cut out with a knife. In experiments in which cultures are to be exposed to accurate doses of X-radiation, it is advantageous to use agar sheets 3 mm thick, in order to minimize "back scattering" of radiation from the metal grid.

The gas chamber (shown black in Fig. 1) is machined out of a length of 3 inch diameter aluminium bar. The plate glass lid and the silicone-rubber sealing ring are held on by an external screw clamp. Figure. 2 shows a convenient arrangement in which the clamps for 6 chambers are permanently mounted on a common baseboard. The chambers can be used in an incubator, but it is much more convenient to have them on a table in a small dust-free room maintained at 37ºC which also contains the gas cylinder and gas line. A removable Perspex diaphragm divides the chamber into an upper compartment (35 ml) which is the culture chamber proper and a lower compartment (150 ml) which is the gas reservoir.

Four 1 mm diameter holes in the diaphragm are quite sufficient to maintain gaseous equilibrium between the two compartments under all conditions of culture. The gas mixture, which is normally per cent CO_2 in oxygen, enters by a rubber tube attached at gas inlet and leaves by a similar tube attached at

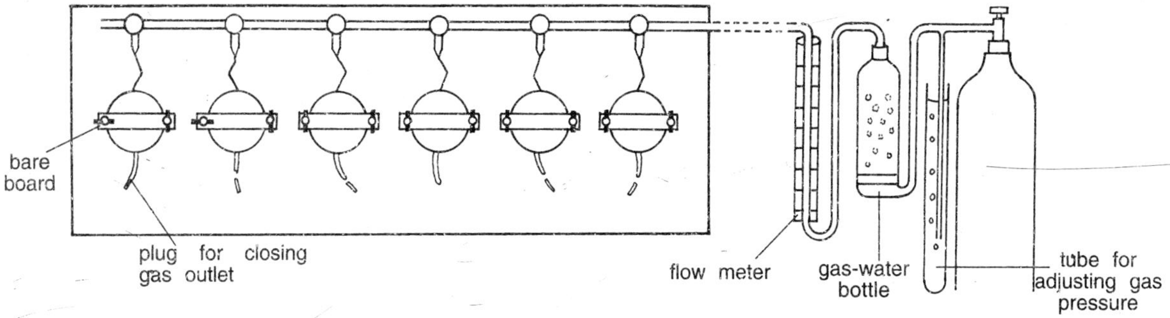

Fig. 2. Arrangement of tissue culture chambers in a six chamber assembly. The lid of each chamber is held by a perpex or Lucite bar which is screwed on a bare board.

gas outlet. These tubes and all other rubber tubing used in the gas line and also the sealing ring are made of "translucent silicone rubber" (Esco Rubber Ltd., London, N.16), which is non-toxic and can be sterilized by dry heat. If ordinary rubber is used it absorbs oxygen at a surprising rate and a considerable negative pressure develops. The standard rate of gas flow is 75 ml min, measured by a Rotameter Flowmeterand adjusted by raising or lowering tube (Fig. 2). Sometime before the experiment, the empty chamber (i.e. without culture dish) is sealed up and gas is passed through it at this rate for 10 minutes after which the outlet is closed with a glass plug. This is sufficient to displace all the air. Then the time arrives to insert the culture dish (with cultures already planted) the gas flow is restarted before the chamber is opened. Under these conditions gas is passing upwards through the holes all the time and there is no possibility of air getting into the lower compartment. After the lid is closed the gas flow is continued for a further 4 minutes, which is sufficient to displace all the air from the upper compartment. In the same way the gas flow is restarted before opening the chamber for manipulations such as changing the medium or removing cultures.

The total gas span, with dish and medium in place, is 170 mt Twenty organ cultures produce about 2 ml of CO_2 per day, by respiration and glycolysis, and consume about 1.5 ml of oxygen, so, if the chamber is left for 3 days, the CO_2 should rise from 5 to 8.5 percent and the oxygen fall from 95 to 92.4 percent. In practice, the CO_2 does not rise so much as this, probably because some escapes by diffusion through the silicone rubber. The chambers are normally opened every 3 days for the purpose of changing or reconditioning the medium. This involves 5-10 minutes re-gassing every third day, which is usually all that is required. The perspex chambers originally used had to be regassed twice a day.

The apparatus is cleaned and sterilized as follows. The aluminium chambers, lids, sealing rings and gassing attachment tubes are sterilized at 110^0 C for 1 hour. The Perspex diaphragms are rinsed in ether and put in a sterile box. The culture dishes and all other glassware used for culture work or medium-making are scrubbed out with a mildly abrasive cleaning compound rinsed in hot water, immersed in nitric acid overnight, then well rinsed in glass distilled water, dried and sterilized. The stainless steel grids are briefly boiled in 10 percent sodium carbonate, rinsed, immersed in pure nitric acid overnight then rinsed, dried and sterilized at 110^0C for 1 hour. The lens paper is washed in 4 changes of Ether A.R., followed by glass distilled water 12 changes and overnight, after which it is dried, cut to size and sterilized at 110^0C, During and after cleaning, the grids and paper are handled only with sterilized forceps.

It may be mentioned that the gas chambers, made of aluminium, can also be made of stainless steel or perspex, but not of brass.

Synthetic Medium

Several culture media are available nowadays. A simple medium called TACPI consists of inorganic salts, glucose, 19 amino acids, cocarboxylase, p-aminobenzoic acid and insulin, together with choloramphenicol as antibiotic and phenol red as indicator. This medium has now been modified as follows (i) seven amino acids have been modified, the remaining 12 being those which Eagle and co-workers found essential for the maintenance of a variety of human cell lines *in vitro* (ii) the concentrations of the 12 amino acids have been reduced to approximate those found optimal by Eagle et al., except that 0.3 mM cysteine has been used in place of 0.05 mM cysteine; (iii) the concentration of phosphate has been increased from 1 mM to 3 mM in the light of the work of Waymouth; (iv) thiamine is used instead to cocarboxylase, because it is obtained in purer from (v) in TACPI the tryptophane must have been destroyed during heat sterilization of the stock solution; this is now avoided. The new medium is called T8 and its composition is given in table 1. The medium is made up, just before use, from, the following five stock solutions each of which contains the constituents mentioned at 20 times the concentration given in table 2.

Solution AA contains all the amino acids except cysteine. The tyrosine should be dissolved in the final volume of glass distilled water first, heated to about 90^{0}C to facilitate solution. Then add the remaining amino acids, introducing the tryptophane last when the solution is cool.

Solution S. NaCl, KCl, $CaCl_2$, $MgSO_4$

Solution BP. $NaHCO_3$, Phenol red.

Solution PIC. p-Aminobenzoic acid, insulin, chloramphenicol ("Chloromycetin", crystalline). In addition, 0.3 ml N.HCl per 100 ml of solution is added to dissolve the insulin.

Solution GPTC. Glucose, NaH_2PO_4

Solution BP is put up in 3 ml amounts in small ampoules made from 8 mm bore hard-glass tubing. The ampoules are sealed off and then sterilized at 105°C for 1 hour. The other four solutions are sterilized by suction through No. "5 or 3" porosity sintered-glass filters and stored in hard glass test tubes with silicone rubber stoppers. Solution GPTC is made up freshly on each occasion; solution PIC should not be more than a month old, but the other three solutions can be stored for at least 6 months at room temperature without deterioration. To make up 10 ml of medium, 0.5 ml volumes of each of the five stock solutions are added to 7.5 ml of fresh glass distilled water, equilibrated with 5 percent CO_2 at 37°C, the pH is 7.6.

Animals

It has been found by experience that, for cultures, organs should approximately be spherical, the diameter must not exceed about 2 mm, otherwise necrosis occurs in the centre from lack of oxygen. So it is desirable, in theory, to select animals in which the organ in question is about 2 mm in size and can be cultured whole. In practice, however, this is not always feasible, for organs such as lung, liver and kidney that will always be too large to use whole. Furthermore we have found in the case of organs with fairly uniform histological pattern, such as thyroid,prostate, ovary and lymph node, that no better results are to be obtained by culturing the whole organ of a small animal than by using a one half or quarter piece cut from the organ of a larger animal.

Table 2. **Composition of medium T8**

	mM/l	mg/100 ml		mM/l	mg/100 ml
NaCl	104	610	L-Lysine HCl	0.2	3.6
KCl	6	45	DL-Methionine	0.05[a]	1.5
$CaCl_2$	2	22	DL-Phenyl-Alanine	0.1[a]	3.3
$MgSO_4.7H_2O$	1	25	DL-Threonine	0.2[a]	4.8
$NaH_2PO_4.2H_2O$	3	45	L-Tryptophane	0.02	0.4
$NaHCO_3$	33.5	282	L-Tyrosine	0.1	1.8
Glucose	22	400	L-Valine	0.2	2.3
L-Arginine HCl	0.1	2.1	Thiamine HCl	0.05	1.7
L-Cysteine HCl	0.3	4.7	p-Aminobenzoic acid	0.25	3.5
L-Histidine HCl	0.05	1.0	Insulin	0.001	5.0
L-Isoleucine	0.2	2.6	Chloramphenicol	0.1	3.0
L-Leucine	0.2	2.6	Phenol red	0.03	1.0

In our experience the 4 week-old rat, weighing about 60 g, is the most useful animal, and most of the work has been done with it. In this animal the adrenal, pituitary, pineal, parathyroid, ovary and lymph nodes can be used whole, and cultures of narrow tubular organs, such as ureter, ductus deferens, and uterine horn, can be of unlimited length. The adult mouse appears to be equally suitable. **Richter** has used adult bats, which have conveniently small organs. For certain organs rats of 10, 20 or 200 g have been used. Apart from convenience of size, we have usually found no difference in the cultural behaviour of organs taken from rats of different age, ranging from 1 week to 3 months.

Procedure

The empty culture chambers are set up at 37^0C and filled with 5 percent CO_2 in oxygen as already described. The culture dishes, each containing a grid, are set out in the culture room, each one in a petridish. The required volume of medium is made up, allowing 6 ml for each chamber and an extra 5 ml for dissection, etc. Medium is now pipetted into each dish, at one side of the grid. After about 5 ml has been added it rises enough to wet the underside of the grid at one corner. Addition is now continued, drop by drop, until, spreading across the underside of the grid, the medium just reaches the opposite corner. This is the correct volume of medium to use and no further adjustment is required. With it, the cultures will be wet enough for nutritional purposes and will not wash off if the dish is tilted. A piece of lens paper is then carefully lowered onto each grid. If, in any chamber, it is planned to remove some of the cultures before others, it is best to have the lens paper in several strips so that one strip with its attached cultures can be removed without disturbing the others. It is necessary to make sure that the paper is thoroughly wet and that no air remains entrapped beneath it. The prepared culture dishes can now be left in the petri dishes for up to 2 hours if necessary.

The animal (rat or mouse) is anaesthetized, outside the culture room, with a 50 percent CO_2 - 50 percent O_2 mixture. It is then killed and bled out, by decapitation if no organs from the head and neck are needed, or by opening the chest and cutting the heart if the head and neck is required. By means of rubber bands attached to the feet, the animal is firmly extended on and fastened to a metal plate (15 × 10 cm). The whole animal is then liberally swabbed with 80 percent alcohol and passed into the culture room through a service hatch.

The skin is widely deflected, with instruments kept in a beaker of 80 percent alcohol. Then, with fresh sterile instruments, the organ or organs are freely exposed but not touched. The organ is now flooded with a few drops of medium, dissected free with fresh instruments and transferred to a pool of medium in a cavity slide. When the organs required for one chamber have been collected, they are cleaned free of fat and connective tissue with two cataract knives. Small organs such as liver and lung must be cut into suitably-sized pieces with the cataract knives. The cultures are then transferred to the lens paper and arranged in some sort of order which is recorded, so that each one in individually identifiable. It is wise to cut off the top left-hand corner of the lens paper, to preserve orientation. The best instrument for lifting the cultures is a "spud" made by mounting a platinum wire in a glass rod and hammering out the end to make a flat spoon about 3 mm diameter.

The gas flow through the chamber is now restarted, the dish is inserted, and the flow continued for a further 4 minutes. The chamber can now be left for three days, after which the medium must be either "changed" or "reconditioned".

To "change" 4 ml the medium, removed and 4 ml of fresh medium added. It appears, however, that deterioration of the medium after three days is due to two factors only-exhaustion of glucose and increased acidity from accumulation of lactic acid. This can be rectified by adding isotonic glucose and isotonic $NaHCO_3$ to the medium, a procedure which we call "reconditioning" the medium. We have found in fact that, over a 9 day culture period, rather better results are obtained by reconditioning the medium every 3 days than by changing it. A 5.5 ml volume of medium detaining the medium every 3 days than by changing it. A 5.5 ml volume of medium is normally reconditioned by adding 0.2 ml of 5.83 percent glucose and 0.5 ml of 1.36 percent $NaHCO_3$ and then, after mixing, removing 0.7 ml of medium. This increases the glucose concentration by 175 mg/100 ml and the $NaHCO_3$ by 100 mg/100 ml.

When the cultures are to be studied histologically, the lens paper is lifted off with cultures attached and placed in formol-sublimate fixative (9 vols. of 6 percent $HgCl_2$, 1 vol. of precipitate – free 40 percent formaldehyde) for 2 hours. After washing, the cultures are gently detached from the paper, dehydrated in 2-ethoxyethanol (cellosolve) and embedded and cut in ester wax. For cultures of average size it is appropriate to use 8 changes of 2-ethoxyethanol (total time 3 hours) and 2 changes of ester wax, 20 mins each. The cultures are usually sectioned in the vertical plane; if the top of each is lightly touched with Indian ink just before fixation, the ink is visible in the final section and identifies the top side of the culture.

Growth Media for Mammalian Cell Culture

This section describes growth media, supplements, and digestion solutions for the preparation of primary cells for culture and for the propagation and culture of continuous and primary mammalian cell lines. Although most labs use commercially available media preparations for tissue culture, we have included media recipes that are intended as a reference guide for manipulating tissue culture conditions. Be sure that repeated use of a common stock of these solutions does not result in contamination. Aliquots will help avoid this problem.

DMEM prepared from powdered medium

Powdered medium	13.4 g
1.5 M HEPES (pH 7.45)	10 ml
$NaHCO_3$	1.2 g
Distilled H_2O to make a total volume of 1 liter	

The resulting pH is 7.3. Sterilize by filtering through a sterile D.2-l1m filling bell filter. Divide into 100- to 250-ml aliquots. This medium can be stored for up to 6 months at 4°C.

DMEM can also be purchased as a solution, but it is less expensive to make it.

I × antibiotics/antimycotic (sterile 100× penicillin-streptomycin/amphotericin B stock solution) Medium is completed by the addition of antibiotics/antimycotics and serum, the type and concentration appropriate to the cell line used.

This medium can be stored for up to 6 months at 4°c.

EBSS (with pH adjusted to 1.0 with CO_2 gas)

Component	EBSS# I	EBSS #2
HEPES	2.38 g	0.476 g
Glucose	1.26 g	0.252 g
$NaH_2PO_48H_2O$	0.07 g	0.014 g
NaCl	3.4 g	0.68 g
KCl	0.2 g	0.04 g
$MgSO_47H_2O$	0.18 g	-
$NaHCO_3$	1.1g	0.22 g
BSA	1.5 g	0.3 g
$CaCl_2$ (anhydrous)	0.1 g	-
DNase I	-	0.05 g
Ultrapure (Milli-Q) H_2O		
to total volume of	500 ml	100 ml

Add all components except the BSA to the appropriate volume of ultrapure H_2O and mix well. Add the BSA to a small volume of this mixture and allow it to sit for 5- 10 minutes. When the BSA is dissolved, mix it with the remaining solution. Adjust the pH of the bicarbonate-buffered EBSS with CO_2 as follows: Place a small chip of dry ice in a 500-ml Erlenmeyer flask containing a small volume of H_2O. Stopper the flask with a rubber cork that has tubing attached to a glass-rod outlet. Attach a sterile pasteur pipette to the tubing and insert its tip into the EBSS for 2-4 minutes to adjust the pH.

Sterilize the solution by filtering small volumes through sterile *0.2-l1m* filters and large volumes through sterile *0.2-J.lm* filling bell filters. This solution can be stored for up to 1 month at 4°c.

Freezing medium

Growth medium (RPMI, DMEM, etc.)	7 ml
FBS	2 ml
Glycerol or DMSO	1 ml

The concentration of glycerol or DMSO can vary from 5% to 20%. The volume of growth medium should be adjusted to accommodate changes in the amount of cryoprotectant used.

G418 Gentamicin sulfate

Purchase as Geneticin, an impure preparation. Different batches will need to be titrated.

HAT medium

Add L-glutamine (lOOx stock solution) to a final concentration of Ix if it is not already included in the DMEM or if the DMEM has been stored. We recommend adding the L-glutamine just before use.

10-20% FCS (sterile stock solution)

I× HT (sterile 1O0x stock solution)

Ix Aminopterin (sterile 1O0x stock solution)

Ix PSN antibiotic mixture (sterile 100x stock solution)

This medium can be stored for up to 6 months at 4°C.

HBSS

In 1 liter of distilled H_2O, prepare fresh from chemicals:

8 g/liter NaCl
400 mg/liter KCI
60 mg/liter KH_2PO_4 monobasic
47.86 mg/liter Na_2HPO_4 anhydrous
1000 mg/liter glucose anhydrous
350 fig/liter $NaHCO_3$
Autoclave to sterilize.

Saline/EDTA buffer plus glucose for isolation of germ cells and tissue culture

	g/100 ml in 2x glass-distilled H_2O
EDTA (disodium salt)	0.02
NaCl	0.80
KCl	0.02
Na_2HPO_4 (anhydrous) KH_2PO_4	0.115
Glucose	0.02
Phenol Red	0.02

The final EDTA concentration is 0.02%. Check that pH is 7.2. Filter-sterilize or autoclave (121°C, 15 psi for 15 minutes). Store at room temperature. The glucose can be omitted for tissue culture alone.

N2 Supplement

insulin stock (SO mg/IO ml of 0.01 N HCI)	1 ml
progesterone stock (63 mg/100 ml of absolute ethanol)	1 ml
putrescine stock (161 mg/10 ml of MilliQ H_2O)	1 ml
selenium dioxide stock (330 Jlg/1O0 ml of MilliQ H_2O)	1 ml
transferring	100 mg
MEM	96 ml

Filter-sterilize. Stock solutions can be kept at -20°C for 6 months.

0.25% trypsin in tris-saline for tissue culture MME

	g/100 ml
NaCl	8.00
KCl	0.40
Na_2HPO_4	0.10
Glucose	1.00
Trizma base	3.00
Phenol Red	0.010
Penicillin G	0.060 (final conc. 100 U/ml)
Streptomycin	0.100
Trypsin	2.5 g (dissolve in small volume of H_2O before adding)

Trypsin stock solution for tissue culture 0.25% trypsin 1:250 in Tris-saline (or any other well-buffered isotonic salt solution). Addition of antibiotics is optional. Adjust pH to approximately 7.6. Filter-sterilize and aliquot into sterile containers. Store at -20°e. This stock is diluted 1:4 insaline/ EDTA before use.

Trypsin *Ix working solution (0.05%)*

trypsin/EDTA 10x stock	100 ml
NaCl	7.1 g
KCl	0.4 g
Glucose	1.0 g
$NaHCO_3$	0.35 g
1 % Phenol Red	1 ml
H_2O	900 ml

Adjust pH to 7.2.

Trypsin/EDTA 10x stock

trypsin (1:250)	5.0 g
EDTA • tetrasodium salt	2.0 g
H_2O	100 ml

Most Commonly Used Media and Solutions for Bacteria

Liquid media

This section contains recipes for the most commonly used bacterial media and solutions. All recipes are for 1 liter of medium, unless otherwise specified. A protocol for preparing stab cultures is included at the end of the section. Be sure that repeated use of a common stock of these solutions does not result in contamination. Aliquots will help to avoid this problem.

λ Diluent per liter:

1 M Tris-HCl (pH 7.5)	10 ml
$MgSO_47H_2O$	2 g
H_2O to 1 liter	

LB medium

Combine the following in 0.9 liter of H_2O:

Bacto tryptone	109
Bacto yeast extract	5 g
NaCl	10 g

Shake until the solutes have dissolved. Adjust the pH to 7.0 with 5 N NaOH (~0.2 ml). Adjust the volume of the solution to 1 liter with deionized Hp. Sterilize by autoclaving for 20 minutes at 15 psi on liquid cycle.

LB broth + antibiotic
Using sterile technique, add 1 ml of 10 mg/ml antibiotic to 1000 ml of *cool* LB broth. Swirl to mix. Store at 4°C (3 months).

Maltose
Maltose, an inducer of the gene *(lamB)* that codes for the bacteriophage A receptor, is often added to the medium during growth of bacteria that are to be used for plating bacteriophage ë. Add 1 ml of a sterile 20% maltose solution for every 100 ml of medium.

Make up a sterile 20% stock solution of maltose as follows:

maltose 20 g
H_2O to 100 ml

Sterilize the solution by filtration through a 0.22-micron filter. Store the sterile solution at room temperature.

M9 *Minimal* medium
Per liter:

To 750 ml of sterile deionized H_2O (cooled to 50°C or less), add:

5× M9 salts	200 ml
sterile deionized H_2O to 1 liter	
1 M $MgSO_4$	2 ml
20% solution of the appropriate carbon source (e.g., 20% glucose)	20 ml
1 M $CaCl_2$	0.1 ml

If necessary, supplement the M9 medium with stock solutions of the appropriate amino acids.

5 × M9 salts are made by dissolving the following salts in deionized H_2O to a final volume of 1 liter:

$Na_2HPO_47H_2O$	64 g
KH_2PO_4	15 g
NaCl	2.5 g
NH_4Cl	5.0 g

The salt solution is divided into 200-ml aliquots and sterilized by autoclaving for 15 minutes at 15 psi on liquid cycle.

Note: The $MgSO_4$ and $CaCl_2$ solutions should be prepared separately, sterilized by autoclaving, and added after diluting the 5x M9 salts to 1 liter with sterile deionized H_2O. Glucose should be sterilized by filtration before it is added to the diluted M9 salts.

NZCYM medium
To 950 ml of deionized H_2O, add:

NZ amine	10 g
NaCl	5 g
Bacto yeast extract	5 g
casamino acids	1 g
$MgSO_47H_2O$	2 g

Shake until the solutes have dissolved. Adjust the pH to 7.0 with 5 N NaOH (~0.2 ml). Adjust the volume of the solution to 1 liter with deionized H_2O. Sterilize by autoclaving for 20 minutes at 15 psi on liquid cycle.

NZ amine: Casein hydrolysate enzymatic.

***NZYM* medium**
NZYM medium is identical to NZCYM medium, except that casamino acids are omitted.

NZM medium
NZM medium is identical to NZYM medium, except that Bacto yeast extract is omitted.

SM
This buffer is used for storage and dilution of bacteriophage A stocks.

NaCl	5.8 g Per liter
$MgSO_47H_2O$	2 g Per liter
1 M Tris-HCl (pH 7.5)	50 ml Per liter
2% gelatin solution	5 ml Per liter
H_2O	1 liter

Sterilize the buffer by autoclaving for 20 minutes at 15 psi on liquid cycle. After the solution has cooled, dispense 50-ml aliquots into sterile containers. SM may be stored indefinitely at room temperature.

Note: A 2% gelatin solution is made by adding 2 g of gelatin to a total volume of 100 ml of H_2O and autoclaving the solution for 15 minutes at 15 psi on liquid cycle.

SOB medium
To 950 ml of deionized H_2O, add:

Bacto tryptone	20 g
Bacto yeasfextract	5 g
NaCl	0.5 g

Shake until the solutes have dissolved. Add 10 ml of a 250 mM solution of KCl. (This solution is made by dissolving 1.86 g of KCl in 100 ml of deionized H_2O.) Adjust the pH to 7.0 with 5 N

NaOH (~0.2 ml). Adjust the volume of the solution to 1 liter with deionized H_2O. Sterilize by autoclaving for 20 minutes at 15 psi on liquid cycle. Just before use, add 5 ml of a sterile solution of 2 M $MgCl_2$. (This solution is made by dissolving 19 g of $MgCl_2$ in 90 ml of deionized H2O. Adjust the volume of the solution to 100 ml with deionized H_2O and sterilize by autoclaving for 20 minutes at 15 psi on liquid cycle.

SOC medium

SOC medium is identical to SOB medium, except that it contains 20 mM glucose. After the SOB medium has been autoclaved, allow it to cool to 60°C or less and then add 20 ml of a sterile 1 M solution of glucose. (This solution is made by dissolving 18 g of glucose in 90 ml of deionized H_2O. After the sugar has dissolved, adjust the volume of the solution to 100 ml with deionized H_2O and sterilize by filtration through a 0.22-micron filter.)

Terrific broth

To 900 ml of H_2O, add:

Bacto tryptone	12 g
Bacto yeast extract	24 g
Glycerol	4 ml

Allow the solution to cool to 60°C or less, and then add 100 ml of a sterile solution of 0.17 M KH_2PO_4, 0.72 M K_2HPO_4. (This solution is made by dissolving 2.31 g of KH_2PO_4 and 12.54 g of K_2HPO_4 in 90 ml of H_2O. After the salts have dissolved, adjust the volume of the solution to 100 ml with H_2O and sterilize by autoclaving for 20 minutes at 15 psi on liquid cycle.)

TM

Per liter:

1 M Tris-HCl (pH 7.5)	50 ml
$MgSO_4 7H_2O$	2 g
H_2O to 1 liter	

Sterilize the buffer by autoclaving for 20 minutes at 15 psi on liquid cycle. After the solution has cooled, dispense 50-ml aliquots into sterile containers. TM may be stored indefinitely at room temperature.

2x YT medium

Combine the following in 0.9 liter of H_2O:

Bacto tryptone	16 g
Bacto yeast extract	109
NaCl	5 g

Adjust the pH to 7.0 with 1 N NaOH (-1 ml) if desired. Adjust the final volume to 1 liter with H_2O.

Note: For agar plates, include 12 g of Bacto agar per liter. For top agar, include 7 g of Bacto agar per liter.

Agar medium for plating bacteria

Prepare liquid media according to the recipes given above. Just before auto claving, add one of the following:

Bacto agar (for plates)	15 g/liter
Bacto agar (for top agar)	7 g/liter
agarose (for plates)	15 g/liter
agarose (for top agarose)	7 g/liter

Sterilize by autoclaving for 20 minutes at 15 psi on liquid cycle. When the medium is removed from the autoclave, swirl it gently to distribute the melted agar or agarose evenly throughout the solution. Be careful! The fluid may be superheated and may boil over when swirled. Allow the medium to cool to 50°C before adding thermolabile substances (e.g., antibiotics). To avoid producing air bubbles, mix the medium by swirling. Plates can then be poured directly from the flask; allow about 30-35 ml of medium per 90-mm plate. To remove bubbles from medium in the plate, flame the surface of the medium with a bunsen burner before the agar or agarose hardens. Set up a color code (e.g., two red stripes for LB-ampicillin plates; one black stripe for LB plates, etc.) and mark the edges of the plates with the appropriate colored markers.

When the medium has hardened completely, invert the plates and store them at 4°C until needed. The plates should be removed from storage 1-2 hours before they are used. If the plates are fresh, they will "sweat" when incubated at 37°C. This allows bacterial colonies or bacteriophage plaques to spread across the surfaces of the plates and increases the chances of cross-contamination. This problem can be avoided by wiping off any condensation from the lids of the plates and then incubating the plates for several hours at 37°C in an inverted position before they are used. Alternatively, the liquid can be removed by shaking the lid with a single, quick motion. To minimize

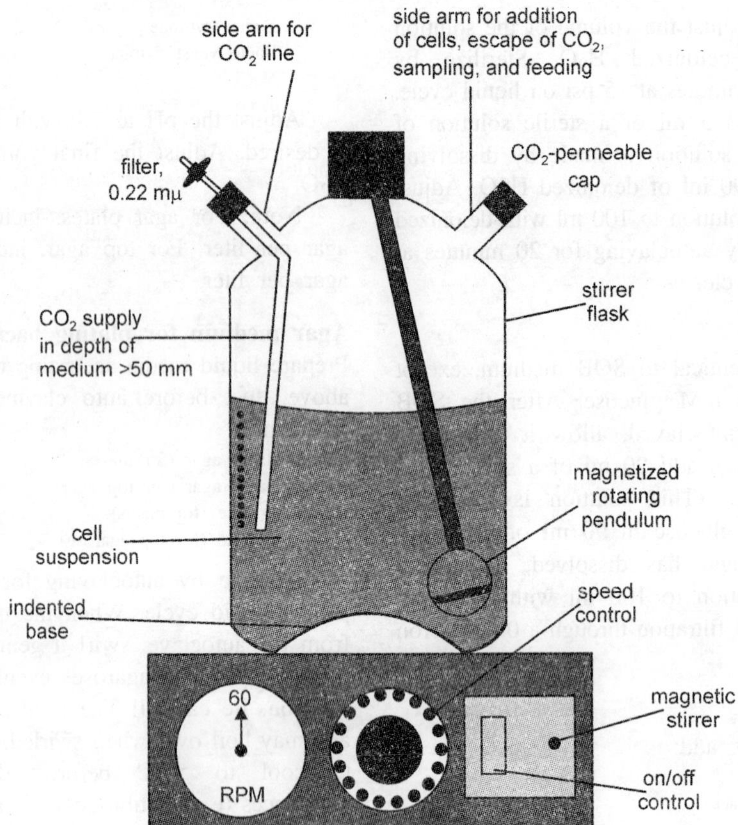

Fig. 3. Cross-sectional diagram of a stirrer vessel on a magnetic stirrer. The side arm at top right is used to add cell suspension and collect samples; it has a permeable cap to allow escape of CO_2. Filtered CO_2 in air is supplied via a filter to the side arm at top left; it is required if the depth of the culture medium exceeds 50 mm. Agitation is achieved by a magnet, enclosed in a glass pendulum, and is driven by the magnetic stirrer at 60rpm.

the possibility of contamination, hold the open plate in an inverted position while removing the liquid from the lid.

Adding antibiotic

Antibiotic is usually added to plates prior to pouring. In a pinch, antibiotic-containing plates can be quickly made by evenly spreading 200 111 of 10 mg/ml antibiotic on the surface of an **LB agar plate**. Allow the antibiotic to absorb into agar for 10-20 minutes before using. Outdated antibiotic plates can be refurbished in this manner.

Directions for the preparation of stock solutions of antibiotics are provided in Section 1 of this book.

Histotypic culture

It is possible to create the cell-cell interactions by growing, cell cultures to high densities. This can be achieved in several ways for example by growing cells in **filter well insert**, by growing cells as stirred aggregates known as **spheroids** on agar or agarose in a multiwell plate or growing cells on the outer surface of perfused microcapillary bundles where the cells are seeded in the outer chamber holding the hollow fibres and medium is pumped through the fibres from a reservoir.

Organotypic culture

When two or more different cell types are cocultivated, the process is known as organotypic culture. Culture of **skin** cells is a classic example of organotypic culture. For example, epidermal epithelium can be maintained in coculture with dermal fibroblasts embedded in collagen. The requirement for **collagen** is similar to many specialized culture which require elements of the extracellular matrix such as collagen, laminin, fibronectin for proliferation and differentiation.

Monolayer and suspension cultures

Some cells will grow readily in suspension, either spontaneously (**murine ascite tumors**) or by mechanical stirring (**e.g., HeLa cells**). Suspension cultures can be propagated in large bulk without elaborate mechanisms for increasing the surface area. Gas exchange is improved when the depth of the medium exceeds 50 mm by sparging the medium with a mixture of 5% CO_2 in air.

There are a few advantages in using suspension cultures. They can be scaled up easily, deliver a large bulk of cells at one time and do not need trypsin for harvesting the cells from the culture. They can be maintained in a steady state of growth by regulating the cell proliferation and by withdrawl of surplus cells. Such cultures are called as **biostats or vivostats**.

Culture vessels

Cell cultures are usually grown in disposable plastic flasks, petri dishes, or multiwell plates that have been treated with plasma discharge or some similar process to create a net negative charge on the surface of the flask. Flasks are preferable for long term propagation, dishes for cloning and multiwell plates for replicate sampling. Where a large number of cells are required (1×10^9), roller bottles or **multisurface propagators** are required for attached cells and large fermenters for suspension grown cells.

Electrofusion

Electrofusion is an alternative method for protoplast fusion that involves two steps. In the first, protoplasts are placed in a medium of low conductivity between two electrodes (platinum wires arranged in parallel on a microscope slide). A high frequency alternating field (0·5 to 1·5 MHz) is applied between the electrodes, which cause the protoplasts to align in a process known as **dielectrophoresis**. In the second step, one or more short (10–200 μs) direct current pulses (of 1–3 kV cm^{-1}) are applied, which cause pores to form in the membranes of protoplasts and allow fusion to take place where there is close membrane contact. This technique allows a higher degree of control over the fusion process than chemical methods do and consequently is becoming more widely used.

Fusion is a random process and the result of a fusion treatment can be a mixture of unused homokaryon parental protoplasts, fused homokaryons and fused heterokaryons. Following fusion, heterokaryons containing nuclei of both species in a common (mixed) cytoplasm regenerate a new wall. Nuclear fusion, if achieved will result in a somatic hybrid cell which must be totipotent, if hybrid whole plants are to be produced. Various techniques have been devised for identification and recovery of somatic hybrids, which are frequently based on complementation of biochemical mutants. Morphologically distinct or fluorescently labelled protoplasts can also be identified under an inverted microscope and removed with micromanipulation. Fluorescence activated cell sorting methods may also be used for separating different protoplast populations.

Protoplasts were used for early genetic transformation experiments because of the relative ease of infection with *Agrobacterium tumefaciens*. In this case, sterile protoplasts were suspended at 25°C in a buffered plasmid preparation (concentration 10 μg poly-L-ornithine cm^{-3}. After incubation, which is conducted under vaccum, protoplasts are washed and plated onto an appropriate selection medium. Protoplasts may also be transformed using direct DNA injection either by electroporation, or by liposome invasion or by bombardment.

The proliferation of animal cells in culture has many applications including their use as model systems for biochemical, physiological and pharmacological studies and the production of growth factors, blood factors, monoclonal antibodies, interferons, enzymes, vaccines and hormones. A

Table 3. **Some applications of plant cell and tissue culture.**

System	Process investigated
Protoplasts	
Nicotiana tabacum	Cell wall regenerations; clonal propagation of mutant plants; interspecific hybrids; uptake of Rhizobium; homologous and heterologous gene expression.
Solanum tuberosum	Somaclonal variation in cultivar *Russet burbank*; genetic transformation using Ti plasmid; transformation by cocultivation of protoplasts with isolated *Agrobacterium tumefaciens* cells; direct protoplast transformation.
Arabidopsis thaliana	Intergeneric hybridization, model for molecular biological investigations.
Glycine max	Isolation of viable bacterioids from root nodule protoplasts, molecular model for investigating nitrogen fixation.
Cell suspensions	
Acer pseudoplatanus	Control of cell division and expansion in single cells, batch and continuous cultures, with monitoring of associated biochemical changes.
Daucus carota	Somatic embryogenesis in higher plants
Nicotiana tabacum	Industrial fermentation of biomass for tobacco industry; ubiquinone production; selection, regeneration and sexual transmission in regenerates resistant to the herbicide pidoram
Digitalis purpurca	Biotransformation of digitoxin in digoxin
Catharanthus roscus	Ajmaladne and serpentine production
Lithosphermum crythrorhizon	Commercial shikonin
Callus	
Phasecolus vulgaris	Physiology and biochemistry of differentiation *Vicca faba* Cytogenetic studies indicating chromosome instability
Elaeis guinensis	Cloning of oil palm plantlets and crop improvement *Solanum tuberosum* Somaclonal variation
Nicotiana tabacum	Shoot regeneration following exposure to electric currents
Anther and microspores	
Brassica napus	Embryogenesis from cultured microspores
Vitis vinifera	Transformation and regeneration of grapevine
Nodal stem segments	
Baciopa monnicra	Micropropagation of a medicinal plant
Embryos	
Papaver somniferum	Plant breeding; direct pollination of excised ovules to overcome prezygotic barriers to fertility
Hordeun vulgare	Production of mutants resistant to lysine analogues
Meristem	
Solannum tuberosum	Elimination of potato virus X by thermotherapy followed by plantlet regeneration
Chrysanthemum morifolium	Breeding of radiation induced mutants
Leaf discs	
Brassica napus	Transformation using *A. tumerfaciens* of glyphosphate resistance genes
Lycopersicum esculentum	Transformation using *A. tumerfaciens* of antisene genes to inhibit fruit ripening

brief outline of some of the specific uses of particular animal cell and tissue cultures is given in table 5.

Ames Test

The Ames test *(Salmonella typhimurium* reverse mutation assay) is a bacterial short-term test for identification of carcinogens using mutagenicity in bacteria as an endpoint. It includes mammalian metabolism to activate promutagens. A high but not complete correlation has been found between carcinogenicity in animals and mutagenicity in the Ames test. The latter detects mutations in a gene of a histidine-requiring bacterial strain that produces a histidine-independent strain. The Ames test is one of the most frequently applied tests in toxicology. Almost all new pharmaceutical substances and chemicals used in industry are tested by this assay. The Ames test is named after Bruce N. Ames, University of California, Berkeley, who developed this mutagenicity test.

Table 4. **Strengths and weaknesses of animal cell and tissue culture.**

Strengths

Range of cell types in culture is now very large including genetically defined clones. Ready availability of media, cells and culture vessels from commercial suppliers. Methods for isolation of primary cells and storage of cell lines is now well documented. Viability and physiology of tissue is easily monitored.

Increased control of environmental variables, e.g. temperature, pH, medium constituents. Ease of application of test compound with improved tissue specificity and easier recovery of metabolites.

Large scale replication of experiments may be performed readily in small space and short time.

Scale of experimentation in model system is from single cell to organ.

Scale up offers scope for biotechnology.

Reduction of animals killed for experimentation/bioproducts processing e.g. in cytotoxicity testing and antibody production.

High batch to batch consistency when compared with sources for isolation of serum proteins.

Weakness

Method may be considered to be too specialized and laborious for routine use.

Resources needed are expensive, e.g. fetal calf serum.

Lack of *in vitro.*

Table 5. **Some applications of animal cell and tissue culture.**

Baby hamster kidney (BHK) cells	Large scale production of foot and mouth vaccines WI38 (ex human embryo lung tissue) Production of rubella vaccine
Simian kidney epithelial cells	Production of polio vaccines
Murine lymphoblastoid cells	Production of histocompatibility (H-2^K) and differentiation specific (Thyol) antigens
Myeloma cell lines	Production of monoclonal antibodies
T-helper cells	Production of lymphokines
Leukocytes	Production of α-interferon
Diploid fibroblasts	Production of β-interferon
B or T lymphocytes	γ-interferon
Procine kidney cells	Production of urokinase

Principle and Tester Strains

Several histidine-requiring bacterial strains of *Salmonella typhimurium* are used for mutagenicity testing. Each tester strain contains a different type of mutation in the histidine operon (Table 6). Because of this mutation, the tester strain is not able to form colonies on agar without or with only very low histidine content. If a mutation is induced in this histidine requiring strain that generates a histidine-independent strain, for instance by restoration of the wild-type gene (Figure 6), it will gain the ability to form colonies also on minimal agar. Since a mutation restores the histidine-independent wild-type phenotype, the Ames test is classified as a "reverse" mutation assay.

Approximately 109 bacteria are incubated with a single concentration of a test substance. Although the probability for reversion to the wild-type is extremely low for a single bacterium, the extremely high **number** of exposed bacteria results in a high probability that a mutagen will cause a reverse mutation to the histidine prototroph.

Some mutagens induce exclusively specific types of mutations that can be classified as base exchange and frameshift mutations. The set of *tester* strains shown in Table 6 includes different mutations in the histidine operon that combined are able to detect most (probably >85 %) of all genotoxic carcinogens. In order to increase their ability to detect mutagens, the Ames *tester* strains also contain other mutations. One mutation *(rfa)* causes partial loss of the lipopolysaccharide barrier. As a consequence, the permeability of the cell wall to large molecules is increased. Another advantage of *rfa* is that this mutation leads to completely nonpathogenic bacteria. *UvrB* indicates a deletion of a gene required for DNA excision repair, resulting in increased sensitivity in detection of many carcinogens. The deletion excising the *uvrB* gene extends also through the gene required for biotin synthesis. Thus, they also require biotin for growth. Some **tester** strains (TA98,

Table 6. **Genotypes of commonly used *Salmonella typhimurium* tester strains.**

Strain	*Mutation*	Lipopolysaccharide *barrier*	*DNA* repair		Resistance	
			uvrB	pKM101	*Ampicillin*	*Tetracycline*
TA 98	Frameshift in *hisD3052*	*rfa*	-	+	R	S
TA 100	Base substitution in *hisG46*	*rfa*	-	+	R	S
TA 102	Base substitution in *hisG428*	*rfa*	+	+	R	R
TA 1535	Base substitution in *hisG46*	*rfa*	-	-	S	S
TA 1537	Frameshift in *hisC3076*	*rfa*	-	-	S	S

[a]All strains were originally derived from *Salmonella typhimurium* LT2. *hisD3052,* mutation in the *hisD* gene coding for histidinol dehydrogenase; hisG46, mutation in the hisG gene coding for the first step in histidine biosynthesis; *hisG428,* TA 102 contains A-T base pairs at the site of the mutation in *hisG* in contrast to TA 100 and TA 1535 that contain G-C base pairs at the site of mutation; *rfa,* mutation that causes a strong reduction in the lipopolysaccharide layer; *uvrB,* a gene involved in DNA excision repair; pKM 101, plasmid that increases chemically induced and spontaneous mutagenesis by enhancement of error-prone DNA repair; R, resistant; 5, sensitive.

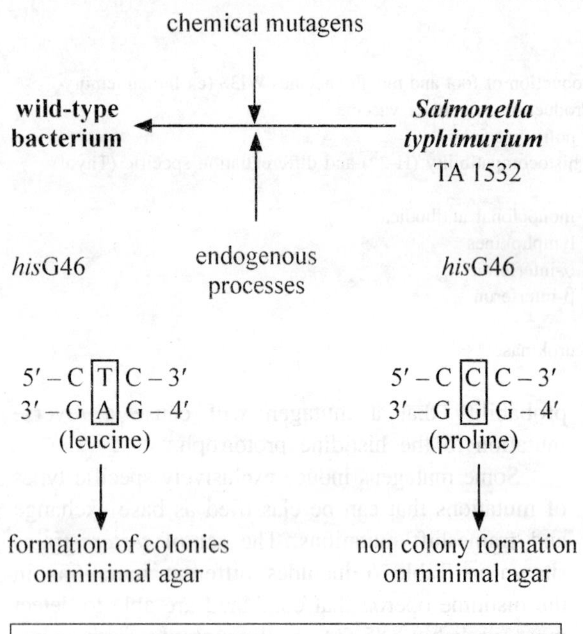

Fig. 4. Genetic basis of the Ames test shown for test strain *Salmonella typhimurium* TA 1535. TA 1535 carries an A to G point mutation compared with the wild-type bacterium. This point mutation causes an amino acid exchange (leucine versus proline) in the histidine operon (*hisG46*). As a consequence, TA 1535 is not able to perform histidine biosynthesis., A G to A point mutation restores the wild-type gene and produces a bacterium that is able to form a colony also on minimal agar, containing only very small concentrations of histidine.

TA1OO, TA1O2) contain the plasmid pKM101, which confers ampicillin resistance and increases the sensitivity to mutagens by enhancement of error-prone DNA repair. Bacteria lack most of the enzymes required for the activation of promutagens to mammalian carcinogens. A metabolically active fraction of mammalian liver homogenate is therefore added in the Ames test.

Specific Techniques

Two versions of the Ames test are usually applied (Figure 5): the plate incorporation assay, where bacteria and test substance are mixed and immediately given onto the agar, and the preincubation assay, where bacteria and test substance are incubated for 1 h at37°C before plating them on agar (Fig. 5). The preincubation version is more sensitive for some compounds, but also more laborious. In toxicological routine, a negative result in the plate incorporation assay has to be confirmed in a second series; the first may be a plate incorporate, the second a preincubation assay. Recently, a new version of the Ames test, 'Ames II, has been developed as a microwell fluctuation test in contrast' to the standard plate or preincubation test. Ames II allows automated, high-throughput screening, requiring only very small amounts of test substance.

Metabolizing System: Rat Liver S9 Mix

Since most carcinogens are not carcinogenic directly, but are active only after metabolism, the compounds are tested in the Ames test in the presence of a mammalian metabolizing system as well as directly. The 9000 supernatant fraction ('S9'; see **Figure 6**) of liver homogenate from rats treated with substances causing a strong induction of many xenobiotic metabolizing enzymes (e.g., Aroclor 1254 or a

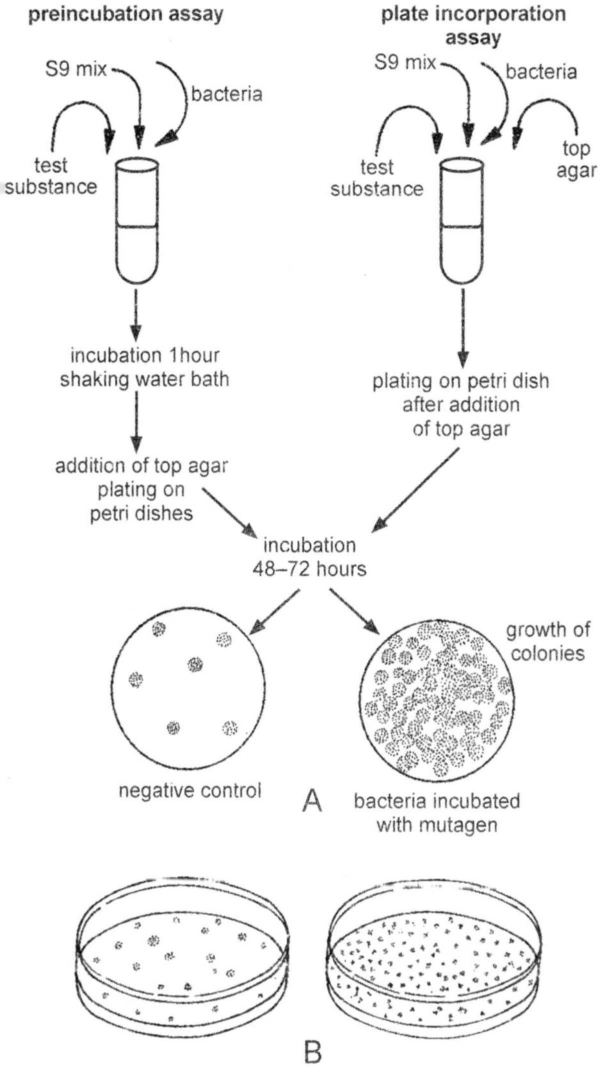

Fig. 5. (A) Ames test procedure. All incubations are performed with and without addition of rat liver 59 mix (see Figure 3). (B) A typical result of an Ames test with tester strain TA 98 without 59 mix. Only a small number of revertants can be observed in the solvent control (left side). Colonies on control dishes are a consequence of spontaneous mutations due to endogenous processes, such as generation of reactive oxygen species and physical instability of DNA. Addition of a mutagen, such as 10 ìg benzo [a] pyrene-4,S-oxide per plate dramatically increases the number of revertants (right side).

combination of naphthoflavone and phenobarbital) in combination with an NADPH-generating system have been shown to be very favorable for activation. NADPH is required because it represents a cofactor for cytochrome P450-dependent monooxygenase activity. Liver S9 is highly active in carcinogen metabolism, since the liver represents the most important organ for the metabolism of most foreign compounds.

Guidelines for Interpretation of Ames Test Data

There are several criteria for determining a positive result, including a reproducible increase in the number of revertants or a dose-related increase in mutations. A positive result in the Ames test will usually initiate additional investigations by other mutagenicity assays including also mammalian cells. If the positive result is confirmed, most pharmaceutical companies will terminate further development of a drug. However, an Ames-positive substance is not necessarily harmful to humans. Although the Ames test is a useful tool in screening for potential carcinogens, often false-positive results are obtained. It is generally accepted that a substance may be used clinically even if the Ames test is positive, when the positive effect is due to a mechanism not relevant for humans and, ideally, if additional mutagenicity tests with mammalian cells *in vivo* and *in vitro,* tests for chromosomal aberrations, and animal carcinogenicity studies with two species were negative.

Mechanisms causing false-positive results may be: (1) differences between bacteria and mammalian cells concerning metabolism and DNA repair; (2) differences between rat and human liver, since rat liver S9 mix is used in the standard Ames test; and (3) differences between liver homogenate preparations such as S9 mix and intact hepatocytes. The latter is due to the loss of barrier effects in homogenate by destruction of the cell membrane and loss of phase II metabolizing enzymes owing to dilution of cofactors. Thus, one should bear in mind that the Ames test is an artificial system and does not necessarily reflect the *in vivo* situation. This is illustrated by the observation that the endogenous tripeptide glutathione and the amino acid cysteine both are positive in the Ames test under specific conditions (Glatt *et al.,* 1983).

Performance and interpretation of Ames test results have been standardized by international guidelines, such as those of the Organization for Economic Cooperation and Development (OECD

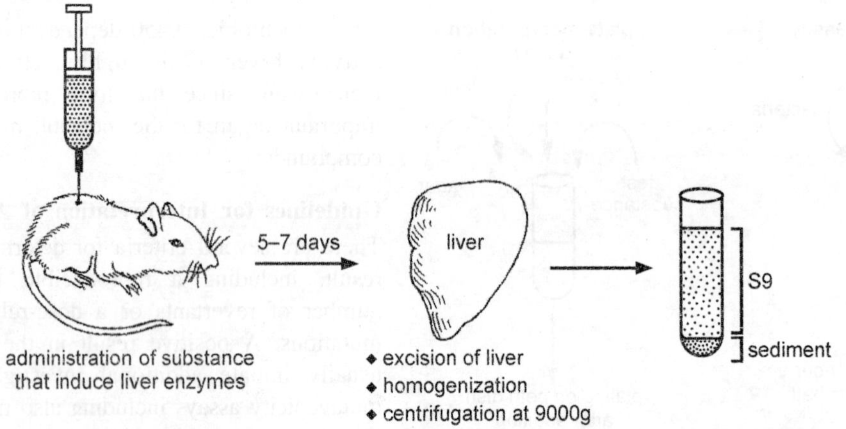

Fig. 6. Preparation of rat liver S9 mix. After centrifugation of liver homogenate at 9000, the supernatant (S9) is used as a metabolizing system in the Ames test. S9 contains microsomes and cytosol and therefore all microsomal and cytosolic xenobiotic metabolizing enzymes. In contrast, the sediment containing cell membranes and lysosomes is discarded. An NADPH (cofactor for cytochrome P450-dependent monooxygenase activity)-generating system is added to S9 to form the "S9 mix."

Guideline 471) and the International Conference on Harmonization (ICH).

Future Prospects

The Ames test is a sensitive tool in screening for potential genotoxic carcinogens. However, despite the high correlation, a positive result is difficult to interpret for the individual case in question, because a mutagen in the Ames test is not necessarily harmful to humans. These problems can be alleviated in future. It has been shown clearly that the use of intact cells instead of S9 mix improves the correlation between carcinogenicity and mutagenicity data (Dtesch *et al.,* 1987). Since cryopreserved human hepatocytes are now available, they can be used as a metabolizing system instead of rat S9 mix (Hengstler *et al.,* 2000). This gives a possibility to test whether a positive result in the standard rat S9 Ames test is also relevant to humans.

Flow Cytometry

Flow cytometry has been used to analyse microorganisms since the 1940s but the majority of the work has been done in the last 20 years. Early work was largely a proof-of-principle. The majority of flow cytometers even today are designed for the analysis of animal cells. Since animal cells are typically 10-15 μm in diameter and bacteria are ~1μm in diameter, bacteria are towards the lower detection threshold of many instruments. There are many examples in the literature of flow cytometry being used to detect target cells against a background of other cell types or particulates – for example detection of bacteria against a background of soil particles or detection of wild yeast against a background of commercial brewing strains of yeast. So What is flow cytometry? Well to break the term down, cytometry is a technique for making measurements on cells. These are the kind of measurements that you might be more familiar with doing via microscopy – in basic terms things like measuring the size of cells or making observations about the presence or absence of cellular characteristics such as uptake of a stain. At the measurement point the cells pass through a beam of light from a laser or a mercury arc lamp. When light interacts with cells several things can happen.

For the purposes of flow cytometry, there are 2 important types of interaction – **Light scattering** and **fluorescence**. In the simplest case the light can simply be reflected off the surface of the cell. When this happens the wavelength and energy of the light are unchanged. However the angle that the light travels is changed. When there is no cell present laser light travels in a straight line, when a cell or other particle is present some of the light is deflected. By placing detectors at specific angles around the measuring point the scattered light can be detected. Light scattered in the forward direction (i.e. only deflected slightly from the uninterrupted path of the laser) gives an indication of the size of the scattering particle. Light scattered at wider angles gives some information about cell structure or granularity but is generally more informative in animal or plant cells than in bacteria.

In the second case – fluorescence – light is absorbed by substances either on the cell surface or inside the cell. Some of the energy from that light is re-emitted via other means such as heat loss. The remainder is re-emitted as light. However because of the reduction in total energy emitted as light, there is also a wavelength shift so the emitted light is of a different wavelength i.e. a different colour to the laser light. This means that it can be separated by optical filters and quantified.

This is perhaps clearer if we look at the spectrum of light in the context of the electromagnetic spectrum. The visible spectrum fits in between the ultraviolet and infrared. Light energy is linked to its wavelength so short wavelength light such as UV or purple has a higher energy and a shorter wavelength than red or infrared radiation. When higher energy light such as UV, purple or blue light is put into a cell, some of the energy is lost as heat. The remainder is remitted as light a few nanoseconds later however due to energy loss it is moved to the right of this chart and so the wavelength will be longer. The emitted light will be redshifted and the difference between excitation wavelength and emission wavelength is known as the **Stokes shift**.

So to make flow cytometric measurements we need a method for delivering cells one at a time to the measuring point. At the measuring point we need to have optical components to illuminate the cells and to collect and quantify changes in the light due to scattering and/or fluorescence.

This is achieved by having a fluidic system that delivers the sample either via a pump, syringe or displacement by positive air pressure. The cell sample is carried inside a sheath fluid that acts to constrain the cells to the centre of the stream via a process known as hydrodynamic focusing – this ensures reproducible sample delivery. At the measurement point the cells pass through a beam of light from either a laser or an arc lamp. As discussed light will be scattered by the cell and in some cases autofluorescence from cellular pigments or fluorescence from added stains will also be produced. A series of optical filters will split the light into discrete bands. Dichroic filters are selective mirrors that let light longer than a specified wavelength through while reflecting shorter wavelength light. Bandpass filters allow light between a given upper and lower threshold through while preventing transmission of other wavelengths.

Advantages of Flow Cytometry

So what are the advantages of flow cytometry over these more conventional methods?

(1) The fluidics system of the flow cytometer delivers cells to the measuring point one at a time so data are collected for individual cells. This means that differences between members of a population can be observed giving us knowledge of the heterogeneity of the sample.

(2) Secondly the technique is very rapid. Typical instruments such as the research instruments that use make measurements at 100-500 cells per second. Specialised high-throughput instruments can make these measurements at 10000+ cells a second.

(3) Thirdly since very sensitive electronic detectors are used to measure the intensity of scattered light or fluorescence at a given wavelength, different intensities of light scattered fluorescence can be distinguished. By calibrating an instrument with samples of known size or fluorescent intensity, it is possible to obtain quantitative measurements.

(4) Fourth, flow cytometric measurements can be made on several different characteristics of each cell. Multiparametric measurements are useful because you can correlate the different characteristics and define subpopulations and/or distinguish between different cell types. Typical commercial flow cytometers allow 5-10 different parameters (e.g. size, protein content, DNA content, lipid content, antigenic properties, enzyme activity etc) to be collected for each cell, creating a multidimensional representation of a population.

(5) Finally, some specialised instruments (cell sorters) are able to physically separate cells on the basis of their properties. Cells may be bulk-sorted for biochemical analysis in order to gain an understanding of how different cohorts of cells vary with respect to a character of interest. Alternatively, in some instruments, individual cells can be sorted into microtitre plates or onto agar plates for recovery and growth. This has particular advantages in molecular biology for isolating mutants, and can be used in strain improvement programmes in industrial microbiology.

(6) Biochemical measurements on single cells to determine for example protein, lipid or nucleic acid content can be useful to determine subpopulations with different characteristics. With industrial strains producing products of commercial interest it is sometimes possible via autofluorescence or following appropriate staining, to identify cells in a population that produce an unusually high amount of product. This, coupled with cell sorting, has obvious commercial advantages.

(7) There is currently an increased interest in the detection of specific microorganisms in air samples collected in a variety of environments. This is because of the need for a system to detect potential biowarfare or bioterrorism attacks. FCM has been used to detect biowarfare agents and biowarfare simulants in the laboratory and during field trials. The most credible threat is usually considered to be anthrax. The reason for this is that the causative agent *Bacillus anthracis* forms spores which are resistant to UV, desiccation and heat and therefore suitably stable for dissemination in the environment. Spores can generally be distinguished from other microorganisms since fluorescent stains do not penetrate the spore coat effectively. Fluorescently-tagged antibodies can be used with FCM to identify target microorganisms in about 5 minutes. Detection and viability assays can be combined to determine the extent of any threat. The availability of portable flow cytometers that can be operated remotely is one possible method for biowarfare detection.

Stains

Certain dyes such as propidium iodide (PI) are normally prevented from entering the cell by the presence of an intact cell membrane. However when the cell dies the membrane will begin to deteriorate and the dye can enter. Therefore dead cells will be stained with the fluorescent dye while live ones will remain unstained.

Other dyes such as Rhodamine 123 are accumulated by live cells. This is an active process that can only be carried out by live cells. Therefore live cells will be more brightly fluorescent than dead ones.

A third class of dyes monitor metabolic activity. For instance fluorescein diacetate (FDA) is a non-fluorescent molecule that is taken up by cells. Esterase enzymes in the cell cleave the molecule releasing fluorescein which is fluorescent. So again live cells will be more fluorescent than dead cells.

Here are the results obtained by mixing live and dead yeast cells and staining with Propidium iodide.

On the x-axis from left to right we have increasing fluorescence, on the y axis we have the number of cells with a particular fluorescence value. There are two clear subpopulations.

In the case of live cells the membrane prevents the PI from entering the cell so the cells have very little fluorescence.

With dead cells PI can freely enter the cells due to membrane damage and so the cells are more fluorescent.

While I mentioned that FDA could be used to indicate viability, it can also be used as a gene reporter. The gene for the esterase enzyme can be introduced down-stream from a gene promoter of interest, enzyme activity then indicates that the gene is switched on. This means that heterogeneity of gene expression within a population can be monitored and thus flow cytometry has a growing role in molecular biology.

FCM in Microbiology

Another useful tool for the molecular biologist is the development of green fluorescent protein. This was originally isolated from the *Aequorea Victoria* jellyfish but has been manipulated for use as a gene reporter in microbial, plant and animal cells. The original protein has been modified by mutation to produce an enhanced, brighter variant and also to produce a range of proteins with different colours of fluorescence.

This means that the expression of several different genes can be monitored simultaneously in individual cells.

An alternative approach is to use dye-tracking technology to select novel strains. This has been done with the yeast *Saccharomyces cerevisiae* Mating parental strains and screening the hybrids produced is used to obtain strains with desirable industrial traits. However when the parental strains and the hybrids are all capable of growth on the same medium, separating the novel strains from the parental strains can be a problem. In the research laboratory the introduction of genetic markers (such as antibiotic resistance) is often used to enable separation of the hybrids from the parental strains. For instance resistance to antibiotic A is introduced to one strain and resistance to antibiotic B is introduced to the second strain. Only cells that have hybridised successfully will be able to grow on a medium containing both antibiotics. However the use of antibiotics in industrial processes is undesirable because they may affect fermentation performance. Also since yeast is often used in food manufacture it is obviously best to avoid the use of antibiotics and antibiotic-resistant strains. To overcome these problems Bell and colleagues used FCM combined with cell tracking dye technology. Following the loading of one parental strain with a green dye and the other with an orange dye, the yeast cells were mated and flow cytometry was performed. A small 1% subpopulation of the 2 million cells analysed were fluorescent at both green and orange wavelengths, indicating that mating had taken place. These cells could be separated from the parental population by cell sorting based on the dual-stained phenotype. When the isolated cells were cultured the cell tracking dyes were diluted out by cell division because at each division the dye is split between the 2 daughter cells. After a few generations the tracker dyes are diluted to extinction and thus have no lasting effect on the isolates.

So to conclude FCM is a very powerful technique with many advantages over conventional techniques. Most importantly heterogeneity of a cell population can be rapidly quantified. Generally speaking, if you can find a fluorescent stain that gives a signal that is correlated with the characteristic you are interested in then FCM can be used to measure it.

Important Questions

1. Describe suitable methods for the following :
   (i) Microbial cell culture, (ii) Plant cell culture, (iii) Animal cell culture.
2. Give a detailed account of the methods used for organ culture.
3. Describe the methods of mature organ culture with special reference to mammals.
4. Describe briefly the following:
   (i) Electrofusion, (ii) Culture vessels, (iii) Bioconversion, (iv) Ames test.
5. Discuss the advantages of flow cytometry.

3 Basic Requirements in a Biological Laboratory

As in all sciences, there is a need for basic equipment (instruments, tools, glassware and miscellaneous items) which should be present in any biological laboratory. Basic requirements of a laboratory for microscopic examination, isolation or culturing and identification of a microorganism, study their structure, function and application, and for routine analysis are listed below.

Instruments and Appliances

(1) Bunsen burner or spirit lamp
(2) Laminar flow safety hood
(3) Microscope and immersion oil
(4) Water bath
(5) Oven
(6) Incubators
(7) Refrigerator
(8) Autoclave
(9) Hotplate/Heater
(10) Tripod with asbestos mat
(11) Centrifuge
(12) pH meter
(13) Spectrophotometer
(14) Quebec colony counter
(15) Camera lucida
(16) Photomicrographic camera
(17) Balances

(18) Homogenizers for grinding of specimens
(19) Constant temperature water-bath

Tools

(1) Transfer needle
(2) Inoculating loop
(3) Dissecting needles
(4) Forceps
(5) Scissors
(6) Hemostat
(7) Ocular micrometer
(8) Stage micrometer
(9) Burette setup
(10) Thermometers

Glassware

(1) Petri dishes
(2) Conical flasks
(3) Culture tubes without screw caps
(4) Screw-capped tubes for media
(5) Durham fermentation tubes
(6) Beakers
(7) Funnels
(8) Graduated cylinders
(9) Graduated pipettes
(10) Capillary pipettes
(11) Dropper bottle for staining reagents
(12) Screw-capped bottles for stock reagents
(13) Glass microscope slides
(14) Depression (concave) slides
(15) Glass cover slips

Miscellaneous

(1) Culture media
(2) Test tube rack
(3) Cotton plugs
(4) Wooden sticks, with and without cotton swabs
(5) Rubber bulb for pipettes
(6) Stains and staining apparatuses
(7) Glass marking pen
(8) Tape for labels and for sealing plates
(9) Nail polish/wax for sealing microscope mounts
(10) Disinfectant
(11) Discard containers
(12) Facilities for disinfecting hands
(13) Distilled water
(14) Syringes and needles

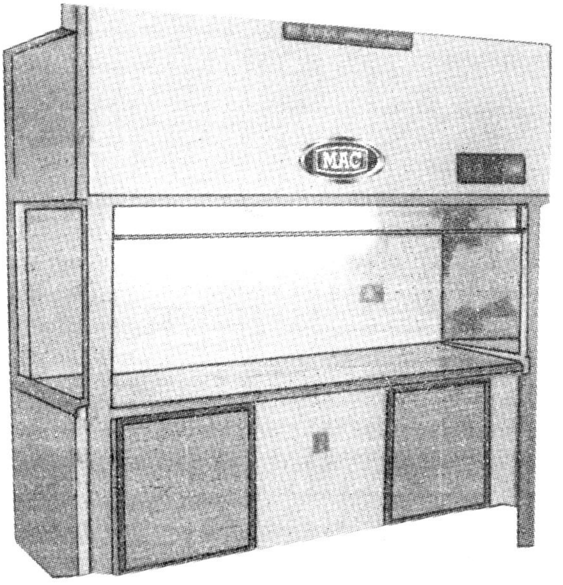

Fig. 1. Laminar flow hood.

(15) Butter paper
(16) Blotting paper and lens tissue
(17) Rubber bands
(18) Muslin/cheese cloth
(19) Pipette can
(20) Petri dish can
(21) Cotton or gauze masks

Instruments and applicances etc. have been described here in detail :

Bunsen burner

The **Bunsen burner** (named after R.W. Bunsen) is a type of gas burner with which a very hot, practically nonluminous flame, the temperature of which reaches 1,8700C at its hottest point, is obtained by allowing air to enter at the base and mix with the gas. The Bunsen burner or spirit lamp is used to sterilize inoculating loops/needles before they are inserted into cultures. It is also used for flaming the mouths of test tubes, media containing flasks and other glass apparatuses to avoid contamination by other microorganisms. Sterilization is done with dry heat. **Incineration** (sterilization procedure by which contaminated particles are burned to ashes) in a flame is perhaps the most rigorous of all heat treatments for sterilization. The materials are placed for a few seconds in a very hot (800°C) flame that results in complete sterilization.

Laminar Flow Hood

The **laminar flow hood** (Fig. 1) is used for reducing the danger of infection while working with infectious microorganisms and for preventing contamination of sterile materials. It works on the principle of application of **high-efficiency particulate air (HEPA) filters** (fiberglass filters) instead of **membrane filters** (membrane filters are thin pieces of synthetic material, usually cellulose acetate or polycarbonate, that contain very small openings or pores, so small that microbial cells cannot pass through them in air filtration. Room air is filtered before entering the working chamber and moves in a single direction.

Autoclave

The **autoclave** is an apparatus in which saturated steam under pressure effects sterilization (autoclaving). The pressure increases the boiling point of water, thereby increasing the temperature to which water can be heated (Table 1). Cells are destroyed by the higher temperature and not by the pressure. Most of the organisms are killed at 121°C (*i.e.* 151 b/in^2) in 15 minutes. Sterilization in an autoclave is done with saturated steam under pressure.

Saturated steam is the water vapour at the temperature at which it is produced. Tremendous amounts of heat energy are transferred from the steam to the object when saturated steam condenses on the surface of the cooler objects. **Saturated steam heats an object about 2500 times more efficiently than does hot air at the same temperature.** Autoclave is the most efficient and common instrument used for sterilizing solid and liquid media for microbial cultures, heat stable liquids-usually the common media ingredients, heat resistant instruments and equipment, glassware and rubber products. Scalpels and other sharp metal instruments are damaged by constant flaming and are usually sterilized by autoclaving. **Autoclaving is not recommended for oils, powders, heatsensitive fluids and plastics** (that melt).

Table 1. **Relationship between pressure and temperature of steam in an autoclave.**

Pressure in pounds per square inch (psi) (free flowing steam)	Temperature in °C
0	100·0
1	102·3
3	105·7
5	107·8
7	111·7
9	114·3
10	115·6
12	118·6
15	121·0
18	124·3
20	126·0
25	130·0
30	135·0

An autoclave is a double-walled cylindrical metallic vessel, made of thick stainless steel or copper, one end of which is open to receive the material to be sterilized. Autoclave lid is provided with pressure gauge for noting the pressure, steam cock (exhaust valve) for air exhaustion of the chamber. Autoclave is provided with controls for adjusting the pressure and temperature and a safety valve to avoid explosions. The articles to be sterilized are kept loosely in a basket, provided with holes all around, for the free circulation of the steam. To increase

Fig. 2. Autoclave.

the area for the materials to be sterilized, metallic separators, having holes can be used.

The **pressure cooker** is a suitable alternative to an autoclave. It is a closed vessel usually made of steel or aluminium in which sterilization is accomplished with saturated steam under pressure. The built pressure inside the vessel increases the temperature of water and vaporizes it to steam: at temperature above 100°C.

Oven

An **oven** is based on the principle where sterilization in accomplished by dry heat or hot air. Dry heat of a given temperature is not nearly as effective a sterilizing agent as moist heat of the same temperature, in other words, the sterilization process in an oven is longer than autoclaving. This is because sterilization by heat is primarily a process of coagulation of proteins and for protein coagulation to occur easily sufficient moisture must be present. Dry heat removes water from microorganisms while moist heat adds water to them. In addition, moist heat has greater penetrating power than dry heat.

Hot-air ovens are most commonly used for sterilizing glassware like petridishes, test tubes, pipettes metal instruments that can tolerate prolonged heat exposure, oils, powders, waxes and other articles that are either spoiled or not effectively sterilized by the moist heat of the autoclave. Sterilization is accomplished by exposure of items to 150°–180°C for 2 to 4 hours.

An oven consists of an insulated cabinet which is held at a constant temperature by means of an electric heating mechanism and thermostat. It is fitted with a fan to keep the hot air circulating at a constant temperature and thermometer for recording the temperature of the oven. For proper circulation of the hot air the shelves are perforated. For normal sterilization work, the oven should be operated at 160°C and most glassware will require a period of two hours for total sterilization. A schedule of time and temperature for sterilization with dry air is given in table 2.

An **incubator** is very similar to an oven in construction and consists of an insulated cabinet fitted with a heating element at the bottom. The temperature of the incubator is maintained at the desired level by an automatic device called thermostat which cuts the connection off when the temperature reaches the point for which the thermostat is set, and turns it on again when the temperature falls slightly below that point. The incubator is properly ventilated by the perforated shelves. They are provided with double doors, the inner one made of glass so that the contents of the incubator may be viewed without admitting outside air. An incubator is used for the **incubation** (culturing of microorganisms at a constant temperature favorable to the growth and development) of various microorganisms. Most incubators use dry heat for maintaining temperature. Moisture can be supplied by placing a beaker of water in it to retard dehydration of the medium, during the growth period of microorganisms. Some incubators are provided with fluorescent light arrangement to provide light to microorganisms which require light for sporulation and/or growth.

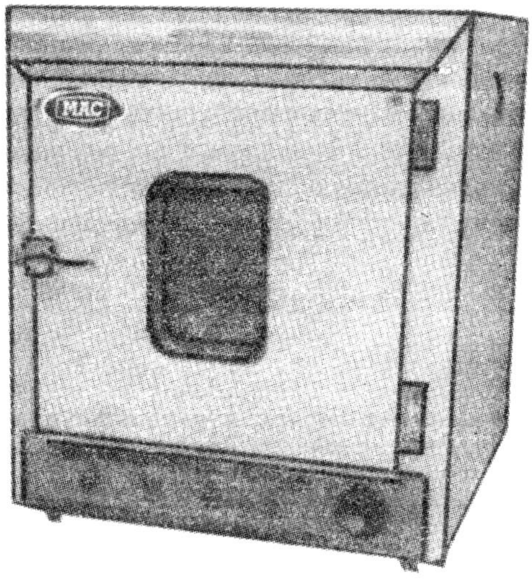

Fig. 3. Oven.

***Table 2.* Schedule of sterilization.**

Temperature (°C)	Time
120	480
140	180
150	150
160	120
170	60
180	20

Kjeldahl Apparatus

The Kjeldahl method was designed for the determination of the nitrogen content of a compound but may be used to determine the protein content of a sample provided that the proportion of nitrogen in the protein is known. Protein determinations are complicated by the presence of nitrogen from non-protein sources. The simplest way of eliminating this source of error is to precipitate the proteins using a suitable method and determine the nitrogen content of the precipitate.

All the nitrogen-containing compounds are oxidized to ammonia by heating the sample with concentrated sulphuric acid together with a catalyst, usually cupric ions although mercuric ions and metallic selenium have been used. Potassium or sodium sulphate is usually included to increase the boiling point of the mixture although excessive heating must be avoided to prevent decomposition of the ammonium sulphate. This digestion stage is important and usually takes several hours during which the sample initially turns brown or black and sulphur dioxide fumes are given off. The solution eventually clears and heating should be continued for about a further 2 hours.

The cooled mixture is transferred to a steam distillation flask and after making the mixture alkaline with excess sodium hydroxide the ammonia is distilled into a receiver flask (Fig. 4). Ammonia is trapped in a boric acid solution and the ammonium ions are titrated directly with a standard hydrochloric acid solution. Although boric acid is the most convenient, it is possible to trap the ammonia in a known volume of standard hydrochloric acid and back-titrate the residual acid with a sodium hydroxide solution. The advantage of the latter method is that the detection of the end-point of the titration (a strong acid and a strong base) is easier than that for the ammonium borate and hydrochloric acid titration.

The calculation is based on the fact that 1 atom of nitrogen will result in the formation of 1 mole of ammonia which will subsequently require 1 mole of acid. Hence:

$$1.0 \text{ mol HCl} = 14\text{g nitrogen}$$

If A ml of acid solution containing B mol^{-1} was required to neutralize the ammonia formed from

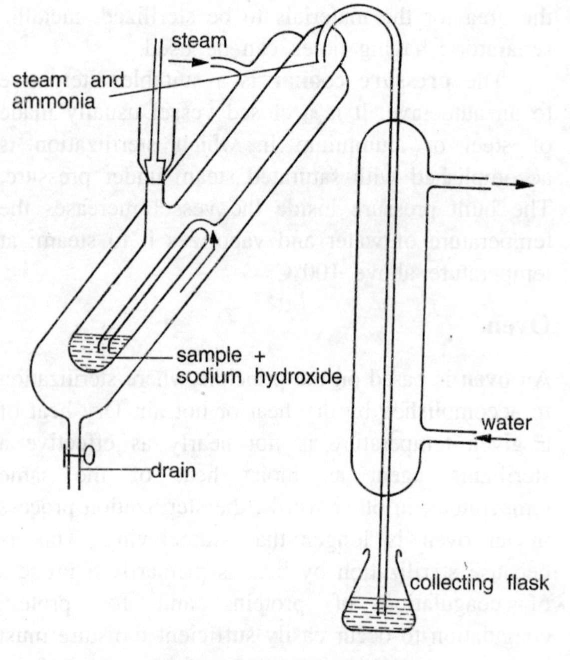

Fig. 4. Kjeldahl apparatus.

a given amount of sample the amount of nitrogen present in the sample was:

$$\frac{14}{1000} A \text{ x } B \text{ gram}$$

and the amount of protein from which this nitrogen was derived:

$$\frac{14}{1000} A \text{ x } B \text{ gram } \frac{100}{16} \text{ gram}$$

The Kjeldahl method is recognized as a reference method for protein quantitation and although tedious and cumbersome it is capable of a high level of precision, a coefficient of variation of less than 1% being feasible. It is also extremely accurate provided that the proportion of nitrogen in the protein sample is known and the complete recovery of nitrogen can be assured. This can be checked by recovery experiments and for most examples it is very high although care must be exercised during the digestion stage of the process.

Fermenter (Bioreactor)

Chin Weizmann with his associate in Great Britain during the first world war (1914–1918) developed a process for the production of acetone by deep

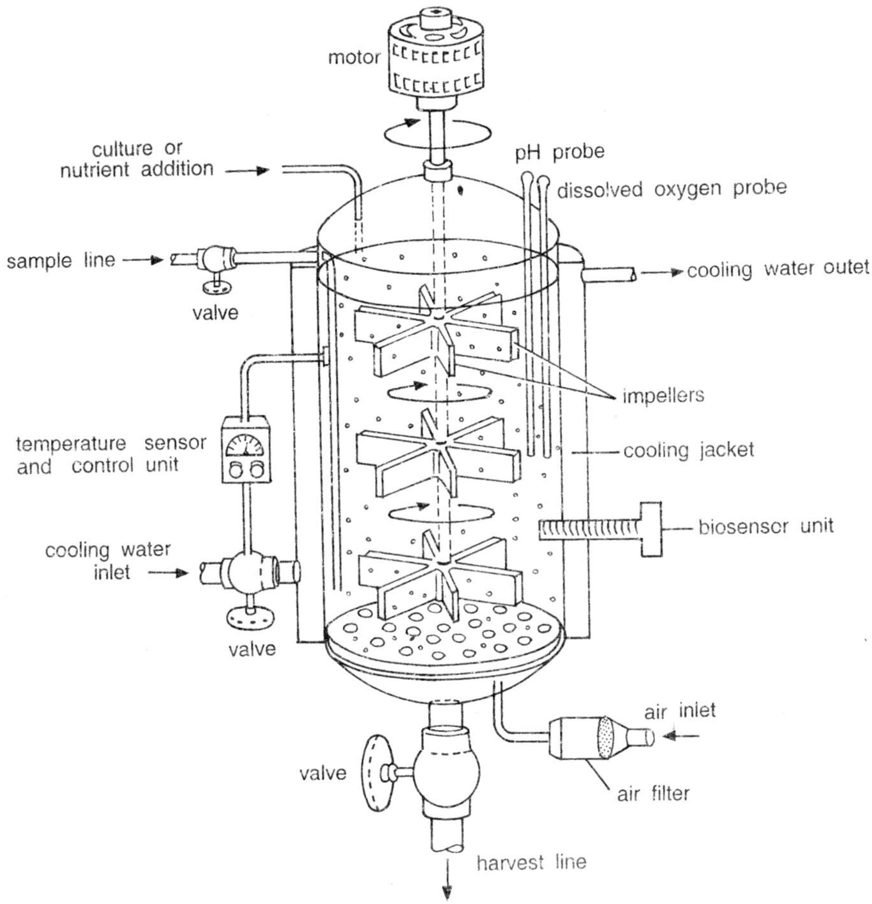

Fig. 5. A schematic diagram of an industrial fermenter for mass culturing of micrograniśms.

liquid fermentation using *Clostridium acetobutylicum.* This work led to the eventual use of first truly large scale aerobic fermenter in central Europe in 1930s for the production of compressed yeasts. The main function of a fermenter is to provide a controlled environment for the growth of microorganisms or animal cell, to obtain a desired product.

Fermenters, often referred to as stirred tank reactors are typically vertical, essentially closed, cylindrical steel vessels in which aerobic and anaerobic fermentations can be carried out either in batch culture or in continuous culture, for industrial use, especially in batch culture or in continuous culture. For industrial use, especially in pharmaceutical industry, the most versatile bioreactor (fermenter) is the simple stirred, aerobic fermenter for the culturing of microorganisms. These instruments are equipped to add nutrients and cultures, to remove product under aseptic conditions, and to aerate, stir and cool the mixture automatically (Fig. 5). Biosensors and infrared (near IR or Fourier transform) monitoring can provide real-time information on the course of fermentation. **Stirred fermenters** can range in size from 3 to 4 liters or larger, depending on production requirements. Fermenter for laboratory experiments range from 1 to 20 litre and are made of glass and stainless steel. For larger volume they are only made of stainless steel. Figure 4 illustrates the design of a typical large-scale stirred fermenter. Important features of fermenter design include provision for: (i) the vessel should be capable of being operated aseptically for a number of days and should be reliable in long term operations; (ii) a system of

Fig. 6. Constant temperature water bath.

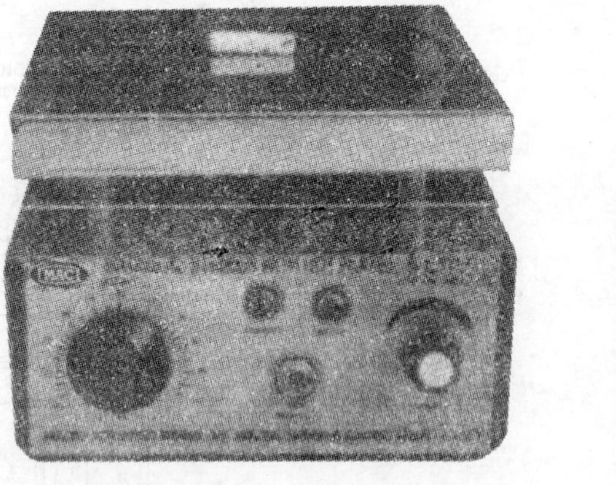

Fig. 7. Hot plate.

temperature control for adequate heat transfer from the culture; (iii) efficient mixing of the culture; (iv) efficient oxygen-to liquid transfer; (v) adaptability to a range of operating conditions; (vi) provided with a system of pH monitoring or control; (vii) suitable for a range of processes; and (viii) ease of scale-up from the laboratory or pilot stage to industrial use. These factors largely determine the economics of a fermentation and the type of a fermenter required for a particular purpose.

Constant Temperature Water Bath

A **constant temperature water bath** (Fig. 6) is an insulated metal maintains the temperature at the desired level. There are racks for holding test flasks. The bath is filled with water until it rises almost to the top of the racks. A glass beaker on a tripod and an asbestos with a source of heat beneath it can be used as a **water bath**.

Shaking Water-Bath

The **shaking water-bath** is a thermostatically controlled apparatus used for the cultivation of microorganisms in a broth medium. It is better than an incubator because it provides a rapid and uniform transfer of heat to the culture vessel and its agitation provides increased aeration, resulting in acceleration of growth and production of enzymes.

Hot Plate

The **hot plate stirrer** is an extremely useful aid in making media as well as to stir without heat to make suspensions. It is fitted with the stirrer and heat controls. Stirring is done by the creation of a magnetic field, which causes the bar magnet (Teflon coated) kept in the container to spin resulting in the stirring of the medium.

Quebec colony counter. The (Fig. 8) is an electronic apparatus used to count the number of colonies in a plate. A petri dish fits into the recess in the platform. The plates are counted on an

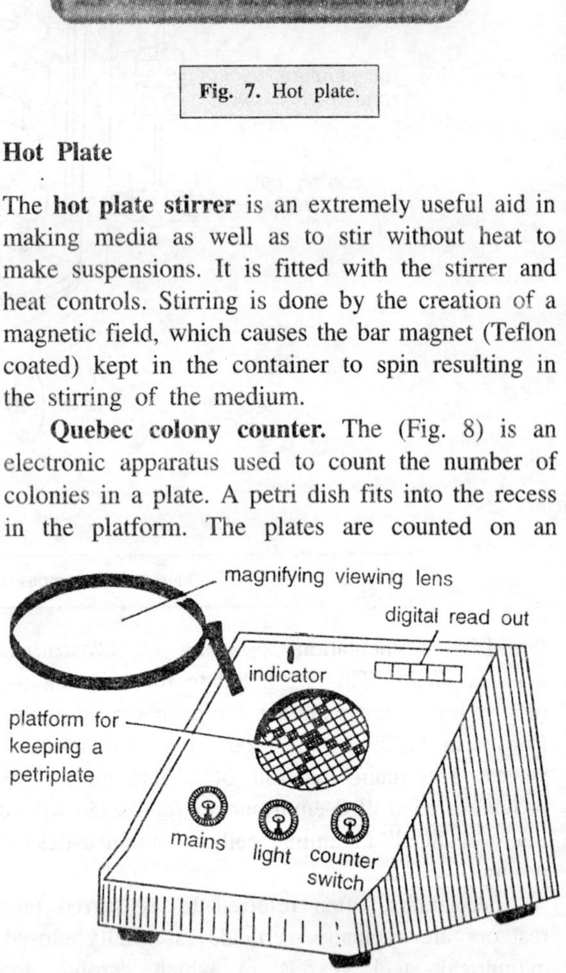

Fig. 8. Quebec colony counter used for counting the colonies of microorganisms.

illuminated screen, illuminated from beneath with a large magnifying lens which provides XI5 magnification.

The **refrigerator**, a basic requirement in a biology laboratory, is used for storing solutions, homogenates, samples and stock cultures of microorganisms at 4°C to save subculturing every few days. When cultures are stored at low temperatures, microorganisms are fairly inactive and will not suffer damage due to the evaporation of the medium. It is also used to store sterile media to prevent dehydration and to serve as a repository for thermolabile solutions, serums, antibiotics and biochemical reagents.

Fig. 9. Centrifuge.

Centrifuge

The **centrifuge** is an apparatus that rotates at high speed and separates substances/particles on the basis of mass and density by means of centrifugal force. The centrifugal force is noted in **revolutions per minute** (rpm) of angular speed. A centrifugal force is noted in revolutions per minute revolved by an upright motor. Generally four metal cups/containers are attached to the head for holding tubes or other containers of the material from which the particulate matter is to be separated. During centrifugation, liquid containing particulate matter is kept in the tubes, runs at a particular speed and when centrifugation is completes, the particulate matter gets settled at the bottom of the tubes (Fig. 9). Various types of centrifuge commonly used are **low-speed (clinical centrifuge)**, **high-speed** or **super-speed** and **ultracentrifuges**. The highest speed limit of low-speed, high speed and ultracentrifuges are 5000 rpm, 18000 rpm and 20000 to 60000 rpm respectively. These are used for separation of particles dispersed in a suspended matter, separation of mixtures of liquids varying in their density or solids from liquids or concentrating microorganisms in various samples for enzymatic studies (see chapter-7).

Spectrophotometer

A **spectrophotometer** (Fig. 10) or colorimeter is an instrument used for counting population of bacteria, based on the principle of turbidity determination. Turbidity or optical density is the cloudiness of the suspension or a solution. The more turbid a suspension, the less light will be transmitted through it. In other words, the amount of light absorbed and scattered is proportional to the mass of cells in the light path. As bacteria grow in a broth, the clear broth becomes turbid. Since the turbidity increases as the number of cells increase, this observation is used as an indicator of bacterial density in the broth. Turbidity is also useful for standardizing the population densities of bacterial cultures of clinical significance.

pH Meter

The **pH meter** (Fig. 11) is used to determine the pH (acidity or alkalinity of a solution) of solutions of unknown pH as well as for setting of pH of various media used for the cultivation and testing biochemical activities of microorganisms. pH is expressed as a number from 0 to 14. **The number is an expression of the concentration of hydrogen ions (^+H) in the solution – the higher the concentration the more acidic the solution.** The value is the negative exponent of the $H^+ = 0.000001$ (10^{-6}) M, the pH is 6. Pure water has a pH of 7 (i.e. neutral). pH values less than 7 indicate increasing acidity whereas values above 7 indicate increasing alkalinity. Growth and the survival of microorganisms is greatly influenced by the pH of the environment and all organisms differ as to their requirements. The specific range for bacteria is between 4 to 9 with the optimum being 6.5 to 7.5. Fungi prefer an acidic environment with optimum being 4 to 6.

Fig. 10. Spectrophotometer.

The measurement of pH with pH meter is done electrometrically and the measurement of pH depends upon the development of a membrane potential by a glass electrode. The **glass electrode** (see chapter- 15) consists of an internal sealed tube with a metallic tip (typically of silver chloride) and an external tube that contains a standard solution. A pH sensitive glass bulb forms the immersion tip of the electrode. The potential of the glass electrode is proportional to the pH of the solution in which it is immersed. In addition to the glass electrode, a pH meter consists of another electrode, the **reference electrode**. The only purpose of this electrode is to complete the measuring circuit with a device that is not sensitive to any of the ions in the solution. The reference electrode consists of a metallic internal element-typically of mercury-mercurous chloride (calomel) or silver chloride-immersed in an electrolyte, usually a saturated solution of potassium chloride. The function of electrolyte is to form a conductive salt bridge between the metallic element and the sample solution in which the two electrodes are placed. To keep stable electrical communication between the internal metallic element and the sample solution, a liquid junction is present in the tip of the outer body of the reference electrode. This junction consists of an extremely small hole through which electrolyte solution streams continuously into the solution to be measured.

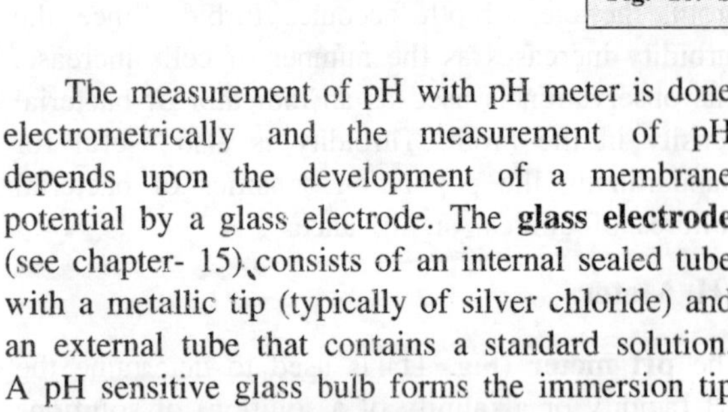

Fig. 11. pH meter.

The pH meter is equipped with a temperature-compensation circuit for introducing a known potential to balance out the potential caused by different sample temperatures. The instrument is also provided with a standardizing potential which is used to balance the circuit to indicate the correct pH of the standard used as a reference to measure the pH of a sample solution.

The procedure for the determination of pH with a simple laboratory pH meter is as follows.

(1) Set the temperature compensation dial to proper setting (i.e. room temperature or temperature of the solution).

(2) Immerse the two electrodes in a standard buffer solution of known pH (say pH 4.0).

(3) Using the standardization knob, set the meter reading to the proper pH i.e., 4.0).

(4) After these calibration steps, replace the buffer with the sample solution of unknown pH.

(5) Read the pH directly from the scale of the pH meter in millivolts or in pH units.

Photomicrographic camera (or photomicroscope)

A **photomicrographic camera** (or **photomicroscope**) is an assembly of a microscope having an illuminator and a camera for producing a photomicrograph. The **photomicrographs** (i.e. enlarged pictures/photographs of minute objects taken through a microscope) are of great value to biologists. This is taken by the application of the mechanism of photographic reproduction to the microscope. A photomicrograph affords more clarity and precision than an ordinary drawing by hand and gives an easily preserved visual record of microscopic findings and renders a wealth of microscopic material available for future study (Fig. 12).

The term **microphotograph** is at times incorrectly used for photomicrograph. The two terms are separate and should be distinguished. **Microphotograph means a small photograph the details of which can be seen clearly only with the help of optical enlargement**.

The **camera lucida** is an attachment of the microscope that enables one to draw clear-cut and simple, but exact outline sketches of objects seen under the microscope. Reflecting prism and a mirror are the two essential parts of a camera lucida. The *prism* surface is silvered except in a particular area in the center, which coincides in position with the ocular lens. The **mirror**, which is adjustable, is inclined at 45° both to the desk and prism. It is attached to the body tube of the microscope. The

Fig. 12. Photomicrographic apparatus.

formation of the image of the object results by the joint action of prism and the mirror. The light rays starting from an object are, deflected at 90° by the mirror and projects an image on the desk. When a sheet of paper is placed on the desk where the image falls, an outline is drawn with the help of a pencil point as the observer visualizes both the images of the object and the pencil point. **Magnification of the image formed on the sheet can also be drawn**, if the slide is replaced with the stage micrometer and the distance between the two points of known value (in μm) can be represented by a line.

Broths

The **broths** are used for growth and maintenance of cultures of bacteria. **Liquid media**, also called broths contain only nutrients dissolved in water. Microorganisms grow while submerged in water. **Nutrient broth** and **trypticase soy-broth** are the two commonly used media in microbiological laboratories: Broths are prepared by dispensing 5 ml. of the liquid medium (i.e. without agar) into each test tube, capped or plugged with plastic cap or cotton plug and autoclaved at 121°C for 15 minutes, allowed to cool to room temperature and stored.

Agar Slats

The **agar slats** are used for maintaining pure cultures of micro-organisms for subculturing purposes. These are prepared by pouring solid media in test tubes while in the liquefied state, which are then allowed to harden in the slanted position. Agar slats provide more surface area for growth to the microorganisms than agar deep tubes and are easier to store and transport than petri plates. Moreover, in a slat, the sloped surface is easier to streak than a horizontal surface. They are also less readily contaminated.

The **agar deep tubes** are prepared by adding the melted medium in culture tubes where agar is allowed to harden in the bottom of test tubes in the upright position. These are used for the study of gaseous requirements of the microorganisms, to grow bacteria that prefer less oxygen than is present on the surface of the medium as well as for preparing agar plates.

Agar Plates

The **agar plates** are prepared by pouring the melted (100°C) and cooled (45.5°C) liquified media into sterilelpetri dishes that provide large surface areas. These are used for the isolation and study of microorganisms. Agar plates, after solidification of the agar medium, are to be kept in an inverted position (i.e. top down) to prevent dropping down of water vapours on to the hardened agar surface.

A **pipette** is made of either glass or plastic drawn out to a tip at one end (lower side). They are calibrated and used for sterile transfers of known volumes of liquids.

Inoculating loops and **inoculating needles** are the most commonly used tools for aseptic transfer. An inoculating loop consists of an insulated handle provided with screw device at the top which holds a heat resistance ichrome or platinum wire, approximately three inches long. The wire end is bent round to form a loop. The **inoculating straight needle** is similar to the loop, but the holder contains a straight piece of wire instead of a loop. They are sterilized by heating or flaming in the blue (hottest) portion of the Bunsen burner flame or electric incinerator until it is red hot. The loop is mainly used to transfer (sub-culture) from liquid culture, the liquid drop being held across the loop area by surface tension. An inoculating needle is used to transfer culture of microorganisms growing on solid medium in colonial forms.

Important Questions

1. Enumerate and describe the instruments that are needed to establish a biological laboratory.
2. Describe the tools and appliances that are needed in a biological laboratory.
3. Write briefly on the following:
   (i) Spectrophotometer, (ii) pH meter, (iii) Photo micrographic equipment, (iv) Broth, (v) Agar slats.

4 Fixation

If a piece of tissue is cut or removed from a living or recently dead organism, it will soon undergo marked changes. If left in the air, it will loose water by evaporation and shrink; if left in a fluid, it is likely to undergo osmotic swelling or shrinkage. If these distortions are prevented, it will still be subject to attack by bacteria and moulds. Even if these are excluded by asepsis, the tissue will gradually fall to pieces by self digestion or autolysis. Cells contain enzymes, collectively known as "**cathepsin**", capable of dissolving their own protein constituents when they die.

To preserve a piece of tissue one requires a **fluid** that will not shrink or swell or dissolve or distort; will kill bacteria and moulds; and will render the autolytic enzymes inactive. This fluid is called a **preservative**. A fixative must do everything that a preservative does, but in addition it must modify the tissues in such a way that they become capable of resisting subsequent treatments of various kinds.

Not every tissue-constituent requires fixation, and some are not capable of being fixed. Chitin, and certain inorganic crystals are examples of hard stable substances not at all subject to distortion or decay.

Fixation can be activated by heat, but this method is seldom used except for blood films. Most fixatives are solids used in aqueous solution, but some are organic liquids that can be used without dilution. All fixatives fall easily into two groups according to their obvious reactions with soluble proteins i.e. coagulant fixatives and non coagulant fixatives.

Coagulants

1. Ethanol (ethyl alcohol). C_2H_5OH. A light, colourless fluid, miscible with water in all proportions. Standard concentration, undiluted (absolute).

2. Mercuric chloride. $HgCl_2$. Colourless crystals, soluble in water at about 7%. Standard concentration, saturated aqueous solution.

3. Chromium trioxide. CrO_3. Brownish-red crystals, giving a strongly acid solution in water, in which it is extremely soluble. Standard concentration, 0·5% aqueous

Non-Coagulants

1. Formaldehyde. HCHO. Colourless gas, very soluble in water. Standard concentration, 4% aqueous.

2. Osmium tetraoxide. OsO_4. Pale yellow crystals, soluble in water at about 7%. Standard concentration, 1 % aqueous.

3. Potassium dichromate. $K_2Cr_2O_7$. Orange-red crystals, giving a weakly acid solution in water, in which it is soluble at about 10%. Standard concentration, 1·5% aqueous.

4. Acetic acid. $H_3C.COOH$. Colourless liquid, miscible with water in all proportions. Standard concentration, 5%.

Small pieces of tissues are best fixed by direct immersion. Perfusion technique can also be used for fixation. The purpose of fixation is usually to stabilize the tissues so that they retain as nearly as possible the form they had in life.

Chemistry of Fixation

The best method of fixation for each particular organ/tissue is of paramount importance and, whatever fixatives are applied it is essential to know as precisely as possible their effect on the reactive groups of various tissue components. The most important of these components are the proteins, lipids and sugars. Different fixatives will react with these groups in a different way. Important reactions of aldehyde fixatives, metal complexes and vapour fixatives are discussed below.

Chemistry of Fixation

Aldehyde Fixatives

Formalin. Formaldehyde exists in aqueous solutions principally in the form of its monohydrate, methylene glycol, $CH_2(OH)_2$ and as low molecular weight polymeric hydrates or polyoxymethylene glycols, HO. (CH_2O). H. The reactions of formaldehyde with tissue proteins are numerous and complex, since it can combine with a number of different functional groups, in many cases forming **bridging links** between them. To this function of forming links between adjacent protein chains formalin owes its success as a polymerizing fixative. The most frequently encountered reaction of formaldehyde is its addition to a compound containing a reactive hydrogen atom with the formation of a hydroxymethyl (methylol) compound.

$$RH + CH_2O \rightarrow R.CH_2(OH)$$

Methylene bridge. The compound is usually reactive also and it may condense with a further H atom to form a *methylene bridge* ($-CH_2-$) in the manner illustrated below.

$$R.CH_2(OH) + HR' \rightarrow R\text{-}CH_2\text{-}R' + H_2O$$

These methylene bridges, as the above reaction suggests, are readily ruptured by hydrolysis. Many of the combinations of formaldehyde with tissue proteins are reversible by the simple-process of washing or, for instance, by the application of dimedone.

Cross-linking. Another essential feature of formaldehyde fixation is the formation of cross-links between protein end groups. Any compound which produces this effect whether used as a fixative or not, is described as bifunctional. The groups particularly involved in the fixation of proteins by formaldehyde are **amino**, **imino** and **amido, peptide**, **guanidyl**, **hydroxyl**, **carboxyl**, **SH** and **aromatic** rings. Methylene bridges may be formed between two similar groups, say NH_2, or between NH_2 and peptide (CONH), or between NH2 and NH, to quote a few examples.

It is clear that in using neutral 10 per cent formalin at room temperature, and even more so at 4°C we are making relatively little use of its capacity to form addition compounds and bridges. Moreover, a high proportion of those initially formed are too labile to withstand washing. Unfortunately we do not know precisely which groups are responsible for the irreversible reactions.

Acrolein. This compound, acrylic aldehyde, $H_2C{=}CH.\ CHO$, is a bifunctional aldehyde used in the tanning industry which is capable of introducing more cross-links than formaldehyde, under optimum conditions (**Bowes, 1963; Cater, 1963**). It is unpleasant to use and unstable at alkaline pH levels so it is little used as a routine fixative. The **tanning** (fixative) effect of acrolein is due to its hydrogen atoms adjacent to the double bond, since it is abolished by the introduction of ethyl and propyl groups in the 2- and 3-positions of the molecule.

Glutaraldehyde. Glutaric dialdehyde, $(CH_2)_3CHO.CHO$, is more properly aepresented by the following structural formula.

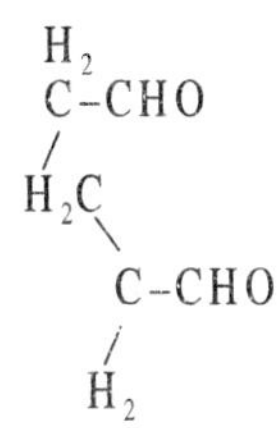

Glutaraldehyde

It was first used in the leather industry as a tanning agent (**Seligsburger and Sadlier, 1957; Fein** and **Filachione, 1957**). **Sabatini, Bensch and Harrnett (1963)** showed that it was a better preservative of structure and enzyme activity than any other of the 9 aldehydes tested. Studies carried out by Bowes (1963) indicated that glutaraldehyde was the most efficient cross-linking agent.

It is clearly not always possible to draw conclusions directly from tanning experiments but the remarkable effectiveness of glutaraldehyde is apparent and it is obvious that we have here a fixative capable of far more variety in application than formaldehyde. It is widely used as a fixative for electron microscopical studies.

Metallic Ions and Complexes

Metallic complexes also precipitate proteins. In histology and histo-chemistry we are mainly concerned with osmium, mercury and chromium salts.

Chromium. Chromium salts have the property of forming complexes with water of the type Cr-O-Cr, and these complexes combine with the reactive groups of adjacent protein chains to bring about a binding effect similar to that of formalin. The main affinity of chromium is for the carboxyl and hydroxyl groups of protein. Hexavalent chromium has been shown to be bound by egg albumin in decreasing amount as the pH is changed from 4 to 7.35.

Mercury. Salts of mercury are much more commonly employed in histological fixatives and in many institutions the routine fixative is a mercurial one. Histochemical studies may be called for when no material other than that fixed with mercury (formal-mercury) is available. It is therefore important to consider the effect of salts of this metal on the tissues, and particularly on the proteins. In general, Hg^{++} behaves like other metallic ions in combining with the acid groups of proteins, especially carboxyl and hydroxyl, and the phosphoric acid of nucleoproteins. It differs from chromium in not forming complexes capable of binding together adjacent protein chains and also from the majority of metals in one important respect. This is its selective affinity for thiol (SH) groups. If a very small quantity of a mercuric salt is added to a protein containing reactive thiol groups it will react with these in preference to any others, and the stability of the mercury sulphur bond is greater than that between mercury and any other grouping. The reactions which take place are given below.

$$RSH + HgCl_2 \leftrightarrow RSHgCl + HCl \text{ and}$$
$$RSHgCl + RSH \leftrightarrow (RS)_2\,Hg + HCl$$

The second reaction is a slow one and probably of little importance in histological fixation. Both reactions are reversible, but while the second can be reversed by any reaction which forms an un-dissociated mercury complex, the first is only reversed by reagents such as cysteine which form equally stable mercury derivatives.

Osmium. The so-called osmic acid was first employed by **Schultze** and **Rudneff in 1865** and since then osmium tetroxide (OsO_4) has been in general use as a cytological fixative. Its use in histology has been limited due to its poor penetrating qualities, but its current pre-eminence in the preparation of tissues for electron microscopy has brought about a revival of interest in the mechanism by which it acts as a fixative. Our knowledge of this process is still scanty and unsatisfactory in many respects. However, its reactions with lipids, proteins, amino acids and sugars are discussed below.

Reactions of Osmium Tetroxide With Lipids

Saturated fats do not react but unsaturated fats reduce OsO_4 with the formation of black compounds containing osmium or its hydroxide.

Whatever the nature of the reaction of unsaturated fats with OsO_4 polymerization will occur if, there are a number of unsaturated chains in the molecule. It may also occur when, there are a number of unsaturated bonds in a single chain. **Finean (1954)** used buffered OsO_4 at pH 7.0 to fix sciatic nerve and observed an increase in intensity and a change in relative intensity of the bands in its low angle X-ray diffraction pattern. He suggested that the monoethanoid fatty acids of the myelin sheath were the main site of its action. Alcohol normally extracts the lipids of the myelin sheaths completely. After OsO_4 fixation it no longer does this and it is often assumed that binding of lipid to protein has occurred.

Discussing the mechanism of fixation of lipids with OsO_4 **Bahr (1954)** had suggested that the reaction of lecithin was a double effect involving both the unsaturated fatty acid and the choline, or cholamine residue in the molecule. Investigations by **Khan *et al.* (1961)** confirmed the involvement of the polar groups of lecithin as well as its double bonds and further work supporting Bahr's concept was reported by **Riemersma** and **Booij (1962)**. These authors showed, in the first instance that the amount of OsO_4 bound by lecithin corresponded to the number of double bonds available. Secondly, they showed that so-called tricomplex formation (staining of lecithin with the acid dye Brilliant scarlet 3 R after blocking the lipid phosphate groups with uranyl ions) was progressively reversed by reaction with OsO_4. The probable mechanism of tricomplex formation involves binding of the dye by the choline (quaternary ammonium) groups of the lipid after removing interference by its anionic (phosphate) groups. At the same time Riemersma and Booij observed that after reaction with OsO_4 the affinity of lecithin for a basic dye, Brilliant green, was greatly increased. This was considered to be due to reaction with lipid phosphate groups after removal of interference by the quaternary ammonium groups.

Much of the work discussed above has important implications for the electron microscopist in that it explains why the latter observes that the deposition of osmium in lipid micelles occurs at the site of the polar groups and not at the original site of reaction in the hydrophobic interior of the micelles. This is shown below in figure 1, which indicates diagrammatically the two possible sites of osmium deposition.

Reactions With Lipoproteins

Quantitative determinations of the OsO_4 lipoprotein interaction were made by **Hayes *et al.* (1963)**, using the X-ray fluorescence technique and serum lipoprotein fractions. These workers showed that nearly all of the reaction occurred with lipid rather than protein and that as the percentage of the latter increased the uptake of osmium decreased. Recovery of fatty acids from fixed lipoproteins was limited but the results showed that unsaturated fatty acids were preferentially involved in the fixation process.

Reactions With Proteins, Amino-acids and Sugars

OsO_4 forms gels with albumin, globulin and fibrinogen. The clear gel which forms relatively slowly with albumin is regarded as an indication of fine micellar or even unimolecular binding. The opaque gel formed with globulin and fibrinogen, on the contrary, is held to indicate some coarser type of binding.

Three types of reactions are known to occur with OsO_4:

(1) the formation of a black precipitate with watery solutions of OsO_4 (unsaturated lipids, SH groups, etc.):
(2) the formation of a black precipitate with OsO_4;
(3) oxidation by OsO_4 without the formation of a visible precipitate.

Alcohol and Acetone

These two protein precipitants have been used as "fixatives" especially for enzymes because, in spite of the morphological disturbances which they create in the tissues, they leave the reactive groups of enzymes to a large extent in their original state.

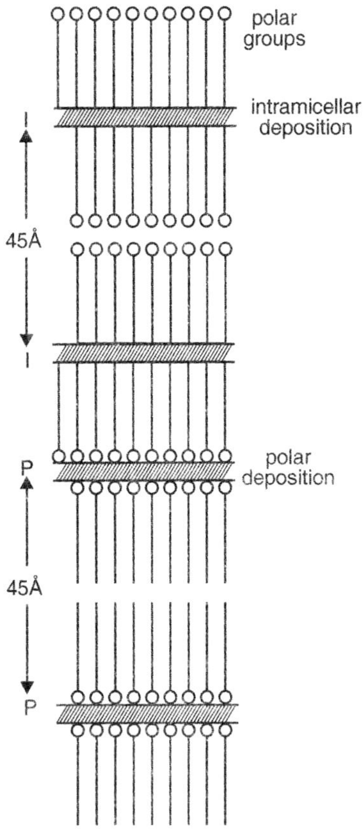

Fig. 1. Sites of osmium dioxide deposition in lipid micelles.

Unfortunately very little is known about the exact effect of alcohol and acetone on proteins. In general, however, denaturation of a protein by precipitation may change the reactivity of its groups in three ways:

(1) by rendering parts of the molecule inaccessible to various reagents;
(2) by altering the rate at which such reagents diffuse into the protein; and
(3) by bringing into proximity previously separated groups in the protein molecule, thus producing new stereochemical relations.

The effects of denaturation are to some extent reversible and many of the original properties of the protein are sometimes regained when the denaturing agent is removed. The mucoproteins of the anterior pituitary gland, for instance, are entirely soluble in water after precipitation by brief treatment with alcohol, and after treatment with acetone the alkaline phosphatase of various tissues is still soluble to some extent in dilute solutions of alcohol. Other effects are apparently irreversible, such as the partial inactivation of most enzymes. It is not known whether this is due to a chemical effect on their reactive groups or to one of the denaturation factors mentioned above.

The cross linkages which bind protein chains together are of several types. It has been suggested that alcohol acts by turning the protein chains outwards (away from each other), breaking the hydrogen bonds and salt links and thus revealing the end groups of the side chains to a varying extent. The precise mechanism and the extent of liberation of side chains are largely unknown.

Chemical Actions of Vapour Fixatives

Use of vapour fixatives is a practice of long standing in histology and cytology. Its use has been confined mainly to formaldehyde and OsO_4, usually applied to smears or sections at 37°C or lower. The motive for employing vapour as opposed to liquid fixatives has been the desire to retain soluble materials *in situ* by converting them to insoluble products before they come into contact with water or non-aqueous solvents.

Each study shows the effectiveness of "**hot**" vapour fixation applied to freeze-dried tissues. Comparisons were made between formaldehyde, acrolein, glutaraldehyde, OsO_4, chromyl chloride, cyanuric chloride, and a number of volatile metal derivatives. The important agents are briefly considered below.

Formaldehyde

Freezedrying and formaldehyde gas treatment can be recommended for any type of histochemical work where formaldehyde fixation is permissible. The usual source of monomeric formaldehyde is heated para-formaldehyde and, where the moisture content of the environment has been found to be critical, the polymer should be stored before use in an environment with strictly controlled humidity.

Other Aldehydes

The two reagents most often used are acrolein and glutaraldehyde. The later is supplied as a 25% aqueous solution so that if the vapour is required the aldehyde must first be extracted into ether or liquid paraffin. Glutaraldehyde has little fixing (cross-linking) effect in the absence of water vapour, unlike formaldehyde, and a high temperature (60°C) is required for effective fixation in a short period.

Osmium Tetroxide

At 37°C the vapour pressure of this reagent is absolutely sufficient. It penetrates very rapidly into freeze-dried blocks of tissue and one hour or less is usually adequate.

Chromyl Chloride

Sufficient vapour pressure is available at 37°C. This fixative presumably acts as chromic acid by combination with water vapour and, possibly, with bound water also.

$$2CrO_2Cl_2 + 3H_2O \rightarrow H_2Cr_2O_7 + 4HCl$$

Tissues treated with chromyl chloride vapour alone are rendered extremely brittle and almost impossible to cut after any known embedding process. If it follows formaldehyde, however, this type of post-chromation can be extremely valuable.

Alcohol

Ethanol vapour at 60°C has a pronounced denaturating effect on freeze-dried tissues and polysaccharides like glycogen become less soluble than in control tissues. No real indications for the use of ethanol vapour are forthcoming and other alcohols seem not to have been tested.

Practical Fixative Solutions

Primary Fixatives

The only primary fixatives that are commonly used without the admixture of other primaries are formaldehyde and osmium tetroxide. Solutions of these fixatives are called as **simple fixatives. Fixative mixtures** contain two or more primary fixatives.

On the contrary, they were put together in a hit-or-miss fashion. In several cases the formula was relegated to a footnote, with no indication of any reasons governing the choice or concentration of the ingredients. Some of these empirical fluids gave good results and found favour, others did not. A process of natural selection of almost random variations resulted in the survival, on the whole, of the fittest; though many that are used are superfluous. To understand the action of fixative mixtures, a careful study of a few valuable primary fixatives should be made.

Formaldehyde in Simple Fixatives

Formaldehyde is generally dissolved in a solution of an indifferent salt. The latter is used at a concentration that gives the same osmotic pressure as the body-fluids of the organism from which a part is to be taken for fixation, or at a concentration slightly less than this. The following is suitable for the tissues of most vertebrates other than elasmobranchs, and for many terrestrial and fresh-water invertebrates:

Distilled water	...	83 ml
Sodium chloride, 10% aq.	..	7 ml
Formalin		10 ml

Add powdered calcium carbonate in the fluid.

In this and other formulae, the word 'formalin' means the commercial fluid containing formaldehyde at approximately 40% w/v. In the fixing solutions given here, formaldehyde is therefore used at its standard concentration.

For the tissues of marine invertebrates, one may dilute formalin with 9 times its volume of sea-water. The pH of the fluid is 7.6.

There can be no doubt that non-fixative salts improve fixation by formaldehyde and certain other primary fixatives. Since they are used at concentrations that give about the same osmotic pressure as the body-fluids of the organism, the fixative solution as a whole is hypertonic. One would therefore expect the latter to cause shrinkage: in fact, however, the virtue of non-fixative salts is that they **reduce** shrinkage.

Formaldehyde is much used in these simple solutions in histochemical studies, especially of lipids. To make sure that phospholipids will be fixed, the tissue may be 'postchromed'. After quite short fixation (6 hours) in the formaldehyde solution, it is transferred (without washing) to a solution of potassium dichromate. A solution of this salt maintained at saturation in an incubator at 37°C is suitable.

For some reason, not yet satisfactorily explained, it is helpful to add sucrose to formaldehyde solutions in electron-microscopical studies. It may be added at 7.5% w/v or thereabouts.

Osmium Tetroxide in Simple Fixatives

Osmium tetroxide gives excellent results when unmixed with other primary fixatives, provided that a suitable embedding medium, such as methacrylate, is used. Gross shrinkage and distortion occur if tissues fixed in this way are embedded in paraffin. Osmium tetroxide has been and is enormously used in electron-microscopical studies. It is generally believed that osmium tetroxide fixes best for electron-microscopical studies if the solution is buffered with **Michaelis's** buffer at about pH 7.4, but there is evidence from several sources that a simple 1 % w/v solution in distilled water works as well.

We turn now to fixative mixtures.

Fixative Mixtures

The great majority of fixative mixtures fall into one or other of four groups. Fifteen of the most valuable are listed here.

Group A. Coagulant + acetic acid. These are primarily fixatives for micro-anatomy and histology. Examples: **Clarke, Zenker.**

Group B. Coagulant + non-coagulant + acetic acid. These are mostly fixatives for detailed histology and general cytology: many are used in the study of chromosomes. Examples: **Flemming's strong fluid, Allen's 'B.15', Bouin, Heidenhain's 'Susa', Hermann (mammalian formula), Sanfelice.**

Group C. Coagulant + non-coagulant. These are routine fixatives for cytoplasmic inclusions. Examples: **Helly, Champy, Flemming without acetic, Mann, Zenker without acetic.**

Group D. Non-coagulants only. This is a small group, adapted to the study of cytoplasmic inclusions. Examples: **Altmann, Regaud.**

It is curious that so many valuable fixative mixtures contain one or more coagulants. This is probably connected with the predominance of paraffin as an embedding medium. Group D is likely to come to the fore in the future, as new plastics replace paraffin; but it remains to be seen whether any non-coagulant is as useful as chromium trioxide in the fixation of chromosomes for optical microscopy.

Clarke's Fluid

Absolute ethanol	3 vols
Acetic acid (glacial)	1 vol

Wash out in absolute ethanol.

The formula for this fixative was given by the English neurologist no less than 35 years before **Carnoy**, the celebrated Belgian cytologist, first published it. In the intervening period it was familiar in microtechnique as **die Clarke'sche Vorschrift.** This is the most ancient of all fixative mixtures commonly used in microtechnique today.

The advantage that may be gained by mixing certain primary fixatives cannot be more vividly illustrated than by a consideration of Clarke's Hardy centenarian. By themselves, ethanol and acetic acid are both very bad fixatives, but each compensates neatly for the defects of the other. The shrinkage that ethanol alone would cause is offset by the swelling action of acetic acid; the latter stabilizes nucleoproteins, which are left unfixed by the former; acetic acid fixes neither cytoplasm nor nuclear sap, but both are fixed by ethanol (the former in a rather coarse coagulum). The mixture is useful in routine microanatomy and histology applicable also in histochemistry whenever it is desirable to avoid additive fixation and the resultant shift in the iso-electric points of proteins; glycogen is preserved, but not fixed. The fluid is a solvent of many lipids; for this reason, and because it coagulates rather coarsely, it is unsuitable for the study of most cytoplasmic inclusions.

Zenker's Fluid

Distilled water	100 ml
Mercuric chloride.	5 g
Potassium dichromate	2.5 g
Sodium sulphate	1 g

To 20 ml, add 1 ml of glacial acetic acid immediately before use. (pH 2.5)

Short fixation (3 to 6 hours) is best, since certain dyes do not work well when it is prolonged. The reason for this has not been explained. Wash overnight in running water.

Zenker's fluid is chosen as next example after Clarke's fluid because it is one of the best fixatives for use in routine histology and in preliminary work with unknown tissues in biological microtechnique of all kinds. It contains two protein coagulants (mercuric chloride and acidified potassium dichromate) and a substance that opposes shrinkage (acetic acid). No non-coagulant fixative of protein is included in the mixture. Sodium sulphate is an 'indifferent' salt; its effect in this mixture is uncertain.

The ground cytoplasm and certain cytoplasmic inclusions are far better preserved by Zenker than by most routine fixatives. The fine texture of the protein coagulate is probably due to the mercuric chloride, which also ensures easy dyeing. Acidified potassium dichromate favours the action of acid dyes, which give much more brilliant effects than after Clarke.

Flemming's Strong Fluid

Distilled water.	0.8 ml
Chromium trioxide, 5 % aq.	0.3 ml
Osmium tetroxide, 2 % aq.	0.4 ml
Acetic acid, 20% aq.	0.5 ml or less

As a general rule, use the full concentration of acetic acid. Wash out for several hours in running water or repeated changes.

Since 2 ml of the mixture are sufficient for the fixation of the small pieces of tissue that should be used, it is desirable to follow the formula given above. There is then no wastage of the extremely expensive osmium tetroxide. The fluid made up in this way has the same composition as that which results from the use of Flemming's own formula.

Flemming contains a trio of ingredients that are found over and over again in successful mixtures; namely

(1) one or more coagulants of protein (in this case chromium trioxide);

(2) a non-coagulant fixative of protein (in this case osmium tetroxide);

(3) acetic acid.

One might suppose that the best results would be given by non coagulate fixatives, in the absence of coagulants; but tissue that has been treated with no other fixative of protein than a non-coagulant does not give ready access, to paraffin, and the preparation of good paraffin sections is often difficult. This particularly applies to osmium tetroxide. The spongework produced by coagulants provides spaces into which melted paraffin can enter. Beyond this, coagulants give the best fixation of chromosomes, and chromium trioxide is pre-eminent in this respect. If, however, no non-coagulant fixative of proteins is included, the spongework tends to be unduly coarse, and cytoplasmic inclusions are distorted mechanically or even destroyed. The coagulants and. non-coagulants thus 'compensate for one another's defects.

The chief effect of acetic acid in these mixtures is the prevention of excessive shrinkage. Tissues fixed in acetic acid alone swell, but are greatly shrunken on subsequent dehydration. If, however, they are stabilized in the swollen condition by the simultaneous action of a fixative for proteins, the shrinkage seen in the final preparation is far less. When acetic acid is used in mixtures at 5 % or thereabouts, there is no necessity to add an indifferent salt. Acetic acid also plays a part in the fixation of nucleoprotein, but this is not important when the coagulant is chromium trioxide.

Helly's Fluid

Distilled water	100 ml
Mercuric chloride	5 g
Potassium dichromate	2.5 g
Sodium sulphate	1 g

To 10 ml of fixative add 0.5 ml of formalin (neutralized by powdered calcium carbonate) immediately before use. (pH 3.7.)

Fix overnight and wash for several hours in running water, or leave for 24 hours, between fixation and washing, in a saturated aqueous solution of potassium dichromate maintained at 37° C. Dehydrate through grades of ethanol, with iodine treatment.

The fixative is one of the most valuable in the routine study of cytoplasmic inclusions in paraffin sections. It contains a coagulant and a non-coagulant fixative of protein (mercuric chloride and formaldehyde respectively), and also an important fixative of many lipids (unacidified potassium dichromate). It is uncertain whether the indifferent salt (sodium sulphate) plays a useful role in the mixture.

Helly is not nearly so similar to Zenker as the list of its constituents might suggest. Formaldehyde and unacidified potassium dichromate are profoundly different in their effects on tissues from acetic acid and acidified potassium dichromate.

Mercuric chloride and formaldehyde, acting in conjunction, fix ground cytoplasm smoothly, giving just sufficient sponginess to allow easy penetration by paraffin. The constituents penetrate well and it is not necessary to use very small pieces.

Post chroming is useful in studies of mitochondria. The latter are usually well fixed, though those of mammalian liver tend to shorten and round up.

Altmann's Fluid

Osmium tetraoxide	2 % aq.
Potassium dichromate	5 % aq.
pH 4.0.	

Use pieces of tissue 2 mm or less in thickness. In studies of mitochondria fix for 24 hours (postchroming is unnecessary). Wash out overnight in running water.

Altmann was the first serious student of mitochondria, though he did not know them under this name. The distinguished Leipzig cytologist was mistaken about the nature of these cytoplasmic inclusions, which he regarded as 'elementary organisms', living within the cell; but he designed a fixative that is still one of the best for showing them in preparations for optical microscopy.

The fluid differs from the mixtures already described and from the great majority of fixative mixtures used in microtechnique, in containing no coagulant. Ground cytoplasm is therefore fixed very homogeneously. The cytoplasmic inclusions maintain their form, partly because they are not distorted by coagulation of the surrounding ground cytoplasm, partly because both the constituents of the fluid are lipid-fixatives. The dichromate, a stronger oxidizer than osmium tetroxide, prevents excessive blackening of the tissues and gives easy colouring by acid dyes; unfortunately it dissolves nucleoprotein, and the fixative is not adapted to studies of nucleus or chromosomes.

The disadvantage of this fixative is that it does not give ready access to melted paraffin. Embedding often results in shrinkage and distortion, the tissue cracks, and sections are difficult to flatten.

Ammonium dichromate may be substituted for potassium dichromate in this solution. The pH of 'NH_4-Altmann' is slightly more acid. The ammonium salt differs curiously from the other. Mitochondria are not well fixed at the surface of the piece of tissue, but in the interior they are better fixed than by potassium dichromate: filamentous ones retain their form, instead of shortening and thickening. For this reason it is best to cut out rather larger pieces of tissue when the ammonium salt is to be used.

Freeze-Drying

Chemical fixation does offer certain advantages, but for many cytochemical and histochemical studies, this process was found to be disadvantageous. The brief disadvantages of chemical fixation are —

(1) the loss of soluble substances e.g. lipids, proteins, polysaccharides and inorganic material
(2) displacement of cell constituents by diffusion
(3) denatratuion of proteins
(4) chemical alteration of reactive groups
(5) destruction or inactivation of enzymes

To overcome these problems, freeze drying method was developed. According to **Mann** (1902), the preparation of tissues for microscopical research by drying is the oldest of all methods. He describes that Leuwenhoek in 1720 used to cut sections of muscles prepared according to this method. **Altman** (1890) used to maintain small dried tissues in vacuo at –30°C. **Gersh** (1932) produced perhaps the first functional freeze-drying apparatus. The earlier type of apparatus and the theory and practice of tissue freeze-drying were ably described in an excellent monograph by **Neumann** (1952). An account of application of freeze-drying in biological research was given by **Bell** (1955).

Principle and practice of freeze-drying

The process of freeze-drying involves following steps

(1) Initial freezing or quenching
(2) Subsequent drying

(3) Embedding
(4) Post fixation
(5) Sectioning and mounting
(6) Final treatment before examination

1. Quenching process. This is the initial step of rapid freezing of the tissue sample. It stops all chemical reactions and autolysis. Prevention of sub-mortem changes and diffusion are the two major advantages of this technique. However, the greatest disadvantage is the formation of ice crystals from the unbound water in the cytoplasm of the cells and the subsequent precipitation of materials dissolved in such water at the boundaries of the ice crystals. In practice, a rapid rate of cooling is desirable. The ability to do this depends on thermal conductivity of the liquid used for freezing. In early experiments **Gersh** used liquid air (–195°) for quenching bath. Ethyl alcohol cooled at –100°C in place of liquid air was recommended by **Scott** (1933). **Hoerr** (1936) introduced crude isopentane cooled to –165°C with liquid nitrogen. Various other fluids have been employed for cooling viz: isopentane mixed with dry butane, a mixture of propane and isopentane and pure propane. **Boll** (1952) recommended Arcton –6(I.C.I. Ltd.), known as Freon-22 in United States as a safe quenching agent with liquid oxygen. Later Freon-22 was found to be more efficient than Freon-12. Rapid freezing with liquid helium-II has also been recommended for electron microscopical observations. The size of the sample and the temperature of the quenching are important in freeze drying.

2. Eutectic phenomenon. In general when a mixture of two liquids is cooled one of the components will freeze out first, thus concentrating the other. By this process the freezing point is lowered and if cooling is continued the temperature is finally reached when both components freeze out simultaneously and the whole mass then solidifies without further fall in the temperatures. This point is called as eutectic point. Eutectic is a Greek term (eu = easily and tectic = melt). **Bayliss** (1915) was the first to stress on eutectic point. Measurement of eutectic temperature is made by a process described as thermal analysis. The eutectic temperature is defined as the maximum temperature at which crystallization can be achieved.

Fig. 2. Thermoelectric Freeze-Dryer showing complete assembly with resin embedding accessory.

3. The drying process. The process of drying of solid frozen block of tissue can be considered under following headings —

(a) Heating
(b) Vapour transfer
(c) Vapour removal

(a) Heating. It is easy to maintain temperature much lower than eutectic point during drying. Practical requirements dictate that although the temperature must be sufficiently low to prevent melting it must be sufficiently high to allow drying within a reasonable period. Several methods are available for achieving the optimum results. In older types of freeze drying apparatus heating is done by cooling bath. This process maintains a temperature between –30°C and –78°C. Modern freeze dryers employ the principle of heating by radiation. This is generally supplied electrically. Other dryers are called as thermoelectric dryers.

(b) Vapour pressure. When a sample is freeze dried, dried tissue appears first at the surface of the specimen. As drying proceeds this outer shell becomes progressively thicker. All water vapour produced by sublimation of ice must diffuse through this dried barrier layer to reach the surface. The force that drives water vapor from drying boundary to the tissue surface is vapour pressure which is a concentration gradient. It is thus necessary to produce a high vapor pressure at the boundary and low vapour pressure at the surface. This process removes water molecules as soon as they arrive.

*(c) **Vapour removal.*** The removal of water molecules from the surface of the drying specimen depends on the identical force responsible for vapour transfer. Therefore, it is necessary to have a high vapour pressure at the drying boundary and low vapour pressure at the surface. This objective is achieved by means of a vacuum system containing water traps.

Modern Type of Tissue Dryers

Commercially designed freeze dryers are now available that offer simplicity in operation and reliability. A few of them are described below —

(1) Cold finger dryer-derives its energy for sublimation by radiation of heat from the environment.

(2) The cold hand dryer-uses radiant heat supplied electrically through a wire spiral surrounding the specimen tray.

(3) The type of tissue dryer-was designed particularly for plant materials. Heat is provided by an electrical unit adjusted near to the sample holder.

(4) Thermoelectric tissue dryers - employ heat received through radiation as well as conduction. Vapour gradient is measured by vaccum and by placing a P_2O_5 trap a short distance away from the drying tissue.

Embedding

Freeze dried specimen are customarily embedded in paraffin. At the end of the drying stage, we are left with an almost completely water free specimen at a temperature of –40°C and pressure of a 0.001 Torr. The most convenient procedure is to allow the dried tissue to reach the room temperature while still under vaccum and then to admit air and to transfer them from the chamber to a pot of melted wax in a conventional vaccum embedding bath. Transferring cold tissue directly into wax at 56°C causes appreciable shrinkage. Some workers advise the use of celloidin alone or in combination with paraffin as the alternate embedding media. Carbowaxes and resins and liquid paraffin are also sometimes used.

Post-Fixation

Treatment of freeze dried sample with a suitable fixative is called as post fixation. Several agents viz: absolute alcohol, osmium tetraoxide, formaldehyde, glutaraldehyde and hydroxy acetaldehyde have been used as fixatives for light microscopical studies. Result of post fixation are much better at light microscopy but unsatisfactory for electron microscopy.

The following fixatives and metallic vapours have also been tested.

Formaldehyde	= 37°, 60°, 70°, 80°
Glutaraldehyde	= 37°, 60°, 70°, 80°
Acrolein	= 37°, 60°
Osmium tetraoxide	= 37°, 60°, 70°
Chromyl chloride	= 37°, 60°, 70°
Molybdenum hexacarbonyl	= 37°, 60°

The most useful practice is to cut the paraffin-embedded tissues on a standard bench type of microtome. Until 1960, it was customary to cut sections on a freezing microtome. The advent of thermoelectric cooling for block holders and knives has made it easy to apply suitable cooling to any microtome.

We now suppose that the material quenched in section-1, dried in section-2, and embedded, and cut in the form of a 6-8 μ thick section on an albuminized slide with the wax still *in situ,* there remains only the final treatment before it can be brought to the microscope for examination.

Final Treatment Before Microscopy

For optimum observations, various possibilities can be considered

(1) Examination of unfixed material, in inert media, by physical methods.

(2) Examination of unfixed material by micro-incineration or by treatment with buffer extraction etc.

(3) Examination after post sectioning fixation by conventional histological and histochemical techniques.

(4) Examination after pre-embedding fixation by physical and chemical techniques.
(5) Examination by autoradiographic techniques

Cryopreservation

Cryopreservation can be defined as a procedure of preserving the cells or a group of cells (serum, organ, embryo, callus) for storage at a temperature colder than –80°C and warming to body temperature. All steps in this process are optimized to provide survival of sufficient cells to achieve a specific task such as impregnation of a female with cryopreserved sperm.

General Principles of Cryopreservation

Successful cryopreservation programms depend on successful cooling of the organ/embryo to subzero temperatures (–196°C) followed by subsequent thawing of the cryopreserved material to room temperature prior to transfer. First, the cells are cooled to approximately –7°C in cryoprotectant medium, a temperature at which both cells and medium are not frozen. Next, extracellular ice formation is initiated by seeding the solution, bathing the sample with a needle or forcep cooled to –196°C. As the temperature continues to decrease, exosmosis continues as a result of the osmotic gradient created by the nonpermeating cryoprotectants and the rising sodium concentration in the extracellular media. A sufficiently slow cooling velocity is required for intracellular exosmosis to occur. Exosmosis minimizes intracellular ice crystal formation and membrane damage. In the mouse embryo, 90% of the original intracellular water concentration must move to the extracellular space to avoid potentially lethal intracellular ice formation. Once the temperature reaches –130°C, all chemical reactions cease and the cryopreserved samples are then kept in long-term storage at –196°C. The pregnancy rates for cryopreserved embryos stored in liquid nitrogen do not appear to diminish even after upto 60 months of storage.

Recrystallization and osmotic shock during thawing are the major steps leading to successful thawing procedures. Recrystallization and osmotic shock are highly dependent on the thawing rate, which is pre-determined by the cooling velocity: rapid cooling- rapid thawing or slow cooling-slow thawing. The size of crystals formed during cooling is directly related to the cooling rate and amount of intracellular hydration. For this reason, when cooling of the sample is carried to –30°C to –40°C followed by a plunge into liquid nitrogen, a rapid thawing protocol (200–500°C per minute) is required to prevent the fusion of small ice crystals that may be present into large crystals (rapid cooling plunge-rapid thawing). When the slow cooling is continued to –60°C or lower, slow thawing rates (25°C per minute) are necessary in order to prevent osmotic shock to the extensively dehydrated cells (slow cooling-slow thawing).

Cryoprotectants

Permeating cryoprotectants are small molecules which allow intracellular fluid to be supercooled to temperatures between –5°C and –15°C without forming ice crystals. In this temperature range ice crystals begin to form in the external media, but the intracellular fluid remains unfrozen. Cooling below –15°C uniformly results in intracellular ice formation. The process of seeding involves a controlled reduction in the freezing process between –5°C and –8°C, at which time the introduction of a seed crystal causes a rapid formation of ice crystals in the medium. The cessation of cooling during seeding allows additional intracellular water to equilibrate with extracellular water through exosmosis. The intracellular dehydration during cooling inhibits ice crystal formation and potential freeze injuries. Nonpermeating cryoprotectants are used to osmotically remove intracellular water for replacement with permeating cryoprotectants during cooling and additionally to prevent osmotic shock by controlling the intracellular rehydration of the cells during thawing.

1. Permeating agents. Permeating cryoprotectants include glycerol, di-methyl sulfoxide, and 1,2-propanediol. Permeating cryoprotectants enter the cells of the sample/embryo with a developmental stage specifically and vary in their diffusion properties. 1,2-Propanediol is most effective for the freezing of pronucleate oocytes and two to four-cell stage preembryos. Dimethyl sulfoxide appears to be best suited for later stages of cleavage. Glycerol is appropriate for blastocyst cryopreservation. A stepwise declining dilution of cryoprotectants in the thawing protocol helps reduce the osmotic shock of the thawed embryos.

2. Nonpermeating agents. Nonpermeating cryoprotectants are typically larger molecules such as sucrose and are used to osmotically remove water from the blastomeres, thus allowing cryoprotectants to replace the water inside the cells. They are also useful in the stepwise rehydration of cells to avoid osmotic shock from rapid rehydration. The nonpermeating molecule also aids in removal of the permeating cryoprotectant by creating a hyperosmotic medium.

Cryopreservation Techniques

Cryopreservation techniques for embryos are generally classified as follows: (i) slow cooling-slow thawing, (ii) rapid cooling-rapid thawing, (iii) vitrification, and (iv) ultrarapid freezing.

1. Slow cooling-slow thawing. This technique requires a programmable biological freezer. With this method, organs are loaded into vials after equilibration with a cryoprotectant solution and then cooled at a rate of 0.5-2°C per minute down to –1°C. Seeding is then induced and a holding period of 5-15 min allows equilibration of the temperature. There is a slight increase in temperature during seeding due to the release of latent heat during ice formation. Intracellular and extracellular water also equilibrate during this time period through exosmosis. Thereafter, embryos are cooled to –60°C or lower at a rate of 0.3–0.5°C per minute before being transferred to liquid nitrogen. Frozen embryos must be slowly thawed at a rate of less than 25°C per minute to prevent osmotic shock.

2. Rapid cooling-rapid thawing. This technique involves the equilibration of samples with a cryoprotectant solution, seeding at –1°C, and a holding period of 5-15 min as in the slow cooling-slow thawing protocol. In this technique, however, cooling is terminated at –30 to –40°C and the embryos are then plunged into liquid nitrogen for rapid cooling to –196°C. Thawing is therefore performed rapidly (200-500°C per minute) to prevent recrystallization.

3. Vitrification. Vitrification eliminates the need for a controlled biologic freezer. In this technique, cryoprotectants are added at 0°C in a high concentration (40% weight/volume). These concentrations are cytotoxic at room temperature. This technique capitalizes on partial dehydration of cells in the high concentrations of cryoprotectants (6-8 M) before rapid freezing into a glassy, vitreous state. Thawing is done rapidly in ice-water temperature at a rate of 200-500°C per minute to avoid devitrification of the glassy solution, at which time serial dilutions remove the cryoprotectants. Within certain limits, the faster the temperature is changed, the lower the concentration of viscosity required and vice versa. This method avoids ice crystal formation but retains the complications of toxicity by cryoprotectants, osmotic shock, and fracture damage associated with all cryopreservation techniques.

4. Ultrarapid freezing. This method, originally developed for oocyte cryopreservation, is thought to result in less damage to the zona pellucida than that seen with the slow cooling-slow thawing protocol. In this technique, serial equilibrations of embryos in high concentrations of DMSO (3-5 M) supplemented with sucrose (0.3-0.5 M) are required. The embryos are then plunged into liquid nitrogen. Thawing is done in a warm water bath (approximately 500°C per minute). Both these techniques and vitrification are currently used in various research protocols.

Quality Control

Quality control is a major key to success in any cryopreservation programme. Feedback on the cryopreservation procedure is delayed until thawing occurs; therefore, any errors in processing must be corrected immediately to avoid continued suboptimal outcomes. It is recommended that all aspects of the cryopreservation program be double-checked by a second member of the laboratory staff. All equipment must be checked routinely and have appropriate monitors and alarms. All aspects of the cryopreservation programme should be documented in log books. Seeding temperatures are logged daily for each run. Additionally, it is recommended that freezing and thawing media and procedures be tested each week in a mouse two-cell embryo toxicity bioassay. Backup systems for the cryopreservation programme include emergency power sources, a secondary liquid nitrogen source, and a backup freezing unit. Alarms must be monitored for refrigerant leakage, temperature variations, and fire and water damage. A laboratory contact for security personnel must be established, a disaster management plan should be developed, and an accessible duplicate inventory storage list should be maintained off the laboratory premises. Manufacturer's technical support and maintenance numbers and a secondary source of refrigerant must be readily available and should be included with the backup inventory storage list.

Clinical Applications of Cryopreservation

The first delivery resulting from cryopreservation of human embryos was reported in 1985. In the 3 year period 1987-1990, more than a 600% increase in the number of cryopreserved embryos was recorded in the United States. For ethical, financial, and medical reasons, the use of embryo cryopreservation in assisted reproduction continues to increase rapidly throughout the world.

1. As an adjunct to *in vitro* fertilization. The ability to store excess embryos increases the efficiency and minimizes the risks associated with *in vitro* fertilization (IVF). Multiple series document the improved overall IVF pregnancy rates per retrieval provided through the transfer of cryopreserved embryos. Cryopreserved embryo transfer not only adds a 6% or greater improvement in the ongoing pregnancy rate per retrieval but also this is accomplished at a cost between 25 and 45% of the cost of any other assisted reproductive technologies. By limiting the number of fresh embryos transferred, the multiple gestation rate and its attendant obstetrical risks can also be reduced. Restriction in the number of fresh embryos transferred in some countries has made cryopreservation an integral component of successful IVF programs.

2. Avoidance of ovarian hyperstimulation syndrome (OHSS). The most significant complications of therapies that use controlled ovarian hyperstimulation are multiple pregnancies and ovarian hyperstimulation syndrome (OHSS). Severe OHSS may be associated with massive ovarian enlargement, intravascular volume depletion, ascites, pleural effusions, and electrolyte and coagulation disturbances. Improved methods and expertise in. monitoring follicular development and estradiol response in women treated with gonadotropins have resulted in the virtual elimination of the risk of mortality; however, the risk of morbidity due to OHSS remains. This risk is particularly noted in patients with polycystic ovarian syndrome who conceive in the treatment cycle. It has been recognized that the incidence of this complication has not been eliminated with the use of GnRHa protocols for ovarian stimulation. A number of therapeutic approaches have been used in an attempt to reduce the incidence and severity of OHSS in patients considered to be at risk. Continuation with the inherent risks, cancellation of the cycle, "coasting," and cryopreservation have become the options available to these patients. Cryopreservation and a delayed primary transfer of embryos results in an acceptable pregnancy rate which rivals fresh transfer rates in published reports and eliminates the risk of OHSS.

3. Oocyte and embryo cryopreservation for women with cancer. Recently, the application of cryopreservation technologies has extended to women who face the loss of gonadal function. Extirpative gonadal surgery, chemotherapy, and radiation therapy for patients with various cancers have become increasingly successful, and sustained remissions are common. The price for these successes has been acute toxicity and, in the long-term, infertility due to gonadal failure. Oocyte banking and embryo cryopreservation for women with various cancers has been the natural consequence of the technological advances in cryopreservation. As sperm banking through cryopreservation has been successfully implemented in men for many years, oocyte banking and maturation techniques will eventually be common place.

4. An adjuvant to preimplantation genetic diagnosis. The number of diseases capable of being diagnosed through molecular biological techniques is expanding. While some of these diagnoses can be made rapidly with precision, the ability to remove time constraints through embryo biopsy and cryopreservation until all diagnostic work is completed will expand the utilization of preimplantation genetic diagnosis.

5. Predicting the ability to cryopreserve successfully. The ovarian response to various stimulation protocols, patient age, endometrial receptivity, and number of embryos transferred affect the success of cryopreservation.

6. New developments : blastocyst cryopreser -vation. Recently, cryopreservation of cocultured human blastocysts has been shown to produce acceptable pregnancy rates. The use of cryopreserved blastocysts for patients undergoing IVF-ET yields cryosurvival rates of over 80%, the ability to transfer embryos in over 90%, and ongoing pregnancy rates of nearly 20%. It appears that GnRHa down regulation hormone replacement transfer cycles result in higher pregnancy rates. Although there may be fewer preembryos to cryopreserve by continuing culture until the blastocyst stage, those remaining appear to be of good quality for cryopreservation and can be successfully thawed and transferred.

Safety

The incidence of birth defects and prenatal and obstetrical risks associated with pregnancies resulting from the transfer of frozen embryos are no different than those of normally conceived pregnancies. Programmes are encouraged to monitor the outcomes of these pregnancies.

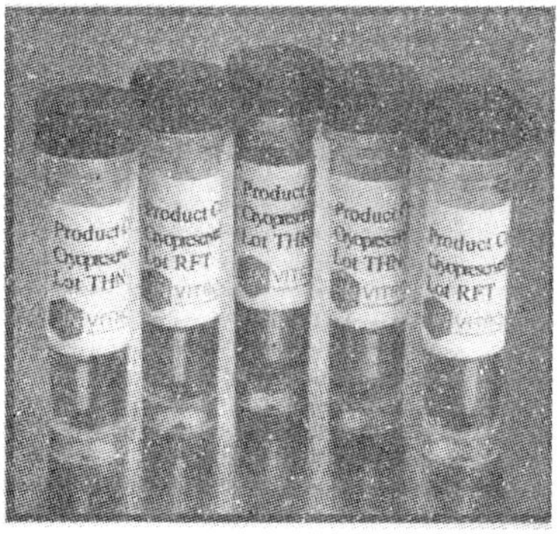

Fig. 3.

Cryopreserved Hepatocytes

Cryopreserved hepatocytes from human, cynomolgus monkey, beagle dog, New Zealand white rabbit, Sprague-Dawley rat, Wistar rat, ICR/ CD-1 mouse, marmoset monkey, Gottingen minipig, and Dunkin-Hartley guinea pig are commercially available. New cryopreserved human lots are added frequently. Cryopreserved hepatocytes perform coupled phase I and II metabolism and are a powerful tool for studying and comparing the species-specific metabolism, toxicity of many drugs and chemicals. Cryopreserved hepatocytes are stored at less than -150^{0}C to assure the long term viability of these cells. They can be procured from in vitro technologies **GmBH (www. invitrotech.de)**.

Important Questions

1. Explain briefly the process of freeze-drying.
2. What do you understand by cryo-preservation? Discuss general principles and applications of cryo-preservation.
3. Write short notes on the following :
   (i) Fixation, (ii) Post fixation, (iii) Cryo-protectants, (iv) Vitrification.
4. Discuss in details the chemistry of fixation.
5. Write short notes on the following:
   (i) Vapour fixatives, (ii) Methylene bridges, (iii) cryopreserved hepatocytes.

5

Histological Methods

A sample of a plant/animal origin needs to be fixed, dehydrated, cleared, embedded, sectioned and stained before final examination through a microscope.

Fixation

As discussed in the preceding chapter, fixation of a sample is the first and most important step in microscopical examination. After being removed from an animal/plant, a tissue or organ is cut into pieces. These are placed in a fixative for suitable time at room temperature or at 4°C in a refrigerator. Commonly used fixatives are 4-10% formalin, aqueous or alcoholic Bouin, acetic alcohol formalin, Cornoy's fluid. The purpose of fixation is to preserve normal morphology of the tissue and prepare it for further processing.

Dehydration

After fixation, the next step is to remove the fixative. The aqueous fixative may be removed by washing the fixed tissue in running water. Alcoholic fixative are removed by washing the tissue in 70% alcohol several times.

Removal of fixative is followed by dehydration. Dehydration is performed by transferring the sample through a series of alcohols of increasing concentrations upto 100% alcohol.

Clearing

Dehydration is followed by clearing. Several clearing agents such as xylene, toluene and benzene can be used. These agents are miscible with alcohol as well as paraffin wax. This intermediate step is essential before infiltrating the dehydrated tissue with paraffin because alcohol and paraffin do not mix.

Embedding

Cleared tissue is embedded in a suitable embedding medium. Paraffin wax is the most preferred medium. Several plastics are also available nowadays and they offer better sections. Paraffin embedding is carried out in an oven at a temperature just above the melting point of the paraffin. When infiltration is complete, the specimen is transferred to an embedding mold of fresh paraffin which is allowed to harden. Then the mold is removed and excess paraffin is trimmed away.

Microtomy

The trimmed block of paraffin is then fixed on a block holder. This block holder is then secured to the microtome and oriented appropriately with respect to the knife. With each revolution of the microtome handle, the specimen moves through the blade and a section of desired thickness is produced. Each successive section adheres to the preceding are forming a continuous ribbon. The ribbon is cut into small piece and transferred onto clean albuminized slides. The ribbon is flattened by putting a few drops of water. These floating sections are stretched using a hot plate or warming table.

Staining

Next, the paraffin is removed with xylene or another appropriate solvent and the specimen is rehydrated. It is then stained, dehydrated, cleared (made transparent) with xylene, covered with a suitable mounting medium, and topped with a cover-slip. Various stains are available to the histologist. **Hematoxylin and eosin** (H&E) is a frequently used combination of stains. Hematoxylin imparts a purple color to substances, but must be linked to a metallic salt called a mordant before it can function effectively. This combination, called a lake, carries a positive charge and behaves as a basic (cationic) stain. The lake combines electrostatically with negatively charged radicals such as phosphate groups of nucleoproteins. Substances that become colored by a basic stain are said to be basophilic. Methylene blue, toluidine blue, and basic fuchsin are basic stains. Unlike hema-toxylin, these stains have molecules that carry a positive charge of their own and do not require a mordant. Acidic (anionic) stains carry a negative charge and color cell or tissue components that bear positive charges. Eosin is an acid stain. It imparts an orange or red color to acidophilic substances. Other commonly used acid stains are **orange G**, **phloxine**, and **aniline blue**.

In addition to the widely used H & E staining procedure, numerous other stain combinations and techniques are available. Some are especially useful for identifying certain tissue elements. For example, trichrome procedures such as Mallory's and Masson's specifically stain collagenous fibers within connective tissue. Orcein and Weigert's resorcin fuchsin are stains used to color elastic fibers, providing a means of distinguishing them from other fibrous elements. Reticular fibers and nervous tissue components such as neurons, myelin, and cells of the neuroglia can be stained by procedures employing the use of silver. There are also special histochemical and immuno histochemical procedures that make possible the localization of various carbohydrates, lipids, and proteins found in tissue. Stains such as Wright's and--Giemsa's (Romanovsky stains) are available for differentiating the various cells found in blood and bone marrow.

Stains

The question is often asked, "What are biological stains and how do they differ from dyes?" Dyes are colored substances, generally aromatic organic compounds, used for imparting color to fabrics, paper, leather, wood, oils, fats, waxes and other products as well as for producing color in plant and animal tissues to study their gross and microscopic structure and nature. However, stains are uncolored organic and inorganic reagents which produce colors in these tissues. We now define staining as any means of conferring a color reaction on tissue elements and their stainable contents, metabolic, functional or pathological. The reagents themselves may be colored or uncolored, organic or inorganic.

Although we can observe, by phase contrast microscopy, we are now vastly dependent on stains to discern clearly the morphologic and tinctorial details to which we have become accustomed. Very little use of stains occurred before the 1860s, although long wood and cochineal were known to Robert Hooke (1660), who actually studied dyed wool and hair microscopically. Leeuwenhoek in 1714 used saffron to improve the visibility of muscle fibers under his microscope (Conn, 1948). Raspail (1825) employed iodine to demonstrate plant vascular tissue. According to Gertz (1916), Hartig used phytolocca as a nuclear stain in 1850. The first useful employment of hematoxylin was made by Bohmer's (1865). Ranvier (1875) enumerated only 6 synthetic dyes used in histology. Among them was quinoline blue with which he stained intraepithelial fat droplets and peripheral nerve myelin blue- the first lysochrome staining of fats- over 20 years before Daddi's (1896) introduction of Sudan III. Ferrocyanide staining of tissue iron, first noted by Grohe (1861) was really put on a working basis by Perls (1867) and Quincke added the sulfide reaction in 1880, Macallum the hematoxylin reaction in 1897. Meanwhile the acid and basic nature of various aniline dyes was realized and they were widely employed for the staining of cytoplasm and nuclei, respectively.

The first dyes used by microscopists as stains were all natural dyestuffs: saffron, Leeuwenhoek, 1714; phytolacca or pokeberry juice, Sarrabat, Hartig, 1850; carmine, Goppert and Cohn, 1849, Corti, 1851, Hartig, 1854-1858; hematoxylin, Bohmer, 1865. According to Farrar (1974) synthetic dyes appeared in the textile industry in 1835-1862. The case of orchil or French purple has been urged as the first synthetic dye. It was prepared as early as 1300 by air oxidation of orcinol in the lichen *Roccella* in the presence of ammonia from fermented urine (Farrar, 1974). Saxe blue (indigocarmine, C.I. 75781; Natural Blue 2) was prepared by Barthin in 1740 by treating indigo with highly concentrated sulfuric acid, and dyed wool blue. Rosolic acid (Runge) and rufigallic acid (Robiquet) appeared in the 1830s. Fritzsche produced murexide and picric acid about 1840 and both were used as textile dyes for silk and later wool; chrysamic acid (Kurtz) was made about 1850. Prout made murexide with nitric acid or uric acid; it was produced commercially by 1855. Then in 1856 Perkin produced aniline purple or mauve. Williams produced a diquinoline "cyanin" dye about the same time and Verguin made magenta in 1858.

Gierke (1984), in his historical discussion of staining, stated that the history up to his day was divided into three periods, each occupying a decade. The first decade, the 1850s, was characterized by a few important but unrelated discoveries which ended in the work of Gerlach, each investigator followed up accidental observations on the staining powers of carmine and the other well known dyes of those days. After Gerlach's work, the development of the technic in the 1860s was more rapid and depended less upon chance success by the individual investigator; the effort was made to use similarly all the dyes and metallic colors then available. The next decade would have had much less left to develop in this line if it had not been that by this time the great variety of aniline dyes was available and microscopists were constantly finding new uses for them. Gierke wondered if there would be any opportunity for equal development during the 10 years to follow his paper.

Uses of Stains

Only a brief summary of the uses of stains is given here. More detailed citations are given under the discussion of the individual dyes. Certain very general texts of the subject are also useful; among those which have proved most valuable sources of the information are: Mann (1902), Ehrlich et al. (1903, 1910), Krause (1926-1927), Lee (1937 and earlier editions), McClung (1950 and earlier editions).

Staining of Animal Material

Although many of the earlier uses of stains were botanical, modern histological technic was first developed on animal material. As a result the first extensive use of stains was in animal histology. It is still true that there are many more staining procedures developed in animal histology than in plant histology, and that many more dyes are thus employed in the former field than in the latter.

In animal histology one, two, three, and occasionally four or more dyes designed primarily to differentiate nuclei from cytoplasm of cells, permit distinctions between the various types of tissues. Best known of these are the various procedures calling for hematoxylin, sometimes alone and more often with a counterstain, such as eosin Y, Congo red or safranin; the hematoxylin-eosin combination is in such general use that it is commonly referred to as the "H and E stain" or more concisely "H & E." Although these hematoxylin procedures have received many modern refinements, they date back to the 19th century and still bear the names of Weigert, Benda, Heidenhain, Delafield, Harris, and Mayer, who did their main work in the 1880s and 1890s. Also included among the general tissue stains are various combinations of basic dyes such as crystal violet, methylene blue or one of the azures, with some contrasting acid dye such as eosin Y; the former to stain the nuclei, the latter, the cytoplasm of the cells.

Somewhat more specialized in their application are the **connective tissue stains**. The distinction between them and the general tissue stains is more or less arbitrary, particularly because some procedures that bring out connective tissue and elastin to good advantage are also fine general tissue stains. The grouping can, however, be made in a rough way and for practical purposes is rather convenient. These stains fall into two groups: the order of mixtures of picric acid with various blue, red and green acid dyes, the latter by the use of mordanting with phosphomolybdic or phosphotungstic acid just before the final fiber stain, usually with a blue or green acid triarylmethane dye. The first of these stains was Jullien's (1872) picroindigocarmine, the most used of this group has been Van Gieson's (1889) picro-acid fuchsin, and one of the more precise of the latter combinations is Lillie's (1951) allochrome procedure, a combination of the periodic acid Schiff method to show basement membranes with a picromethyl blue for fine collagen fibrils. The phosphomolybdic and phosphotungstic aniline blue stains originated by Mallory (1900) have also been widely used as triple or "trichrome" stains for collagen, muscle and nuclei. The Masson, "tri-chrome" and Heidenhain (1916) "azan" methods with many variations have likewise enjoyed much popularity. Other dyes have been substituted for aniline blue, which was a mixture of water blue and methyl blue, with good results. Specific stains for elastic fibers are often included in both groups of technics, thus giving rise to "quadruple" or tetrachrome stains. Besides these procedures, Mallory's phosphotungstic acid hematoxylin, Mann's methyl blue eosin and many modifications of Maresch's (1905) application of Bielschowsky's ammonical silver for reticulum can be included as connective tissue methods.

A third important group of methods in animal microtechnic includes those for **neurological staining**. These methods are very numerous and all highly specialized any of them (as is true of some methods for demonstrating connective tissue) are not actually dyeing procedures, but depend on the use of silver salts with which tissue elements are impregnated so that the desired structures are made visible when the salts are converted into metallic silver.

In addition to these three groups of staining procedures in animal histology, there are stains for other types of tissue and body fluids. Fats, for example, are stained by special oil soluble dyes, such as Sudan IV and by special procedures not using solvent dyes. Blood has its own special methods of staining, most of which depend on the use of compound stains, prepared by allowing eosin or a related dye to react upon a mixture of dyes of the methylene blue group; such compound dyes are also useful in staining bone marrow. Bone has its own special methods, many of which depend on the use of alizarin red **S, Kernechtrot** and related dyes, are particularly valuable by demonstrating bone in small specimens that have been cleared by treatment in alkali.

Histochemistry

Many of the above mentioned specialized staining methods might yield actual chemical information as to the nature of cell constituents, but were, in general, not thought of under that term. Some theories of staining do postulate chemical affinities to explain differential staining; but they do not go very far in the matter, chiefly because stains are ordinarily applied to fixed tissue, whose chemical nature is often quite specifically altered by the prestaining preparation procedures. The introduction, however, of rapid freezing methods is now enabling histochemists to avoid chemical fixation and is giving them material for study which can be compared critically with chemically fixed or denatured tissue. Also, their study of enzymes on the one hand and their identification of the individual nucleic acids on the other are gradually giving them criteria to show which stains or other reagents are actually specific for definite cytochemical ingredients. Especially important has become the use of the Schiff reagent (fuchsin-sulfurous acid), after periodic or chromic acid, in identification of mucopolysaccharides. Developments in histochemistry were so rapid that predictions were hard to make.

Plant Histology

A rough classification of the common plant histological methods can be made by recognizing general tissue stains and stains for woody tissue. This grouping is no more absolute, however, than the separation between general tissue stains and connective tissue stains in animal histology. Probably the most frequently used dye in botanical microtechnic is hematoxylin, which is employed in a number of procedures either for general tissue or woody tissue. Another very valuable dye is safranin which is one of the best nuclear stains employed in botanical work; with- a green or blue counterstain, very effective pictures are obtained.

Various combinations of stains have been employed for certain more highly specialized purposes, such as staining fungi in tissues, or for demonstrating pollen tubes in the style. For such purposes as this, numerous dyes have been called for, such as thionin, orange G, Martius yellow, malachite green, acid fuchsin, methyl green, carmine, basic fuchsin and lacmoid. It is nevertheless true, that there is by no means such a variety of staining procedures in plant histology as in the zoological field.

Plant Cytology

Although the statement just made is true in the general histological field, it cannot be made in regard to cytology. The earliest cytological work was done with plant material, probably because of the greater ease with which rapidly dividing cells (meristematic tissue) can be obtained from plants than from

Late Prof. H. J Conn,
The founder of Biological Stain Commission

animals. As a result considerable variety of procedures are available in plant cytology. Best known among them, undoubtedly, are: the variations of the hematoxylin methods; the **Flemming triple stain**, which calls for crystal violet, safranin and orange G; and the acetocarmine method employed for fresh smears of anthers. There are numerous special combinations of crystal violet and safranin, each with particular counterstains designed to bring out certain desired effects.

It is interesting to note that, although there are many dyes used in both plant and animal microtechnic, there are others that are important in one of these fields but not in the other. Thus carmine and safran in are pre-eminently botanical stains, methylene blue a very important zoological stain that is hardly ever employed by the botanist.

Microbiology

Another very important field in which biological stains are employed is the study of bacteria and other microorganisms such as fungi and protozoa. The dyes thus used are somewhat limited in number, methylene blue, crystal violet and basic fuchsin satisfying most of the bacteriologist's needs. It is very interesting, however, to note that these three dyes, which are pre-eminently bacteriological stains, are by far the largest sellers of any of the biologicals.

In microbiology dyes are used not only as stains but as constituents of culture media. They are thus employed either as indicators or for their bacteriostatic effects; sometimes they even serve in the differentiation of species.

A comparatively new field now is **bacterial cytology**. As in the case of histochemistry, development in this field has been made possible by improved methods of fixation. The conventional method of rendering bacterial cells stainable was merely to dry them on a slide, a process which distorts the cell and makes internal structure quite difficult to demonstrate. Such crude fixation methods are now being replaced, for all delicate work, with others that cause less distortion; and gradually bacterial cytology is being revealed. There are difficulties still to be surmounted; artifacts and true nuclear structures are sometimes difficult to tell apart, and misinterpretations are frequently made. Nevertheless, the field is being rapidly explored, and the subject of bacterial cytology is no longer so highly speculative as it was a comparatively few years ago.

Bacteriological staining methods (outside of cytology) can be divided into two groups: stains for bacteria in dried films; and stains for bacteria in tissue. The former consist of very simple procedures, ordinarily; about the most complicated of them is Gram's iodine stain which calls for crystal violet and a counterstain; some species of bacteria retaining the violet stain, others, taking the counterstain. The stains for bacteria in tissue are essentially histological methods, many of them very similar to those used for general animal tissue; their main purpose, however, is not the differentiation between different tissue elements but that between bacteria and the tissue in which they are located.

An important aspect of bacterial staining is the laboratory diagnosis of disease. In numerous diseases, of which tuberculosis and diphtheria are the most conspicuous examples, staining procedures play a prominent role in diagnosis; in the case of tuberculosis diagnosis, fluorochrome dyes are proving valuable information.

Classification of Stains

Dyes are sometimes classed in two groups, the natural and the artificial or synthetic. The former class is now of relatively smaller importance from the standpoint of the manufacturer and the textile dyer; for the synthetic dyes far out-number them and the advancement of science is gradually making it possible to produce many of the formerly natural dyes by artificial means (e.g., indigo, orcein). It just happens that one or two natural dyes, the derivatives of cochineal and logwood extract are among the most valuable biological stains; but the natural dyes in general are so few in number that they can be practically disregarded in considering the general chemical nature of dyes.

Because the first synthetic dyes were produced from aniline all of this class are often called "aniline dyes," although there are now a large number of them which bear no relation to this compound and are not derived from it. Therefore the term was replaced by the then more correct term "coal tar dyes" since this was the main source. Latterly petroleum refinery products have come to greatly exceed coal tar as a source of organic compounds and dyes and we now tend to speak simply of "synthetic" dyes. In view of the current depletion rate of petroleum, the geologically more abundant coal may again become a principal sources.

The cytological stains are solutions of those aromatic organic compounds, which impart colour to the objects. These have two kinds of active chemical groups namely:

1. The chromophoric group. These groups impart colour to the dyes (stain) and include carboxyl group (-COOH), azo group (-N=N-), nitrogroup (-NO_2), indamin group (-N=) and quinoid group 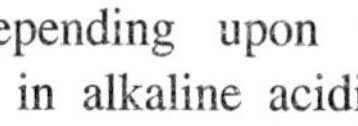 etc.

2. The auxochoromic group. These provide the dye an ability to attach to the tissue or the material. They dissolve and dissociate in water. Stains containing hydroxyl group (-OH) belong to auxochromic group.

Depending upon whether the stain imparts colour in alkaline acidic or neutral conditions, the stains can be classified into three categories:

1. Basic stains. The chromophoric group of basic stains is cationic (basic) in nature and stains in alkaline medium only. The basic stains are used to stain nucleus and chromosomes particularly the nucleic acids. Basic fuchisn, crystal violet, methyl green, methylene blue, safranine, azures and acridine red are basic dyes. These combine with –NH_2 group.

2. Acidic stains. The chromophoric group of acidic stain is acidic in nature. These contain nitro (-NH_2) and quinoid groups. These combine with the protein structures of the cell at a low pH by their hydroxyl (-OH), carboxyl (-COOH) or sulfonic (-HSO_4) groups. Picric acid, acid fuschin, methyl blue eosin, orange G, congo red, aniline blue are acidic dyes.

3. Neutral stains. The neutral stains have the properties of acidic as well as that of basic stains e.g. neutral red.

4. Nitroso dyes. The nitroso dyes are produced by the action of nitrous acid on phenolic compounds, according to the equation.

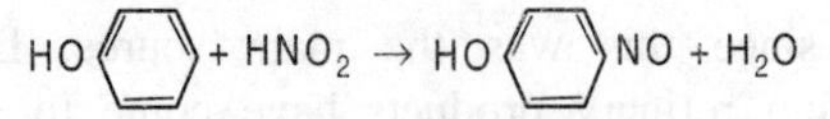

p-Nitrosophenol

The fact, however, that the quinine oxime produced by the action of hydroxylamine on p-quinone according to the equation,

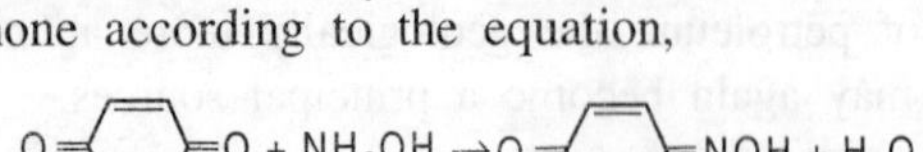

p-quinone oxime

Is identical with the nitrosophenol produced as shown above, shows that in all probability the substances can react as quinine oximes, which better accounts for their behavior as dyeing agents since the quinine ring

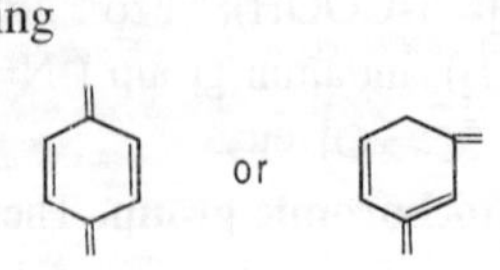

Occurs frequently in other dyes and a chromophore.

The examples are fast green O, Naphthol green Y, Gambine R, Naphthol green B.

5. Nitro dyes. In this group the chromophore is NO_2. It is of such a strongly acid character that all the dyes of this group are acid dyes. The examples are picric acid, nitrophenols, victoria yellow, picryl sulfonic acid.

Azo group. The azo group are characterized by the chromophore –N=N– joining benzene or naphthalene rings, (I) It is possible for the azo group to occur more than once in a molecule, forming the disazo dyes, thus (II).

I II

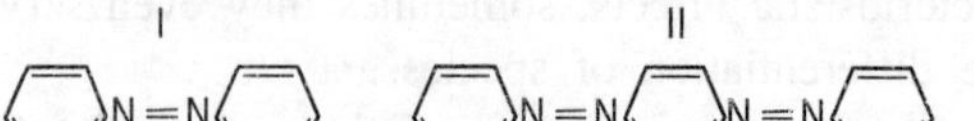

Similarly dyes with three or four azo groups are known. The azo chromophore is distinctly basic; but not sufficiently so to make the dyes basic when they contain hydroxyl groups. Those containing amino groups are of course, distinctly basic.

The position of the hydroxyl or amino group on a benzene ring in relation to the azo group is important. Ordinarily they are in the **para** position to each other (III).

III

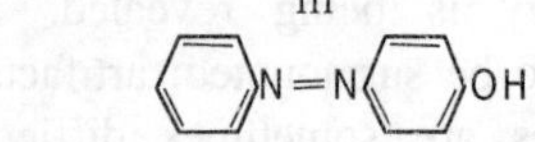

Michaelis (1901) proposed that only those azo dyes which lacked an ionizable group could serve as specific fat stains. He stained that when the phenolic or naphthol hydroxyl was in a position **ortho** to the **azo** group a quinonoid shift occurred, thus preventing ionization (I→II).

I II

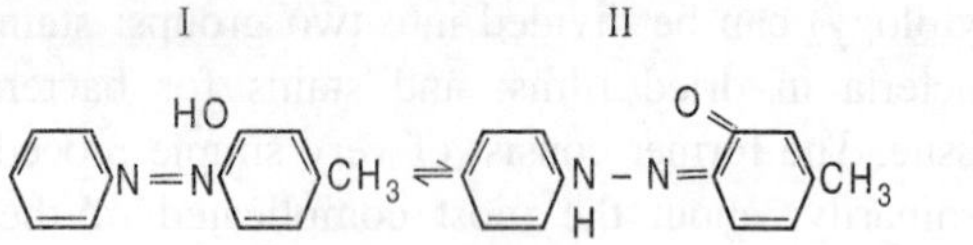

III

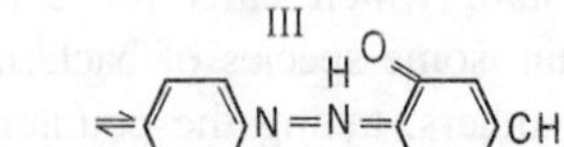

Of the phenol group, and that with p-phenols and α-naphthols the azo compound remained alkali soluble, in contrast to o-phenol and β-naphthol azo dyes, which were alkali insoluble. Thus benzene azo-p-cresol acts as a fat stain, but benzene azo-o-cresol does not. This theory was widely accepted. The formation of the quinonization product has been modified to include a pentavalent nitrogen (III above). These formulations were not accepted by the **Colour Index**.

6. Monoazo dyes. Examples are orange G, Aniline yellow, fast green GBC, Janus green, Nubian yellow.

7. Diazo and polyazo dyes. This diazo dye of orange brown color is insoluble in water, soluble in alcohol, acetone, fat solvents, oils, fats and waxes, slightly soluble in aliphatic hydrocarbons. Its lighfastness is very good and it resists heating at 120°C. It should serve well as a fat stain.

Examples are Janus yellow, fast brown, thiazin brown R, Blue block N, Bismark brown Y, Benzo orange R, sudan N, oil red O.

8. Diazonim and tetrazolium salts. The diazonium and tetrazonium salts have the same basic structure, and are considered in this section. They are salts of a theoretical base R-N^{+}=N (or R-N=NOH). These bases are usually quite unstable, and in many instances their simple halides are also, though some reasonably stable chlorides and acid sulfates exist. Combinations as double salts of zinc chloride, boron trifluoride, sodium bisulfate, and naphthalene-1,5-disulfonic acid are the usual commercially available salts, and many keep fairly well even with (dry) room temperature storages. Solution stability, especially in the alkaline range, is generally brief.

Examples are fast scalet GG, fast brown RR, fast orange GR, fast red GG, fast garnet GC, fast blue B.

9. Xanthenes and acridines. The group of compounds known as xanthene dyes comprises a number of basic and acid dyes. They are derivatives of the compound xanthene:

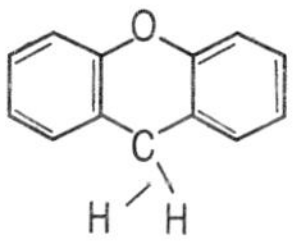

The xanthene dyes fall into three major classes, the fluorenes or amino xanthenes, the rhodols or aminohydroxyxanthenes, and the fluorones or hydroxyxanthenes. The chromophore of the aminoxanthenes is the resonance hydrid:

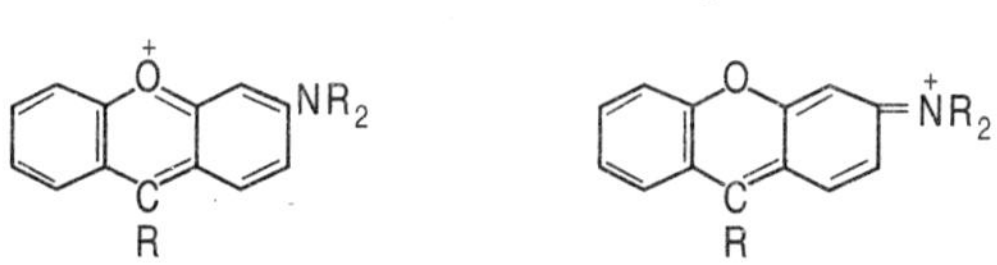

In the hydroxyxanthenes the chromophore is the quinoid product:

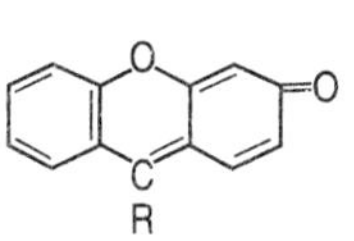

In both of the above R may be hydrogen, alkyl, or aryl. When the R on the methane carbon is aryl, the dyes present certain analogies with the triarylmethane group although they possess the pyran ring.

The **Colour Index** divides the fluorenes into five classes: pyronins, succineins, sacchareins, rosamines, and rhodamines. Of these classes the first, second, fourth, and fifth have representatives among commonly used biological stains.

Pyronins include pyronin Y, succineins, sulforhodamine B, rhodamine G, Rho dols include rhodamine 12 GM, Fluorones include rosamines, fluorescein.

10. Natural dyes. The group of natural dyes is shrinking, as many of them are now being produced synthetically. For example madder, a dyestuff used in ancient Egypt and Libya, the Libyan women dyed their goatskin caps with it (Herodotus IV-189). It has been now replaced by its principal derivatives the anthroquinone dyes alizarin and purpurin, produced synthetically. Indigo formerly produced in Europe from wood *(Isatis tinctoria)* and other plants of the genera *Indigofera*, *Polygonum*, and *Lonchocarpus*, is made synthetically except in a few primitive areas. Orcein, now made from the oxidation of orcinol in the presence of ammonia and consisting of oxazin and oxazone dyes, is now considered, in that group which was formerly prepared from lichens, *Lecanora* and *Roccella* sp.

Remaining to be considered are a number of dyes whose structure is now more or less well known, but whose synthesis is either not yet achieved or not practiced on a commercial scale. The most important for the biologist in this group are cochineal and carmine, hematoxylin and brazilin, morin, and tetracycline. Others less used are saffron, berberin, curcumin, alkanna, and maclurin.

11. Neutral stains. The other major class of bicolored dye combinations are, the neutral stains in which one of the component dyes is acid and stains cytoplasm,-the other basic coloring nuclei, cartilage, mast cells, and acid mucins.

The simple aniline dyes, as we saw earlier often owe their value as biological stains to their acidic (anionic) or basic (cationic) character. The acid dyes that owe this property include phenol, sulfonic acid or carboxylic acid groups. These usually exist in commerce as sodium, potassium, ammonium, or sometimes calcium salts. The basic dyes are chlorides, acetates, bromides, or sulfates usually of immonium bases. In both cases, the dye or color ion is the weaker of the pair the mineral or organic acid, the metal or ammonium ion being stronger.

Mechanism of Staining

It is a well known fact that proteins, certain polysaccharides and nucleic acids have the property of ionization. But the ionisation of proteins depends upon pH of the medium. At pH values above isoelectric point, acid groups become ionized and below isoeletric point, all the basic groups dissociate. Thus at a pH above isoelectric point, the proteins react with basic dyes and exhibit basophilic property. At pH value below isoelectric point, the proteins react with acidic dyes and exhibit acidophilic property. The intensity of staining depends upon the degree of acidity or alkalinity of the medium. The basophilic or acidophilic property of cell components also depends on the fixative used.

Acidophilic and Basophilic Tissues

The objects, tissues or cell components which are stained with acidic dyes are known as acidophilics where as those stained with basic stains are basophilics. The cytoplasm and its components are acidophilic and the nucleus, chromosomes and DNA are basophilic.

Metachromasia

Some basic dyes stain certain cell components with a colour totally different from their original colour. This property of stains is called metachromasia. **Toluidine blue**, **azure-A** and **thionine** are metachromatic stains which react with muco-polysaccharides, nucleic acids and certain acid lipids and stain them in different colours. For example, toluidine blue stains nucleus bluish green and cytoplasm pinkish or purple.

Mordants and Lakes

Certain dyes can stain the proteins and the cytoplasm only when their action is supplemented by some metal or **metallic compounds** which is capable of combining both with the protein of the cell and the dye. Such metals or metallic compounds are called mordants. The mordant is usually a double salt of potassium or ammonium with aluminium or ferric sulfate. The combination of mordant and dye is called lake. NH_4 So_4 (iron alum) is the most common mordant used with haematoxylin and carmine.

Staining for Light Microscopy

The selection of a stain for the study of cells under light microscope depends upon the nature of material to be studied, the type of fixative used, and the chemical reactivity of the dye. The concentration of the dye and the temperature and pH at which it is most effective are also to be considered. The cytoplasmic proteins and carbohydrates are stained with acidic stains while the nucleus and chromosomes etc. are stained with basic dyes.

Staining of Lipids and Steroids

Lipids might be stained in frozen sections or in sections of freeze dried specimens infiltrated with carbowax by using any of these dyes – Sudan dyes, fluorescent dyes, aqueous, nile blue, etc. In second method lipids may be made insoluble first and then stained with dichromatie, osmium, Ca and Cd solutions.

Staining with Fluorescent Dyes

These dyes are used in very low concentrations and the time for staining is also very short. The florescence can be attached in extreme dilution. Thus the identification of **riboflavine**, vitamin A and thiamine in the lowest concentration is very easy. The most commonly used basic dyes are **berberine**, **acridine orange** and **yellow**, **coriphosphine**.

Staining for Electron Microscopy

Usually no stains are required for electron microscopy, because the image is photographed in black and white. For obtaining better contrast following methods are used:

1. Heavy metal shadow casting. The material is deposited with vapours of heavy metals like **platinum**, **chromium** or **ceranium** from side and a shadow is formed on the other side. This is known as heavy metal shadow casting.

2. Negative staining method. For studying virus and macromolecules, the specimen is embedded in a droplet of some electron dense medium like **phosphotungstate**. The material penetrates into all empty spaces between the macromolecules. The spaces filled with electron dense material appear dark, while the biological macromolecules appear electron transparent.

3. Electron staining. The heavy atoms of osmium tetraoxide, **lead, uranyl etc.** act as electron stains and combine selectively with certain regions of the cells and appear darker.

Vital Staining

Vital staining is the staining of living cells and the stains used are called a vital stains. The common vital stains are janus green B, neutral red, methylene blue, and trypan blue. The vital staining can be done by dissociating the living cells from the body and keeping them in stain (**supravital staining**) or by injection of the dye into the living organism (**intravital staining**). Vital staining demonstrates the cytoplasmic structure by specific staining of cellular components for example staining of mitochondria by janus green.

Cytochemical Stains

Certain stains are very specific and stain specific cellular components. The staining depends upon the chemical composition or the enzymatic activity of the component. Therefore, cytochemical stains are used to test the presence or absence of specific organic compounds and their localization in the tissue or cells.

[I] Cytochemical Demonstration of Proteins

Two types of proteins are found in the cell—the acidic proteins and basic proteins. Both the proteins can be demonstrated in the same material and such a material is said to demonstrate total proteins. Certain stains can specifically stain the acidic proteins and the others only the basic proteins but fast green is a stain which can be used to demonstrate the total proteins or only the basic protein. Fast green is a disodium salt of paradibenzyl diethyl diamine parahydroxy triphenyl trisulfonic acid aldehyde. Other reactions specific for proteins are:

1. Million reaction. The stain used is a nitrous mercuric reagent which reacts with the tyrosine groups and forms a red precipitate.

2. Diazonium reaction. The stain used is a diazomium hydroxide which reacts with tyrosine, tryptophan and histidine groups.

3. Sakaguchi test. The stain is an alkaline mixture of a-naphthol and sodium hypochlorite. It stains arginine group.

[II] Cytochemical Demonstration of Nucleic Acids

There are several stains specific for nucleic acids. Some of them (toluidene blue, methyl green pyronin etc.) impart differential colours to DNA and RNA. Some (**Feulgen**) are specific for DNA and some (azure B) are specific for RNA.

1. Feulgen reaction for DNA. The Feulgen reaction was discovered by Feulgen and Rossenback (1924) for demonstrating the presence of DNA. It is based on the old and popular **Schiff's reaction** known for testing the presence of aldehyde group.

2. Demonstration of nucleic acids with methyl green pyronin. Methyl green pyronin is a complex of two stains- methyl green which stains DNA green and pyronin which stains RNA pink or red.

3. Demonstration of nucleic acids with toluidine blue. Toluidene blue is another stain for the localization of DNA and RNA. DNA is stained bluish green and RNA deep violet.

[III] Cytochemical Demonstration of Lipids

The lipids of cells can be stained by those dyes which are soluble in fat. **Sudan black B** is the most common stain used for staining phospholipids and golgi complex. Osmium tetraoxide and Sudan red are other dyes for staining lipids.

[IV] Cytological Demonstration of Carbohydrates

Starch, cellulose, mucoproteins and chitin etc. are all stained with Schiff's reagent with suitable modifications.

Chemistry of Staining

General principle underlying biological staining methods present two basic ideas:

In all staining methods the important questions to be asked are: why do any tissue components stain? Why do some components remain stained while all components are not stained?

Possible answers to these questions can be derived from recognition that when staining a smear or sections, we are dealing with two phase systems (i) solid phase (ii) soluble phase, These methods depend upon selective uptake of reagents and selective loss of products from the tissue. These uptakes and losses depend upon chemical affinity and rate factors.

Factors Contributing to Chemical Affinities

We know that all dyes have a tendency to form aggregates. A major contribution to dye/reagent tissue affinity, when using organic reagents from solutions is the hydrophobic binding. This binding means that any staining system between the hydrophobic groups such as phenyl alanine or tryptophan to bring together the molecules even though initially dispersed in an aqueous environment. This process occurs due to chemical thermal dynamics – a process which involves the increase in entropy of the system due to properties of the solvent. This phenomenon becomes more important as the hydrophobic character of substrate and reagent becomes more marked. We can consider an example of staining of elastic fibres either by dyes or **tetrazoium salts** which contains a biphenyl system.

Regarding the affinity between dyes, we may consider metachromatic dyes. These dyes are classic examples having spectral properties unlike those of monomeric dyes:

1. Vanderwaal's forces. They are the reactions most common among dye - tissue attraction. They occur between tissue and reagents at varying degrees. They occur quite frequently when a close reagent – substrate contact is possible. This is important because Vanderwaals attraction are polar forces all of which become stronger as the **polarsibility** of molecules increases. These forces are potent for a short distance only. They are non ionic and quite suitable for hydrated substances. They are usually expected to play a role in staining but this may be with low molecular weight dyes and polar substrates.

2. Coulombic attractions. These are most widely acknowledged reagent-tissue interactions, also termed as salt linked or electrostatic bonds. They arise due to electrostatic attractions for example between of basic dyes and tissue structures which are rich in phosphated DNA and RNA. It may be emphasized that these interactions are important for all ionic reactions. Even if the tissue substrate remains unchanged, it acquires anionic nature in the process of staining for example **PAS or Best carmine** method for glycogen.

3. Hydrogen bonding. This is a localized bond formed when a hydrogen atom exists in between two electronegative atoms like oxygen and nitrogen. It is also known as a covalent binding to one of them. It is really a source of tissue affinity when aqueous solvents are used. In non-aqueous solution also hydrogen bonding plays a significant role for example in Best carmine method in glycogen where methyl alcohol is used as a solvent.

4. Covalent bonding. These bonds are formed when tissue and reagents act as a source of affinity to each other. We meet this kind of bonding in classical method viz: Feulgen method and mercury orange method. Details of the reactions involved further show that covalent bond leading to mode of action of modern dyes are widely supposed to attach to tissue as metal tissue covalencics. Recent researches, however, have failed to support this traditional concept. It seems that modern dyes are usually large sized and consequently **Vanderwaal's forces** and **hydrophobic bonding** can make large contributions to dye tissue affinities.

Why do the Stains Remain in a Tissue?

We know that a mounting medium has a low affinity for stains and organic pigments. Consequently hydrophilic media are used as mounting material. Modern dyes once formed in the tissues are non readily removed by processing fluids. They are mounted in non-aqueous media otherwise the diffusion of dye will occur. Conversely nonionic dyes are mounted in aqueous media.

Why the Stains are not Taken up by Every Part of Tissue (Differential Dyeing)?

The answer to this question lies in variations observed between reagent tissue affinities. e.g. non-ionic, Sudan dye has affinity for a fat droplet but not for surrounding proteins. In practice, the stain conditions are manipulated to maximize such affinities. The basic dyes must be applied from neutral or acidic solutions. An another fashionable manipulation is to change the concentration of inorganic salt in dye bath. It is considered by many workers that critical electrolytic concentration plays an important role. However, when the dye – tissue affinity are the same, the uptake of reagents or loss of reagents might not be the same in two structures. The rate of reaction or reagent uptake can be brought to optimum by choosing the coloured derivative which is covalently bound in reaction e.g. in PAS reaction the oxidation by periodic acid can oxidize a variety of chemical structures in addition to aldehydes.

Should be chosen as such, the aldehyde generation may be fast and specific. Sometimes these methods become complicated due to certain factors. Any factor affecting the rate of reaction can alter the staining pattern. Finally a reagent may stain a variety of structure and colours. These can occur both with dyes and with reactive stains. An example of **polychromasia** with a reactive stain arises in use of amino brown anthrapine sulphonic acid as a thiol reagent. Although nucleophils can react with two reagents give rise blue reagent and only the thiol group look orange.

Modifications Prior to Staining

Such modifications are in the processes of fixation as well as during extraction techniques which finally alter staining patterns. Fixation of the tissue may cause loss of tissue components during processing and staining and also during the formation of geometrical component. The first point to know this is that different components are retained in tissues at a different degree of fixation and that different fixations exert these differences. Nothing can be stained in tissues which can not be retained, e.g. lipids, are well stained in fixation with osmium tetraoxide but poorly with formalin. Proteins are well preserved by formalin but are lost after osmium tetraoxide fixation.

During staining, it has been observed that HCHO, OS_2O_3 induce basophilia where as HCHO increases tissue acidophilia. These differences show causes – effect system. It becomes important to choose a right fixative and dye at optimum temperature and pH.

Interpreting Sections

One must know the gross structure of an organ before a histologic section from it can be comprehended. It is also helpful to know how the section was cut, that is, whether it was a cross section (x.s.), a longitudinal section (R.S,), or an oblique slice through the organ. Was the cut made through the entire organ or only through a portion of it? Frequently, prepared slides are labelled indicating the particular orientation of the section. This is not important in an asymmetric organ such as the spleen or liver because their appearance would be unaffected by the direction of the cut, Conversely, the small intestine is radially symmetrical and its appearance is affected by the direction of the cut.

The three-dimensional structure of organs and their components must also be considered when examining a histologic preparation. Cells are three-dimensional objects differing in size and shape. For example, some are long and thin, some cuboidal, and others ovoid. They may have a random or specific arrangement within an organ. How they appear depends on their shape, as well as how they were cut. Imagine how the spindle-shaped and tall columnar cells shown in figure 1A would look if sectioned in various planes. Note that the nucleus may or may not be included in a particular cut through a cell. The histologist examines multicellular structures having a wide variety of shapes. Some are hollow, some branch repeatedly, some open onto surfaces, etc. Figure 1, B and C, and figure 2 show a variety of three-dimensional structures and how they would appear if cut at different levels. Examine these carefully. They will help you to understand situations you will encounter on actual slides.

Helpful Hints

Be sure that the lenses of your microscope are clean before you begin examining slides. Use a piece of lens paper or a soft, clean cloth such as an old (but clean) linen handkerchief. If the lenses have been coated with oil or another substance, remove it using lens tissue moistened sparingly with a glass cleaner such as windex. Slides should also be cleaned using a soft, dust-free cloth or tissue moistened with glass cleaner. Every microscope should have a pointer in the ocular. This is usually supplied by the manufacturer, but can be made from a short piece of hair. The latter is cemented into

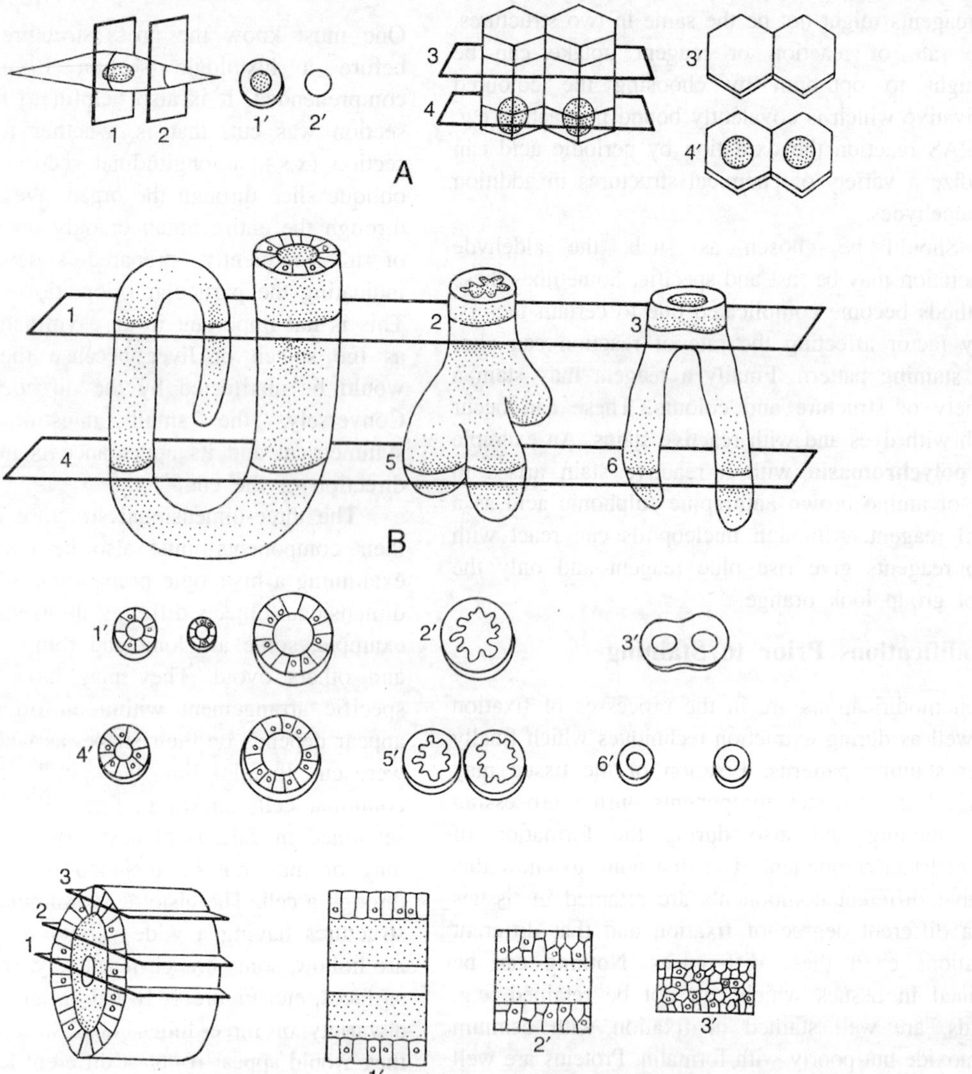

Fig. 1. A slice, indicated by numbered planes, taken through two different types of cells would appear as identified by the prime numbers. Only if the plane of the cut passes through the nucleus will the latter be seen, B and C. Planes of section taken from different levels in four separate multicellular objects are illustrated. Note how the appearance of sections varies with the level of the cut.

place inside the ocular with a drop of quick-drying glue or nail polish. Without a pointer, it is not possible to accurately indicate an object in the microscope field for another observer.

Before beginning a section at the microscope, make sure that the fine-adjustment knob is near the middle of its range of rotation. If you do not, you may find that the knob is at the limit of its excursion when you are busily making observations. At that point, you must correct it carefully.

It is also a good habit to examine your slide with the unaided eye before placing it on the stage of your microscope. If you do so, you will gain information about the gross aspects of the specimen and be more likely to center it properly over the light source. Centering is especially important for small specimens that might otherwise be difficult to locate. Also, make sure that you put the slide on the stage with the cover glass uppermost. If the slide is upside down, you will not be able to focus on it with the high-power lenses. Do not snicker. We have seen this happen often in the teaching laboratory.

It is always a good idea to start your observations using the lowest power objective available on your microscope. This is usually 4X lens. The field of view will be large, enabling you to locate regions of special interest more easily. When you locate something you wish to examine at a higher magnification, center the object in the middle of the field of view. Then, when you change to a stronger lens, the object should be somewhere in the field.

Binocular microscopes often have atleast one ocular that can be adjusted to accommodate your vision. It is important that you adjust this properly if you want to have a comfortable, headache-free session at the microscope. Assuming that your microscope is of the binocular type and that it has at least one adjustable ocular, you should first bring the specimen into focus with the ocular that is not adjustable by using the fine adjustment knob. When you have done this, focus the other eye using the adjustable ocular. Use of this procedure will ensure a proper focus for both eyes and prevent eye strain.

Bright, even lighting is absolutely essential to effective microscopy. The best way to achieve this is to use Kohler illumination. This can be obtained with any microscope that is equipped with both a condenser aperture diaphragm (the one in the condenser) and a field diaphragm (the one in the light source). If you have such an instrument, proceed as follows:

(1) Center the light source, using the directions you received with the microscope.
(2) Open both the field and aperture diaphragms fully.
(3) Raise the condenser to its uppermost position.
(4) Place a specimen on the stage and focus on it using the 10X objective.
(5) Close the field diaphragm so that its leaves are clearly imaged in the field of view.
(6) Center the image of the diaphragm by manipulating the condenser centering screws, then open the field diaphragm until its leaves disappear just beyond the edge of the field of view.
(7) Remove an ocular and, while looking into the back aperture of the objective, close the aperture diaphragm completely and then open it until it is about 75% of being fully open.

You now have Kohler illumination. If you want to increase or decrease the light intensity, use the rheostat or neutral-density filters, but do not adjust the condenser aperture diaphragm or field diaphragm. If the aperture diaphragm is open to excess, the image will lack some contrast and be flooded with light. If it is closed too far, there will be a loss of resolution and increase in contrast. This increase in contrast is often confused with sharpness or high resolution; this is a common error in microscopy. All of the above adjustments (except for centering the light source) must be made each time, a different objective is used.

If your microscope lacks a field diaphragm, you will not be able to obtain Kohler illumination. You can still acquire good and useful lighting, however. Place a specimen on the stage, open the aperture diaphragm fully, and adjust the light intensity with the rheostat so that it is comfortable for your eyes. Be sure that the condenser is raised to its highest position, or close to it, when you do this. Now, remove an ocular and look at the back aperture of the objective. Close the aperture diaphragm fully and then open it until it is about 75% of being fully open. This will provide proper lighting for most purposes. If you should need more or less illumination, make adjustments only with the rheostat or neutral density filter; do not use the aperture diaphragm.

To get the most from a specimen, you must avoid being a passive microscopist, that is, one who finds an object and then stares at it admiringly without making further adjustments of the focus. Get into the habit of focusing continuously with the fine adjustment as you peruse a slide, because even though a tissue section may be only a few micrometers thick, the depth of field of the higher power objectives may be less than the thickness of the specimen. Therefore, if you do not focus repeatedly as you examine a preparation, you will certainly miss seeing structural detail that might be important to your work.

You might like to return to a particular location on your slide preparation at a future time. Remembering landmarks in the vicinity of the object of interest will aid you in locating the object later. A more expedient way of relocating structures is by using verniers, which are mounted on both the X and Y axes of the mechanical stage. A vernier consists of two, parallel, graduated, sliding scales, one long and one short. The smaller scale is 9 millimeters (mm) long and is divided into 10 subdivisions (0 to 10). The larger scale is several centimeters (cm) long and is graduated in millimeters, for example, 0 to 80 or 100 to 160. To relocate an object on a slide, you must first center it in the microscope field. Once this has been done, you establish its location by reading each of the verniers (X and Y). For example, the 0 point on the small scale of the vernier on the X axis might be located somewhere between lines 42 and 43 on the larger scale (Fig. 2). To determine its specific location, find the line on the small scale that coincides exactly with a line on the longer scale. Then count, on the smaller scale, the number of spaces between 0 and the point of coincidence. This number is your decimal point. In the example given the decimal is 0·6 and you should read 42·6 as the vernier value. Do the same for the other vernier (Y) and record the numbers for both. In future, if you want to return to the same location, simply secure the slide to the mechanical stage and move the stage controls until the verniers are adjusted to the numbers you previously recorded. These manipulations will have returned the slide to its former

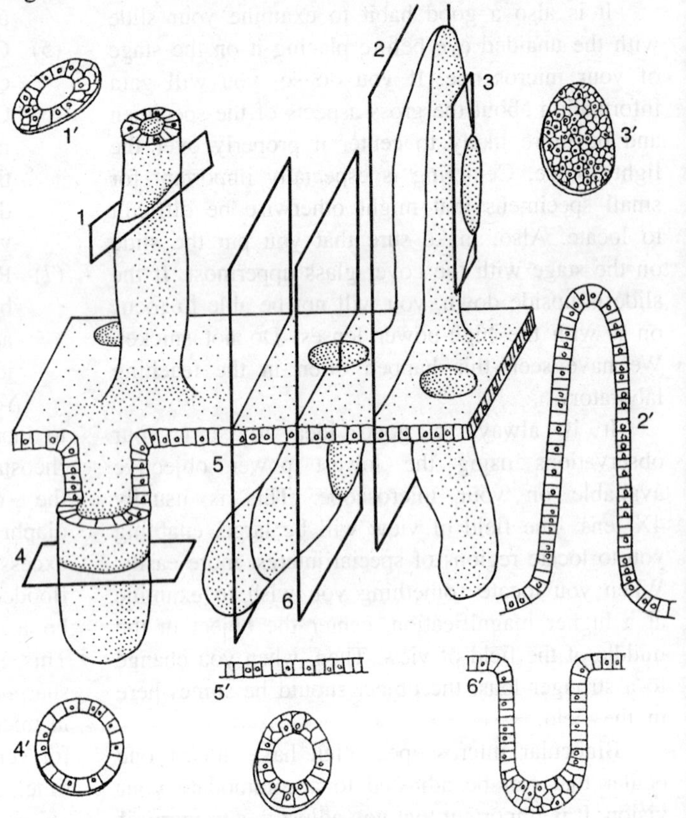

Fig. 2. The prime numbers illustrate sections resulting from transverse (4), oblique (1), and longitudinal (2, 3, 5, 6) cuts made through a plate of cells bearing hollow projections (above plate). Plane 3 differs from the others because it passes only through the cellular wall of a projection, and not the lumen; therefore, section 3′ appears as a plate of cells rather than a hollow structure. You should also be aware that structures may often appear unrelated to a surface or another object, when in fact they are. Compare planes 5 and 6 with sections 5′ and 6′, where continuity of the invagination with the surface is evident only in 6 and 6′. While not apparent from a single section, such continuity would be evident if an uninterrupted series of sections through the entire invagination were made and examined.

position, and the object you are looking for should be somewhere within the microscope field.

By knowing the approximate diameter of a red blood cell in a section you can estimate the size of other tissue components. Therefore, it is useful to know that in tissue sections prepared by the paraffin method the average size of erythrocytes for each of the following animals is as follows —

Goat—2·4 μm diameter (smallest erythrocytes of the domestic mammals)

Dog—4·9 μm diameter (largest erythrocytes of the domestic mammals)

Chicken—9·4 mm long

Each average value is based on a total of 20 to 30 cells that were measured from five different slide preparations of tissues embedded in Paraplast X- TRA (Monoject Scientific, Division of Sherwood Medical, St. Louis, MO 63103).

Artifacts

Folds, knife marks, stain precipitate, spaces (where none belong), shrinkage, and air bubbles are examples of commonly occurring imperfections seen in slide preparations. They were introduced during processing and are called artifacts.

Important Questions

1. Describe the entire process of preparation of a paraffin section.
2. Describe the process of staining of a paraffin section.
3. How will you find out the section prepared by you is :
   (i) Cross section, (ii) Longitudinal section.
4. Classify and discuss the major properties of stains or dyes.
5. Discuss in details the mechanisms of staining.
6. Explain briefly the chemistry of staining.
7. Write short notes on the following :
   (i) Azo dyes, (ii) Metachromasia, (iii) Mordants and lakes, (iv) Cytochemical stains.

6

Microscopy

Microscopy is defined as a lens or combination of lenses used to magnify and observe near objects so that details invisible to the naked eye can be revealed. At the beginning of the **Age of Enlightenment**, magnifying property of an optical lens was already known and such lenses were used by various scientists in Europe resulting in the invention of the telescope and of the 2-stage microscope. These developments initiated a period of discoveries in the microscopic field mainly by Anthony van **Leeuwenhoek** (1632-1723), **Robert Hooke** (1635-1703), **Marcello Malpighi** (1628-1694) and **Jan Swammerdam** (1937-1680). These followed an interval of almost 150 years during which owing to the lack of further development of the instruments, hardly any scientific discoveries were made but a "microscopic delectation of the mind and the eye", became known.

On the realization of important optical principles and the progressive mastery of the design of instruments for astronomy and navigation, the barriers of difference in the traditional theoretical and practical thinking were broken. The demands for instruments for research in astronomy and microscopy grew with the blossoming of natural sciences. Increasing interest, following **French Revolution**, in medical sciences during first half of the 19th century, led to the realization that microscope is capable of revealing more than entertaining spectacles and curiosities. Although the first functional microscope was produced by a Dutchman **Zacharias Janssen** in the first decade of the sixteenth century, the present design of light microscope emerged only in the twentieth century. Advent of electron microscopy about midway through the century greatly extended out powers of visual resolution. Today a variety of microscopes are available to a biologist. Basic principles, designs of these microscopes and applications are discussed below in detail.

Light Microscopy

All optical instruments including the eye, depend upon a physical parameter known as resolution. **Resolution** of the unaided human eye is about 0.1 mm (100μ). In other words, two objects within 100μ of each other appear to be in contact. The minimum distance at which they are resolvable as separate entities is explained by Abbe's relationship.

$$d_0 = \frac{0 \cdot 6\lambda}{n \sin \alpha}$$

where

d_0 = minimum distance

λ = wavelength of radiation

n = refractive index between the specimen and the first lens

$n \sin \alpha$ = numerical aperture

Abbe's relationship makes it clear that high resolution in a microscope can be achieved by manipulating these variables i.e. wavelength of illuminating radiation, the refractive index and the aperture. 85° is the limit of aperture of a good optical microscope. Refractive index is easy to alter, but only within narrow limits, n for air is 1, whereas transparent oils have an n upto 1·5, accounting for the popularity of the oil immersion lenses of modern microscopes.

Thus, a good light microscope with a numerical aperture of 1.4 and using light at the short and of the visible spectrum (0·4 μ or 400 nm) will resolve two points at about 0·17μ separation. This is immensely better than the unaided eye. The resolving power of a lens can be expressed as follows —

$$RP = \frac{0 \cdot 6\lambda}{n \sin \alpha}$$

Thus resolving power of a low power, high power and oil-immersion objectives can be calculated as follows —

$$\text{RP for low power objective} = \frac{550 \text{ nm}}{2 \times 0 \cdot 25} = 1100 \text{ nm} = 1 \cdot 1 \ \mu\text{m}$$

$$\text{RP for high power objective} = \frac{550 \text{ nm}}{2 \times 0 \cdot 65} = 423 \cdot 07 \text{ nm} = 0 \cdot 42 \ \mu\text{m}$$

$$\text{RP for an oil immersion objective} = \frac{550 \text{ nm}}{2 \times 1 \cdot 25} = 220 \text{ nm} = 0 \cdot 22 \ \mu\text{m}$$

Depending upon the lens system, microscopes are of two types (i) simple microscope and (ii) compound microscope. A simple microscope consists of a single lens system while a compound microscope consists of two or more lens systems. Depending upon the source of illumination, the microscope can be classified as —

(1) Light microscope
 (i) Bright field microscope
 (ii) Dark field microscope
 (iii) Ultraviolet microscope
 (iv) Phase contrast microscope
 (v) Fluorescent microscope
(2) Electron microscope

A comparison of the major features of various kinds of microscopes is given in the table 1.

Bright-field Compound Microscope

The bright-field compound microscope (**microscope that uses a direct light source for illumination**) is a type of microscope, which is most commonly used for general laboratory observations. It consists of a series of two lens system between the eye and the object and a direct light source (sun and mirror or lamp) where light shines directly on the specimen, and dark objects in a bright field is observable.

A typical bright-field microscope (Fig.1) consists of four basic parts :

(1) The **base** to provide firm support and stability to the microscope;
(2) The **stage**, which is a flat platform that holds the slide in position;
(3) The **arm** which is movable, used for carrying the microscope and can be set in a comfortable position for the worker; and
(4) The **body tube** for transmitting the magnified image.

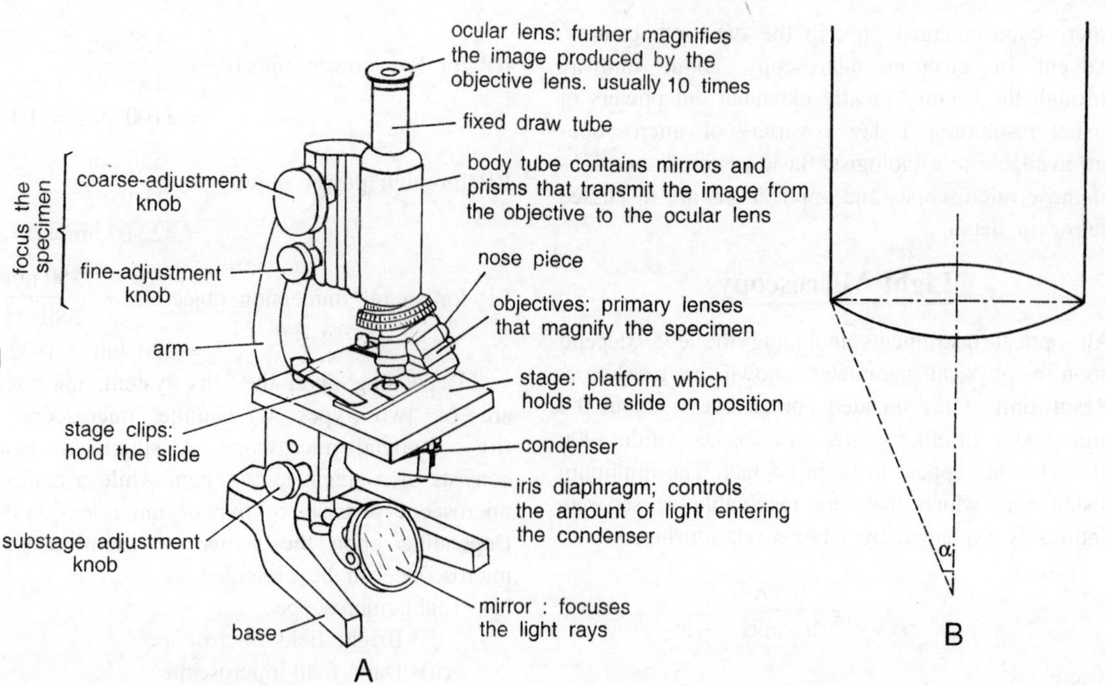

Fig. 1. The monocular compound bright-field (or light) microscope. (A) The principle parts and their function (B) A diagrammatic representation of numerical apearture.

The **optical system** consists of two series of lenses, the objective lens and ocular lens (eye piece). The upper end of the body tube holds the ocular lens (10×–15×) through which the image is viewed. The lower end of body tube which is lodged close to the object being examined is fitted with a rotating nose piece holding generally three objective lenses, which provide magnification powers of 10X, 40X and 100X. The greatest magnification achievable by most standard bright-field microscope is 10 X 100 = 1000X. The resolution of such a microscope is 0·00027 mm (0·27 μm), about one-thousandth the thickness of a human hair.

The stage may have two clips or a mechanical stage, which moves by means of adjustment knobs, to hold the slide. Attached to the stage is the substage consisting of a condenser, an iris diaphragm and a mirror. The condenser consists of several lenses that concentrate light on the slide. The iris diaphragm controls the angle and amount of light used. The mirror reflects light from the source of illumination via the condenser. **The concave side of the mirror is used for natural day light (sunlight) and the flat side for the artificial light (e.g. lamp)**. More recently designed microscope has a built-in light source which simplifies light focusing.

The coarse (larger) and fine (smaller) focus **adjustment knobs** are used for focusing the image of the specimen. The coarse adjustment which raises or lowers the base tube, is used for focusing the low-power objective and the fine adjustment, is used for focusing high-power and oil-immersion objectives. The area seen through a microscope is known as the **field of vision**.

A microscope possessing a single ocular lens is called a monocular microscope and that possessing two ocular lenses is called a **binocular microscope**.

Requirements

- ➔ Bright-field (light) microscope
- ➔ Light source
- ➔ Lens paper, Immersion oil
- ➔ Xylol
- ➔ Prepared slide of an organism

Table 1. **Comparison of five types of microscopes.**

Microscope	Maximum useful magnification	Appearance of specimen	Common uses	Advantages	Disadvantages
1. Bright-field	1000 ×	Specimen stained or unstained; bacterium generally stained and appear in stain.	Observing stained specimen; sections microbes, colour of	Easy to use; readily available; allows staining reactions to be interpreted.	Lack of contrast; inability to resolve very small bacteria and viruses; introduction of artifacts during staining procedures.
2. Dark field	1000 ×	Generally unstained; appears bright or "lighted" in an otherwise dark field Bright and coloured'	Viewing unstained cells not observable with bright field microscope	Allow living microbes to be viewed e.g. spirochetes.	Staining reactions cannot be sued for examining stained specimens.
3. Fluorescence	1000 ×	Colour of the fluorescent dye	Detecting specific infectious agents in tissue, detecting immunological reactions	Rapid identification of infectious microorganism	Specimens that naturally fluoresce or which are stained with a fluorescent dye are only observed.
4. Phase-contrast	1000 ×	Structures varying degrees "darkness'	Observing living unstained cell; revealing intracellular structure	Enhances subcellular anatomy; allows observation of motility, phagocytosis and biological activities.	Inability to evaluate staining reactions.
5. Electron	1,00,000 ×	Viewed on fluorescent screen	Examination of viruses and ultrastructure of cells; diagnosis certain virus diseases and cancers; detecting certain giant molecules	Allows viewing of objects too small to be observed by light microscopy.	Very expensive; only killed specimens are observed; introduction of artifacts in the specimen during harsh preparation procedures.

Procedure for Microscope Operation

(1) Remove the microscope from the cabinet by grasping the microscope arm firmly with the right hand and the base with the left hand and carry close to the body and gently keep it on the laboratory table in an upright position.

(2) Place the microscope with its arm facing the user approximately 15 cm from the edge of the laboratory table.

(3) Clean the lenses of the microscope with lens paper before using it. Remove oily substances from glass parts by wiping with a lens paper moistened with xylol. But it is to be removed immediately with lens paper dipped in 95% alcohol and the lens is later on wiped dry with a fresh lens paper.

(4) If the microscope does not have a built-in-light source place the microscope in front of a microscope lamp.

(5) Place the slide on the microscope stage and secure it with stage clips or other means provided.

(6) Adjust the mirror so that the flat side reflects the light into the barrel of the microscope.

(7) Bring the low power (10×) objective in position by rotating the nose piece.

(8) Look through the eye piece/eye pieces and raise the condenser until there is a minimum illumination i.e. light is seen as a circle in the center of the field called **"a bright full moon"**.

(9) Raise the condenser up to the stage with the help of the condenser adjustment knob.

(10) Look through the ocular, keeping both eyes open, bring the specimen into sharp focus by using fine-adjustment knob.

(11) Adjust iris diaphragm to produce optimum illumination.

(12) When the image comes into focus with the low-power objective, the nose piece is rotated to the next lens (i.e., 40 × or 100 ×) by simply swinging the objective desired into place, without raising the body tube. Only slight adjustment of the fine-adjustment knob will bring the object into sharp focus because all objectives are parafocal.

(13) When using the oil-immersion objective, swing the high-power objective partially out of way and place a drop of immersion oil on the area of the slide you are observing and bring the oil-immersion objective into position.

(14) Now look through the eye piece and focus the object with fine-adjustment knob.

(15) Before putting the microscope to its cabinet, after completion of the exercise, move the nose piece to bri·· a low-power objective into position, clean the oil from the immersion lens using a special lens paper and also clean off the slide with a tissue paper (Fig. 2).

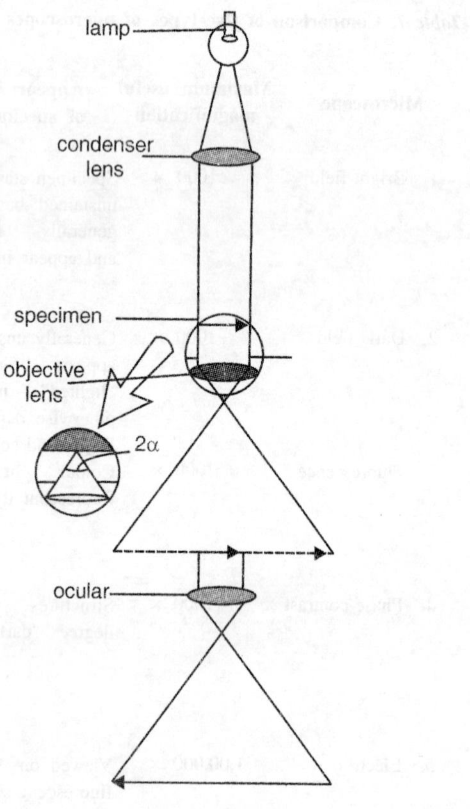

Fig. 2. The light microscope. Note the aperture angle, α, which is related to the resolving power by equation. When using an oil immersion lens, the space between the specimen and the objective lens (circled) is filled with transparent oil.

Phase Contrast Interference Microscopy

These microscopical methods have been developed using special optical techniques. Their basic principle lies on the fact that although biological structures are highly transparent to visible light, they cause phase changes or retardations in transmitted radiations.

For example, a ray of light can be adjusted to pass through a material which does not absorb light (A) and a material which absorbs light (C). In A, the wave of light is thrown over a material which has different refractive index than the medium in passing through this object, the amplitude of the wave is not changed but the velocity is altered. When the refractive index of the material is higher than the medium, it causes delay or retardation in the transmittance of light (Fig. 3).

In phase contrast microscope, special objectives are used to intensify small phase differences. The lateral plane of the objective and central plane of the objective are adjusted to retard or advance the wavelength of light by additional ¼ wavelength (1/4 λ) with respect to central light and by an annular phase plate that introduces ¼ wavelength variation in the back focal plane of the objective. This phenomenon is called as phase effect. The **phase effect** results from the interference between the direct geometric image given by the central part of the objective and lateral image, which has been retarded, or advanced to a total ¼ wavelength.

In bright or negative contrast, the two sets of rays are added and the object appears brighter than the surroundings. **In dark or positive contrast**, the two sets of rays are subtracted making the image of the object darker than the surroundings (Fig. 3). A transparent object thus appears in various shades of gray, depending on

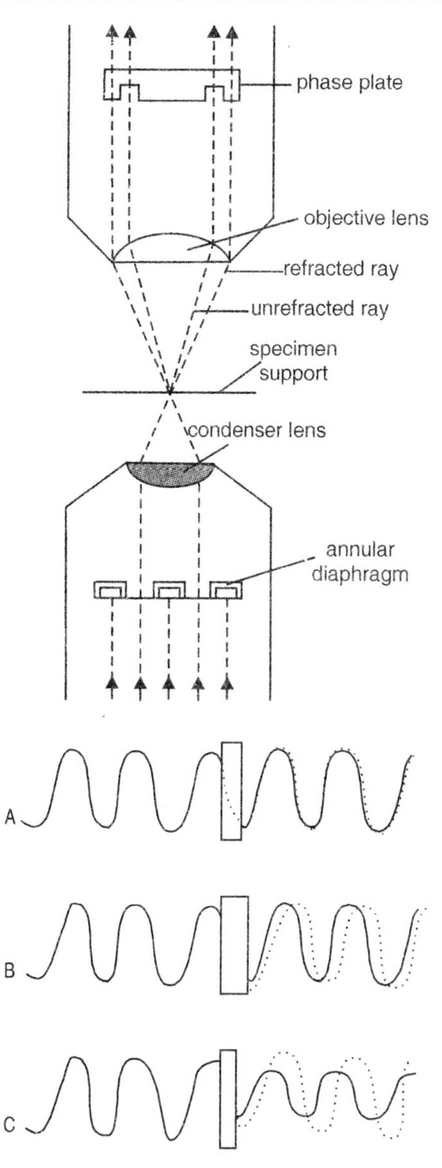

Fig. 3. Diagram of the phase contrast microcope. Rays that pass through a region of changing refractive index will be refracted and after passing through the phase plate, will cause interference with unrefracted rays. This produces a halo effect, increasing contrast and making it easier to observe unstained, living cells.

its thickness and the difference between the refractive indices of the object and the medium.

Applications. Phase contrast microscopy is used in routine to observe living cells and tissues, microbes and parasites and has been found useful in observing cells cultured *in vitro* during mitosis.

Interference Microscopy

The interference microscope works on the principle similar to that of phase contrast microscope but it offers additional advantage of giving quantitative data. It detects small and continuous changes in refractive index whereas phase microscope reveals only sharp boundaries. The variations in phase can be transformed in coloured images that a living cell may resemble a stained preparation.

Nomarski interference. This technique is used to give the image a characteristic effect that is better than the phase contrast image. Observations on cell division are generally made using this technique.

Ultra-Microscopy

This technique is also called as dark field microscopy. It works on the principle that light can be scattered at boundaries between regions having different refractive indexes. Certain modifications are made in the ordinary microscope. An ordinary condenser is replaced by one that illuminates the object obliquely. Use of dark field condenser does not allow the light to enter the objective directly. Therefore, the object appears bright in scattered light and the background remains dark.

Dark field microscopy allows the detection of objects smaller than those seen with the ordinary light microscope. However, it can not resolve such objects.

Polarization Microscopy

Certain components of cells and tissues show particular behaviour when examined under polarized

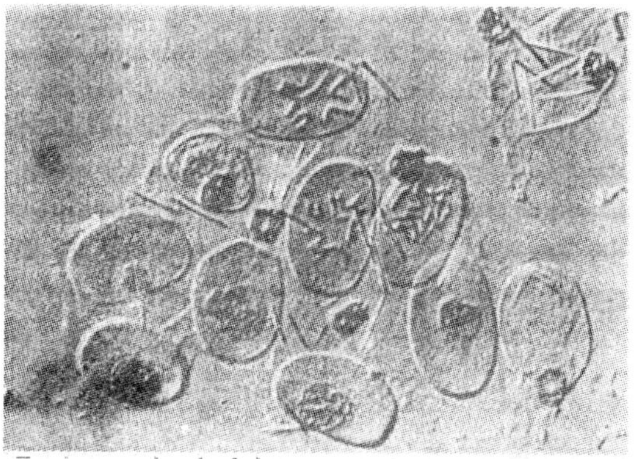

Fig. 4. *Tradescantia virginica* mother pollen dividing interference (contrast) 2000 ×.

light. When polarized light is propagated through a component material with the same velocity, independent of the impringing direction, they are called as **isotropic**. Such structures have the same index of refraction in all directions. However, certain structures affect the velocity of light. Such objects are called **anisotropic** or **birefringent** (two different indexes of refraction).

For example, connective tissue fibres are birefringent if the index of refraction is greater along the length of fibre than in the perpendicular plane and non birefringent in the opposite case.

Birefringence (B) forms the principle of a polarization microscopy. It may be expressed quantitatively as the difference between the two indexes of refraction (N_e–N_O). Thus $B = N_e - N_O$

In practice, these differences result into retardation of polarized light. This retardation depends upon the thickness (t) of the specimen. Therefore,

$$B = \frac{\lambda}{t}$$

A polarizing microscope is equipped with two additional devices i.e. the polarizer and the analyzer both of which can be prepared from a Polaroid film *or* from Nicol prisms of calcite. The polarizer is placed below the substage condenser whereas the analyzer is placed above the objective lens.

Fluorescence Microscopy

Fluorescence microscopy dates from about 1904 when **Kohler** reported observing fluorescence of tissues under ultraviolet radiation in a microscope. **Coons** (1941) introduced the fluorescent antibody technique with a consequent revolution in immunology. Development of instrumentation, of staining methods, and of applications has been rapid during past few years. The basic technique of fluorescence microscopy have been described by **Price** and **Schwartz** (1956), **Haitinger** (1959) **Holborow** (1970).

Basic Principles

Essentially, fluorescence is an optical phenomenon in which light is absorbed by a substance, known as **fluorophore**, and is instantaneously re-emitted as light of a larger wavelength. This change in

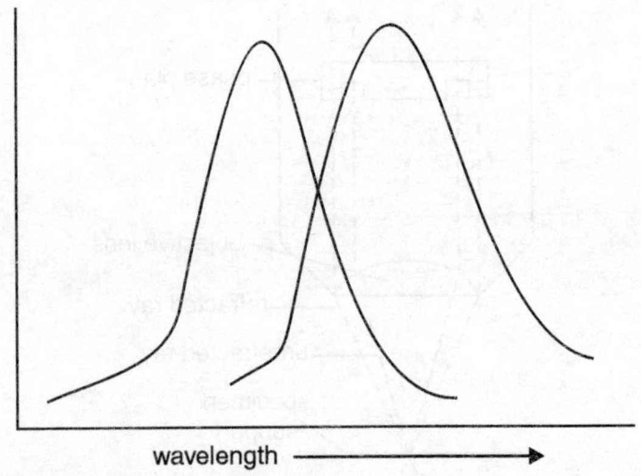

Fig. 5. Excitation (left) and emission spectrum of a typical fluorophore.

wavelength is known as **Stokes shift**. On absorption of light, the fluorophore molecules become excited that is to say their electronic state is changed to an excited state. When this excited molecule returns to ground state, the surplus energy is dissipated as heat, emitted as fluorescence or utilized in a photochemical reaction. The spectral characteristics of a typical fluorophore are shown in Figure 5. For a pure substance, the emission spectrum is independent of the wavelength used for excitation. The fact that the emitted light is of a longer wavelength than that used for excitation forms the basis of fluorescence microscopy.

Design of a Fluorescence Microscope

This microscope differs from the conventional microscope. Two filters are used in this microscope. A primary (excitation) filter is placed somewhere between the light source and the specimen. The filter allows light only over a comparatively narrow band of wavelength corresponding to the excitation peak of the fluorophore being observed.

The secondary filter or **barrier filter** is intended to prevent light of the excitation wavelength from reacting the observer's eye. It is placed between the object and eye (Fig. 6).

The usual optical arrangement of a fluorescence microscope is such that the fluorescent specimen microscopy is capable of revealing the presence of a very small quantity of fluorophore which will stand out against the dark background. It is the extreme sensitivity of the fluorescence technique which gives

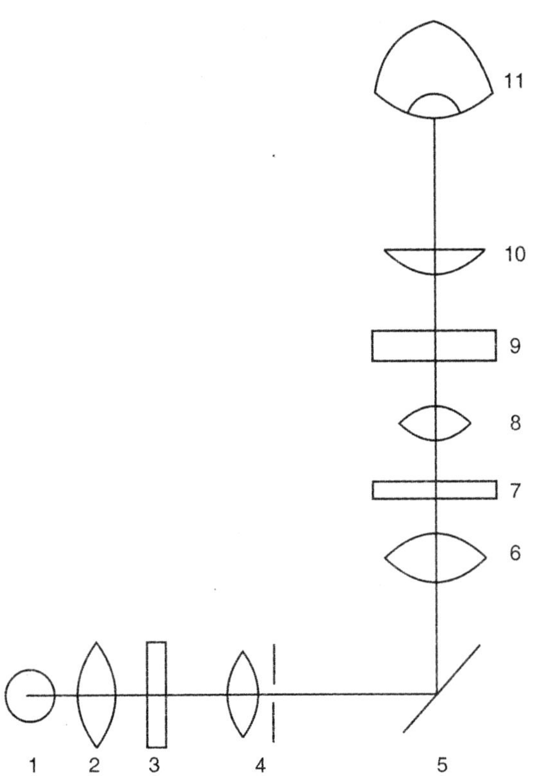

Fig. 6. Optical diagram of a fluorescence microscope using dia-illumination or dark-ground illumination. 1 lamp, 2 collector lens, 3 excitation filter, 5 field lens and diagphragm, 5 substage mirror, 6 condenser, 7 object (fluorescent), 8 objective, 9 barrier filter, 10 ocular, 11 observer's eye or camera.

it great value in immunofluorescence and for other purposes requiring the demonstration of small amounts of substances.

The apparent colour and contrast of a fluorescent specimen depends not only upon the filter system but also upon the characteristics of the observer's eye (or photographic film).

Applications

Fluorescence techniques can be applied to all kinds of biological material. A major advantage of fluorescence microscopy is its very high sensitivity. Particles below the resolution of light microscope can be viewed by fluorescent microscope. Opaque objects or relatively opaque objects such as very thick sections can also be examined by fluorescence microscopy using an epi-illiuminator. The basic type of fluorescent material that can be studied in tissues are listed in the following table.

Table 2. **Strongly autofluorescent substances which may occur in tissues. (all proteins are to some extent autofluorescent).**

Substance	Fluorescence Colour
Collagen fibres	blue-green
Elastic fibres	blue-green
Protein bound $NADH_2$	blue
Vitamin A	red
Lipofuscin	orange
Porphyrins	red

Electron Microscopy

Electron microscopy developed along with light microscopy or optical microscopy. Optical microscopy could function under certain limits of resolution. In the light microscope, magnification is largely determined by the objective and a maximum magnification of 100 or 120X can be achieved. Since the ocular lens can increase this image only 5 to 15 times, a total useful magnification of 500 to 1500X can be achieved.

In practice there were no lenses that could be used to focus very short wavelengths. To overcome this problem **Dr. Ruska** (University of Berlin) discovered electron optical system that led to this well established science of electron microscopy (EM) in 1931.

In EM, charged particles such as electrons respond to magnetic fields. Since particles also exhibit wave properties, focusing them with magnetic lenses produces an image. If a metal filament is placed in vaccum tube and heated, it emits electrons that can be accelerated by an electrical potential and tend to follow a straight path with properties similar to those of light. Like light, the stream of electrons has a corpuscular and vibratory character but the wavelength can be expressed by the equation

$$\lambda = \frac{12 \cdot 3}{\sqrt{E}} A^{\circ}$$

Where E is the voltage through which the electron is accelerated. Electrons at 50,000 volts have a wavelength of 0·05 A°. This value does not offer improvement in resolution because numerical aperture of electron microscope is much smaller than that of light microscopes. Therefore, magnetic coils are used which act as a condenser. Electrons are focused on the plane of the object and then are deflected by another magnetic coil which acts as an objective lens and gives a magnified image of the object. This is received by a third magnetic lens which acts as an ocular or projection lens and again magnifies the image from the objective. The final image can be observed on a fluorescent screen or recorded on a photographic plate.

In the EM the resolving power is so high that a wide range of magnifications can be attained by introducing one or more intermediate lenses. Direct magnifications as high as 1,000,000X may thus be obtained and the micrographs further enlarged photographically to 10,000,000X or more depending upon the resolution achieved.

The Scanning Electron Microscope (SEM)

Although, scanning instruments were available by the mid 1940s, biologists found the ways to use this technique by 1960s. In scanning microscope, the beam of electrons are allowed to move back and forth across the specimen. As electrons strike the specimen, they may be scattered or secondary electrons may be knocked from the sample. These electrons, in either case, are collected by a photomultiplier tube. Other types of radiation can also be induced in the specimen and detected. Crevices will produce fewer detectable electrons, whereas projections will be highlighted. These variations are used to modulate the beam sweeping across the picture tube, thus producing an image.

With the scanning EM, surface view of a specimen is obtained by using the secondary

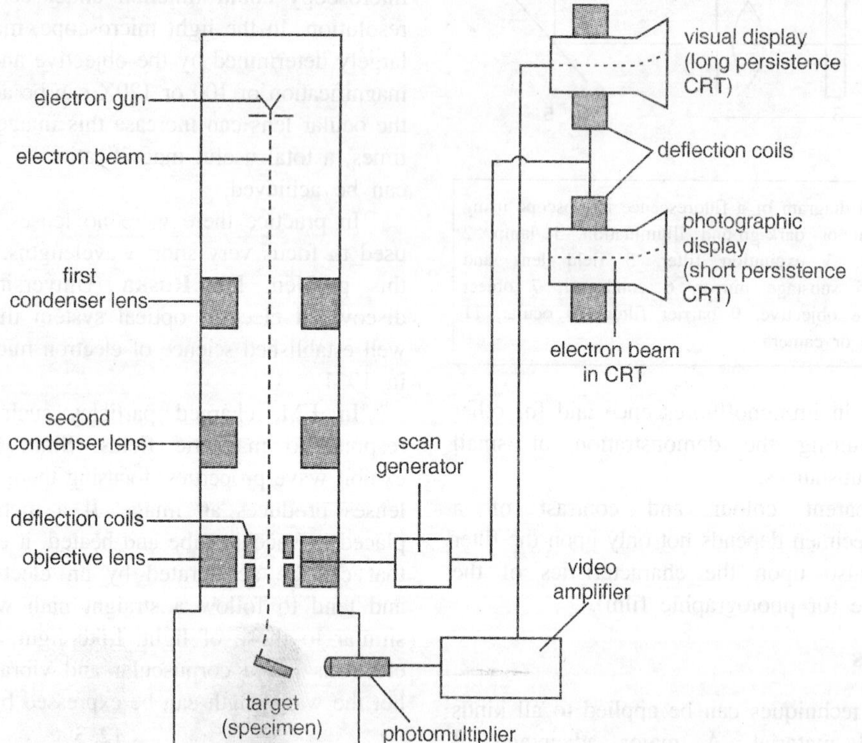

Fig. 7. The Scanning Electron Microscope. The beam is swept back and forth across the specimen in synchrony with a beam moving across the face of a television picture tube. Radiation (scattered or secondary electrons, etc.) from the sample is used to modulate the observation beam, producing variations in brightness.

electrons emitted from primary electron beam that interacted with the surface of the specimen.

The Transmission Electron Microscope (TEM)

The optics of TEM are, in principle, very simpler to those of the light microscope, except that the TBM uses a beam of electrons rather than a beam of light. The principle components of this microscope can be summarized as follows —

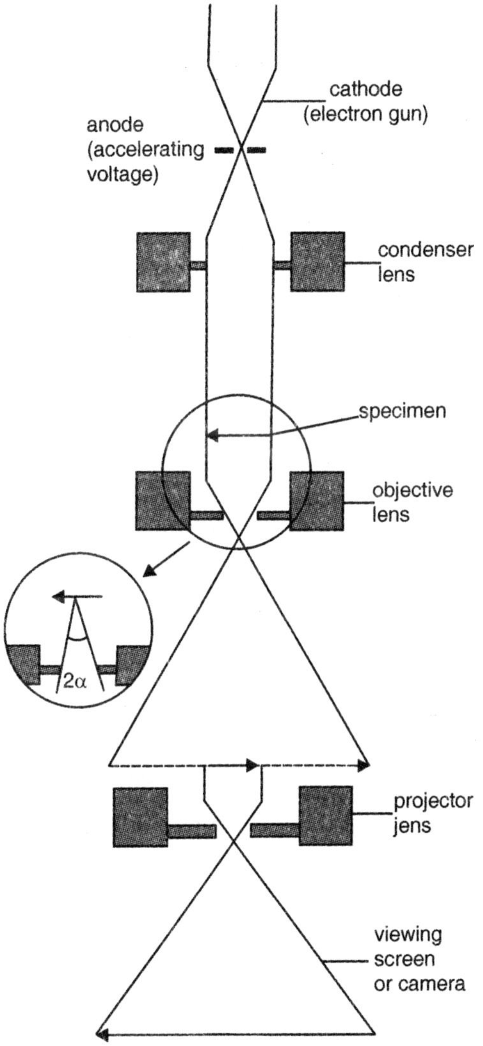

Fig. 8. The Electron Microscope. Compare with Fig. 7. The entire column, from filament to screen, is maintained in a very high vacuum. Note the small aperture angle, greatly enlarged in this drawing.

(1) A heated tungsten filament that emits electrons (cathode)

(2) There is an anode toward which the electrons are attracted

(3) A potential difference between the cathode and the anode imparts an accelerating voltage of between 20,000 and 200,000 volts to the electrons creating the beam

(4) The beam thus emerging from the electron gun (the cathode and anode assembly) is condensed into a nearly parallel beam at the specimen by the condenser lenses, and after passing through the specimen, the beam is projected as the magnified image of the object.

(5) Specimen onto the fluorescent screen by the objective and projector lenses.

(6) The specimen for TEM are cut into ultrathin sections using ultramicrotome. In case the sections are not thin, the electrons would simply be stopped and no image would be formed.

When electrons impinge on the section, portions of the section through which electrons have passed appear bright in the fluorescent screen while portions of the specimen that have absorbed or scattered electrons because of their inherent density or because of heavy metals added during specimen preparation appear dark.

Scanning Transmission Electron Microscopy (STEM)

Recently, a combination of the scanning and the transmission EM has been developed in the so called STEM. The STEM uses a thin electron beam (a few A° in diameter) to scan the specimen. The electrons that are scattered are collected and analyzed by special detector and the image obtained is displayed on a television screen.

The STEM, is particularly useful for observing the biological specimens. Due to the high contrast thus obtained, it is possible to study unstained proteins molecules and to obtain a more reliable image than those stained by heavy metals.

Confocal Microscopy

Confocal microscopy, now a well established tool, complements both light and electron microscopy. Due to its high temporal resolution it allows the visualization of living as well as fixed tissues and cells and therefore, dynamic processes can be examined and analyzed as and when they occur. The basic principle of confocal microscope is to eliminate the scattered, reflected or fluorescent light from out-of-focus planes by making the illumination, specimen and detector all have the same focus, i.e. they are confocal. In fact, this microscope can image only very thin optical sections, on which the beam is focused. Confocal microscope is often designed to scan in a raster pattern over the sample in which the microscope illuminates one spot at one time, scanning the spot along parallel lines in the focal plane. Faster scanning is done by using the lasers as the illumination source. They provide an intense beam of monochromatic radiation that can be condensed onto a small spot. Hence many confocal microscopes are laser scanning confocal microscopes (LSCM).

Applications of (LSCM). (1) determining the location of proteins, lipids and nucleic acids, cytoskeletal structures and organelles within the cells using dyes like phalloidin and lectins.

(2) observing ionic fluctuations such as calcium and magnesium within the cells.

(3) measuring membrane potential using fluorescent dyes.

(4) to make four dimensional imaging of macromolecules.

Atomic Force Microscopy

Binning and colleagues in 1986 invented atomic force microscopy (AFM). It has the resolution power in the micrometer to subnanometre range. This imaging technique has the ability to image both **insulating** and conducting surfaces in a variety of environments. It has facilitated imaging of a variety of materials including proteins, lipids and DNA. In addition to its imaging abilities, AFM can be used to probe spatial variations in surface properties such as adhesiveness and elasticity.

AFM in its most basic form measures the topography by moving a probe across the sample to feel and record the contours of the sample. Key element in this technique is the sensor known as cantilever. The cantilever is usually formed by one or more beams of silicon or silicon nitride that is 100 to 500 μm long and 0·5 to 5 μm thick. Mounted on the end of the cantilever is a sharp tip that is used to sense a force between the sample and tip. For normal topographic imaging, the probe tip is brought into continuous or intermittent contact with the sample and **raster** scanned over the surface. AFM uses special type of scanners known as piezo-electric scanners. Fine motion piezo electric scanners are used to generate topographic images and force measurements. A piezo-scanner is a device that moves by a microscopic amount when a voltage is applied across its electrodes. These scanners can translate in three directions (X, Y or Z axis). They are available in different sizes to allow maximum scan ranges of 0.5 to 125 μm in the *X* and *Y* axis and several microns in the vertical Z axis.

AFM has been used to investigate micro filtration (pores 10 μm – 0·1 μm), ultrafiltration (pores 0·1 μm-5 nm) and nanofiltration (pores <=1 nm) membrane surface structure. Earlier AFM studies used the contact mode technique where the tip intimately traces the topography of the sample surface. Recent development of "non contact mode" of operation that allows the tip to respond to attaractive vander Waal interactions is proving useful for the study of membranes.

The AFM software allows quantitative determination of the diameter of pores by use of the images in conjunction with digitally stored line profiles. The simultaneous use of images and profiles greatly facilitate identification of the individual pores. In conclusion, AFM has provided the membrane technologist with valuable analysis of membrane surfaces not only through its powerful imaging capabilities identifying device quantifying surface interactions such as adhesion thus AFM is an essential tool for the membrane biologist.

Cryoelectron Microscopy
(Low temperature electron microscopy)

Low temperature electron microscopy was initially developed to avoid water loss from hydrated samples which occurs at room temperature in the high vacuum of the conventional electron microscope. The development of this technique for visualizing frozen hydrated tissues and macromolecules has been a boon for studying their structures in a state that closely resemble their native condition. Basic principle of examining frozen hydrated specimens is

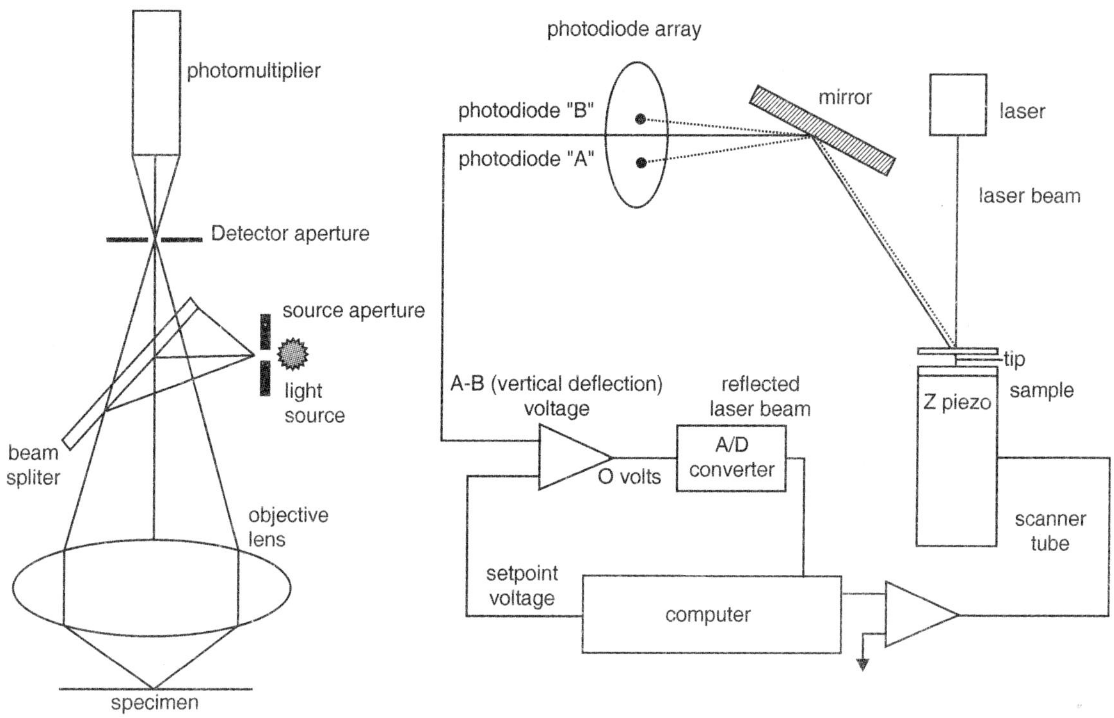

Fig. 9. Confocal imaging.

the preservation of the environment by rapid freezing. Rapid freezing causes the water of the specimen and its environment to be trapped in a vitreous (amorphous or glass like) state. This vitreous state prevents damage to the specimen caused by the formation of ice crystals when the specimen is frozen more slowly. These samples retain high structural integrity. However, it is crucial to preserve the specimen below –140°C because vitreous substances crystallize above this temperature.

A wide range of frozen sample have been examined by cryo-electron microscopy, however, workers have mainly studied macromolecules and their assemblies hydrated and frozen on thin films. Cryosection of biological tissues have not been studied that extensively. The first published reports dealt with the structure of viruses and produced their 3-D reconstructions at relatively low resolution. By combining cryoelectron microscopy with X-ray crystallography overall architecture of large complexes could be obtained. The examples include 3-D structure of Rhinovirus 14, DNA fragments and ribosomal t-RNA of *E. coli.*

Low temperature SEM has also been used in environmental mineralogy.

Sample preparation for cryo-electron microscopy is a critical process. The methods of sample preparation are described below.

Image Analysis and Video Microscopy

A union of optics with electronics strictly speaking of the microscope with the television camera and the electronic evaluation instrument has made it possible to fulfill the long standing demand for automatic image analysis. An image processing system is a tool for extracting additional information from an image. The system comprises following components.

(1) A monochrome video camera or digital camera
(2) A frame grabber or digitizing board
(3) A computer
(4) A storage display and printing device

Video camera converts light into electrical signal. CCD (charged couple device) cameras use an assay of solid state light sensitive charge coupled

Table 3. **Methods of specimen preparation in Cryoelectron microscopy.**

Frozen Hydrated Specimens	**Dry Specimen Previously Frozen**
1. **Vitrified film of ice** A thin layer of macromolecules in aqueous suspension is rapidly frozen by plunging in a cryogen, eg., ethane, and transferred to a cryoelectron microscope.	1. **Freeze drying** Cells or tissues are frozen, then lyophilized. The remaining material is dried and stabilized for transfer to a conventional electron microscope. Alternatively, a replica is made.
2. **Frozen section** Cells or tissues are rapidly frozen by contact with a cold metal block, sometimes under high pressure, then sliced into thin sections at <-160°C. Subsequently, sections are transferred to a cryoelectron microscope.	2. **Freeze fracture** Cells or tissues are frozen, then fractured. A replica of the fractured surface is made.
	3. **Freeze etching** Freeze fracture followed by freeze drying.
	4. **Freeze substitution** Tissues are frozen, then the ice is replaced at low temperature by an organic solvent. Conventional plastic embedment follows.
	5. **Cryoimmunohistochemistry** Tissues are first chemically fixed, then infused with a cryoprotectant and frozen for sectioning. Immunolabelling of the thawed sections follows.

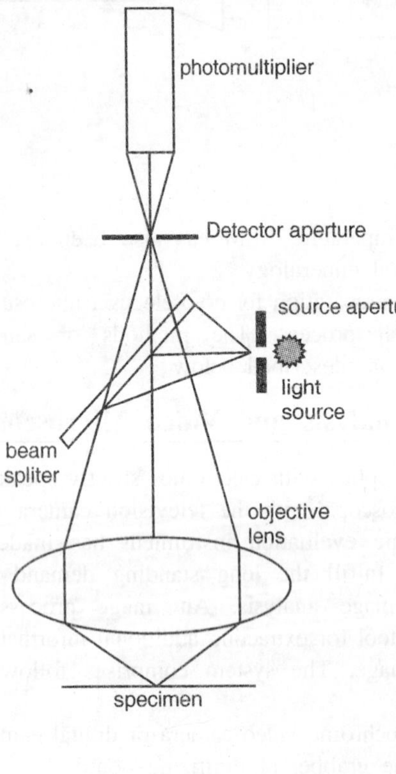

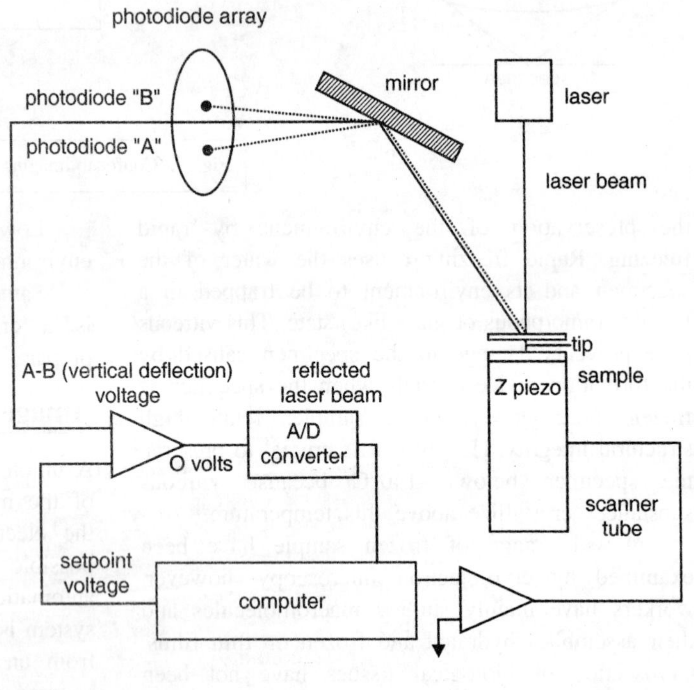

pro = processed image, sync = synchromiser, raw = raw image, VTR = video tape recorder, ODR = optical disc recorder

Fig. 10. Image analysis system.

cells. Nowadays charge injection devices (CIDs) are also available that offer certain advantages over the CCD cameras. Most video systems utilize a camera with a CCD that has a resolution of 750×500 pixels or about 400,000 pixels.

The frame grabber is basically an analog-to-digital converter optimized for digitizing (capturing) video signals. On command, it digitizes one complete video image. Then the captured image is transferred to the computer memory for processing.

The computer running an image analysis programme comprises the heart of an imaging system. Desktop computers, are the most common and cost effective platforms for these systems since they are inexpensive and are supported by the widest variety of frame grabber boards and image analysis software.

The image storage device of an imaging system should have sufficient capacity so that large number of images can be stored and should be fast enough to transfer the images from and to the computer. Most of the systems use PC monitor and its SVGA graphics adapter for this purpose. The 14"/15" color SVGA monitor has 1024 × 768 pixel resolution. Various print technologies such as dye sublimation, laser and inkjet printer are available now. The inkjet and laser printers provide good print quality at about 600dpi resolution. Inkjet printers are economical but slower in printing speed. Video printers can provide hardcopy directly from a video source.

Telemicroscopy

The requirement of remote imaging studies over a WAN or internet emerged from the great promised advantages of internet revolution. The WAN allows effective sharing or offering of services by laboratories equipped with costly facilities like SEM/STEM. Scientists thus collaborate using this technique. A remote operator is trained to control and adjust the microscope and communication system. Once the initial setup is completed to the satisfaction of remote operator located at a desired region, internet offers access to the microscope.

With the advent of wireless, battery operated and processor embedded cameras, other applications of this technology like telemedicine, telesurgery, machine diagnostics and process monitoring have also emerged.

Optical Characterization and Imaging of Biological Tissues

The non-invasive monitoring of physiological parameters and early diagnosis of pathological changes in tissues are of paramount importance for the examination of organs as well as for other medical routines. X-radiation has often been applied in the diagnosis of skeletal abnormalities, some soft tissue lesions in the chest and coronary blood vessels (angiography), breast-cancer screening (mammography) and reconstruction of tomographic images (X-ray CT), etc. However, due to the ionizing nature of radiation, its use for continuous monitoring or frequent screening is not recommended. On the other hand, magnetic resonance imaging, position emission tomography, radionuclide imaging, etc. are prohibitively expensive and require contrast agents for which many people are allergic. Ultrasonography, based on the variation of acoustic impedance, is often applied in tissue characterization and imaging, but precise localization of abnormalities in tissues at times is difficult due to similar acoustic characteristics. During the onset of pathological changes in tissues, the variation in refractive index is more pronounced compared to that in acoustic impedance. Therefore, optical techniques, due to their nonionic, noninvasive, quantitative and relatively inexpensive qualities, emerge as a natural choice of alternative diagnostic modality.

Laser radiation possesses nearly single frequency, high degree of temporal and spatial coherence, enormous intensity and highly plane-polarized characteristics. When a laser beam is incident on a thick tissue surface such as the human arm, due to mismatch in refractive index at the air-tissue interface, a part of this is backscattered, whereas the remaining part is absorbed in the tissues. Due to high scattering and low absorption, the penetration of light within the 'therapeutic window' (600-1300 nm) is more, which also leads to high backscattering from the surface after deep penetration. The spatial distribution of the backscattered and transmitted components contains information on the metabolic, physiologic or possibly structural status of tissues. Optical reflectance imaging of tissues, a novel concept in diagnostic medicine, is applied to determine the variation in internal structure of tissues. The images of tissues as obtained on the surface of the human hand and forearm, reconstructed by diffuse backscattered radiation, show the compositional variation in tissues below the skin, whereas the contribution due to skin pigmentation at all locations in healthy skin tissues remains constant. These images are in qualitative agreement with the perfusion images as obtained by laser Doppler flow meter.

Principle

The variability of scattering in biological tissues is attributed to the absorption (μ_a) and reduced scattering (μ'_a) coefficients. In contrast to their direct measurement by double integration spheres on tissue slices, these parameters for intact organs and phantoms are generally determined by indirect techniques, which involve the experimental measurement of spatial variation of reflectance on the tissue surface and matching of this curve by interactive procedure either based on optical diffusion the ory or Monte Carlo procedure. Recently, by measuring the surface reflectance profiles and matching them with those obtained by Monte Carlo simulation, we have determined the variability of optical parameters at various regions of the human forearm and their images are reconstructed. Such a procedure could further be applied to characterize healthy and diseased tissues.

The transmitted component, after passing through thinner, complex tissues (finger) and thicker, soft tissues (breast, neonatal head, testis, etc.), also contains information on selective absorption by the internal tissue constituents. The cigar-shaped scattered volume within a tissue in a given span of time, contains all possible paths of photons. Through the development of short laser pulses and fast detecting system, it has been possible to detect the partially coherent photons and suppress photons that have experienced excessive scattering. This effect has further been minimized by techniques such as time-resolved profile, modified tomographic reconstruction and by reducing the effect of background heterogeneity.

The detection of tumour in human breast is one of the 1 major objectives of the 1 optical techniques. The various developments of optical tomography include its applications to tissue-equivalent phantoms. For direct applications to detect breast tumour the techniques based on optical tomography (OT) and frequency domain optical mammography (FDOM) are developed. In OT, the breast is placed between the laser source and detectors for tomogram reconstruction, whereas in FOOM the breast is sandwiched between two optical plates and the transmitted laser light is scanned by a set of photo detectors. As the latter technique presents the three-dimensional breast structure in two dimensions, the actual shape and size of the inclusions could not be well determined. Recently, using three-dimensional OT of tissue phantoms we have shown that these details could be obtained from the sequence of tomograms of the phantoms. But inclusion of optical fibres either to deliver laser light from the laser source to optical head or to collect transmitted intensity data leads to loss of power or intensity, which is also affected by the optical characteristics of fibres.

The incidence of breast cancer is on the increase internationally. The procedures applied for early detection of tumour and routine examination of breast may save many precious lives. Hence the objectives of the present work are not only to provide the procedure to characterize the biological tissues in terms of their optical parameters, but also to present our techniques for reflectance imaging of tissue abnormalities below the tissue surface and tomographic imaging of compositional variation in breast phantoms and biological tissues.

Multi-slice Optical Tomography System

The scheme of the laser multi-slice tomography system is shown in Figure 11. This primarily consists of four subsystems: laser system, optoelectronic system, mechanical system, and data acquisition and image reconstruction system.

The laser system consists of a laser diode (LD), driven by the laser diode driver operating at 830 nm with maximum power 100 mW. The laser beam is collimated by diffraction limited aspheric collimation optics, encased in the collimation tube. This laser beam is expanded into a thin sheath of thickness 1.0 mm by a rod lens system.

The opto-electronic system consists of an array of 16 photodiodes which detect the laser radiation after passing through tissue or tissue-phantom. These photodiodes are of high-speed and low-noise characteristics with good sensitivity (0.9) at 830 nm. The laser source with lens system was placed on one arm of the mechanical scanner assembly, while the photo-detector array was mounted in front of it in a fan-beam configuration. Both the laser system and detector array were placed horizontally on the circumference of a circle of radius 80.0 mm. The angle subtended by the fan-beam configuration was 600 and the angle between two adjacent detectors was 4°. The linear distance between two successive photodiodes on the array ring was 10.42 min. The current outputs from the photodiodes were converted into their corresponding voltages by a current-to-voltage convener.

The mechanical system consisted of three stepper motors, SM1, SM2 and SM3, to carry out upward and downward, rotational and pitch movements of scanning assembly, respectively. The movement of the gears G1 and G2 was controlled by SM3, which varied the separation between laser diode and photodiode array. The stepper motor motion was controlled by a three-axis motion controller card which generated the control sequence. These control signals were amplified by a stepper motor driver card, designed to obtain multiple trans-axial projections at a given height to construct the tomogram. For tomographic reconstruction, the breast phantom was mounted in the phantom holder (PH) and placed at the centre of the laser-photodiode assembly after adjusting the pitch by SM3 and height by SM I. The scanner head was moved by SM2 to take hundred projections (step angle 3.6°) at a given height of the phantom. The same procedure was repeated to obtain projections at various heights. The entire mechanical system was fabricated in steel and painted black to prevent any stray reflections of laser light.

Data, in the form of projections, were acquired by a 16-channel, 16-bit resolution, high-speed data acquisition card and stored in the computer for further processing. Each projection consisted of 16 samples. The projection data of 100 projections at a given height were in the form of an array of 100 × 16. The stored data were preprocessed to remove any noise in the dataset and then interpolated to 64 datapoints from 16 measured outputs of photodiodes. The cross-section of the object was obtained by convolution-back projection algorithm 28.

Prior to tomogram reconstruction of an object, a blank run (without breast phantom BP) to capture the dark current in the photodiodes in dark environment was conducted. The dataset was subtracted from the input array of 100 × 16 phantom data matrix (background subtraction). The noise in the subtracted dataset was median-filtered (3 × 3 window) and interpolated to 100 × 64 data set. Each projection $R_{\beta i}(\gamma)$ was sampled with a sampling interval of angle θ. If n denotes integer values and θ_i represents the angles at which projections are taken, then $R_{\beta i}(n\theta)$ denotes the fan-beam projection. For each projection, the modified projection $R_{\beta i}(n\theta)$ was obtained as

$$R'_{\beta i}(n\theta) = R_{\beta i}(n\theta) \; *D* \cos(n\theta) \qquad (1)$$

where D is the distance of the source from the origin O. n = 0 corresponds to the ray passing through the centre of the object.

Filtered projection was obtained by convoluting each modified projection $R'_{\beta i}(n\theta)$ with the impulse response of a filter function $g(\theta)$,

$$Q_{\beta i}(n\theta) = R'_{\beta i}(n\theta) * g(n\theta) \qquad (2)$$

Finally, the reconstructed image was obtained by

$$f(x,y) = \Delta b \sum_{i=1}^{M} (1/L^2 (x,y, \beta\iota) \times Q_{\beta\iota} (g')) \qquad (3)$$

where γ is angle of the fan-beam ray that passes through the point (x, y) and; M is the total number of angles; L the distance from the source S' to that point (x, y).

When the computed value of γ' did not correspond to one of the (nθ) for which $Q_{\theta i}$ is known, an interpolation (linear) was performed. The reconstructed images were displayed with 256 grey levels. The raw image is generally associated with noise and poor contrast. Therefore, details of the image may not be clearly delineated. To overcome this, the images obtained by the present technique should be processed by histogram equalization, smoothening, image segmentation, edge detection and contour extraction.

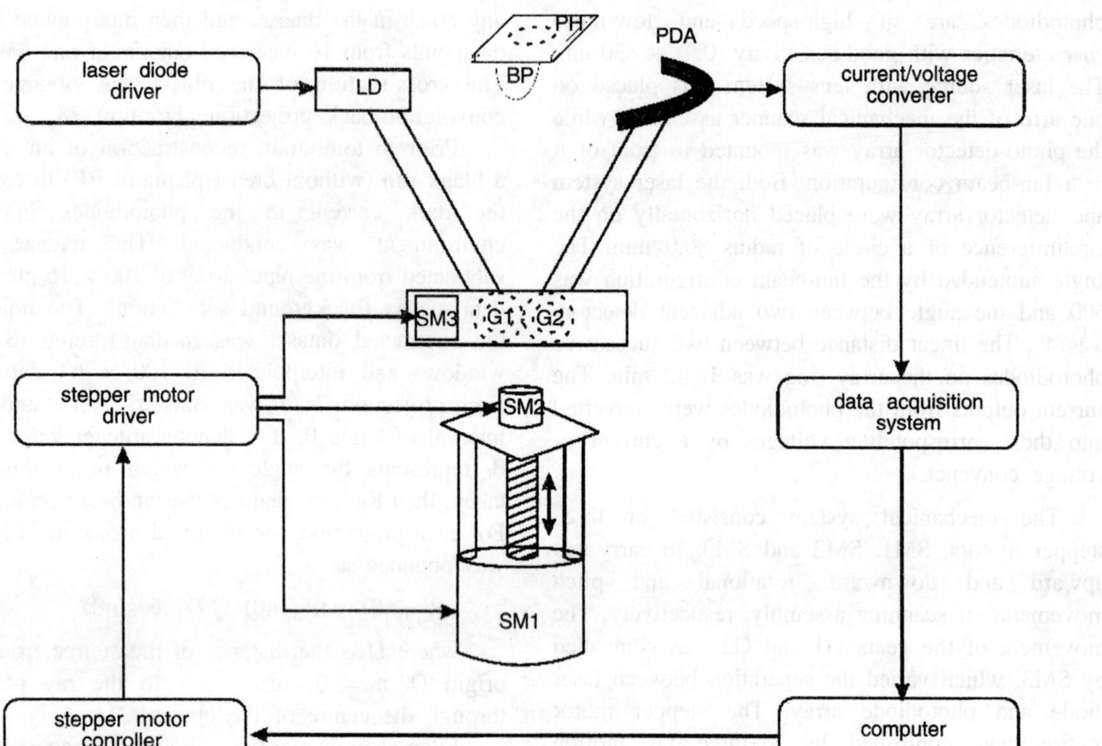

Fig. 11. Components of an optical tomography system.

Applications

In conclusion, the principal motive behind the development of optical tomography, which is cost-effective compared to time-resolved and frequency-domain techniques, is to provide a safe and effective method of detecting and specifying diseases in the breast and other soft-tissue structures. Applications of this system to tissue-phantoms and biological tissues show that the present technique could be employed to detect structural changes. This technique is sensitive to detect changes in absorption coefficient and the minimum size of the inclusion detected in a 50 mm diameter slice. Due to its simplicity and versatility, this may prove to be an ideal system for structural analysis of soft tissues. Optical parameters quantify the tissue changes, whereas reflectance imaging could further provide data on variability of tissue composition below the skin over an entire organ.

Advantages and Disadvantages of Three Types of Microscopy

Although resolution of the transmission electron microscope is generally superior for the present time at least to that of the scanning electron microscope, and enormously greater than that of the light microscope, resolution is not the only criterion that affects the usefulness of these instruments. In fact, each of the three microscopes just described has applications in which it is clearly preferable to the others.

The traditional light microscope is easy to use and ignores the presence of water. All electron microscopes, on the other hand, are complicated by comparison, require more elaborate sample preparation, and can normally examine only dried specimens placed in a vacuum chamber. The latter restriction results the fact that an electron beam is scattered by air or water, although the mega volt electron microscopes have a beam that can penetrate thin layers of liquid, making it possible to observe some living specimens. In general, however, we can say that while light microscopes can easily be used to examine living objects, electron microscopes, with a very few exceptions, can only examine cells that are killed, fixed (i.e., chemically stabilized) and stained.

In addition, the ability of the light microscopist to perceive color is an important asset, for variations in color either the natural color of the specimen and its components, or a wide variety of stains can impart considerable information. In contrast, the transmission electron microscope is decidedly monochromatic. The ability of the scanning microscope to use several different kinds of radiation from the specimen provides some of the advantages of color, but it is a weak substitute for the countless clues to which the human eye is sensitive.

The scanning electron microscope, as it is commonly used, images surface features, as electrons do not pass through the specimen. This factor is the source of both its strengths and its weakness. Neither of the other instruments, which depend primarily on transmitted radiation are particularly good at visualizing surface, although surface features can be of considerable interest. The advantage of the scanning microscope in this application is its impressive depth of field at least 300 times greater than that of optical instruments.

Another advantage of the scanning electron microscope is the facility with which magnification can be changed without refocusing. For example, an operator can pick out an interesting area from a wide field at 50X, and then merely turn a knob to examine a portion of it at 50,000X. The ease with which this change can be accomplished is a result of the magnification being determined simply by the ratio of the movement of the scanning beam to that of the display beam.

When sample preparation time is critical (e.g., a pathologist's examination of a tissue while the surgeon waits by the operating table for a decision), the light microscope has no serious rival. In addition, the variety of molecular stains available for light microscopy give it a versatility unmatched by the other instruments. On the other hand, when details of intracellular structures are to be examined at the submicron level, only the transmission electron microscope can be used. But when surface features are important, particularly when small features of varying depth are to be studied, the scanning electron microscope is the instrument of choice.

Sample Preparation

Light Microscopy

The amount of information obtained from a microscope depends in large measure on how the specimen is prepared. Samples for the light microscope are commonly fixed (with alcohol, formalin, osmium salts, formaldehyde, and so on) to make their protein components insoluble and stable to subsequent procedures, then air dried and treated with a stain having an affinity for the structure to be examined. To ensure even penetration of the stain, the specimen is usually first embedded in paraffin (to provide support) and cut into thin sections. The paraffin is dissolved again with xylol before staining. Some of the dyes in common use are eosin, hematoxylin, aniline blue, crystal violet, methylene blue, methyl green, fuchsin, Congo red, rose Bengal, and so on. Although most stains are specific for proteins, some are specific for nucleic acids (e.g., Feulgen's procedure for DNA, which uses a fuchsin derivative); others are specific for lipids and still others stain starches.

For rapid preparation of specimens, paraffin embedding may be replaced with rapid freezing in liquid nitrogen. Sections may be cut from a frozen specimen, dried by sublimation (freeze-drying) to preserve structural features and to avoid the flattening effect imposed by surface tension when specimens are air dried, and then stained in the usual way.

Electron Microscopy

The purpose of using stains is to improve the contrast between specimen and environment. The wide variety of stains available for light microscopy has no counterpart in electron microscopy. There are, however, several different techniques by which samples are prepared for the electron microscope, each of which has its own advantages. The five most common are thin-sectioning, negative staining, metal shadowing, freeze- fracture, and whole mounts.

A brief description of each follows in order to better understand the illustrations used later.

(1) Thin-sectioning refers to the use of an ultramicrotome to remove slices that are only a few hundred angstroms thick. To withstand the passage of the diamond or glass knife without tearing, the specimen is first embedded in a hard plastic, such as epoxy resin, which is allowed to penetrate the sample before being polymerized. Sections are floated from the knife onto the surface of water and picked up by touching them with a copper grid (200-300 wires/inch) that has been coated with a thin plastic or carbon membrane as a support.

(2) Thin-sectioning eliminates overlying and underlying structures that would otherwise confuse the image. However, stains must be incorporated into the tissue to improve contrast, since the structures left in these very thin sections would not otherwise scatter electrons differently enough to be seen. Typical stains are salts of tungsten, manganese, uranium, osmium, etc. all of which provide electron-dense heavy metal atoms to scatter electrons.

(3) Negative staining differs from positive staining in that the specimen itself is unstained. Rather, it is embedded in a dense substance, usually phosphotungstic acid ($H_3PW_{12}O_{40}$), which is chosen for its extremely high electron density and consequent ability to scatter the beam. The portions of the specimen that exclude phosphotungstic acid transmit electrons readily, so that their image can be seen. Because the stain penetrates various openings and crevices, some fine structure can often be observed. The technique is used mostly with viruses and other particulate material.

(4) Heavy metal shadowing is used to provide a relief of the object being examined. If metal deposition is carried out from one direction only, one side of the object will be coated while the other is not. Electrons pass readily through the area of lighter metal content, less readily through the plane on which the particle sits, and are scattered most severely by the side of the particle on which metal has accumulated. As a result, the particle appears as if it had been viewed in strong light.

In other cases, the specimen is rotated constantly while metal deposition is taking place, so that no shadows are created. Instead, metal builds up on all sides of particle, making it stand out above the background. This technique is often used with DNA, which by itself is a filament only about 20Å thick. After "rotary shadowing", it has a diameter of a couple of hundred angstroms, and is therefore readily visible.

The layer of metal cannot be ignored when shadowed specimens are examined; it not only increases the overall size, but it may obscure some of the smaller features.

(5) Freeze-fracture is carried out by rapidly freezing the sample and then sectioning it in a vacuum while still at –100°C, The knife does not cut cleanly under those conditions, but tends to fracture the specimen along lines of natural weaknesses such as the middle of a membrane running parallel to the cut. After fracture, the sample may be left in the vacuum long enough to allow some water to evaporate from and shrink softer tissues, a process called etching. The exposed face is then shadowed with metal to provide the necessary contrast, later, the organic material (ie. the specimen itself) is removed by acids to leave a metal replica for examination in the electron microscope. Much detail is retained in the replica, providing out best look at certain internal features of cells and the only way of seeing the face and internal features of a membrane.

(6) Whole mounts are often used to examine chromosomes and other relatively thick objects that can be isolated free of debris. As the name implies, the specimen is neither sectioned nor stained. Thick areas scatter electrons more strongly than thin area, providing enough contrast to form an image. In fact, since scattering of the beam is directly proportional to the electron density of the sample, and hence to its mass, proper calibration allows estimates of specimen mass to be obtained from the image.

Samples for the scanning electron microscope are usually prepared by chemical fixation or freeze-drying to preserve shape, followed by shadowing with a layer of heavy metal. The latter step provides

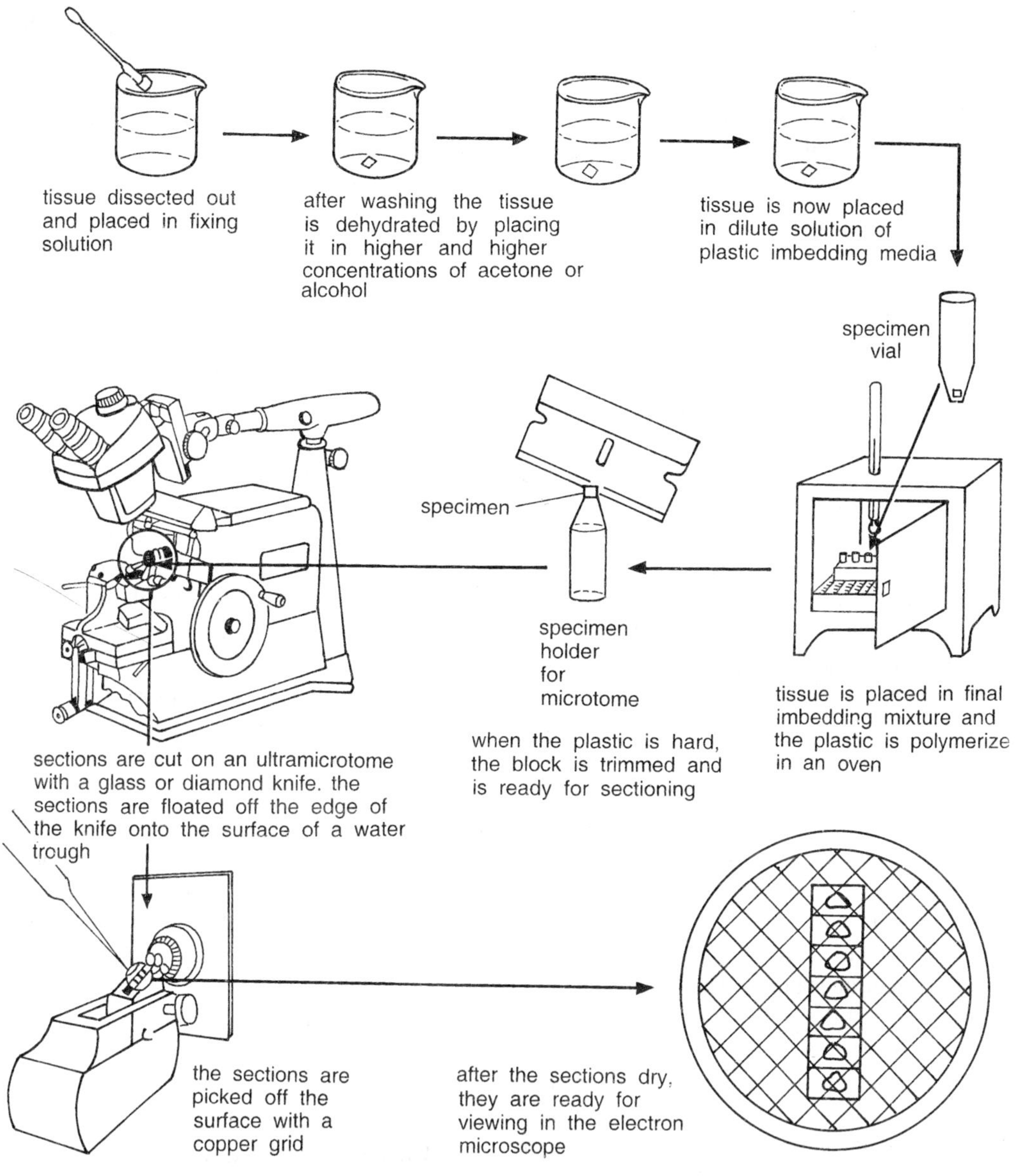

Fig. 12. Preparation of ultra thin sections for transmission electron microscopy.

a conductive surface to drain off captured electrons that would otherwise cause distortions by deflecting the incoming beam. (Charge buildup can be a problem in transmission electron microscopy, too, though the thinner specimens transmit, rather than collect, most of the beam).

Tissue Preparation for Transmission Electron Microscopy

1. Primary fixation e.g. Glutaraldehyde (formaldehyde also used). Glutaraldehyde not only stabilizes the fine structure and prevents gross distortion during embedding, but also increases the permeability of the tissues to the embedding media. The tissue can be left in the fixative for many hours without deterioration. Presently glutaraldehyde is considered to be the most efficient and reliable aldehyde for fixing biological materials.

2. Secondary fixation in osmium tetroxide (OsO_4). Glutaraldehyde fixed tissues fall to show cellular membranes. These difficulties are overcome by post fixation by osmium tetroxide. Post fixation not only adds contrast and develop membranous sharpness, but also stabilize the fine structure already maintained by glutaraldehyde so that it can withstand embedding in plastics (resins). O_SO_4 is not only a fixative but also an electron stain and this is a special advantage. It is non-coagulant type of fixative, i.e., it is able to stabilize some proteins by transforming them into clear gels without destroying many of the structural features. The proteins of the tissue that are stabilized by this fixative are prevented from being coagulated by alcohols during dehydration. It is recognized to be most versatile fixative known for preserving the cytoplasmic details. The quality of tissue preservation obtained through fixation with a mixture of glutaraldehyde and osmium tetraoxide has not been surpassed by any other fixation combination. But the tissue has to be cut into small pieces 1 mm^3. Unlike most polar oxidizing agents it is able to penetrate both hydrophilic and hydrophobic lipids. The duration taken for satisfactory fixation is 1-2 hrs for the above tissue. The ideal temperature is 0-4°C since autolytic activity is reduced at low temperature.

3. Preparation of OsO_4. For most purpose 2% solution having a pH of 7·2 to 7·4 with 0·3 M osmolarity is recommended (in phosphate buffer) usually it is available in crystal form in 1 gm packing in small glass ampules. It is volatile and poisonous when the ampule is broken. The fumes are injurious to eyes and nose. The reagent is a strong oxidizing agent and is readily reduced by the presence of organic matter and exposure to light. The solution is prepared in amber coloured bottle and covered by aluminium foil to prevent it from light and is stored in refrigerator.

4. Washing. After primary fixation the tissue must be washed properly prior to post fixation in OsO_4. Otherwise traces of glutaraldehyde can produce a fine dense precipitate of reduced osmium. The washing is done by the same buffer of the fixative. Generally two or three quick rinse in the buffer for a period of 15 minutes are adequate.

5. Dehydration. The aim of dehydration is to remove all the free water from the fixed and washed tissue and to place it in an organic solvent such as acetone or ethanol. Acetone a non-reactive solvent causes less shrinkage of the tissue than does ethanol. Acetone has also the advantage of not being reactive with any OsO_4, which is left in the tissue. Also there is no indication of any chemical interaction between epoxy monomers (embedding agents) and acetone. After acetone treatment the amount and nature of phospholipids remain unaltered. Só acetone can be safely used for dehydration. The typical procedure is as follows—

(1) Washing in buffer solution
(2) 30% acetone - 5-10 minutes
(3) 60% acetone – – do –
(4) 90% acetone – – do –
(5) 100% acetone (2 changes) – – do –

On the other hand when ethanol is employed for dehydration the use of a transitional solvent is necessary as most resins are not miscible with ethanol. To remedy this difficulty propylene oxide was introduced (transitional solvent). It dissolves resins more readily than ethanol.

6. Infiltration. It is known that a complete and uniform penetration of tissue specimens by a suitable embedding medium is prerequisite for satisfactory sectioning on the ultramicrotome. Infiltration is accomplished by gradually decreasing the concentration of the solvent and proportionately increasing the concentration of the embedding medium. A typical routine procedure is given below —

(1) Last change in 100% acetone (dehydration)
(2) 100% acetone and plastic (or resin) 1 : 1 – 30 minutes
(3) 100% acetone and plastic 1 : 3 – 30 minutes
(4) Plastic mixture
(5) Leave plastic mixture to polymerize

Final embedding is most conveniently done in predried gelatin or polyethylene capsule. The capsule containing the embedding mixture and the tissue blocks are polymerized in an oven for 12 hrs at 45°C followed by a final treatment at 60°C until polymerisaion is complete (mostly 36-48 hrs).

7. Embedding materials (Resins).

(1) Epon 812 (2) Araldite 502
(3) Maraglas 655 (4) Methacrylate

8. Sectioning. Automatic ultramicrotomes are used with glass or diamond knives. Glass knives are freshly prepared and are very successful in cutting sections even upto 50Å to several microns of thickness. Also diamond knives are used for continuous sectioning, while glass knives are frequently changed depending on sharpness.

The ultramicrotomes operate on the principle of either thermal or mechanical feed. The knives are fixed at a clearance angle of 4-8 degrees for successful sectioning. The sections are collected in troughs or boats containing water and acetone mixture. Under optimal operating conditions, sections in long unbroken ribbons can be easily obtained. Cutting speed and section thickness can be varied while cutting is in progress. Normal section thickness varies in the range of 600Å – 800Å.

9. Specimen block. Trimming and preparation of the block face. A block should be trimmed always after it is mounted in the chuck (block holder).

10. Preparation of troughs. Troughs are either ready made that can be fixed on the knife or electric adhesive type can be used to make a trough.

(a) Floatation fluid. 10-20% acetone is used in the troughs as floatation fluid on the surface of which ultra thin section float in the form of a ribbon.

(b) Section collection. This is collected on copper grids.

(c) Staining. Different parts of an electron micrograph are recognizable because they differ in contrast, and contrast in turn is a result of differential electron opacity. Deposition of heavy metal ions i.e. uranium and lead in sufficient quantities help to obtain better contrast and resolution.

11. Commonly used stains.

(1) Uranyl acetate
(2) Lead acetate
(3) Lead citrate
(4) Uranyl magnesium acetate
(5) Uranyl nitrate
(6) Phosphotungstic acid (PTA)
(7) OsO_4 is also a stain

Freeze-fracture Electron Microscopy

History and Principles

Freeze-fracture electronmicroscopy has been firmly established as a major technique in ultrastructure research for well over 30 years. Although elements of the technique in emerging form can be traced back to the 1950s, it was not until the 1960s that images of such persuasive beauty were obtained that its potential captured the imagination of the cell biologists of the day. Initially, interpretative controversies held up the application of freeze fracture but, once these had been resolved, the technique flourished during the 1970s and 1980s, providing advances in our understanding of the structural organization of membranes and organelles that were impossible to achieve by conventional thin-section electron microscopy (EM). Currently, a revival of interest has taken place with the development of effective approaches in freeze-fracture cytochemistry, providing new tools to address hitherto unresolved questions in cell biology.

The critical feature of the freeze-fracture technique on which its success depends is the tendency of the fracture plane to follow a plane through the central hydrophobic core of frozen membranes, splitting them into half-membrane leaflets. The resulting en face views of membranes give spectacular three-dimensional perspectives of cellular organization and details of membrane structure at macromolecular resolution. Of particular importance is the technique's ability to reveal the distribution and organization of integral membrane proteins as intramembrane particles in the membrane plane.

Methodology

There are four essential steps in making a freeze-fracture replica:

(1) rapid freezing of the specimen,

(2) fracturing the specimen,

(3) making the replica of the frozen fractured surface by vacuumdeposition of platinum and carbon and

(4) cleaning the replica to remove all the biological material. In addition, the freezing step is commonly preceded by pretreatment, and an optional etching step may be interposed between fracturing and making the replica.

The standard method of rapid freezing is to immerse swiftly a suitably mounted sample into a liquid coolant (e.g., subcooled liquid nitrogen). Unfortunately, most biological samples frozen in this way show ice crystal damage at the ultrastructural level unless they are treated beforehand with a cryoprotectant. The most commonly used cryoprotectant is glycerol. As exposure to glycerol (or other cryoprotectants) may lead to artifacts in membrane structure, the standard practice is to carry out chemical fixation with glutaraldehyde first. Resorting to these pretreatment steps falls short of the ideal of directly freezing cells from the living state, a limitation that has been one of the driving forces in the development of more specialized ultrarapid freezing techniques.

Fracturing the frozen specimen is usually carried out under vacuum by using a liquid-nitrogen-cooled microtome blade or by breaking the frozen specimen apart in a hinged device. In some simple versions of the technique, fracturing is carried out with a razor blade under liquid nitrogen at atmospheric pressure. Making the replica involves two steps, shadowing and backing. In the standard procedure, oblique, unidirectional shadowing is carried out by evaporating a fine layer of platinum–carbon onto the specimen; this is followed immediately by a strengthening (backing) layer of electron-lucent carbon, evaporated from above. The topographical features of the frozen, fractured surface are thus converted into variations in thickness of the deposited platinum layer of the replica.

After the replica has been made, the sample is brought to atmospheric pressure and allowed to warm to room temperature. The biological material is removed from the replica using sodium hypochlorite solution, chromic acid or other cleaning agents. After washing in distilled water, pieces of replica are mounted on grids for examination in the transmission electron microscope.

Freeze Etching

The term "freeze etching" is sometimes used synonymously with "freeze fracturing." This usage, which arises for historical reasons, is to be discouraged. "Etching" is defined as removal of ice from the surface of the fractured specimen by vacuum sublimation (freeze drying), before making the replica. In the early days of the technique, it was thought that the planar aspects viewed in replicas represented true surfaces of membranes, exposed by removal of ice—hence the technique was originally designated "freeze etching". However, it was subsequently conclusively demonstrated that the planar membrane views (fracture faces) so characteristic of the technique are revealed just as effectively when freeze fracturing is carried out in the absence of etching; moreover, in suitably prepared samples, a narrow margin representing the true surface of the membrane (alongside the fracture face) is exposed specifically by etching. Thus, "freeze fracture" is the preferred term for the technique in its standard form, where the major features of relief observed in the replica are generated by the splitting of membranes.

The traditional etching step, when executed after fracturing standard glycerol-treated specimens, does not lower the ice table sufficiently to reveal underlying structural detail because glycerol cannot be removed by vacuum sublimation. Only small ice crystals that have been broken apart by the fracture plane are removed; etching is halted once the surrounding glycerol eutectic is reached. Consequently, etching has little effect other than giving the cytoplasmic, nuclear and extracellular matrix a fine granular texture. In a few specific instances, etching may help reveal some extra detail, but for most glycerol-treated specimens, etching is redundant. When applied to non-glycerol-treated specimens, however, etching (or freeze-drying) is a valuable method in its own right for exposing the natural surfaces of membranes or other cellular components, and it is to such applications that the term "etching" should be confined. To be effective in this mode, the etching period is typically longer than that traditionally applied, and the specimens are frozen directly in distilled water, dilute buffer or buffer mixed with methanol.

Ultrarapid Freezing

Although a few types of specimen of low water content can be successfully frozen by standard plunge freezing without prior cryoprotective treatment, in most instances direct freezing requires ultrarapid freezing techniques. These techniques are designed to improve the cooling rate of the sample sufficiently that the ice crystal damage normally encountered in non-pretreated specimens is avoided. The principal ultrarapid freezing techniques are

(1) optimized plunge freezing,
(2) jet freezing,
(3) spray freezing and
(4) freezing by impact against a coldmetal block

A further technique, high-pressure freezing, reduces ice crystal size by subjecting the sample to high pressure, rather than by enhancing the cooling rate. Apart from their value in etching applications, these techniques have been successfully applied to examine cell and membrane structure in samples frozen directly from the living state and to capture sequential dynamic cellular events. They are, however, more challenging to perform than conventional immersion freezing and require more specialized equipment. The effectiveness of etching in imaging surface structure is exemplified by the combination of metal-block-impact ultrarapid freezing, extended etching and low-angle rotary shadowing, a technique dubbed the "quick-freeze/deep-etch technique". Brief or deep etching, or complete freeze-drying, may also be applied to rapidly frozen but unfractured specimens, with either unidirectional or rotary shadowing to visualize surface detail, providing superior structural preservation to that of metal-carbon replicas of critical point-dried or air-dried samples.

Freeze-Fracture Cytochemistry

Freeze fracture and associated techniques provide a wealth of unique structural information, but the potential scientific value of this information initially remained limited by the lack of effective means to identify the chemical nature of the transmembrane proteins (rendered visible as intramembrane particles) and other structural features viewed in replicas. The successful combination of cytochemistry with freeze fracture remained an eagerly sought but elusive goal for several decades. Significant progress came with the introduction of "fracture-label" and "label-fracture" techniques in the 1980s and, building on these, the technique of applying SDS treatment in place of the standard replica cleaning procedure followed by immunogold labeling. In this last procedure, the SDS removes the bulk of the biological specimen from the replica but leaves attached to it a very fine layer of macromolecules whose epitopes are preserved for immunogold labeling. The layer of biological molecules is so fine that it does not obstruct the electron beam when the replica is viewed in the electron microscope, and the gold markers are sufficiently electron-dense that they are sharply defined against the replicated background. Glutaraldehyde fixation of samples has to be avoided (to preserve epitopes for labeling at the end of the procedure) either by applying ultrarapid freezing or simply omitting the fixative and using very brief glycerol treatment. Freeze-fracture cytochemistry has now come of age, and is currently contributing to new advances in our understanding of the functional morphology of membranes and organelles.

Protocol

A large range of different apparatus and machines has been developed for undertaking freeze fracture since the technique's inception. In most laboratories, freeze fracturing and freeze etching are undertaken using a purpose-built machine rather than simpler equipment. The most popular machines in the heyday of freeze fracture were the various models marketed by Balzers (now Bal-Tec), and active practitioners in the field today generally still use these machines, purchased in the 1970s and 1980s. Balzers machines account for the majority of published freeze-fracture results and are the most likely to be encountered by the intending practitioner. Accordingly, the protocol presented here takes the user through the steps of carrying out freeze fracture using a typical Balzers machine of the period, the BAF 400. Although some of the detail is specific to this machine, the principles and many parts of the procedure are common to freeze fracture in general. The protocol should thus prove useful, with some adaptation, to users of other purpose-built freeze-fracture machines.

Important Questions

1. Describe the components of a light microscope. Discuss the procedure of its operation.
2. Write an essay on fluorescent microscopy.
3. What is the principle of electron microscopy? Discuss the basic instrument of scanning electron microscopy. Describe its applications in biology.
4. What do you understand by transmission electron microscope (TEM)? Discuss its principle, design & applications.
5. Write briefly on the following:
   (i) Confocal microscopy, (ii) Atomic force microscopy, (iii) Cryo-electron microscopy, (iv) Telemicroscopy, (v) Multi sliced optical tomography system, (vi) Freeze fracture electron microscopy.

7

Centrifugation

Biological molecules have different mass, shape and density. **Thomas Graham** (1861) classified all substances into two groups, crystalloids and colloids. When in solution, crystalloids can be separated through a parchment membrane whereas colloids can not. According to modern principle, colloidal solutions, instead of being solutions of particular types of matter, are solutions with a characteristic kind of structure. The smallest particle that can be seen with a high power light microscope has a diameter of 200 mμ. Electron microscope can observe particles with diameter as small as 10 mμ. When the size of particles of a solute are larger than 200 μm they are said to be in suspension. If a solution of these particles is left to stand, they tend to sediment under the influence of gravity. The process is called as **sedimentation**. Smaller particles do not sediment but can be filtered. However, still smaller particles are not retained by filter paper but they are too large to pass through a semipermeable membrane. When these colloidal particles are separated from crystalloids by selective diffusion through a semipermeable membrane, the process is called as **dialysis**. When traces of electrolytes are removed by this process, it is called as **electrolysis**. If a solution containing colloidal particles is forced through a suitable membrane by pressure, the membrane becomes an ultrafilter, and colloidal particles are separated. This process is called as **ultrafiltration**. Furthermore, it is possible to prepare membranes containing pores of desired size so that colloidal particles of any particular size may be separated from smaller particles as well as from material in true solution.

Svedberg (1920) found out that the rate of velocity at which a given particle sediments is proportional to the force applied. The particle will sediment more rapidly when the force applied is greater than the gravitational force of the earth. This concept forms the principle of centrifugation that can be defined as "a technique often employed during isolation or analysis of various cells, organelles and biopolymers including proteins, nucleic acids, lipids or carbohydrates dissolved or dispersed in biologically relevant solvents". This technique is also applicable to synthetic macromolecules dispersed or dissolved in nonaqueous organic solvents.

In this technique, the sample (comprising a liquid phase and a solute) is placed in a centrifuge tube which is spun in centrifuge rotor. The centrifugal force created by the spinning rotor causes the solute to sediment out of the solution at the base of the tube (Fig. 1).

Principle of Centrifugation

Sedimentation of the solute at the base of the tube is a function of a series of complex interacting factors related to the properties of the solute and the system. The centrifugal force applied to the sample is equal to gravitational force (acceleration) and is measured in gravities (G)

$$G = \omega^2 r$$

where

ω = is angular velocity in radians per second

r = is the radius of rotation in centimeters

It is more usual to monitor the speed of a centrifuge in terms of revolutions per minute than in radians per second

Hence

$$RCF = G = \frac{(2\pi \text{rpm})^2}{60} r \times g^{-1}$$

where

RCF = relative centrifugal force

2π = one revolution of the rotor

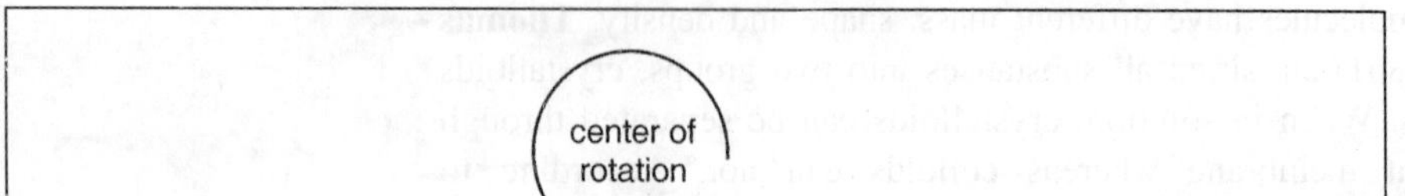

Fig. 1. A schematic diagram of a centrifugation experiment.

g = radians per second

For a particle to sediment, it must displace the equal volume of the solvent from beneath it. This can only be achieved by centrifugation if the mass of the particle is greater than the mass of the solvent displaced.

$$\text{Net force} = (M_p - M_s)\ \omega^2 r - fv$$

where

M_p = mass of particle

M_s = mass of the equal volume of solvent

fv = friction

It is convenient to classify particles by their rate of sedimentation per unit centrifugal field, a parameter known as sedimentation coefficient (s),

A Svedberg unit (S) is defined as sedimentation coeffecient of 1×10^{-13} seconds,

Types of Centrifuges

Different types of centrifuges are available now for different purposes. Generally they are classified into four groups: the bench centrifuges, large capacity refrigerated centrifuges, high speed refrigerated centrifuges and ultracentrifuges.

Small Bench Centrifuge

Simplest centrifuges that are used to separate erythrocytes, coarse precipitates and cells are known as bench or laboratory centrifuges. They have a speed ranging from 4000 to 6000 RPM and a relative centrifugal force of 3000 to 7000 g. They can be operated at ambient temperature (Fig. 2).

Small samples are sedimented nowadays with microfuges that after a speed of 8000-13000 RPM and relative RCF of approximately 10,000 g. They sediment small volumes (250 mm^3 to 1·5 cm^3) of material in 1 or 2 min. Blood samples are sedimented in routine using these microfuges.

Fig. 2. Bench centrifuge.

Fig. 3. A refrigerated centrifuge.

Large Refrigerated Centrifuge

These instruments can work at a speed of 6000 RPM and produce a maximum relative centrifugal field of 6500 g. Their rotor chamber is refrigerated.

Rotor	RPM	RCF ×g
12 × 1·5 ml Angle	20,000	26,600
10 × 8 ml Angle	16,000	21,750
6 × 30 ml Angle	12,000	12,880
20 × 5 ml Angle	17,000	22,620
9 × 1·5 ml Swing out	10,000	9,620
24 × 1·5 ml Angle	17,500	23,970
4 × 30 ml Angle	16,500	20,100
4 × 50 ml Angle	13,000	14,200
24 × 05 ml Angle	20,000	26,600

Fig. 4. Different types of rotor heads, corresponding RPM and RCF.

Swinging type or fixed angle rotors can be interchanged and accommodate 10, 50 and 100 cm^3 tubes. They are often used to collect substances that sediment rapidly, (Fig. 3) erythrocytes, nuclei, chloroplasts, yeast cells and bulky precipitates.

High Speed Refrigerated Centrifuge

As the name suggests, these centrifuges can attain a speed of 25,000 RPM and a centrifugal field of 6000 g. Interchangable rotor heads can be used to accommodate desired volume of the sample. They have a total capacity of up to 1.5 cm^3. They are generally used to collect micro-organisms, cellular debris, large cellular organelles and precipitated proteins. However, viruses and smaller organelles viz: ribosomes can not be separated by these centrifuges (Fig 4).

Ultracentrifugation

These instruments operate at a speed of 60,000 to 100,000 RPM. Despite the high speed, technique is very gentle and provides a valuable method for the separation of large labile molecules or particles. The technique can be further divided into two categories—

1. Preparative ultracentrifugation. In these centrifuges, rotors can spin to a maximum speed of 80,000 RPM and can produce a centrifugal field upto 600,000g. They are equipped with a refrigeration unit. Temperature is monitored by an infrared sensor. An overspeed control system prevents the operation above the rated speed. Rotor imbalance is electronically controlled. Rotor chambers are always enclosed in heavy armour plating. Preparative centrifugation is routinely employed in isolating, separating and purifying a variety of biological and cellular/subcellular components (Fig. 5).

(a) Differential centrifugation. In differential centrifugation, the material containing different fractions (tissue homogenate) is divided centrifugally into a number of fractions by increasing the applied centrifugal field. The centrifugal field, at each stage,

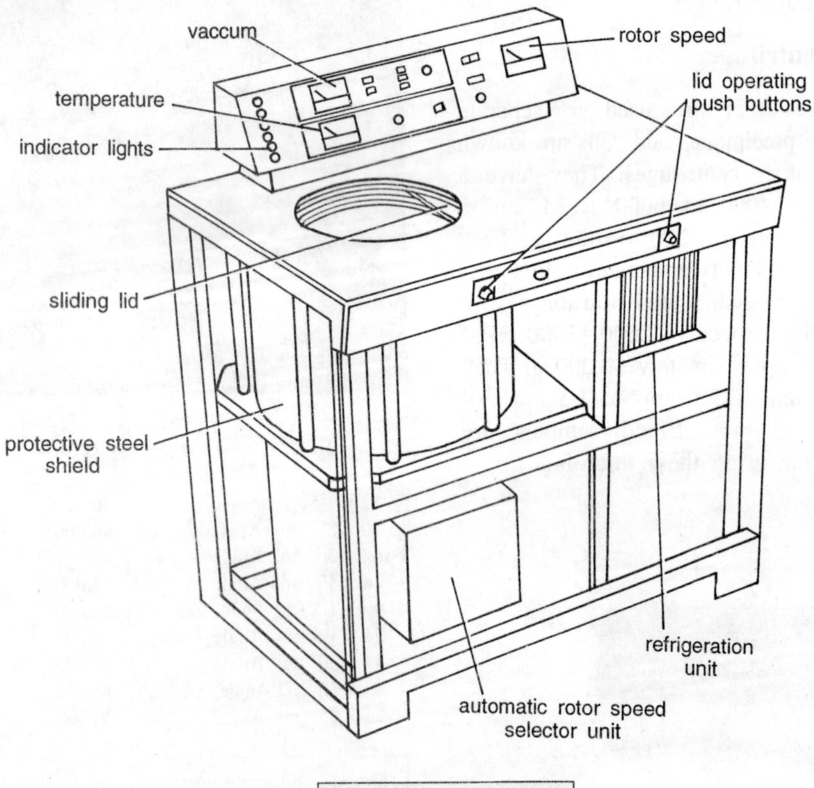

Fig. 5. An ultracentrifuge.

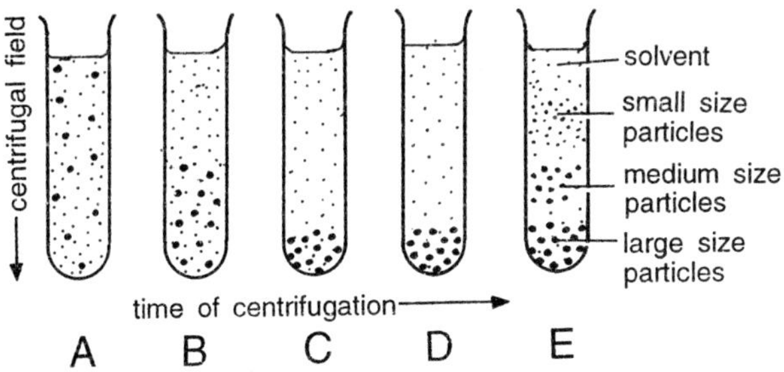

Fig. 6. Differential sedimentation of a particulate suspension in a centrifugal field. (a) Particles are uniformly distributed throughout the centrifuge tube (b) to (c) Sedimentation of particles during centrifugation is dependent upon their size, shape and density.

is selected to allow a particular fraction to sediment. The process begins with the preparation of tissue homogenate in a suitable medium e.g. distilled water, saline solution or sucrose. All particles in the homogenate, at this stage, are homogenously distributed through out the centrifuge tube at their respective sedimentation rates and a pellet is formed at the bottom of the centrifuge tube. This pellet of a particular fraction is removed and the resulting supernatant is centrifuged at a higher speed to separate medium sized particles and so on. The scheme of differential centrifugation is described by the following flow chart (Fig. 7).

The separation achieved by differential centrifugation may be improved by repeated (two or three times) resuspension of the pellet in homogenization medium and recentrifugation under the same conditions as in the original pelleting. Further centrifugation of the supernatant in gradually

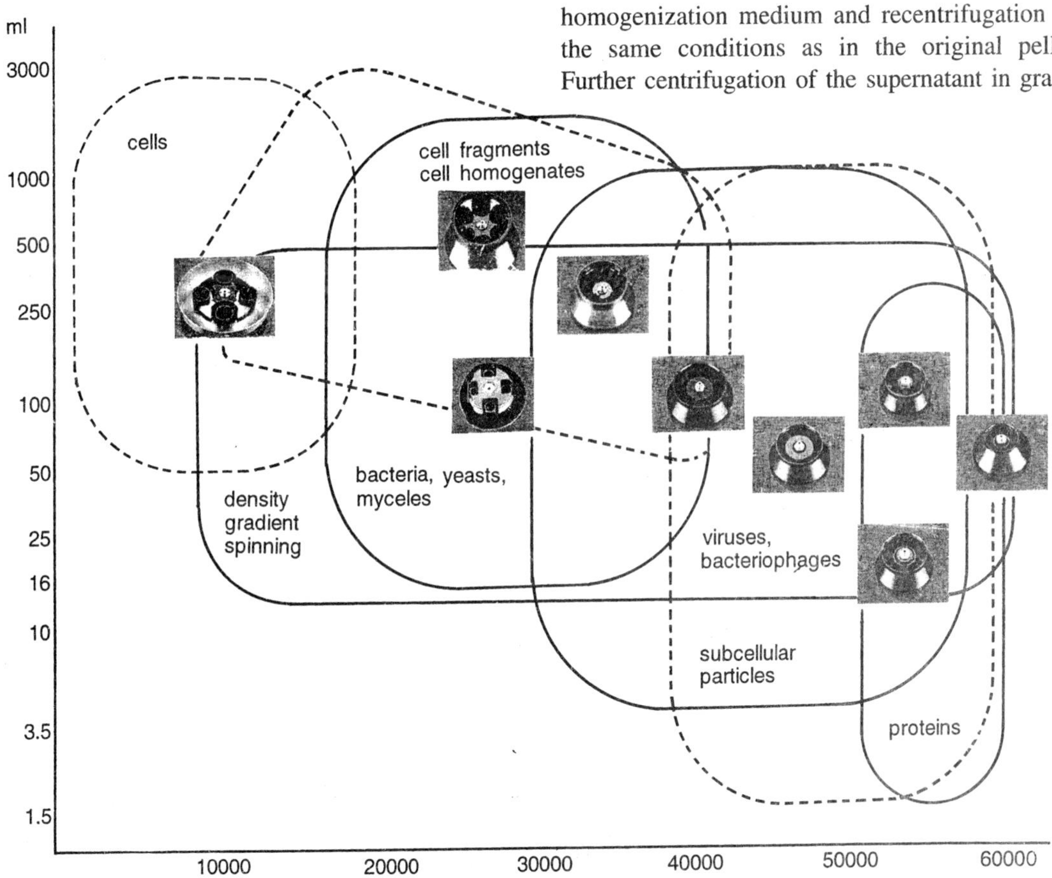

Fig. 7. Figure demonstrates the capabilities of the centrifuge for separation tasks in biological sciences. It depicts the application range of the various rotors of the centrifuge based on typical sample volumes and g-force ranges for the most important sample materials. A typical application for the high capacity rotors holding up to 3000 ml will be pelleting large particles such as cells or particulate materials. The most versatile rotor model 18·50 covers an extermely wide application range with its 700 ml capacity. It focuses mainly on processing subcellular particles.

increasing centrifugal fields results in the sedimentation of the intermediate and finally the smallest and least dense particles. At present, differential centrifugation is probably the most commonly used method for the isolation of cell organelles from homogenized tissue samples.

(b) Density gradient centrifugation. When a quantitative separation of all the components present in a mixture of particles is required, techniques of density gradient centrifugation are applied. There are two methods of density gradient centrifugation i.e. **zonal technique** and **isodensity methods**.

(i) Moving zone centrifugation. This technique is based on the differences in the size, shape and density of the particles, the density and viscosity of the medium and the applied centrifugal field. Since similar types of biological particles are often similar in shape and their densities fall into a relatively narrow range, maximum density of the gradient is chosen not to exceed the densest particle to be separated. Zonal technique is used for the separation of a wide range of particles and macromolecules, e.g. mitochondria, nuclei, ribosomes and proteins. Lysosomes and peroxisomes which have different densities but are similar in size are not efficiently separated by this technique. This technique may be used for bulk preparative work using a zonal rotor which is filled with a solvent gradient while running at a low speed.

(ii) Iso-density methods (Isopycnic centrifugation). This technique is used to separate particles of similar size but of different density, buoyant density of the particle and not on its shape and size. The method is a combination of sedimentation and flotation, achieved by using a density gradient which straddles the density of sediment until they reach a solvent zone with the same density. This results in the development of a zone for each type of particle (p) present in the sample. Hence, soluble proteins, which have a very similar density (e.g. p = 1·3 g cm^{-3} in sucrose solution), can not usually be separated by this method, whereas subcellular organelles (e.g. Golgi apparatus (p = 1·11 g cm^{-3}), mitochondria (p = 1·19 g cm^{-3}) and peroxisomes (p = 1·23 g cm^{-3}).

During centrifugation, sedimentation of the particles occurs until the buoyant density of the particle and the density of the gradient are equal. At this point of isodensity no further sedimentation occurs though centrifugation may continue. Thus the process can further be divided into two types.

(i) Preformed density gradients. Here the centrifuge tube is filled with a solvent in a graded range of concentrations prepared from mixtures of two different stock solutions which determine the limits of the gradient. Solutions of either sucrose or caesium chloride are generally used and the sample is layered on the surface and centrifuged. Under the influence of the centrifugal force, each component will move to an area of isodensity.

(ii) Equilibrium density gradients. This is a method for the separation of molecules with very similar densities and depends upon the formation of a density gradient by the effect of centrifugal force on the supporting solute molecules, but because of their low mass, the technique demands a long period of centrifugation (2-3 days). The gradient forms and the molecules are separated into zones simultaneously during the long period of centrifugation.

2. Analytical ultracentrifugation. These instruments are operated at a very high speed approaching to almost 70,000 RPM (500000g). In addition to a motor, rotor contained in a protective chamber that is refrigerated and evacuated, an optical system is also provided. This optical system allows the sedimenting material to be observed during the duration of centrifugation. By this method, the concentration distributions in the sample can be observed at any time during centrifugation.

Three types of optical systems are available in the analytical centrifuge.

(1) Light absorption system

(2) Schlieren system

(3) Rayleigh interfermetric system

Rotors of these centrifuges are also specially designed. Simplest type of rotor has two cells - the analytical cell and the counterpoise cell. The counterpoise cell counterbalances the analytical cell. A wide variety of cells are available with capacity ranging between 0·4 and 1·0 cm^{-3}. Analytical cells to be used with **ultraviolet light absorption optical system and the Schlieren optical system** have a single 2" or 4" sector shape and an optical pathlength varying from 12 mm to 30 mm. Double sector cells are also available. They allow the measurement of differences in sedimentation coefficients and diffusion coefficients (Fig. 8).

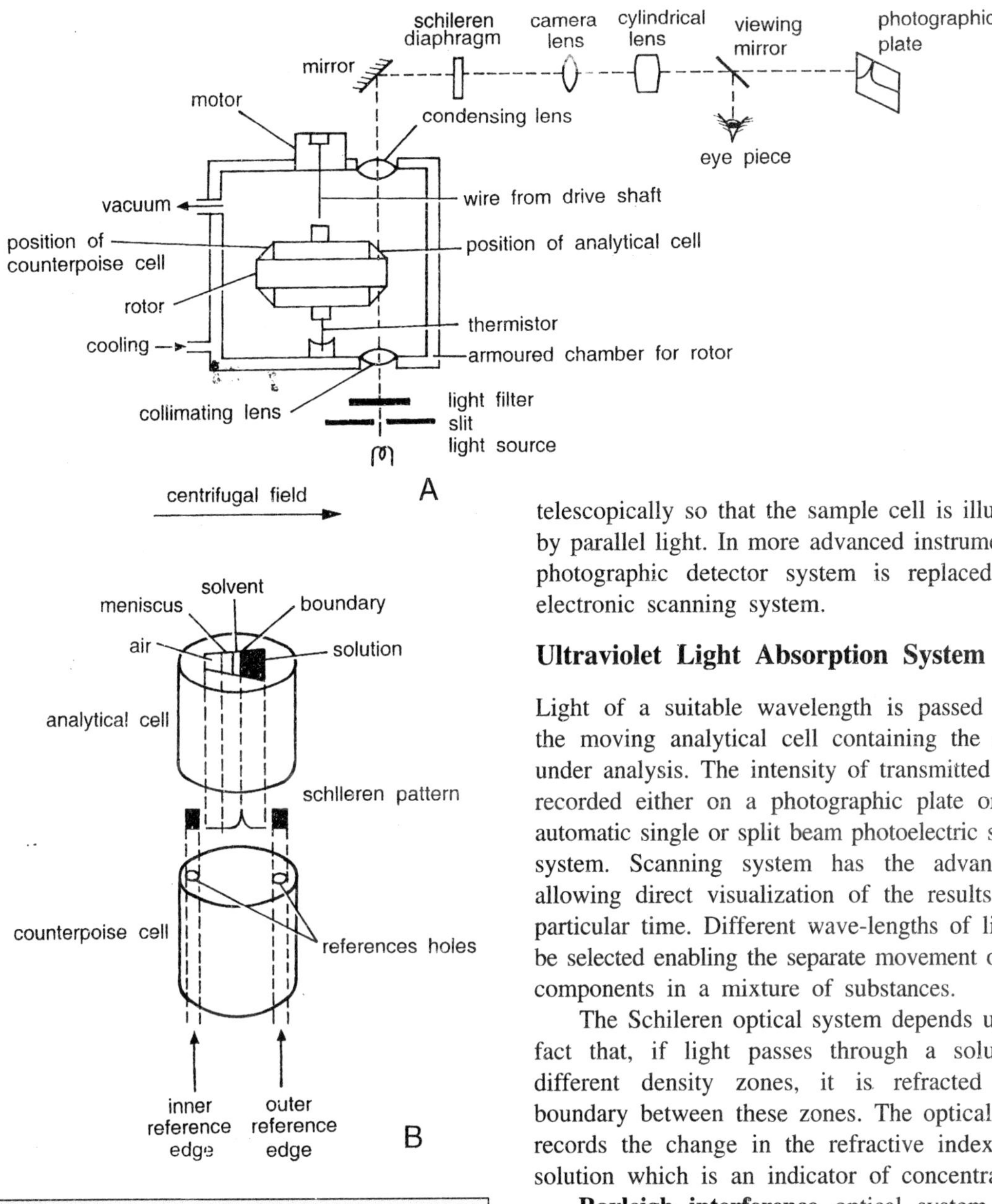

Fig. 8. Diagram of (a) an analytical ultracentrifuge system with a Schlieren optical system and (b) a single sector analytical cell and a counterpoise cell.

Analytical cells have upper and lower plane windows of optical grade of quartz or synthetic sapphire. The latter is used with interference optics.

The rotor chamber of these centrifuges contain an upper condensing lens together with a camera lens focuses light on to a photographic plate whereas the collimating lens adjusts the light telescopically so that the sample cell is illuminated by parallel light. In more advanced instruments, the photographic detector system is replaced by an electronic scanning system.

Ultraviolet Light Absorption System

Light of a suitable wavelength is passed through the moving analytical cell containing the solution under analysis. The intensity of transmitted light is recorded either on a photographic plate or by an automatic single or split beam photoelectric scanning system. Scanning system has the advantage of allowing direct visualization of the results at any particular time. Different wave-lengths of light can be selected enabling the separate movement of single components in a mixture of substances.

The Schileren optical system depends upon the fact that, if light passes through a solution of different density zones, it is refracted at the boundary between these zones. The optical system records the change in the refractive index of the solution which is an indicator of concentration.

Rayleigh interference optical system uses a double sector cell. One sector contains the solvent while the other contains the solution. The optical system measures the difference in refractive index between the reference solvent and the solution by the displacement of interference fringes caused by liquid columns, each fringe tracing the curve of the refractive index gradient against distance in the cell. Since the position of the fringes is determined by solute concentration, it is possible to measure the concentration of solute at any point along the cell.

Applications of Analytical Centrifugation

[I] Determination of relative molecular mass

During ultracentrifugation, when the frictional force equals the centrifugal force and the particle achieves maximum velocity, the relative molecular mass (*Mr*) of the particle may be represented by the Svedberg equation:

$$Mr = \frac{RT_s}{{}^r D(1-\bar{v}p)} \times \frac{S}{D}$$

where

S = is the sedimentation coefficient,

R = is the gas constant,

T = is the absolute temperature in K,

D = is the diffusion coefficient,

ρ = is the density of the solvent,

v = is the partial specific volume of the solute.

The partial specific volume is the increase in the volume of a solution caused by the presence of the solute and is defined as the volume occupied by 1 kilogram of the solute in 100 kilograms of the solution. The value may be calculated using the densities of both the solvent (ρ) and the solution (ρs).

$$\bar{v} = \left[\frac{\frac{100}{\rho_s} - \frac{(100-n)}{\rho}}{n} \right]$$

where n is the percentage concentration of the solute in the solvent (w/w).

The value of the partial specific volume for proteins is approximately 0·7 while for nucleic acids the value varies around 0·5.

The sedimentation coefficient may be determined by measuring the velocity of the particle at a fixed centrifuge speed (ω, in radians per second) and, from a series of observations, plotting the logarithm of the distance moved (x) against the time taken in second (t). The relationship is expressed by the equation —

$$s = \frac{l_n x}{\omega^2 t} = \frac{2 \cdot 303 \log_{10} x}{\omega^2 t}$$

and the value for s can be calculated from the slope of the resulting graph. Although relative molecular mass may be calculated using the Svedberg equation, the calculations are complicated by difficulties in determining the diffusion coefficient and correcting for differences in viscosity and temperature. For these reasons the sedimentation coefficient of a particle is often used instead of its mass, the two being proportional to one another.

An alternative method for the determination of the relative molecular mass involves a technique known as meniscus depletion. If a homogeneous sample is centrifuged at a speed greater enough to cause the particles to move away from the meniscus resulting in a solute concentration of zero at the meniscus and producing a concentration gradient due to the solute, the relative molecular mass is proportional to the slope of a plot of the logarithm of concentration against the distance squared. This relationship is not absolute and depends upon measurements being taken early in the process and assumes that the density of the solution is constant throughout the solution despite the very slight concentration gradient which does develop. The concentration of solute may be determined from the steepness of the interference fringes formed in a Rayleigh pattern.

$$RMM = \frac{4{\cdot}606\ RT}{(1-\bar{v}\,\rho)\omega^2} \times \frac{\log \text{concentration}}{(\text{distances})^2}$$

[II] Estimation of purity of macromolecules

These instruments are also used in determining the purity of DNA preparations, viruses and proteins. The first requirement is the assessment of homogeneity.

Homogeneity can be presumed only through the absence of detectable heterogeneity. Homogeneity is usually recognized by a single sharp symmetrical sedimenting boundary throughout the duration of sedimentation velocity experiment. Impurities in the preparation are displayed as additional peaks.

[III] Determination of conformational changes in macromolecules

Conformational changes in macromolecules e.g. DNA can be determined by analytical centrifugation. DNA may exist as single or double strands, each of which may be either linear or circular in nature.

When exposed to a variety of agents, drugs or chemicals or elevated temperature, DNA molecules may undergo a number of reversible or irreversible changes. These changes may be ascertained by examining differences in the sedimentation velocity of the sample. Similarly, confirmation changes of allosteric proteins and disaggregation into subunits (protomers) may readily be studied by analytical centrifugation.

Precautions

A centrifuge user should strictly observe the following precautions :

(1) Manufacturer's manual should be strictly followed.

(2) Lid of the rotor chamber should remain locked during operation.

(3) Rotor speed should not exceed the assigned speed.

(4) Attention should be given to imbalance detectors.

(5) When zonal rotors and continuous flow rotors are used, the moving rotors should not be touched and loose clothing should be avoided.

(6) To avoid the rotor failure, manufactures instructions regarding rotor care and use should always be followed.

(7) When centrifugation of hazardous substances like pathogenic microorganisms, infectious viruses, carcinogenic, corrosive, and radioactive material is to be made, samples should be kept in air-tight, leak- proof containers.

(8) Rotors should be stored in proper containers.

Important Questions

1. What do you understand by centrifugation? Discuss the principle of centrifugation. Describe different types of centrifuges.
2. What is ultra centrifugation? Discuss different methods of ultra centrifugation and their applications.
3. What is analytical ultra centrifugation? Discuss the principle, instrument design and applications of analytical centrifugation.
4. Write briefly on the following:
   (i) Centrifugal and centripetal force, (ii) Differential centrifugation, (iii) Density gradient centrifugation.

8

Spectrophotometry

For millions of years, light has defined the life of *Homo sapiens sapiens.* Through, photosynthesis light has given us food, energy and atmosphere. And using light we communicate information, see the big objects far from us through telescope and small objects through microscope. From where does light get this transcending power? It took nearly a millennium until **James Clark Maxwell** in 1864 told the world that light is made of waves of disturbances of electric and magnetic fields. Maxwell's equations predict the correct high speed of light (c = 300,000 km/s). In elucidating that light is an electromagnetic wave, Maxwell unified the important work of **Michael Faraday** (1791-1867) on electricity and magnetism and of **Thomas Young** on the wave nature of light. As a wave, light has a wavelength (λ) and frequency ($\Upsilon = c/\lambda$). This is true for all waves of electromagnetic spectrum from radio waves to X-rays.

The interaction of electromagnetic radiation with matter is essentially a quantum phenomenon and is dependent both upon the properties of radiation and the material involved. Measurement of the intensity and wavelength of radiation which is either absorbed or emitted provide the basis for sensitive methods of detection and quantitation of a matter.

In 1905, **Albert Einstein** recognized the implications of quantiztation for light – it is made of a stream of particles and comes as bundles of energy, called by **G . N. Lewis** as **photons**.

Energy associated with the radiation can be mathematically related to the waveform. A waveform can be defined at least in two different ways.

Wavelength (λ) is defined as the distance between successive peaks and is measured as nanometer (10^{-9}m). One nanometer is equivalent to 10Å.

The frequency of radiation (Υ) is defined as the number of successive peaks passing a given point in 1 second. Hence the relationship between two units of measurement is –

$$\Upsilon = \frac{1}{\lambda}$$

The visible region of the **spectrum** extends approximately over the wavelength range of 400-700 nm. The shorter wavelength being the blue end and the longer end wavelength the red end. Wavelengths between 200 – 400nm comprise the near ultraviolet region of the spectrum and wavelengths above 700 nm to approximately 2000 nm, the near infrared region.

Energy associated with a particular waveform is directly related to the frequency of the radiation and therefore, inversely related to the wavelength that can be calculated using the following equation —

$$E = hv = \frac{hc}{\lambda}$$

Where

h = Planck's constant ($6{\cdot}624 \times 10^{-34}$ Js^{-1})

λ = wavelength of radiation

c =speed of light ($3{\cdot}0 \times 10^{10}$ cm s^{-1})

while the energy associated with a waveform is related to its wavelength, the intensity of the radiation is related to its amplitude.

A study of the wavelength or frequency of radiation absorbed or emitted by an atom or molecule will give information about its identity and this technique is known as **qualitative spectroscopy**. Measurement of the total amount of radiation will give information about the number of absorbing or emitting atoms or molecules and is called as **quantitative spectroscopy**.

Beer-Lambert Relationship

Ultraviolet and visible light spectroscopy follow a principle known as Beer-Lambert law. It is a combination of two laws. Lambert's law states that the proportion of radiant energy absorbed by a substance is independent of the intensity of the incident radiation.

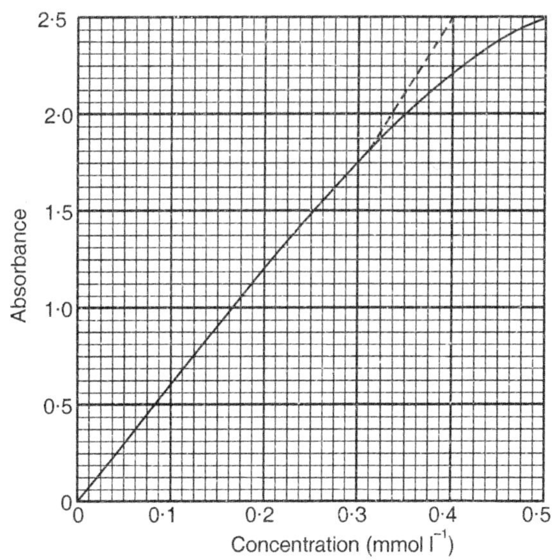

Fig. 1. Molar absorption coefficient of nicotinamide adenine dinucleotide (reduced) (NADH). The Beer-Lambert relationship is true up to an absorbance value of 1·8 with the instrument used. The molar absorbance can be calculated from the slope of the straight line

Beer's law states that the absorptions of radiant energy is proportional to the total number of molecules in the light path. Beer's law describes the basic relationship between the concentration of the absorbing substance & the measured value of absorbed radiation. **Lambert's law** is of major significance in the manner in which measurements are made and the fact remains that the given sample always absorbs the same proportion of the incident radiation regardless of intensity.

It is not possible to measure directly the amount of radiation absorbed by a partially transparent substance. It is usually determined by measuring the difference in intensity between the radiation falling on the sample (incident radiation, Io) and the residual which finally emerges from the sample (transmitted radiation, I). Thus transmittance, T can be expressed as —

$$T = \frac{I}{I_0}$$

A 100% value of T represents a totally transparent substance with no radiation being

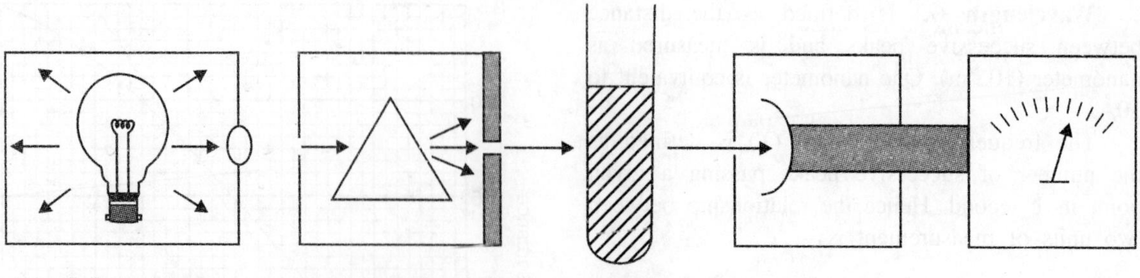

Fig. 2. Components of a spectrophotometer.

absorbed and a zero value of T represents a totally opaque substance, which in effect represents complete absorption. For immediate values we can define the absorbance (A) or extinction (E) which is given by the logarithm (base 10) of the reciprocal of the transmittance.

$$A = E = \log (1/T) = \log (I_0/I)$$

It is now possible to define Beer-Lambert law in simple terms that it states that absorbance is proportional to both the concentration of absorber and thickness of the layer as —

$$A = E_\lambda cl$$

Where E_λ is the molar extinction coefficient for the absorber at a particular wavelength λ, c is the concentration of absorbing solution and l is the pathlength through the solution (or thickness).

Deviation From the Beer-Lambert Law

The Beer-Lambert equation expresses the linear relationship between the concentration of the sample and the absorbance value recorded. However, this relationship is experimental one and not a fundamental law of nature and as a result the linearity is only true under certain limiting conditions.

The basic assumption that the difference between incident and transmitted radiation is a measure of the absorbed radiation is not completely true because incident radiation may not appear in the transmitted from for other reasons besides absorption. A certain amount of radiation will be reflected from the surface of the sample holder or absorbed by the material of the cell is composed. The sample may also be dissolved in a solvent which itself may also be absorbed or reflect radiation.

Hence,

Incident radiation (I_0) = absorbed + transmitted (I) + other losses

For these reasons, radiation transmitted by a blank sample is measured and considered as effective incident radiation. The blank is identical to the test sample but does not contain the test substance.

$$\text{Blank reading} = I_0 - \text{Other losses}$$

Hence,

$$\text{Absorbance} = \text{blank} - \text{transmission } (I)$$

Instrumentation

A wide range of instruments are available for measuring the absorbed radiation. A simple instrument which is designed to measure the intensity of a beam of light and usually does so by comparing it with some reference source of radiation is called as **photometer**. However, an instrument which is capable of splitting the incident radiation into a spectrum and is used to identify the individual wavelengths is known as **spectrometer**. Whereas a **spectrophoto-meter** is an instrument which combines both of these functions. It is capable of producing radiation of defined wavelength and subsequently measuring the intensity of that radiation.

The basic design of a spectrophotometer is illustrated by figure 2. Light from the lamp pass through a monochromatic device at a selected wavelength. After passing through the sample, light is measured by a suitable photoelectric detector.

Intensity of the initial radiation is controlled either by an attenuator which is often a simple shutter system or by changing the operating voltage of the lamp. The geometry of the light path is controlled by a series of lenses of focussing mirrors. The degree of sophistication of the instrument and the quality of the results depend upon the individual components and the optical design but the basic method is similar. Prepare a set of standards and produce a concentration versus absorption calibration curve, which is linear because it is a Beer-Lambert law for all the instruments. The usual procedure is to measure absorbance and the concentration interpolated from the linear region of the plot. Interpolation is critical and following precautions should be observed —

(1) One should never extrapolate beyond the region for which any instrument has been calibrated.

(2) Observations taken beyond colour-regent limit, does not follow **Beer-Lambert** relationship and a plate is formed. This phenomenon is called as **Job effect**.

(3) Accuracy of the instrument is not uniform throughout the transmission range. The final measurement involves a galvanometer. The errors at low and high absorbance can be large due to the nature of galvanometer. Therefore, analysis should be designed to give absorbance in the middle range of transmission scale.

The characters of individual components of a spectrophotometer are described below—

Source of Radiation

The tungsten lamp is a reliable source of radiant energy in the visible region of the spectrum. The usual source of ultraviolet radiation is hydrogen or deuterium discharge lamp or the mercury vapour lamp. All ultraviolet sources must be covered with quartz or silica glass windows. **Blackbody** radiators are used as sources of infrared radiation. **Nernst glower** is most frequently used. It consists of a hollow rod made up of oxides of **zirconium**, **yttrium** and **thorium**. When heated it emits instance continuous infrared radiation.

Monochromators

There are several devices designed to produce radiations of limited wavelength range. They may be simple prisms, glass filters, interference filters or diffraction gratings. Silica or quartz prisms are used for ultraviolet region of the spectrum while glass is used for visible region. **Rock salt prisms** are necessary for infrared spectrophotometry.

Detectors

Detectors function on the principle that absorption of radiation results in the displacement of electrons and hence in the development of a potential difference between two electrodes. Two types of detectors e.g. **photovoltaic** and **photoconductive** are used in spectrophotometry. Photovoltaic detectors are used in visible and ultraviolet spectrophotometers whereas infrared spectrophotometry uses photoconductive detectors.

Optical Systems

The optical systems are usually either prisms which are used to split the multiwavelength radiation into its components by refractions, or gratings which achieve the same thing by diffraction. A basic photometer (Colorimeter) is a single beam instrument. It allows only one light path and the instrument is standardized using a blank solution, which is replaced with a sample to obtain a reading. In a double beam instrument, the radiation is split into two beams one passing through the sample to the detector and one through the blank. A series of **half mirrors** may be used permitting both light paths to work simultaneously or alternatively the beam may be chopped mechanically, deflecting a beam of radiation alternately along each light path. The detector receives alternate pulses of radiation and it produces alternating electrical signals.

Optical Materials

The sample is kept in tubes or cuvettes. They are the integral part of the spectrophotometer. Normal silicate glass will only transmit radiation between 350 nm and 3 μm, therefore, its use is restricted to the visible and near infrared region of the spectrum. Materials suitable for ultraviolet region include **quartz** and **fused silica**. In infrared spectrophotometry, samples are often dissolved in suitable organic solvent e.g. carbon tetrachloride or carbon disulphide.

Applications of Spectrophotometry

Applications of spectrophotometry :

(1) It is used to make quanlitative as well as quantitative analysis.
(2) Substances in pure state and in biological mixture can be analyzed.
(3) Substances with overlapping spectra such as chlorophyll a and chlorophyll b may be estimated.
(4) Difference between two absorption spectra may be obtained.
(5) The binding of monoclonal antibody with its antigen may be monitored using second order differential spectroscopy.
(6) Valuable structural studies may be performed on biological macromolecules such as proteins and nucleic acids.

Atomic Spectroscopy

The method described above deal essentially with molecular spectroscopy. However, it was recognized that metals when heated emit radiation. Subsequently methods of their analysis were developed that use the wavelength of emission for quantitative analysis. Emission spectroscopy is frequently encountered as "**flame emission photometry**", which is restricted to visible region of the spectrum and to those elements which can be excited at the temperature of the flame. This principle is used in estimating trace elements by flame emission spectroscopy.

Flame Emission Photometry

A flame photometer (Fig. 3) is designed to cause atomic excitation and subsequently measure the intensity of the emitted radiation. A monochromator differentiates between the emission of the test element and other radiation from the flame.

The flame combines two functions. It is a source of radiation and carries the atomized sample. The flame temperature should be high enough to excite the atoms under investigation, the hotter the flame the greater the proportion that will be excited.

The sample is taken to the atomizer where it is covered into an aerosol. From atomizer, it goes to an expansion chamber where large droplets settle out and atoms are left as the finely distributed gas. In practice only a small part of the sample (about 5%) is used. Remaining 95% drains out of the system.

No special monochromators are required for flame photometry. Any one of the monochromators described for absorption metres may be used. Many instruments use filters, however, the use of interference filters improves the specificity of analysis.

Quantitative methods used in flame emission spectroscopy are not absolute, because an unknown proportion of the sample will reach the flame and subsequently emit radiation. Hence it is essential to construct a calibration curve for any analysis.

Atomic Absorption Spectrophotometry

An atom comprises a nucleus surrounded by electrons. Every element has a specific number of electrons. When energy of a right magnitude is supplied to an atom, this energy is absorbed by the atom and outer electrons get excited. This process is called as excitation. As this state is unstable, the atom will immediately return to ground state and the electron will return to initial orbital state vadiating the amount of energy initially absorbed. This process is called as decay.

If light waves of the specific wavelength impinges on a free ground state atom, the atom may absorb the light and enters into the excited state. This process is known as atomic absorption and can be illustrated as follows —

As the number of atoms in the light path increases, the amount of light absorbed increases

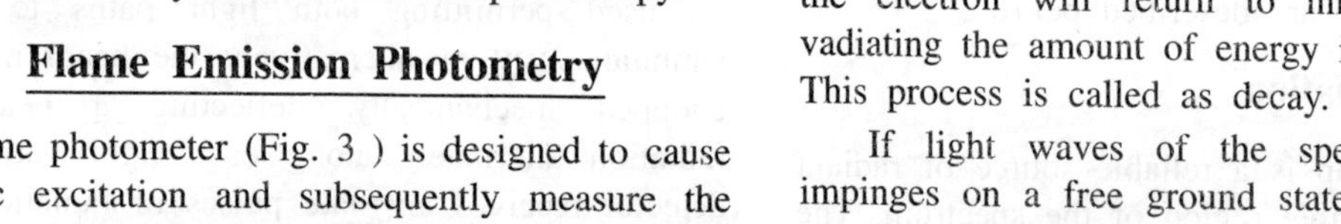

Fig. 3. Excitation of an atom.

in a predictable way. Therefore by measuring the amount of light absorbed, a quantitative determination of the amount of analyte element present can be made.

Principle of Atomic Absorption Spectroscopy

The basic principle of atomic absorption spectroscopy is the absorption of energy by ground state atoms in the gaseous state forms. When a solution containing metallic species is introduced into a flame, the vapour of metallic species is obtained. Some of the atoms may be raised to an energy level sufficiently higher to emit the characteristic radiation of the metal but large percentage of metal atoms remain in non-emitting ground state. These ground atoms are receptive of light radiation of their own specific resonance wave length. When a light of this wavelength is allowed to pass through a flame having atoms of metallic species, part of that light will be absorbed and the absorption will be proportional to the density of atoms in the flame.

If the light at the resonance wavelength of initial intensity I_0 is focused on the flame cell containing ground state atoms, the initial light is decreased by an amount determined by the atom concentration in the flame cell. The light is then directed onto the detector where reduced intensity, I is measured. The amount of light absorbed in determined by comparing I to I_0.

Instrumentation of Atomic Absorption Spectrophotometer

The typical atomic absorption spectrophotometer consists of following main components —

(1) Radiation Source
(2) Chopper
(3) Sample cell/burner
(4) Gases for flame
(5) Nebulizer
(6) Monochromator
(7) Detector
(8) Amplifier
(9) Readout ssystem
(10) Hydride generation system (optional)
(11) Graphite furnace (optional).

1. Radiation source. The radiation source should emit stable intense radiation of the element to be determined, usually the resonance line of the element. These resonance line should be narrow compared to the width of the absorption line to be measured and there should not be interference from other spectral lines which are not resolved by spectrophotometer.

The problem of using such narrow spectral line has been solved by adopting **Hollow Cathode Lamp** (HCL) as radiation source. The cathode of the Hollow Cathode Lamp is cup shaped generally constructed of the highly pure metal or it may be constructed from an inert element into which the desired element or its salt is kept. The anode is generally a tungsten wire. The lamp envelop is made from the glass and filled with neon or argon gas at low pressure (1 to 5 torr). In the high pressure the discharge tend to be unstable while in low pressure the vaporization of hollow cathode metal increases and operating temperature also increase. The neon or argon gas performs three functions.

(1) It is the main source of current carrying capacity in the hollow cathode.
(2) The atoms from the surface of cathode are dislodged by it.
(3) It is primarily responsible for excitation of the ground state metal atoms.

When a DC voltage of 300-500 volts is put across the anode and cathode, the atoms of the filled gas undergo ionization at the anode and rapidly attracted by the cathode. The fast moving ions strike the surface of cathode and physically

Table 1. **Gas composition and temperature for the analysis of elements.**

Gas mixture	Temperature required	Elements analyzed
1. Air-Propane	About 1800^0C	Cu, Pb, K, Na, Zn, and Mg in sample solution
2. Air-Acetylene	About 2300^0C	30 elements including above elements
3. N_2O-Acetylene	About 3000^0C	Al, Si, V and Ti and 67 other elements. It is used where air-propane, air acetylene flames are not satisfactory.

displace the surface metal atoms of the cathode into neon/argon gas. The collision of vaporized metal atoms from the cathode with energetic filled gas ions results in excited metal atoms emitting the characteristic spectrum of the metal used for construction of the cathode. For example copper cathode emit the copper spectrum, zinc cathode will emit zinc spectrum. The emission spectrum from cathode lamp is a sharp line narrow spectrum, which is completely absorbed by the atoms and detection/ measurement of that atom is done by atomic absorption.

Apart from hollow cathode lamp, gaseous discharge lamp are also used as radiation source. These lamps contain an inert gas at low pressure and a metal salt and known as the "**Arc Lamp**". These lamps are used in estimation of alkali metals, like zinc, cadmium and mercury.

2. Chopper. The rotating wheel interposed between hollow cathode lamp and flame is known as chopper and it breaks the steady light from the lamp into an intermittent or pulsating light. The chopper provides pulsating current to the **photocell**. There is also a steady current caused by light emitted by a flame but only pulsating current is amplified and recorded. Thus absorption of light is measured without interference from the light emitted by flame itself.

3. Production of atomic vapours (burner + sample cell). ***(a) Burner.*** The sample is reduced to atomic state to achieve absorption by atom utilizing flame, which converts the liquid sample into gaseous state and also converts molecules entities into an atomic vapour. The burner used in atomic absorption spectrophotometry are of two types. (i) **total consumption burner**, (ii) **pre-mixed burner**.

In total consumption burner the sample solution, the fuel gases and oxidizing gases are passed through separate passage to meet at the opening of the base of the flame. As the sample containing metallic element enters the flame region, the flame breaks up the liquid sample into droplets which are then evaporated or burnt leaving the residue, reduced to atoms. In these burners, fuel gases are oxygen with hydrogen or acetylene and these provide very hot flames. In addition these burners are noisy and its efficiency are not very good. Liquid droplets are preheated through which liquid is evaporated leaving the residue. The **conduction**, **convection** and **diffusion** of radicals in this region initiate the combustion. The sample residue is burnt later to produce atoms. The premixed burners are very suitable for atomic absorption studies of metals of group IA, IB and IIB of periodic table together with Ga, In, TI, Pb, Te, Mn, Ni and Pb.

(b) Optical system atomization cell (sample cell). In atomic absorption spectrophotometer, the basic purpose of the optical system is to gather light from source, direct through the sample, and then direct it into the monochromator.

In atomization cell, a flame burns at a long slit and it is usually about 10 cm long and 0·5 mm wide. When sample is being atomized, the absorbing atoms are distributed along the length of the flame. Atoms have extremely narrow absorption lines and there are few problems of background absorption involving spectral interferences.

(1) Un-dissociated molecular forms of matrix materials have broad banded absorption spectra.
(2) Tiny solid particles in the flame may scatter light over a wide wavelength region, when this non specific absorption overlaps the atomic absorption wavelength of the analyte, background absorption is present.

For the point of safety, cost or convenience, air-propane, air acetylene and nitrous oxide acetylene gases are used for flame. Generally the choice of gas mixture will depend on the temperature required as depicted in table below for compound dissociated and or the chemical characteristics of the elements being determined.

The decomposition of compound in the flame is assumed to proceed directly following desolation. The high temperature will cause the reaction to proceed one step further. For example —

$$Pb(NO_3)_2.H_2O \longrightarrow Pb(NO_3)_2 + H_2O$$

$$Pb(NO_3)_2 + O \longrightarrow PbO + NO$$

$$PBO \longrightarrow Pb + O$$

4. Nebulization of liquid. Before the liquid sample enters into the burner, it is converted into small droplets. This method of formation of small droplets from the liquid sample is called nebulizaiton. The common method of nebulization is by use of a gas moving at high velocity called

pneumatic nebulization. The conversion of liquid sample into fine droplets through atomization is accomplished in five successive stages.

Stage I	–	Nebulization
Stage II	–	Droplet precipitation
Stage III	–	Mixing
Stage IV	–	Desolation
Stage V	–	Compound decomposition

5. Monochromator. In atomic absorption measurements the most monochromators are prism and gratings. The functions of monochromator is to isolate a single atomic resonance line from the spectrum of lines emitted by hollow cathode lamp. In the commercial packaged AAS system the monochromator is having about ½ m focal length with line reciprocal dispersion in the range 16-35 Å/mm.

The monochromator is infact an adjustable filter which selects a specific narrow region of the spectrum for transmission to the detectors and rejects the wavelengths out this region. The ability to discriminate between **different wavelength** (the resolution) is thus a very important characteristic of monochromator.

The isolation of required portion of spectrum is being universally accomplished by grating monochromator. The grating consists of usually about 500 to 3000 grooves/n. Slit width is an important determinant of monochromator performance because the width of the slit controls the resolution of adjacent wavelength. The shape of the groove known as the blaze determines the distribution of energy.

6. Detector. For atomic absorption spectroscopy, the photomultiplier tube is most suitable detector having good stability in case stable power supply is used. It works satisfactorily and enables to compare intense line in a satisfactory manner.

In **photo-multiplier tube** (PMT) there is an evacuated envelope which encases photocathode, a series of electrodes called dyodes and an anode. The photocathode fixed to the terminal end of the power supply.

The photomultiplier tube produces an electrical signal which is proportional to intensity of light at the wavelength, which has been isolated by the monochromator. The electrical signal is then amplified and used to provide a quantitative measurement absorption.

7. Amplifier. The electric current from the photomultiplier detector is fed to the amplifier which amplifies the electric current many times. Generally, lock-in amplifier are preferred which are provided a very narrow frequency band pass and help to achieve and excellent signal to noise ratio. The signal from photomultiplier tube is led to an AC amplifier to modulate the energy source. The modulated signal finally enters the **synchronous detector**. At the same time, the signal from a reference source (usually a flashlight bulb) is modulated at exactly the same frequency as the signal from the photo multiplier tube undergoes by passing through an AC amplifier.

The modulated reference signal also enters the synchronous detector through phase shifter. The two signals are combined in a synchronous detector to produce sum and difference frequencies. The sum frequency will be twice the chopping frequency and the difference frequency will be zero. Thus the difference frequency will be a DC signal when the signal from synchronous detector are allowed to pass through a low pass RC filter. It removes the 'sum frequencies' and a DC difference signal is amplified by a DC amplifier and then goes out to the read out system.

8. Read out system. The readout system of an atomic absorption spectrophotmeter constitutes the technical system by which the electrical signals from the photomultiplier are translated into analog or digital display readings corresponding to the analytical results. Modern atomic absorption instruments are now available with inbuilt facilities for presenting results in digital form. A **chart recorder** can be used to make a permanent tracings of the analog signals.

9. Hydride generation system. In hydride generation, the gaseous hydrides of certain metals (such as arsenic, selenium, antimony) are chemically produced by the addition to **sodium borohydride**. When the sample vapor is atomized in the flame or heated cell, a peak signal is produced, the height of which is proportional to the amount of analyte in the sample.

$$NaBH_4 \longrightarrow AsH_3 \text{ (metals hydride)}$$

10. Graphite furnance atomic absorption. Since the graphite furnace required only a few microlitres of samples, this technique can be used in solutions where only a small amount of sample is available. With this device many elements can be determined at lower concentrations than what can be detected by flame atomic absorption. The graphite furnace is a flameless sampling device. The energy required for atomization is supplied by passing a high electric current through a graphite tube into which the samples have been placed. The furnace is aligned in the sampling area of the spectrophotometer in such a way that the light from the spectral lamp will pass through the centre of the graphite tube. By controlling the amount of current blow, the temperature of the tube can be adjusted to any desired level upto a maximum of about 3000°C. By circulating the water through the housing the outside temperature of the furnace is kept at a safe level, and after atomization the graphite tube is rapidly cooled to room temperature where it is ready to accept the next sample. To prevent tube destruction at high temperatures, from air oxidation, an inert gas purge of the graphite tube is provided.

Single and Double Beam Atomic Absorption Spectrophotometer

The atomic absorption spectroscopy employs both single and double beam atomic absorption spectrophotometer. In single beam instruments, a light source is placed ahead of the flame, when there is no sample in the flame, the output of the detector amplifier unit is arranged to give full deflection. After this the sample solutions sprayed into the flame and the output of the detector amplifier is recorded. The main disadvantage of single beam is low stability.

In double beam atomic absorption spectrophotometer, the stability is increased as the chopped beam from the hollow cathode lamp is divided into two; one part goes to the flame while other part by-passes it. After recombination, the two beams pass through monochromator to a detector and read out system. The advantage of double beam AAS equipment is that there is no effect of lamp drift and there is no change in detector sensitivity with time.

Atomic Absorption Spectrophotometer–Makes and Models

About eleven different makes of standard AAS systems are available in the Indian market. Varying options are available for different systems but mostly these AAS system are automated compatible with IBM-PC controlled system. In atomic absorption spectrophotometer main facilities include 'Flame' as well as 'Graphite Tube' atomization, vapor generation systems.

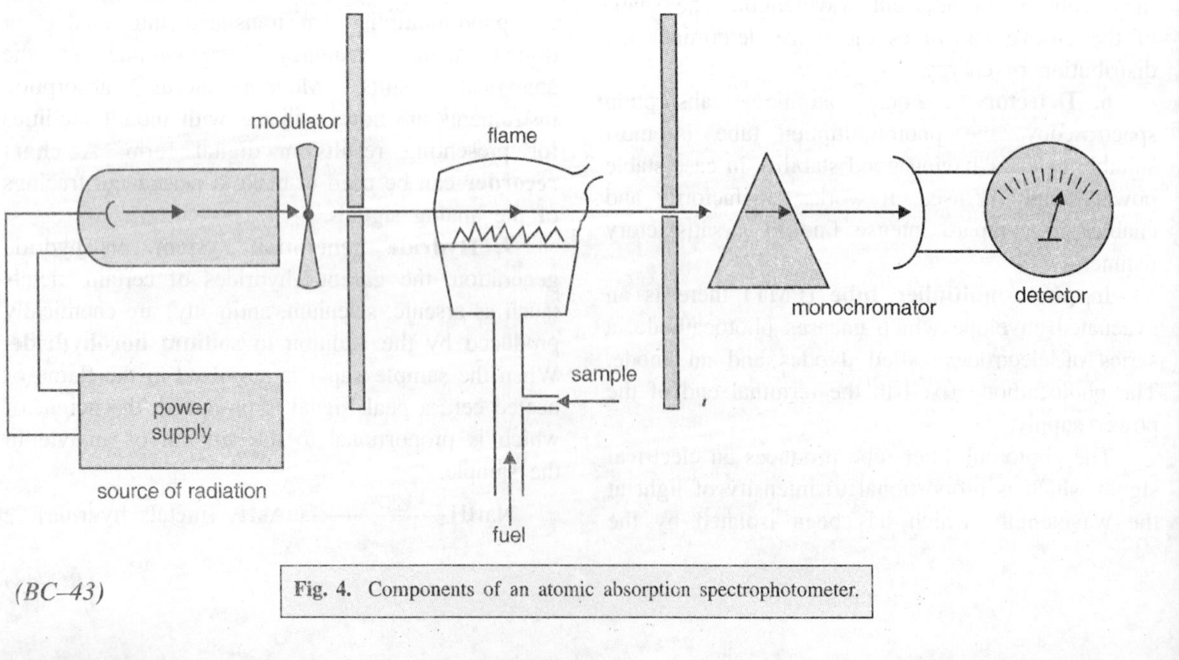

Fig. 4. Components of an atomic absorption spectrophotometer.

Advantages and Disadvantages of AAS

Advantages. (1) Atomic absorption spectroscopy is most powerful technique for the quantitative determination of trace elements in liquid.

(2) Total metal content of the sample can be estimated.

(3) AAS can be used for the estimation of 60-70 elements including rare earth metals in concentration range from traces to micro-quantities.

(4) A particular element can be estimated in presence of many other elements. There is no need to separate the test element from the mixture of other elements present in the sample

Disadvangates. (1) During analysis, separate hollow cathode lamp (HCL) is required for each element.

(2) The estimation of metal species like aluminium, titanium, tungsten, molybdenum, vanadium and silica can not be made as these elements give rise to oxides in the flame.

(3) In aqueous solution, the predominant anion effect the signal to a negotiable degree.

Spectrofluorimetry

Luminiscense is one of the oldest analytical technique having been first observed by **Monardes** in 1565 from an extract of *Ligirium nephiticiem*. **Sir David Brewster** noted red emission from chlorophylls in 1833 and **Sir Stokes** described the mechanism of emission and absorption process in 1852. Biologists have long been aware of the fluorescence assay and were amongst the first to utilize it.

Fluorescence — A fluorescent, compound absorbs ultraviolet and visible light and the molecule comes to an excited state. The phenomenon of light emission during the process of returning to the ground state is called fluorescence.

In other words, when the emission of light is instantaneous, the phenomenon is known as **fluorescence**. When emission occurs after some lag period, it is known as **phosphorescence**. **Luminescence** is the general term applied to the absorption or emission of radient energy.

Fluorescence emission has three principles —

(1) Molecules enter an excited state after absorbing ultraviolet or visible light. Then molecules come to an unstable state of high energy (excited singlet state, S1).

(2) Electrons loose excess energy as vibration energy and reaches the lowest level of excited singlet state.

(3) Fluorescence emission occurs when electrons lose energy and reaches ground state.

Fluorescence intensity is determined by the following five factors —

(1) Stronger the light, the greater is the fluorescence intensity (I_0).

(2) The ratio of photons emitted and absorbed is known as quantum efficiency (Q).

$$Q = \frac{\text{emitted photons}}{\text{absorbed photons}} = \phi$$

For fluorescent compound $\phi = 0$

(3) The expression of the absorbed fluorescent molecule by the incident light is known as molar absorption coefficient (ε).

(4) Fluorescent intensity is proportional to concentration (c) for low densities. However, for high concentrations, the proportional relationship breaks down. This is known as **quenching**. Quenching occurs mainly because the incident light is absorbed in the light path.

(5) Sample thickness and length of the incident light also determine fluorescence intensity.

When all the above factors are summarized, following equation can be drawn

$$F = [I_0 \ (1 - 10^{-\varepsilon CB})] \ [\phi]$$

Where I_0= incident radiation, ε = molar absorbality, c =molar concentration, B = path length of the cell and ϕ is quantum efficiency.

The spectrofluorimetric estimations are most accurate at very low concentrations whereas absorption spectrophotometry is least accurate at these concentrations.

Principle

A solution containing the molecules of interest is irradiated with light of a selected wavelength (the excited wavelength) and is absorbed returning to their original state releasing their absorbed energy in the form of radiant energy at longer wavelength (the emission wavelength). This energy falls on the

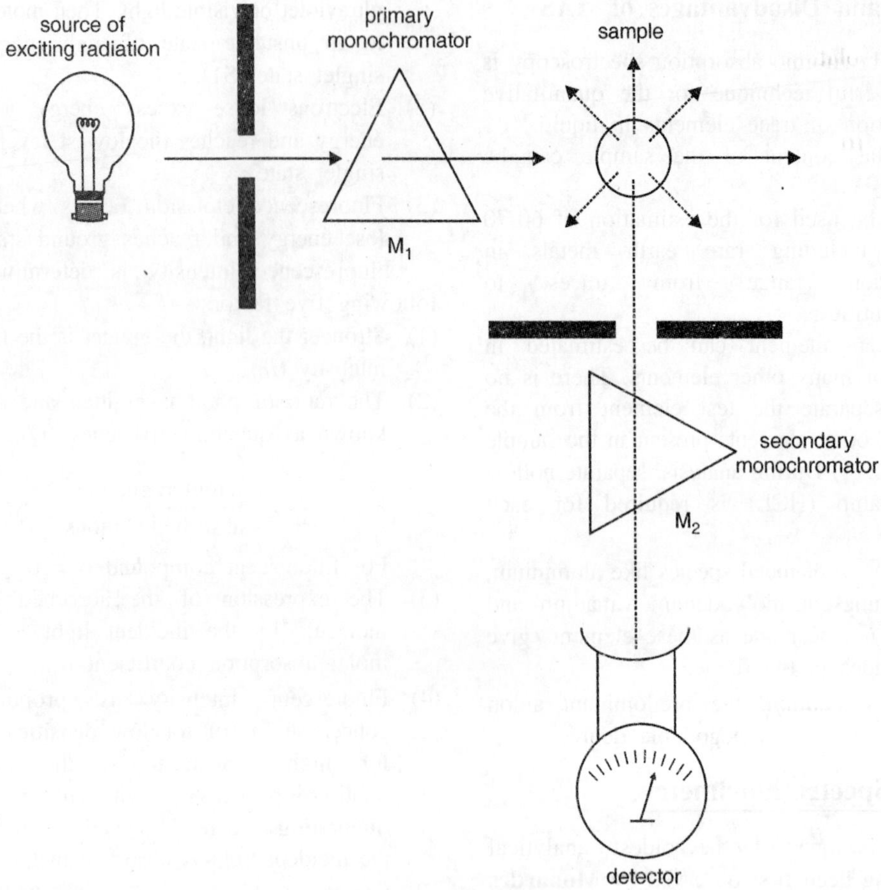

Fig. 5. Fluorimeter design.

sensitive photo detector such as photomultiplier — where it is converted to a signal for feeding to a readout device.

Instrumentation

A basic spectrofluorometer is equipped with following components.

(1) The Radiation source — Source of radiation is generally a mercury lamp or xenon arc lamp.

(2) Monochromators — Two monochromators are employed, the first (M_1) is used for selecting the excitation wavelength. Fluorescence emission occurs in all possible directions and one direction (90°) is chosen and the second monochromator (M_2) is used for the determination of the fluorescent spectrum.

(3) The detector — It is usually a sensitive photocell, for example a red sensitive photomultiplier for wavelengths greater than 500 nm. Temperature control is required for accurate work as the intensity of the fluorescence may vary between 10% to 50% for a change in temperature from 10°C to 25°C.

Principle of Operation

The primary light source is a Xenon Arc Lamp, whose output passes into the first monochromator (excitation) that disperses the light and provides monochromatic radiation to excite the sample. The excited sample becomes the source for the second monochromator (emission). A fluorescence spectrophotometer can provide two kinds of spectra, excitation and emission for any fluorescent sample. Detector is placed at the right angles to the samples and 37ºC for the turbid solutions or solid samples. Flourescence measurements usually are made by reference to some arbitrarily chosen standard. A plot of fluorescence intensities against concentration of the reference solutions furnishes the calibration curve which should obey Beer's Law.

Fluorescence in Medicine and Biology

1. Fluorescence in organic products. (amino acids, amines and their metabolites). The various amino acids give rise to large number of metabolic products. Some amino acids are inherently fluorescent and can therefore be detected fluorometrically without the need for chemical modification.

Example. aromatic amino tyrosine, tryptophan, kynurenine etc.

Certain amino acids have a characteristic structures which permit them to react with specific reagents to yield fluorescent derivatives.

Example : Histidine and related imidazoles yield highly fluorescent derivatives upon reaction with σ-phthalaldehydes.

In a mixture of amino acid derivatives, chromatographic separations would then be required for individual assay.

2. Proteins. Proteins are classified into two categories for fluorescence purposes.

(a) Class A. Those containing phenylalanine and tyrosine but no tryptophan.

(b) Class B. Those containing tryptophan as well as tyrosine and phenylalanine. Fluorescence assay has been applied in many ways to studies concerning. (i) the chemical composition of proteins, (ii) the physiochemical properties of proteins and other macro molecules, (iii) the interaction of proteins with one another and with smaller molecules.

The fluorometric procedures are developed to determine amino acid composition of a protein.

Example. Aromatic amino acids tyrosine and tryptophan in protein hydrolysates.

3. Vitamins. Vitamins were the first group of biologically important compounds assayed fluorometrically. This is because many of them are aromatic structures containing substituent groups.

Example. Riboflavin; Excitation at 470 nm; emission at 525 nm

Some can be converted to such structures by simple procedures.

Example. Thiamine itself does not possess appreciable fluorescence, but it is readily oxidized to fluorescent product thiochrome excitation at 365 nm; emission at 435.

4. Enzymology. Because of the remarkable sensitivity, fluorometry is particularly suited to studies related to enzymes and coenzymes within organs and individual cells. Many of the fluorometric procedures for enzyme assay are based on the changes in oxidation and reduction.

Example. Hydrolysis of a-naphthyl phosphate by serum alkaline phosphatase at pH = 10 with excitation at 335 nm shows fluorescence at 455 nm, but the acid phosphatase necessitates alkalization of the reaction mixture before fluorometric assay.

5. Nucleic acid components. The fluorescence properties of purines and pyrimidine bases, as well as. DNA and RNA are of extreme interest for the performance of molecular biological studies.

Example. Adenine at pH 1·3 shows fluorescence at 365 nm when excited at 265 nm.

Similarly thymine of pH 7 shows fluorescence at 338 nm when excited at 270 nm.

6. Alkaloids. Many fluorometric methods have been developed for the determination of several alkaloids.

Example. Caffeine being florescent in cyclohexane solution, fluoresces maximally at around 303 nm when excited at 270 nm in neutral aqueous solution.

7. Fluorescence in inorganic substances. Fluorescence analysis of inorganic substances consists of various methods of these compounds. Both inorganic and organic reagents can be used for the determination of the inorganic substances. These methods are generally very sensitive and have detection limits (100 – 0.1 ppb) compared to methods based on absorption.

Example. Arsenic in 7·6 M HBr shows fluorescence at 690 nm when excited at 350 nm.

Aluminium with morin reagent shows fluorescence at 500 nm when excited at 430 nm.

8. Fluorescence in drugs.

(a) Analgesics. A simple, sensitive and specific method was proposed for the fluorometric determination of morphine and quinine extracted from the biological material (urine, plasma, tissue

homogenate) Quinine can be determined in 0.1 N H_2SO_4 at an excitation wavelength of 350 nm and emission of 450 nm.

*(b) **Antibiotics.*** Tetracycline was determined fluorometrically in blood serum of man and animals by incubating the serum with beryllium ions and measure fluorescence at 460 nm. The method at pH 7·0 was accurate to 0·01µg/ml serum.

Ampicillin forms a strongly fluorescent yellow product in acid solution during hydrolysis at elevated temperatures. The quantity and rate of formation of fluorescent material are enhanced appreciably by formaldehyde and fluorescent product exhibits extraction properties of an organic acid. In alkaline solution the fluorescent compound has excitation and emission maximum at 346 and 422 nm.

*(c) **Cardiovascular drugs.*** A fluorometric procedure has been developed based on the reaction of fluorescamine in aqueous media at a pH of 7·5 to form a fluorophor with activation and emission wavelength of 400 and 485 nm respectively. The fluorimetric methods are found to be sensitive over diazodisation methods.

*(d) **Alkaloids.*** Reserpine, an important agent in the treatment of hypertension, can be determined fluorometrically based on the reaction with nitrous acid, producing a yellow fluorescence. The fluorescence can be measured at 510 nm when excited at 390 nm.

*(e) **Muscular relaxants.*** A method sensitive for chlorzoxazone, a skeletal muscle relaxant, based on the fluorescence in chloroform is found suitable for the determination of the drug in biological fluids and is also useful for the analysis of tablets. The fluorescence can be measured at 310 nm when excited at 286 nm.

Microspectrofluorimetry

In this technique, a microscope is combined with a spectrofluorometer equipped with fibre optics to enable the examination of single bacterial cells binding fluorescent antibodies and also the fluorescent intensity of subcellular structures. The extra amount of nucleic acid that tends to be present in malignant cells will take up more fluorescent probe like acridine orange than the normal cells. This observation may be used to detect malignant cells in a biopsy sample.

Luminometry

Chemi- and bioluminescence measurements have become extremely popular in recent years. They are often used to determine the amount of a specific unknown present in a sample, and in the last decade, have become extremely important in the study of gene expression and gene regulation. **Chemiluminescence is** the light emitted by a chemical reaction and bioluminescence is a type of chemiluminescence in which the chemical reaction is catalyzed by an enzyme.

Measurement of light from a chemical reaction is highly useful because the concentration of an unknown can be inferred from the rate at which light is emitted. The rate of light output is directly related to the amount of light emitted and accordingly, proportional to the concentration of the luminescent material present. Therefore, light measurement is a relative indicator of the amount of luminescent material present in the sample of interest.

Instrumentation

Light, as we see it, consists of billions of tiny packets of energy called photons. Photons, packets of light, emitted from bioluminescent and chemiluminescent reactions are typically measured using a luminometer. Luminometers are simple, relatively inexpensive instruments designed to measure sample light output. Light output is measured by integrating, or measuring the area under the chemical reaction's light emission curve for a set period of time. All luminometers consist of a sample chamber, detector, signal processing method, and signal output display. Figure 6 shows a typical luminometer.

Sample Chamber

The luminometer sample chamber, which holds a test tube, microplate, or other type of sample container, presents the luminescent sample to the detector. The chamber must be sealed from ambient light in order to minimize potential interferences. The sample chamber should be positioned as close to the detector as possible to maximize optical efficiency. High optical efficiency is desirable for an optimum signal-to-noise ratio, which allows rapid and precise measurements.

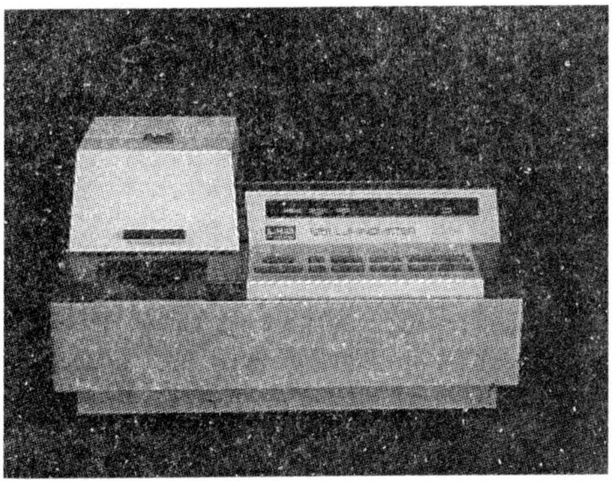

Fig. 6. A luminometer.

Detector

Photodiodes and photomultiplier tubes (PMTs) are the detection devices commonly found in inexpensive commercial luminometers. Improvements in photodiodes have made them effective for some applications, however PMTs continue to be the detector of choice for measuring extremely low levels of light.

PMTs function such that an incident photon triggers an amplified cascade of electrons. This amplification is very fast and essentially free of externally generated electrical noise. It is the PMT's quick response and amplification that make it extremely useful for luminescence measurements.

PMTs are positioned either to the side ("side-on" configuration) or underneath ("end-on" configuration) the sample cell. The bottom-viewing or end-on configuration of the photomultiplier tube ensures uniformity of light collection from even the smallest sample.

Photon Counting *vs.* Current Measuring

Most of today's commercial luminometers are either photon-counting or current- measuring in their signal processing and readout design. A photon-counting luminometer counts individual photons with a PMT and a current-measuring luminometer measures the electrical current that results when photons strike the PMT. Because not all of the light emitted from the sample is directed toward the PMT, neither a photon-counting or current-measuring luminometer detects all of the photons from the sample. Both photon-counting and current-measuring instruments have a response that is proportional to the sample light output. A photon counter will read in "photons per second", while a current-measuring luminometer will read in arbitrary light units, usually referred to as "relative light units" or RLUs. When comparing readings between these two types of instruments, reading ratios and hence, concentrations will be identical; however, due to different methods of measurement, the actual numeric output will be different.

Standards and Instrument Calibration

Analytical standards for luminescent analyses are solutions containing known concentrations of the analyte under study. They are used for final calibration of an analytical luminescence procedure. The reagent systems for bio- and chemiluminescent reactions tend to be far more complex than those used for spectrophotometric and fluorometric analyses and, therefore, require more careful control. This problem is a primary concern of reagent manufacturers. They must produce a uniform product. Manufacturers have found that the best comparison standard is a stable light source with a light output comparable to that of the bio- or chemiluminescent reaction which can be installed in place of the cuvette in the sample chamber. There are three basic approaches to this problem: use radioactive material in a scintillation cocktail, use a simple and stable chemiluminescent reaction as a standard, or use a secondary light standard. Storage, disposal, handling problems, limited lifetime, and the fact that no two standards have the same output are well known problems with radioactive materials. If a simple chemiluminescent reaction is used as a standard, it must be well characterized and be of consistent quality and purity. Also, it should be insensitive to temperature, quenching, and solvent viscosity.

Applications

Luminometry, the analytical technique used to measure chemi- and bioluminescent reactions, has several advantages over other analytical techniques. Extraordinary sensitivity, a wide dynamic range, inexpensive instrumentation, and the emergence of novel luminescent assays make this technique very popular.

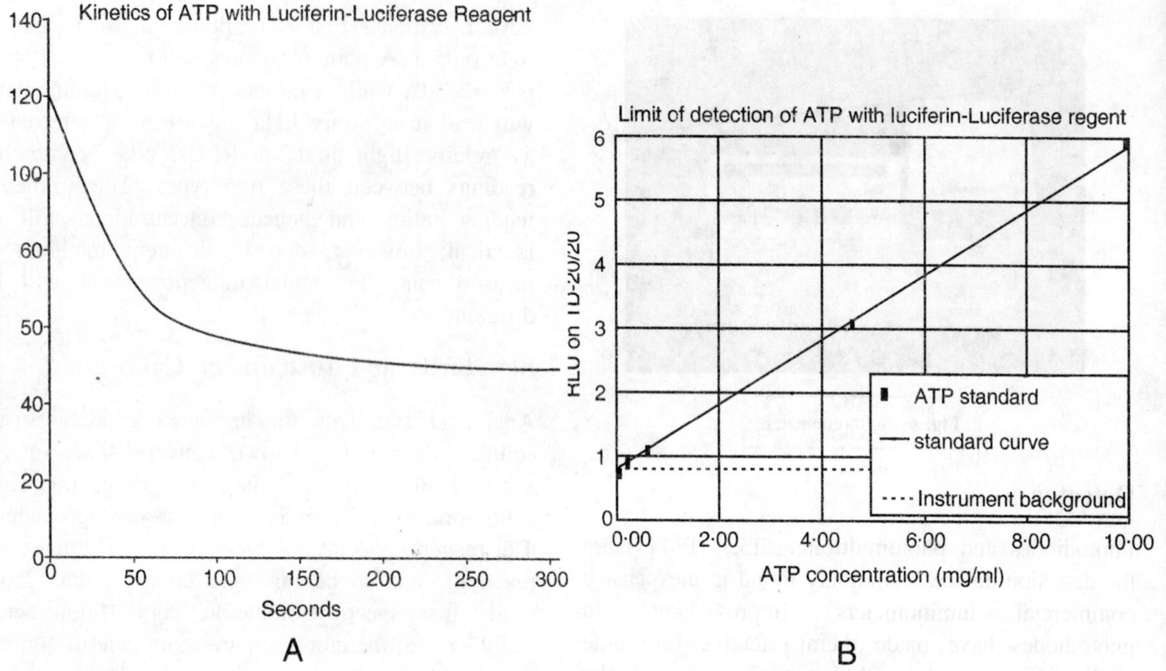

Fig. 7.

Superior sensitivity and low background distinguish luminometry from other analytical methods. Luminometry is up to 100,000 times more sensitive than absorption spectroscopy and is at least 1,000 times more sensitive than fluorometry. A well-designed luminometer can detect as little as 0.6 picograms of adenosine triphosphate (ATP) or 0.1 fentograms of luciferase, two common luminescent analytes. The **ATP/luciferin-luciferase reaction** and its lower limit of detection are shown in Figures 7A and 7B.

In luminescence, there are two components of light that reach the detector. The first component is proportional to the concentration of the limiting reactant in the chemiluminescent reaction. The second component, known as background, is an approximately constant light level due to various factors such as the phosphorescence of plastics, impurities in the reagents, etc. This background light component is much lower in luminometry than in other analytical techniques such as spectrophotometry and fluorometry.

Wide dynamic range and low instrument cost are also distinct advantages of luminometry. Samples can be measured across decades of concentration without dilution or modification of the sample cell. Figure 9 covers over 5 decades of luciferase measurement using Turner BioSystems' TD-20/20 Luminometer.

On a final note, the use of luminometry in research and quality control has increased dramatically in recent years. Advances in molecular biology and an increased interest in ever-more-sensitive assays have led to the development of novel luminescence systems for a wide variety of applications in genetic research, food technology, and environmental monitoring.

Numerous bioluminescent and chemiluminescent reactions are studied using luminometry. Luminometry is commonly used in biotechnology research, environmental testing, and industrial applications. The most widely used applications are the measurement of gene expression using reporter gene assays and the determination of intracellular ATP.

Reporter gene assays. Molecular and cellular biologists use reporter genes to study gene expression and regulation. Reporter genes are

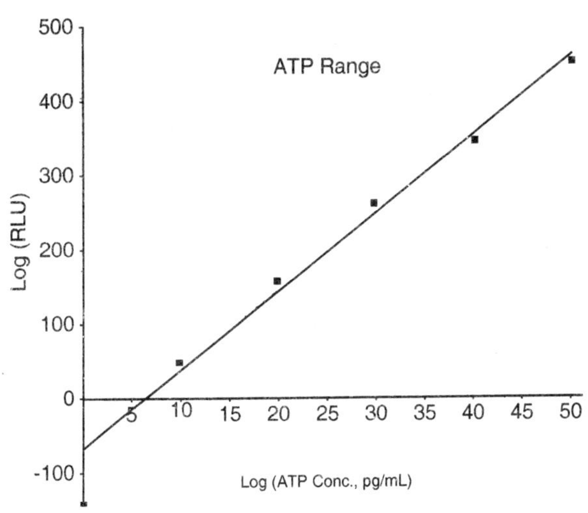

Fig. 8.

introduced into cellular DNA and used to associate a specific molecular event with a measurable property. In this case, the molecular events involve gene function and the measurable property is luminescence. There are several luminescent reporter genes currently on the market. These include firefly luciferase, β-galactosidase, β-glucuronidase (GUS), alkaline phosphatase, and human growth hormone (hGH). Luminometry is ideal for gene expression studies because of its extraordinary sensitivity, low cost, speed, and ease of use.

ATP determinations. All living cells contain ATP. ATP can be extracted from cells and assayed with firefly luciferase. In this luminescent reaction, ATP is the limiting reagent. Therefore, the light reaching the luminometer's photomultiplier tube is proportional to the amount of ATP in the sample and, correspondingly, to the number of cells from which it was extracted. ATP luminometric assays have been used for decades. The speed and sensitivity of luminometry make it an ideal technique for ATP determinations. ATP measurements are used in:

- ***Microbial detection in water, foods and pharmaceuticals.*** The lumin-ometric assay for ATP measures all the micro-organisms present in a sample. This principle has been used to measure bacterial contamination in both drinking water and industrial water used for oil field injection, cooling systems, and paper processing. Luminometric ATP determinations have also been used for the microbiological control of pharmaceuticals, cosmetics, milk, and various other foods.
- ***Biomass estimations.*** Micro-biologists use ATP determinations to measure total live biomass in soil and sediments. Related studies include determining the effect of pollutants on fresh water and marine micro-organisms.

Variables

In order to effectively use chemiluminescent reactions for quantitative chemical analysis, the analyst should have an understanding of the key experimental variables affecting luminescence measurements. Variables worth discussing include sample volume, rates of reaction, concentration of reactants, reagent injection and mixing, cuvette material and size, and temperature control and extraneous light.

Infrared Spectroscopy

Basic Technique

Electromagnetic radiation in the wavelength range of 800 nm to 1000 is called as infrared radiation. This range can be subdivided into the near-IR region (0.8 to 2 μm), the middle or fundamental IR region (2 to 15 μm) and the far-IR region (15 to 1000 μm). The middle fundamental IR region is the one that provides the greatest amount of information for the elucidation of molecular structure. Most IR spectrophotometers are designed to carry out measurements in this wavelength range.

On absorption of IR radiation a change in the vibrational energy occurs in the ground state of the molecule. All molecules have a large number of accessible vibrational and rotational energy levels with a correspondingly large number of allowed transitions. The energies of these transitions are strongly influenced by molecular structure. Thus, IR spectra are unique and ideally suited for the identification of xenobiotics, drugs, and other organic substances. A typical IR spectrum of the antibacterial drug sulfacetamide is illustrated in Figure 9.

For energy to be transferred from the radiation source to the molecule, the frequency of vibration of both must coincide, and energy transfer must be accompanied by a change in the dipole moment of

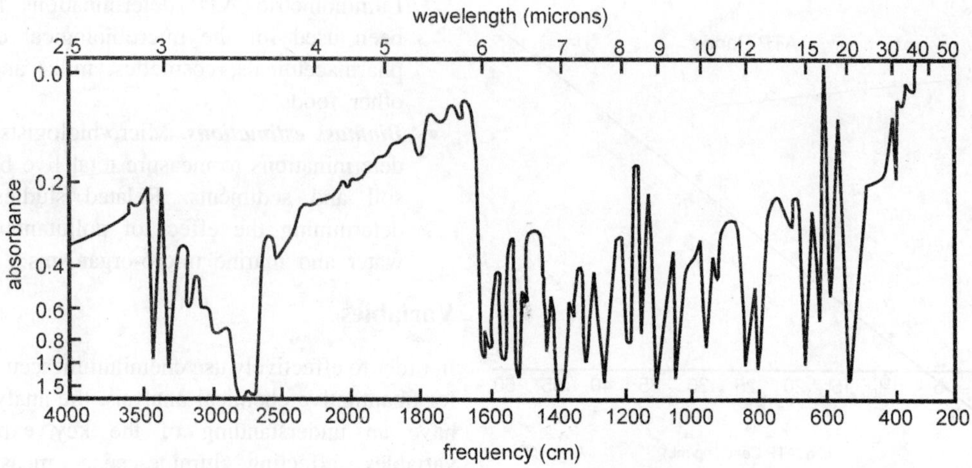

Fig. 9. Infrared spectrum of sulfacetamide.

the molecule. Molecules that contain certain symmetry elements will display more simplified spectra; for example, the *C=C* stretching vibration of ethylene and the symmetrical C–H stretching of the four C–H bonds of methane do not produce an absorption band in the IR region. For nonlinear polyatomic molecules, the number of fundamental modes of vibration is 3n – 6 (3n – *5* for linear molecules), where *n* is the number of atoms. Certain groups within a molecule, such as –OH, –C = O, –NH_2, – CN and –CC– have characteristic absorption frequencies known as **group frequencies**. These frequencies are generally independent of the structure of the rest of the molecule and can therefore be used diagnostically to confirm the presence of the functionality in a molecule of unknown structure.

In practice, it is usually not possible to observe the calculated number of peaks in the spectrum of a known compound. This may be due to the superimposition or coalescing of absorptions that are too close to be resolved. A fundamental band may be too weak to be observed. Alternatively, additional (nonfundamental) bands may be observed that are either overtones and harmonics that occur with greatly reduced intensity or combination and difference bands.

Molecules have two types of fundamental vibrations. Stretching occurs when the distance between two atoms increases or decreases but the atoms remain in the same bond axis. Polyatomic molecules may produce asymmetric stretching vibrations (Fig. 10). Bending or deformation occurs when the position of the atom changes relative to the original bond axis.

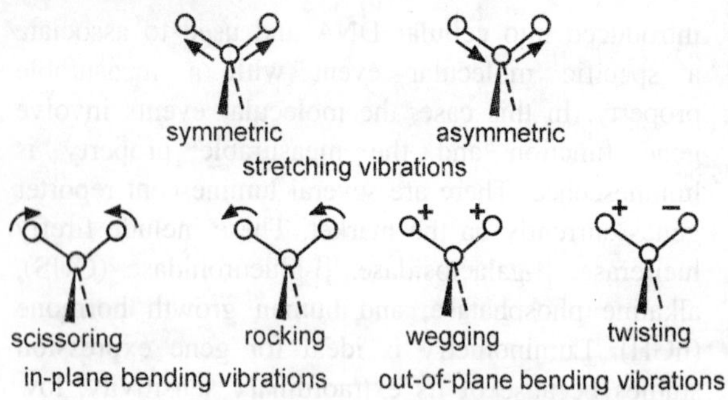

Fig. 10. Infrared vibration modes of groups of atoms (+ and – refer to vibrations above and below the plane of the paper, respectively).

The stretching frequency (v) of a bond is related to the masses of the two atoms involved (*Ma* and *Mb,* in g), the velocity of light (r), and the force constant of the bond (*k.* in dynes cm′). An approximate value for the stretching frequency can be calculated from the following equation :

$$\nu \text{ (in cm}^{-1}\text{)} = \frac{1}{2\pi c}\sqrt{\frac{k}{M_a M_b/(M_a+M_b)}}$$

Note that the force constants for sp^3, sp^2, and sp bonds have values of 5. 10, and 15 × 10^5 dynes

cm^{-1}, respectively Infrared spectra are usually recorded as plots of sample absorbance (or percent transmittance) vs. wavelength or frequency in reciprocal cm (wavenumbers). The relationship between wavelength and wavenumber is :

$$\text{wavenumber } (cm^{-1}) = \frac{1\times10^4}{\lambda(\mu m)}$$

Unlike UV and visible spectra, IR spectra are by convention plotted with zero absorbance (or 100% transmittance) at the top of the spectrum—that is, in an inverted mode relative to UV-visible spectra.

Qualitative Uses and Interpretation of Spectra

The complexity in the IR spectra of organic molecules is a valuable tool that can be used for the unambiguous identification of unknown compounds if an authentic standard is available. If all the bands in the IR spectrum of the unknown structure are identical in all respects (i.e., in their wave number value and their relative intensity) when compared with an IR spectrum of an authentic standard, then the two compounds are identical. The region 1430 to 910 cm^{-1} contains many absorptions caused by bending vibrations as well as absorptions caused by C-C, C-O, and C-N stretching vibrations. As a molecule has many more bending vibrations than stretching vibrations, this region of the IR spectrum is particularly rich in absorption bands and shoulders and has been termed the **fingerprint region**. Although similar molecules may show very similar spectra in the region 4000 to 1430 cm^{-1}, there will nearly always be discernible differences in the fingerprint region. Spectral comparisons are best carried out in the solution state. Compounds can often be prepared in different polymorphic forms, both crystalline and amorphous, depending on the conditions of crystallization. Polymorphic forms of the same compound may show significant differences in the fingerprint region of the spectrum; therefore, if spectral comparisons are to be made in the solid state, then both the unknown and an authentic standard should be recrystallized from a specific solvent in the same manner.

A second important use of qualitative IR spectroscopy is that it gives structural information about an unknown molecule. The previously mentioned group frequencies, together with frequencies of other characteristic bands, can be utilized in the form of comprehensive frequency correlation charts which have been compiled for easy reference. This type of compilation is invaluable as a means of confirming the presence or absence of a particular functionality in an unknown structure. In this respect, the region between 4000 and 1500 cm^{-1} is probably easier to interpret than that between 1500 and 650 cm^{-1}, as the latter includes many skeletal vibrations, typical of molecules as a whole, which are not diagnostic.

Instrument Considerations

Dispersive IR Spectrophotometers

The instrument design of a typical double-beam recording IR spectrophotometer is shown in Figure 11. The beam chopper, which is a rotating mirror, permits radiation passing alternately through sample cell and solvent cell to reach the IR detector. The difference in absorption by solute and solvent is measured as an alternating electric current from the thermocouple. The system operates on the optical null principle with the recorder pen linked mechanically to a "comb" (not shown), which is placed across the solvent cell beam and moved by a servomechanism to reduce or increase the solvent cell-beam intensity. The servomechanism is actuated by the amplified thermocouple output to make the solvent beam intensity equal to the solution beam intensity, which reduces the detector output to zero or the null point. The spectrum can be scanned through various wavelengths by rotation of the prism in synchronization with the motion of the recorder drum or chart. Most modern instruments now utilize a diffraction grating in place of the prism. Sodium chloride prisms can be used for the entire region from 4000 to 650 cm^{-1} but suffer from the disadvantage of low resolution at 4000 to 2500 cm^{-1}. The use of a grating monochromator provides a better overall resolution throughout the range 4000 to 625 cm^{-1}.

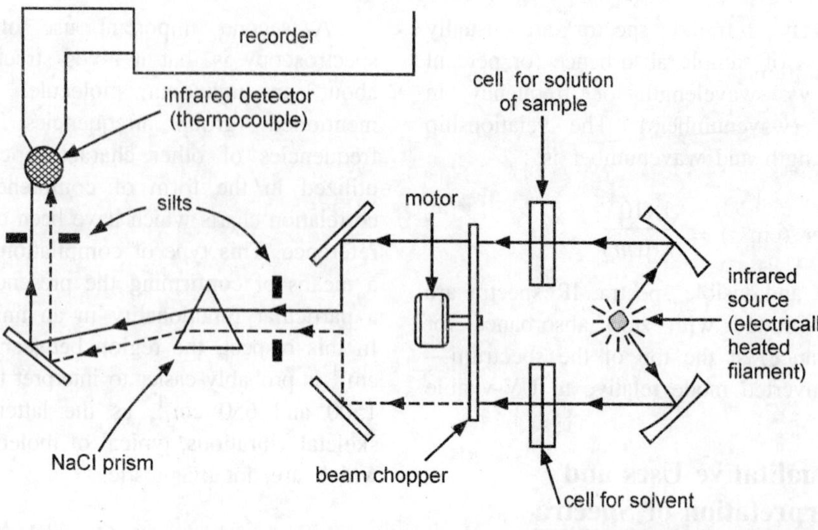

Fig. 11. Schematic representation of a double-beam recording infrared spectrophotometer.

Fourier Transform IR Spectrometers

Fourier transform (FT) IR spectrometers are widely used in chemical analysis. The FT-IR spectrometer is built around an interferometer rather than a monochromator (Figure 12). The beam from the light source passes through the chopper and is collimated and directed to the beam splitter via mirror C. The beam splitter is a half-silvered mirror that reflects 50% of the incident light onto movable mirror F and allows 50% to pass through fixed mirror E. The beams reflected from mirrors F and H are then combined at the beam splitter so an interference pattern results, and this is focused by mirror G onto detector. The sample to be analyzed is located in the combined beams between spectral filter H and the detector.

The interferogram of the source is obtained by driving the moveable mirror over a fixed distance and determining the interference pattern as a function of path length difference traveled by the light beams in the two arms of the interferometer. Each frequency of light that passes through the interferometer produces its own interference pattern. Because all of the frequencies generated are observed all at once by the detector, the spectrum is said to be multiplexed, and no grating is required to disperse the radiation. The increased energy reaching the detector allows the relatively rapid accumulation of data, so repetitive scans can be carried out.

Extensive data analysis must be undertaken to extract the frequency information from the interferogram. The principle computation required is Fourier transformation of the interferogram. Because data that have been transformed to the frequency

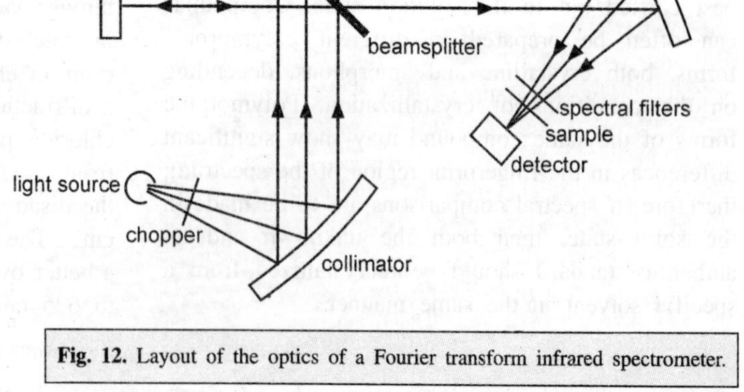

Fig. 12. Layout of the optics of a Fourier transform infrared spectrometer.

domains are available in digital form manipulations such as substitution of solvent background and smoothing are simplified.

Fourier transform-IR analysis offers considerable advantages over conventional prism or grating instruments. The S/N under the conditions of the FT experiment is increased from the conventional apparatus by $/V^{1/2}$, where N is the number of resolution elements in the spectrum; thus, for a 1000-cm^{-1} scan with 2-cm^{-1} resolution, the S/N advantage is $(1000/2)^{1/2}$, or about 22. These high S/N values permit the accurate subtraction of backgrounds due to liquid H_2O. Accordingly, one principle application of FT-IR spectrometry is in the acquisition of protein spectra in aqueous media. In terms of sample preparation and analysis time, FT-IR is considered to be a truly high-throughput analytical technique.

Quantitative analysis of compounds by 1R spectrophotometry utilizes the same basic principles involved in UV and visible spectrophotometry; however, the complexity of the spectra obtained allows the selection of several bands for quantitative work. Generally, the selection of a fairly strong band for each component in a mixture is made so no interference occurs between components. The areas of absorption bands are typically integrated; however, with sharp TR bands, peak heights may also be used for quantitative calculations. A calibration curve of absorbance vs. concentration can then be constructed. If Beer's law is obeyed, a direct comparison of the sample absorbance with that of a standard can be made.

In IR studies, very short path lengths (0.025 to 0.1 mm) are used, and solution concentrations of analytes are often in the 10% region. All solvents absorb in some part of the IR spectrum. Given this high concentration of solute, the accurate cancellation of solvent absorption is difficult to achieve. For this reason, the baseline technique is usually applied (Fig. 13). This technique assumes that absorption due to solvent (or a second component) is constant or varies linearly with wavelength over the region of the absorption band. The determination of small amounts of impurities or low amounts of solutes in a preparation can also be improved by introducing the major component, or the solvent, into the reference beam of the spectrophotometer, thereby compensating for the absorption of this component.

Due to the higher concentrations of samples required for IR analysis, deviations from Beer's law are encountered much more frequently in IR spectrophotometry than in UV and visible spectrophotometry; thus, significant intermolecular hydrogen-bonding effects may be observed that increase as the concentration of the solute increases. Notably, the absorbance at the Xmax of a free OH group actually decreases with increasing concentration of the analyte.

Sample Preparation and Sample Cells

Although IR spectra have been obtained on materials in every physical state from solids to gases, most analyses are carried out on the neat liquid analyte, solutions of the analyte in organic solvents, suspensions, Nujol suspensions, and KBr discs. Solution spectra are preferred for quantitative analysis, as errors arising from nonhomogeneous samples and pathlengths are minimized. KBr discs are often used for qualitative analysis because subtle structural differences such as polymorphism can often be observed in this medium. Cells for quantitative

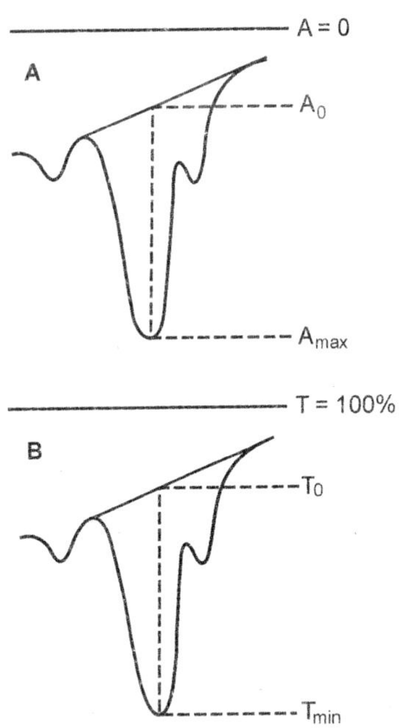

Fig. 13. Measurement of infrared band intensities using the baseline technique. (A) When the scale is linear in absorbance, peak absorbance = $A_{max} - A_0$. (B) When the scale is linear in transmittance, peak absorbance = $-\log(T_{min}/T_0)$.

IR analysis of solutions consist of a pair of sodium chloride plates with a thin metal spacer between them. This unit is housed in a metal frame along with protective washers. The plate spacing is ~10~^{2} cm. Considerable care in handling and storing the IR cells should be exercised, because the windows are easily fogged by traces of moisture and are easily scratched. When not in use, cells should be stored in a desiccators.

Neat liquids and Nujol suspensions or mulls for qualitative analysis are usually placed as a drop on an unmounted circular sodium chloride plate, and a second plate is pressed on top until the liquid is spread into a thin film with a thickness on the order of 1 × 1(H to 50 × K)^4 cm. The plates are held in a frame while the spectrum is scanned. Nujol mulls are prepared by grinding the solid analyte in a small mortar with mineral oil until a milky emulsion is obtained. Other suspending agents such a perfluorokerosene, hexachlorobutadiene, or other heavy liquids can also be used. The spectrum obtained with mulls will consist of bands from the analyte superimposed upon bands from the mulling agent. The C-H regions of the spectrum will be obscured when mineral oil mulls are used, and the C—F or C-Cl regions will be obscured when the halogenated mulls are used.

Qualitative analysis of solid analytes is typically performed using KBr discs. Here, the analyte (0.3 to 9 mg) is ground with 300 mg of spectral-quality KBr (-400 mesh). Between 100 and 300 mg of the grind is then pressed into pellets or discs at between 20,000 and 100,000 psig using a stainless steel die and a vacuum pump. The finished pellet is transparent and produces excellent spectra. Unlike mulling agents, KBr does not contribute extraneous bands in the IR spectrum; however, KBr is slightly hygroscopic and may pick up moisture during the disc preparation. This will lead to characteristic water bands at 3300 and 1640 cm^{-1}.

Applications of Infrared Spectroscopy

High signal-to-noise spectra and sophisticated data reduction techniques have made FT-IR a versatile, high-throughput analytical technique. Advances in the acquisition of FT-IR spectra from preparations such as monolayers, tissues, and samples *in situ* include fiberoptical waveguides for beam handling and remote held sensing. Metabolic fingerprinting, a process where crude metabolite mixtures are rapidly screened and analyzed by multivariate mathematical models, is central to metabolomic studies. FT-IR is critical to these studies, wherein mixed sample

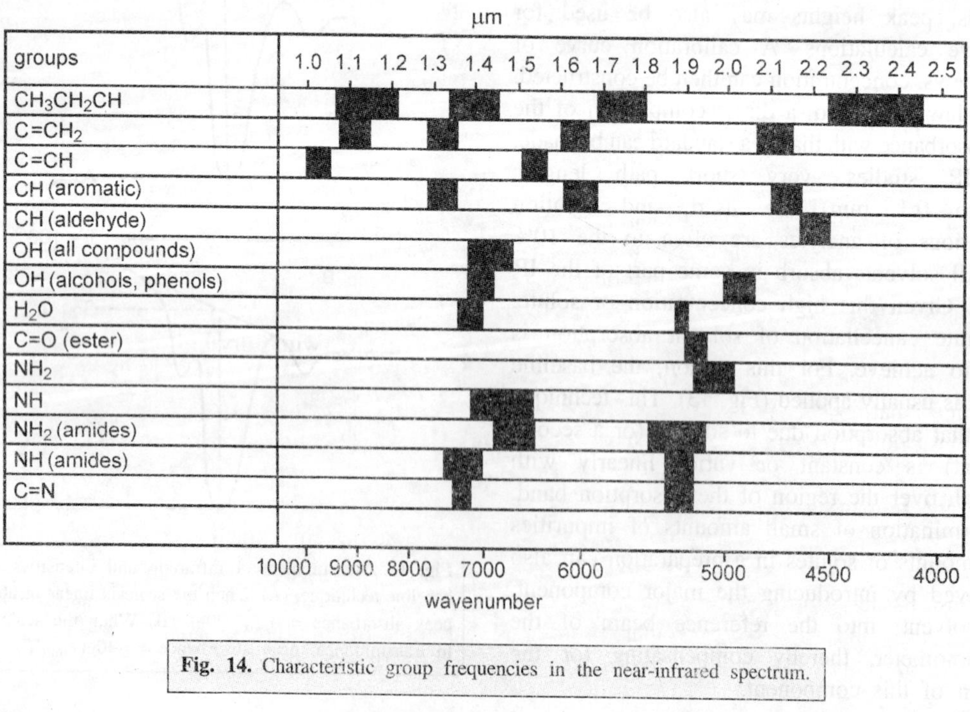

Fig. 14. Characteristic group frequencies in the near-infrared spectrum.

profiles are correlated to biological origin, metabolic status, and exposure to chemical or environmental stimuli.

Near-infrared spectroscopy is particularly useful as a noninvasive *in vivo* analytical tool. Virtually every organic compound has a near-IR spectrum that can be measured. Near-IR spectra consist of overtones and combinations of fundamental mid-IR bands. These IR spectra are characterized by good penetration of light into tissues and a high capacity to identify organic compounds. Figure 14 illustrates some of the structural moieties that can be determined by near-IR and their absorption characteristics.

The application of *in vivo* FT-IR microspectroscopy in the diagnosis of disease has been reviewed. FT-IR spectroscopy is used for studying human arteries, cancers and tumors, and brain tissues from stroke and Alzheimer's patients. Wetzel et al. utilized FT-IR microspectroscopy for deuteration studies investigating the metabolic activity in various layers of the cerebellum. Some specific examples of the use of FT-IR spectroscopy in disease diagnosis and toxicological research are described below :

Analysis of Solid Human Tumor Cells by FT-IR Microspectroscopy

Early detection of human tumors often allows for a higher survival rate. Cells from normal and neoplastic human lung tissue have been analyzed by means of FT-IR microspectroscopy. Reliable spectra that can differentiate between normal and neoplastic cells may be obtained. Neoplastic cells show an increase in the intensity of the bands corresponding mainly to the PO. Symmetrical and asymmetrical vibrations (1080 to 1540 cm^{-1}) of DNA compared to normal cells. This analytical method may be useful for recognizing early neoplastic transformation that is usually not possible with traditional procedures. Similar results have been observed in the FT-IR spectra of sections of normal and malignant human colon tissues and in other malignant tissues such as stomach, esophagus, skin, liver, cervix, and vagina. The results suggest that, in cancerous tissues, most PO, groups become hydrogen bonded and the intermolecular packing among $PO2^-$ groups becomes closer. Nucleic acids may be the molecules primarily responsible for the observed changes in the vs($PO2^-$) and vas($PO2^-$) bands.

Analysis of Stroke-Induced Changes by Near-Infrared Spectroscopy

Historically, Near-IR spectroscopy has been used to monitor fat and protein in agricultural products. Near-IR spectroscopy is also well suited for animal work because tissue penetration by near-IR light is good, excellent S/N values can be obtained in near-IR measurements, and discrimination between various types of tissue constituents is possible because the near-IR signals arise from combinations and overtones of the fundamental IR bands of these constituents. The gerbil brain is an established animal model of stroke. The gerbil skull is relatively thin, making near-IR spectroscopy of the brain readily achievable *in vivo* with common spectrometers of moderate light intensity. In addition, the gerbil brain is enriched in polyunsaturated fatty acids. Dramatic changes occur in fatty acid metabolism during the ischemia and reperfusion stages. Near-IR techniques have been used to examine stroke-induced changes in the lipids and proteins of whole gerbil brains. The changes are parallel to the hypothesized series of free-radical and altered enzymatic events that occur during transient ischemia and reperfusion in the human brain.

To understand the early changes in lipid and protein metabolism following stroke and trauma, animal models have been developed to recreate these changes. The examination of whole brains has been made possible by a combination of hardware modifications and mathematical techniques designed to make the sample presentation to the spectrometer quite reproducible. A refrigerated sample compartment with dry nitrogen purge can be constructed for analysis of whole frozen brains. The cooled compartment enables repeated scans of frozen brains to be collected over time without thawing. The spectrophotometer itself can be purged with dry nitrogen gas, eliminating spectral artifacts associated with lipid/protein oxidation and atmospheric water vapor or other gases. A geometric noise filter removes spectral variations arising from positional variation of the brain. The BEST and extended BEST algorithms, which scale spectral vectors in multidimensional hyperspace with a directional probability, can be used with a supercomputer to analyze the spectra collected.

In addition to changes observed in stroke, age-related changes occur in the polyunsaturated fatty acid pool and in the state of protein oxidation within the central nervous system. Near-IR spectral analysis has many applications to aging and stroke research, including :

- Determination of age from brain spectra
- Prediction of short-term memory deficit from the spectra of injured brains
- Simultaneous multi-component analysis of lipids and proteins
- Quantification of edema
- Transcranial scanning of the brain *in vivo*

Near-IR scanning of brains *in vivo* simplifies the testing of antiepileptic drug candidates by reducing the number of subjects required, by allowing each subject to be used as its own control, and by eliminating variance due to outlier subjects, such as those that have had a stroke before the experiment.

Near-Infrared Fiberoptics as Arterial Probes for Studying Cardiovascular Disease

Another tool for studying mechanisms of toxicology couples near-IR with fiberoptic arterial probes. Fiberoptic catheters have been used to locate atherosclerotic lesions, but the techniques merely distinguish lesions from healthy arterial tissue. Near-IR fiberoptics may be used to spatially map lesions and their chemical constituents. Chemical analysis of lesions *in vivo* permits the kinetic study of atherogenesis and contributes to the understanding of lesion formation and growth. The chemical imaging power of this technique permits the testing of hypothetical mechanisms of lesion formation, growth, and regression, including those involving toxic injury and antioxidant protection.

Applications in Toxicological Studies

Infrared spectroscopy is extensively employed in toxicological research. The toxic effects of selenium exposure on the external cell membranes of living bacteria may be efficiently analyzed by FT-IR directly in the biomass. FT-IR spectroscopy was employed to assess the hepatotoxic effects of a single dose of carbon tetrachloride in rat liver. Dynamic chemical changes in liver samples were monitored over time by analyzing the IR spectra in the lipid (1800 to 1000 cm^{-1}) and C-H stretching (3000 to 2400 cm^{-1}) regions and comparing them to untreated controls. Changes in band shape and intensity were correlated with toxicity. To develop a high-throughput metabolomic toxicology assay, researchers hypothesized that FT-IR could be used to detect differences between urine collected from rats treated with lipopolysaccharide, a potent inflammatory agent, and urine obtained from untreated controls. In addition, cotreatment with ranitidine, a drug often associated with idiosyncratic hepatotoxicity, was performed to determine whether or not the FT-IR method would be useful for predicting this idiosyncratic toxicity. The results of this pilot study suggest that similar methods might be applied for the rapid metabolomic screening of drug toxicity. In the occupational and environmental toxicology settings, FT-IR analysis may be useful for the continuous monitoring of the presence of airborne toxins. Over a 2-year period, 39 selected air toxins were measured at 11 different petrochemical sites using open-path FT-IR. The data enabled the researchers to calculate the hazard indices for both acute and chronic health effects attributable to these toxins over time and by location, thereby estimating potential health risks to workers.

Specialized Instrumentation

Several modified approaches for performing IR spectroscopic imaging microscopy have been developed. One instrument integrates an acoustic-optic tunable filter (AOTF) and charge-coupled device (CCD) detector with an infinity-corrected microscope for operation in the near-IR spectral regions. Images at moderate spectral resolution (2 nm) and high spatial resolution (1 μm) can be rapidly collected. Data can be presented with 128 × 128 pixels. The CDD is a true imaging detector, with wavelength selection provided by the AOTF and quartz tungsten halogen lamp to create a tunable source. The instrument can be utilized for both absorption and reflectance spectroscopies.

Synchrotron FT-IR (SFT-IR) microscopy, which does not require sample mounting or specialized preparation, has been used to probe the molecular responses to toxic injuries in intact, living cells. SFT-IR allows the observation of several types of molecular responses and lesion development induced by stressors such as radiation and toxic compounds in the same cell over time. Real-time changes in nucleic acids and proteins in live human cells treated with dioxin were studied using this technique.

Portable FT-IR units arc available and broadly deployed for field use. Potential applications include the rapid detection of toxins and suspected bioterror agents at remote locations. To evaluate the utility of these portable systems for the field-based characterization of biological threats, a series of peptide and nonpeptide toxins were analyzed and compared to libraries of known spectra. In the case of pure compounds, this spectral searching technique allowed the researchers to discriminate between aflatoxin, mycotoxin, and strychnine at a 99% conlidence level. Nonpeptide toxins were readily identified in chemical mixtures, and peptides such as ricin were correctly identified in mixtures at a *959c* confidence level. FT-IR analysis is being rapidly developed as a versatile tool for onsite identification of chemicals, toxins, and biological threats.

Raman Spectroscopy

The discovery of the Raman effect is undoubtedly one of the greatest scientific achievements in the last century. It originated from India, but fast spread all over the world. As a result, Dr. C.V. Raman was awarded a Nobel Prize in 1930. Raman spectroscopy was introduced in Japan in the early 1930s that played a crucial role in the discovery of the rotational isomerism (**trans** and **gauche**) of the C-C single bond by Mizushima and co-workers (1934). This discovery was an immediate and distinct product of Raman spectroscopy that was followed by many others.

Since the early 1930s, there has been a long tradition of Raman spectroscopy at the Department of Chemistry, School of Science, The University of Tokyo. Hamaguchi did his first Raman experiment in 1968, 40 years after Raman's discovery, in the laboratory of Takehiko Shimanouchi. The laboratory had a newly constructed laser Raman spectrometer as well as an old, traditional Raman spectrograph with a large mercury lamp. An NEC He-Ne laser, a Spex double monochromator and a Hamamatsu photomultiplier were utilized with a laboratory-made lock-in amplifier using bulbs. It took tens of minutes to scan a Raman spectrum, several orders of magnitude longer than it does today, with a multichannel Raman spectrometer.

Raman spectroscopy has witnessed several dramatic developments in the field, viz. resonance Raman spectroscopy, nanosecond and picosecond time-resolved Raman spectroscopy, nonlinear Raman spectroscopy, and time- and space-resolved Raman spectroscopy.

Raman spectroscopy is closely related to infrared spectroscopy. in that the information about molecular vibrational frequencies provided by the latter technique is of the same kind as that provided by the Raman vibrational spectrum. In molecules with a center of symmetry, however, vibrational transitions that are allowed in the IR spectrum are forbidden in the Raman effect, and *vice versa,* providing useful information about molecular symmetry. Structurally symmetrical diatomic molecules such as H and O, are also electrically symmetrical and do not give IR absorption spectra. These molecules do afford Raman spectra due to excitation of symmetrical vibrations. In a molecule such as tetrachloroethylene ($CCl_2=CCl_2$), the double-bond stretching frequency is symmetrical and the molecule does not show a double-bond stretching frequency in the IR spectrum; however, this vibration appears strongly in the Raman spectrum of tetrachloroethylene and provides evidence of a symmetrical structure (Figure 15). Thus, the two techniques are complementary to each other.

The Raman effect is a scattering process in which the interaction between photon and the molecule occurs in a very short period of time, and the Raman peaks obtained correspond to photons that have bounced inelastically off the molecule. The Raman spectrum arises as a result of the light photons being captured momentarily by molecules in the sample and giving up (or gaining) small increments of energy through changes in the molecular vibrational and rotational energies before being emitted as scattered light. These changes in vibrational and rotational energies result in changes in wavelength of the incident light. The convention in Raman spectra is to quote the positions of

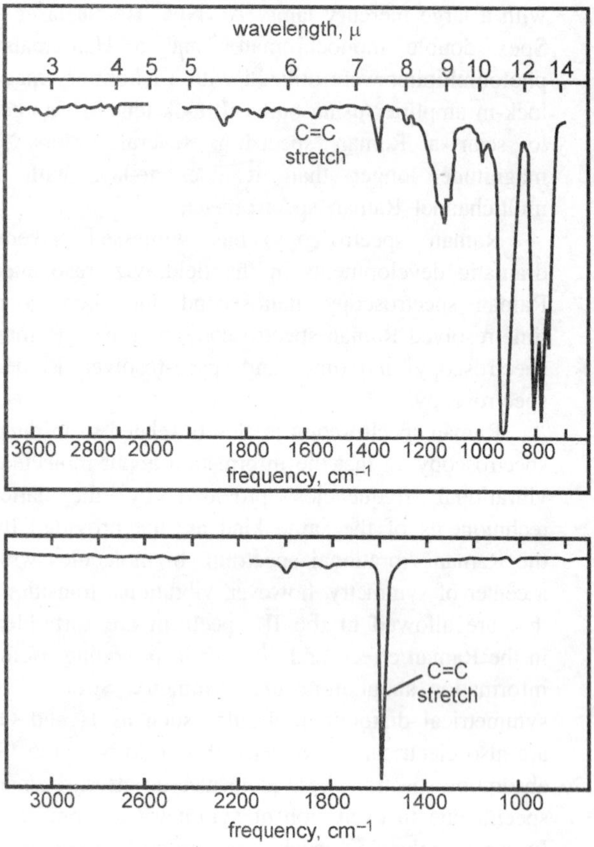

Fig. 15. Infrared (top) and Raman (bolloni) spectra of tctrachloroethylene.

vibrational peaks as the difference between the absolute wavenumbers of the exciting line and the absolute wavenumbers of the resulting scattered photons. The Raman effect is extremely weak, and only a minute portion of the incident photons are useful emergent photons; thus, relatively high-power lasers must be used to create a high photon flux. Sophisticated optical and electronic equipment is also required to detect the scattered photons.

One of the major advantages of Raman spectroscopy is that spectra may be obtained for molecules in aqueous solutions, as water has a weak Raman spectrum that interferes only minimally with the spectrum of the solute. Analyte concentrations in the range of 0.1 to 0.01 *M* in water are normally used. In resonance Raman spectroscopy, concentrations of chromophoric molecules in the range 10^{-4} to 10^{-6} *M* can be used, making this technique particularly useful for biochemical studies.

(BC–43)

Basic Optics of the Raman Experiment

In a standard Raman experiment, intense monochromatic radiation provided by a continuous-wave laser is focused onto or into the sample. Some of the resultant scattered light is collected by optics and directed to a dispersing system that is usually a monochromator. The monochro-mator separates the scattered light on the basis of frequency, and these frequencies are then detected and recorded either by single-channel (scanning) or multichannel detection. Figure 16 illustrates the optics involved in a conventional Raman experiment.

Sampling Techniques and Problems

Samples for Raman spectroscopy may be examined in any physical state. Liquid samples are usually measured in a quartz (1-cm) cuvette similar to the type used in fluorescence spectroscopy; however, because the incident laser beam travels longitudinally down the length of the liquid column, the cell bottom must be transparent. Capillary cells are often used for biological samples, especially when material is limited in availability. Single crystals and fibers can be analyzed by mounting on a goniometer head. Solid crystalline or polycrystalline materials can be pressed into pellets, prepared as KBr discs, or packed into capillary microprobes. Samples in the form of thin films can also be examined. Potential problems include the breakdown of photolabile analytes during laser irradiation. This can be reduced or eliminated for liquid samples by utilizing a spinning cell, a cell in which the liquid sample is continually moved through the laser beam, or a cell in which the liquid is continually stirred with a magnetic stirrer. These procedures reduce the build-up of degradation products usually observed with static sample analysis. In Raman spectroscopy, it is important for the analytes to be optically homogeneous, especially in the case of biological samples. Particulate matter in solutions should be removed either by centrifugation or filtration; otherwise, hot spots may occur in the sample on irradiation, leading to possible degradation. Luminescence, which may often obliterate the Raman effect, may occur if the sample or an impurity in the sample has a chromophore. Luminescence can often be reduced

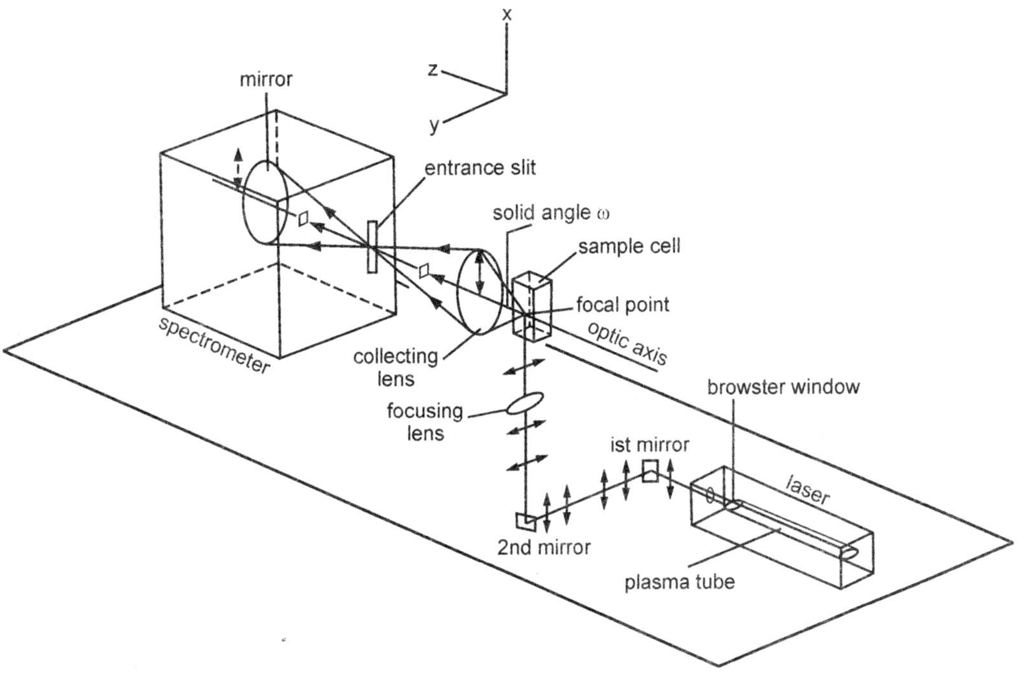

Fig. 16. Optics of a conventional Raman spectrometer.

or climinated by changing the wavelength of excitation or adding a quenching agent such as KI.

Conformation of protein by Raman spectroscopy

Protein molecules are classical examples of the application of Raman spectroscopy to biomolecules. This technique can probe structural details such as average peptide backbone conformation, as well as the side chains of some amino acids, such as tyrosine and tryptophan. Protein spectra are usually obtained in the 450- to 650-nm region. UV-excited resonance Raman spectra of proteins containing aromatic amino acids of interest is often conducted with excitation below 300 nip. The normal Raman spectrum of proteins contains diagnostic amide I (C=O stretch) and amide III (N-H in-plane bending) bands that can be utilized to characterize the secondary structure of the protein or peptide backbone. Table 10 gives approximate positions for the amide I and amide III bands in both the 1R and Raman spectra of various polypeptide conformations. Characterization of the secondary structure of a protein depends on the determination of characteristic amide I and III frequencies in the Raman spectrum for a-helical, fl-sheet and random protein conformations. This is often achieved by using polypeptide models and proteins of known conformation. Figure 16 illustrates the Raman spectra, run in water, of native and denatured ribo-nuclease A and shows the change in the amide III band in the disordered protein.

Resonance Raman Labels

Resonance Raman labels are chromophores that have been carefully designed to mimic natural biochemical components and that are themselves biologically active molecules. They provide detailed vibrational and electronic spectral data when in the vicinity of a biologically important site. Extrinsic protein-bound chromophores such as methyl orange bound to bovine serum albumin have been studied in detail. Other systems that have been studied include protein ligand interactions, such as drug-enzyme and hapten-antibody complexes where the drug or hapten is the chromophoric resonance Raman label. This method is useful for studying enzyme-substrate complexes and can provide vibrational spectra of the substrate during enzyme catalysis.

Table 10. **Approximate Positions (cm^1) of the most Intense Amide I and Amide III Bonds in Raman Spectra and the Amide I Band in IR Spectra for various polypeptide conformations**

	Amide 1		Amide III
Conformation	Raman	Infrared	Raman
α-Helix	1645-1660	1650,00	1265-1300
β-Sheet	1665-1680	1632.00	1230-1240
Unordered	1660-1670	1658.00	1240-1260

Structural Analysis of RNA and DNA by Raman Spectroscopy

Analysis of polynucleotides by Raman spectroscopy affords bonds (~30) primarily attributable to purine or pyrimidine ring modes. In addition, the phosphate group shows interesting features in the spectrum. The sugar moieties in DNA and RNA molecules and the related polynucleotides are poor Raman scatterers. From the Raman spectrum it is possible to obtain a semiquantitative estimate of the relative population of bases in the polynucleotide molecule. Base protonation in DNA has been studied using Raman spectroscopy. Metal-nucleotide binding has also been investigated. The mode of binding of ions such as Ca^{2+}, Mg^{2+}. Co^{2+}, Cu^{2+} and Mg^{2+} to adenosine triphosphate over a wide pH range has also been studied. Raman spectroscopy can detect the disruption of base-pairing and base-stacking interactions. In Figure 17, raising the temperature of poly(rA)-poly(rU) from 32°C to 82°C results in thermal disruption of the helix. Important features in the difference spectra are the radical changes in the carbonyl region (1650 to 1700 cm^{-1}) due to the disruption of H bonding in the Watson-Crick model. Phosphate backbone conformation in nucleic acids has also been studied by monitoring the -O-P-O- symmetrical stretching vibration (800 cm^{-1}) and the $-PO^2$ symmetrical stretch motion (1100 cm^{-1}). The interaction of nucleic acids with proteins is an area of active study; for example, the stabilizing effect of the viral capsids on the secondary structure of the viral RNA has been investigated. Also, Raman data on DNA-histone interactions have indicated that the sites of DNA-protein interactions are probably located in the grooves running along DNA.

Determination of Membranous Lipids by Raman Spectroscopy

Raman spectroscopy is ideally suited for the study of lipids and membranes and has some advantages over other techniques. The analysis time frame of fractions of a picosecond provides instant snapshots, thereby eliminating the line broadening commonly seen in magnetic resonance spectra. No probe molecule is required, and both gel and liquid-crystal hydrocarbon regions can be monitored. The most useful regions are 1000 to 1150 cm^{-1} (C-C accordion stretch) and the 2800 to 3000 cm^{-1} (C-H stretching

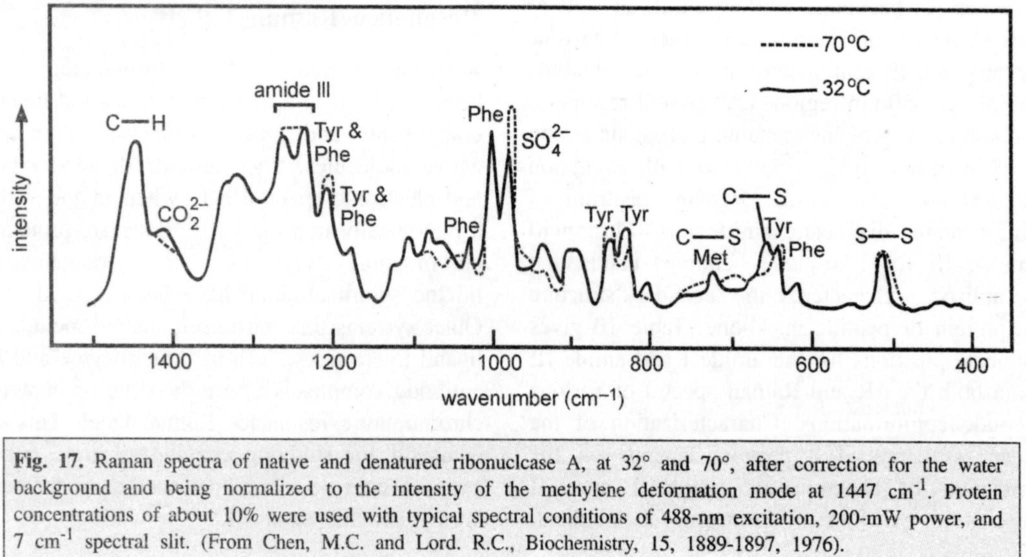

Fig. 17. Raman spectra of native and denatured ribonuclcase A, at 32° and 70°, after correction for the water background and being normalized to the intensity of the methylene deformation mode at 1447 cm^{-1}. Protein concentrations of about 10% were used with typical spectral conditions of 488-nm excitation, 200-mW power, and 7 cm^{-1} spectral slit. (From Chen, M.C. and Lord. R.C., Biochemistry, 15, 1889-1897, 1976).

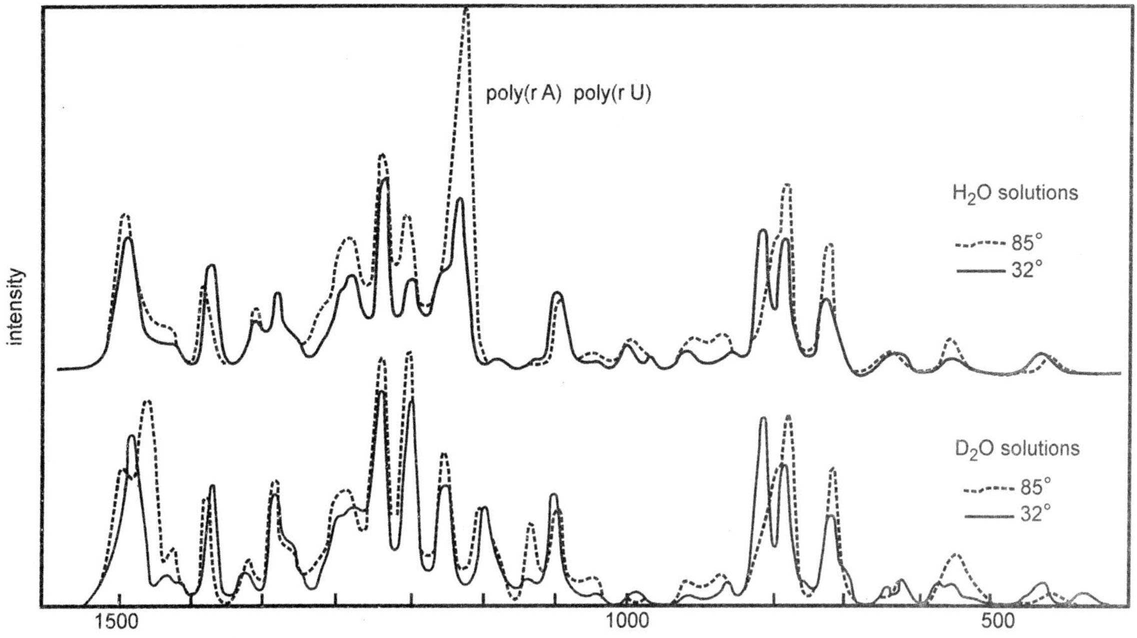

Fig. 18. Raman spectra of H_2O and D_2O solutions of poly(rA)-poly(rU) at 32° and 85°C. The background of Raman scattering by the solvent has been subtracted from each spectrum. (From Laflcur, L. *et. al., Biopolymers*, 11. 2423-2437, 1972).

mode). Transitions from gel to liquid-crystal in membranes are indicated by marked changes in the bands assigned to the C-C stretch mode, and the C-H stretch region is extremely sensitive to conformational change within the individual fatty acid chains.

Applications

Raman spectroscopy has become the tool of choice for many chemical and biological applications. Extremely sensitive to minute structural changes, Raman techniques require minimal sample preparation and are extensively employed in noninvasive studies. Raman microspectroscopy also offers high spatial resolution for analyzing discrete regions of biological matrices. These characteristics make Raman spectroscopy particularly useful for exploring biological processes in living tissues and in individual living cells and organelles. Continuous Raman spectroscopy monitoring of living A549 human lung cells was employed to evaluate the effects of nonionic surfactant exposure on biochemical processes and the sequence of events in cell death. The molecular mechanisms of cell death were strongly associated with specific decreases in Raman peaks associated with nucleic acids and proteins. Western blotting analysis supported the conclusions derived from the Raman spectroscopy data. Raman spectroscopy analysis of specific, time-dependent biochemical changes might be applied to tissue engineering and high-throughput toxicity screening.

Evans and colleagues combined coherent anti-Stokes Raman scattering (CARS) with video-rate microscopy for real-time monitoring of dynamic processes in lipid-rich tissues of living mice. CARS imaging of the methylene stretching vibrational band afforded exceptional subcellular resolution in tissues such as adipocytes, corneocytes, and the sebaceous glands. Important processes such as *in vivo* cellular transport, xenobiotic diffusion, and transcorneal absorption might be monitored using the CARS method.

Several reports on the biomedical applications of *in vivo* Raman spectroscopy (TV-RS) have been published. These include the *in vivo* diagnosis of certain diseases in their very early stages. *In vivo* Raman scattering has been explored as a means of measuring levels of the antioxidant molecules lutein and zeaxanthin in the retina of young and older adults. The results indicated that the concentration of these protective pigments decreased with increasing age, even in normal eyes. The authors suggest a role for Raman screening of retinal carotenoid levels in populations at risk for macular degeneration, a leading cause of blindness. The potential use of IV-RS for diagnosing arterial disease and cancer in gynecological tissues, soft tissues, breast, colon, bladder, and brain has been discussed by Manoharan et al. (1996), Lawson et al. (1997) reviewed the application of Raman spectroscopy to the study of human arteries, tumors, gall- stones, hair, and nails. Brain tissues have also been investigated using FT-Raman spectroscopy, and spectra from the cerebral cortex, cerebral white matter, caudate-puta-men, thalamus, synaptosomal fraction, and myelin fractions have been recorded. Brain tumors have also been studied using FT-Raman spectroscopy.

Ong et al. (1999) studied the substantia nigra of the rostral mid-brain in monkeys using Raman microspectros-copy to determine differences between white and gray matter. As compared to the laser spot size of 20 im in IR micro-spectroscopy, the 1-ìm laser spot size in Raman micro-spectroscopy afforded much greater spatial resolution in sample analysis. The white and gray matter could be clearly distinguished and their relative proportions evaluated from Raman frequencies in the 3000-cm^{-1} region.

Singer and coworkers evaluated Raman confocal microscopy as a means of assessing environmental pollutant bioavailability and toxicity in a cell culture system. Phenanthrene, dodecane, 3-chlorobipheny and pentachlorophenol (four common environmental pollutants) were detected and quantified using this potential pollution bioassay.

Along with IR spectrometers, portable Raman spectrometers have also been developed for remote field use. Raman analysis with portable instrumentation was used in a blind field test to analyze a matrix of 58 unknowns for comparison with a standard hazardous materials response library of known spectra. Despite the inclusion of multiple solvents and compounds with uncata-logued spectra, over 97% of the samples were correctly identified with no false positives. Free-base crack cocaine and its hydrochloride salt were readily identified and distinguished from common street adulterants using fiberoptic Raman spectroscopy.

Raman spectroscopy systems have been developed for the detection of toxins associated with bioterrorism including chemical and microbial weapons. The capacity of a human-lung-cell-based Raman spectroscopy system to detect and differentiate between sulfur mustard and ricin exposure was assessed non-invasively over time. Differences in cellular Raman spectra correlated with characteristic changes in cellular biochemistry and structure. Damaged cells were detected with high sensitivity and specificity, and toxic agent identification was reasonably accurate for ricin (71.4%) and sulfur mustard (88.6%).

Surface Plasmon Resonance (SPR) Spectroscopy

The term biosensor was introduced around 1975, relating to exploiting transducer principles for the direct detection of biomolecules at surfaces. Currently the most prominent example of a biosensor is the glucose sensor, reporting glucose concentration as an electronic signal, e.g. based on a selective, enzymatic process. Application of SPR-based sensors to biomolecular interaction monitoring was first demonstrated in 1983 by Lundstrom's pursuit towards physical Introduction to Surface Plasmon Resonance methods for label-free, real-time detection of biomolecules. The intrinsic properties of the molecules, e.g. mass, refractive index and/or charge distribution were probed using ellipsometry, refractometry, surface plasmon resonance, photothermic detection methods and others. Wood observed a pattern of "anomalous" dark and light bands in the reflected light, when he shone polarized light on a mirror with a diffraction grating on its surface. Physical interpretation of the phenomenon was initiated by Lord Rayleigh (1907), and further refined by Fano (1941), but a complete explanation of the phenomenon was not possible until 1968, when Otto (1968) and in the same year Kretschmann and Raether (1968) reported the excitation of surface plasmons. Application of SPR-based sensors to biomolecular interaction monitoring was first demonstrated by Liedberg et al. (1983).

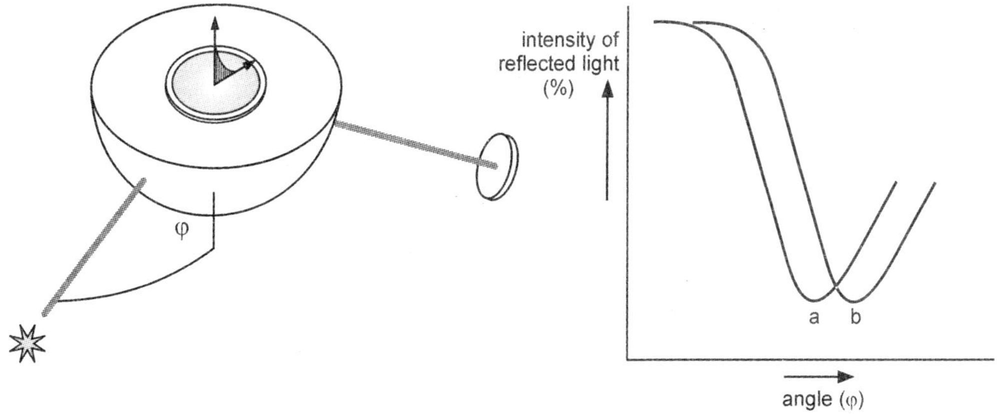

Fig. 19. Schematic experimental set-up of surface plasmon resonance excitation. A sensor chip with a gold coating is placed on a hemisphere (or prism). Polarized light shines from the light source (star) on the sensor chip. Reflected light intensity is measured in the detector (disk). At a certain angle of incidence (j), excitation of surface plasmons occurs, resulting in a dip in the intensity of the reflected light (a). A change in refractive index at the surface of the gold film will cause an angle shift from a to b.

A simple Experiment

Consider the experimental set-up depicted in Figure 19. When polarized light is shone through a prism on a sensor chip with a thin metal film on top, the light will be reflected by the metal film acting as a mirror. On changing the angle of incidence, and monitoring the intensity of the reflected light, the intensity of the reflected light passes through a minimum (Fig. 19, line a). At this angle of incidence, the light will excite surface plasmons, inducing surface plasmon resonance, causing a dip in the intensity of the reflected light. Photons of polarized light can interact with the free electrons of the metal layer, inducing a wave-like oscillation of the free electrons and thereby reducing the reflected light intensity.

The angle at which the maximum loss of the reflected light intensity occurs is called resonance angle or SPR angle. The SPR angle is dependent on the optical characteristics of the system, e.g. on the refractive indices of the media at both sides of the metal, usually gold. While the refractive index at the prism side is not changing, the refractive index in the immediate vicinity of the metal surface will change when accumulated mass (e.g. proteins) adsorb on it. Hence the surface plasmon resonance conditions are changing and the shift of the SPR angle is suited to provide information on the kinetics of e.g. protein adsorption on the surface.

From Dip to Real-Time Measurement

Surface plasmon resonance is an excellent method to monitor changes of the refractive index in the near vicinity of the metal surface. When the refractive index changes, the angle at which the intensity minimum is observed will shift as indicated in Figure 20, where (a) depicts the original plot of reflected light intensity vs. incident angle and (b) indicates the plot after the change in refractive index. Surface plasmon resonance is not only suited to measure the difference between these two states, but can also monitor the change in time, if one follows in time the shift of the resonance angle at which the dip is observed.

Figure 20 depicts the shift of the dip in time, a so-called sensorgram. If this change is due to a biomolecular interaction, the kinetics of the interaction can be studied in real time.

How to Construct an SPR Assay?

Now we have a basic understanding of the surface plasmon resonance signal and how to measure it in time. We know that the sensor surface needs to be modified to allow selective capturing and thus

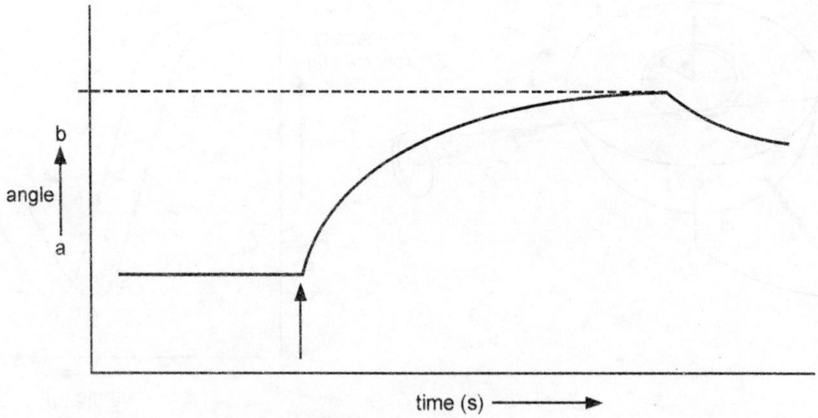

Fig. 20. A sensorgram : the angle at which the dip is observed vs. time. First, no change occurs at the sensor and a baseline is measured with the dip at SPR angle (a). After injection of the sample (arrow) biomolecules will adsorb on the surface resulting in a change in refractive index and a shift of the SPR angle to position b. The adsorption–desorption process can be followed in real time and the amount of adsorbed species can be determined.

selective measurement of a target compound. In the following, we are going to learn more about an SPR measurement. First, the steps of an SPR assay will be discussed from immobilization through analysis to regeneration in a measurement cycle. Next, we get acquainted with a typical calibration curve, followed by examples of assay formats. Finally, a short outlook is provided on the basics of the instrumentation.

The Steps of an Assay

In the simplest case of an SPR measurement, a target component or analyte is captured by the capturing element or so-called ligand (Figure 21). The ligand is permanently immobilized on the sensor surface previous to the measurement. Various sensor surfaces with immobilized ligands are commercially available.

In the simplest case, the event of capturing the analyte by the ligand gives rise to a measurable signal, this is called direct detection. Figure 22 shows the sensor signal step-by-step in the measurement cycle with direct detection. Each measurement starts with conditioning the sensor surface with a suitable buffer solution (1). It is of vital relevance to have a reliable baseline before the capturing event starts. At this point, the sensor surface contains the active ligands, ready to capture the target analytes. On injecting the solution containing the analytes (2), they are captured on the surface. Also other components of the sample might adhere to the sensor surface; without a suitable selection of the ligand, this adherence will be non-specific, and thus easy to break. At this step, adsorption kinetics of the analyte molecule can be determined in a real-time measurement. Next, buffer is injected on to the sensor and the non-specifically bound components are flushed off (3). As indicated in the figure, the accumulated mass can be obtained from the SPR response (ΔR). Also in this step, dissociation of the analyte starts, enabling the kinetics of the dissociation process to be studied. Finally, a regeneration solution is injected, which breaks the specific binding between analyte and ligand (4). If properly anchored to the sensor surface, the ligands remain on the sensor, whereas the target analytes are quantitatively removed. It is vital in order to perform multiple tests with the same sensor chip to use a regeneration solution which leaves the activity of the ligands intact, as the analysis cycle is required to take place repeatedly for hundreds, sometimes even thousands of times. Again, buffer is injected to condition the surface for the next analysis cycle. If the regeneration is incomplete, remaining accumulated mass causes the baseline level to be increased.

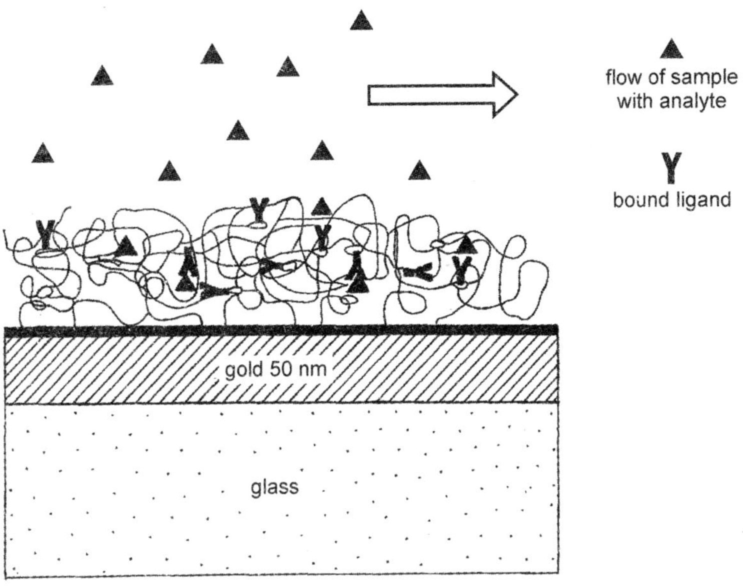

Fig. 21. Schematic representation of direct detection: the analyte is captured by the ligands (Y) immobilized on the sensor surface. Accumulation of the analyte results in a refractive index change in the evanescent field shifting the SPR angle. Here the ligand is immobilized in a hydrogel.

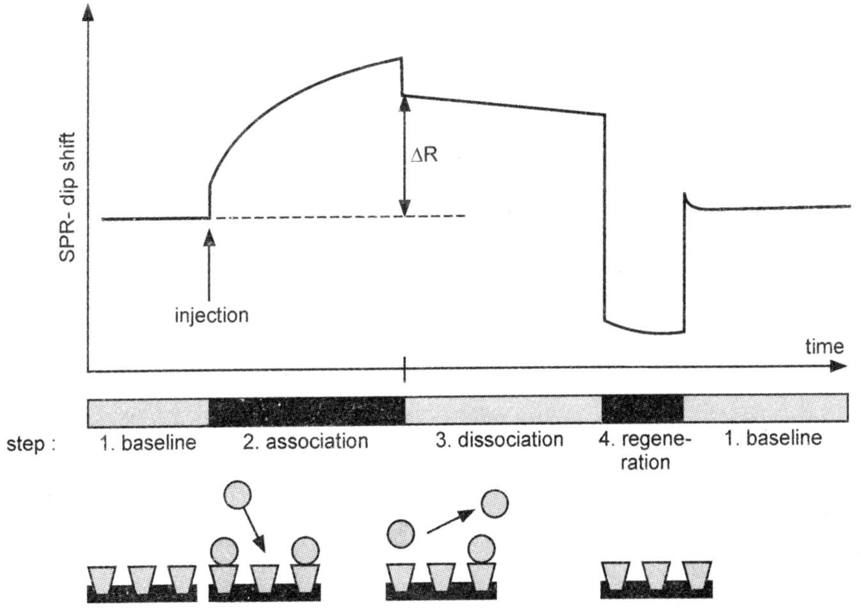

Fig. 22. Sensor gram showing the steps of an analysis cycle: 1, buffer is in contact with the sensor (baseline step); 2, continuous injection of sample solution (association step); 3, injection of buffer (dissociation step); DR indicates the measured response due to the bound target compound; 4, removal of bound species from the surface during injection of regeneration solution (regeneration step) followed by a new analysis cycle. A bulk refractive index shift can be observed at t1.

Often SPR measurements are carried out to determine the kinetics of a binding process. For realistic results it is vital to prevent immobilization from changing the ligand in a way that would influence its strength or affinity towards the target component. In addition, kinetic experiments can provide information on the thermodynamics, e.g. on the binding energy of processes.

Calibration Curve

Apart from kinetic and thermodynamic studies, SPR measurements can also be used for the determination of the concentration of the analyte in a sample (quantitative analysis). In this case, first different concentrations of the analyte are applied in separate analysis cycles. The sensorgrams measured at different concentrations give an overlay plot similar to that depicted in Figure 23, with the plateaus of the association step increasing at increasing analyte concentration. A calibration curve can be constructed by plotting the response (ΔR) after a certain time interval (t1) versus concentration. When analyzing samples with an unknown concentration of the analyte, usually multiple dilutions are made, for example 10, 100 and 1000 times, or for more accurate determinations serial dilutions by a factor of 2. If the concentration of the analyte in the sample is very high, the undiluted sample will yield results on the upper plateau range of the calibration curve. The diluted solutions, however, might yield points along the lower, concentration-dependent sections of the calibration curve and the concentration of the analyte can be determined.

As mentioned above, SPR sensing means detection of refractive index changes at the sensor surface, which in practice translates to the amount of mass deposited at the sensor surface. Direct detection is only possible if the capturing event of the analyte brings about measurable refractive index changes. This is easier to achieve if the molecular weight of the analyte is high (i.e. around 1000 Da or higher). However, for small molecules to produce a measurable refractive index change, large numbers would be required, making the analysis intrinsically less sensitive. If the analyte is a small molecule (MW<1000 Da), often direct detection is not viable.

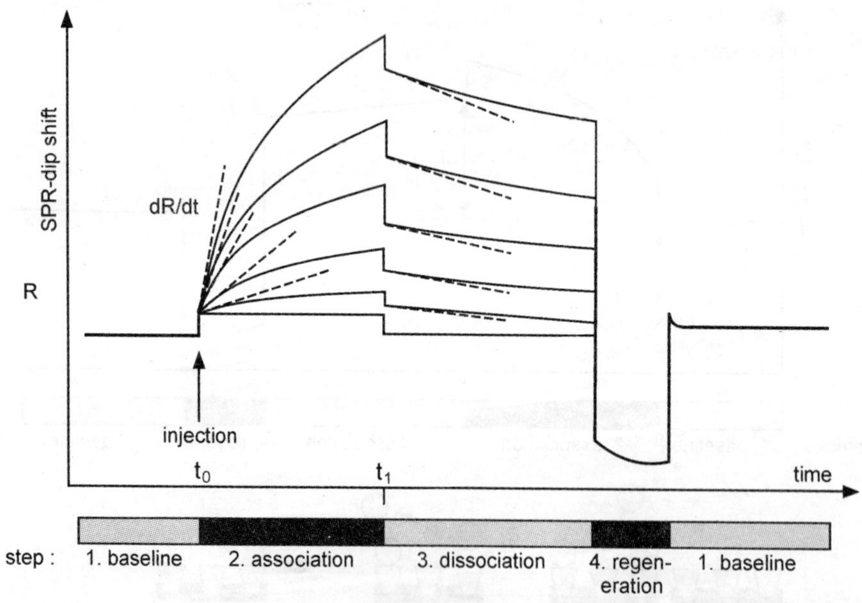

Fig. 23. Typical overlay plot of sensorgrams from serial diluted analyte concentrations. Just after injection at t0 a sample specific binding of the analyte occurs and mass transport to the surface is rate limiting and linearly dependent on the concentration. From the slopes of a positive control (dR/dt), the concentration of an unknown sample can be determined. During the association phase the number of unbound ligand molecules decreases and dissociation takes place. The off-rate constant or dissociation constant (kd) can be determined after injecting dissociation buffer at t1.

Detection of small molecules can be carried out using a different strategy. Most often, small molecules are detected in a sandwich, competition or inhibition assay format. In all assay formats, not only the lower detectable concentration is limited, but also the physical number of immobilized elements on the sensor surface, which provides a maximum limiting value.

Basics of Instrumentation

SPR instruments comprise three essential units integrated in one system: optical unit, liquid handling unit and the sensor surface. The features of the sensor chip have a vital influence on the quality of the interaction measurement. The sensor chip forms a physical barrier between the optical unit (dry section) and the flow cell (wet section).

SPR instrumentation can be configured in various ways to measure the shift of the SPR-dip. In general, three different optical systems are used to excite surface plasmons: systems with prisms, gratings and optical waveguides. Most widespread are instruments with a prism coupler, also called "Kretschmann configuration". In this configuration, which is shown in Figure 19, a prism couples p-polarized light into the sensor coated with a thin metal film. The light is reflected on to a detector, measuring its intensity, using a photodiode or a camera. In instruments with a grating coupler, light is reflected at the lower refractive index substrate. In practice, this means that light travels through the liquid before photons generate surface plasmon waves as in ellipsometric instruments. Besides the grating couplers, some instruments apply optical waveguide couplers or measure the SPR wavelength shift as a result of the biomolecular interaction process.

All configurations share the same intrinsic phenomenon: the direct, label-free and real-time measurement of refractive index changes at the sensor surface. SPR sensors offer the capability of measuring low levels of chemical and biological compounds near the sensor surface. Sensing of a biomolecular binding event occurs when biomolecules accumulate at the sensor surface and change the refractive index by replacing the background electrolyte. Protein molecules have a higher refractive index than water molecules ($\Delta n \approx 10^{-1}$). The sensitivity of most SPR instruments is in the range $\Delta n \approx 10^{-5}$ or 1 $pgmm^{-2}$ of proteinous material. Often in real-time biosensing absolute values are not a prerequisite, only the change is monitored as a result of biospecific interaction at the sensor surface. A detailed description of commercial instruments is given in figure mentioned below (Figure 24).

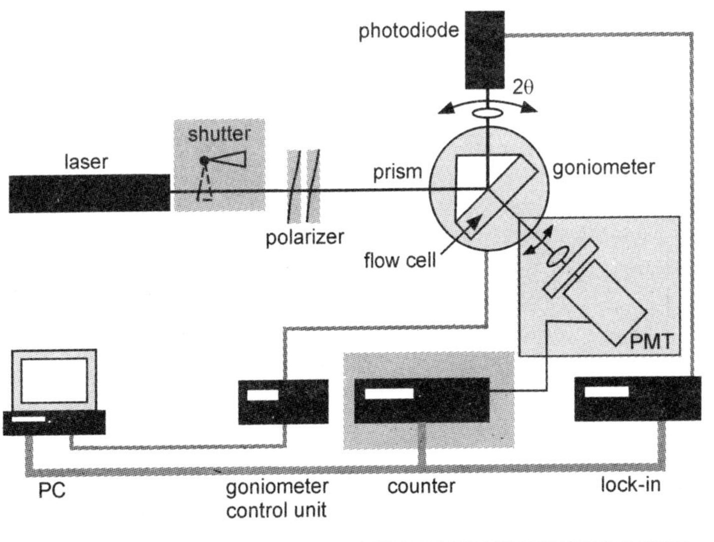

Fig. 24. A typical surface plasmon fluorescence spectroscopy setup. The fluorescence components are highlighted in gray.

Applications of SPR

Along with its increased use and application in biological, medical and physical sciences, SPR continues to evolve as an elegant and powerful analytical method with unique capabilities. In addition to all of the advantages previously known, such as label-free, real-time, and surface-sensitive detection, new aspects of SPR and SPR imaging are being explored and developed with great creativity. In particular, major trends seem to be present in the development of combined techniques (SPR-MS, ESPR, SPFS, etc.), use of new materials (classified substrates, polymers, etc.), and development of new methods (nanoparticle amplification, enzymatic amplification, TM receptors in tethered membranes, etc.). Together, these developments constitute a major thrust forward that could eventually make the use of SPR as common as that of fluorescence for surface-interaction analysis and biosensing. The future outlook for research with SPR, in our opinion is a bright one.

Important Questions

1. Define spectroscopy. Discuss the basic design of a spectrophotometer and applications of spectrophotometry.
2. What do you understand by atomic absorption spectrophotometer? What are the components of atomic absorption spectrophotometer? Discuss its applications.
3. What is spectrofluorimetry? Discuss its principle, instrument design and applications.
4. Describe the principle and applications of luminometry.
5. What are the advantages of luminometry over conventional spectrophotometry?
6. Write briefly on the applications of luminometer.
7. Write briefly on the following :
   (i) Beer-Lambert relationship, (ii) Luminometry, (iii) Flame emission photometry, (iv) Imfrared resononce spectrophotometry.

1. Describe the principle, instrument design and applications of Raman spectroscopy.
2. Write briefly on the biomedical applications of Raman spectroscopy.
3. Describe the principle, instrument design and applications of surface plasmon resonance spectroscopy.
4. Discuss the principle, instrument design and applications of infra-red spectroscopy.
5. Write short notes on the following :
   (i) Fingerprint region; (ii) Dispersive IR spectrophotometers; (iii) Fourier transform spectrometers; (iv) Applications of IR spectroscopy in Toxicology.

Mass Spectrometry

9

Mass spectrometer is an analytical tool used for measuring the **molecular weight** (MW) of a sample. For large samples such as **bio-molecules**, molecular weights can be measured to within an accuracy of 0.01% of the total molecular weight of the sample i.e. within 4 Daltons (Da) or atomic mass units (amu) of 40,000 Da. This is sufficient to allow minor mass changes to be detected, e.g. the substitution of one amino acid for another or a post-translational modification. For small organic molecules the molecular weight can be measured to within an accuracy of 5 ppm, which is often sufficient to confirm the molecular formula of a compound, and is also a standard requirement for publication in a chemical journal.

Structural information can be generated using certain types of mass spectrometers, usually tandem mass spectrometers, and this is achieved by fragmenting the sample and analyzing the products generated. This procedure is useful for the structural elucidation of organic compounds, for peptide or oligonucleotide sequencing, and for monitoring the existence of previously characterised compounds in complex mixtures with a high specificity by defining both the molecular weight and a diagnostic fragment of the molecule simultaneously e.g. for the detection of specific drug metabolites in biological matrices.

Simplified Schematic of a Mass Spectrometer

Mass spectrometers can be divided into three fundamental parts, namely the ionization source, the analyzer, and the detector (Fig. 1).

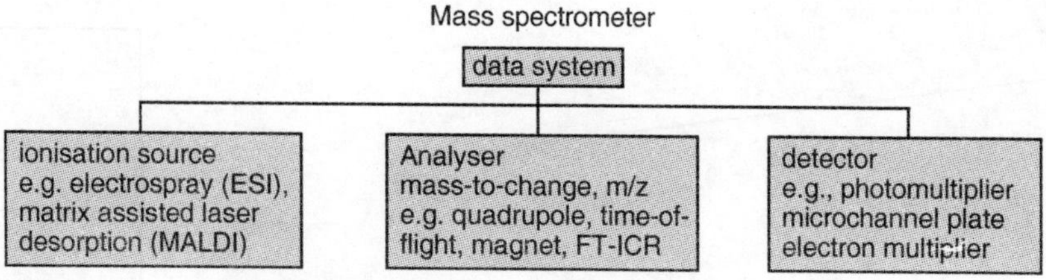

Fig. 1. Components of a mass spectrophotometer.

The sample under investigation has to be introduced into the ionization source of the instrument. Once inside the ionization source the sample molecules are ionized, because ions are easier to manipulate than neutral molecules. These ions are extracted into the analyzer region of the mass spectrometer where they are separated according to their **mass (m) -to-charge (z) ratios (m/z)**. The separated ions are detected and this signal sent to a data system where the m/z ratios are stored together with their relative abundance for presentation in the format of a m/z spectrum.

The analyzer and detector of the mass spectrometer, and often the ionization source too, are maintained under high vacuum to give the ions a reasonable chance of traveling from one end of the instrument to the other without any hindrance from air molecules. The entire operation of the mass spectrometer, and often the sample introduction process also, is under complete data control system.

Sample Preparation

The method of sample introduction to the ionization source often depends on the ionization method being used, as well as the type and complexity of the sample.

The sample can be inserted directly into the ionization source, or can undergo some type of chromatography en route to the ionization source. This latter method of sample introduction usually involves the mass spectrometer being coupled directly to a high pressure liquid chromatography (HPLC), gas chromatography (GC) or capillary electrophoresis (CE) separation column, and hence the sample is separated into a series of components which then enter the mass spectrometer sequentially for individual analysis.

Methods of Sample Ionization

Many ionization methods are available and each has its own advantages and disadvantages.
The ionization method to be used should depend on the type of sample under investigation and the mass spectrometer available. Ionization methods include the following :

Atmospheric Pressure Chemical Ionization	(APCI)
Chemical Ionization	(CI)
Electron Impact	(EI)
Electrospray Ionization	(ESI)
Fast Atom Bombardment	(FAB)
Field Desorption / Field Ionization	(FD/FI)
Matrix Assisted Laser Desorption Ionization	(MALDI)
Thermospray Ionization	(TSP)

The ionization methods used for the majority of biochemical analyses are Electrospray Ionization (ESI) and Matrix Assisted Laser Desorption Ionization (**MALDI**).

With most ionization methods there is the possibility of creating both positively and negatively charged sample ions, depending on the proton affinity of the sample. Before starting on an analysis the user must decide whether to detect the positively or negatively charged ions.

Electrospray Ionization

Electrospray Ionization (ESI) is one of the Atmospheric Pressure Ionization (API) techniques and is well-suited to the analysis of polar molecules ranging from less than 100 Da to more than 1,000,000 Da in molecular weight (Fig. 2).

During standard electrospray ionization on the Platform II mass spectrometer, the sample is

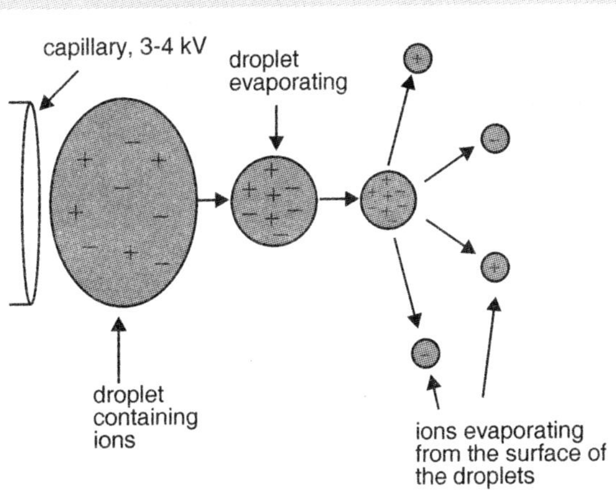

Fig. 2. Scheme of electron spray ionization.

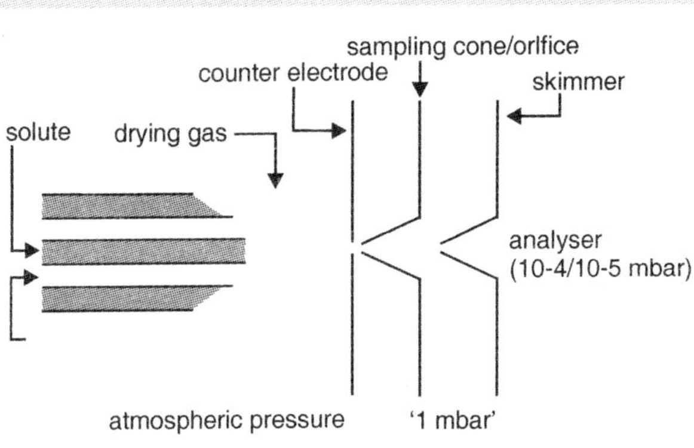

Fig. 3. Standard electrospray ionization source (platform-II).

dissolved in a polar, volatile solvent and pumped through a narrow, stainless steel capillary (75 – 150 μm i.d.) at a flow rate of between 1 μL/min and 1 ml/min. A high voltage of 3 or 4 kV is applied to the tip of the capillary, which is situated within the ionization source of the mass spectrometer, and as a consequence of this strong electric field, the sample emerging from the tip is dispersed into an aerosol of highly charged droplets, a process that is aided by a co-axially introduced nebulising gas flowing around the outside of the capillary. This gas, usually nitrogen, helps to direct the spray emerging from the capillary tip towards the mass spectrometer. The charged droplets diminish in size by solvent evaporation, assisted by a warm flow of nitrogen known as the drying gas which passes across the front of the ionization source. Eventually charged sample ions, free from solvent, are released from the droplets, some of which pass through a sampling cone or orifice into an intermediate vaccum region, and from there through a small aperture into the analyzer of the mass spectrometer, which is held under high vaccum. The lens voltages are optimised individually for each sample (Fig. 3).

A small volume (1-4 μl) of the sample dissolved in a suitable volatile solvent, at a concentration of ca. 1–10 pmol/μl, is transferred into a miniature sample vial. A reasonably high voltage (ca. 700 – 2000 V) is applied to the specially manufactured gold-plated vial resulting in sample ionization and spraying. Desolvation is followed by ion extraction through the sampling cone, which is situated at 90o to the original flow of solute and solvent, and then through the extraction cone (another 900 turn) into the analyzer for separation and analysis of the ions according to their m/z ratios, as with standard ESI-MS. The two right-angled bends in the ionization source have led to its name of Z-spray.

The flow rate of solute and solvent using this procedure is very low, 30 – 1000 ml/min, and so not only is far less sample consumed than with the standard electrospray ionization technique, but also a small volume of sample lasts for several minutes, thus enabling multiple experiments to be performed. A common application of this technique is for a protein digest mixture to be analysed to generate a list of molecular weights for the components present, and then each component to be analysed further by tandem mass spectrometric (MS-MS) amino acid sequencing techniques.

ESI and **nanospray ionization** are very sensitive analytical techniques but the sensitivity deteriorates with the presence of non-volatile buffers and other additives, which should be avoided as far as possible.

In **positive ionization** mode, a trace of formic acid is often added to aid protonation of the sample molecules; in **negative ionization** mode a trace of ammonia solution or a volatile amine is added to aid deprotonation of the sample molecules. **Proteins and peptides** are usually analysed under **positive ionization** conditions and **saccharides and oligonucleotides** under **negative ionization** conditions. In all cases, the **m/z** scale must be **calibrated** by analysing a standard sample of a similar type to the sample being analysed (e.g. a protein calibrant for a protein sample), and then applying a mass correction. *(BC–43)*

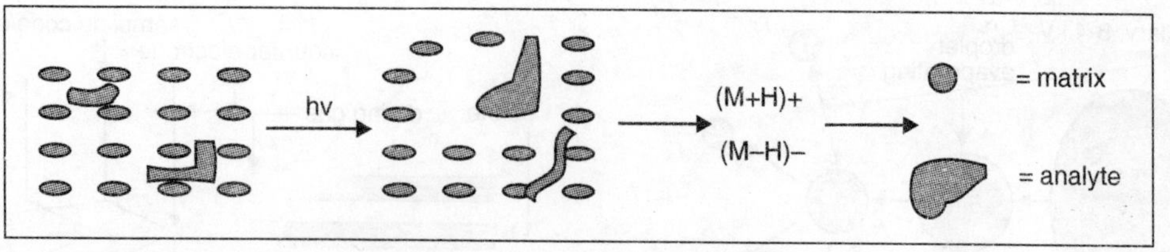

Fig. 4. Simplified scheme of MALDI.

Matrix Assisted Laser Desorption Ionization (MALDI)

The sample to be analysed is dissolved in an appropriate volatile solvent, usually with a trace of trifluoroacetic acid if positive ionization is being used, at a concentration of ca. **10 pmol/μL** and an aliquot (**1-2 μL**) of this removed and mixed with an equal volume of a solution containing a vast excess of a matrix. A range of compounds is suitable for use as matrices: **sinapinic acid** is a common one for **protein** analysis while **cyano-4-hydroxycinnamic acid** is often used for **peptide** analysis. An aliquot (1-2 μL) of the final solution is applied to the sample target which is allowed to dry prior to insertion into the high vacuum of the mass spectrometer. The laser is fired, the energy arriving at the sample/matrix surface optimised, and data accumulated until a m/z spectrum of reasonable intensity has been amassed. The time-of-flight analyzer separates ions according to their **mass(m)-to-charge(z) (m/z)** ratios by measuring the time it takes for ions to travel through a field free region known as the flight, or drift, tube. The heavier ions are slower than the lighter ones.

The m/z scale of the mass spectrometer is **calibrated** with a known sample that can either be analysed independently (external calibration) or pre-mixed with the sample and matrix (internal calibration).

Simplified Schematic of MALDI-TOF Mass Spectrometry (Linear Mode) (TofSpec)

MALDI is a "soft" ionization method and so results predominantly in the generation of **singly charged molecular-related ions** regardless of the molecular weight, hence the spectra are relatively easy to interpret. Fragmentation of the sample ions does not usually occur.

In **positive ionization** mode the **protonated molecular ions** ($M+H^+$) are usually the dominant species, although they can be accompanied by salt adducts, a trace of the doubly charged molecular ion at approximately half the m/z value, and/or a trace of a dimeric species at approximately twice the m/z value. Positive ionization is used in general for **protein** and **peptide** analyses (Fig. 4).

In **negative ionization** mode the **deprotonated molecular ions** ($M-H^-$) are usually the most abundant species, accompanied by some salt adducts and possibly traces of dimeric or doubly charged materials. Negative ionization can be used for the analysis of **oligonucleotides** and **oligosaccharides** (Fig. 5).

Positive or Negative Ionization

If the sample has functional groups that readily accept a proton (H^+) then positive ion detection is used *e.g.* **amines $R\text{-}NH_2 + H^+ \rightarrow R\text{-}NH_3^+$ as in proteins, peptides.**

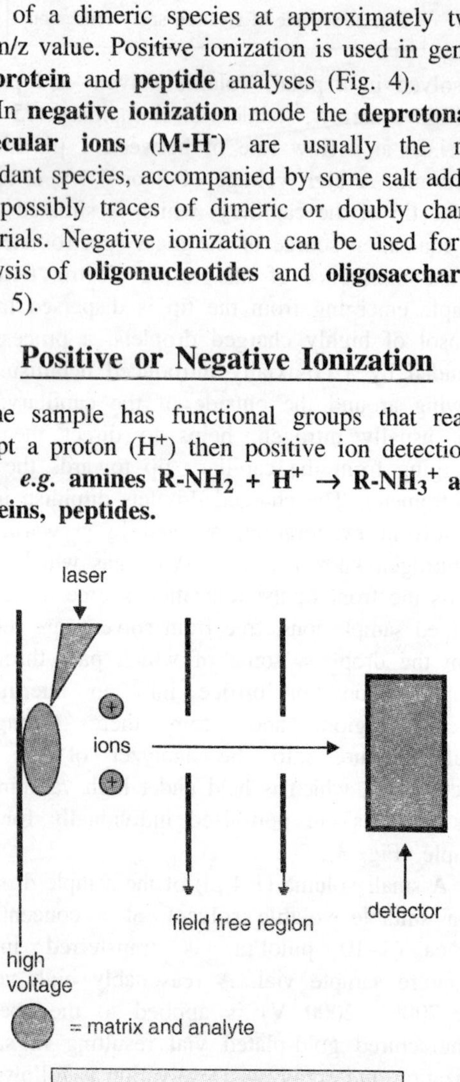

Fig. 5. Positive ionization technique.

If the sample has functional groups that readily lose a proton then negative ion detection is used *e.g.* **carboxylic acids R-CO_2H → R-CO_2^- and alcohols R-OH → R-O^- as in saccharides, oligonucleotides**

Analysis and Separation of Ions Present in the Samples

The main function of the mass analyzer is to separate, or resolve, the ions formed in the ionization source of the mass spectrometer according to their mass-to-charge (m/z) ratios. There are a number of mass analyzers currently available, the better known of which include quadrupoles, time-of-flight (TOF) analyzers, magnetic sectors, and both fourier transform and quadrupole ion traps.

These mass analyzers have different features, including the m/z range that can be covered, the mass accuracy, and the achievable resolution. The compatibility of different analyzers with different ionization methods varies. For example, all of the analyzers listed above can be used in conjunction with electrospray ionization, whereas MALDI is not usually coupled to a quadrupole analyzer.

Tandem mass spectrometers are instruments that have more than one analyzer and so can be used for structural and sequencing studies. Two, three and four analyzers have all been incorporated into commercially available tandem instruments, and the analyzers do not necessarily have to be of the same type, in which case the instrument is a hybrid one. More popular tandem mass spectrometers include those of the quadrupole-quadrupole, magnetic sector-quadrupole, and more recently, the quadrupole-time-of-flight geometries.

Detection and Recording of Sample Ions

The detector monitors the ion current, amplifies it and the signal is then transmitted to the data system where it is recorded in the form of mass spectra. The m/z values of the ions are plotted against their intensities to show the number of components in the sample, the molecular weight of each component, and the relative abundance of the various components in the sample.

The type of detector is supplied to suit the type of analyzer; the more common ones are the photomultiplier, the electron multiplier and the micro-channel plate detectors.

Tandem Mass Spectrometry

Tandem mass spectrometry is used to produce **structural information** about a compound by

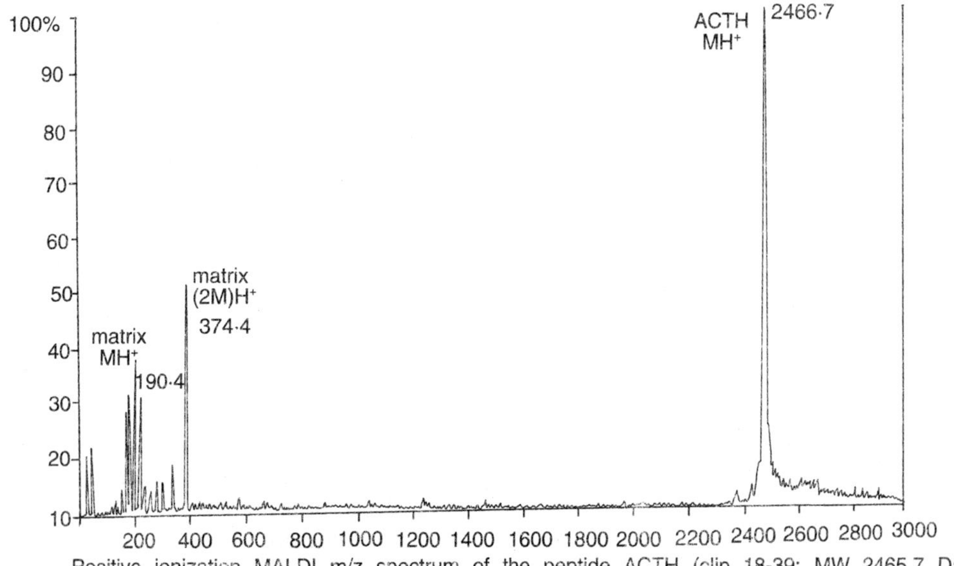

Positive ionization MALDI m/z spectrum of the peptide ACTH (clip 18-39; MW 2465.7 Da) using ±-cyano-4-hydroxycinnamic acid as matrix.

Fig. 6. M/Z spectrum of the peptide ACTH.

fragmenting specific sample ions inside the mass spectrometer and identifying the resulting fragment ions. This information can then be placed together to generate structural information regarding the intact molecule. Tandem mass spectrometry also enables specific compounds to be detected in complex mixtures on account of their specific and characteristic fragmentation patterns.

A **tandem mass spectrometer** is a mass spectrometer that has more than one analyzer, in practice usually two. The two analyzers are separated by a collision cell into which an inert gas (e.g. argon, xenon) is admitted to collide with the selected sample ions and bring about their fragmentation. The analyzers can be of the same or of different types, the most common combinations being:

- **quadrupole - quadrupole**
- **magnetic sector – quadrupole**
- **magnetic sector – magnetic sector**
- **quadrupole – time-of-flight.**

Fragmentation experiments can also be performed on certain single analyzer mass spectrometers such as ion trap and time-of-flight instruments, the latter type using a post-source decay experiment to effect the fragmentation of sample ions.

Proteomics by Mass Spectrophotometry

Peptides fragment along the amino acid backbone to give sequence information. Peptides ca. 2500 Da or less produce the most useful data.

The amount of sequence information varies from one peptide to another. Some peptides can generate sufficient information for a full sequence to be determined; others may generate a partial sequence of 4 or 5 amino acids.

A protein digest can be analysed as an entire reaction mix, without any separation of the products, from which individual peptides are selected and analysed by the mass spectrometer to generate sequence information.

About 4 μL of solution is required for the analysis of the digest mixture, with a concentration based on the original protein of ca. 1-10 pmol/μL. MS-MS sequencing is a sensitive technique consuming little sample.

Sometimes the full protein sequence can be verified; some proteins generate sufficient information to cover only part of the sequence. 70 - 80% coverage is reasonable.

Often a sequence "tag" of 4/5 amino acids from a single proteolytic peptide is sufficient to identify the protein from a database.

The final point in this summary means that mass spectrometers have been found to be extremely useful for **proteomic** studies, as illustrated below.

The **proteomics procedure** usually involves excising individual spots from a **2-D gel** and independently **enzymatically digesting** the protein(s) contained within each spot, before analysing the digest mixture by mass spectrometer in the manner outlined above. Electrospray ionization or MALDI could be used at this step.

The initial **MS spectrum** determining the **molecular weights** of all of the components in the digest mixture can often provide sufficient information to search a **database** using just several of the molecular weights from this **peptide map.**

If the database search is not fruitful, either because the protein has not been catalogued, is previously uncharacterised, or the data are not accurate or comprehensive enough to distinguish between several entries in the database, then further information is required.

This can be achieved by sample clean-up and then **MS-MS** studies to determine the amino acid sequences of the individual proteolytic peptides contained in the digest mixture, with which further database searching can be carried out

Uses of Mass Spectrometry

Mass spectrometers are used in industry and academia for both routine and research purposes. The following list is just a brief summary of the major mass spectrometric applications:

⇒ **Biotechnology**: the analysis of proteins, peptides, oligonucleotides

⇒ **Pharmaceutical**: drug discovery, combinatorial chemistry, pharmacokinetics, drug metabolism

⇒ **Clinical**: neonatal screening, haemoglobin analysis, drug testing

⇒ **Environmental**: PAHs, PCBs, water quality, food contamination

⇒ **Geological**: oil composition

How Can Mass Spectrometry Help Biochemists?

⇒ **Accurate molecular weight measurements:** sample confirmation, to determine the purity of a sample, to verify amino acid substitutions, to detect post-translational modifications, to calculate the number of disulphide bridges

⇒ **Reaction monitoring:** to monitor enzyme reactions, chemical modification, protein digestion

⇒ **Amino acid sequencing:** sequence confirmation, *de novo* characterisation of peptides, identification of proteins by database searching with a sequence "tag" from a proteolytic fragment

⇒ **Oligonucleotide sequencing:** the characterisation or quality control of oligonucleotides

⇒ **Protein structure:** protein folding monitored by H/D exchange, protein-ligand complex formation under physiological conditions, macromolecular structure determination

Important Questions

1. Describe the principle and function of mass spectrophotometer.
2. Write short notes on:
   (i) Electro Spray Ionization; (ii) Matrix Assisted Laser Desorption Ionization; (iii) Tandom mass spectrometry; (iv) Applications of mass spectrophotometry.

10 Electron Spin Resonance and Nuclear Magnetic Resonance Spectroscopy

All substances are magnetic. Magnetism arises from the motion of charged particles. This motion is controlled by internal forces in a system. These forces exist in the form of chemical bonds. These bonds are responsible for adjusting the pair of electrons carrying opposite charges. When two electrons are present in the same atomic orbit, they spin in opposite directions as a result any magnetic effect is effectively neutralized. Similarly protons of the nucleus of an atom do not show any overall magnetic effect. However, in certain situations, electrons may become delocalized. These unpaired electrons or protons will impart, a magnetic moment to the species which will act in a manner comparable to the magnet. Moreover, it can interact with an applied magnetic field, if any. Such interactions form the basis of magnetic resonance spectroscopy.

Thus electron magnetic resonance (EMR) refers to the spectroscopy of unpaired electrons. Some aspects of this technique are termed as electron spin resonance spectroscopy (ESR) and **electron paramagnetic resonance spectroscopy** (EPR). A paramagnetic material is one that can be attracted by an external magnetic field, magnetic field, whereas a diamagnetic substance is rejected. It is the number of nucleons (protons + neutrons) that determine whether a species will exhibit nuclear paramagnetism or not. Certain metals such as iron, cobalt and nickel are the extreme case of paramagnetism that is termed as ferromagnetism.

Electron Spin Resonance and Spin-trapping

Electron spin resonance (ESR) is a technique that can be applied to study free radicals, since it detects the presence of unpaired electrons. An unpaired electron has a spin of either + ½ or – ½ and behaves as a small magnet. If it is exposed to an external magnetic field, it can align itself either parallel or anti-parallel (in opposition) to that field, and thus can have two possible energy levels. If electromagnetic radiation of the correct energy is applied, it will be absorbed and used to move the electron from the lower energy level to the upper one. Thus an absorption spectrum is obtained, usually in the microwave region of the electromagnetic spectrum. For reasons that need not concern us, ESR spectrometers are set up to display **first-derivative spectra**, which show not the absorbance but the **rate of change of absorbance**, i.e. a point on the derivative curve corresponds to the gradient (slope) at the equivalent point on the absorption plot.

The condition to obtain an absorbance is:

$$\Delta E = g\beta H$$

where Δ is the energy gap between the two energy levels of the electron, H is the applied magnetic field, and β a constant known as the **Bohr magneton**. The value of g (the '**splitting factor**') for a free electron is 2·00232 and nearly all biologically important radicals have values close to this. Thus, if this equation is obeyed, an absorption spectrum results. For a single electron this can be crudely represented as follows —

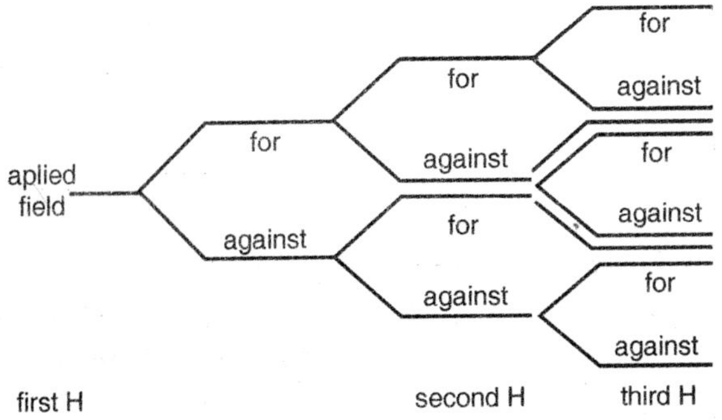

but, if presented as its first derivative (as ESR machines do) it will appear as —

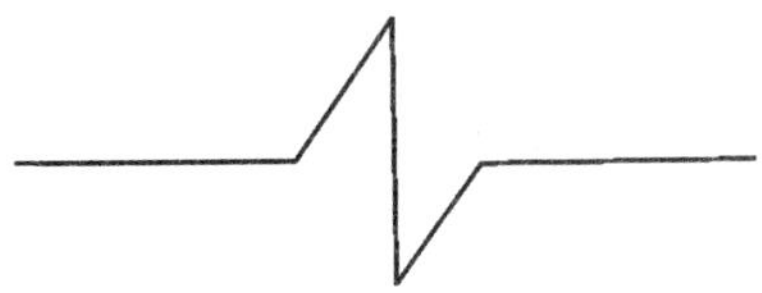

A number of atomic nuclei, such as those of hydrogen and nitrogen, also behave like small magnets and will align either parallel or antiparallel to the applied magnetic field. Thus in a hydrogen atom the single unpaired electron will actually see two different magnetic fields: the one applied plus that from the nucleus, or the one applied minus that from the nucleus. Thus there will be two energy absorptions and the single line becomes a doublet, i.e. or, as more usually  presented, If the unpaired electron 'sees' two

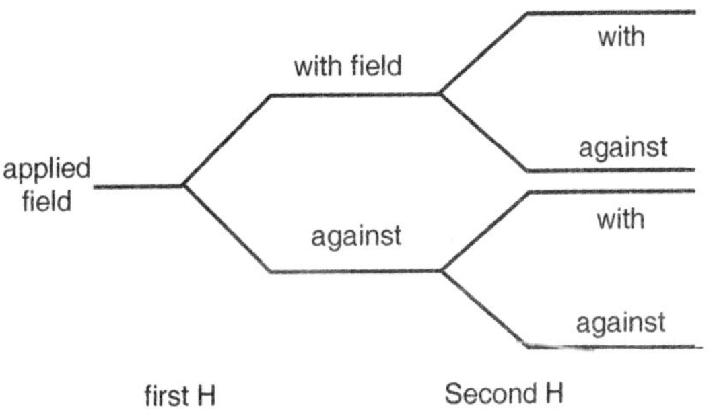

hydrogen nuclei, each can be aligned in the same way with the applied field, in opposite i.e.

Give a three-line spectrum in which the intensities are in the ratio 1:2:1, i.e.

In the **methyl radical**, CH_3, the unpaired electron on the carbon can see three hydrogen nuclei and the ESR spectrum contains four lines. Remembering that the field of each hydrogen nucleus can align for or against the applied magnetic field, a 'tree' diagram like that above can be used to predict the spectrum i.e.

or

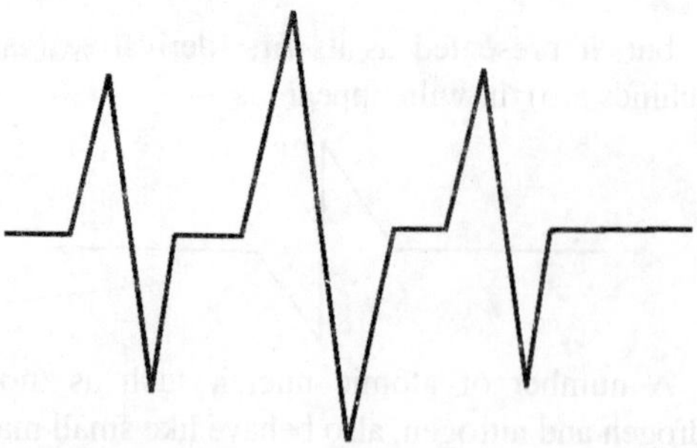

which therefore consists of four lines with intensity ratios 1:3:3:1.

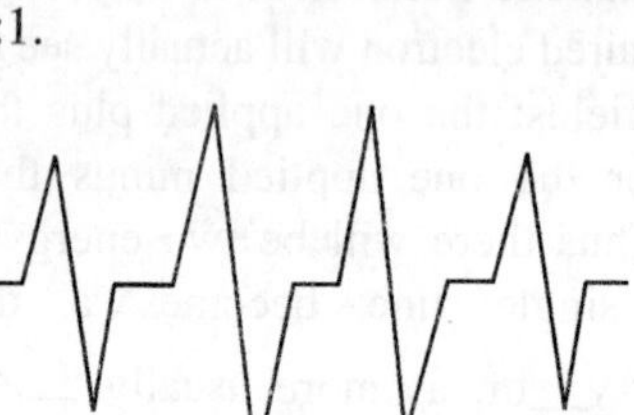

The number of lines in the ESR spectrum of a radical is called the **hyperfine structure** and is often very large in complicated radicals containing many nuclei. A radical can be identified from its ESR spectrum by looking at the g value, hyperfine structure, and line shape.

ESR is a very sensitive method and can detect radicals at concentrations as low as 10^{-10} mol^{-1}, provided that they stay around long energy to be measured. For very unstable radicals, a number of techniques are available to detect their presence. One can use flow systems whereby the radicals are continuously generated in the spectrometer so as to maintain a steady-state concentration. Another approach is to generate the radical in a frozen transparent solid matrix which prevents it from colliding with other species and undergoing reaction. Such a 'rapid-freezing' technique was used in 1969 by **P.F. Knowles** and others in England to identify the superoxide radical being produced in an enzyme-catalyzed reaction (xanthine oxidase catalyzing the oxidation of xanthine) by observing its ESR spectrum. By allowing the matrix to warm up, reactions of the radical can then be observed.

Another approach is **spin trapping**. A highly reactive radical, difficult to observe by normal ESR, is allowed to react with a compound to produce a long-lived radical. Reaction of nitroso compounds

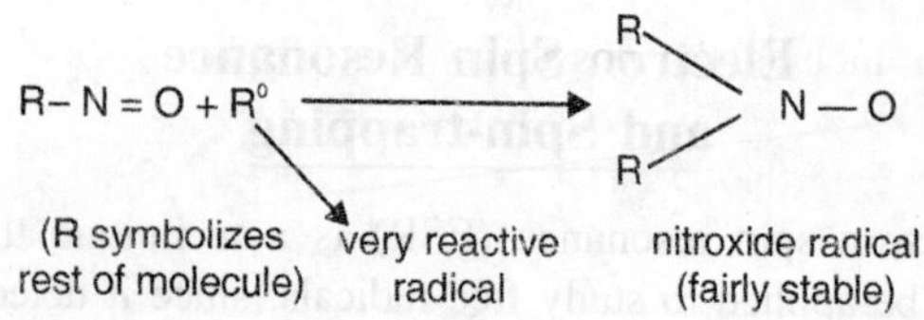

(R=NO) with radicals often produces nitroxide radicals that have a long lifetime.

Nitrones ($R=N^{+}-O^{-}$) also produce nitroxide radicals in a similar reaction.

Spin-trapping methods have often been used to detect the presence of superoxide and hydroxyl radicals during lipid peroxidation. Table 1 shows some of the trapping molecules that have been used, **DMPO (5,5-dimethylpyroline-N-oxide)** being especially popular. The 'ideal' trap should react rapidly and specifically with the radical one wants to study, to produce a product that is stable and has a highly characteristic ESR spectrum. It is also worth noting that if a biological process is dependent on, say, hydroxyl radicals, then addition of a trap that reacts with such radicals will inhibit the process to an extent that depends on how much trap DMPO inhibits ethanol oxidation by the MEOS system as it removes the $OH^{\bullet}$% required. None of the spin-type used at present is ideal, although better ones are being developed. For example, DMPO reacts with both $OH^{\bullet}$% and O_2^- radicals to form products with different ESR spectra (Fig.1). The second-order rate constants for the reactions are very different however, approximately 10 M^{-1} s^{-1} for O_2^- and $3{\cdot}4 \times 10^9$ for OH. Unfortunately, the product of reaction of DMPO with O_2^- is unstable and decomposes to form the same product as is given by direct reaction with OH. One way around this problem is to add ethanol to the system. If the OH signal observed was due to a reaction of DMPO directly with OH, then ethanol scavenges OH and should abolish the signal. Further, the reaction of OH with ethanol produces a hydroxyethyl radical that reacts with DMPO to give another adduct with a different ESR spectrum. This spectrum should be observed as the OH signal disappears. If however, the signal arose from decomposition of a O_2^- adduct then ethanol should have no effect, since it does not react with O_2^-. This is by no means the only 'artefact' identified in the use of DMPO, however, other include the possibility that decomposition of the DMPO–OOH adduct (formed by reaction with O_2^-) into the DMPO to a system producing O_2^- might cause small amounts of OH to be formed.

Since the trapping molecules commonly used (Table 1) are commercially available, any laboratory with access to ESR facilities can carry out spin-trapping experiments and 'identify' all sorts of oxygen and organic radicals in biological systems.

Aromatic hydroxylation (i.e. compounds containing benzene rings) react extremely rapidly with hydroxyl radicals, the first product being a **hydroxycyclohexadienyl** radical, e.g. for benzene.

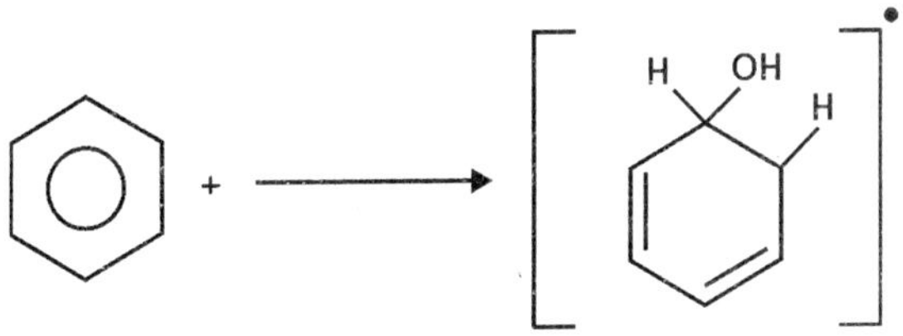

Such radicals can undergo several reactions, e.g. to give a product that can decompose under appropriate conditions to give biphenyl, or undergoing a disproportionation reaction to give a mixture of phenol and benzene

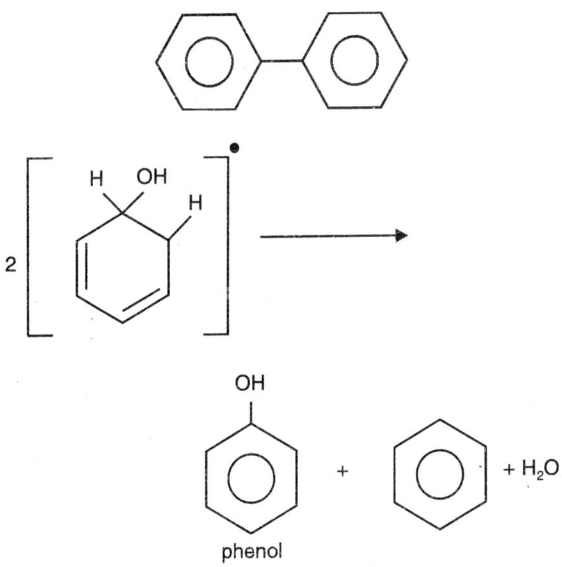

Disproportionation is any reaction in which one molecule is reduced and an identical molecule oxidized. In this case one radical molecule is being reduced to benzene and another oxidized to phenol.

The attack of OH upon phenol itself produces a mixture of hydroxylated products, the 1,3-product being found in much smaller yields than is the 1,2- or 1,4-product.

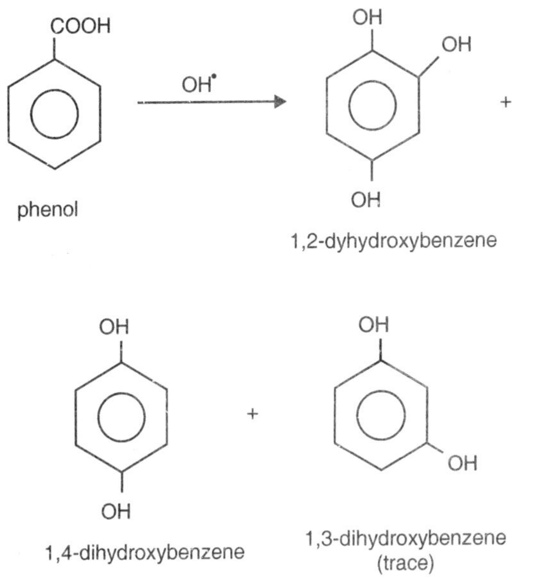

If 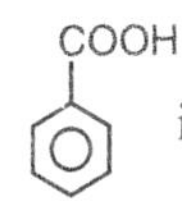 is used, one of the side reactions results in loss of the carboxyl group as carbon dioxide with probable formation of phenol, although this is likely to be only a minor reaction pathway.

The formation of hydroxylated products from aromatic compounds has been used to detect the formation of hydroxyl radicals in several biochemical systems, the products being identified either by gas-liquid chromatography, by 'colour reactions', or by their fluorescence spectra. An alterative approach has been to add benzoic acid labelled with the isotope ^{14}C in the carboxyl group, and measure the production of radioactive $^{14}CO_2$ by radiochemical techniques. Table 2 shows the former method being used to detect hydroxyl radicals produced during the oxidation of xanthine catalyzed by the enzyme xanthine oxidase.

Conversion of Methional and Related Compounds Into Ethane Gas (C_2H_4)

This assay method, developed in Professor Fridovich's laboratory in the USA, was the first

Table 1. **A selection of the 'spin traps' that have been used in biological systems**

Name	Abbreviation	Structure
tert-Nitrosobutane (nitroso-*tert*-butane)	tNB (NtB)	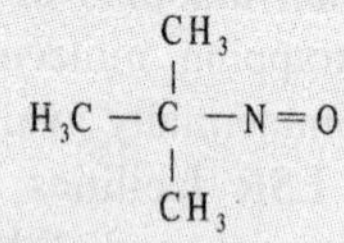
α-Phenyl-*tert*-butylnitrone	PBN	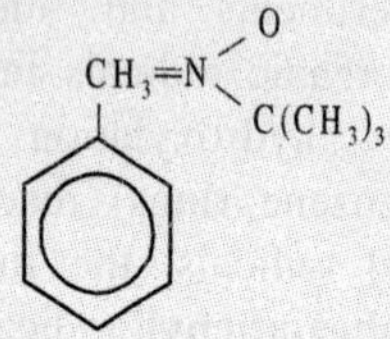
5,5,-Dimethylpyrroline-*N*-oxide	DMPO	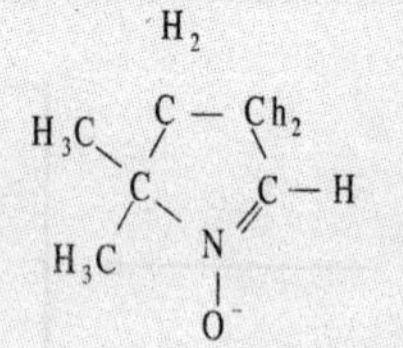
tert-Butylnitrosobenzene	BNB	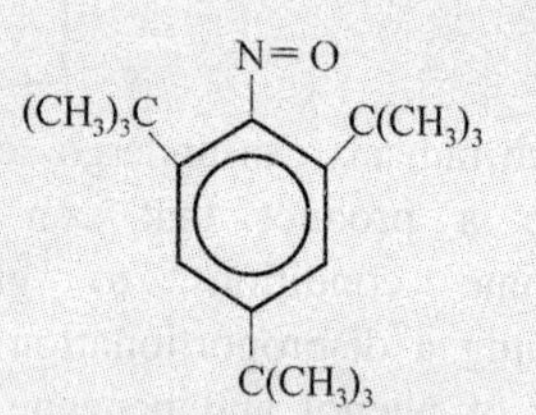
α-(4-Pyridyl-l-oxide)-*N*-terit-butylnitrone	4-POBN	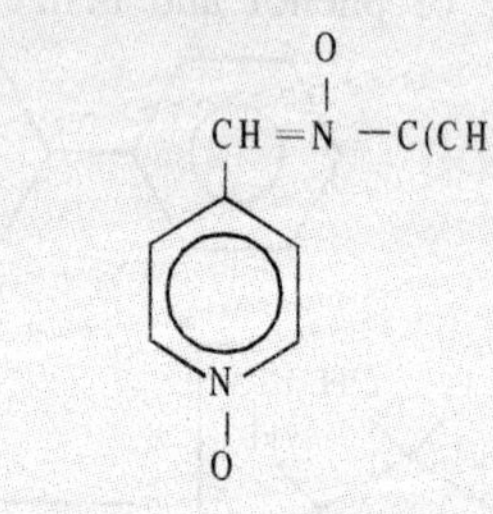

used to show formation of hydroxyl radicals in a biological system. Methional, which has the structure $CH_3 - S - CH_2 - CH_2 - CHP$, reacts with hydroxyl radicals in a very complex series of reactions to form ethane ($H_2C - CH_2$) gas, which may be measured by gas-liquid chromatography. The amino acid methionine and the compound KTBA (2-keto-4-thiomethylbutanoic acid) also release ethane upon exposure to hydroxyl radicals. Ethane formation from these compounds is not specific as a test for the hydroxyl radical since there are several other oxidizing radicals that can convert them into ethane. However, Fridovich's group showed that formation of ethane in the system that they studied was inhibited by compounds that react with the hydroxyl radical in the way expected from their known rate-constants. If the ethane formation is due to OH, then addition of, say sodium formate at a concentration that competes with methional for the OH should decrease ethane formation. Addition of an equal concentration of ethanol should inhibit more, and urea, which reacts only slowly with OH should have little inhibitory effect. If the ethane formation is inhibited by OH scavengers to extents that can be correlated with known rate-constants for reactions of these compounds with OH then it can probably be attributed to OH.

Table 2. **Formation of hydroxyl radicals during the oxidation of xanthine by xanthine oxidase.**

Reagent added	Rate constant for reaction with OH (M^{-1} s^{-1})	Amount of hydroxylated products formed (n moles)	Percentage inhibition of hydroxylation
None	–	102	–
Mannitol (2nM)	2.7×10^9	64	37
Sodium formate (5 nM)	2.7×10^9	49	52
Thiourea (5 mM)	4.7×10^9	24	76
Urea (5 mM)	$< 7.0 \times 10^5$	102	0

Other methods

Hydroxyl radical reacts with many other compounds to give products that can be easily detected. It is essential that 'scavenger' experiments be performed to show whether or not the radical producing the product is indeed OH or something else.

Instrumentation

As shown in the following figure, the ESR spectrophotometer is equipped with electromagnets, a monochromatic system to produce microwave radiation and a cathode ray oscilloscope is used as a recorder. The electromagnetic field generated by the electromagnets can be manipulated in the range of 50 to 500 millitesla, and variations of less then 1 in 10^6 are required for highest accuracy. The monochromatic microwave radiation is produced using a **Klystron oscillator**, the wavelength being in the range of 3×10^{-2} m (9000 MHz).

The sample are required to be in the solid state; hence biological samples are usually frozen in liquid nitrogen. In ESR the differential spectrum is obtained. This means a difference between absolute reduced spectrum minus the absolute oxidized spectrum (dA/dH). Hence a figure similar to that as shown in following figure is obtained. This shape is called a 'line' in ESR spectroscopy. The presence of a few unpaired electrons in a molecule results in the formation of several (about 10) lines which are irregularly paced.

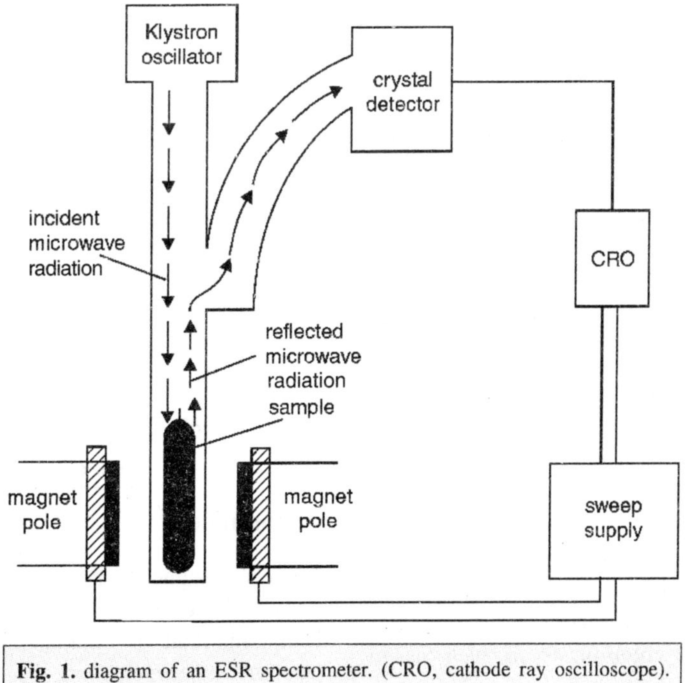

Fig. 1. diagram of an ESR spectrometer. (CRO, cathode ray oscilloscope).

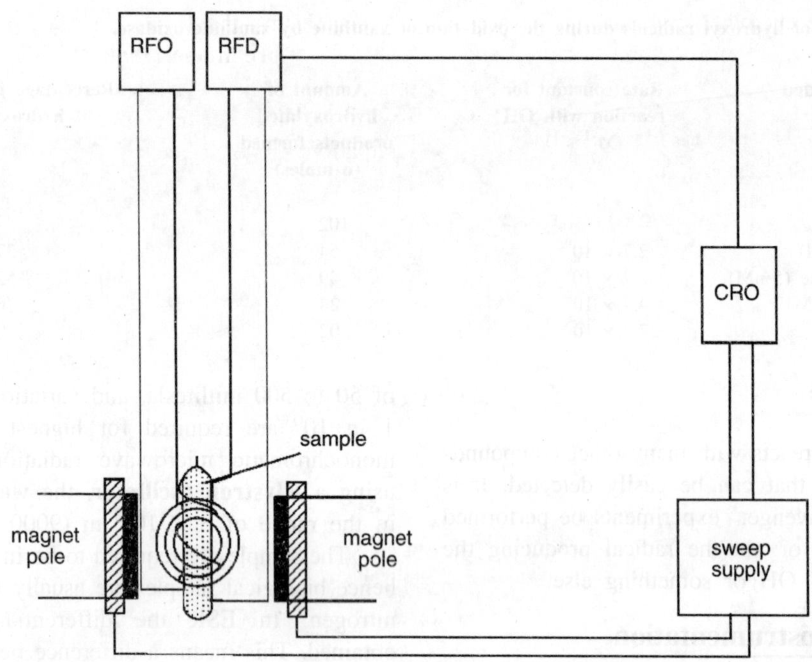

Fig. 2. Diagram of an NMR spectrometer. CRO, (cathode ray oscilloscope), RFO, (radio frequency oscillator) RFD, (radio frequency detector).

Applications

ESR techniques are used, nowadays, in biological, biochemical, enzymological, pharmacological, toxicological and cancer biology studies. A few examples of its application can be described as follows—

(1) ESR spectrophotometry is widely used in determining the generation of free radicals. Metabolism of several drugs, chemicals, carcinogens etc. in the microsomes of liver generate free radicals e.g. superoxide anion, nitric oxides (NO), hydrogen peroxide etc. Since they are unstable, spin trapping is used to make them stable using compounds such as 5,5-demethylpyroline N-oxide (DMPO).

(2) It is one of the main methods used to study the metalloproteins particularly those containing molybdenum, (xanthine oxidase), copper (cytochrome oxidase) and iron (cytochrome, ferredoxin). The appearance and disappearence of their ESR signals are used to monitor their activity in the multienzyme systems of their mitochondria and chloroplasts as well as in isolated enzymes.

(3) ESR spectrophotometry is used in membrane studies as well. Intramolecular motions and lateral diffusion of lipids through the membrane may be observed and measured. Spin trapping in such studies is made using 2,2,6,6-tetramethyl piperidine-1-oxyl (**TEMPOL**).

(4) Phosphorescent molecules may also be studied by ESR. This data is complimentary to that obtained by ultraviolet region of the spectrum.

(5) It has been found that, free radicals initiate the formation of neoplasia. Chemical carcinogenesis is also attributed to free radicals. These free radicals are monitored by ESR.

(6) Irradiated food shifts can also be monitored for residual free radicals.

Nuclear Magnetic Resonance Spectroscopy

Introduction

Nuclear Magnetic Resonance spectroscopy is a powerful and theoretically complex analytical tool. It is important to remember that, with NMR, we perform experiments on the **nuclei** of atoms, not the electrons. The chemical environment of specific nuclei is deduced from information obtained about the nuclei.

Nuclear Spin and the Splitting of Energy Levels in a Magnetic Field

Subatomic particles (electrons, protons and neutrons) can be imagined as spinning on their axes. In many atoms (such as ^{12}C) these spins are paired against each other, so that the nucleus of the atom has no overall spin. However, in some atoms (such as ^{1}H and ^{13}C) the nucleus does possess an overall spin. The rules for determining the net spin of a nucleus are as follows:

(1) If the number of neutrons **and** the number of protons are both even, then the nucleus has **NO** spin.

(2) If the number of neutrons **plus** the number of protons is odd, then the nucleus has a half-integer spin (i.e. 1/2, 3/2, 5/2)

(3) If the number of neutrons **and** the number of protons are both odd, then the nucleus has an integer spin (i.e. 1, 2, 3)

The overall spin, I, is important. Quantum mechanics tells us that a nucleus of spin I will have $2I + 1$ possible orientations. A nucleus with spin 1/2 will have 2 possible orientations. In the absence of an external magnetic field, these orientations are of equal energy. If a magnetic field is applied, then the energy levels split. Each level is given a **magnetic quantum number, m**.

Energy levels for a nucleus with spin quantum number 1/2

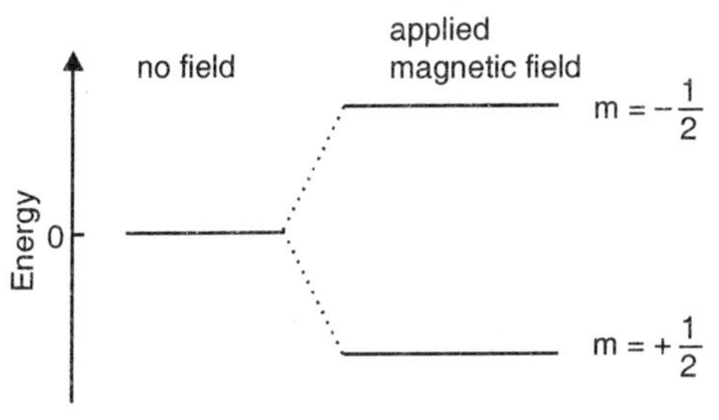

When the nucleus is in a magnetic field, the initial populations of the energy levels are determined by thermodynamics, as described by the Boltzmann distribution. This is very important, and it means that **the lower energy level will contain slightly more nuclei than the higher level**. It is possible to excite these nuclei into the higher level with electromagnetic radiation. The frequency of radiation needed is determined by the difference in energy between the energy levels.

Calculating Transition Energy

The nucleus has a positive charge and is spinning. This generates a small magnetic field. The nucleus therefore possesses a magnetic moment, μ, which is proportional to its spin, I.

The constant, γ, is called the **magnetogyric ratio** and is a fundamental nuclear constant which has a different value for every nucleus. h is Plancks constant.

$$\mu = \frac{\gamma I h}{2\pi}$$

The energy of a particular energy level is given by;

$$E = -\frac{\gamma h}{2\pi} mB$$

Where B is the strength of the magnetic field **at the nucleus**.

The difference in energy between levels (the transition energy) can be found from

$$\Delta E = -\frac{\gamma h B}{2\pi} mB$$

This means that if the magnetic field, B, is increased, so is ΔE. It also means that if a nucleus has a relatively large magnetogyric ratio, then ΔE is correspondingly large.

The Absorption of Radiation by a Nucleus in a Magnetic Field

In this discussion, we will be taking a "classical" view of the behaviour of the nucleus - that is, the behaviour of a charged particle in a magnetic field.

Imagine a nucleus (of spin 1/2) in a magnetic field. This nucleus is in the lower energy level (i.e. its magnetic moment does not oppose the applied field). The nucleus is spinning on its axis. In the presence of a magnetic field, this axis of rotation will *precess* around the magnetic field;

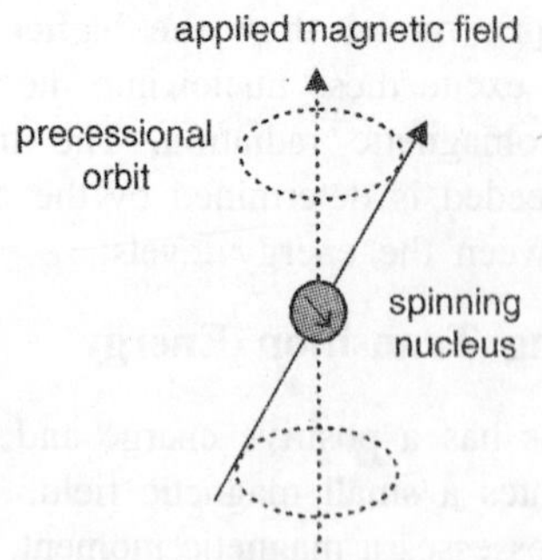

The frequency of precession is termed the **Larmor frequency**, which is identical to the transition frequency.

The potential energy of the precessing nucleus is given by;

$$E = -\mu\ B\ \cos\ \theta$$

where θ is the angle between the direction of the applied field and the axis of nuclear rotation.

If energy is absorbed by the nucleus, then the angle of precession, θ, will change. For a nucleus of spin 1/2, absorption of radiation "flips" the magnetic moment so that it **opposes** the applied field (the higher energy state).

It is important to realise that only a small proportion of "target" nuclei are in the lower energy state (and can absorb radiation). There is the possibility that by exciting these nuclei, the populations of the higher and lower energy levels will become equal. If this occurs, then there will be **no** further absorption of radiation. The spin system is **saturated**. The possibility of saturation means that we must be aware of the relaxation processes which return nuclei to the lower energy state.

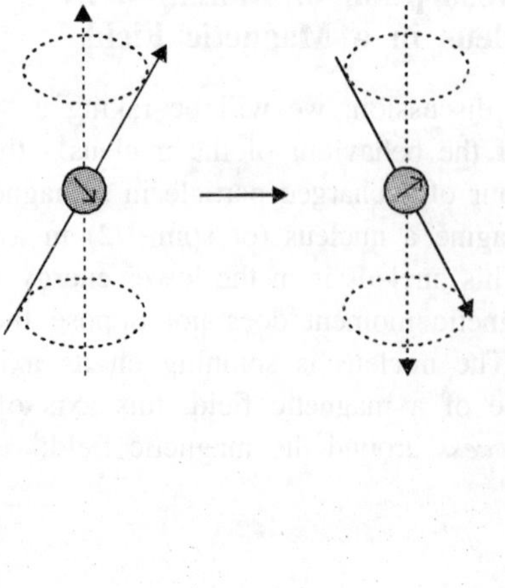

Relaxation Processes

How do nuclei in the higher energy state return to the lower state? Emission of radiation is insignificant because the probability of re-emission of photons varies with the cube of the frequency. At radio frequencies, re-emission is negligible. We must focus on non-radiative relaxation processes (thermodynamics!).

Ideally, the NMR spectroscopist would like relaxation rates to be fast - but not too fast. If the relaxation rate is fast, then saturation is reduced. If the relaxation rate is too fast, line-broadening in the resultant NMR spectrum is observed.

There are two major relaxation processes;

- Spin – lattice (longitudinal) relaxation
- Spin – spin (transverse) relaxation

Spin–Lattice Relaxation

Nuclei in an NMR experiment are in a sample. The sample in which the nuclei are held is called the **lattice**. Nuclei in the lattice are in vibrational and rotational motion, which creates a complex magnetic field. The magnetic field caused by motion of nuclei within the lattice is called the **lattice field**. This lattice field has many components. Some of these components will be equal in frequency and phase to the Larmor frequency of the nuclei of interest. These components of the lattice field can interact with nuclei in the higher energy state, and cause them to lose energy (returning to the lower state). The energy that a nucleus loses increases the amount of vibration and rotation within the lattice (resulting in a tiny rise in the temperature of the sample).

The relaxation time, T_1 (the average lifetime of nuclei in the higher energy state) is dependant on the magnetogyric ratio of the nucleus and the mobility of the lattice. As mobility increases, the vibrational and rotational frequencies increase, making it more likely for a component of the lattice field to be able to interact with excited nuclei. However, at extremely high mobilities, the probability of a component of the lattice field being able to interact with excited nuclei decreases.

Spin–Spin Relaxation

Spin – spin relaxation describes the interaction between neighbouring nuclei with identical processional frequencies but differing magnetic quantum states. In this situation, the nuclei can exchange quantum states; a nucleus in the lower energy level will be excited, while the excited nucleus relaxes to the lower energy state. There is no **net** change in the populations of the energy states, but the average lifetime of a nucleus in the excited state will decrease. This can result in line-broadening.

Chemical Shift

The magnetic field at the nucleus is **not** equal to the applied magnetic field; electrons around the nucleus shield it from the applied field. The difference between the applied magnetic field and the field at the nucleus is termed the **nuclear shielding**.

Consider the s-electrons in a molecule. They have spherical symmetry and circulate in the applied field, producing a magnetic field which opposes the applied field. This means that the applied field strength must be increased for the nucleus to absorb at its transition frequency. This **upfield shift** is also termed **diamagnetic shift**.

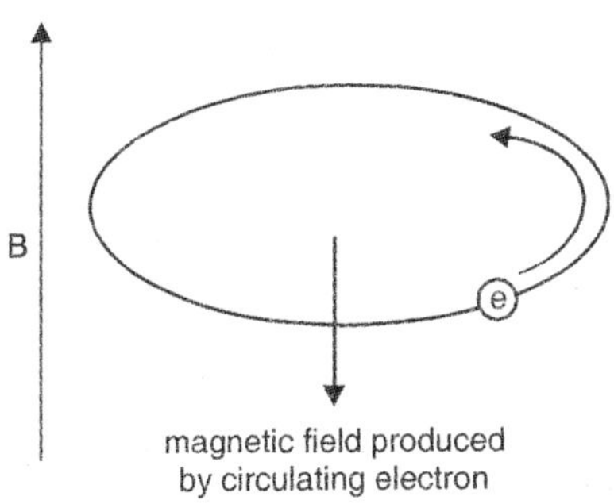

Electrons in p-orbitals have **no** spherical symmetry. They produce comparatively large magnetic fields at the nucleus, which give a **low field shift**. This "deshielding" is termed **paramagnetic shift**.

In proton (^1H) NMR, p-orbitals play no part (there aren't any!), which is why only a small range of chemical shift (10 ppm) is observed. We can easily see the effect of s-electrons on the chemical shift by looking at substituted methanes, CH_3X. As X becomes increasingly electronegative, so the electron density around the protons decreases, and they resonate at lower field strengths (increasing δ_H values).

Chemical shift is defined as **nuclear shielding / applied magnetic field.** Chemical shift is a function of the nucleus and its environment. It is measured relative to a reference compound. For ^1H NMR, the reference is usually tetramethylsilane, Si $(CH_3)_4$.

Spin–Spin Coupling

Consider the structure of ethanol;

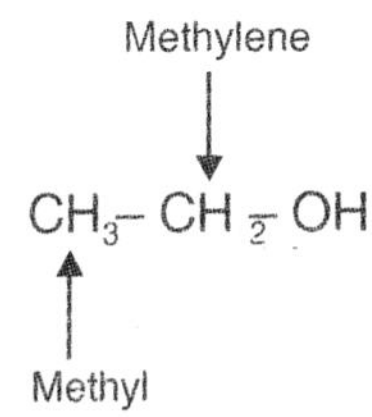

The ^1H NMR spectrum of ethanol (below) shows the methyl peak has been split into three peaks (**a triplet**) and the methylene peak has been split into four peaks (**a quartet**). This occurs because there is a small interaction (**coupling**) between the two groups of protons. The spacings between the peaks of the methyl triplet are equal to the spacings between the peaks of the methylene quartet. This spacing is measured in Hertz and is called the **coupling constant, J**.

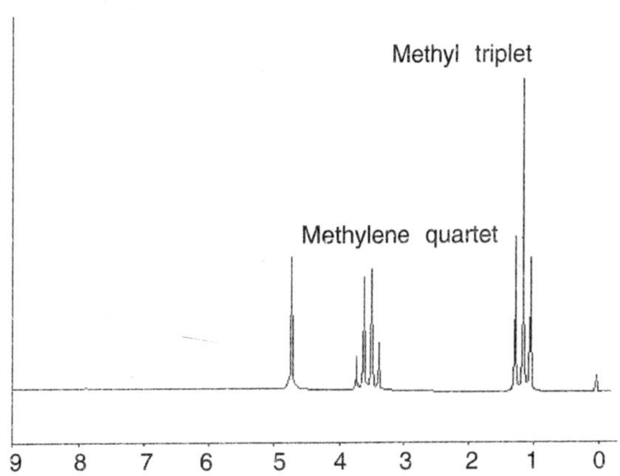

To see why the methyl peak is split into a triplet, let's look at the **methylene** protons. There are two of them, and each can have one of two possible orientations (aligned with or opposed against the applied field). This gives a total of four possible states;

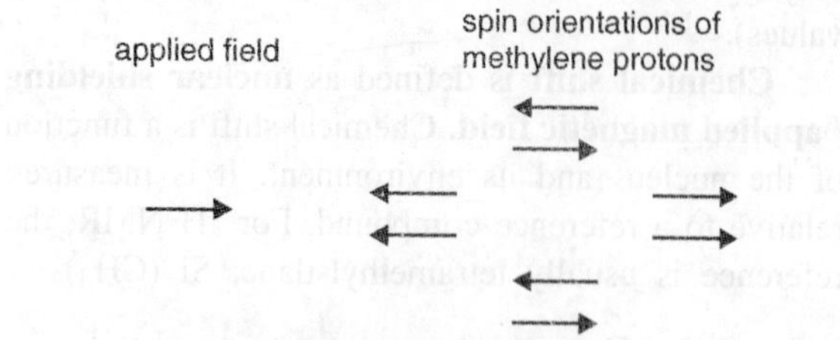

In the first possible combination, spins are paired and opposed to the field. This has the effect of reducing the field experienced by the **methyl** protons; therefore a slightly higher field is needed to bring them to resonance, resulting in an upfield shift. Neither combination of spins opposed to each other has an effect on the methyl peak. The spins paired in the direction of the field produce a downfield shift. Hence, the methyl peak is split into three, with the ratio of areas 1:2:1.

Similarly, the effect of the methyl protons on the methylene protons is such that there are eight possible spin combinations for the three methyl protons;

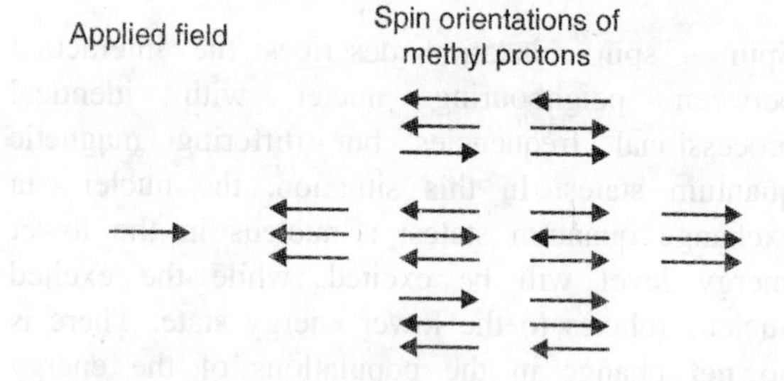

Out of these eight groups, there are two groups of three magnetically equivalent combinations. The methylene peak is split into a quartet. The areas of the peaks in the quartet have the ration 1:3:3:1.

In a **first-order** spectrum (where the chemical shift between interacting groups is much larger than their coupling constant), interpretation of splitting patterns is quite straightforward;

- The multiplicity of a multiplet is given by the number of equivalent **protons** in **neighbouring** atoms plus one, i.e. **the n + 1 rule**
- Equivalent nuclei do not interact with each other. The three methyl protons in ethanol cause splitting of the neighbouring methylene

Fig. 3. 500 MHz FT-NMR Spectrometer, Bruker DRX 500.

protons; they do not cause splitting among themselves

- The coupling constant is not dependant on the applied field. Multiplets can be easily distinguished from closely spaced chemical shift peaks.

Instrumentation

Instrument design of NMR spectrophotometer is more or less similar to ESR instrument. It is comprised of the following —

(1) A sample tube
(2) Radio-frequency oscillator
(3) Radio-frequency detector
(4) Cathode ray oscilloscope

Instead of Klystron oscillator, two sets of coils, a transmitter and receive of the appropriate radio frequency (RF) are used.

Samples in solutions are contained in sealed tubes which are rotated rapidly in a cavity to eliminate irregularities and imperfections. This process helps in creating a uniform signal which is received by the receiver and recorded.

Sophisticated electronics and advanced computer technology is used nowadays in solid state, high field and multidimensional NMR to be performed. These methods allow even difficult analysis to be made.

Applications

Most of the observations by NMR are made in solution. To remove the effects of solvent, deuterated solvent is used. Important applications of NMR are described below.

(1) Molecular structure and confirmational changes of molecules can be determined by NMR.
(2) The technique along with infrared and x-ray diffraction data is used in molecular modeling methods using sophisticated computer techniques.
(3) High resolution protein structures for example antiviral protein BDS-1, the $C3_a$ and $C5_a$ inflammatory proteins, plastocyanin, thioredoxin, epidermal growth factor and the interleukins have been elucidated by NMR.
(4) The technique has been applied to study enzyme kinetics e.g. trypsin, chymotropsin, papain, pepsin, thermolysin, adenylate and pyruvate kinases, alkaline phosphatase, ATPase and ribonuclease, both *in vivo* and *in vitro*.
(5) Structural studies on both DNA and RNA can be made under different experimental conditions viz: drug-DNA interaction, DNA-binding proteins.
(6) Interactions between proteins and lipid bilayers in membranes have been observed to predict their possible biological functions. e.g. bacteriorhodopsin, rhodopsin, phase coat proteins and alamethicin.
(7) Intracellular and extracellular inorganic phosphate concentrations may be measured in living cells and tissues.

NMR spectroscopy is used in several other studies. The examples described above indicate that a wide variety of structural, kinetic and molecular dynamic studies are possible through NMR spectroscopy.

Important Questions

1. What are electron spin resonance and electron magnetic resonance?
2. Discuss the principle of electron spin resonance spectroscopy and its applications.
3. Describe the instrument design of NMR spectroscopy and its applications.
4. Write short notes on :
   (i) Spin trapping methods, (ii) Bohr magnaton, (iii) DMPO.

11 X-Ray Diffraction

In 1912 **Knipping** and **Frinedrich** in Laue's laboratory performed the first X-ray diffraction experiment with a crystal. Their result showed at the same time that X-rays behave as waves and that crystals display a high degree of order in arranging their atoms, ions or molecules. The crystal acts as a three-dimensional grating and diffracts X rays just as visible light is diffracted by an optical grating. Since 1912, **X-ray crystallography** has had an enormous impact on chemistry and biology. At first, great triumphs were obtained in the field of inorganic chemistry. The structures of simple ionic compounds and of complex structures, like the silicates, became understood, and ionic radii could be measured with high accuracy. Unlike inorganic compounds that are mainly ionic, organic compounds consist of molecules. The intensity of the beams diffracted by organic compounds is relatively low and, in the beginning, progress was slow in determining their structures. However, the introduction of improved hardware and **Fourier analysis** solved the problem, and now the X-ray structure determination of a small or medium-sized organic molecule is an easy job, at least when good quality crystals are examined.

Only a few decades ago, virtually nothing was known about the three-dimensional structures of nucleic acids, proteins, and polysaccharides. Today, largely as a result of the technique of x-ray diffraction, many of these molecules are understood at a level of detail that would have surprised the biochemists of 1950. The method is complicated and it is possible to give only a brief introduction here, describing what is measured and what can be obtained.

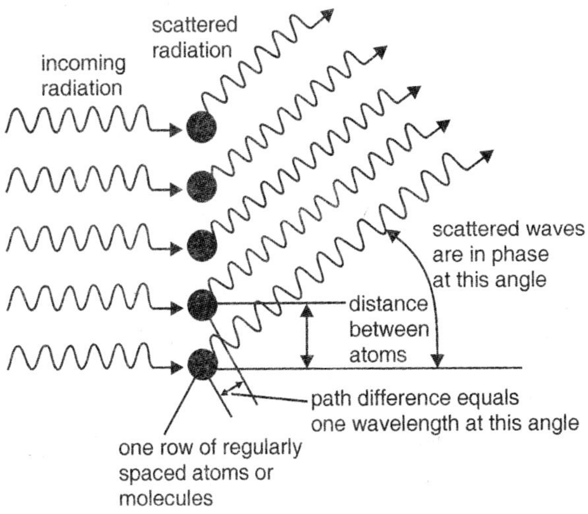

Fig. 1. Diffraction from a very simple structure – a row of atoms or molecules.

When a radiation is allowed to pass through a regular, repeating structure, **diffraction** is observed. This means that radiation scattered by the repeating elements in the structure shows reinforcement of the scattered waves in certain specific directions and weakening of the waves in other directions. A simple example is given in Figure 1, which shows radiation being scattered from a row of equally spaced atoms. Only in certain directions will the scattered waves be in phase and therefore constructively interfere with (reinforce) one another. In all other directions they will be out of phase and destructively interfere with one another. Thus, a diffraction pattern is generated. For the diffraction pattern to be sharp, it is essential that the wavelength of the radiation used be somewhat shorter than the regular spacing between the elements of the structure. This is why x-rays are used in studying molecules, since x-rays typically have a wavelength of only a few tenths of a nanometer. If the regular spacing in the object being studied is large (as in a window screen), we can observe exactly the same phenomenon with visible light, which has a wavelength thousands of times longer than x-rays. We will find that a point source, seen through a window screen, gives a rectangular diffraction pattern of spots.

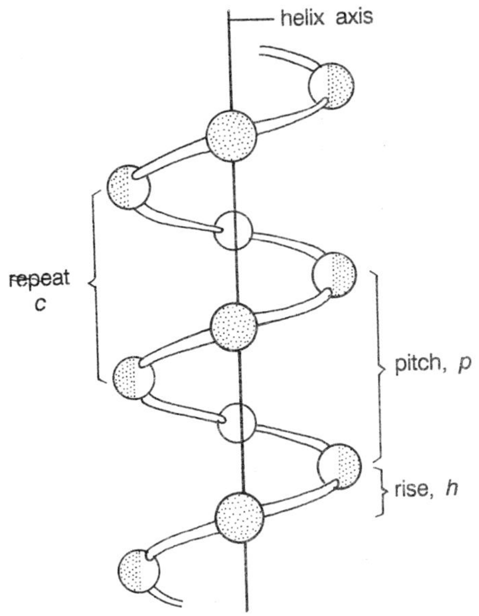

Fig. 2. A simple hellcal molecule.

The rule relating the periodic spacings in object and diffraction pattern is simple : short spacings in the periodic structures correspond to large spacings in the diffraction pattern, and vice versa. In addition, by determining the relative intensities of different spots, we can tell how matter is distributed within each repeat of the structure.

Fiber Diffraction

We consider first the diffraction from helical molecules, aligned approximately parallel to the axis of a stretched fiber. A helical molecule, like the one shown in Figure 2, is characterized by certain parameters:

The repeat (c) of the helix is the distance parallel to the axis in which I the structure exactly repeats itself. The repeat contains some integral number (n) of polymer residues. In Figure 2, $n = 4$.

The pitch (p) of the helix is the distance parallel to the helix axis in which the helix makes one turn. If there is an integral number of residues per turn (as here), the pitch and repeat are equal.

The rise (h) of the helix is the distance parallel to the axis from the level of one residue to the next,

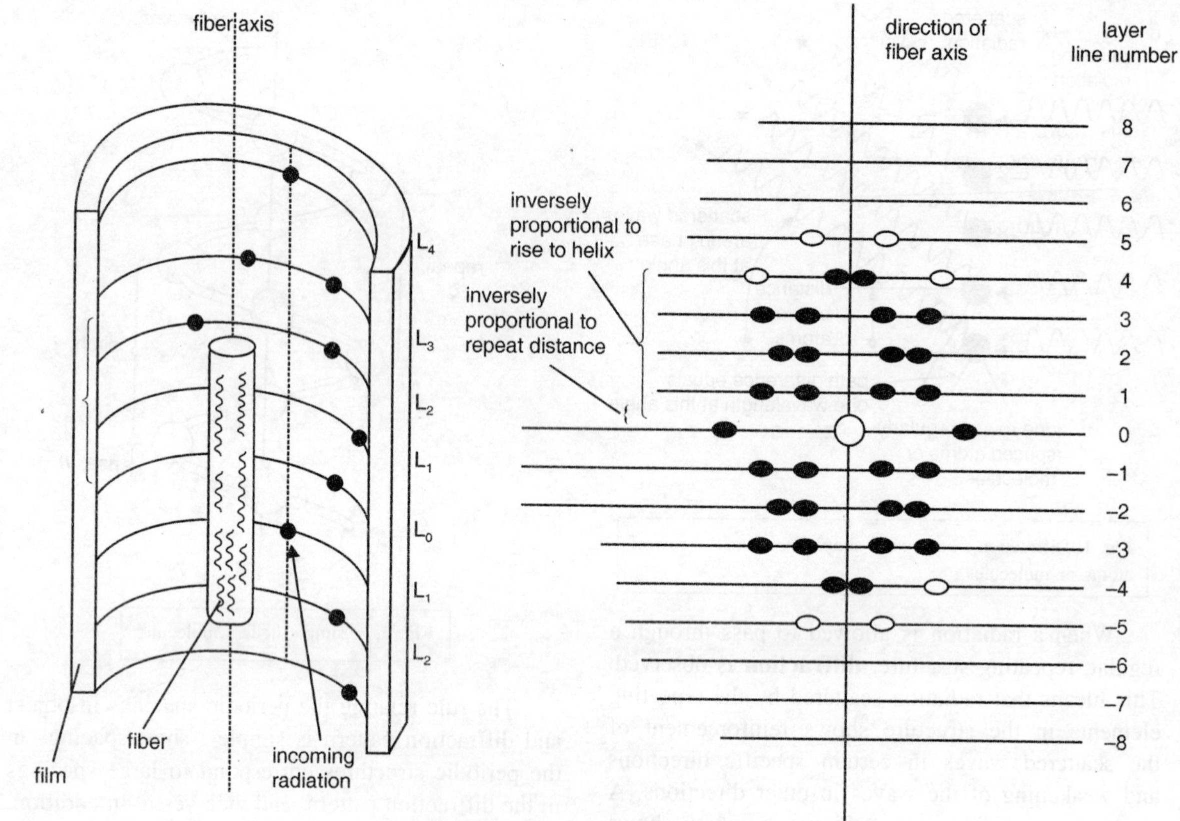

Fig. 3. Diffraction from fibrers (A) A fiber in an x-ray beam. (B) The diffraction pattern.

so **h = dn**. If we think of a spiral staircase as an example of a helix, the rise is the height of each step and the pitch is the distance from where one is standing to the corresponding spot directly overhead.

Suppose we wish to investigate a polymer with the helical structure shown in Figure 2. A fiber is pulled from a concentrated solution of the polymer. Stretching the fiber further will produce approximate alignment of the long helical molecules with the fiber axis. The fiber is then placed in an x-ray beam, and a photographic film is positioned behind it, as shown in Figure 3a. The diffraction pattern, which consists of spots or short arcs, will look like that in Figure 3b. It can be read as follows: According to the mathematics of diffraction theory, a helix always gives rise to this kind of cross-shaped pattern. Therefore, we know we are dealing with a helical structure. The spots all lie on lines perpendicular to the fiber axis; these are called layer lines. The spacing between these lines is inversely proportional to the repeat of the helix, *c*, which in this case equals the pitch. Note that the cross pattern repeats itself on every fourth layer line. This repetition pattern tells us that there are exactly 4.0 residues per turn in the helix. Thus, the rise in the helix is c/4. This is the kind of evidence that told **Watson** and **Crick** that B-DNA was a helix with 10 residues per turn.

The information above is given directly by the pattern. To find out exactly how all of the atoms in each residue are arranged in each repeat, a more detailed analysis is necessary. Usually, a model is made using the correct repeat, pitch, and rise. Model making is simplified because we know approximate bond lengths and the angles between many chemical bonds. The model must also be inspected to see that no two atoms approach closer than their vander Waals radii. From such a model, the intensities of the various spots can be predicted. These predictions are compared with the observed intensities, and the model is readjusted until a best fit is obtained. The initial determination of the structure of DNA was done in just this way. As one can see from Figure 4, real fiber diffraction patterns are not as neat as the idealized example, mainly because of incomplete alignment of the molecules.

Crystal Diffraction

To study molecular crystals such as those formed by small oligonucleotides, molecules like tRNA, and globular proteins, one faces a rather different problem from the study of helical fibers and proceeds in a quite different way. A schematic drawing of such a crystal is shown in Figure 4. The repeating unit is now the unit cell, which may contain one, two, or more molecules. The unit cell may be thought of as the basic building block of the crystal. Repetition of the unit cell in three dimensions (marked by arrows on the figure) creates the whole crystal. A simple two-dimensional analog of the crystal unit cell is the repeating pattern in wallpaper. No matter how random a wallpaper pattern may seem, if you stare at it long enough, you can always find a unit that, by repetition, fills the entire wall. Just as in fiber diffraction, passing an x-ray beam through a molecular crystal produces a diffraction pattern.

The pattern shown in Figure 5 was obtained from a crystal of a small DNA. Again, the spacing of the spots allows us to determine the repeating distances in the periodic structure — in this case the *x, y,* and *z* dimensions of the unit cell labelled *a, b,* and *c* in Figure 4. But the important information in crystal diffraction studies is just how the atoms are arranged within each unit cell, for that arrangement describes the molecule. Again, this information is contained in the relative intensities of the diffraction spots in a pattern like that shown in Figure 5, But in crystal diffraction, more exact

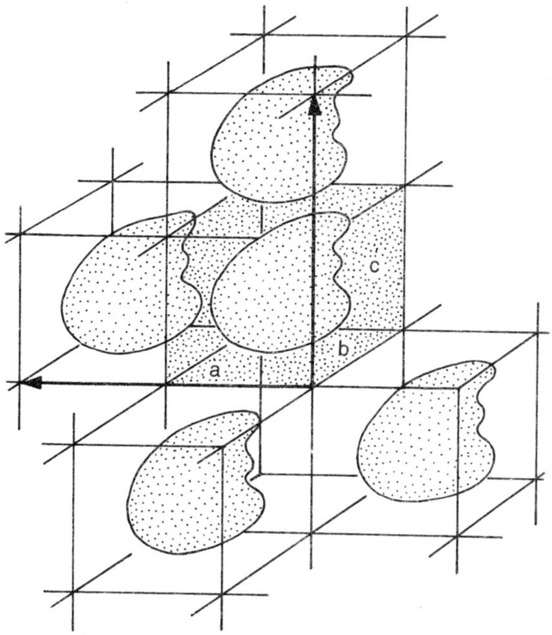

Fig. 4. Scheme drwaing of a molecular crystal.

information can be extracted than from a fiber diffraction pattern, because the corresponding molecules in each unit cell of the crystal are of the same shape and are oriented in the same way. In fiber diffraction, the helical molecules may all have their long axes pointed in the same direction, but they are rotated randomly about these axes. This difference in exactness of arrangement can be appreciated by comparing the sharpness of the crystal diffraction pattern shown in Figure 5 with the fiber pattern depicted in Figure 4.

After obtaining the diffraction pattern from a molecular crystal, the experimenter measures the intensities of a large number of the spots. If the molecule being studied is a small one, it is possible to proceed in much the same manner as with fiber patterns. A structure is guessed and expected intensities are calculated and compared with the observed intensities. The structure is refined until the relative intensities of all spots are correctly predicted. However, such a procedure won't work with a molecule as complex as the tRNA, there is simply no way to guess such a structure.

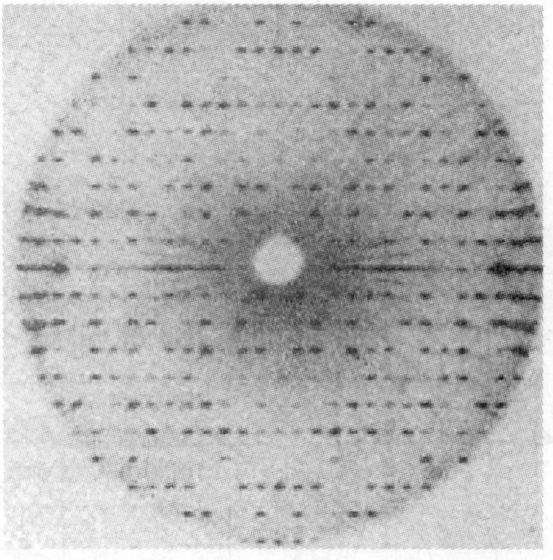

Fig. 5. Diffraction pattern produced by a molecular crystal of a small DNA.

Why not proceed directly from spot intensities to the structure? The difficulty is that some of the information contained in the spot intensities is hidden. To greatly simplify a complex problem, we may say that it is as if the quantities that the experimenter needed in order to deduce the structure (which are called structure factors) were the square roots of the intensities. *If the intensity has a value of, say, 25, the investigator knows that the number needed is +5 or - 5. But which? This sort of quandary is the essence of the **phase problem**, which prevented progress in large-molecule crystallography for many years. One way of solving the problem was discovered in the early 1950s. Suppose a heavy metal atom can be introduced into some point in the molecule in such a way that the molecule and crystal are otherwise unchanged. This process is called an isomorphous replacement. Now suppose the heavy metal contributes a value of +2 to the structure factor for the spot we were just discussing. If the original value was +5, its new value is +7 and its square is 49. If the original value was –5, the value now becomes ~3 and its square is 9. The investigator takes a diffraction photograph of the crystal with the heavy metal inserted. If the new crystal has an intensity 1 of 9 for this spot, the original structure factor must have been – 5 not +5. Although an oversimplification, this example gives the essence of the method.

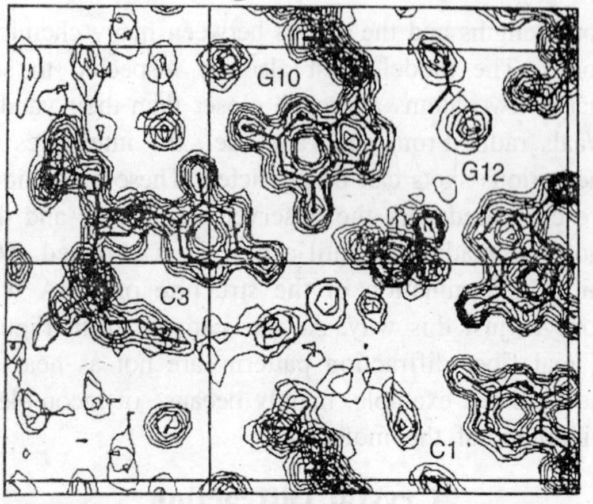

Fig. 6. Part of an electron density map derived from the DNA crystal diffraction pattern.

Usually multiple isomorphous replacements are necessary to determine the phases of the structure factors.

Given structure factors for all of the spots, the investigator can calculate the positions of all atoms in the unit cell. What is actually calculated is an electron density distribution (Fig. 6), but this amounts to the same thing, for regions of high electron density are where the atoms are. In the particular view shown in Figure 6, we are looking at a two-dimensional "slice" through the three-dimensional electron density distribution.

It is now appropriate to review the steps that must be taken to determine the three-dimensional structure of a macromolecule from crystal diffraction studies:

(1) Obtain satisfactory crystals. This step is often the hardest part of the procedure, for the crystals must be of good quality and at least a few tenths of a millimeter in minimum dimension. Crystals that are too small will not give sharp diffraction patterns. Getting macromolecules to crystallize well is still more of an art than a science.

(2) Record the diffraction pattern from the crystal, and measure the intensities of many of the spots.

(3) Find some way to make isomorphous replacements in the molecule. Usually two or more replacements are required.

(4) Repeat steps 1 and 2 for each isomorphous derivative.

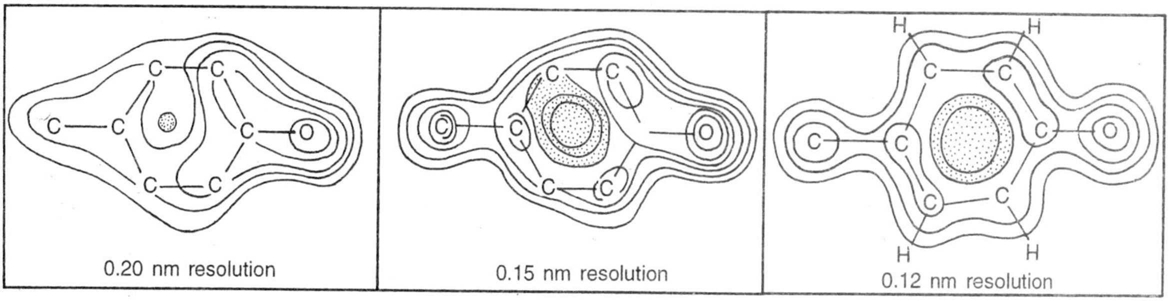

Fig. 7. Effect of increased resolution on molecular details observed by x-ray diffraction.

(5) Calculate structure factors and, from them, the electron density distribution. These calculations are usually done on a large computer.

In most cases, the investigator will first carry through this analysis with a relatively small number of spots. This procedure will give a **low-resolution** structure. If all is going well, more spots will be measured and the calculations refined to give higher resolution. With the best crystals, it is now possible to obtain resolutions of about 0.10 nm. This resolution is sufficient to identify individual groups and even some atoms and to show how they interact with one another. The detail in the phenolic ring of a protein side chain revealed at different resolutions is shown in Figure 7.

Most of the detailed three-dimensional structures of biological macromolecules shown in this book have been determined by x-ray diffraction studies of crystals. At present, hundreds of such structures are known. This knowledge represents an enormous amount of labor in many laboratories, but the results allow us to understand macro molecular function at a level that would have been unbelievable only a short time ago.

Fig. 8. X-ray diffraction spectrophometer.

Instrument

The beams diffracted by crystals of small compounds are usually detected and measured with a **diffractometer**. Using this instrument, the crystal can be rotated around three or four axes and can reach nearly every orientation. The diffracted beams are measured with a photon counter. Because the beams are measured one after the other, this process is slow and not very suitable for protein crystals where thousands of beams must be measured. Protein crystallographers prefer an instrument that has one or more axes to orient the crystal and is equipped with an **area detector** on which hundreds or thousands of diffracted beams are registered nearly simultaneously. A popular type of the imaging plate is covered with phosphorescent material. After registration, the information collected on the imaging plate is replaced by a laser and read with a **photomultiplier**.

Applications

Protein crystallography is the youngest branch of X-ray crystallography. It started in 1934 when **Bernal** took the first X-ray diffraction picture of a protein crystal, first a crystal of pepsin, soon followed by a crystal of insulin. These observations showed that even these large molecules are nicely ordered in their crystals and that their structures might be solved. This was not an easy problem, however, and it took twenty years to find a solution. Surprisingly, it could be done by a technique already successfully applied for small organic compounds: the method of isomorphous replacement in which a heavy atom is attached to the protein structure. It was **Perutz**' achievement to show that the method could also be used for proteins and that the heavy atoms cause a much larger change in intensity than initially expected. Because of the rather primitive instrumentation, progress was slow at first. With the introduction of more sophisticated instrumentation and structures are being published with ever increasing speed. They are collected in the Protein Data Bank, Brookhaven National Laboratory, Upton, NY 11973-5000, USA.

Important Questions

1. Describe in details the process of X-ray diffraction with special reference to its applications.
2. Differentiate between the fiber diffraction and crystal diffraction with suitable examples.

Chromatography

12

The term chromatography is derived from two Greek words **Khromatos** (color) and **graphs** (written). The International Union of Pure Applied Chemistry (IUPAC) has further defined chromatography as —

"**A method, used primarily for separation of the components of a sample in which the components are distributed between two phases, one of which is stationary, while the other moves. The stationary phase may be a solid or a liquid supported on a solid or a gel. The stationary phase may be packed in a column, spread as a layer, or distributed as a film, etc. In these definitions chromatographic bed is used as a general term to denote any of the different forms in which the stationary phase may be used. The mobile phase may be gaseous or liquid**".

Russian botanist **Mikhail Tswett** in 1906 coined this term chromatography that now implies the separation of components present in a mixture by partition between two phases, one of which stationary and the other is mobile. Tswett (1872-1919) was the first scientist to report that chlorophyll was not a single compound and separated plant pigments using a column of calcium carbonate. In principle, chromatographic separations are based on polarity. Applications of different chromatographic methods depend upon the number of phases available. Figure 1 describes these methods in which the polarity of the test molecule plays and important role.

The basis of **chromatography** is the partition or distribution coefficient (Kd) which describes the way in which a compound distributes itself between two immiscible phases. For example, the concentration of a compound in two immiscible phases A and B, the value for this coefficient is a constant at a given temperature

$$\frac{\text{Concentration in phase A}}{\text{Concentration in phase B}} = \text{Kd}$$

Distribution coefficient is defined as the total amount of substance present in one phase divided by the total amount present in other phase.

The successful chromatographic separation of individual components present in a mixture depends upon the selection of appropriate chromatographic methods, followed by the optimization of the experimental conditions associated with the separation. Chromatographic separations can be achieved by selecting a suitable method.

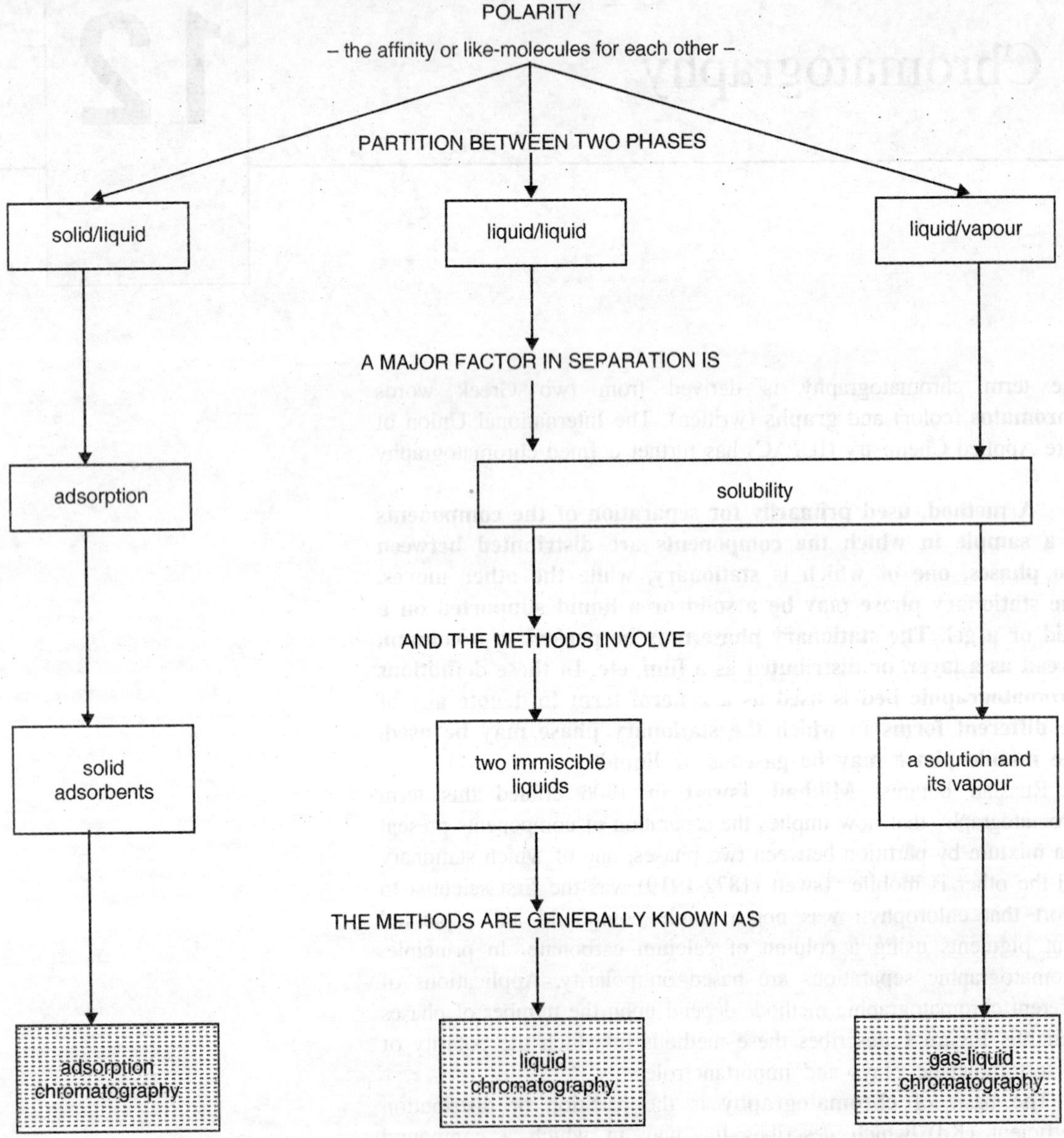

Fig. 1. Separation methods in which the polarity of the test molecule plays an important part.

Liquid Solid Chromatography (Adsorption Chromatography)

[I] Column chromatography

When a solution of polar compound is in contact with a finely divided solid such as charcoal or silica, fairly extensive adsorption takes place on the surface of the solid. The majority of the adsorbants are polar, either acidic (e.g. silica) or basic (e.g. alumina). A large surface area is required.

Such separations can be achieved by using glass or metal columns. This process is also known as **column chromatography**. Stationary phase attached to a suitable matrix is packed into a column. Mobile phase is allowed to pass through a column either by gravity force by using a pumping system or applied gas pressure (Fig. 2 & Fig. 3).

A typical column chromatographic system consists of a column, a mobile phase reservoir and delivery system, a detector for identifying the separated compounds, a recorder and a fraction collector. Each separated analyte is represented by a peak on the chart recorder and the fraction collector allows each analyte to be collected separately for further study.

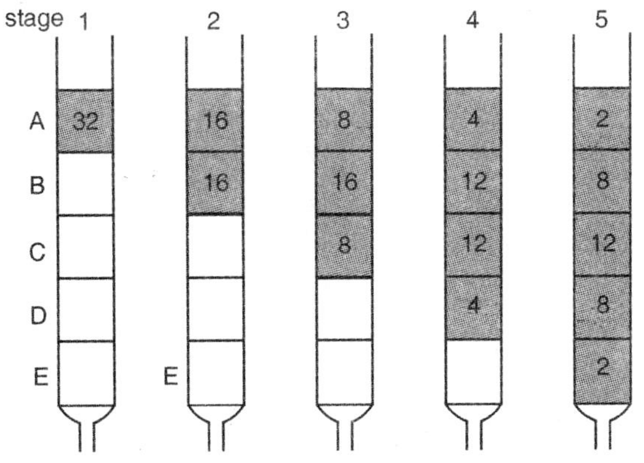

Fig. 2. Principle of Column Chromatographic Separation.

[II] Thin layer chromatography

Chromatographic developments greatly accelerated after the famous paper of **Martin** and **Synge** that appeared in 1941. They provided a theoretical framework for the basic chromatographic process. Martin and Synge were awarded noble prize for this work in 1952. In late 1950s the field of thin layer chromatography was born and became so popular that it largely replaced the older technique of paper chromatography.

In thin layer chromatography – a layer of the adsorbent (silica) is allowed to spread over an inert, flat support usually glass, aluminum or rigid plastic film. The plates are then dried in an oven and stored in a desicator. Commercially prepared plates are also available. Samples ranging between 1 to 20 'd' are applied to these plates with the help of a capillary or micropipette. After the samples have been applied and dried, the plate is kept in a tank which contains the solvent. It is essential to saturate the atmosphere of the tank with solvent vapour. When the solvent has moved to the top of the plate (10-20 cm), the plate is removed, solvent front is marked and the plate dried quickly. The separated bands are viewed under ultraviolet light or stained using a suitable reagent. Test spots are by comparing their migration with that of a reference sample. It is possible to identify a component using a specific colour reagent. The R_f value (rate of flow) is a measure of the movement of a compound compared with the movement of the solvent.

$$R_f = \frac{\text{Distance compound has moved from the origin}}{\text{Distance solvent has moved from the origin}}$$

Selection of the proper solvent depends upon the type of separation desired. In choosing the solvent, reference may be made to one of the "elutropic" series published for use with either column, paper or thin layer chromatography. Such a series is shown in Table 1.

Spots can be visualized by spraying ninhydrin. The addition of fluorescent chemicals e.g. rhodamine fluorescein in trace quantities permit the ultraviolet examination of spots. Radioactively labeled materials can be located by exposure of an x-ray film to the chromatoplate and subsequent development.

***Table 1.* Elutropic solvent series.**

1.	Petroleum ether	8.	Chloroform
2.	Cyclohexane	9.	Diethyl ether
3.	Carbon tetrachloride	10.	Ethyl acetate
4.	Trichloroethylene	11.	Acetone
5.	Toluene	12.	n-propanol
6.	Benzene	13.	Ethanol
7.	Dichloromethane	14.	Methanol

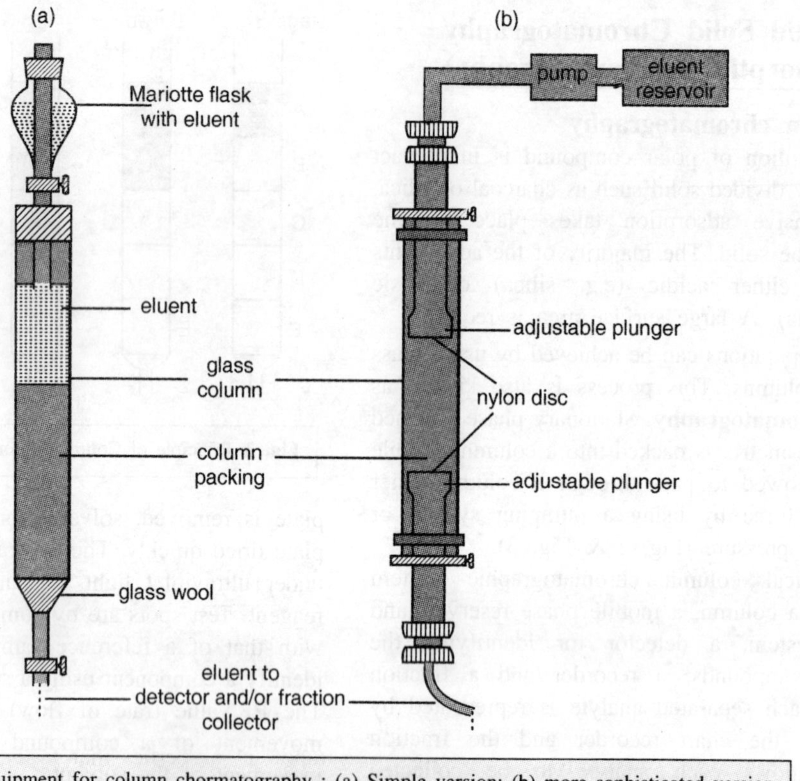

Fig. 3. Equipment for column chormatography : (a) Simple version; (b) more sophisticated version.

Liquid-liquid Chromatography

In its simplest form, liquid-liquid chromatography involves two solvents which are immiscible. The partition of a solute between two immiscible liquid phases provides the basis of separation. Since the polarity of both solute and solvent are important factors in determining the solubility of the solute, polar solutes will dissolve more readily in polar solvents than in non polar solvents.

Paper Chromatography

It is the simplest and commonst form of liquid-liquid chromatography. Whatman filter paper or commercially prepared cellulose plates are used for chromatographic separation. The basic principle of this procedure was described for the first time by **Consden**, **Gordon** and **Martin** (1944). A small drop of solution containing the mixture of compounds (amino acids) is applied on the filter paper and allowed to evaporate to dryness. This piece of filter paper is placed in a tank containing a suitable solvent. The solvent is allowed to flow slowly along the filter paper over the spot, either by capillary action (ascending) or aided by gravity (descending). The substances in the initial spot are extracted by the flowing solvent and carried along the filter paper to an extent which appears related to their distribution between the free and bound solvent phase of the filter paper. After the solvent has moved for a suitable distance along the paper, the paper is removed, freed of excess solvent by drying and subjected to suitable tests to locate the various amino acids present in the sample.

An improved procedure of paper chromatography is so called two-dimensional chromatography. Here the sample spot is applied in one corner of the square of filter paper. The solvent carries the sample along one edge of the paper. Excess solvent is removed by drying. Now the paper is turned 90° and a second solvent is allowed to flow across the filter paper at right angles to the direction of flow of the first solvent. The second solvent is then removed by drying and substances are located by suitable staining. While paper chromatography has been superseded by other procedures, it is still when a compound is detected by colour reaction, its intensity may be used to determine the quantity of the compound. The separate compound may be extracted from the filter paper by a suitable solvent in a pure solution.

High Performance Liquid Chromatography (HPLC)

Modern liquid chromatography (HPLC) was introduced in the early 1970s permitting the efficient separation of a wide range of compounds. It has emerged as the most popular, powerful and versatile technique for faster and better resolution of particles. For efficient separations, it is essential to have very small and regular shaped support media (column), a supply of mobile phase (sample) pumped at a pressure which is adequate to give a suitable constant flow rate through the column and a convenient and efficient detection system.

The apparatus required consists of five basic components (Fig. 4).

[I] Columns

Stainless steel columns are generally used for HPLC. They can sustain the pressure of upto $5{\cdot}5 \times 10^7$ Pa (~8000 lbf in^{-2}). The length of these columns generally vary from 15-50 cm whereas they have a diameter of 1 to 4 mm. Preparative columns having the internal diameter upto 25 mm are also available commercially. Porous plugs of stainless steel or teflon are used in the ends of the column to retain the packing material.

HPLC columns are packed with a specific packing material. Structure and dimensions of the packing material are important in achieving efficient separation. They are of three types.

1. Pellicular material. These are porous particles coated onto an inert solid core such as glass bead of about 40 μm in diameter.

2. Bonded material. Here the stationary phase is chemically bonded onto an inert support such as silica.

3. Microporous material. Here the micro pores ramify through the particles which are generally 5 to 10 μm in diameter.

4. Selection of columns. While HPLC techniques were initially developed as liquid-liquid chromatographic methods, the difficulties in maintaining a stationary phase were significant, therefore chromatographic media were developed in which the stationary phase is chemically bonded to the surface. In selecting a column material for the separation of a specific substance, physical characteristics of the molecule are to be considered. The polarity and solubility of the molecule are two important properties that further help in classifying the chromatography as —

(a) Adsorption chromatography. This technique is based on the polarity of the samples, Samples with polar groups are retained longer by a polar adsorbent whereas nonpolar analytes interact better with a nonpolar stationary phase. In this technique the analyte remains in contact simultaneously with both the stationary phase and the mobile phase.

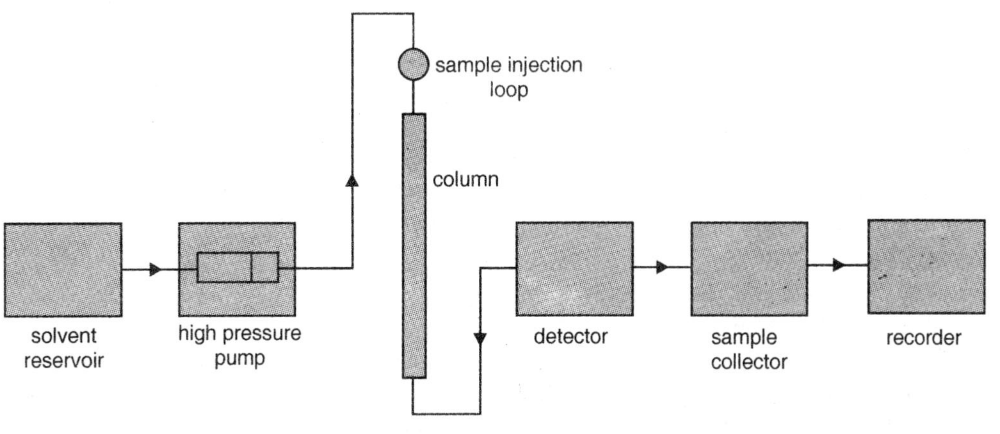

Fig. 4. Diagram of the components of an isocratic HPLC system.

(b) Partition chromatography. Partition chromatography is based on the differences in the partition coefficient of the sample between the mobile and the stationary phases. There is a competition for neutral analytes between the mobile and the stationary phase.

(c) Ion-exchange chromatography. This technique is based on the electrostatic interaction between a charged solute and an oppositely charged solid stationary phase. Separation in ion exchange chromatography is achieved by the differing affinities of ions in solution for oppositely charged ionic groups in the stationary phase.

[II] Solvent delivery system

It includes a pump which delivers the appropriate solvent from a reservoir at a pre-selected rate. A single solvent system is known as **isocratic system**. However, when it is desirable to use a mixture of solvents, the procedure is known as **gradient elution**. Pumping systems for delivery of the mobile phase are one of the most important features of HPLC. Good pumping systems are that it should be capable of outputs of atleast 5×10^7 Pa and ideally there should be no cyclical variations in pressure (pulses). There must be a flow capability of atleast 10 cm^3 min^{-1} and 100 cm^3 min^{-1} for preparative separations. Various pumping systems are available that operate on the principle of constant pressure or constant displacement.

[III] Detectors

HPLC system require very small amount of sample. Therefore, a detector of very high sensitivity is required. These detectors are based on the principle of **ultraviolet visible spectrophotometry**. These may operate at fixed wave length selected by interference filters or desired wavelength can be selected by using monochromators. Wavelengths in the range of 190-350 nm are frequently used. They have a sensitivity as low as 0·001 **absorbance units for full scale deflection** (**AUFS**).

Fluorescent samples can be detected using fluorescent detectors. This type of detectors are very important for HPLC systems.

Certain systems use electrochemical detectors. They are employed to measure the electroactive species. These detectors are of two types i.e. amperometric and coulometric, the principles of which are similar. They employ a flow cell which is fitted with two electrodes- a stable counter electrode (Agi/AgCl or calomel), and a working electrode which is highly polarisable. A constant potential is applied to the working electrode at such a value that, as an analyte flows through the flow cell, molecules at the electrode surface undergo either an oxidation or a reduction resulting into a current flow between two electrodes. Compounds like-hydrocarbons, amines, amides, phenols, catecholamines, and quinolines undergo oxidation whereas compounds that undergo reduction include esters, olefins, ketones, aldehydes, ethers azo nitro compounds. The electrochemical detector has been particularly useful in the assay of catecholamines, vitamins and antioxidants.

HPLC can also be coupled with mass spectrometer. More recently, HPLC has been interfaced with NMR spectroscopy to give structural information about the analytes that is complimentary to that obtained by HPLC - mass spectroscopy.

Applications of HPLC

(1) Virtually types of biological molecules can be assayed or purified using HPLC.

(2) Separation of proteins can be made using fast protein liquid chromatography (FPLC).

(3) Micropore columns allow the analysis using a very small amount of sample.

Gas-Liquid Chromatography (GLC)

Majority of non polar and polar compounds can be qualitatively and quantitatively analyzed by a technique known as GLC. Principle of separation is the - difference in the partition coefficients of the volatilized compounds between the liquid and gas phases as the compounds are carried through the column by the carrier gas.

Preparation of the Sample

The sample for GLC is dissolved in a suitable solvent such as acetone, heptane or methanol. Chlorinated organic solvents are generally avoided as they can contaminate the detector. The sample in very small quantities viz. 0.1 to 10 mm^3 of solution is injected onto the column using a micro syringe through a septum in the injection port that is attached to the top of the column. The injection region of the column is maintained at a temperature higher than the column itself. It is necessary for the rapid and complete volatilization of the sample. Many commercial instruments possess automated injection system.

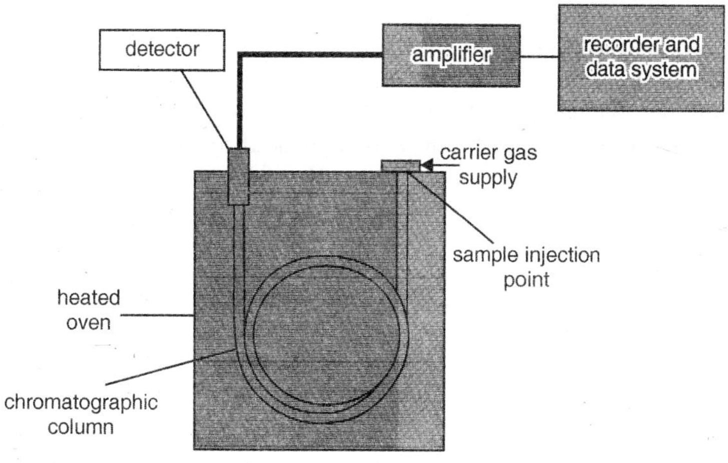

Fig. 5. Diagram of a GLC system.

[I] Columns

Columns used in GLC are made up of glass or steel. They are 1 to 3 metres long and possess an internal diameter of 2 to 4 mm. An inert carrier such as nitrogen, helium or argon is passed through the column. It makes the mobile phase of the system whereas materials such as silicone grease supported by inert granule solid make the stationary phase. The column is maintained in an oven at a high temperature to ensure that the compounds to be separated are maintained in a vapour state.

Capillary columns are also used in GLC. They are made up of glass or metal. Their length is about 100 m and the diameter lies between 0.03 to 1.0 mm. They are of two types i.e. wan coated open tubular (WCOT) columns and support coated open tubular (SCOT) columns.

[II] Detectors

Several types of detectors viz: flame ionization detector (**FID**), nitrogen phosphorus detector (**NPD**) and the electron capture detector (**ECD**) are used in GLC systems.

FID can detect almost all organic compounds and in very small quantities e.g. µm. A mixture of hydrogen and air is introduced into the detector to give a flame. The jet of this flame works as one electrode while the other electrode is brass or platinum wire mounted near the tip of the flame. When the sample components pass out from the column, they are ionized in the flame, resulting into an increased singal being passed to the recorder.

The NPD is similar to FID in design. It is also known as thermoionic detector. It has excellent selectivity towards nitrogen and phosphorus containing compounds. It is widely used for the analysis of organophosphorus pesticides.

The ECD responds particularly to halogen containing compounds. It is used in the analysis of polychlorinated compounds such as pesticides, DDT, dialdrin and aldrin. It has a very high sensitivity. The detector employs a radioactive source (^{63}Ni) for ionizing the column gas. When an electron capturing compound emerges from the column the ionized electrons are captured, the current drops and this change in the current is recorded by recorder.

More recently GLC spectrophotometer, has been linked to other types of detectors viz: infra-red, nuclear magnetic resonance spectrophotometer and an atomic emission spectrometer.

Applications of GLC

Prior to the invention of HPLC, GLC was probably the most commonly used form of chromatography. Nowadays, its use is mainly confined to volatile, non-polar compounds that do not need derivatization. Samples are characterized by their retention time relative to the reference compound. A widely used method for quantitative analysis is the retention of a compound relative of n-alkanes. Modern GLC systems with data processing facilities have the capacity to calculate Rf values automatically.

Chromatofocusing

In ion-exchange chromatography, a technique similar to that of iso-electric focusing is used for separation of proteins. It works on the pH gradient principle. A linear pH gradient is generated in the column by manipulating the high buffer capacity of the ion-exchanger pre-equilibrated to a particular pH. The pH at the top of the column and at the bottom of the column develops a gradient of 3 to 4 pH units. When a protein sample is introduced to this pH gradient with a buffer whose pH is similar to that prevailing at the top of the A column, it will migrate down to the column as a cation, encountering an increasing pH, until it reaches a pH corresponding to the isoelectric point. Just beyond this point, it will behave as an anion and shall bind to the positive groups of the exchanger. The protein will continue its movement down the column until once again it encounters pH slightly above its isoelectric point. Thus in a mixture of proteins, each molecule would elute corresponding to it iso-electric point. More proteins can be added at the top of the column during elution. They will automatically catch up the initial protein thereby producing a focusing effect. This effect is called **chromatofocusing**. It gives good resolution of complex mixtures of proteins provided they have discrete iso-electric point.

Analysis of Organic Oollutants by Gas Chromatography

Gas chromatography (GC) is the most common analytical technique for the quantitative determination of organic pollutants in aqueous and nonaqueous samples. In environmental analysis, a very low detection limit is required to determine the pollutants at trace levels. Such low detection can be achieved by sample concentration followed by cleanup of the extract to remove interfering substances.

Aqueous samples containing volatile organics can be directly analyzed by GC (without any separate sample extraction steps) interfaced with a purge and trap setup. The analytes in the sample are concentrated by the purge and trap technique, (as discussed in the following section), prior to their analysis by GC or GC/MS. The volatile organics in soils, sediments, and solid wastes may be analyzed in a similar way by subjecting an aqueous extract of the sample to purge and trap concentration. Alternatively, the analytes may be thermally desorbed from the solid matrices and transported onto the GC column by a carrier gas.

At the outset, one must understand certain principles of GC to assess if it is a proper analytical tool for the purpose. If so, how to achieve the best separation and identification of component mixtures in the sample with reasonable precision, accuracy, and speed? And what kind of detector and column should be selected for the purpose? It is, therefore, important to examine the type of compounds that are to be analyzed and certain physical and chemical properties of these compounds. Information regarding the structure and the functional groups, elemental composition, the polarity in the molecule, its molecular weight, boiling point, and thermal stability are very helpful for achieving the best analysis. After we know these properties, it is very simple to perform the GC analysis of component mixtures. To achieve this, just use an appropriate column and a proper detector. Properties of columns and detectors are highlighted below in the following sections.

Efficiency of the chromatographic system can be determined from the number of theoretical plates per meter. Although this term primarily describes the property and resolution efficiency of a column, other extra column variables, such as the detector, inlet, injection technique, and the carrier gas velocity can also affect the theoretical plates. It is calculated from the following equation:

$$\text{Theoretical plates/m} = \frac{5 \cdot 54\left(\frac{t}{w}\right)^2}{L}$$

where t = retention time of the test compound, w = width of the peak at half height, and L = length of the column (m).

The number of theoretical plates also depend on the partition ratio k of the test compound and its solubility in the liquid phase. Substances that have higher k values have lower plate numbers. Greater plate numbers indicate greater resolution or better separation of the component mixture.

Selection of Column

A variety of GC columns are commercially available to meet the specific purpose. Selection of columns, their stationary phases, inside diameters, lengths, and the film thickness are briefly discussed below.

A capillary column is usually preferred over packed column for better resolution and lower detection limit. Efficiency of a column to separate organic compounds depends on the stationary phase and the polarity of the analyte molecules. The polarity of the phase, therefore, is the most important characteristic in selecting a column. While a nonpolar phase most effectively separates nonpolar molecules, a polar phase is required to achieve the separation of polar compounds. Aliphatic hydrocarbons containing C-H single bonds are all nonpolar compounds while those containing C=C double bonds, such as olefins and aromatics, are polarizable compounds. On the other hand, organic compounds containing oxygen, nitrogen, sulfur, phosphorus, or halogen atoms should exhibit greater polarity. Examples of such polar compounds include carboxylic acids, ketones, aldehydes, esters, alcohols, thiols, ethers, amines, nitroaromatics, nitrosamines, nitriles, halocarbons, PCBs, and organic phosphates. An increase in polarity reduces the thermal stability of the stationary phase. Therefore, a phase of least polarity should be selected, whenever possible, to enhance the life of the column. Table 1 lists the polarity of various stationary phases of common capillary GC columns.

Capillary columns are composed of fused silica which has shown remarkable properties of inertness and efficiency in chromatographic analysis. Glass capillaries and stainless steel are sometimes used too; but their applications are nowadays limited.

The inside diameter of the capillary column is another major factor that often dictates the separation of components. The narrowbore columns with internal diameter (ID) 0.20, 0.25, and 0.32 mm provide the best separation for closely eluting components and isomers. The smaller the ID, the greater is the resolution. On the other hand, a major disadvantage of such a narrow bore column, however, is its low sample capacity [i.e., the quantity of sample that can be applied without causing the peak(s) to overload]. Wider bore columns of 0.53 and 0.75 mm ID do not have this problem. These wider columns have greater sample capacity than narrowbore columns but relatively lower resolution capacity. Such widebore columns, however, are better suited for environmental samples that often contain pollutants at high concentrations. In addition, widebore columns of 0.53 and 0.75 mm ID provide sufficient sensitivity for minor components peaks without being overloaded with the major components. The sample capacity of a column may further be

Table 1. **Polarity of Stationary Phases**

Polarity	Stationary phase	Examples of GC-columns
Nonpolar	Polydimethylsiloxane	AT-1, BP-1, OB-1, OC-200, HP-1, OV-1, OV-101, RSL- 160, Rtx-1, SF-96, SP2100, SPB-1, ULTRA-1
	Polyphenylmethylsiloxane	AT-5, BP-5, OB-5, HP-5, MPS-5, OV-73, RSL-200, Rtx-5, SE-52, SPB-5, ULTRA-2
Intermediate	Polyphenylmethylsiloxane MPS-50, OV-17, RSL300,	AT-20, BP-10, OB-17, HP17, Rtx-20, SP-2250, SPB-20
	Polycyanopropylphenyl-dimethylpolysiloxane	AT-1301, OB-1301, Rtx-1301
	Polycyanopropylphenyl-methylsiloxane	AT-1701, OB-1701, GB-1701, OV-1701, Rtx-1701, SPB-1701
Polar	Polytrifluoropropylsiloxane QF-1, RSL-400, SP-2401	AT-210, OB-210, OV-210,
	Polyphenylcyanopropyl-methylsiloxane	AT-225, OB-225, HP-225, OV-225, RSL-500, Rtx-225
	Polyethyleneglycol	AT-WAX, BP-20, Carbowax 20M, CPIWAX 51, OB WAX, HP-20M, Stabilwax, Supelcowax 10, Superox II
Very polar (acidic)	Polyethyleneglycol ester	AT-1000, FFAp, Nukol, OV351, SP-1000, Superox-FA

Table 2. **Separation efficiency and sample capacity of GC columns of varying internal diameters (ID)**

Column ID (mm)	Sample capacity	Separation Efficiency (theoretical plates/m)[a]	Carrier gas flow rate, optimum (cc/min)
		Capillary	
0.20	10-30	5000	0.4
0.25	50-100	4200	0.7
0.32	400-500	3300	1.4
0.53	1000-2000	1700	2.5
0.75	10,000-15,000	1200	5
		Packed	
2.0	20,000	2000	20

Note: The data presented are for a 60-m capillary column and a 2-m packed column. a Numbers are rounded off. The higher this number, the greater is the resolution efficiency.

increased by temperature programming. It also depends on the polarity of the components and the phase-the polar phase has a high capacity for polar components, while the nonpolar phase has a high capacity for nonpolar components.

The stationary phase can be bound to the tubing either as a physical coating on the wall, or can be chemically immobilized. The former type phases are called nonbonded phases, while the chemically bound phases, cross-linked within the tubing are known as bonded phases. The latter is preferred because it can be used at high temperatures with less bleeding and can be rinsed with solvents to remove nonvolatile substances that accumulate on the column.

The film thickness of the stationary phase is another major factor that should be taken into account for column selection. A thicker film increases the resolution on a nonpolar column, but decreases the same on a polar column. It also increases the sample capacity, retention of sample components, and therefore, the retention time and the temperature at which the components would elute from the column-and the column bleed. Thus, it has both advantages and disadvantages. Use a thicker film (>1mm) to analyze gases or substances with low boiling points or to analyze highly concentrated samples. On the other hand, a thin film (0.25 mm) should be used to analyze compounds with high boiling points (>300°C) and should be employed with a shorter column (10 to 15 m length). Film thickness of the stationary phase and the column ID are interrelated, as follows :

$$\text{Phase ratio, } \beta = \frac{\text{column radius } (\mu m)}{2 \times \text{Phase thickness } (\mu m)}$$

Columns with equal beta value (β) will provide similar separations under the same analytical conditions. For example, a capillary column with 0.32 mm and 0.8 mm phase film thickness could be substituted with a column of same phase with 0.53 mm ID and 1.3 mm film thickness to produce very similar separation. Standard film thickness (0.25 to 0.8 mm) should, however, work for most chemical analyses.

Separation of closely eluting components can be efficiently achieved on a longer column. The greater the length of the capillary column, the higher is its resolution efficiency. On the other hand, the long column enhances the time of analysis, increasing the retention times of the components. As mentioned earlier, high resolution can also be attained with narrow bore columns. Therefore, optimizing the column length and ID can provide good separation in the desired analysis time.

Detectors

Selection of GC detectors is very crucial in chemical analysis. Flame ionization detector (FID) and thermal conductivity detector (**TCD**) can be used for all general purposes. The detection limits for analytes, however, are high, especially for the TCD. The latter is commonly used for gas analysis.

When using FID, aqueous samples can be directly injected onto the GC without any sample extraction. The detection limit of an analyte, however, in such a case would be much higher (low ppm level) than what is desired in environmental analysis. When appropriate sample concentration steps are adopted, organic compounds in aqueous and solid matrices and air can be effectively determined at a much lower detection level. Carbon disulfide is commonly used in the air analysis of many organics by GC-FID.

Halogen specific detectors, such as electron capture detector (ECD) and Hall electrolytic conductivity detector (HECD) show the best response to compounds that contain halogen atoms. Most nitrogen-containing organics can be determined by nitrogen-phosphorus detector (NPD) in nitrogen mode while organophosphorus compounds can be analyzed by the same detector in phosphorus specific mode. Flame photometric detector (FPD) is also equally efficient for determining phosphorus compounds. FPD, however, is primarily used to analyze sulfur-containing organics. Photoionization detector (PID) is sensitive to substances that contain the carbon-carbon double bond such as aromatics and olefins, as well as their substitution products.

Calibration

Prior to the analysis of the unknown, a calibration standard curve is prepared by running at least four standards. There are two ways in which calibration is performed: external standard method and internal standard method. External standard method involves preparation of a calibration curve by plotting area or height response against concentrations of the analyte(s) in the standards. The calibration factor is then calculated as the ratio of concentrations to areaheight response and should be constant over a wide range of concentrations. To determine the concentration of the analyte in the unknown sample (extract), the response for the unknown should be compared with that of the standards within the linear range of the curve. Alternatively, an average of response ratios may be calculated which is compared with the response of the analyte. A single point calibration may be used if the area height response of the analyte is within 20% of the response of the standard.

The internal standard method is more reliable than the external standard method. Equal amounts of one or more internal standards are added onto equal volumes of sample extracts and the calibration standards. The response factor (RF) is then calculated as follows:

$$\text{RF} = \frac{A_s \times C_{is}}{A \times C}$$

where A_s and A_{is} are the area (or height) response for the analyte and the internal standard, respectively; while $C.$, and Cis are their concentrations. Thus, RF for analytes may be determined by running standard solutions of the analytes containing internal standards. If the RF values over the working range of concentrations fall within:!: 20% relative standard deviation, an average RF value should be used in the above equation to determine the concentration of the analytes in the sample. Alternatively, a calibration curve may be plotted between response ratio (A_s/A_{is}) vs. RF. The concentration of the analyte is usually expressed in m.g/L. All concentration terms including those of the calibration standards and internal standards must be in the same unit.

Calculations

The concentration of an analyte in an aqueous or nonaqueous sample may be calculated by one of the following methods:

External Standard Calibration

The areaheight response for the analyte peak is compared with that of the standards from the calibration curve or from the calibration factor.

$$\text{Concentration, mg/L} = \frac{A_{unk} \times Q_{std} \times V_{tot} \times D}{A_{std} \times V_{inj} \times V_{sample}}$$

where A_{unk} = Area count or peak height of the analyte

Q_{std} = Amount of standard injected or purged in ng

V_{tot} = Volume of total extract in µ.L

D = Dilution factor, dimensionless

A_{std} = Area or peak response for the standard

V_{inj} = Volume of extract injected in µ.L

V_{sample} = Volume of sample extracted or purged in mL

For nonaqueous samples, the concentration of the analyte is calculated' in the same way except that weight of the sample W is substituted for the volume of the sample, V_{sample} Thus,

$$\text{Concentration, } \mu g/kg = \frac{A_{unk} \times Q_{std} \times V_{tot} \times D}{A_{std} \times V_{inj} \times W}$$

The concentration calculated above is on the sample "as is" and not as dry weight corrected. Concentration on a dry weight basis may be calculated by dividing the above result with the percent total solid expressed in decimal.

Routine Analysis

Routine GC analysis for environmental samples involve running one of the calibration check standards before sample analysis to determine if the area or height response is constant (i.e., within 15% standard deviation of the response factor or calibration factor, and to check if there is a shift in the retention times of the analytes' peaks. The latter can occur to a significant degree due to any variation in conditions, such as temperature or the flow rate of the carrier gas. Therefore, an internal standard should be used if possible in order to determine the retention time shift or to compensate for any change in the peak response. If an analyte is detected in the sample, its presence must be ascertained and then confirmed as follows:

(1) Peak matching of the unknown with the known should be done, additionally, at a different temperature and/or flow rate conditions.

(2) The sample extract should be spiked with the standard analyte solution at a concentration to produce a response which is two-to-three times the response of the unknown peak.

(3) The identification of the peak must be finally confirmed on a second GC column. This may be done either after performing steps 1 and 2 or by injecting the extract straight onto the second column (confirmatory GC column) without going through steps 1 and 2.

In addition to determining the presence or absence of pollutants of interest in the sample, the routine analysis must include quality control/quality assurance tests to determine the precision and accuracy of the test results and any possible source of errors such as sample contamination, absence of preservative, or exceeding of sample holding time.

Affinity Chromatography

This technique, in principal, does not rely on physical properties of the molecules to be separated. Instead, biological properties of molecules are used to achieve separation and purification. It was originally developed for the purification of enzymes. However, nowadays it is used to separate nucleotides, nucleic acids, immunoglobulins, membrane receptors and even to whole cells and cell fragments.

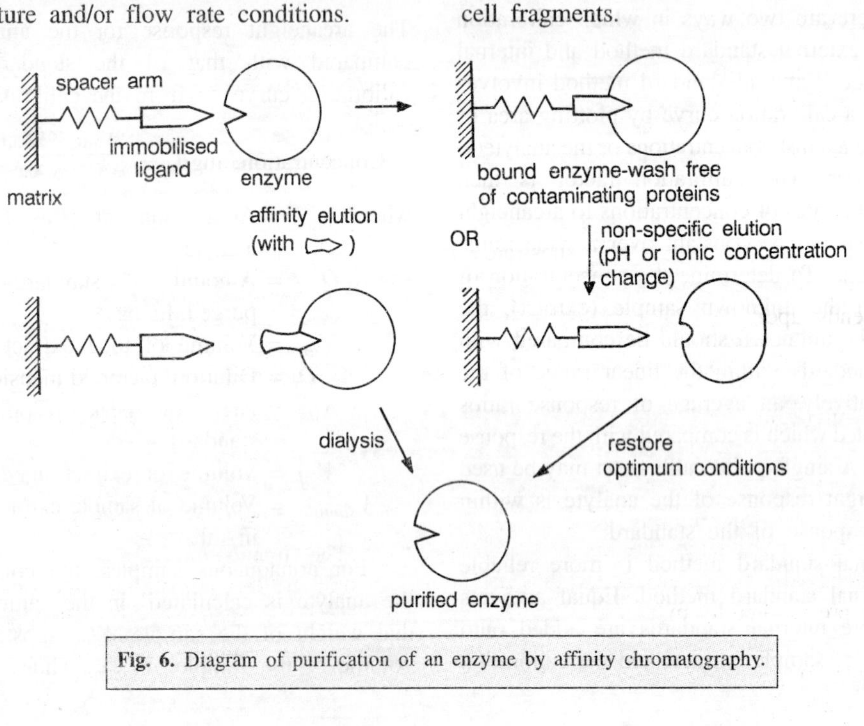

Fig. 6. Diagram of purification of an enzyme by affinity chromatography.

Table 2. **Examples of group-specific ligands commonly used in affinity chromatography.**

Ligand	Affinity
Nucleoitides	
5`-AMP	NDA$^+$-dependent dehydrogenases, some kinases
2`5`-ADP	NADP$^+$-dependent dehydrogenases
Calmodulin	Calmodulin-binding enzymes
Avidin	Biotin-containing enzymes
Fatty acids	Fatty-acid binding proteins
Heparin	Lipoproteins, lipases, coagulation factors, DNA Polymerases, steroid receptor proteins, growth factors, Serine protease inhibitors
Proteins A and G	Immunoglobulins
Concanavalin A	Glycoproteins containing α-D-mannopyranosyl and α-D-glucopyranosyl residues
Soybean lectin	Glycoproteins containing N-acetyl-α-or (β)-D-glactopyranosyl residues
Phenylboronate	Glycoproteins
Poly (A)	RNA containing poly (U) sequences, some RNA specific proteins
Lysine	rRNA
Cibacron Blue F3G-A	Nucleotide-requiring enzymes, coagulation factors

$$\underset{\text{Macromolecule}}{M} + \underset{\text{Ligand}}{L} \underset{R-1}{\overset{k+1}{\longleftrightarrow}} \underset{\text{Complex}}{ML}$$

In principle, a mixture containing the specific compound to be purified is added to an immobilized ligand. The compound binds reversibly to the specific ligand that is attached to the insoluble matrix (Fig. 6).

All other compounds are washed away and the compound is subsequently recorded by displacement from the ligand.

In this method, it is essential to know the primary structure and biological specificity of the compound, to be purified. Thereafter the separation conditions are planned. For example in the case of an enzyme, the ligand may be the substrate, an inhibitor or an allosteric activator. Success of the method depends upon the reversible formation of the complex on the numerical values of the first order rate constants i.e. k + 1 and k – 1.

Column procedure are more successful than batch type methods. Certain alternative methods have recently been developed for large scale separations. They include —

1. Affinity precipitation. In this procedure, a ligand is attached to a soluble carrier that can be subsequently precipitated by making a change in the pH.

2. Affinity partitioning. In this method, the ligand is attached to a water soluble polymer such as polyethylene glycol. A partition between aqueous polymer phase and pure aqueous phase is created.

Procedure of Affinity Chromatography

It is similar to that used in other forms of liquid chromatography. It requires the selection of a suitable matrix. In practice, particles that are uniform, spherical and rigid are used. Commonly, agarose, dextrans, polyacrylamide gels, polystyrene, cellulose, porous glass are used.

Next step involves the selection of the ligand. In practice ligands of absolute selectivity are used. Alternatively, it is possible to select a ligand that displays group selectivity. The most common method of attachment of the ligand to the matrix involves the preliminary (CNBr). Alternatively, bis-epoxides, N – N' -disubstituted carbonimides, sulphonyl chloride, sodium periodate and dichlorotriazines can be used. Many preactivated matrixes prepared using these reagents are available commercially. Examples of certain ligands are given in following Table 2.

The ligand treated matrix is packed into a column. Buffers containing cofactors viz: metal ions are necessary for ligand-macromolecule interaction. Once the sample has been introduced and macromolecule bound, the column is eluted with more buffer to remove non-specifically bound contaminates. The purified compound is recovered from the ligand by specific or nonspecific elution. Non-specific elution can be done either by changing the pH or ionic strength.

Applications of Affinity Chromatography

The process has number of applications viz —

(1) A wide range of enzymes, proteins, receptor proteins and immunoglobulins can be purified by affinity chromatography.

(2) Messenger RNA is isolated by selective hybridization on poly (U) sepharose 4B - by exploiting the poly (A) tail.

(3) Immobilized single stranded DNA can be used to isolate complimentary RNA and DNA.

(4) It can be used in the separation of a mixture of cells into homogeneous populations.

Important Questions

1. Explain the term chromatography. Discuss different methods used in adsorption chromatography.
2. Discuss the principle instrument and applications of high performance liquid chromatography (HPLC).
3. Give detailed account of the process of gas liquid chromatography (GLC).
4. Write short notes on :
   (i) Column chromatography, (ii) Thin layer chromatography, (iii) Affinity chromatography, (iv) Chromatofocusing.

13 Electrophoresis

Electrophoresis, initially described by **Arne Tiselius** in 1937, is the process by which charged particles move through a media in the presence of an electric field at a given pH. The charged particles move at a constant velocity. The electric force *(Eq)* is equal to the friction force or viscous drag *(fv)* as defined by the relationship.

$$Eq = fv$$

where E is the strength of electric field (volts per centimeter), q is net charge of particles (electrostatic units), f is the frictional coefficient (a function of shape and size of the particle), v is the velocity of the particle (centimeters per second).

Ohm's law states that voltage (v) and current (I) are related by the following relationship, where R is the resistance.

$$v = IR$$

The electric field strength (E) is kept constant, then the velocity (v) of the particle depends on its net change (q) and its frictional coefficient (f). The frictional coefficient is directly proportional to the radius of a spherical particle with equivalent hydrodynamic properties.

$$v = Eq/f$$

Many biological molecules, such as amino acids, peptides, nucleotides, and nucleic acids possess ionisable groups and therefore at any given pH, they exist in solution as electrically charged species either as cations (+) or anions (–). Under the influence of an electric field, these charged particles will migrate either to the cathode or to the anode, depending upon the nature of their net charge. This

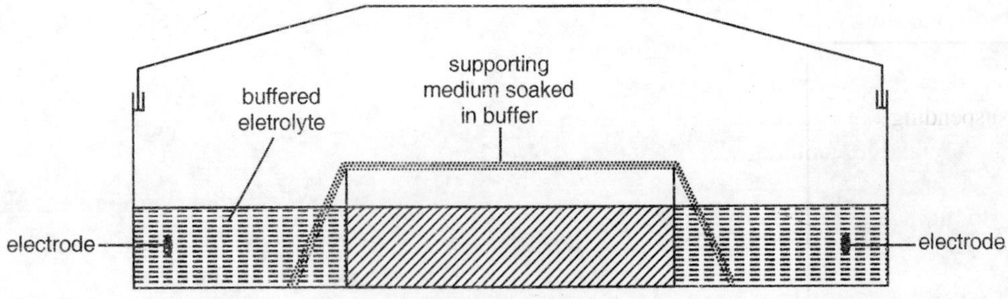

Fig. 1. An electrophoresis tank.

phenomenon is known as **electrophoretic mobility** (μ), which is the ratio of the velocity of the ion to field strength (*v/E*). When a potential difference is applied, molecules with different overall charges will begin to separate owing to their different electrophoretic mobilities. Even the molecules with similar charges will begin to separate, if they have different molecular sizes, since they will experience different frictional forces.

Some electrophoretic methods rely on different charges on molecules, while other methods exploit differences in molecular sizes. Electrophoresis can thus be treated as the complete form of electrolysis. The separated samples are then located by staining with an appropriate dye or by using autoradiography.

Instrumentation

A wide range of **electrophoretic equipment** is available and while it varies considerably in appearance, each has a common basic design. It consists of two items i.e. electrophoretic tank and a power supply. Vertical or horizontal electrophoretic tanks are commercially available. A well designed tank includes a cover to present evaporation of the buffer. A stabilized voltage supply is necessary and safety devices on the whole equipment are essential to prevent accidents, particularly when high voltages are used.

Electrophoretic mobility of the sample is allowed on a **supporting medium**. Several supporting media are available nowadays. It can be a filter paper, cellulose acetate membrane, agarose gei and polyacrylamide gels (Fig. 1).

Filter Paper

Filter paper has been an extremely useful and convenient medium for many years. It is still the most appropriate medium for high voltage electrophoresis. However, there are certain shortcomings. The random structure of the paper tends to result in irregularities in the separation patterns. Secondly relatively polar nature of cellulose shows some absorptive effects giving a significant degree of "failing" of separated zones. Thirdly diffusion of sample results into the broadening of zones.

Cellulose Acetate Membrane

Cellulose acetate membrane (**CAM**) was introduced as a better supporting medium as it contained more regularly defined pore structure. Separation could be made in 1-2 hrs. Absorptive effects were minimum. Small amount of the sample was required. Membrane could also be made transparent for densitometry either by soaking in an oil or organic solvent. However, CAM still showed electroendosmotic effects.

Gel

A variety of gels have been used in order to develop preparative techniques and to eliminate some of the disadvantages of the solid support media. Purified agar is used at a concentration of $10gl^{-1}$ in a buffered electrolyte and the samples are introduced in a small well or through cut out of the gel. **Agarose** a linear polysaccharide (molecular mass about 12000), is made up of the basic repeat unit agarobiose which is made up of galactose and 3,6 anhydrogalactose. Agarose is generally used at concentrations between 1% to 3%. Agarose gels are formed by suspending dry agarose in aqueous buffer, then boiling the mixture until a clear solution is formed. This is poured and allowed to cool to room temperature to form a rigid gel. Agarose gels are used for the electrophoresis of both proteins and nucleic acids.

Starch Gel

All the media described above have a large pore size which does not interfere with the separation process but starch and polyacrylamide gels have a restricted pore size and show a molecular sieving effect. The starch gel is also prepared by heating starch in the appropriate buffer in a boiling water bath until the mixture becomes translucent. A vaccum is applied to the flask to remove air bubbles and the solution is quickly poured into a heated tray and allowed to cool to form a gel about 5 mm thick.

Polyacrylamide Gel

Polyacrylamide shows many advantages over starch gel because of its synthetic nature & pore size. The gel is formed by the polymerization of two monomers, acrylamide and a cross linking agent **N, N-methylene-bis-acrylamide**. Acrylamide gels are defined in terms of the total percentage of the acrylamide present. Pore size in the gel can be varied by changing the concentrations of both acrylamide and bis-acrylamide. Acrylamide concentration may vary from 3% to 30%. Low percentage acrylamide are used to separate DNA. Gels between 10% and 20% are used in SDS-gel electrophoresis.

Polymerization of the gel may be achieved either by ultraviolet photo activation with riboflavin or preferably using ammonium persulphate as a catalyst. It is necessary to include an initiator for the reaction, TEMED (tetra methyl ethylene diamine) being commonly used.

Polyacrylamide gel electrophoresis (PAGE) is performed either in cylindrical glass tubes or in flat beds. The method is compatible with other electrophoretic techniques but care must be taken to keep the current low to prevent any significant heating effect.

Electrophoresis of Proteins

Separation of proteins possessing different molecular size or molecular mass can be conveniently done through electrophoresis. Sodium dodecyl sulphate-polyacrylamide gel electrophoresis (**SDS-PAGE**) is the most widely used method for analysis of protein mixtures qualitatively. Samples to be run on SDS-P AGE are boiled for 5 minutes in sample buffer containing p-mercaptoethanol and SDS. The mercaptoethanol reduces disulphide bonds that are holding the tertiary structure of the protein and SDS denatures the protein. An ionisable tracking dye usually the bromophenol blue is mixed with the sample buffer. Once the sample is loaded current is passed through the gel. This forces all the ionic species to migrate. The negatively changed protein-SDS complexes now continue to move towards anode. After the dye has reached to the bottom of the gel the current is turned off and the gel is removed from between the glass plates and shaken in an appropriate stain solution (Coomassie Brilliant Blue) for a few hours and then washed in destain solution overnight. The destain solution removes unbound background dye from the gel. Stained proteins are observed as clear blue bands. A typical gel would take 1 to 1½ hour to prepare and set, 8 hours to run at 30 mA and have a staining time of 2 to 3 hours with an overnight destain. Vertical slab gels are invariably run since it allows upto 20 different samples to be loaded onto a single gel. A typical SDS-polyacrylamide gel is shown in Figure 2.

The molecular mass of a protein can be determined by comparing the mobility with those of a number of standard proteins of known molecular mass that are run on the same gel. By plotting a graph of distance moved against log molecular mass for each of the standard protein, a calibration curve can be constructed. The distance moved by the unknown sample is then measured and then its log molecular mass can be determined from the calibration curve.

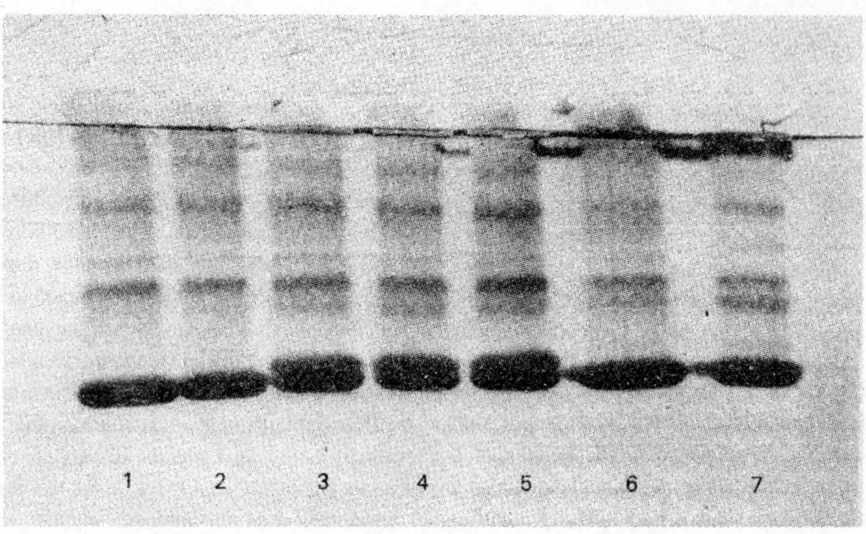

Fig. 2. Starch gel electrophoresis of human serum proteins. Samples 1 and 2 are normal while samples 3, 4 and 5 show an extra band adjacent to the normal albumin which is due to the presence of bis-albumin. Sample 7 contains a myeloma protein which has remained near the origin.

Electrophoretic Separation of Enzymes

SDS-PAGE system is most frequently used to separate proteins, however, this method is of no use in the separation of enzymes, since enzyme (protein) is denatured in SDS-PAGE procedure. These polyacrylamide gels are used again but the SDS is absent. The enzyme of interest is identified by incubating the gel in an appropriate substrate solution so that a coloured product is produced at the site of the enzyme.

Iso-Electric Focusing

Electrophoresis depends primary upon the charge carried by a molecule but at its iso-electric pH a molecule will not migrate in an electric field. If electrophoresis is performed in an electrolyte which has a pH gradient, molecules will migrate to the point where the pH of the solution is the same as their isoelectric pH and remain there as long as the gradient and potential differences are maintained. This forms the basis of iso-electric focusing technique (Fig. 3).

This method is quite suitable for the separation of amphoteric substances such as proteins because it is based on the separation of molecules according to their isoelectric points. At this point the molecule carries no net charge and is therefore electrophoretically immobile. The method has a high

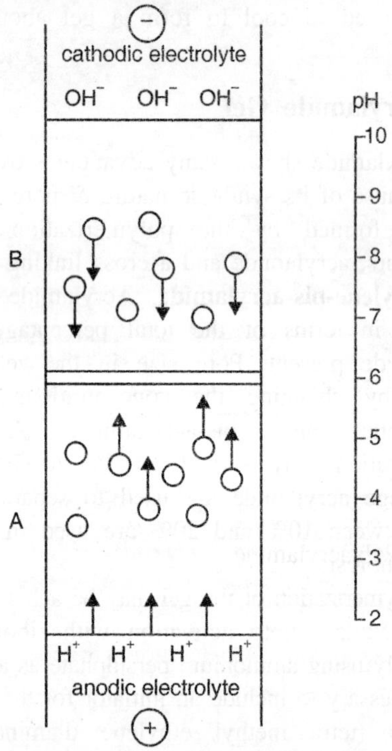

Fig. 3. Iso-electric focusing. A protein which has an iso-electric pH of 6, in position A in the pH gradient is on the acid side of its iso-electric pH and will carry a positive (H^+) charge. It will migrate electrophoretically towards the cathode. In position B, the charge on the protein will be negative and it will migrate towards the anode. In both cases, movement is towards its iso-electric pH position, where it will remain.

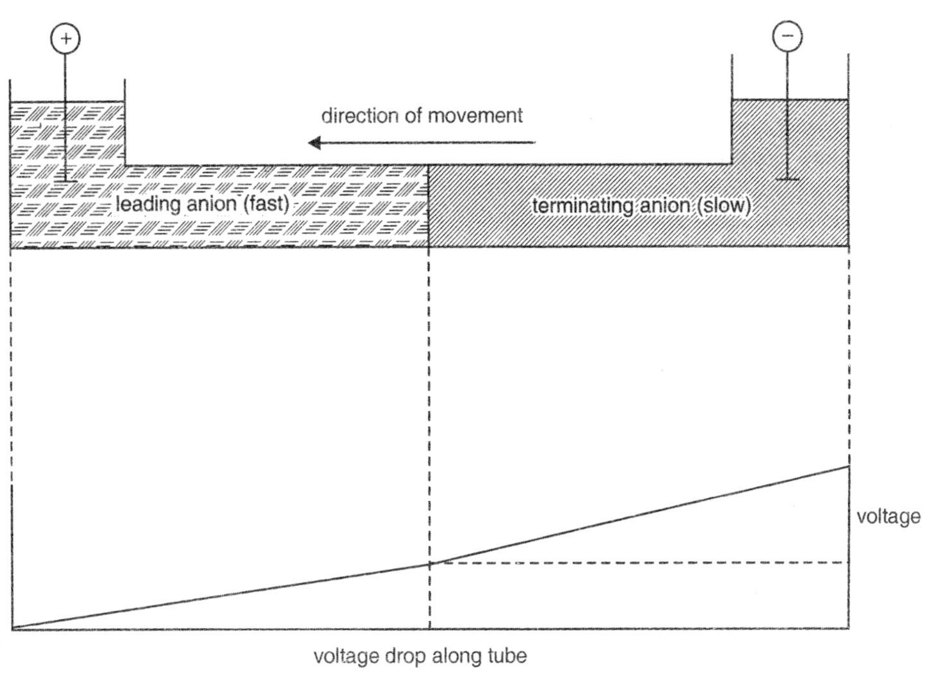

Fig. 4. Isotachophoresis. The spontaneous development of different voltage gradients across the two electrolyte solutions has the effect that both types of anion migrate at the same velocity.

resolution being able to separate proteins that differ in their isoelectric points by as little as 0·01 of a pH unit. Separation is achieved by applying a potential difference across a gel that contains a **pH gradient**. The gel of compounds known as ampholytes are complex mixture of synthetic polyamino polycarboxylic acids. Ampholytes can be purchased in different pH ranges covering a wide range of pH 3 to 10 or a narrow range between pH 7-8. Bio-Lyte and pharmalyte are available commercially.

Polyacrylamide gels (4%), agarose or IEF gels are used in this process. An IEF gel can be prepared by mixing the IEF gel, ampholyte of a suitable pH and riboflavin. This mixture is poured over a glass plate which contains a space. The second glass plate is placed on the first plate to form a gel cassette. These plates are placed in front of a bright light. The photo-decomposition of riboflavin generates a free radical which initiates polymerization. Once the gel has set, the glass plates are separated allowing gel to remain stuck to one plate. The thick strips of filter paper are wetted in phosphoric acid (the anode) and sodium hydroxide (cathode) and laid along the long length of each side of the gel and potential difference applied. Under the effect of this potential difference, the ampholytes form a pH gradient between the anode and cathode. Then the power is turned off and samples are soaked in the sample squares of filter paper that are laid on the gel. A voltage is again applied for about 30 min to electrophorese the sample off the paper and into the gel. Proteins that are initially at a pH below their isoelectric point will be positively charged & will migrate towards the cathode. As the migration will proceed, the positive charge on the protein will decrease correspondingly until eventually the protein arrives at a point where the pH is equal to its isoelectric point. Similarly proteins with a negative charge will move forwards the anode until they reach the isoelectric point and become stationary. Following electrophoresis, gels are first washed in the fixing solution (eg. 10% (v/v) trichloroaetic acid). This process precipitates the proteins in the gel. The gel is stained with Coomassie Brilliant Blue R--250 prepared as 0.1% (45:45:10 by vol.). Staining in most gels is completed in 2 hours. Destaining is done by mild agitation overnight in the same acid methanol solution. Other widely used protein stains are Ponceaus and amido black.

IEF is particularly useful in determining the microheterogenity in a protein. For example a protein may show a single band on a SDS-gel but may show three bands on an IEF gel. The technique is particularly useful in separating isoenzymes.

Isotachophoresis

Isotachophoresis is also known as displacement electrophoresis. In this process, the electrolyte between two electrodes is not a uniform single solution but a discontinuous sequence of different electrolyte solutions, ions of which all migrate at the same velocity. Under identical conditions of concentration and velocity, different ions have different electrophoretic mobilities and to cause all the ions to move at the same speed, a different voltage gradient is required for each group of ions. These different gradients develop spontaneously during the electophoretic process.

Istotachophoresis is generally performed in narrow tubes with electrodes at either end. For the separation of a particular type of ion e.g. an anion- two buffered electrolyte solutions are selected which have different anions but a common cation with a buffering capacity. One of the anions termed as leading electrolyte shows a greater mobility, than the other known as terminating electrolyte showing slower mobility. Thus a sharp boundary separating two solutions is created. A sample containing various anions is introduced in between the leading and the terminating electrolyte. These ions will move at a speed which depends upon their ionic mobility and the voltage gradient. A test ion which is in the terminating electrolyte will move quickly because of the higher voltage but when it moves into the leading electrolytes, it will slow down because of the lower voltage gradient. As a consequence the ions will move into zones in decreasing order of their ionic mobilities and a voltage pattern will develop along the tube to maintain a constant velocity of all ions. This forms the basis of qualitative or preparative form of isotachophoresis.

Quantitative Estimation of Proteins

Quantitative analysis of proteins through electrophoresis can be made by scanning densitometry. In a densitometer, stained portion of the gel is passed over a beam of laser light. In this' process a certain amount of light is transmitted. Thus a graphic presentation of protein zones (peaks of absorbance) against the distance migrated is produced. The peak areas are calculated to obtain quantitative data. An alternative and much cheaper way of obtaining such data is to carefully cut out the stained bands of interest, remove the dye by shaking overnight in a known volume of 50% pyridine. The colour thus released is measured spectrophotometrically.

Recently gel-documentation systems have been developed that are replacing the scanning densitometers. These systems comprise a video-imaging unit, attached to a dark room equipped with a transilluminator. Gel images can be stored on the computer, enhanced accordingly and printed as required on a thermal printer.

Electrophoresis of Nucleic Acids

The genomes of even the most simple organisms are extremely complex and the analysis of complex genomes remains one of the great challenges of Biology. By the early 1970s, it had been found that restriction endonucleases could be used to cut large DNA molecules into smaller fragments and then agarose or polyacrylamide gel electrophoresis could be used to separate these fragments according to their size. DNA size is measured in terms of base pairs (bp) or kilo-base pairs (kbp). Plasmid DNA-pBR-322 has 4·36 kbp. Single stranded DNA is referred in terms of nudeotides (nt). Since the charge per unit length in any given fragment of DNA is the same, all DNA molecules should move towards anode with the same mobility under an applied electric field. However, separation in Agarose gels is achieved due to resistance to their movement caused by the gel matrix. It will be difficult to larger molecules to pass through the gel whereas the small molecules will be relatively unhindered. In this process, the gel concentration is to be carefully selected. Gels containing 0·3% agarose will separate double stranded DNA between 5 and 60 kb size whereas 2% gels are used for samples between 0·1 and 3 kb. Many laboratories use 0·8% gels which are suitable for separating DNA molecules ranging between 0·5 to 10 kb.

DNA gels are run in submerged gels using horizontal submarine system. Agarose gel is prepared by boiling agarose in buffer. It is poured on a plastic or glass plate surrounded by a wax or adhesive tape or a plastic frame to provide a gel a depth of about 3 mm. The gel is placed in the electrophoresis tank, covered with a buffer and samples loaded by directly injecting the sample into the well. Samples are prepared by dissolving them in sucrose, glyaxalol or ficoll which makes the solution dense and allows it to sink to the bottom of the well. A suitable dye such as bromophenol blue is also included in the sample solvent. General purpose gels are generally 25 cm long and 12 cm wide and are run on a voltage gradient of about 1·5 vcm^{-1} overnight.

Thereafter, DNA in the gel is stained and visualized. Staining is performed by ethidium bromide. The gel is rinsed gently in a solution of ethidium bromide (0·5 $\mu g\ cm^{-1}$) and then viewed in ultraviolet light (300 nm) using a transilluminator. It is essential to protect the eyes by wearing goggles or helmet plastic mask (Fig. 5).

Southern Blotting

E.M. Southern (1975) developed a technique for- transferring single stranded DNA and denatured double stranded DNA from an agarose gel to a nylon membrane or nitrocellulose filter. The blotted DNA is tightly bound to the membrane but can still hybridize to labelled nucleic acid probe. Following steps are involved in southern blotting (Fig. 6).

(1) Preparation of DNA samples for electrophoresis
(2) Agarose gel electrophoresis
(3) Preparation of agarose gel for blotting
(4) Blotting
(5) Fixing the DNA to the membrane

There are a number of different ways to perform a southern blot.

- Capillary blotting
- Electrophoretic transfer (electroblotting)
- Vacuum blotting
- Positive pressure blotting

All these methods are suitable for blotting agarose gels. However, capillary blotting is by far the most popular method for blotting agarose gels.

Applications of southern blotting. Southern blotting has many applications in molecular biology research. It is used in important steps of gene cloning projects. Genomic DNA, containing the gene to be cloned is blotted and hybridized to identify one or

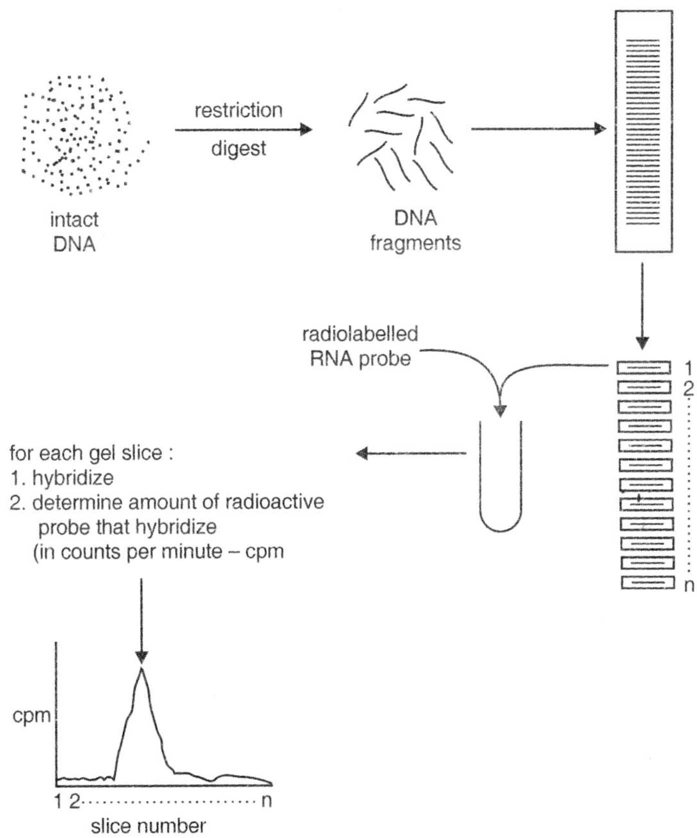

Fig. 5. Electrophoresis of DNA.

more restriction fragments containing the desired gene. A second application of southern blotting is in restriction fragment length polymorphism (RFLP) analysis, which is important in several contexts including construction of genome maps.

Electrophoresis of RNA (Northern Blotting)

Electrophoresis of RNA is usually carried out in agarose gels and the principle of separation is similar to that of DNA. However, the most important difference is that RNA molecules are single stranded rather than double stranded. Secondly, RNA is much more prone to degradation by enzymes than DNA. A third difference between RNA and DNA is that RNA is much more sensitive to hydrolysis by acid or alkali.

Since southern blotting is used to detect specific DNA molecules, a number of workers modified this technique to detect RNA. The resulting procedure was named as northern blotting by molecular biologists.

Northern blotting allows to determine whether a particular gene probe hybridizes to one or more RNA species in a given cell type. It also allows to determining the length of the hybridizing RNA species and gives an indication of their abundance.

After electrophoresis, the RNA is transferred from the gel to a nylon membrane by diffusion blotting or electroblotting. After transfer, the membrane is either placed in UV-crosslinker or vacuum oven at 80°C to irreversibly attach the RNA to the filter. After pre-hybridization, the filter is exposed to a solution containing a suitable probe and hybridization is begun. Either DNA or antisense RNA can be used as probes. The probe is usually radioactively labelled so that a hybridization signal can be visualized on a film or photoimager system.

Northern blotting has a sensitivity of detection of approximately 1-5 mg of a particular species of mRNA.

The term "reverse Northern", refers to the procedure in which DNAs are attached to a nylon membrane followed by hybridization with labelled

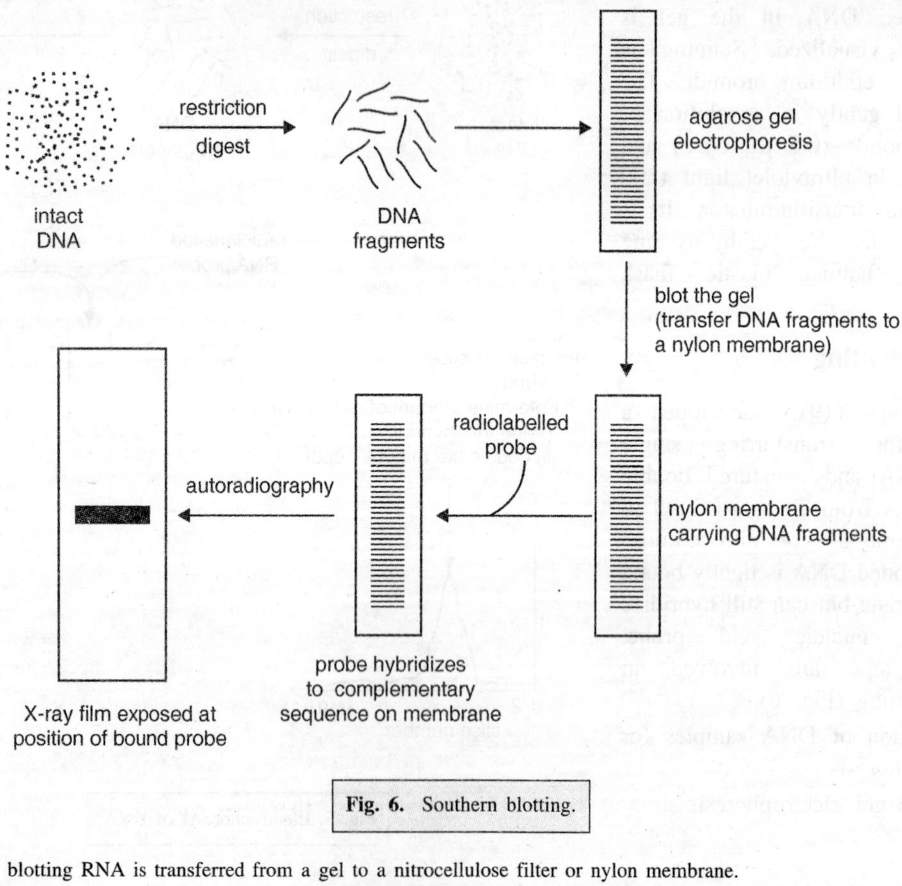

Fig. 6. Southern blotting.

* In northern blotting RNA is transferred from a gel to a nitrocellulose filter or nylon membrane.

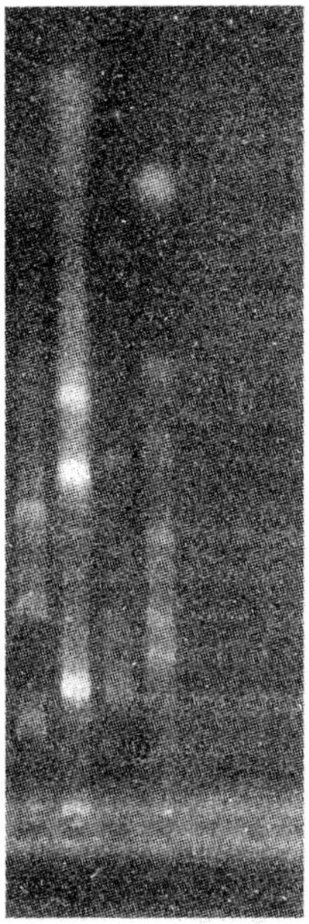

Fig. 7. Gel electrophoresis of RNA in a 1·4% agarose gel. Track 1 is total RNA from the tobacco plant denatured with glyoxal prior to running. Track 2 is the same sample, not denatured. The two faster-running major bands are 18 S and 25 S ribosomal RNA. The slower running major band is nuclear DNA. Tracks 3 and 4 show a mixture of RNA marker fragments, with (track 3) and 4 without (track 4) glyoxal treatment. The sizes of the marker RNA fragments are 0·24, 1·4, 2·4. 4·4, 7·5 and 9·5 kb. Note that, with each sample, denaturation results in lower mobilities for the components of each sample.

RNA probes. This procedure can provide quantitative data regarding mRNA abundance but not on mRNA size.

Western Blotting

More recently, the **"Western blotting"** technique has been developed for transferring proteins from SDS-polyacrylamide gels to nitrocellulose filters so that they can be detected with labeled antibodies or other protein binding molecules. The transfer of proteins from the gel to nitrocellulose can be achieved in one of two ways i.e. capillary blotting or electroblotting. The nitrocellulose with its transferred protein is called as blot. The blot can be further examined to detect a specific protein. DNA sequences that bind nuclear proteins have been identified by transferring double stranded DNA

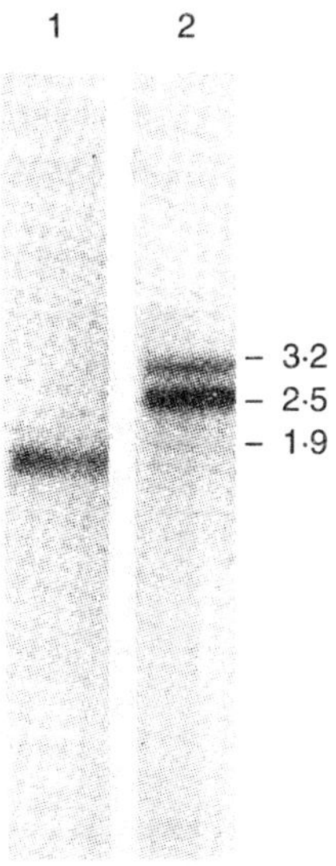

Fig. 8. Northern Blots.

molecules from agarose gels to filters and incubating them with labelled proteins attracted from cell nuclei. This process is called as "south western blotting". A method for blotting polyadenylated m-RNA from agarose gels to cellulose filter paper coupled with polyuridylic acid enjoyed brief fame as **"middle eastern blotting"**.

Capillary Electrophoresis

As the name suggests capillary electrophoresis (CE) is carried out in very narrow bore tubes (internal diameter = 250 μm and external diameter – 300 μm). CE works on the following equation

$$t = \frac{L^2}{\mu v}$$

where t is the migration time for a solute, L is the tube length, μ is the electrophoretic mobility of the sample and v is the applied voltage.

The basic instrument design is shown in Figure 9. Sample is introduced at the anode end of a fused silica capillary tube containing an appropriate buffer through anyone of the following methods.

1. High voltage injection. Here the sample is introduced applying high voltage. The sample reservoir is then removed, buffer reservoir replaced voltage applied and separation is commenced.

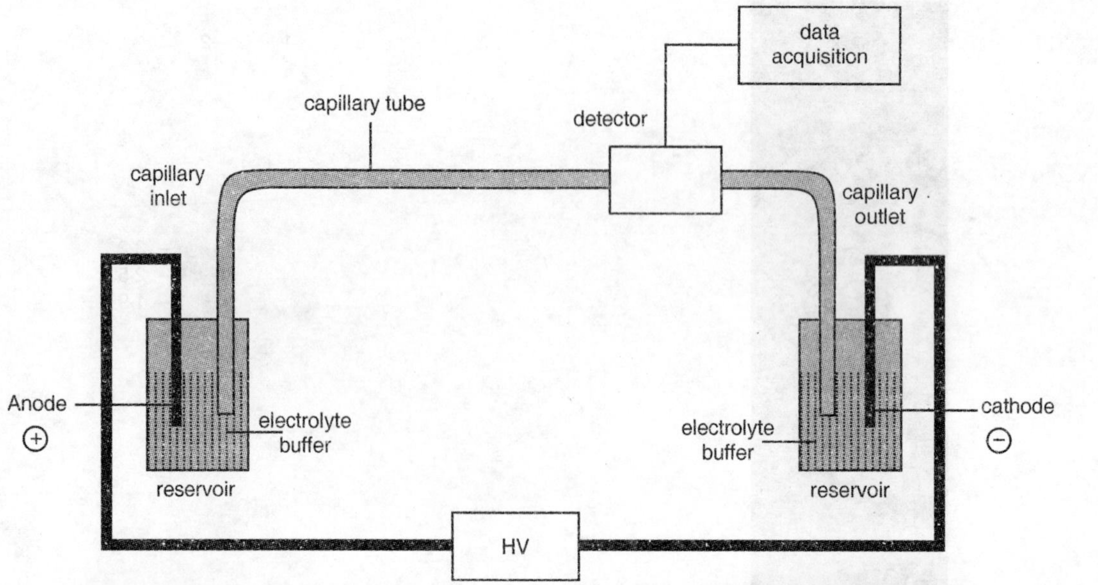

Fig. 9. Diagrammatic representation of a typical capillary electrophoresis apparatus.

2. Pressure injection. In this technique, the capillary is removed from the anode buffer reservoir and inserted through an airtight seal into the sample solution. A pressure by second tube is applied to force the sample into the capillary.

Molecules of the injected sample migrate at different rates along the length of the capillary tube. Negative and positive charged molecules reach the cathode first. As the separated molecules approach the cathode, they pass through a viewing window where they are detected by an ultraviolet monitor that transmits the signal to recorder, integrator or computer. Typical run times are between 10-30 minutes.

A wide range of biological molecules including amino acids, peptides, proteins, DNA fragments, small organic molecules such as drugs and their metabolites can be detected in physiological solutions such as urine or serum. Chiral compounds can also be detected by CE. Point mutation that occur in DNA during a range of human diseases can also be identified by CE.

Important Questions

1. Who described for the first time the process of electrophoresis? What do you understand by electrophoretic mobility? Discuss the procedure of electrophoretic separation of proteins.
2. Give a detailed account of different supporting media used in the process of electrophoresis.
3. Write short notes on the following:
   (i) Iso-electricfocusing, (ii) Isotachophoresis.
4. Describe the process used for the separation of nucleic acids by electrophoresis.
5. Write briefly on the following :
   (i) Southern blotting, (ii) Northern blotting, (iii) Western blotting, (iv) Capillary electrophoresis.

Polymerase Chain Reaction (PCR)

14

There have been a number of key developments in molecular biological techniques; the one that has had the most impact in recent years is the polymerase chain reaction (PCR). One of the reasons for the adoption of FCR is the elegant simplicity of the reaction and relative ease of the practical manipulation steps. The polymerase chain reaction is a technique for quickly "cloning" a particular piece of DNA in the test tube (rather than in living cells like *E. coli*). Unlimited copies of a single DNA molecule can be synthesized from a mixture containing many different DNA molecules.

Kary Mullis invented PCR in 1983. He was awarded the Nobel Prize in Chemistry in 1993 for this achievement. Mullis's aim was to develop a process by which DNA could be artificially multiplied through repeated cycles of duplication driven by an enzyme called DNA polymerase. DNA polymerase occurs naturally in living organisms, where it functions to duplicate DNA when cells divide in mitosis and **meiosis**. Polymerase works by binding to a single DNA strand and creating the complementary strand. In Mullis's original process, the enzyme was used *in vitro*. The double-stranded DNA was separated into two single strands by heating it to 94°C. At this temperature, however, the DNA polymerase used at the time was destroyed, so the enzyme had to be replenished after the heating stage of each cycle. Mullis's original procedure required a great deal of time, large amounts of DNA polymerase, and continual attention throughout the process.

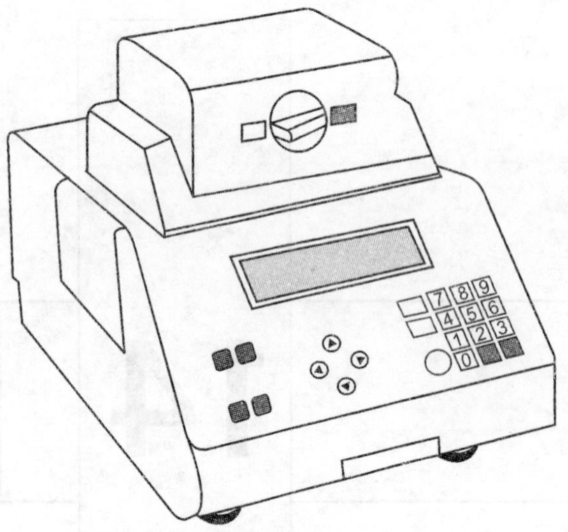

Fig. 1. Thermal cycler.

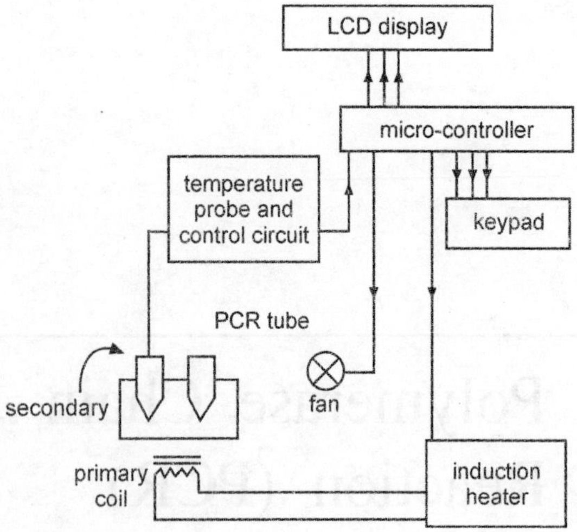

Fig. 2. Block diagram of the various parts of the thermal cycler.

Later, this original PCR process was greatly improved by the use of DNA polymerase taken from thermophilic bacteria grown in geysers at a temperature of over 110°C. The DNA polymerase taken from these organisms is stable at high temperatures and, when used in PCR, does not break down when the mixture was heated to separate the DNA strands. Since there was no longer a need to add new DNA poiymerase for each cycle, the process of copying a given DNA strand could be simplified and automated.

One of the first thermostable DNA polymerases was obtained from *Thermus aquaticus* and was called **Taq. Taq** polymerase is widely used in current PCR practice. A disadvantage of *Taq* is that it sometimes makes mistakes when copying DNA, leading to mutations in the DNA sequence, since it lacks 3′ ~> 5′ proofreading exonuclease activity. Polymerases such as **Pwo** or **Pfu**, obtained from *Archaea,* have "proofreading mechanisms" (mechanisms that check for errors) and can significantly reduce the number of mutations that occur in the copied DNA sequence. However, these enzymes polymerize DNA at a much slower rate than **Taq**. Combinations of both **Taq** and **Pfu** are available nowadays, and provide both high processivity (fast polymerization) and high fidelity (accurate duplication of DNA).

The PCR reaction is carried out in a thermal cycler (Fig. 1). This is a machine that heats and cools the reaction tubes within it to the precise temperature required for each step of the reaction. To prevent evaporation of the reaction mixture, a heated lid is placed on top of the reaction tubes or a layer of oil is put on the surface of the reaction mixture.

A block diagram of the various parts of the thermal cycler is shown in Fig. 2. It consists of the induction heater and its river circuit, a fan for cooling the reaction tubes, a temperature probe and control circuit, and a micro-controller with a keypad and an LCD display for programming the cycling parameters.

Principle and Wroking Mechanism

The purpose of a PCR {Polymerase Chain Reaction) is to make a huge number of copies of a gene. This is necessary to have enough starting template for sequencing.

The DNA sample is heated to separate its strands and mixed with the primers. If the primers find their complementary sequences in the DNA, they bind to them. Synthesis begins (5′ – 3′, as always) using the original strand as the template. The reaction mixture must contain all four deoxyribonucleotide triphosphates (dATP, dCTp *dGTF,* dTTP) and a DNA polymcrase.

DNA Replication (Synthesis)

- A portion of the double heiix is unwound by a helicase.
- A molecule of a DNA polymerase binds to one strand of the DNA and begins moving along it in the 3′ to 5′ direction, using it as a template for assembling a leading strand of nucleotides and reforming a double helix. In eukaryotes, this molecule is called DNA polymerase delta ($).
- Because DNA synthesis can only occur 5′ to 3′, a molecule of a second type of DNA polymerase (epsilon, e, in eukaryotes) binds to the other template strand as the double helix opens. This molecule must synthesize discontinuous segments of polynucleotides {called Okazaki fragments). Another enzyme, DNA ligase I then stitches these together into the lagging strand.

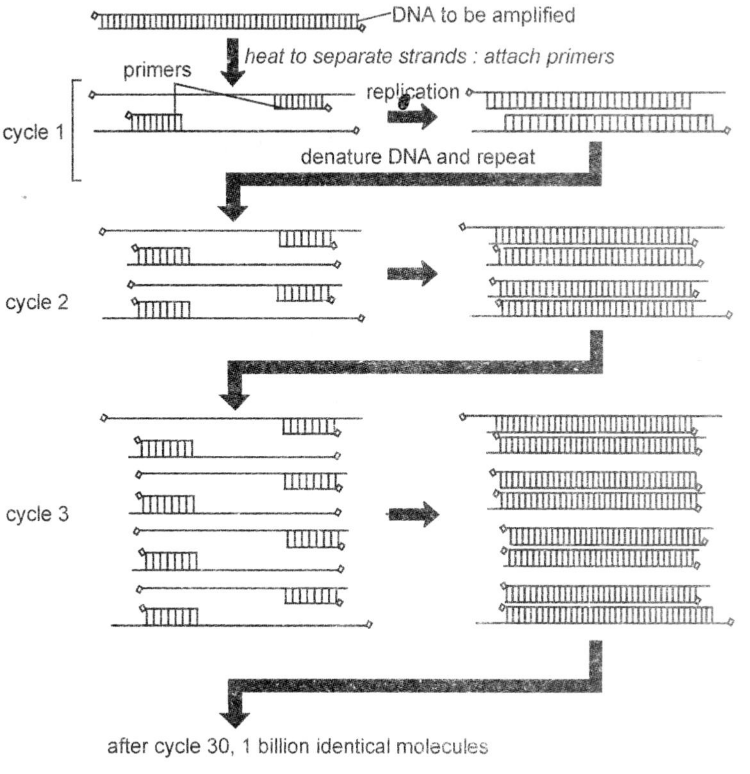

Fig. 3. The cycling reactions in PCR.

Polymerization continues until each newly synthesized strand has proceeded far enough to contain the site recognized by the other primer. Two DNA molecules identical to the original molecule are thus synthesized. Each cycle doubles the number of DNA molecules.

The Cycling Reactions

There are three major steps in a PCR, which are repeated for 30 or 40 cycles. This is done on an automated cycler, which can heat and cool the tubes with the reaction mixture in a very short time.

1. Denaturation at 94°C. During the denaturation, the double strand melts open to single-stranded DNA, all enzymatic reactions stop (for example: the extension from a previous cycle).

2. Annealing at 54°C. The primers are jiggling around, caused by the Brownian motion. Ionic bonds are constantly formed and broken between the single-stranded primer and the single-stranded template. The more stable bonds last a little bit longer (primers that fit exactly) and on that little piece of double-stranded DNA (template and primer), the polymerase can attach and start copying the template. Once there are a few bases built in, the ionic bond is so strong between the template and the primer that it does not break anymore.

3. Extension at 72°C. This is the ideal working temperature for the polymerase. The primers, where there are a few bases built in, already have a stronger ionic attraction to the template than the forces breaking these attractions. Primers that are on positions with no exact match get loose again (because of the higher temperature) and do not give an extension of the fragment. The bases (complementary to the template) are coupled to the primer on the 3′ side (the polymerase adds dNTPs from 5′ to 3′, reading the template from 3′ to 5′ side, bases are added complementary to the template).

After 30 cycles, what began as a single molecule of DNA has been amplified into more than a billion copies (Fig. 3).

Constraints in PCR

Polymerase Errors

Taq polymerase lacks a 3′ to 5′ exonuclease activity. This makes it impossible for it to check the base it has inserted and remove it if it is incorrect, a process common in higher organisms. This in turn results in a high error rate (approximately 1 in 10000 bases). If an error occurs early, it can alter large proportions of the final product. As a result other polymerases are available for accuracy in vital uses such as amplification for sequencing. Some examples of polymerases with 3' to 5' exonuclease activity include **Vent** (*Thermococcus litoralis*), **Pfu** {*Pyrococcus juriosus*) and **Pwo** {*Pyrococcus woesii*).

Size Limitations

PCR works readily with DNA of lengths 2-3 kb, but above this length the polymerase tends to fall off and the typical heating cycle does not leave enough time for polymerization to complete. It is possible to amplify larger pieces (up to 20 kb), with a slower heating cycle and special polymerases.

Non-Specific Priming

The non-specific binding of primers is always a possibility due to sequence duplications, non-specific binding and partial primer binding (leaving the 5′ end unattached). This is increased by the use of degenerate sequences or bases in the primer. Manipulation of annealing temperature and magnesium ion (which stabilize DNA and RNA interactions) concentrations can increase specificity.

Practical Modifications of the PCR Technique

Nested PCR

Nested PCR is intended to reduce the contamination in products due to the amplification of unexpected primer binding sites. Two sets of primers are used in two successive PCR runs, the second set intended to amplify a secondary target within the first run product. This is very successful, but requires more detailed knowledge of the sequences involved.

Inverse PCR

Inverse PCR is a method used to allow PCR when only one internal sequence is known. This is especially useful in identifying flanking sequences to various of genomic inserts. This involves a series of digestions and self ligations before being cut by an endonuclease, resulting in known sequences at either end of the unknown sequence.

RT-PCR

Reverse Transcription PCR is the method used to amplify, isolate or identify a known sequence from the RNA library of a cell or tissues. This is widely used in expression mapping, determining when and where certain genes are expressed.

Asymmetric PCR

Asymmetric PCR is used to preferentially amplify one strand of the original DNA more than the other. It finds use in sequencing where only one of the complementary strands is required for sequencing. PCR is carried out as usual, but with a great excess of the primers for the chosen strand. Due to the slow amplification, many cycles of PCR are required.

Quantitative PCR and Real Time PCR

Quantitative PCR (Q-PCR) is used to rapidly measure the quantity of PCR product (preferably real-time), and thus is an indirect method for quantitatively measuring starting amounts of DNA, cDNA or RNA. This is commonly used for the purpose of determining whether a sequence is present or not, and if it is present, the number of copies in the sample. Quantitative real-time PCR is generally known as ORT-PCR or RTO-PCR.

Touchdown PCR

Touchdown PCR is a variant of PCR that reduces non-specific primer annealing by variation of primer annealing temperature between cycles.

Recent Developments in PCR Techniques

- A more recent method which excludes a temperature cycle, but uses enzymes, is helicase-dependent amplification.
- TAIL-PCR, developed by Liu *et al* in 1995, is the **thermal asymmetric interlaced** PCR.
- Meta-PCR, developed by **Andrew Wallace**, allows to optimize amplification and direct sequence analysis of complex genes.

Applications

Human Health and the Human Genome Project

PCR has very quickly become an essential tool for improving human health and human life. Medical research and clinical medicine are profiting from PCR mainly in two areas: detection of infectious disease organisms, and detection of variations and mutations in genes, especially human genes. Because PCR can amplify unimaginably tiny amounts of DNA, even that from just one cell, physicians and researchers can examine a single sperm, and track down the elusive source of a puzzling infection.

The method is especially useful to detect the AIDS virus : during the first few weeks after infection than the standard ELISA test. PCR looks directly for the virus's unique DNA, instead of the method employed by the standard test, which looks for indirect evidence that the virus is present by searching for antibodies the body has made against it.

PCR can also be more accurate than standard tests. It is making a difference, for example, in a painful, serious, and often stubborn misfortune of childhood, the middle ear infection known as otitis media. The technique has detected bacterial DNA in children's middle ear fluid, signalling an active infection even when culture methods failed to detect it.

Lyme disease, the painful joint inflammation caused by bacteria transmitted through tick bites, is usually diagnosed on the basis of symptom patterns. But PCR can identify the disease organism's DNA contained in joint fluid, permitting speedy treatment that can prevent serious complications.

PCR is the most sensitive and specific test for *Helicobacter pylori,* the disease organism now known to cause almost all stomach ulcers. Unlike other tests, PCR can detect three different sexually transmitted disease organisms on a single swab (herpes, papilloma viruses, and chlamydia) and can even distinguish the particular strain of papilloma virus that predisposes to cancer, which other tests cannot do.

With PCR analysis of cells shed into faeces, premalignant changes in the gastrointestinal tract such as mutations in genes that protect against tumours can be demonstrated. Researchers have also detected potentially metastatic cells in the circulation of patients with newly diagnosed tumours.

PCR can also be used to differentiate mutations in a single gene, each of which can lead to a disorder such as Duchenne muscular dystrophy. It helps doctors track the presence or absence of DNA abnormalities characteristic of particular cancers, so that they can start and stop drug treatments and radiation therapy as soon as possible. And it promises to greatly improve the genetic matching of donors and recipients for bone marrow transplantation.

PCR can even diagnose the diseases of the past. **Hubert H. Humphrey** underwent tests for bladder cancer in 1967. Although the tests were negative, he died of the disease in 1978. In 1994, researchers compared a 1976 tissue sample from his cancer-ridden bladder with his 1967 urine sample, With **the help** of PCR amplification of the small amount of DNA in the 27-year-old urine, they found identical mutations in the p53 gene, well known for suppressing tumors, in both samples. "Humphrey's examination in 1967 may have revealed the cancerous growth if the techniques of molecular biology were as well understood then as they have become," the researchers said.

Historical medical genetics has gone even further back in time with PCR. After the colour-blind British chemist John Dalton died in 1844, some tissue from his eyes was preserved. Dalton had asked for a posthumous investigation of the reason why he confused scarlet with green and pink with blue. A recent examination of DNA taken from that tissue, carefully amplified by PCR, has shown

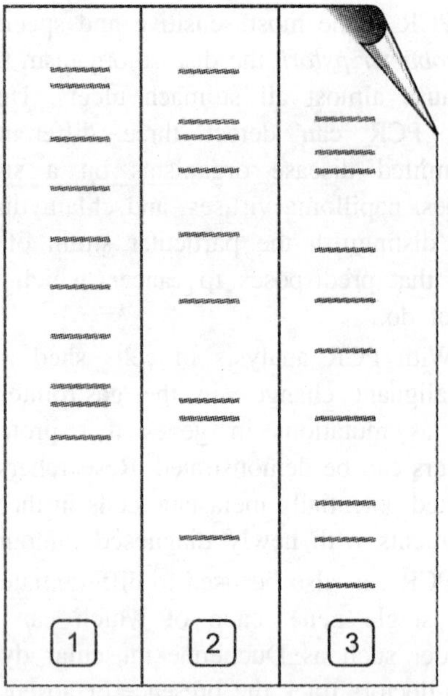

Fig. 4. Electrophoresis of PCR-amplified DNA fragments. (1) Father (2) Child (3) Mother

that Dalton lacked a gene for making one of the three photopigments essential for normal colour vision.

Many of the new genetic tests are the result of the Human Genome Project, the huge international effort to identify and study all human genes. DNA sequencing reveals crucial variations in the nucleotides that constitute genes. These mutational changes produce disease and even death by forcing the genes to produce abnormal proteins, or sometimes no proteins at all. DNA sequencing involves isolating and duplicating DNA segments for nucleotide analysis. Thus PCR is an essential tool for the Human Genome Project because it can quickly and easily generate an unlimited amount of any piece of DNA for this kind of study.

Genetic Fingerprinting

Genetic fingerprinting is a forensic technique used to identity person by comparing his or her DNA with a given sample, such blood from a crime scene can be genetically compared to blood from a suspect. The sample may contain only a tiny amount of DNA, obtained from a source such as blood, semen, saliva, hair, or other organic material. Theoretically, just a single strand is needed. First, one breaks the DNA sample into fragments, then amplifies them using PCR. The amplified fragments are then separated using gel electrophoresis. The overall layout of the DNA fragments is called a **DNA fingerprint**. Since there is a very small possibility that two individuals may have the same sequences, the technique is more effective at acquitting a suspect than proving the suspect guilty.

Figure 4 shows the electrophoresis of PCR-amplified DNA fragments of a father, child and a mother. The child has inherited some, but not all of the fingerprint of each of its parents, giving it a new, unique fingerprint. Although these resulting 'fingerprints' are unique (except for identical twins), genetic relationships, for example, parent-child or siblings, can be determined from two or more genetic fingerprints, which can be used for paternity tests, A variation of this technique can also be used to determine evolutionary relationships between organisms.

Detection of Hereditary Diseases

The detection of hereditary diseases in a given genome is a long and difficult process, which can be shortened significantly by using PCR. Each gene in question can easily be amplified through PCR by using the appropriate primers and then sequenced to detect mutations. Viral diseases can also be detected using PCR through amplification of the viral DNA. This analysis is possible right after infection, which can be from several days to several months before actual symptoms occur. Such early diagnoses give physicians a significant lead in treatment.

Cloning Genes

Cloning a gene, not to be confused with cloning a whole organism, describes the process of isolating a gene from one organism and then inserting it into another organism (now termed a genetically modified organism (GMO)). PCR is often used to amplify the gene, which can then be inserted into a vector (a vector is a piece of DNA which 'carries' the gene into the GMO) such as a plasmid (a circular DNA molecule) (Fig. 5). The DNA can then be transferred into an organism (the GMO) where the gene and its product can be studied more closely. Expressing a cloned gene [when a gene is expressed, the gene product (usually protein or RNA) is produced by the GMO] can also be a way of mass-producing useful proteins, for example medicines or the enzymes in biological washing powders. The incorporation of an affinity tag on a recombinant protein will generate a fusion protein which can be more easily purified by affinity chromatography.

Mutagenesis

Mutagenesis is a way of making changes to the sequence of nucleotides in the DNA. There are situations in which one is interested in mutated (changed) copies of a given DNA strand, for example, when trying to assess the function of a gene or in *in vitro* protein evolution. Mutations can be introduced into copied DNA sequences in two fundamentally different ways in the PCR process. Site-directed mutagenesis allows the experimenter to introduce a mutation at a specific location on the DNA strand. Usually, the desired mutation is incorporated in the primers used for the PCR program. Random mutagenesis, on the other hand, is based on the use of error-prone polymerases in the PCR process. In the case of random mutagenesis, the location and nature of the mutations cannot be controlled. One application of random mutagenesis is to analyse structure-function relationships of a protein. By randomly altering a DNA sequence, one can compare the resulting protein with the original and determine the function of each part of the protein.

Analysis of Ancient DNA

Using PCR, it becomes possible to analyse DNA that is thousands of years old. PCR techniques have been successfully used on animals such as a forty thousand-year-old mammoth, and also on human DNA, in applications ranging from the analysis of Egyptian mummies to the identification of a Russian tsar.

Genotyping of Specific Mutations

Through the use of allele-specific PCR, one can easily determine which allele of a mutation or polymorphism an individual has. Here, one of the two primers is common, and would anneal a short distance away from the mutation, while the other anneals right on the variation. The 3' end of the allele-specific primer is modified, to only anneal if it matches one of the alleles. If the mutation of interest is a T or C single nucleotide polymorphism (T/C SNP), one would use two reactions, one containing a primer ending in T, and the other ending in C. The common primer would be the same. Following PCR, these two sets of reactions would be run out on an agarose gel, and the band pattern will tell us if the individual is homozygous T, homozygous C, or heterozygous T/C. This methodology has several applications such as amplifying certain haplotypes (when certain alleles at 2 or more SNPs occur together on the same chromosome [Linkage Disequilibrium]) or detection of recombinant chromosomes and the study of meiotic recombination.

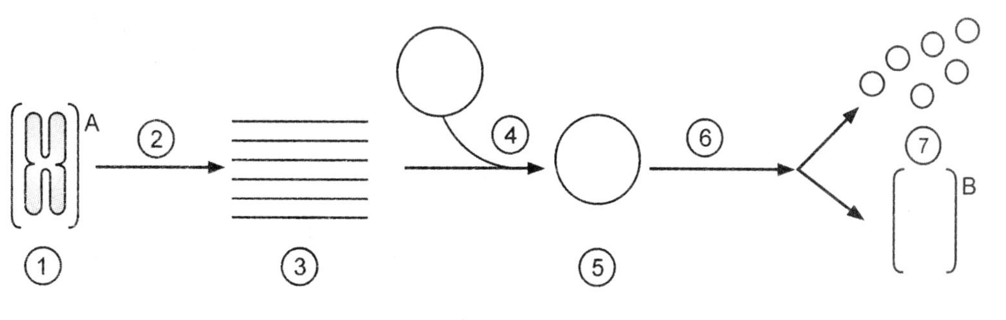

Fig. 5. Cloning a gene using a plasmid (1) Chromosomal DNA of organism A (2) PCR (3) Multiple copies of a single gene from organism A(4) Insertion of the gene into a plasmid (5) Plasmid with gene from organism A (6) Insertion of the plasmid in organism B (7) Multiplication or expression of the gene, originally from organism A, occurring in organism B

Comparison of Gene Expression

Researchers have used traditional PCR as a way to estimate changes in the amount of a gene's expression. RNA is the molecule into which DNA is transcribed prior to making a protein, and those strands of RNA that hold the instructions for protein sequence are known as messenger RNA (mRNA). Once RNA is isolated it can be reverse transcribed back into DNA (complementary DNA to be precise, known as cDNA), at which point traditional PCR can be applied to amplify the gene. This methodology is called RT-PCR. In most cases, if there is more starting material (mRNA) of a gene, then during PCR more copies of the gene will be generated. When the product of the PCR reaction are run on an agarose gel, a band, corresponding to a gene, will appear larger on the gel. By running samples of amplified cDNA from differently treated organisms one can get a general idea of which sample expressed more of the gene of interest.

Important Questions

1. Explain the applications of the following :
(i) PCR; (ii) Nested PCR; (iii) Inverse PCR; (iv) RT-PCR; (v) Asymmetric PCR; (vi) ORT-PCR; (vii) Touchdown PCR; (viii) TA1L-PCR.
2. Explain the principle and working mechanism of PCR. Add a note on its applications.

15 Immunodiagnostic Methods

Nature has equipped man and animals with a system known as immune system so as to protect from infection caused by viruses, bacteria, fungi protozoa and parasitic worms. In addition to these organisms, certain agents like pollen grains, dust particles, xenobiotics and drugs cause allergy. All these agents are foreign to the body. They are called as antigens. Introduction of these antigens into the body triggers an immune response producing antibodies. Those substances which are not capable of initiating an immune response by themselves but after conjugating with a protein may result into the formation of antibodies are called as haptens. Antigen-antibody reactions thus provide the basis of very useful methods of qualitative and quantitative analysis of biological molecules.

The detailed mechanisms of immune response are not fully understood but certain major features are generally accepted. The introduction of an antigen into the susceptible animal results into the proliferation of lymphocytes in the tissues viz: liver, spleen, bone marrow, thymus and lymph nodes collectively known as reticulo-endothelial system. The lymphocytes are a heterogenous group of cells. Those derived from thymus are called as T-lymphocytes. Those derived from Bursa of Fabricius are called as B lymphocytes. In man, bone marrow is the source of B lymphocytes.

An immunologically competent cell, whether T or B lymphocyte is thought to have specific membrane bound receptors. The combination of these receptors with an appropriate antigen stimulates the proliferation of cells resulting in a clone of identical cells, a process known as clonal selection. This process forces the antigen to eliminate by normal cellular processes. If the antigen is a toxic substance, its effect may be neutralized by combination with the antibody.

Antibodies

Antibodies are a group of globular proteins known as immunoglobulins. Immunoelectrophoretic studies have shown that immunoglobulins can be divided into subclasses based on their antigenic nature. These consist of monomers or multimers of a basic four chain, bilaterally symmetrical structure containing two light and two heavy chains. Five varieties of heavy chain (known γ, μ, α, δ and ε chains) occur in higher vertebrates and these determine the class of immunoglobulin (known as IgG, IgM, IgA, IgD and IgE) respectively. In mammals the IgG and IgA are further divided into subclasses. Different species have different type of immunoglobulins. The characteristics of these immunoglobulins are described below —

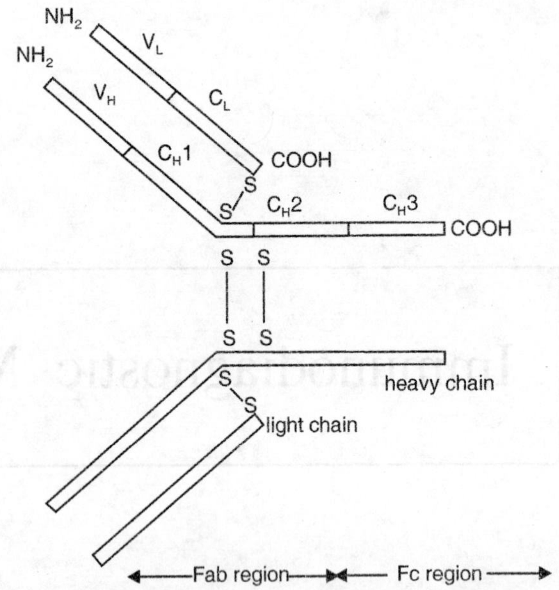

Fig. 1. Basic structure of an immunoglobulin molecule. The basic structure is common to all classes of immunoglobulin and consists of two identical light polypeptide chain and two identical heavy chains linked together by disulphide bonds. The heavy and light chains are divided into variable (V) and constant (C) regions or domains of about 110 amino acids. These are known as V_L and C_L for the light chain and V_H, C_H1, C_H2 etc. for the heavy chain.

Immunoglobulins Classes and Subclasses

The physical and biological characteristics of the five major immunoglobulin classes in the human are summarized in Table 1 and 2. The following comments are intended to supplement this information.

1. Immunoglobulin G. During the secondary response IgG is probably the major immunoglobulin to be synthesized. Through its ability to cross the placenta it provides a major line of defence against infection for the first few weeks of a baby's life which may be further reinforced by the transfer of colostral IgG across the gut mucosa in the neonate. IgG diffuses more readily than the other immunoglobulins into the extravascular body spaces, where, as the predominant species, it carries the major burden of neutralizing bacterial toxins and of binding to micro-organisms to enhance their phagocytosis. The complexes of

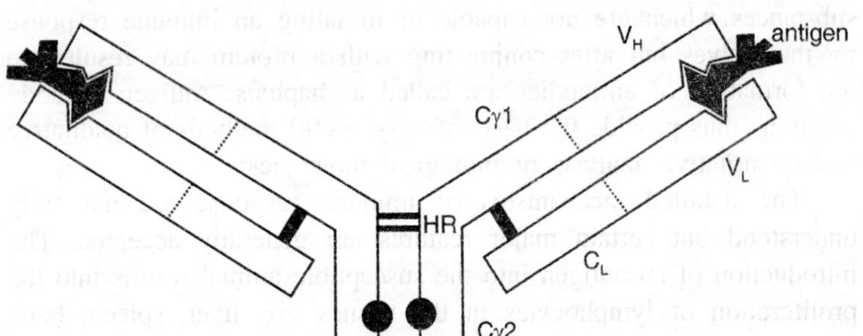

Fig. 2. Structure of IgG. A simple model of IgG_1 showing the various domains of the light and heavy chains. The association of the V_H and V_L domains forms the antigen binding site into which the complementary epitope will fit. The position of the carbohydrate is shown by the black circles and disulphide bonds that join the chains are depicted by black bars. In all IgG molecules there is a hinge region (HR) between the CY_1, CY_2 domains.

Table 1. **Physical properties of major humans immunoglobulin classes.**

Designation	IgG	IgA	IgM	IgD	IgE
Sedimentation coefficient	7S	7S,9S,11S*	19S	7S	8S
Molecular weight	150,000	160,000	900,000	185,000	200,000
Number of basic four-peptide units	1	1,2*	5	1	1
Heavy chains	γ	α	μ	δ	ε
Light chains	$\kappa + \lambda$	$\kappa + \lambda$	$\kappa + \lambda$	$\kappa + \lambda$	$\kappa + \lambda$
Molecular formula !	$\gamma_2\kappa_2$, $\gamma_2\lambda_2$	$(\alpha_2\kappa_2)_{1\text{-}2}$ $(\alpha_2\lambda_2)_{1\text{-}2}$ $(\alpha_2\lambda_2)_2S$* $(\alpha_2\kappa_2)_2S$*	$(\mu_2\kappa_2)_5$ $(\mu_2\lambda_2)_5$	$\delta_2\kappa_2$ $(\delta_2\lambda_2?)$	$\varepsilon_2\kappa_2$, $\varepsilon_2\lambda_2$
Valence for antigen binding	2	2,4	5 (10)	2	2
Concentration range in normal serum	8 – 16 mg/ml	1.4-4 mg/ml	0.5-2 mg/ml	0-0.4 mg/ml	17-450 ng/ml!!
% Total immunoglobulin	80	13	6	0-1	0.002
% Carbohydrate content	3	8	12	13	12

*Dimer in external secretions carries secretory component –S
! IgA dimmer and IgM contain J-chain
!!ng = 10^{-9}g.

Table 2. **Biological properties of major immunoglobulin classes in the human.**

	IgG	IgA	IgM	IgD	IgE
Major characteristics	Most abundant Ig internal body fluids particularly extravascular where it combats microorganisms and their toxins	Major lg in sero-mucous secretions where it defends external body surfaces	Very effective agglutinator; produced early in immune response-effective first line defence vs bacteraemia	Most, if not all, present on lymphocyte surface	Protection of external body surfaces. Recruits antimicrobial agents raised in parasitic infections responsible for symptoms of atopic allergy
Complement fixation					
Classical	+ +	–	+ + +	–	–
Alternative	—	±	–	–	–
Cross placenta	+	–	–	–	–
Fix to homologous mast cells and basophils	–	–	–	–	+
Binding to macrophages and polymorphs	+	±	–	–	–

bacteria with IgG antibody activate complement thereby chemotactically attracting polymorpho-nuclear phagocytic cells which adhere to the bacteria through surface receptors for complement and the Fc portion of IgG; binding to the Fc receptor then stimulates ingestion of micro-organisms through phagocytosis.

In a similar way, the extracellular killing of target cells coated with IgG antibody is mediated largely through recognition of the surface Fcy by NK cells bearing the appropriate receptors. The interaction of IgG complexes with platelet Fc receptors presumably leads to aggregation and vasoactive amine release but the physiological significance of Fc binding sites on other cells types, particularly lymphocytes, has not yet been clarified. Although unable to bind firmly to mast cell in human skin, IgG alone amongst the human immunoglobulins has the somewhat useless property of fixing to guinea-pig skin. The thesis that the biological individuality of different immunoglobulin classes is dependent on the heavy chain constant regions, particularly the Fc, is amply borne out in relationship to the activities we have discussed such as transplacental passage, complement fixation and binding to various cell types, where function has been shown to be mediated by the Fc part of the molecule.

With respect to overall regulation of IgG levels in the body, the catabolic rate appears to depend directly upon the total IgG concentration whereas synthesis is largely governed by antigen stimulation, so that in germ-free animals, for example, IgG levels are extremely low but rise rapidly on transfer to a normal environment.

2. Immunoglobulin A. IgA appears selectively in the sero-mucous secretions such as saliva, tears, nasal fluids, sweat, colostrums and secretions of the lung, genito-urinary and gastro-intestinal tracts where it clearly has the job of defending the exposed external surfaces of the body against attack by microorganisms. It is present in these fluids as a dimmer stabilized against proteolysis by combination with another protein - the secretary component which is synthesized by local epithelial cells and has a single peptide chain of molecular weight 60,000. The IgA is synthesized locally by plasma cells and dimerized intracellularly together with a cysteine-rich polypeptide called J-chain of molecular weight 15000. If dimerization occurred randomly after secretion, dimmers of mixed specificity would be formed which would not be as effective in combining with antigen as those of single specificity which would have a higher effective valency. The dimeric IgA binds strongly to the secretory component precursor present on the surface of the cell in which it was produced and the complex is then actively endocytosed, transported across the cytoplasm and secreted into the external body (Fig. 3).

IgA antibodies function by inhibiting the adherence of coated micro-organisms to the surface of mucosal cells thereby preventing entry into the body tissues. Aggregated IgA binds to polymorphs and can also activate the alternative (Fig. 3), as distinct from the classical complement, pathway which probably accounts for reports of a synergism between IgA, complement and lysozyme in the

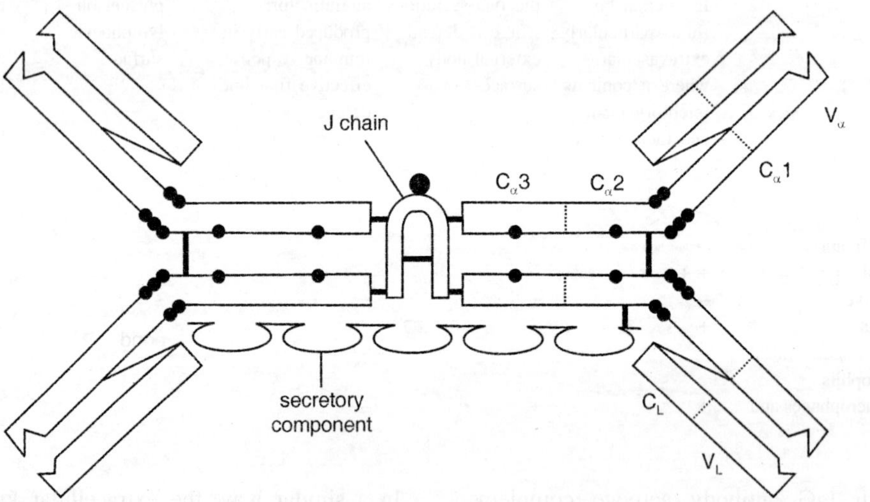

Fig. 3. Structure of secretory IgA. In the dimeric form two IgA molecules are joined together by a J chain. The secretory component is held in place by non-covalent interactions and by a disulphide bond (black bar) to the C_I2 domain. Disulphide bonds also join the light chain to the heavy chain, hold the two heavy chain together and link the J chain to the two IgA monomers. The positions of carbohydrate residues are shown by black circles.

killing of certain coliform organisms. Human plasma contains relatively high concentrations of monomeric IgA and its role still remains a mystery.

3. Immunoglobulin M. Often referred to as the macroglobulin antibodies because of their high molecular weight, IgM molecules are polymers of five four-peptide subunits each bearing an extra CH domain. As with IgA, polymerization of the subunits depends upon the presence of J-chain whose function may be to stabilize the Fc sulphydryl groups during Ig synthesis so that they remain available for cross-linking the subunits to give the structure shown in Figure 4. Under negative staining in the electron microscope, the free molecule in solution assumes a 'star' shape but when combined as an antibody with an antigenic surface membrane it can adopt a 'crab-like' configuration. The theoretical combining valency is of course 10 but this is only observed on interaction with small haptens; with larger antigens the effective valency falls to 5 and this must be attributed to some form of steric restriction due to lack of flexibility in the molecule. IgM antibodies tend to be of relatively low affinity as measured against single determinants (haptens) but, because of their high valency, they bind with quite respectable avidity to antigens with multiple epitopes.

For the same reason, these antibodies are extremely efficient agglutinating and cytolytic agents and since they appear early in the response to infection and are largely confined to the blood-stream, it is likely that they playa role of particular importance in cases of bacteraemia. The isohaemagglutinins (anti-A, anti-B) and many of the 'natural' antibodies to micro-organisms are usually IgM; antibodies to the typhoid '0' antigen (endotoxin) and the 'WR' antibodies in syphilis also tend to be found in this class. IgM would appear to precede IgG in the phylogeny of the immune response in vertebrates.

Monomeric IgM (i.e. a single four-peptide unit) with a hydrophobic sequence stitched into the C-terminal end of the heavy chain to anchor the molecule in the cell membrane, is the major antibody receptor used by B-Iymphocytes to recognize antigen.

4. Immunoglobulin D. This class was recognized through the discovery of a myeloma protein which did not have the antigenic specificity of IgG, A or M, although it reached with antibodies to immunoglobulin light chains and had the basic

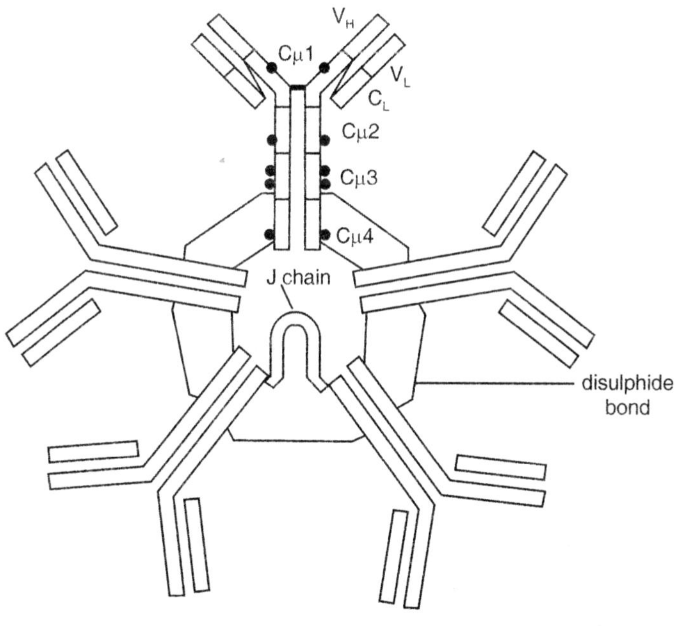

Fig. 4. Structure of IgM. The polymeric form of IgM consists of five monomer subunits joined by disulphide bridges linking adjacent C_r3 and C_r4 domains. A J chain is also present. There is no higher region in the subunits. The position of the carbohydrate is shown by black circles.

Table 3. **Comparison of human IgG subclasses.**

	IgG1	IgG2	IgG3	IgG4
% Total IgG in normal serum	65	23	8	4
Electrophoretic mobility	Slow	Slow	Slow	Fast
Spontaneous aggregation	-	-	+++	-
Gm allotypes	a,z,f,x	N	b0,b1,b3,g,s,t etc.	-
Ga site reacting with rheumatoid factor*	+++	+++	-	+++
Combination with staphylococcal A protein	+++	+++	-	+++
Cross placenta	++	±	++	++
Complement	+++	+++	-	+++
Cross placenta	++	±	++	++
Complement fixation pathway	+++	++	++++	±
Binding to monocytes	+++	+	+++	±
Binding to heterologous skin	++	-	++	++
Blocking IgE binding	-	-	-	+
Antibody dominance	Anti-Rh	Anti-dextran Anti-levan	Anti-Rh	Anti- Factor VIII

*Other rheumatoid factors apparently react with Gm specific sites.

four-peptide structure. The hinge region is particularly extended and although protected to some degree by carbohydrate, it may be this feature which makes IgD, among the different immunoglobulin classes, uniquely susceptible to proteolytic degradation, and account for its short half-life in plasma (2·8 days). An exciting development has been the demonstration that nearly all the IgD is present, together with IgM, on the surface of a proportion of blood lymphocytes where it seems likely that they may operate as mutually interacting antigen receptors for the control of lymphocyte activation and suppression. The even greater susceptibility of IgD to proteolysis on combination with antigen could well be implicated in such a function.

5. Immunoglobulin E. Only very low concentrations of IgE are present in serum and only a very small proportion of the plasma cells in the body are synthesizing this immunoglobulin. It is not surprising, therefore, that so far only six cases of IgE myeloma have been recognized compared with tens of thousands of IgG paraproteinaemias. IgE antibodies remain firmly fixed for an extended period when injected into human skin where they are probably bound to mast cells. Contact with antigen leads to degranulation of the mast cells with release of vasoactive amines. This process is responsible for the symptoms of hay fever and of extrinsic asthma when patients with atopic allergy come into contact with the allergen, e.g. grass pollen.

The main **physiological** role of IgE would appear to be protection of the external mucosal surfaces of the body by local recruitment of plasma factors and effector cells through triggering an acute inflammatory reaction. Infectious agents penetrating the IgA defences would combine with specific IgE on the mast cell surface and trigger the relase of vasoactive agents and factors chemotactic for granulocytes, so leading to an influx of plasma IgG, complement, polymorphs and eosinophils. In such a context, the ability of eosinophils to damage IgG-coated helminthes and the generous IgE response to such parasites would constitute an effective defence.

6. Immunoglobulin subclasses. Antigenic analysis of IgG myelomas revealed further variation and showed that they could be grouped into four isotypic *subclasses* now termed IgG 1, IgG2, IgG3 and IgG4. The differences all lie in the heavy chains which have been labelled γ1, γ2, γ3 and γ4 respectively. These heavy chains show considerable homology and have certain structures in common with each other - the ones which react with specific anti-IgG antisera - but each has one or more additional structures characteristic of its own subclass arising from differences in primary amino acid composition and in interchain disulphide bridging. These give rise to differences in biological behaviour which are summarized in Table 3.

Two subclasses of IgA have also been found, of which IgAl constitutes 80-90% of the totaL The

IgA2 subclass is unusual in that it lacks interchain disulphide bonds between heavy and light chains. Class and subclass variation is also restricted to human immunoglobulins but is a feature of all the higher mammals viz: monkey, sheep, rabbit, guinea-pig, rat and mouse, so far studied.

Immunoassay

Assays employing antibodies for qualitative, semiqualitative and quantitative analyses are broadly termed as immunoassays. In other words immunoassays are methods, utilizing immunological reactions for the analysis of biological molecules. In the past, simple immunoassays were performed *e.g.* determination of blood groups or bacterial agglutination tests. However, in recent times, automated systems for immunological analysis have been developed. The methods generally used today are as follows—

[I] Direct methods
(i) Precipitation, (ii) Agglutination,
(iii) Neutralization, (iv) Complement fixation tests

[II] Indirect methods
(i) Enzyme immunoassays, (ii) Immunofluorescence,
(iii) Radioimmunoassays.

In addition to these tests, allergy testing, human leucocyte antigen typing and immunosensing techniques have also been developed.

Antigen-Antibody Reactions

An antibody combines specifically with the corresponding antigen or hapten in a manner which is very similar to the binding of a enzyme to its substrate and involving hydrophobic and ionic interactions. The bonding between antigen and antibody, however, involves no subsequent chemical reaction and its stability depends upon the complementary shape of the antigen and antibody. In analytical techniques, it is highly desirable to use antibodies which have a high affinity for the antigen. This property is called as **avidity**.

Many antigens are large and may have many antigenic characteristics or **determinants**. Serum taken from an animal that has been immunized against that antigen will contain different antibodies against different antigenic determinants. In such cases, cross reactivity may occur between antigens and antibodies. Therefore, antisera used for analytical purposes should be specific and it is essential that every antiserum should be thoroughly tested prior to its use.

Production of Antibodies

The raising of a specific antiserum by the immunization of an animal involves the parenteral injection of the pure antigen often introduced intramuscularly. A series of injections involving small amounts of antigens are likely to be more effective than a single large injection. An initial injection is normally followed by several booster doses given at two to four week intervals. Too frequent injections may result in an antiserum of reduced avidity.

The selection of animals is very important in raising the antisera. The species to be injected should be different from that from which the antigen has been obtained. The guinea pigs and rabbits are most frequently used for raising the antisera against antigens. Sometimes goats and horses are also used.

Antigens have the ability to initiate an immune response. Usually the antigen is administered with an adjuvant. An adjuvant is a mixture of substances which stimulates an inflammatory response and prevents the rapid removal of the antigen from the tissues by the normal drainage mechanism. FREUND's adjuvant consists of an emulsion of dead mycobacteria in mineral oil but simpler alternatives of aluminium phosphate or hydroxide have similar effect. In order to raise antibodies against a nonimmunogenic molecule (hapten), it is essential to link it to a carrier protein which is capable of initiating a response. Bovine or human serum albumin is used for this purpose. The hapten should be covalently linked with the carrier protein. The process is achieved by using carbodiimide. It results into an amide bond between a carboxyl and amino group on the protein and the hapten. Similarly, glutaraldehyde may be used giving a linkage between the amino-group and a reactive hydrogen.

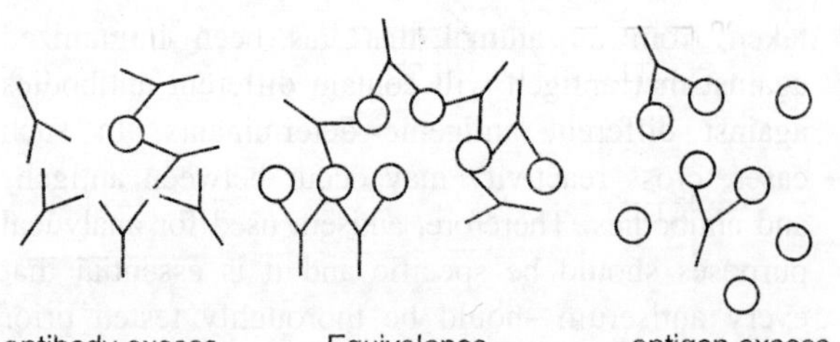

Fig. 5. Diagrammatic representation of immiune complexes formed at varying antigen : antibody ratios. Immunoprecipitation occurs only when an insoluble antigen antibody lattice is formed at the equivalence point.

Immunoprecipitation

Many soluble antigens may be detected and measured by precipitation using antibodies. Antibodies are divalent (IgG) or multivalent (IgM). The antigen, antibody interaction will give rise to an molecular lattice that is too large to remain in solution, so precipitation will occur. The formation of insoluble antigen--antibody complex is very much dependent on their concentration and usually occurs within a narrow range known as the zone of equivalence. Outside the zone of equivalence, the condition known as antigen or antibody excess occurs which results into the formation of small soluble complexes. Immunoprecipitation can be performed in solution or in gels.

Immunoprecipitation in Solution

The precipitation of a soluble antigen by an antibody produces an opalescent solution which can be measured by a photometer or nephelometer. Nephelometer is better than photometer because it measures the scattered light. The extent of light scattered by a turbid solution increases as the wavelength of incident radiation decreases. Generally antigen-antibody complexes are measured in the range of 350 to 400 nm. Nowadays laser nephelometer have been developed to improve the sensitivity. Immunoprecipitation is a valuable

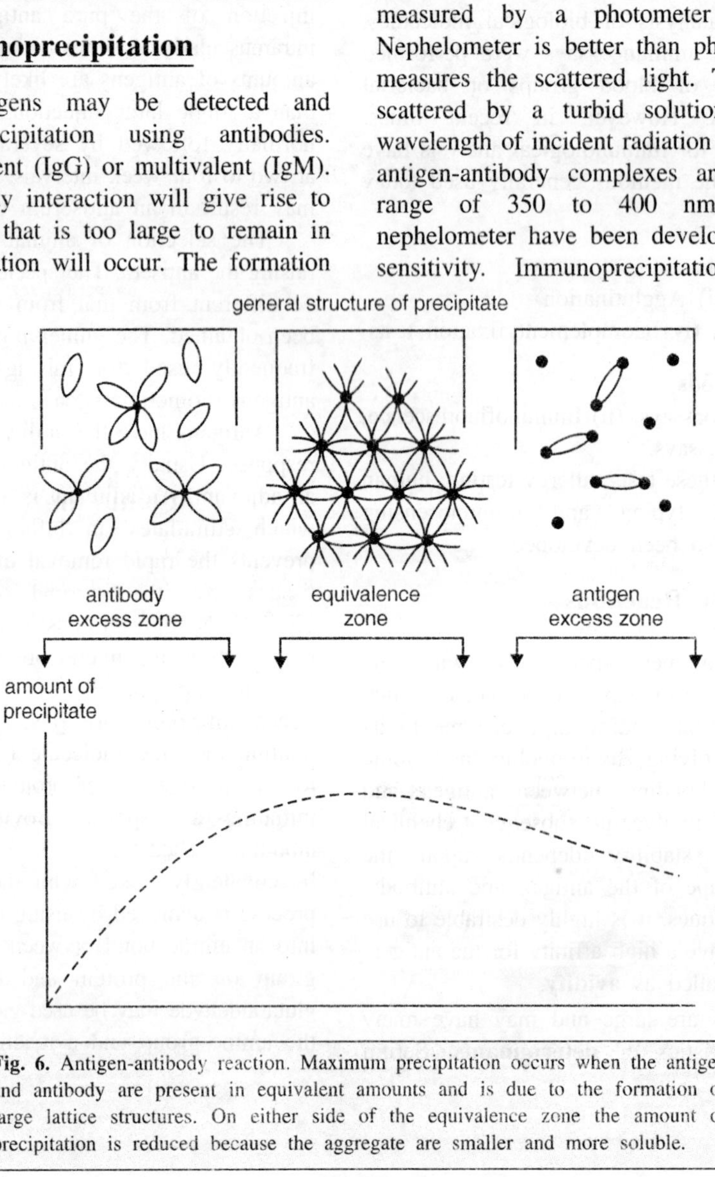

Fig. 6. Antigen-antibody reaction. Maximum precipitation occurs when the antigen and antibody are present in equivalent amounts and is due to the formation of large lattice structures. On either side of the equivalence zone the amount of precipitation is reduced because the aggregate are smaller and more soluble.

technique since it allows the quantitation of a specific protein in the presence of many other proteins.

Immunoprecipitation in Gels

Gels are sometimes used in immunoprecipitation techniques to stablize the precipitate enabling both the position and area of the precipitate to be measured. Precipitation in agar is typically carried out on 2 to 3 mm thick gel cast on microscope glass slides. Warm agar solution is simply poured onto the slide and allowed to set. Wells are made onto the gel using a large bore pipette. In diffusion technique antigen and/or antibody migrate through the gel by simple diffusion. In double diffusion separate wells cut in the agar are filled with antibody and antigen respectively. Both diffuse into and through the agar automatically forming concentration gradients. A precipitin line is formed at the equivalence point. This technique is used to find out the structural similarities or differences between antigens. The area of precipitation is related to the concentration of antigen and in practice the diameter of each ring is measured to the nearest 0.1 mm and a plot of diameter squared against concentration should give a straight line graph (Fig. 7).

Single radial immunodiffusion technique described above offers a sensitive and specific method for the quantitation of individual proteins. However, it is time consuming. Therefore, an electrophoretic technique was developed by **Lauren** (1966). It is called as **rocket electrophoresis**. It involves electrophoretic migration of antigens from wells cut in antibody containing gel. At equivalence rocket shaped precipitation lines are formed, the area under which is proportional to the antigen concentration. The antigen concentration in serum samples can be determined by this technique (Fig. 8).

A calibration curve for the quantitation of unknown samples may be prepared by plotting peak height against the concentration of the antigen. The method shows slightly improved sensitivity to the single radical immunodiffusion technique.

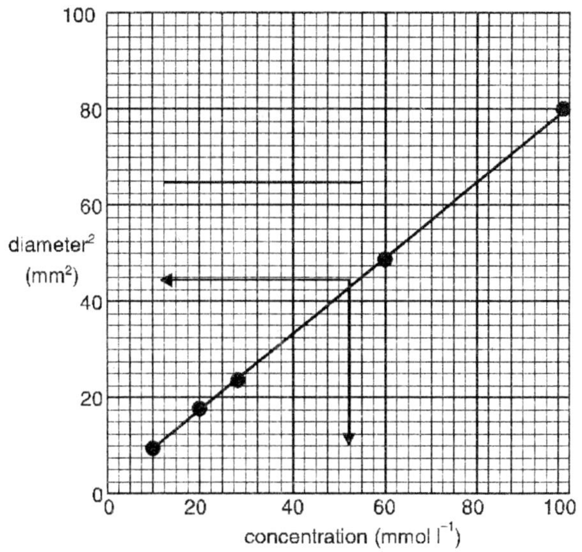

Fig. 7. Quantitation of albumin by single radial immunodiffusion.

A calibration curve for the quantitation of unknown samples may be prepared by plotting peak height against the concentration of the antigen. The method shows slightly improved sensitivity to the single radical immunodiffusion technique.

Radioimmunoassay (RIA)

Radioimmunoassay was developed in 1950 so as to monitor the metabolism of insulin in diabetic patients. Subsequently the method was extended to measure hapten such as drugs and steroid hormones. RIA is more sensitive and specific than chemical methods.

The principle of the technique involves the reaction between the limited amount of a specific antibody with a fixed amount of isotopically labelled antigen and the test sample. When the reaction has reached an equilibrium, the bound and free forms of the labelled antigen are separated from each other and amount of radioactivity in one or both fractions is determined. More recently immuno-radiometric methods have been developed in which the antibody rather than the antigen is labelled.

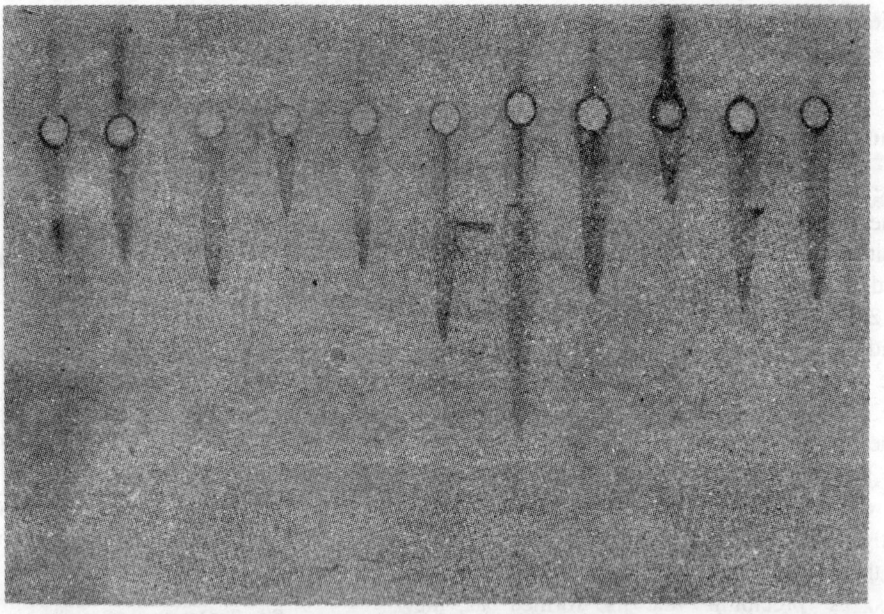

Fig. 8. Rocket elecrophoresis. At pH 8·6 most proteins move towards the anode and precipitation occurs where the antigen and the antibody (in the gel) are in equivalent proportions. The size of the resulting 'rocket'-shaped pattern of precipitate is proportional to the original concentration of antigen. The immunoglobulins show very little electrophoretic mobility at pH 8·6 and so remain in the gel during the process.

How to Label an Antigen?

In this process, a pure sample of antigen is to be obtained or prepared. Often the only source of hormone is the tissue in which it is synthesized. It is to be extracted from the tissue and purified. The purified sample hormone is then labelled with a suitable radioisotope. The choice of isotope is important. Most commonly used isotopes are carbon-14, tritium and the iodine isotopes 125 and 131. Their half life and emission properties are shown by the following Table 4.

Table 4. **Isotopes commonly used in radio immunoassay.**

Isotope	Half life	Emission
Carbon-14	560a	Beta
Hydrogen-3 (tritium)	12.26a	Beta
Iodine-125	60d	Beta & gamma
Iodine-131	8.04d	Beta & gamma

Measurement of beta emission requires liquid scintillation counter whereas gamma emissions are measured with the gamma counters.

Small volumes of the antigen/protein and an appropriate isotope/iodine are mixed in a buffered solution and free iodine is produced by the addition of an oxidizing agent like chloramine T or the enzyme lactoperoxidase. The reaction is stopped after a short time (15-16 seconds) by the addition of sodium metabisulphite. The purity of the labelled antigen is confirmed through electrophoresis.

1. Separation of bound antigen from free antigen. The whole quantitative basis of RIA depends upon the separation of bound and free antigen. Since extremely low concentrations of both reactions are used, antigen-antibody complex does not readily precipitate and a wide variety of techniques have been used to achieve this separation. Several methods are used to separate free from bound antigen (Table 5).

Table 5. **Methods for separating free from bound antigen.**

Method	Example	Comments
Precipitation of proteins	Saturated solution of Ammonium sulphate	Only useful for non-protein antigens, e.g. steroids
Adsorption of free antigen	Dextran-coated charcoal for polar antigens	Non-specific, only suitable
Immunological precipitation of antibodies	Antibodies against the immunoglobulins of appropriate species	Specific, expensive, reliable
Solid phase systems	Cellulose or plastic supports	Simple but usually commercial in origin

(a) Precipitation. Precipitation of the protein is one simple method. Precipitating agents such as solutions of ammonium sulphate, sodium bisulphate, polyethylene glycol and certain organic solvents e.g. ethanol and dioxane are commonly used. The efficiency of precipitation is very dependent upon the concentration of the precipitating agent and affected by factors such as temperature, pH and protein concentration. While such methods are economical, they are also nonspecific and tend to be unreliable.

(b) Adsorption. Adsorption process is particularly useful when polar antigens such as peptide or steroid are to be separated. Particulate charcoal can absorb antibody complex. Charcoal is usually coated with dextran which reduces its adsorption preventing the access of large molecules to the surface by a molecular sieving effect. The reaction time for adsorption is critical. The charcoal is subsequently sedimented by centrifugation and the supernatant that contains bound antigen is removed, the radioactivity in either fraction being measured. Other absorptive agents viz: silica & talc may also be used.

(c) Immunoprecipitation. Bound antigen is separated by a technique called as immuno-precipitation or double antigen technique. It depends upon the precipitation of antigen antibody complex by the addition of an appropriate amount of second antibody directed against the gamma globulins of the animal in which the first antibody was raised. The precipitating antibody is raised in an animal of the different species from that used in the first antibody.

1st antibody system (rabbit) IInd antibody system (goat)

$$Ag + Ab \Leftrightarrow AgAb + \text{antirabbit } \gamma\text{ - globulin}$$

Usually the precipitating antibody is added after the initial reaction has reached an equilibrium and following a further reaction period the mixture is centrifuged and the free antigen decanted with the supernatant fluid. This technique is very specific and can be applied to any antigen antibody system.

(d) Antibody concentration. The avidity of an antiserum is a measure of its ability to bind firmly to the antigen while the concentration is expressed as the titre and measured as the highest point of dilution of the antiserum while it will still give a demonstrable reaction with the antigen the concentration or titre at which an antiserum is used in an assay determines the analytical range and must be appropriate for the amount of labelled antigen, used. Initially, a standard amount of labelled antigen must be selected and in practice the analytical range of a method is approximately one-half to five times the amount of labeled antigen used. Hence if the likely concentration range of test samples is known, a working amount of labeled antigen may be initially selected. The amount of antibody required is then determined by testing decreasing amounts of antiserum against the fixed amount of labelled antigen. This process is called as "titrating the antibody" (Fig 9). the typically S-shaped titration curve from which the dilution of antis erum which will bind 50% of the labelled antigen can be selected.

Assay Procedure

Appropriate small volumes of a diluent buffer, an antibody preparation, a labelled antigen and the test or the standard samples are mixed and allowed to react for a given time at a particular temperature. Subsequently, the two forms of the labelled antigen are separated from each other and the radioactivity, usually of one phase, is measured.

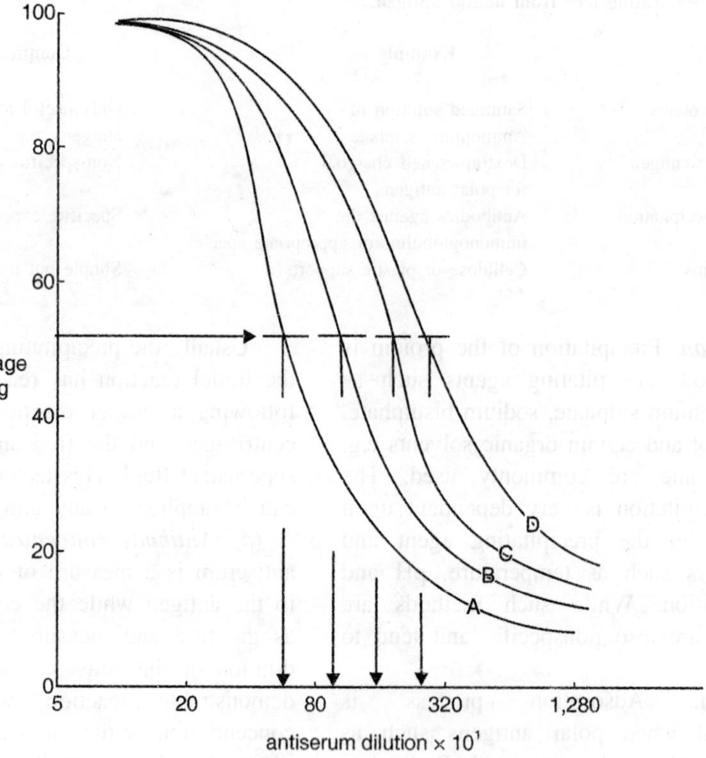

Fig. 9. Radio-imunoassay of insulin-titration of antiserum.

A variety of buffers with pH values varying from 7·4 to 8·6 can be used. They are mixed with bovine or human serum albumin to prevent the adsorption of any of the reactants, particularly the antigen. A bacteriostatic agent such as merthiolate is also incorporated in the buffer when a long reaction time is used.

A calibration curve is plotted from data obtained by analyzing samples containing known amounts in a medium of similar composition to the test samples. Depending upon the method of separation, either the amount of labelled antigen bound by antibody (B) or the amount of free labelled antigen (F) will be measured. Although the ratio of bound or free is the most logical parameter to use, in practice, the other value is calculated by the difference from the total activity. In such cases, it is better to plot the ratio of bound to total (T) activity against the concentration of the unlabelled antigen (Fig. 10).

Radio-immunoassay methods show a high level of sensitivity. Values of coefficient of variation are often in the range of ± 5% and may be as high as ± 10% between assays.

The shelf life of reagents is also limited. The instrument required is expensive.

RIA of Insulin - as an Example

(1) 1·0 ml barbital buffer, pH 7·4 containing 9gl^{-1} NaCl and 3·5 gl^{-1} human serum albumin.

(2) 0·2 ml ^{125}I-insulin containing 2μUml^{-1}

(3) 0·2 ml test or control solution

(4) 0·2 ml antiserum dilution (e.g. 1 in 100,000)

(5) Mix and incubate for 1 hour at 4°C

(6) Add 0·8 ml charcoal (50 gl^{-1}) dextran (5gl^{-1} dextran 50) suspension mix and immediately centrifuge for 15 min at 2000 × g.

Decant the supernatant and count the radioactivity of the supernatant.

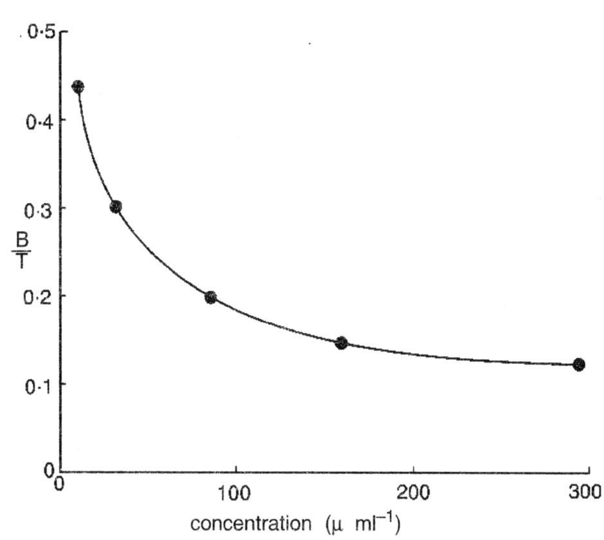

Fig. 10. Radio-immuno assay of insulin-calibration curve.

Enzyme Immunoassay

In enzyme immunoassay, the technique is further divided in two types the heterogenous assay and homogeneous assay. In heterogenous assay, an enzyme label is used as a means of detection and bound and free forms of antigens are separated. The homogeneity does not depend upon the physical separation of two phases because the process of binding to the antibody modifies the activity of the enzyme label, enabling one of the two forms of the label to be detected and measured in the presence of the other.

Heterogenous Assay

Enzyme linked immunosorbent assay (ELISA). The original ELISA was developed along the lines of a solid phase radio-immunoassay replacing the radioactive label with an enzyme. The method involves the binding of an antibody to the walls of a plastic tube. Subsequently, the test and labelled antigens are added which compete for the available antibody. After a prescribed reaction time, the tube is washed to remove all the reagents except those which are bound to the antibody. The amount of enzyme labelled antigen which is bound to the tube wall can be measured by monitoring the enzyme reaction after the addition of a suitable substrate. Under carefully controlled conditions, the amount of product formed is proportional to the amount of enzyme present and inversely proportional to the amount of test antigen.

A key reagent for ELISA is the enzyme conjugate. In most cases, the enzyme is cross--linked covalently to an antibody. The ELISA method is, indeed, adaptable to any legend and receptor pair. The most common enzymes used are alkaline phosphatase and horseradish peroxidase. Enzyme activity is measured through optical absorbance but

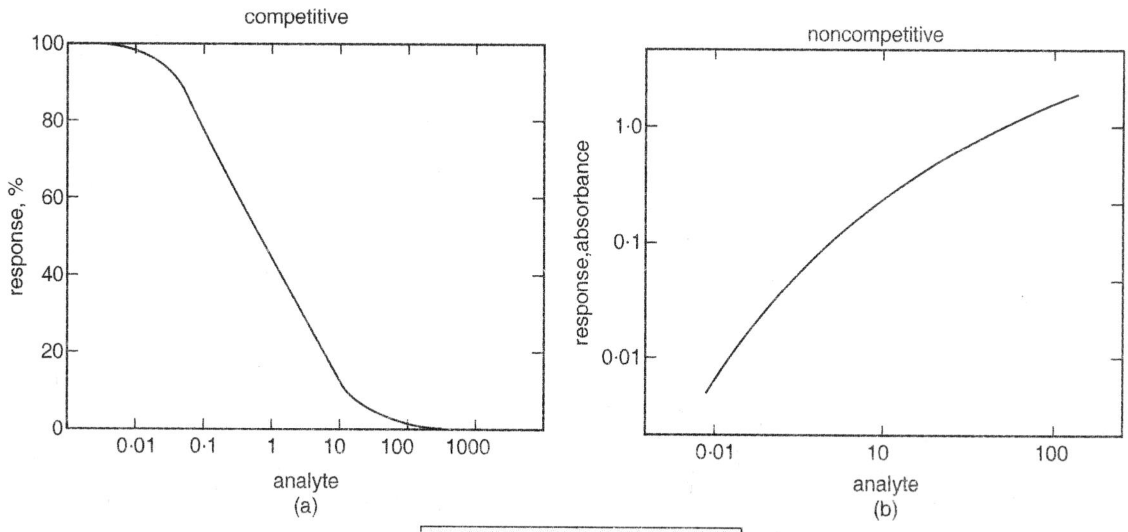

Fig. 11. ELISA standard curves.

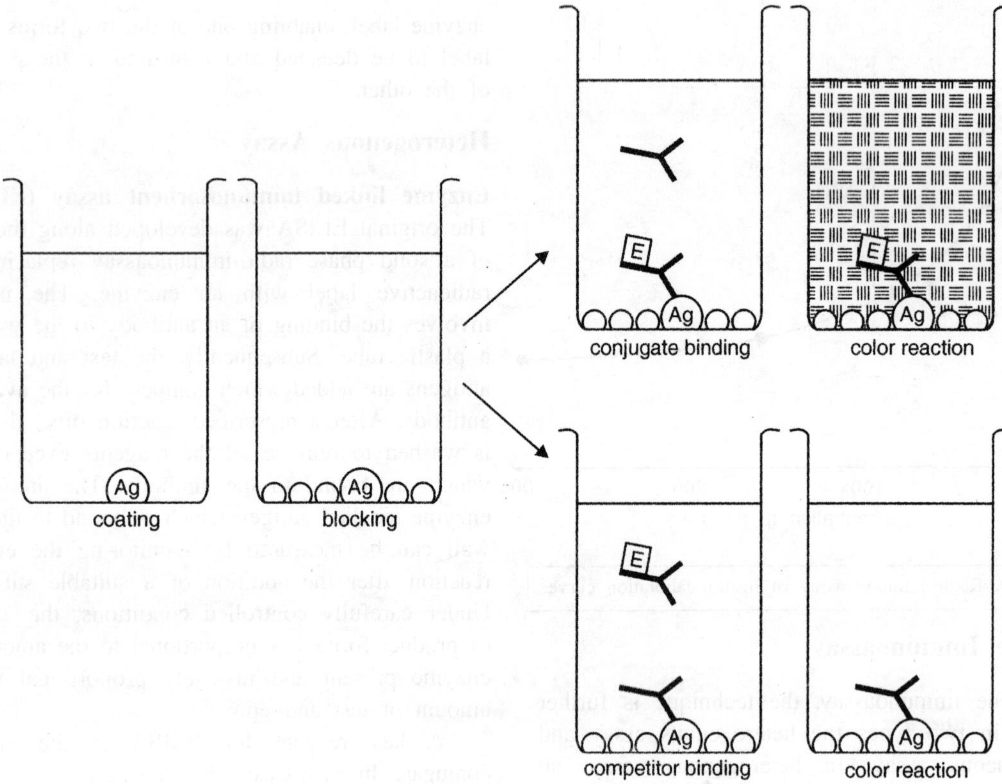

Fig. 12. Competitive ELISA.

fluorescence or chemiluminiscence techniques are also used.

A number of ELISA experiments can be designed, however, simplest and most useful methods are described below.

1. Competitive ELISA. This method begins with adsorption of antigen to the surface of a microtiter plate (Fig. 12). The solution containing antigen is allowed to stand in the wells of the plate. The linkage to the plate is noncovalent but essentially irreversible and the adsorbed antigen is seldom released during subsequent reactions and washing steps. In the second step, a concentrated solution of protein such as serum albumin is used to coat the remaining walls. Thirdly, the plate is washed with a neutral buffer. At the fourth stage, the antibody solutions of unknown concentrations and a series of controls consisting of known quantity of same antibody are mixed with a fixed amount of antibody-enzyme conjugate and added to different walls of the plate. The conjugate binds to the immobilized antigen, so does the unconjugated antibody and binding of each is mutually exclusive. The antigen is allowed to bind for sometime and the plate is washed again. Now the substrate is added to initiate the reaction. The rate of product release or accumulation of the product is determined after a fixed time for unknown and control samples. Reactions in which no unlabelled competitor was added will have the highest absorbance and are taken as 100% response, whereas controls (lacking antigen or conjugate) give the lowest absorbance. This value is treated as 0% response. Data from other controls are plotted in a calibration curve. The value from unknown sample is compared to the calibration curve and the corresponding concentration is read.

2. Indirect ELISA. Indirect ELISA is most common method used to assess the seropositivity of subjects exposed to a variety of pathogens. In this method antigen is immobilized and the plate is

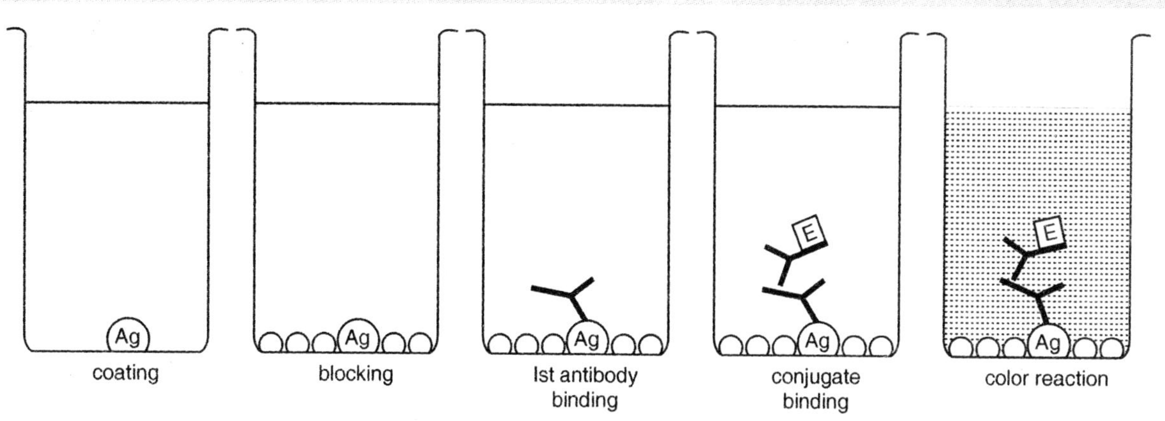

Fig. 13. Indirect ELISA.

blocked. The test sample is added, alongwith controls consisting of antibodies of the same specificity, species and isotype as the test sample. After an interval allowed for antigen binding, the plate is washed and the conjugate added. The antibody used to make the conjugate is typically a polyclonal preparation specific for constant regions of the antibody in the test sample. Finally enzyme activity is assayed as described in the competitive ELISA technique. Control values are plotted on a graph (Fig. 13). In this method, the response increases with increasing amount of analyte and does not necessarily reach a plateau. The concentration curve is interpreted from the calibration curve as described in competitive ELISA technique.

4. Sandwich ELISA. This method, in principle, is similar to the indirect ELISA technique. However, the analyte is usually a nonimmunoglobulin antigen that becomes "sandwiched" between an unlabelled immobilizing antibody and an antibody enzyme conjugate (Fig. 14). The first step in this procedure is to allow the absorption of a specific antibody onto the surface of the assay plate. Now the plate is washed and the test sample is added, alongwith controls consisting of known quantities of the same antibody-enzyme conjugate added. This reagent binds to the immobilized antigen and hence becomes immobilized itself. Design of the sandwich assay is crucial. Use of monoclonal immobilizing antibody is advantageous. After the conjugate is allowed to

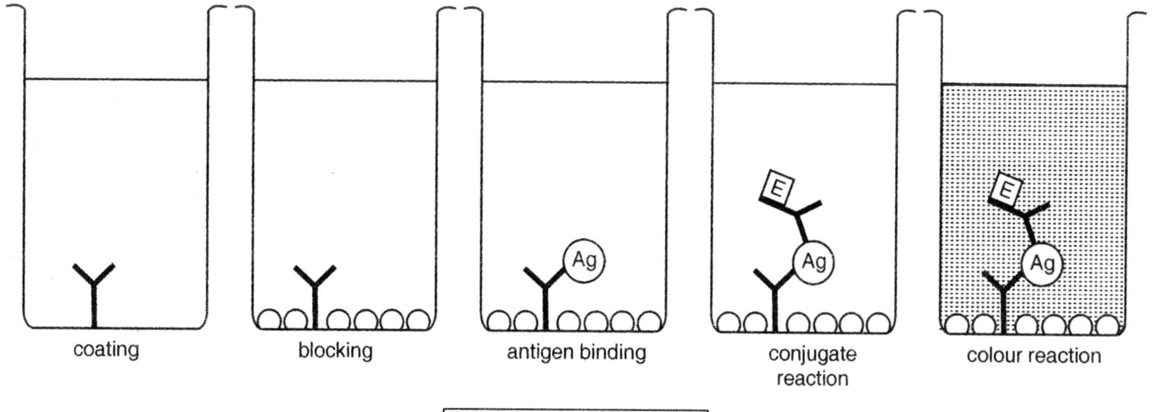

Fig. 14. Sandwich ELISA.

Table 6. **Clinical applications of ELISA.**

Condition diagnosed	Parameter detected or quantitated	Type of assay used
Viral Hepatitis (A and B)	IgM HAV Ab, Total HBc Ab, IgM HBc Ab, HBs Ag, HBs Ab	Immunocapture test One-step competition-test Immunocapture test One-Step "sandwich" test Two step "sandwich" test
HIV infection	Anti-HIV1 Anti-HIV2	One step "sandwich" test One step "sandwich" test
Rotavirus infection	Rotaviral Antigen (Group A)	One step "sandwich" test
Iron deficiency anemia; Polycythemia; Hemolytic anemia; sickle cell anemia; Thalassemia etc.	Transferrin receptor	Direct sandwich test.
Chronic gastritis	IgG Abs to H. Pylori	Sandwich test
Goodpasture's syndrome	Abs to glomerular basement member antigen	Sandwich test
Wagener's granulomatosis and related vasculitic	Anti-neutrophil cytoplasmic Abs	Sandwich test
Pregnancy diseases.	Human Chorionic Gonadotropin (hCG)	Membrane based qualitative ELISA
Colorectal, breast, lung, prostatic pancreatic, ovarian carcinoma	Carcinoembryonic antigen	Sandwich ELISA (Bead test)
Hepatocellular carcinoma; Open neural tube defect	Alpha foetoprotein	Sandwich ELISA (Bead test)

bind, the plate is finally washed and substrate is added to initiate the colour reaction. A calibration curve is formed and sample concentration calculated.

Applications of ELISA

ELISA has numerous clinical and biological applications. It is used in the detection and quantitation of several antigens as well as antibodies. A few of the applications are listed in the following table.

Homogeneous Assay (EMIT)

The word EMIT literally means "Enzyme Multiplied Immunology Technique". This method does not involve a solid phase system but solves the difficulty of separating the bound enzyme labelled antigen by causing the inhibition of enzyme activity in one form or the other. At present, this method is restricted to the quantitation of antigens, being particularly useful in the measurement of drugs (Fig. 15).

The antigen is labelled with an enzyme in such a manner that the enzyme retains its catalytic activity. However on binding with antibody, the enzyme is inhibited. Alternatively, the enzyme labelled antigen may be in an inhibited form but upon binding. Various enzymes viz: lysozyme, malate dehydrogenase, glucose-6-phosphate dehydrogenase can be used as enzyme labels.

Immunofluorescence Techniques

All those assays that employ a fluorophore label are known as fluoroimmunoassay (FIA). In practice FIA are very much similar ELISA and may be divided into two types. In heterogenous assay, the labeled antigen is separated into bound or free forms. Fluorescence associated with one of these two forms is measured in a fluorimeter. Homogeneous assays are those in which the separation is not necessary due to changes in the fluorescent properties occurring when the labelled antigen is bound by the antibody. The commonst system involves the quenching of fluorescence as in the case of the assay of gentamycin with fluoroscein isothiocyanate (FITC). The fluoroscent label must be stable and be easily

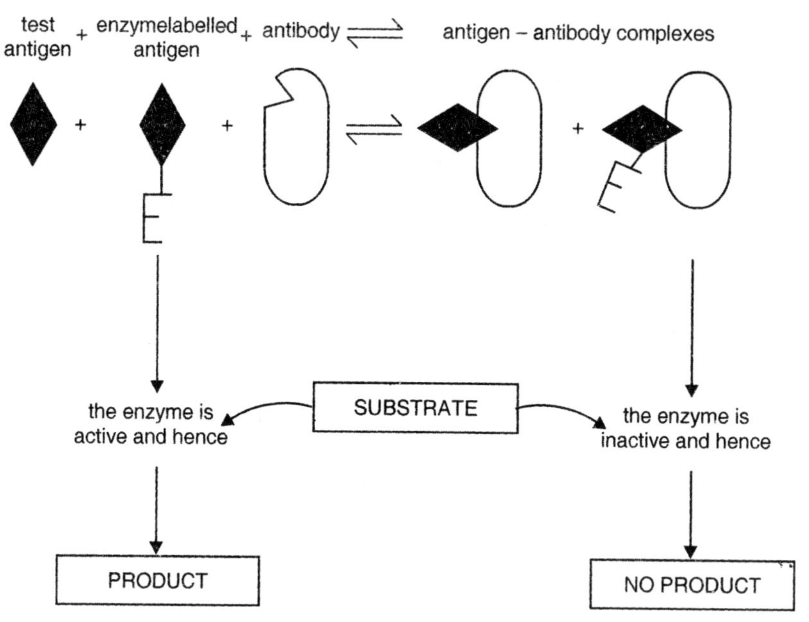

Fig. 15. Enzyme multiplied immunoassy (EMIT). The three reactants, test (or standard) antigen, enzyme-labelled antigen and a limited amount of antibody are allowed to react and reach an equilibrium position. The unbound labelled antigen which remains is the only source of enzyme activity, the bound enzyme being in activated. This free enzyme can be quantitative using a direct kinetic assay method and is proportional to the amount of unabeled antigen originally present.

detectable but must not interfere with the formation of the antigen-antibody complex. A few commonly used fluorescent labels are described in table 7.

Immunocytochemistry

A study of the chemistry of cells and tissue is known as histochemistry. A study of the chemistry of cellular organelle is called cytochemistry. When an antigen-antibody interaction is exploited in such a way that leads to the localization of an antigen *in situ,* the process is called as immunohisto/ cytochemistry. The principle of immunohisto/ cytochemistry is similar to solid phase immunobinding and immunobloting, except that here the antibody is incubated with the sections of tissues mounted on glass slides. In immunocytochemistry the antibody must be conjugated with a fluorescent or enzyme label that gives a fluorescence which is examined under a fluorescent microscope. Light sources include tungsten, quartz-halogen or mercury are lamps for fluorescence microscope.

***Table** 7.* **Fluorescent labels.**

Name	Abbreviation	Excitation wavelength (nm)	Emission wavelength (nm)
1-Anilino-8-napthalene sulphonic acid	ANS	385	471
1-Dimethylaminonaphthalene-5- sulphonic acid	DNS	340	520
4-Phenylspiro-(furan-2(3H)-1-phthalan)-3,3-dione	Fluoran	394	475
Fluorescein isothiocyanate	FITC	492	518
Rhodamine-isothiocyanate	RBITC	550	585

The entire process of immunohistochemistry can be divided into following steps.

(1) Tissue preparation
(2) Staining sequences
(3) Microscopy and photography

Tissue Preparation

Fresh tissues are not rigid enough for sectioning. Therefore they are either fixed in a suitable fixative or processed for frozen sectioning in a cryostat. Several fixatives like formaldehyde, glutaraldehyde, dimethyl superimidate, osmic acid and paraformaldehyde are routinely used in immunocytochemistry.

Staining Sequences

Immunocytochemistry depends on the primary binding of antibodies and not on secondary effects of the bound antibody. The fact that binding has occurred is detected by separation of the specifically bound fluorescent antibody from unbound fluorescent material. The separation depends on two requirements i.e. tissue components should be insoluble during staining and the immunocytochemical reagents should be highly soluble. In principle staining consists of application of a solution containing specific antibody, leaving all nonspecific components of the IgG and of other proteins in solution. These nonspecific components are removed by washing. Staining sequences used in the localization of antigen-antibody reaction in tissues are described below.

1. Direct technique. Tissue antigen binds fluorescein-isothiocyanate (FITC) labelled specific antibody.

2. Indirect technique. In the first step tissue antigen binds specific unlabelled antibody from species "a" (primary antibody). In the second step the bound primary antibody binds FITC-labelled antibody to the immunoglobulin of species "a" produced in species "b" (secondary antibody).

3. Double staining technique. Antigen "a" stains green by binding antibody from FITC labeled antigen "a" and antigen "b" in the same section stains orange red by binding antibody from lissamine rhodamine B200-labelled anti "b".

4. Sequential technique. In the first step antigen "a" binds fluorescent labelled anti "a". The staining pattern is recorded photographically. The fluorescence is destroyed by exposure to full beam of ultraviolet light. In the second step a second antigen "b" binds fluorescein labelled anti "b" and the observation is recorded photographically.

5. FITC-conjugated staphylococcal protein A. This protein is a polyvalent reagent specific for Fc. Hence FITC-conjugated staphylococcal protein may be used instead of the secondary antibody in the indirect technique.

6. Hapten sandwich technique. Tissue antigen binds specific antibody covalently labelled with hapten – FITC labelled antihapten is used as the secondary antibody.

7. FITC-labelled antibody for scanning electron microscopy. Staining is usually carried out at room temperature and the slides are kept in a humid chamber. Reagents are most commonly applied for 30 minutes. Following each reagent, the slides are rinsed in a buffer. PBS pH 7·0 or saline containing 0·05 N Tris buffer pH 7·0 to 7·6 are most commonly used. Many other buffers can also be used. The sections are mounted in polyvinyl alcohol or buffered glycerol.

Microscopy and Photography

Specific fluorescence emission is relatively weak compared to the total light necessary for illumination. Therefore, high-intensity light as provided by the mercury arc high vacuum lamp is a minimum requirement to obtain bright immunofluorescence.

Although fluorescein and rhodamine absorb strongly below 300 nm, optical difficulties of condensing light in this range preclude its routine use. A second absorption maximum for these fluorochromes is too near the emission peak: fluorescence microscopy is sensitive because the emitted light is seen against a dark background. To this end, it is important that only the emitted light is seen and not the illuminating light. Since only part of the illuminating light becomes absorbed, the unabsorbed part must be separated from the emitted light. This separation can not be accomplished if both illuminating and emitted, light have close peaks. Hence, for immunofluorescence with rhodamine and fluorescein, illuminating light in the near-ultraviolet and short-wave blue are commonly used. In this range, both fluorescein and rhodamine absorb though not as efficiently as at shorter or longer wavelengths. Filters are used between the illuminating light and the specimen to provide this range and to cause only minimal tissue autofluorescence.

Secondary filters are placed between specimen and ocular to retain the fluorescence emission light and to cut off any exciting light. Therefore, the secondary filters should cut off the light passed by the primary filter.

When in the double-staining technique it is necessary to contrast the weak rhodamine against the strong fluorescein fluorescence, it is better to excite simultaneously at two wavelengths instead of one, thus being able to independently vary the intensity of the optimal exciting light for rhodamine and that for fluorescein.

With judicious use of filters, it is possible to obtain bright-field fluorescence and still observe fluorescence emission under complete exclusion of illuminating light. However, dark-field illumination greatly simplifies the selection of filters, since even without filters it insures that most of the illuminating light will not reach the ocular, and that only the fluorescence emission light is seen. In practice, dark-field condensers are commonly used in conjunction with filters. Glycerine is used in place of an immersion oil for studies of immunofluorescence under immersion lenses.

Photography is essential, as fluorescence wanes on storage of specimens. This decrease in fluorescence intensity is also an important factor in the technique of photography itself: total light intensity is often low in dark-field microscopy, especially when only a small part of the section is immunofluorescent. Hence, exposure times tend to be long. However, during long exposure time, fluorescence intensity itself fades. Consequently, attempts should be made to use shortest possible exposure times; therefore, with high ASA ratings are recommended. Furthermore, a well-standardized automatic exposure meter is necessary because light measurement is synchronized with the exposure, and any decrease of fluorescence during exposure is automatically compensated for.

When photographing preparations doubly stained with rhodamine- and FITC-conjugated antibodies, it is important to realize that the fluorescein fluorescence is more short lived than the rhodamine fluorescence.

In attempts to preserve FITC fluorescence it is quite common practice to photograph tissue before observing details. When one returns to the tissue after photography, most of the staining may have disappeared, and evaluation will depend entirely on the dark-field -photograph.

Controls

Satisfactory controls require that the microscopic field looks dark except for the faint bluish autofluorescence of tissues. The **staining controls** are as follows:

(1) Exposure to all staining reagents of tissue from the same host known not to contain the antigen under investigation.

(2) In the direct method, preabsorption of the conjugate with homogenate of tissue under investigation.

(3) In the indirect method, preabsorption of the primary antiserum with homogenate of tissue under examination.

(4) In the indirect method, omission of the primary antiserum.

(5) In the direct method, blocking of the reaction with the conjugate by pretreatment with unconjugated serum. The control depends on the fast reaction of antigen with antibody and the relatively slow reverse reaction in most systems. The blocking reaction is favored by low temperature, low concentration of the conjugate, and short exposure time to the conjugate. The inhibition is more likely to be successful if the conjugate is of poor quality, that is of low antibody content. Consequently, entirely non satisfactory blocking control does not necessarily indicate nonspecificity.

(6) In the indirect method, blocking the fluorescence by staining with primary antiserum followed by unlabelled and then labelled secondary antiserum.

The **antibody controls** are as follows —

(1) In the direct method, exposure of the tissue to conjugated normal immunoglobulin or

immunoglobulin of unrelated specificities, or preferably immunoglobulin obtained from the immunized animal prior to immunization (*preimmune* immunoglobulin).

(2) In the indirect method, substitution of the primary antiserum by normal serum or antiserum of unrelated specificity or, preferably, preimmune serum.

(3) In the direct method, absorption of the conjugate with the specific antigen under investigation.

(4) In the indirect method, absorption of the primary antiserum with the specific antigen under investigation.

Absorption is generally done by mixing antiserum with an excess of specific antigen followed by incubation at 1°C for about 24 hours, thus "blocking" the antibodies against subsequent reaction with tissue antigen. A solid-phase immunoabsorbent may be used instead of the soluble antigen. This is the procedure of choice in case of some haptens, such as oxytocin and vasopressin in which reaction of the antibodies with tissue may be of higher affinity than with hapten in solution or in case of immunocytochemistry of receptors, in which admixture of ligand to antibody may enhance rather than inhibit the reaction on the tissue section.

Important Questions

1. What are immunoglobulins? Describe different types of immunoglobulins.
2. What is immunoassay? Describe different methods used for immunoassay.
3. Explain the term radio-immunoassay. Describe different methods used for radio-immunoassay.
4. What is enzyme immunoassay? Discuss the procedure of enzyme linked immunosorbant assay (ELISA).
5. Give a detailed account of immunocytochemical methods used in biological studies.
6. Write briefly on the following :
   (i) Applications of ELISA, (ii) EMIT, (iii) Sandwich ELISA.

Radio-isotopes Techniques

16

Atoms which have the same atomic number and hence are the same element but have different masses, are known as isotopes. Radio-isotopes, or more correctly, radio-nuclides spontaneously and continuously emit characteristic types of radiation. They are particularly useful in analytical biochemistry. This unique nature of the radiation provides the basis for many specific and sensitive laboratory methods (Table 1).

Nature of Radioactivity

The atomic nucleus is made up of protons and neutrons. The number of protons determines the atomic number and hence the identity of an element and is equal to the number of orbital electrons, a feature necessary to ensure the electrical neutrality of the atom. The atomic mass of the nucleus is made up by the additional neutrons which are present.

Hence:

atomic number = the number of protons;
atomic mass = the sum of the number of protons and neutrons.

This information is normally shown as a superscript (atomic mass) and a subscript (atomic number) to the symbol for the element. Hence, ^{14}C represents the isotope of carbon (atomic number 6) with the atomic mass of 14. In practice the subscript is often omitted because the atomic number is unique to the element which is represented by the appropriate letter (e.g. C for carbon). For simplicity in the spoken form and often

Table 1. **Physical data of some frequently used isotopes.**

Element	Symbol	Half-life	Beta emission	Gamma emission
Calcium	^{45}Ca	165 d	+	–
Carbon	^{14}C	5760 a	+	–
Chlorine	^{36}Cl	3 × 105 a	+	–
Cobalt	^{60}CO	5·26 a	+	+
Hydrogen	^{3}H	12·2 a	+	–
Iodine	^{125}I	60d	Electron capture	+
Iodine	^{131}I	8·04d	+	+
Iron	^{59}Fe	45 d	+	+
Magnesium	^{28}Mg	21·4 h	+	+
Nitrogen	^{13}N	600 s	Positron	+
Phosphorus	^{32}P	14·3 d	+	–
Potassium	^{40}K	109 a	Electron capture	+
Potassium	^{42}K	12·4 h	+	+
Sodium	^{22}Na	2·6 a	Positron	+
Sodium	^{24}Na	15 h	+	+
Sulphur	^{35}S	87·2 d	+	–

in the written form, isotopes are often referred to as carbon-14, phosphorus-32, etc.

The stability of the atomic nucleus depends upon a critical balance between the repulsive and attractive forces involving the protons and neutrons. For the lighter elements, a neutron to proton ratio (N: P) of about 1: 1 is required for the nucleus to be stable but with increasing atomic mass, the N : P ratio for a stable nucleus rises to a value of approximately 1·5 : 1. A nucleus whose N : P ratio differs significantly from these values will undergo a nuclear reaction in order to restore the ratio and the element is said to be radioactive. There is, however, a maximum size above which any nucleus is unstable and all elements with atomic numbers greater than 82 are radioactive.

Types of Radioactivity

If a nucleus is too heavy and its atomic number exceeds 82, it may revert to a more stable arrangement by releasing both neutrons and protons. This is effected by the emission of an **alpha particle** which contains two protons and two neutrons and is a helium nucleus, $^{4}_{2}H^{2+}$.

Alpha particles are relatively large particles and are emitted with a limited number of energy levels. They carry a double positive charge and as a result attract electrons from the atoms of the material through which they pass, causing ionization effects. They have an extremely short range, even in air, and as a result present very little hazard as an external source of radiation but their effects within living cells or tissues can be serious.

A nucleus which has an excess of neutrons will undergo neutron to proton transition, a process which may restore the N : P ratio but which requires the loss of an electron to convert the neutron to a positively charged proton and as a result the atomic number increases by one. The particle emitted is a high speed electron known as a negatron (*fr*) and the atom is said to emit **beta radiation**, e.g.

$$^{4}_{2}C \rightarrow ^{14}_{7}N + \beta^-$$

Conversely, nuclei which contain an excess of protons undergo proton to neutron transition with the emission of a positively charged beta particle known as a positron (P+) and with the reduction of the atomic number by one. A positron has only a very short existence, combining immediately with an electron of a nearby atom. The two particles disintegrate in the process with the emission of two gamma rays, e.g.

$$^{11}_{6}C \rightarrow ^{11}_{5}B + \beta^-$$

An alternative mechanism to positron emission, for the conversion of a proton to a neutron, involves a process known as **electron capture** (EC) in which the nucleus captures an orbital electron from an inner shell to restore the N : P ratio. Subsequently, an electron from another orbital falls into the vacancy left in the inner shell and the energy released in the process is emitted as an X-ray, the atomic number again being reduced by one, e.g.

$$^{125}_{53}I + e^- \rightarrow ^{125}_{52}Te + \nu$$

Beta emission from an atom shows a range of energy levels and although the maximum level is characteristic of the isotope, only a small proportion of the emissions may be of this energy. As a result, beta particles show a maximum range in a particular absorbing material with many emissions penetrating considerably less. Penetration distances are about ten times greater than for alpha particles, values of 5 to 10 mm in aluminium being common. Because they

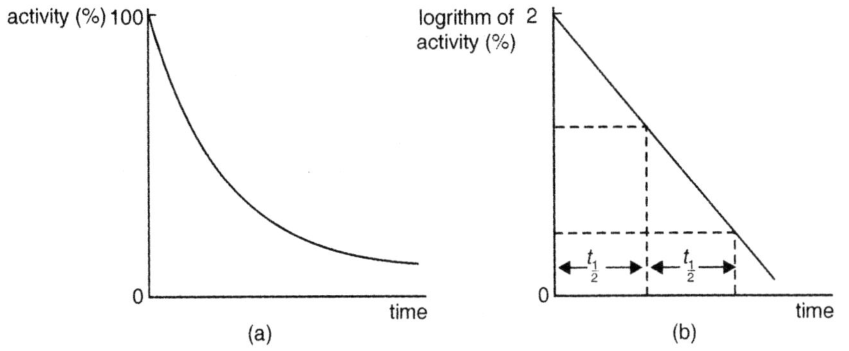

Fig. 1. Radioactive decay. The rate of radioactive decay is proportional to the number of unstable atoms present and although theoretically there should always be some activity left (a), in practice the activity does eventually fall to zero. A plot of the logarithm of the activity against time (b) results in a straight line from which the half-life can be determined.

are light, beta particles are easily deflected by other atoms and are less effective as ionizing agents than are alpha particles.

Although a nucleus may have an N : P ratio in the stable range it is still possible for it to be in an unstable energetic state and to emit energy as protons of magnetic radiation of extremely 'short wavelength known as **gamma** rays. These have neither mass nor charge and as a result cannot cause direct ionization effects but the energy associated with them is absorbed by an atom causing an electron to be ejected which in turn produces secondary ionization effects.

The atoms emitting gamma radiation suffer no change in either mass or atomic number although very few elements emit solely gamma radiation. Sodium-24 $\left({}^{24}_{11}Na\right)$ for example, emits beta radiation (negatron emission) being converted to magnesium-24 $\left({}^{24}_{11}Mg\right)$. It also, however, emits gamma radiation in the process.

In order to handle radio-isotopes safely it is necessary, among other things, to define fairly carefully the penetrating power of the radiation emitted by any isotope. Alpha particles, having only a relatively limited number of energy levels, are absorbed by contact with other atoms and hence it is convenient to define the absorbing power of a material in terms of its equivalent thickness. This is defined as the weight of material per unit area (mg cm^{-2}) necessary to stop the radiation. The thickness required can be calculated by dividing the equivalent thickness by the density of the material.

Beta radiation, because of its wide range of energies, shows an approximately linear relationship between the thickness of the material required to absorb radiation and the logarithm of the activity of the radiation. The percentage of beta particles passing through a given thickness of absorbing material has a sigmoidal relationship to the logarithm of the maximum energy of emission. This information permits the selection of a particular thickness of absorbing material which will totally stop the beta radiation from one source and yet will allow the penetration of a relatively constant proportion of radiation from another source with a higher maximum emission energy.

The absorption of gamma radiation is more difficult to assess and the most convenient means of expressing the absorbing power of a particular material is to quote the half-thickness which is defined as that thickness of material which will reduce the intensity of radiation by one-half.

Radioactive Decay

Radioactive decay is a random process and, as a result, all measurements must involve statistical assessment. The rate at which a quantity of an isotope decays is proportional to the number of unstable atoms present in the sample and a graph of activity against time results in a typical exponential curve. It is because of this that the life span of a radioactive

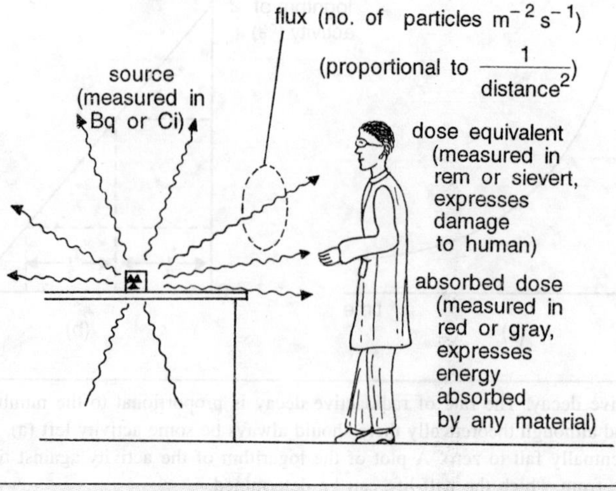

Fig. 2. The relationship between radioactivity of source and absorbed dose.

sample cannot be measured and a more meaningful expression of the rate of decay is provided by the half-life, $t_{½}$ (Fig.1).

The half-life is defined as the time taken for the activity of a sample to fall by half and is independent of the actual activity. It can be determined using the equation which describes the rate of radioactive decay —

$$\log_e \frac{N_t}{N_0} = -\lambda t$$

where N_t = the activity at time t
N_0 = the activity at zero time
λ = the radioactive decay constant
t = time

In its linear form the equation is —

$$\log_e N_t = \log_e N_0 - \lambda t$$

and converting from natural logarithms it becomes:

$$\log_e N_t = \log_{10} N_0 - \lambda t$$

This is the equation for a straight line, the slope being $-0{\cdot}4343\lambda$.

If N_t is made equal to half N_0, then t will equal the half-life ($t_{1/2}$) and the equation becomes —

$$\log_e N_t = \log_{10} N_0 - 0{\cdot}4343\ \lambda t_{1/2}$$

$$t_{1/2} = \frac{0{\cdot}3110}{0{\cdot}4343\lambda}$$

A graph of the logarithm of the activity of the sample ($\log_{10} N_t$) against time (t) will result in a linear plot and the half-life can be determined from the graph either by measuring the time interval between two readings of activity which vary by a factor of two or by using the value for the gradient of the line and substituting in the equation.

$$\text{Half life } (t_{1/2}) = -\frac{0 \cdot 3010}{\text{gradient}}$$

Units of Radioactivity

The basic unit of activity used to be the curie which is based on the activity of 1 gram of pure radium 226 which undergoes $3{\cdot}7 \times 10^{10}$ transformations per second. The curie (Ci) is therefore defined as the quantity of a radioactive isotope which gives 3.7×10^{10} disintegrations per second. With the introduction of SI units the accepted unit of activity is the becquerel (Bq) which is equal to one nuclear transformation per second.

Hence :

$$1 \text{ curie} = 3{\cdot}7 \times 10^{10} \text{ becquerels}$$

The specific activity of an isotope indicates the relative amount of radioactive atoms in a sample and the activity per unit mass or volume is quoted as becquerels per gram (Bq g^{-1}) or millicuries per gram (mCi g^{-1}). A sample in which all the atoms of a particular element are radioactive is said to be carrier-free and is very difficult to achieve in practice.

Safety

Great care must always be exercised in handling radio-isotopes. It is not only the powerful emitters which are dangerous but also weak emitters with long half-lives, e.g. tritium, carbon-14, which may be

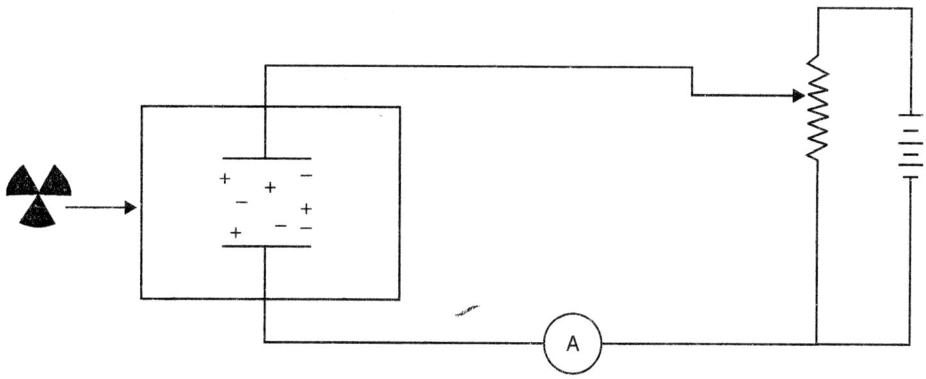

Fig. 3. Detection based on ionization.

incorporated into the body and over a period of time can constitute a serious hazard.

Although there are many regulations regarding the handling and disposal of radio-isotopes, all of which must be fully understood and implemented, there are certain basic 'good housekeeping' principles which can be mentioned here. Laboratory benches should be covered with a waterproof material to prevent absorption of the isotopes by the wood or other material and this must be changed regularly. Everyone handling radio-isotopes should wear protective clothing and disposable gloves. All contaminated glassware should be rinsed in special containers before being washed and it is often advisable to use disposable containers wherever possible.

Methods for Detection and Measurement of Radioactivity

Radiation can be detected in various ways. All these methods depend on its direct or indirect ionization effects. There are three commonly used methods viz: ionization of gases, the excitation of solids or liquids and induction of chemical change. Radioactivity can be measured as number of individual emissions in a unit time or total cumulative effect of all emissions in a given time. In every method, a background count (blank value) is done and the test value corrected for those emissions which are not due to the sample.

Methods Based Upon Gas-Ionisation

When a charged particle passes through a gas, its electrostatic field losses orbital electrons from atoms which are very close to its path. This activity causes ionization of gas. The ability to induce ionization decreases in the order

$\alpha > \beta > \gamma$ (10,000 = 100 = 1)

Therefore an α and β particles may be detected by gas ionization methods, but γ radiations are poorly detected. If ionization occurs between a pair of electrodes, the electrons displaced as a result of ionization will be attracted to the anode and a current will flow between the electrodes. The most commonly used detector of this type is known as Geiger – Muller tube. It consists of a hollow metal cylinder (the cathode) within a glass envelope and a wire (the anode) running along the central axis of the cathode (Fig. 3). The whole tube is filled with the counting gas, often a mixture of neon and argon under a low pressure. Radiation entering the tube causes ionization of the detector gas and as a result a pulse of current flows between the electrodes together with the emission of ultraviolet radiation.

Method Based Upon Excitation

Some substances known as fluors or scintillants, respond to the ionizing effects of α and β particles by emitting flashes of light called scintillations. They do not respond directly to gamma rays, however, they do respond to the secondary ionization effects that gamma rays produce and as a result provide a valuable detection system for all emissions.

Liquid scintillation counters usually consist of two light shielded photomultiplier tubes in between which the sample and a scintillant mixture contained in a glass vessel are placed. A range of scintillants are commercially available each showing particular light emission characteristics. Scintillant 'cocktails' or

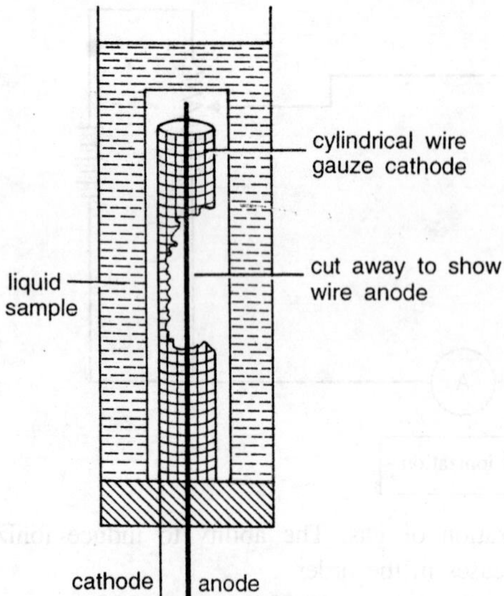

Fig. 4. A Geiger-Muller tube for measuring the activity of liquid samples.

mixtures contain a primary scintillant such as 1-phenyl-4-phenyloxazole (PPO) and often contain a secondary scintillant such as 1, 4, di-2-5 (phenyloxazoyl) benzene (POPOP). They are dissolved in a suitable solvent e.g. toluene or xylene for organic samples and dioxane for aqueous samples.

The number of ionizations or scintillations detected by both types of detectors can be measured electronically and presented either as the total number of counts or as the number of pulses per minute (Fig. 5).

Advantages of Scintillation Counting

The very fact that scintillation counting is widely used in biological work indicates that it has several advantages over gas ionisation counting. These advantages are listed below.

(1) The rapidity of fluorescence decay 10^{-9}, which, when compared to dead time in a Geiger-Muller tube 10^{-4}, means much higher count rates are possible.

(2) Much higher counting efficiencies particularly for low energy β-emitters; over 50% efficiency is routine in scintillation counting and efficiency can rise to over 90% for high energy emitters. This is partly due to the fact that the negatrons do not have to travel through air or pass through an end-window of a Geiger-Muller tube (thereby dissipating much of the energy before causing ionisation) but interact directly with the fluor; energy loss before the event that is counted is therefore minimal.

(3) The ability to accommodate samples of any type, including liquids, solids, suspensions and gels.

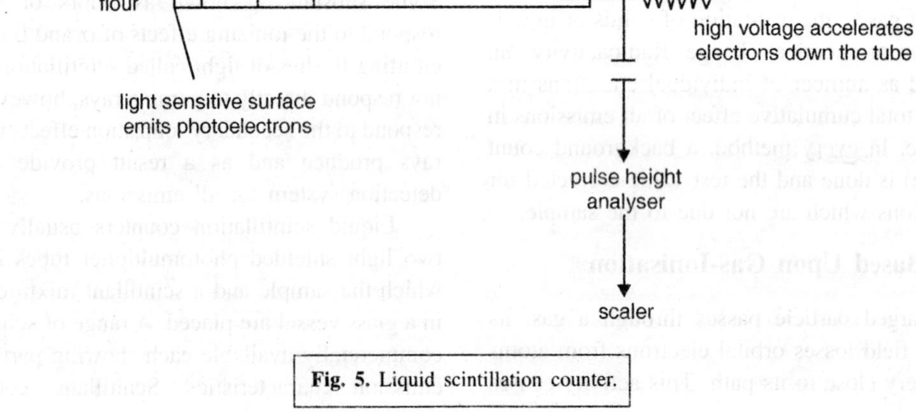

Fig. 5. Liquid scintillation counter.

(4) The general ease of sample preparation (see below).

(5) The ability to count separately different isotopes in the same sample, which means dual labelling experiments can be carried out (see below).

(6) Scintillation counters are highly automated, hundreds of samples can be counted automatically and built-in computer facilities carry out many forms of data analysis, such as efficiency correction, graph plotting, radioimmunoassay calculations, etc.

Disadvantages of Scintillation Counting

It would not be reasonable, having outlined some of the advantages of scintillation counting, to disregard the disadvantages of the method. Fortunately, however, most of the inherent disadvantages have been overcome by improvement in instrument design. These disadvantages include the following.

(1) The cost per sample of scintillation counting is not insignificant; however, other factors including versatility, sensitivity, ease and accuracy outweigh this factor for most applications.

(2) At the high voltages applied to the photomultiplier, electronic events occur in the system that are independent of radioactivity but contribute to a high background count. This is referred to as photomultiplier noise and can be partially reduced by cooling the photomultipliers. Since temperature affects counting efficiency, cooling also presents a controlled temperature for counting, which may be useful. Low noise photomultipliers, however, have been designed to provide greater temperature stability in ambient temperature systems. Also the use of a pulse height analyzer can be set so as to reject, electronically, most of the noise pulses that are of low energy (the threshold or gate setting). The disadvantage here is that this also rejects the low energy pulses resulting from low energy radioac ity (e.g. ^{3}H). Another method of reducing noise, which is incorporated into most scintillation counters, is to use coincidence counting. In this system two photomultipliers are used. These are set in coincidence such that only when a pulse is generated in both tubes at the same time is it allowed to pass to the scaler. The chances of this happening for a pulse generated by a radioactive event is very high compared to the chances of a noise event occurring in both photomultipliers during the so-called resolution time of the system, which is commonly of the order of 20 ns. In general, this system reduces photomultiplier noise to a very low level.

(3) The greatest disadvantage of scintillation counting is quenching. This occurs when the energy transfer process described earlier suffers interference. Correcting for this quenching contributes significantly to the cost of scintillation counting. Quenching can be anyone of three kinds.

(i) *Optical quenching* occurs if in appropriate or dirty scintillation vials are used. These will absorb some of the light being emitted, before it rleaches the photomultiplier.

(ii) *Colour quenching* occurs if the sample is coloured and results in light emitted being absorbed within the scintillation cocktail before it leaves the sample vial. When colour quenching is known to be a major problem, it can be reduced, as outlined later.

(iii) *Chemical quenching,* which occurs when anything in the sample interferes with the transfer of energy from the solvent to the primary fluor or from the primary fluor to the secondary fluor, is the most difficult form of quenching to accommodate. In a series of homogeneous samples (e.g. $^{14}CO_2$ released during metabolism of [^{14}C] glucose and trapped in alkali, which is then added to the scintillation cocktail for counting), chemical quenching may not vary greatly from sample to sample. In these cases relative counting using sample counts per minute can be compared directly. However, in the majority of biological experiments using radioisotopes, such homogeneity of samples is unlikely and is not sufficiently accurate to use relative counting (i.e. counts per minute). Instead, an appropriate method of standardisation must be used. This requires the determination of the counting efficiency of each sample and the conversion of counts per minute to absolute counts (i.e. disintegrations per minute), as described

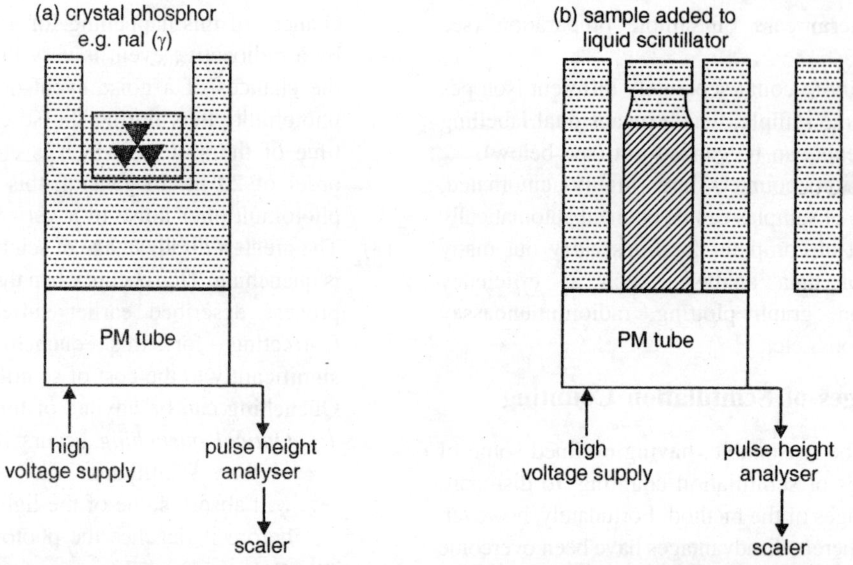

Fig. 6. Diagrammatic illustration of solid (a) and liquid (b) scintillation counting methods.

later. It should be noted that quenching is not such a great problem in solid (external) scintillation counting.

(4) Chemiluminescence can also cause problems during liquid scintillation counting. It results from chemical reactions between components of the samples to be counted and the scintillation cocktail, and produces light emission unrelated to excitation of the solvent and fluor system by radioactivity. These light emissions are generally low energy events and are rejected by the threshold setting of the photomultiplier in the same way as photomultiplier noise. Chemiluminescence, when it is a problem, can usually be overcome by storing samples for some time before counting, to permit the chemiluminescence to decay. Many contemporaneous instruments are able to detect chemiluminescence and substract it or flag it on the printout.

(5) Phospholuminescence results from components of the sample, including the vial itself, absorbing light and re-emitting it. Unlike chemiluminescence, which is a once-only effect, phospholuminescence will occur on each exposure of a sample to light. Samples that are pigmented are most likely to phosphoresce. If this is a problem, samples should be adapted to dark prior to counting and the sample holder should be kept closed throughout the counting process.

Despite all the complications described above, scintillations counters are universal in biosciences departments. This is because the instruments have automated systems for calculating counting efficiency; in other words the instruments do all the hard work!

Sample Preparation

It is impossible here to give details of all aspects of sample preparation for scintillation counting. However, major considerations are outlined below and the reader is referred to books cited in the end of this chapter.

1. Sample vials. In solid scintillation counting, sample preparation is easy and only involves transferring the sample to a glass or plastic vial (or tube) compatible with the counter. In liquid scintillation counting, sample preparation is more complex and starts with a decision on the type of sample vial to be used. These may be glass, low potassium glass (with low levels of ^{40}K that reduce background count) or polyethylene. The last of these types are cheaper but are not suitable for cleaning and reuse, whereas glass vials can be reused many times provided they are thoroughly cleaned. Polyethylene vials give better light transfer and result in slightly higher counting efficiencies, but are inclined to exhibit more phosphorescence than do glass vials. The recent trend is towards minivials, which use far smaller volumes of expensive scintillation cocktails. Modern counters are able to accept many types of vial; the smallest vial possible should be used (within the obvious constraints of sample volume) to save costs and in consideration of environmental issues, as scintillation fluids are toxic. Some counters are designed to accept very small samples in special polythene bags split into an array of many compartments; these are particularly useful to, for example, the pharmaceutical industry where there are laboratories that do large numbers of receptor binding assays.

2. Scintillation cocktails. Toluene-based cocktails are the most efficient, but will not accept aqueous samples, because toluene and water are immiscible and massive quenching results. Cocktails based on 1,4-dioxane and naphthalene that can accommodate up to 20% (v/v) water can be used, but they have largely been phased out due to toxicity. Emulsifier-based cocktails are the most frequently used for counting aqueous samples. They contain an emulsifier such as Triton X-100 and can accept up to 50% water (v/v); however, phase transitions occur from single phase to two phase or gel, as the water content increases. Accurate counting cannot be done if the samples are in the two-phase state. Many ready-made cock-tails are on the market and are sold with precise instructions regarding sample condition.

3. Volume of cocktail. It should be noted that the efficiency of scintillation counting varies with sample volume, though this is less of a problem in modern counters. Nevertheless, care should be taken that sample vials in a given series of counts contain the same volume of sample and that all instrument calibration is done using the same volume as for experimental samples.

4. Overcoming major colour quenching. If colour quenching is a problem it is possible to bleach samples before counting. Care should be taken, however, since bleaching agents such as hydrogen peroxide can give rise to chemiluminescence in some scintillation cocktails.

5. Tissue solubilisers. Solid samples, such as plant and animal tissues, may be best counted after solubilisation by quaternary amines such as NCS solubiliser or toluene. Not surprisingly these solutions are highly toxic and great care is required. The sample is added to the counting vial containing a small amount of solubiliser and digestion is allowed to proceed. When digestion is complete, scintillation cocktail is added and the sample counted. Again, chemiluminescence can be a problem with tissue solubilisers.

6. Combustion methods. A suitable alternative to bleaching of coloured samples or digestion of tissues is the use of combustion techniques. Here samples are combusted in an atmosphere of oxygen, usually in a commercially available combustion apparatus. Thus, samples containing ^{14}C would be combusted to $^{14}CO_2$, which is collected in a trapping agent such as sodium hydroxide and then counted; ^{3}H-containing samples are converted to $^{3}H_2O$ for counting.

As indicated earlier, only important considerations in sample preparation are discussed above and details are not given. However, it is worthy of comment that almost any type of radioactive sample containing (β-emitting istopes can be prepared for counting in a liquid scintillation counter by one method or another, including cuttings from paper chromatographs or membrane filters, again illustrating the versatility and importance of this technique for quantifying radioactivity.

Čerenkov Counting

The Čerenkov effect occurs when a particle passes through a substance with a speed higher than that of light passing through the same substance. If a β-emitter has a decay energy in excess of 0.5 MeV, then this causes water to emit a bluish white light usually referred to as Čerenkov light. It is possible to detect this light using a typical liquid scintillation counter.

Since there is no requirement for organic solvents and fluors, this technique is relatively cheap, sample preparation is very easy, and there is no problem of chemical quenching. Table 2 lists some isotopes that are suitable for this detection method. Most work has been done on ^{32}P, which has 80% of its energy spectrum above the Čerenkov threshold and which can be detected at around 40% efficiency. It may be

Table 2. **Some isotopes suitable for cerenkov counting**

Radioisotope	E_{max} (MeV)	% of spectrum above 0.5 MeV	Counting (%) efficiency
^{12}Na	1·39	60	30
^{12}P	1·71	80	40
^{36}Cl	0·71	30	10
^{42}K	3·5	90	80

noted from Table 2 that, as the proportion of the energy spectrum above 0·5 MeV increases, so too does the detection efficiency.

Autoradiography and its Applications

The basis of autoradiography (or radioautography) is the demonstration of radioactive isotopes in tissue sections by means of their ability to reduce silver grains in a photographic plate, film or emulsion **Loudon** (1904) & subsequently, successful studies with radioactive polonium, lead and phosphorus were made. **Hamilton** (1940) used radioactive iodine in his studies on thyroid gland. After 1940 the practice of autoradiography increased considerably. Substances that were foreign to the tissues like polonium, strontium radium, plutonium, cadmium and gold were localized using this technique. Physiological substances viz: calcium, iron, iodine, proteins, hormone, nucleic acids and metal ions were studied using autoradiography.

Procedure of Autoradiography

The techniques of autoradiography have become more important with recent developments in molecular biology. Details of the procedure are described below.

1. Preparation of sections. Thick frozen sections or paraffin sections of soft tissues may be used. Thin sections give better resolution. For most purposes some kind of fixation is required. The choice of fixative depends upon the nature of the isotope and the tissue component with which it is to be incorporated. For the study of protein bound isotopes, tissues/organs can be fixed in Bouins fluid, neutral formalin or alcohol. Normally, all radioactivity preserved by conventional wet fixatives is protein bound. Unbound isotope in whatever form it has been administered, is totally lost. This process is described as "differential fixation". Freeze dried and paraffin embedded tissue can also be used. Paraffin sections thus prepared are transferred onto glass slides and subjected to the application of photographic emulsion.

Method

(1) Fix small pieces of tissue in absolute alcohol for 1-3 hours.

(2) Clear in benzene, 15 minutes, followed by warm benzene (56°), 15 minutes.

(3) Transfer to four changes of molten paraffin wax (56°), for 30 minutes in each case.

(4) Embed, block and cut sections at 5μ or less and float out on warm water.

(5) Pick up sections on to slides which have previously been dipped in an aqueous solution of 1 per cent gelatin and 0·1 per cent chrome alum, and then allowed to dry.

2. Application of the photographic emulsion. A variety of emulsions are commercially available with different packing densities of the silver halide crystals. X-ray film is generally suitable for macroscopic samples, however, for microscopic observations, very sensitive films are necessary. Following methods are used depending upon the objective of the study.

Contact Method for Autoradiography

In this process, tissue slices or sections are placed in contact with a photographic plate. Contact between sections and the film is maintained for appropriate time. The film is developed afterwards.

Method

(1) Prepare specimen as in Stages 1-5 of the previous method.

(2) Remove wax by immersion in light petroleum.

(3) Bring the section into contact with X-ray film (for highest speed) or fine-grained film (for better resolving power).

(4) Apply even pressure by putting film and specimen into a printing frame, X-ray cassette, or simply by putting a weight on it.

(5) Store in the dark for exposure.

(6) Process the film according to the maker's instructions, paying particularly strict attention to cleanliness throughout.

Mounted Autoradiography

In this technique, the sections are directly mounted on the photographic film/emulsion. Staining is carried out before or after mounting.

This popular technique is based on the use of a thin photographic emulsion on a gelatin base which must be stripped from the plate or celluloid film backing before application.

Stripping Film Autoradiography

Special stripping film for autoradiography is obtainable from a number of suppliers (see table below). The film as delivered is mounted on glass and consists of two layers—μ. thick gelatine facing the glass with a 4μ in thick photographic emulsion upon it. The emulsion is very sensitive to scratching and at all stages careful handling is necessary. Storage in a cold room or refrigerator at 4°C is advisable. Low background is essential to the method and the film must be kept in the shade, even from the recommended dark light, when not actually handled.

Type		Grain size (nm)	Indications
Eastman-Kodak	NTB	290	α and β (low energy)
	NTB2	260	B up to 200 keV
	NTB3	340	High sensitivity
	No-screen	1250	Low resolution
Ilford	G5	270	High resolution
	K2	200	β upto 200 keV
Kodak (UK)	AR10	200	α and β-particles

Application of Film

(1) Cut film in squares with scissors, razor blade or scalpel, allowing for a generous overlap over the edge of the slide; ¼ to ½ inch from the edge of the slide should be discarded. Leave in the dark for 5-10 minutes.

(2) Strip one square slowly, starting at one corner and float on dust-free, fresh distilled water at 23°-25°6, emulsion-side **downwards** for 2-3 minutes. (The water should only be used for one run of coatings.)

(3) Place a deparaffinized slide in the water, section or squash facing upwards, and lift out of the water so that the film covers the specimen.

(4) Dry in front of a fan or hair-dryer at room temperature.

(5) Store in the dark for exposure. (Some workers expose at room temperature, others at 4°. Warm rooms should be avoided.)

(6) Photographic processing should be carried out according to the maker's instructions. Use chemicals of analytical purity dissolved in

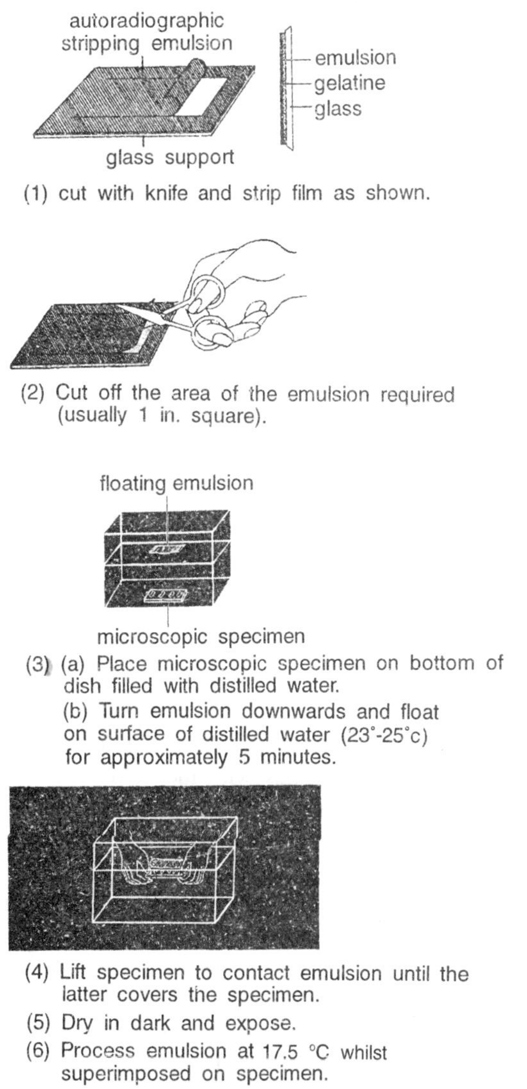

Fig. 7. Method of autoradiography.

distilled water and filtered. All processing should be done at 17·5 ± 0·5°C.

(7) Rinse in distilled water, and in running tap-water if this is sufficiently clear and cool, for one hour, otherwise use 4-6 changes in distilled water.

(8a) For phase contrast microscopy mount in glycerine jelly; glycerogel is suitable for this purpose.

(8b) Staining with haemalum: place moist preparation in celestin blue for 5 minutes, wash briefly and immerse in Mayer's haemalum, 5 minutes.

(9) Differentiate in 1% aqueous HC1 for 16-60 seconds, or until there isminimal staining of the gelatine compatible with retention of nuclear staining.

As an alternative, deparaffinized preparations can be stained before stage 3, by the Feulgen reaction or with Neutral red-Carbol fuchsin (30 ml. 2 per cent Neutral red with 10 ml. Ziehl-Neelsen's carbol fuchsin). Haematoxylin may also be used if hardener and fixer without acetic acid are used in processing. Objections have been made to the use of iron haematoxylins for use at stage 8b since silver is removed by iron salts, especially in acid solution. Removal of silver does not apparently occur with the iron alum-mordanted celestin blue solution recommended above.

1. Dry mounting. In this technique, fresh cryostat sections are cut in the darkroom and picked up on cold coverships coated with stripping film. Freeze drived tissues embedded in silicone plastic have also been used.

2. Coated autoradiography. There are several methods of coated autoradiography. In the first method, sections mounted on slides are covered by a thin layer of photographic emulsion. Photographic emulsion is painted on the sections with the help of a brush or glass rod. Alternatively, the studies are dipped in the emulsion. The liquid emulsion is melted in a waterbath at 40° in diluted or undiluted form. The choice of diluted or undiluted emulsions depends upon the purpose of the investigations. A semiautomatic instrument for dip coating is also available. A third type of method is known as inversion technique. Mounted, unstained tissue sections covered with celloidin are coated with a special emulsion. After exposure and development, the preparation is immersed in water and the emulsion is lifted from the slide with the help of a razor blade, the sections adhered to its under space. It is then inverted and mounted, sections upwards, on a clean slide. Staining is carried out after ward easily.

3. Double labeling (two emulsion technique). In order to distinguish between two types of particles two layers of emulsions separated by a layer of celloidin are applied. By using a tritiated precursor of DNA and ^{14}C labelled precursor of RNA, it was possible to investigate the metabolism of these two substances simultaneously. Many modifications of this technique have been published. Most of them use two successive dipping in the emulsion. However, a few workers have used stripping film first, followed by a treatment with liquid emulsion.

(a) Exposure. Several factors are important in determining the exposure e.g. type of isotope, the dose, the duration of its effect and the type of emulsion. In practice, it is decided by trial and error method. The whole process is normally carried out at 4^0C in a closed box containing Drierite or other water absorbing material.

(b) Development. This is the production of silver grains. A suitable developer is used for a period of 4-6 minutes at 18°. The time of development depends upon the thickness of emulsion, with thick layers, 20-30 minutes may be necessary at 12-14°. After development, washing in water is followed by a treatment in a acid fixer and a final thorough wash in water, provided that the sections have not been prestained.

(c) Staining. Staining can be performed either before application of the emulsion or after development. Stains applied in stage one must be resistant to subsequent procedures. They must not bring the removal or translocation of the isotope and must not cause fogging of the emulsion stains applied at stage two must be able to penetralle the gelatin film without causing damage and loss of silver grains. For post staining haematoxylin and eosin, continue to remain a popular stain. However, many other stains viz: basic fuchsin, toludine blue, methylene blue, azure A and cresyl violet may be applied. Many staining mixtures such as Giemsa, methyl green pyronin and neutral fast red/indigocarmine have also been used.

Quantitative Autoradiography

There are four types of procedures by which the amount of radioactivity in cells and tissues can be calculated:

(1) Grain counting (Andresen *et. al.*, 1952).
(2) Track counting.
(3) Counting of labelled units (e.g. nuclei).
(4) Photometric densitometry.

The first two, and especially the first, are extremely laborious and the third has only limited applications. It would therefore be much preferable to employ the fourth type of method.

An alternative instrument, designed by **Gullberg** (1957) used a direct recording microscope to produce a photometric trace of the density of the grains in an autoradiograph. A flying-spot scanning instrument was described by Tolles (1959) who used photographs different levels combined into a single picture and with the grains converted into lines for photodensitometry.

Electron Microscopical Autoradiography

The methods of EM autoradiography were discussed by **Fromme** (1964) and practical considerations dealt with more fully by the same author (**Fromme**, 1970). Special emulsions with very small silver halide crystals are necessary for EM autoradiography. The most commonly used examples are Ilfored L4 nuclear track emulsion (halide crystal size 120-160 nm), Kodak NTE (30-50 nm), and Gevaert Scientia NUC 307 (70 nm). A fine grain silver bromide emulsion, prepared by van Kleff *et. al.* (1969) was reported to have a mean diameter of less than 10 nm.

The factors involved in EM autoradiography are as follows—

(1) The range of the β-particles in tissue, resin or gelatin.
(2) Geometry: with a monolayer of crystals and a point source of β-particles the probability of a hit on a crystal decreases asthe solid angle from which it is seen by a source.
(3) The shielding of the silver halide crystals away from the source by those which are close to it (thus reducing the probability of finding an exposed grain away from the source).

The combination of these factors results in a distribution curve from which one can predict a resolution of the order of 0·1 μ (with Ilford LV emulsion). Distribution curves were calculated for various distances of source to emulsion and for various grain sizes.

IP Autoradiography System (IPAS)

"Imaging Plate" (IP) is a two-dimensional sensor to detect and store ionization radiation emitted from coated photo-stimulable phosphor. The method for autoradiography by using an Imaging Plate instead of an X-ray film is called "IP-ARG". Bio-Imaging Analyzer is equipped for reading out imaging data of the exposed Imaging Plate, processing the image, such as quantitation, and giving hard-copy printouts. Since "IP-ARG" is about one hundred times more sensitive than X-ray film and superior in quantitation performance, it has rapidly become popular although only a few years have passed since its first introduction into the market.

Important Questions

1. Define radioactivity. How can you classify radioactivity into different types and measure the amount of radioactivity in biological samples?
2. What is autoradiography? Describe different methods used in autoradiography.
3. Write short notes on the following:
   (i) Radioactive decay, (ii) Geiger Muller tube, (iii) Scintillation counting, (iv) Cerenkov counting, (v) Quantative autoradiography (vi) Electron microscopic autoradiography.

17 Electrochemical Techniques & Biosensors

A study of chemical interactions between electricity and matter is known as electrochemistry. A biologist can use electrochemical technique to measure the concentration of a great number of biologically important substances and determine important features of biological environment such as conductivity or pH. Today, a student uses not only the pH electrode but various ions can be measured using ion selective electrodes. Several types of biosensors have been developed for clinical, industrial and environmental applications. Electrochemical analysis of polluted water through HPLC columns is coming up as an alternative to ultraviolet detection techniques.

Principles of Electrochemical Techniques

The general approach to electrochemical techniques involves the use of electrodes to make electrical contact with the solution in arrangements known as electrochemical cells which are of two types:

[I] Electrolytic Cell

When a potential difference is applied across two electrodes dipped into a solution a current will flow between them. The electrical properties of the solution determine the relationship between the voltage applied and the amount of current which flows, a feature which provides the basis for conductimetric and polarographic methods of analysis. In the same way, the total amount of chemical change which takes place at an electrode is related to the amount of current.

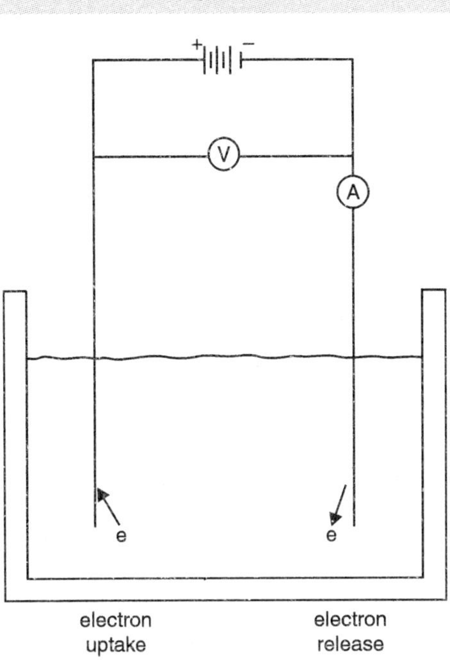

Fig. 1. An electrolytic cell. The current which flows between the electrodes depends not only on the voltage which is applied but also on the electric properties of the solution.

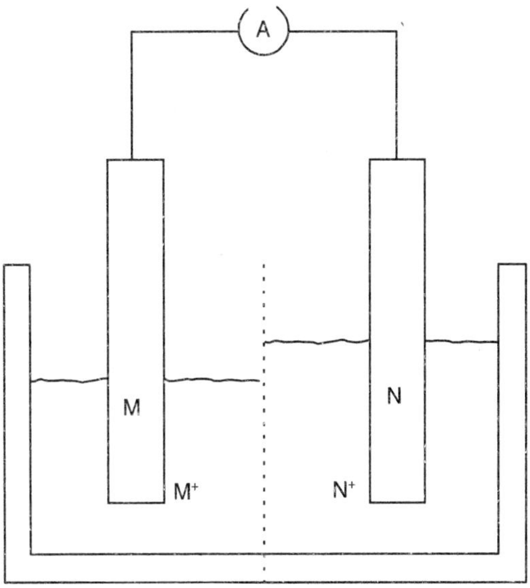

Fig. 2. A galvanic cell. A reaction taking place at the electrodes results in a potential difference developing between the electrodes and in some cases, a measurable current will flow between them.

The measurement of this current forms the basis of coulometric methods of analysis.

Thus electrolytic cells are used in conductimetric, polarographic and coulometric methods of analysis. Well known examples are the electrolytic systems of chlorine and aluminium, electrorefining of copper and electroplating of silver and gold (Fig. 1).

[II] Voltage or Galvanic Cells

In some cells, the chemical nature of electrodes and the solutions results in a chemical reaction taking place at the electrodes with the production of electrical energy (batteries) but without the need for an external voltage.

A restricted form of galvanic cells is used in potentiometeric methods in which no voltage is applied to the cells and no current actually flows between the electrodes (which are said to be unpolarized) but they develop a potential, relative to the solution due to the nature of electrodes and the solution. This potential can be measured and related to the concentration of the ions in the solution. Well known examples of galvanic cells are Zn-MnO_2 cell and rechargeable batteries.

Classification of Electrochemical Techniques

Now we understand that a electrochemical cell can be either galvanic cell or electrolytic cell. Electroanalytical techniques can thus be subdivided into two main groups depending upto the use of these types of cells as follows—

1. Potentiometry. That involves the use of galvanic cells, with the measurement of the potential of an electrode without current flow.

2. Voltametry. That involves the use of electrolytic cells, with the measurement of the current passing through an electrode at constant potential or as the potential varies under potentiostatic control.

Potentiometry

The potential developed by a single electrode in a solution is generated by the tendency of the solution either to donate or accept electrons and can be calculated using the Nernst equation. It describes the behaviour of electrode and can be expressed in the simplest form as follows —

$$E = E_{constant} + \frac{2 \cdot 303\,RT}{nF} \times \log a$$

Where E is the electrode potential at the specified concentration

$E_{constant}$ is the standard electrode potential

R is the gas constant

T is the absolute temperature

n is the number of electrons involved

F is the Faraday constant

a is the activity of the ion

2·303 is the Nernst factor

If the experiment has been made at 25°C, the equation can further be simplified as

$$E = E_{constant} + \frac{2 \cdot 059}{n} \times \log c$$

Where c is the concentration of the ion.

In most biological situations, the concentration of ions are rather low and consequently the activity and the concentration are equal. At higher concentrations, however, the activity becomes less than the concentration. The Nernst equation shows that the electrode response depends on both temperature and the number of changes on the ion.

There can be no chemical reaction in such a system without a complimentary donor or acceptor to complete the process. Each of these electrodes is known as half cell and the potential developed by half cell can not be measured in absolute terms but only compared with that of another half cell. The chemical reaction occurring in half cell is called as half reaction. Any half cell will be able to reduce another half cell which has a lower standard potential. The standard electrode potential is defined as its electrical potential when it is in contact with a molar solution of its ions. Standard electrode potentials of biological interest are described below —

Table 1. **Standard electrode potentials at pH 7·0.**

Half – reaction	E_0'
Oxygen/water	0·81
Ferric/ferrous	0·77
Ferricyanide/ferrocyanide	0·36
Oxygen/hydrogen peroxide	0·30
Cytochrome *c* ferric/ferrous	0·22
Dehydroascorbic acid/ascorbic acid	–0·19
$FAD/FADH_2$	–0·22
$NAD^+/NADH$	–0·32
$2H^+/H_2$	–0·42
Ferrous/iron	0·44

Redox Reactions

Compounds existing in an oxidized and a reduced form can be represented by the following general equation

Oxidized form + ne^- ⇔ reduced form

A mixture of the reduced and oxidized form of a substance (e.g. Fe^{2+}/Fe^{3+} or $NADH/NAD^+$) is known as a redox couple. When an inert electrode (such as platinum) is put into a solution of a redox couple, the metal will become charged and the potential difference created between the metal and the solution can be compared with the steady potential produced by a reference electrode.

Oxidation-reduction (redox) potentials are measured with the standard hydrogen electrode used as a reference electrode and compared with the standard potential (E_0) which is produced by a platinum electrode dipped into 1M concentration of both the oxidized and reduced forms of a substance at 25°C. Redox couples have positive or negative redox potentials depending upon whether they are more oxidized or reduced than the standard hydrogen electrode. Thus the potential of an experimental sample (E) is related to the standard potential (E_0) by Nernst equation (ne).

$$E = E_0 + 2 \cdot 303\ \frac{RT}{nF} \log \left[\frac{(oxid)}{(red)}\right]$$

Application of redox couples. Redox couples are applied in several biological investigations. They are useful in electron transport chain. The change in the color of redox dyes help in making certain

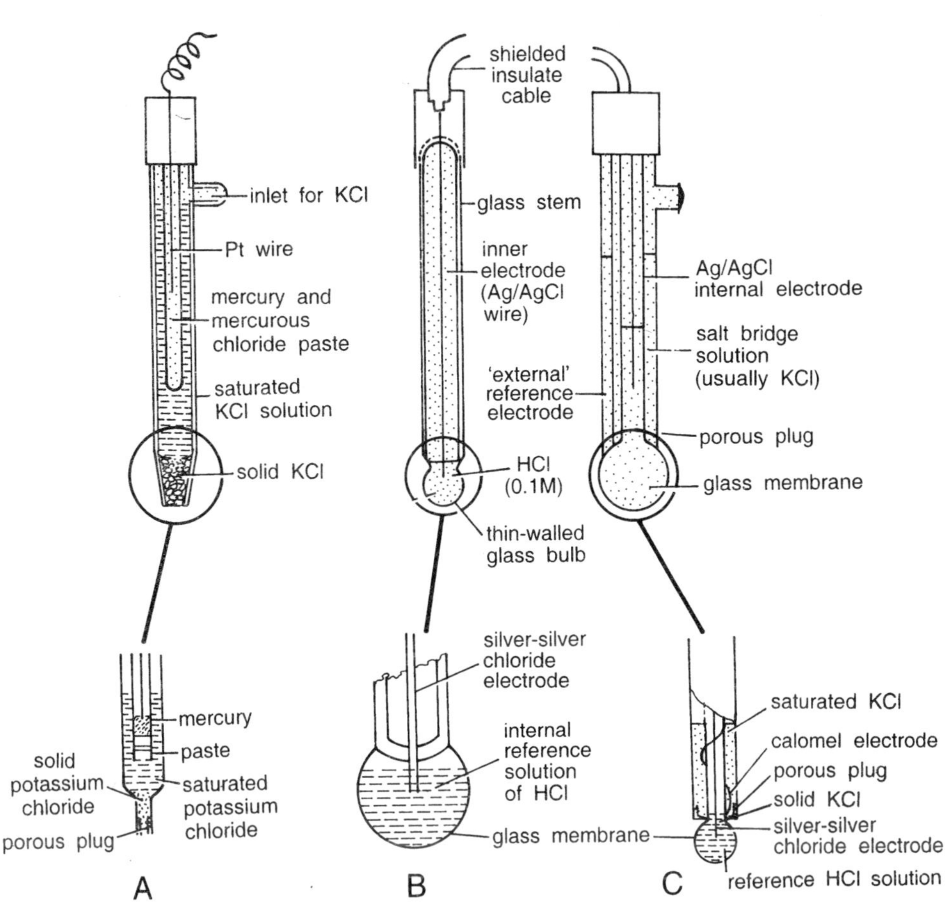

Fig. 3. Electrodes : (A) a calomel reference electrode; (B) glass electrode; (C) a combinatin electrode.

biochemical investigations. The electron transport processes of chloroplasts, mitochondria and bacteria can also be studied using indicator dyes.

Potentiometric Measurements (pH Meter)

Redox measurements are used in determining the pH employing glass electrode. This technique was developed in 1919 and became popular in 1930s after the advent of suitable amplifiers. Today pH meter is an essential tool of a biology laboratory.

A glass electrode consists of a silver chloride electrode in a reference solution of hydrochloric acid ($0{\cdot}1$ mol l^{-1}) contained in a glass membrane. The membrane is made up of a special glass usually a hydrated aluminosilicate containing sodium or calcium ions. It is selectively permeable to hydrogen ions and the potential which develops across the membrane depends upon the hydrogen ion concentration of the test solution compared with the reference acid solution inside the electrode. This potential can be measured against a reference calomal electrode using a high impedance voltmenter. For convenient operation, sometimes the glass electrode is often combined with a reference calomal electrode in a single glass probe. The electrodes must be stored in distilled water between use in order to keep the glass membrane fully hydrated (Fig. 3).

1. Operation of the pH meter. pH meter uses electrodes. These electrodes are available in different shapes and sizes suitable for different applications e.g. measurement of the pH of the blood, flat moist

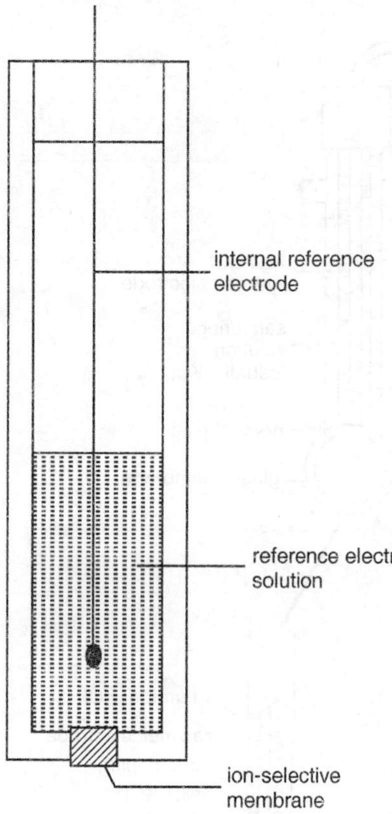

Fig. 4. The basic design of an ion-selective electrode.

surfaces, soil, water and visceral organs. Intracellular pH can also be measured using miniature probes (microelectrodes).

There is an almost linear relationship between potential and pH over the range of 2-10. Calibration of the instrument is essential and may be achieved with either buffers whose pH has been previously measured or solutions of very pure chemicals prepared in specific concentrations e.g. a solution of potassium hydrogen phthalate (0.05 mol l^{-1}) has a pH of 4.00 at 15°C. Temperature control is important and for measurements over a range of pH values, it is necessary to standardize the instruments & on at least two standard buffer solutions which cover the required range.

2. Measurement of pH. A precise measurement of pH of an unknown sample consists of two steps. The first step is to standardize the instrument against a known standard buffer solution at the room temperature. The second step is to measure the pH of the unknown solution. The accuracy of measurement of pH depends on the accuracy of the buffer solution used for standardization and the care taken in setting the 'temperature' compensate control and 'standardize' control.

Standardization Step by Step Procedure

(1) Switch on the instrument
(2) Put the slide switch to 100% SLOPE position.
(3) Set the 'Function' switch to 'Standby' position.
(4) Rinse the electrode pair with distilled water and carefully wipe them with filter paper.
(5) Take the standard buffer solution, say 7.00 pH in a beaker and measure its temperature exactly.
(6) Dip the electrodes into the buffer solution.
(7) Set the 'temperature' control knob to temperature reading obtained in step 5.
(8) Set the 'Function' switch to the 'pH position.
(9) Set the buffer value on digital display to read 7·00 by rotating the 'standardize' control one way or the other.

Now the instrument is standardized against the buffer solution used at the temperature. Put back the 'function' switch to 'STD BY' position. Please **do not disturb** the 'standardize' control till all the pH measurements are completed.

To measure the pH value of the unknown solution. Take out the electrodes from the buffer solution, wash the electrodes with a jet of distilled water and wipe them with filter paper. Dip the electrodes into the unknown solution. Measure the temperature of this solution and set the 'temperature' control to this value. Set the 'function' switch to position 'pH' and read the pH of the unknown solution on digital display.

Ion-selective Electrodes

Recognition of the fact that glass electrode used for measuring the pH is selectively permeable to hydrogen ions, led to the development of a wide range of ion selective electrodes. Ion-selective electrodes respond to the activity of a particular ion. A change in the composition of the glass membrane can change to permeability of the glass to other ions viz: Na^+, K^+, Ca^{2+} and NH_4^+. Glass is the active material within the pH electrode, but

Table 2. **Ion-selective electrodes.**

Test ion	Membrane material	Major interfering ions
Solid state electrodes		
Fluoride	LaF	I^- Br^- Cl^-
Chloride	$AgCl/Ag_2S$	S^- I^-
Bromide	$AgBr/Ag_2S$	S^- I^-
Iodide	AgI/Ag_2S	S^-
Sulphide	AgI/Ag_2S	S^-
Cupric	Ag_2S/CuS	Hg^+ Ag^+
Lead	Ag_2S/PbS	Hg^+ Ag^+
Cadmium	Ag_2S/CdS	Hg^+ Ag^+ Cu^{2+}
Silver	Ag_2S	
Liquid membrane electrodes		
Potassium	Valinomycin in diphenyl ether	
Ammonium	Macrotetrolides in tris (2-ethylhexyl)phosphate	
Calcium	Calcium dialkylphosphate in dioctylphenylphosphonate	
Calcium/ magnesium	Dialkylphosphoric acid in aliphatic alcohol	

modified aluminosilicate glasses, silver sulphide and lanthanum fluoride may be used. In all ion-selective electrodes, basic design of the electrode is similar to pH electrode but nature of the ion selective electrode varies. Membrane material used in certain ion-selective electrodes is described by the following Table 2 —

An electrode may be ion selective but not necessarily ion specific. Many ions can be measured directly by the use of ISEs or indirectly by titration. The response of ion selective electrode is logarithmic, with 10-fold changes in activity giving equal increments on the meter scale. As with pH electrode, the actual potential produced from an ISE is temperature dependent except at the isopotential point which varies depending upon the type of electrode. Therefore temperature compensation is needed. A reference electrode is also needed so that the varying potential of the ISE can be compared with the steady potential protected by reference electrode.

Gas sensing electrodes are used to estimate the concentration of a gas by its interaction in a thin layer surrounding an ion selective electrode, commonly a pH electrode. Carbon dioxide, ammonia, sulphur dioxide and nitrogen oxide can all be measured by their dissolution in a thin layer surrounding a pH electrode.

Recently miniature ion selective electrodes have been developed based on the principle of field effect transistors. These ion selective field effect transistors (ISFETs) are very useful in clinical studies. Multifunctional ISFETs are commericially available to measure pH, Na^+, K^+ and Ca^{2+}.

Applications of Ion-Selective Electrodes

(1) Ion-selective electrodes are easy to use and economical.

(2) They can be used in continuous monitoring experiments.

(3) Microelectrodes can be used to determine the ion contents of cells, muscles and nerves.

Clark Oxygen Electrode

This electrode was developed by **L.C. Clark Jr.** in 1956. It has a variety of biological applications. It consists of a platinum cathode and silver anode, both immersed in the same situation of saturated potassium chloride and separated from the test solution by an oxygen permeable membrane. When a potential difference of 0·6 V is applied across the electrodes such that the platinum cathode is made negative with respect to the silver anode, electrons are generated at the anode and are then used to reduce oxygen at the cathode. The oxygen tension at the cathode then drops and this acts as a sink so that more oxygen diffuses towards it to make up the deficit. Since the rate of diffusion of oxygen through the memberane is the limiting step in the reduction process, the current produced by the electrode is proportional to the oxygen tension in the sample. These reactions may be summarized as —

$$4\ Ag + 4\ Cl \rightarrow 4\ AgCl + 4e^- \text{ (at silver anode)}$$

$$O_2 + 4\ H^+ + 4e^-\ 2 \rightarrow H_2O \text{ (at platinum cathode)}$$

1. How to use the Clark oxygen electrode? The test sample (about 3 cm^3) is placed in the reaction vessel which is separated from the electrode chamber by an oxygen permeable, but ion impermeable membrane. Teflon (12μm thick) is the usual choice of the membrane, however, cellophane, polythene & silicon rubber have also been used with limited success. The electrodes are maintained in

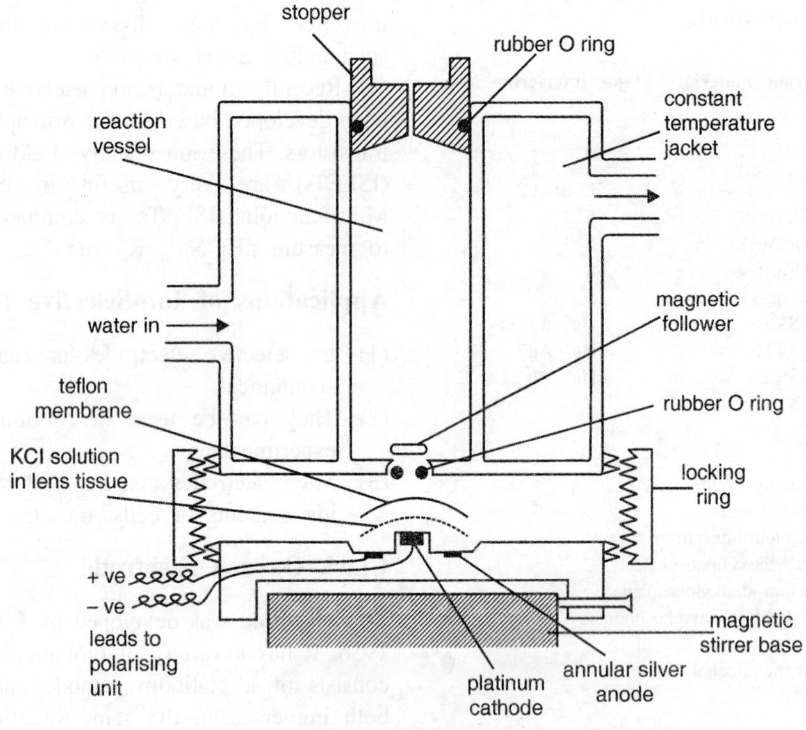

Fig. 5. Section through a Clark oxygen electrode.

electrical continuity with each other via potassium chloride solution. A square piece of tissue paper is immersed in the potassium chloride to provide physical support to thin membrane. A hole of 1 to 2 mm diameter created in the centre allows the platinum cathode to pass through the tissue. The oxygen electrode is mounted over a stirring motor. The contents of the reaction vessel should always be stirred while measuring the oxygen content. Reaction vessel is surrounded by a water jacket. Water is pumped into this jacket through a thermocirculator. The electrode is first calibrated by using calibration solutions. After every use, the apparatus should be thoroughly cleaned (Fig. 5).

2. Applications of the oxygen electrode. Oxygen electrodes are used in all those experiments that measure oxygen uptake and evolution. It has replaced manometric techniques. A few examples of its application are described below—

(1) Oxygen evolution from cyanobacteria, algae, chloroplasts, can be studied using Clark oxygen electrode.

(2) Microorganisms that use oxygen as the terminal electron acceptor of respiratory electron transport can be studied using an oxygen electrode.

(3) Studies on mitochondrial respiration and measurements on oxidative phosphorylation are best done by oxygen electrodes.

(4) When oxygen is involved in an enzyme reaction, enzyme such as glucose oxidase, D-amino acid oxidase and catalase can be studied by using oxygen electrode.

Conductimetry

When two electrodes are dipped in a solution and a fixed voltage is applied, a current flows between them depending upon the conductivity of the solution. This process is known as conductimetry. It allows the quantitative measurement of ions present in a solution.

The principle of conductimetry is based on the current carried by the ions present in a solution.

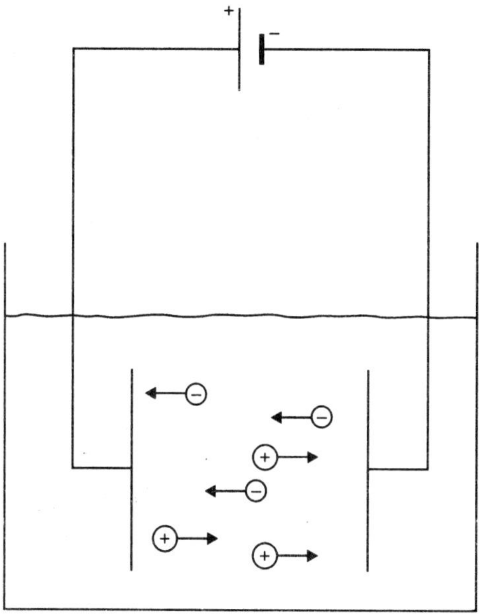

Fig. 6. The conductivity of a solution. The total transfer of electricity is not necessarily shared equally because different ions move at different speeds. The **Kohlrausch** law says that the total conductivity of an electrolyte is the sum of the conductivities of the anions and the cations.

The current is related to the number of ions present in a solution which are related to molar concentration of the compound and the state of its ionization. The anions donate electrons from the cathode. It is the transfer of electrons which determine the amount of flowing current. The current flowing through a conductor is defined by Ohm's law as —

$$\text{Current } (I) = \frac{\text{Voltage applied } (V)}{\text{resistance } (R)}$$

Or in terms of conductance —

Current (I) = Conductance (C) × Voltage applied (V)

Instrumentation

The basic instrument for conductimetric measurements involves a Wheatstone bridge arrangement.

Conductimetric Measurements

The basic instrumentation for conductimetric measurements involves a wheatstone bridge arrangement (Fig. 7). An alternating rather than direct current, is used in order to prevent polarization of the

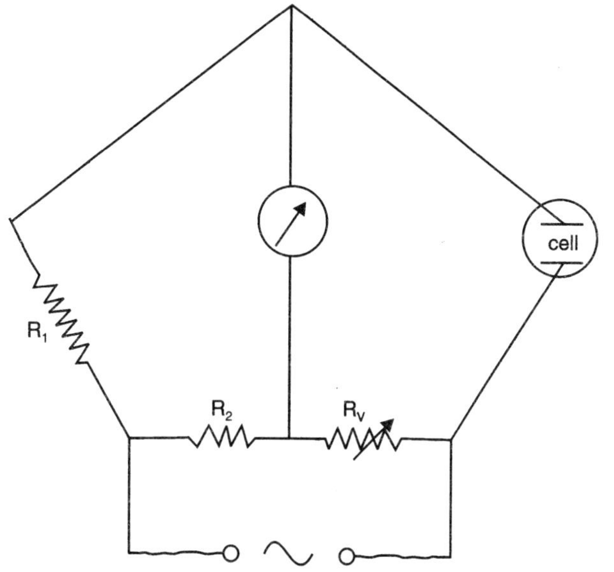

Fig. 7. Wheatstone bridge circuit.

solution (i.e. anions moving to the anode and cations moving to the cathode) and any electrolysis which might result from this polarization. With fixed resistances, R_1 and R_2, the variable resistance R_v is adjusted until no current flows through the galvanometer. Under these conditions :

$$R_1 \times R_2 = R_{cell} \times R_2$$

This gives a value for the resistance of the cell which can be converted to conductance by calculating the reciprocal.

The electrodes of conductivity cells are usually made of platinum coated with platinum black with a known area. Although in many cells the distance between the electrodes is adjustable, for any series of experiments it must be held constant and for many calculations the precise value is required. The cells must be thermostatically controlled because any changes in temperature will cause significant alteration of conductivity values.

Applications of Conductimetric Measurements

Although conductimetry is useful in determining various physical constants, e.g. dissociation and solubility constants, its major analytical application is for monitoring titrations.

When two electrolyte solutions which do not react with each other are mixed, provided that there is

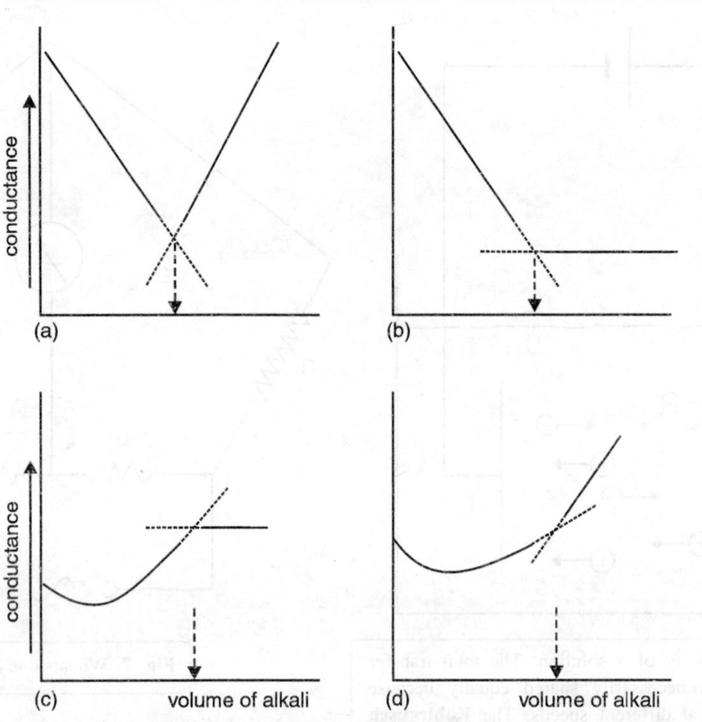

Fig. 8. Conductimetric titration curves. As an acid is titrated with an alkali, so the ionic composition of the mixture changes and is reflected in the conductivity of the solution, (a) A strong acid and a strong base, (b) A strong acid and a weak base, (c) A weak acid and a weak base, (d) A weak acid and a strong base.

no appreciable change in volume, the conductance of the solution will rise because of the increase in the numbers of ions. However, if there is a reaction between the ions, one ion being replaced by another, the conductance of the solution will alter depending upon the relative mobilities of the ions involved. In the reaction

$$A^+B^- + C^+ D^- = AD + C^+B^-$$

in which CD is the titrant, the effect of the reaction is to replace A^+ by C^+ in the solution. If these two ions have different ionic mobilities, the conductance of the solution will change accordingly. This is illustrated in the titration of a strong acid by a strong base, the hydrogen ions are replaced by the cation from the base which will have a smaller ionic mobility and hence a lower conductivity and will result in a gradual fall in the conductance of the solution. However, at the end-point of the reaction, the increasing concentration of hydroxyl ions will result in an increasing conductance (Fig. 8). An extrapolation of the lines before and after the end-point will give an intercept at the end-point.

Conductimetric titrations, particularly when they are automated, are useful if either of the reactants is deeply coloured, so preventing visual monitoring of the tritration using indicators or if both reactants are very dilute.

Coulometric Analysis

Coulometry is an electrolytic method of analysis. In general electrolytic methods have limited applications in analytical biochemistry but they are useful in the analysis of substances which, while not strictly biochemical, are often important in biological and physiological chemistry.

Faraday's laws of electrolysis form the basis of quantitative coulometric analysis. They are:

(1) The weight of substance liberated during electrolysis is directly proportional to the quantity of electricity passed.

Fig 9. A glucometer as a biosensor.

(2) The weights of substances liberated by the same quantity of electricity are in direct proportion to their equivalent weights.

There are two basic types of coulometric analyses using either constant current or constant voltage. In the latter method a voltage is applied which causes the test substance to react at an electrode and the current which flows initially decreases to almost zero as the number of test ions decreases. The total amount of current passed during the reaction can be measured using a coulometer and related to the amount of test substance originally present. Because this method of analysis requires the test substance to undergo a reaction at an electrode it has only very limited biochemical applications, the measurement of oxygen being the main application although the use of the oxygen electrode is very much more appropriate. Such constant voltage techniques are known as coulometric methods.

Biosensors

Biosensor is a device designed to detect molecules with high selectivity. They work on the principle of molecular recognition. The central feature is a selective active surface consisting of a biological material (enzyme, cell or tissue) coupled to an optically or electronically active medium. Suitable transducers convert biochemical interactions to electronic information that can be amplified and translated into a quantitative signal (**Cass**, 1995). A number of biosensors have now been developed for use in the fields of medicine, biotechnology, environmental monitoring and the food industry. Initially miniature biosensors with a single specific function (e.g. measurement of glucose) were developed. However, now they are classified as first, second and third generation instruments depending upon the degree of intimacy between biological catalyst and transducer.

First Generation Biosensors

In such instruments, the biocatalyst within a biosensor responds to the substrate in solution by catalyzing a reaction. For example glucose oxidase will catalyze the following reaction

$$\text{glucose} + O_2 \rightarrow \text{gluconic acid} + H_2O_2$$

This reaction can offer the following information.

(1) The rate of O_2 consumption can be measured with Clark oxygen electrode.

(2) The rate of production of H_2O_2 can be measured by its oxidation at a platinum anode polarized at + 0·7v versus the standard calomel electrode.

(3) The rate of production of gluconic acid can be measured using a pH electrode.

Any one of these three reactions can be used for analysis and the sensor is suitably designed. Glucometer is the most popular biosensor used today to measure glucose in blood samples.

Second Generation Biosensors

An increase in the intimacy between biocatalyst and transducer resulted into the development of second generation biosensors. For example, in this device, the rate of oxidation of glucose is measured by the rate of flow of electrons from glucose to an electrode surface. The reaction can be summarized as follows —

$$\underset{(red)}{\text{Glucose}} + \underset{(ox)}{\text{Go/FAD}} \rightarrow \underset{(ox)}{\text{gluconic acid}} + \underset{(red)}{\text{Go/FADH}_2}$$

$$\underset{(red)}{\text{Go/FADH}_2} + \underset{(ox)}{2M} \rightarrow \underset{(ox)}{\text{Go/FAD}} + \underset{(red)}{2MH + 2H}$$

At the electrode

$$\underset{(red)}{2M} \rightarrow \underset{(ox)}{2M^+ + 2e^-}$$

Where Go/FAD represents the FAD redox center of glucose oxidase in its oxidized form, Go/$FADH_2$ represents the FAD redox centre of glucose oxidase in its reduced form and M is the mediator e.g. ferrocene. The electrons donated to the electrode

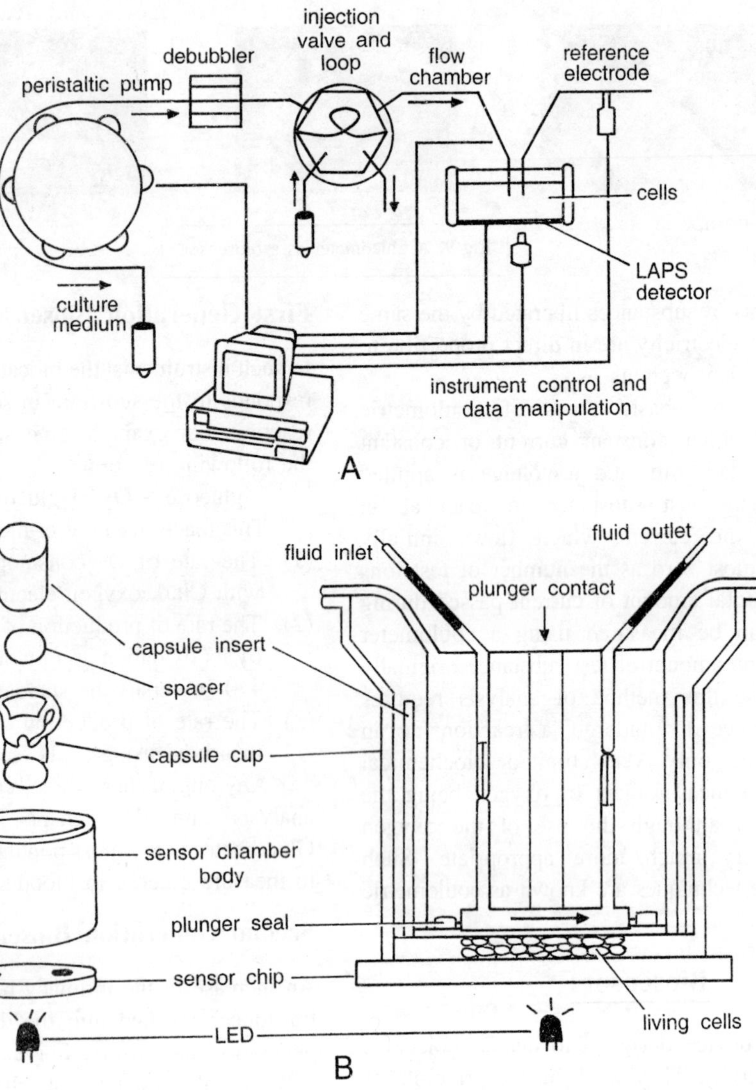

Fig. 10. Cytosensor microphysiometer: **A.** Scheme of the cytosensor. **B.** Cell capsule and sensor.

surface then go to from a current that is proportional to the rate of oxidation of glucose, and hence proportional to the glucose concentration in the blood.

Third Generation Biosensors

These instruments involve more intimate interaction of the biocatalyst and the transducer. A glucose biosensor operating on the principle of second generation instrument in which the enzyme can be directly reduced at the electrode surface (excluding the need of a mediator) would be called as third generation instrument.

Other Biosensor Techniques

Biosensor techniques based on different operating principles could provide complimentary information in particular, the ability to supplement physical binding data with rapidly obtained biological information would be desirable. For such studies, the cytosensor microphysiometer would be an obvious choice.

The cytosensor is a cell based biosensor that detects extracellular acidification after cell stimulation (due to the acidic products of glycolysis, respiration,

ATP hydrolysis), using a potentiometric sensor. By maintaining cells in a low buffer, extremely small quantities of excreted acidic by products can be measured.

Cytosensor

The cytosensor comprises a fluidic system, a tissue cell capsule and pH sensitive silicon sensor which is positioned directly under the cell capsule for the detection of acidic byproducts. The instrument comes in either four or eight channel format allowing simultaneous multichannel analysis. Instruments operation is performed by a PC. Eukaryotic, prokaryotic and adherent and non-adherent cells can be used (typically 50-100,000 cells) by growing or entrapping them on the lower membrane of the capsule. When installed in the instrument the capsule forms the part of a flow cell which can be supplied with culture media and reagents. With flow on (typically 100-140 μl/min), the sensor measures the steady state pH of the infusing medium. The flow is temporarily stopped and the rate of change in pH is measured. The flow is then restarted allowing the cells to return to their baseline conditions.

1. Principle of detection. The surface of sensor (LAPS) is a thin (60-nm) silicon oxynitride insulator containing both hydroxyl and amino functions that can be titrated as a function of pH. An electric field is generated across the silicon by applying a potential and amplitude modulated LEDS under the silicon chip that causes a photocurrent to flow. The magnitude of the current produced at a given voltage depends on the surface change of the silicon oxynitride insulator which in turn depends upon the pH of the culture solution. The major problem with cells is that they have many different surface receptors and hence respond to a range of stimuli.

Table 3. **Reagents for probing signal transduction pathways.**

Pathway	Signal transduction probe	Action
Protein kinase	H-89	Protein kinase A inhibitor
	RpcAMPs	Protein kinase A inhibitor
	PMA	Activator of protein kinase C
	Shingosine	Inhibitor
	Staurospaurine	Nonspecific inhibitor
	Calphostin-C	Inhibitor
	PKC antisense oligonucleotides	Inhibitor
	PD98059	Inhibitor of Erk activation
Tyrosine kinase	Genistein	Inhibitor
	Tyrphostins	EGF receptor inhibitor JAK kinase inhibitors
		Src kinase inhibitors
	PD 153035	EGFR kinase inhibitor
	Herbimycin	Inhibitor
Calmodulin kinase	K252a	Nonspecific inhibitor
Adenylate cyclase	KN62	Inhibitor
	8-bromo AMP	Analogue
	Forskolin	Adenyl cyclase activator
	Dideoxyforskolin	Inactive forskolin analogue
		cAMP analogue
		cAMP analogue
G-protein	8-(4-chlorophenylthio)-cAMP	Nonhydolysable activator
	Cholera toxin	Activator of cAMP pathway[a]
Phosphate	Pertussis toxin	Inhibitor of cAMP pathway[b]
ATPase	Okadaic acid	Inhibitor
	Oubadaine	Na^+/K^+ ATPase Inhibitor
	Bafilomycin	Vasicular H^+ ATPase Inhibitor
	Meprazole	Na^+/K^+ ATPase inhibitor

[a] Activates the stimulatory G-protein (Gs)
[b] Activates the inhibitory G-protein (Gi)

Careful designed control experiments are therefore crucial to the success of this technique.

2. Applications of biosensors. The use of instrumental biosensors in basic research to measure biomolecular interactions in real time is increasing exponentially. Applications include protein-protein, protein-peptide, DNA-protein, DNA-DNA, and lipid-protein interactions. Such techniques have been applied to antigen-antibody, receptor-ligand, signal transduction and nuclear receptor studies.

The cytosensor has been used with many cell types including endothelial, epithelial, fibroblast, muscle, blood, haematopoietic, neuronal, secretory and insect cells. Studies have used endogenous receptors or transfected native, chimeric or mutant molecules. Stimulants like antibodies, hormones, growth factors and cytokines have been studied. Inhibitors like drugs, cytotoxins disinfectants ion-channel blockers have also been studied. A major advantage of cell sensing is that the signal transduction pathways are intact and therefore can be interrogated. Pharmacological studies on second messenger pathways have been performed using a range of specific agonists or antagonists (Table 3).

The cytosensors like SPR biosensors has the potential for ligand searching. In this role, it has been used to support the molecular cloning and expression of a new chemokine receptor gene.

Conclusion

The development of instrumental biosensors capable of analyzing biomolecular interaction in real time has revolutionized the speed and ease with which such interactions can be studied. However, appropriate control experiments should always be carried out. New sensor surfaces or attachment chemistries are likely to be developed further.

Important Questions

1. What is potentiometery? Describe the potentiometric method so as to determine the pH of a solution.
2. What are ion selective electrodes? Discuss their applications.
3. Define conductimetry. Discuss different conductimetric measurements.
4. Write an essay on biosensors.
5. Write short notes on the following:
   (i) Cytosensors, (ii) Clark oxygen electrode, (iii) Coulometric analysis.

Methods of Environmental Analysis

18

Our environment is simple as well as complex. It is simple as long as it remains clean. It gets complex when industrial activities grow. To comprehend this complex nature of environment, we need knowledge of all disciplines of chemical, physical and biological sciences. To devise control measures, we need knowledge of engineering and technology. ~~Thus environmental~~ science and engineering is truly inter-disciplinary in nature. For example, to understand atmosphere we need knowledge of physics and meteorology, for knowing hydrosphere and water we need knowledge of chemistry. The complex behaviour of living organism can be really understood with a knowledge of the life sciences, the interaction in lithosphere can best be understood from principles of earth science, while the entire control mechanism can be devised only with intricate knowledge of engineering and technology. In the process of measurement we collect enormous data, which can be interpreted and understood only if we are conversant with statistical analysis and computer programming.

The control measures for the abatement of pollution cannot be properly devised unless we are aware of the extent or level of pollution. Such level can be ascertained by precise measurement and analysis of the environmental pollution. There are numerous methods for the measurement of pollution. They consist of classical methods of analysis like gravimetric or volumetric methods. These methods are generally applicable at milligram concentrations. Several of the pollutants are present in environment at microgram levels, e.g. dust

Table 1. **Methods of quantitative analysis.**

Name of method	Level of analysis	Range of analysis (gm)
Gravimetry methods	μg	10^{-1}–10^{-3}
Volumetry methods	μg	10^{-1}–10^{-4}
Molecular absorption spectroscopy (UV/visible/infrared)	μg	10^{-3}–10^{-6}
Emission spectroscopy	ηg	10^{-6}–10^{-9}
Atomic absorption spectroscopy	ηg	10^{-6}–10^{-9}
Molecular luminescence methods	ηg	10^{-3}–10^{-9}
Light scattering methods	μg	10^{-3}–10^{-6}
Radioanalytical techniques	ηg	10^{-3}–10^{-9}
Electroanalytical methods	μg	10^{-3}–10^{-6}

and particulate matter, while few metal pollutants like beryllium are having their threshold limiting value as $2\mu g/m^3$. As such spectral methods or electroanalytical methods are best suited in such analysis. Many a times the pollutants are found in association with one another. Under these circumstances determination becomes more complicated. One has to resort to various separation techniques, like chromatography for the isolation of these pollutants. In this chapter, an effort has been made to present a review of various methods utilized for the analysis of the various pollutants. It is presumed that the reader is quite conversant with the basis of these methods. Only, an attempt would be made to highlight applications of these methods in environmental pollution analysis.

Methods for Quantitative Analysis

We have several methods for quantitative analysis of pollutants. These methods are usually applicable when the pollutant is present at milligram (10^{-3}g)n to fentogram concentration (10^{-15}g). Table 1 lists such methods.

Classical gravimetric and volumetric methods can analyze a pollutant up to 10^{-4} g concentration, while analytical absorption or emission spectroscopic method can analyze pollutants to the level of nanogram (i.e. 10^{-9} g) concentration. Other methods involving light scattering or molecular luminescence operate usually up to microgram levels. The radioanalytical or electroanalytical methods can work in the range 10^{-7}-10^{-9} concentration. At this stage, it is worthwhile to make a review of the methods from the point of their end use in pollution analysis.

Gravimetric Method

We use this method only when the pollutant is present in the environment at milligram levels, e.g., the lead candle method for analysis of SO_2 from air is based upon this principle. A candle of PbO_2 on exposure to SO_2 forms $PbSO_4$, which is weighed to find out SO_2 in the air. The method involves simple weighing of PbO_2 and $PbSO_4$ before and after exposure respectively, to find the amount of SO_2 present. The other example is the determination of suspended particulate matter from air. We resort to weighing of particulates deposited on millipore filter paper. This residue is collected by sampling procedure involving high volume sampler. In analysis of water pollution we rarely use gravimetric methods.

Volumetric Methods

Largely these methods are classified into four groups involving acid-base titrations, redox reactions, precipitation methods and complexometric technique. They are used for monitoring of air as well as water pollution, e.g., the acid-base titration with conductance measurement is used for the analysis of SO_2 from air or boron from sample of soil. Simple acid-base titration is also used for ascertaining the acidity or alkalinity of sample of water. The application of oxidation-reduction or redox titration is well known. The Winkler's method for the determination of dissolved oxygen (DO) from water is based upon redox reaction of manganese salt. It is reacted in the presence of oxygen with KI and liberated iodine is titrated with standard $Na_2 S_2O_3$. Many of the organic pollutants from air can be determined by redox titrations. In all these cases, analysis is usually restricted to milligram level. Precipitation titration has wide ranging applications in water analysis, e.g. the determination of dissolved chloride from sample of water can be accomplished by Volhard's method or Mohr's method. Complexometric titrations has maximum utility in pollution analysis. For instance, the hardness of water can be ascertained by titration of calcium or magnesium with EDTA (disodium salt), with suitable metallochromic indicator like Patterson Reed indicator. Similarly, level of iron or manganese from polluted sample of water can be ascertained by complexometric titrations. In comparison to water analysis, the complexometry technique has limited applications in analysis of air pollution. In spite of great advancement of instrumentation and with development of DO (dissolved oxygen) analysers, the Winkler's method with redox titration is still considered to be the best and the most reliable method for analysis of DO, BOD (Biological Oxygen demand) and COD. In fact chemical oxygen demand (COD) for water can be ascertained only by redox titrations involving $K_2Cr_2O_7$, H_2SO_4, KI and $Na_2S_2O_3$.

Ultraviolet and Visible Spectrophotometry

This is perhaps the most popular technique, which has maximum utility in the pollution analysis. The principal reason for such popularity is the easy availability of colorimeters or spectrophotometers. The principle of visual colorimetry also forms the basis of **Ring Oven technique**. Table 2 indicates how UV spectroscopy can be used for the characterization of organic pollutants.

The task is complicated, when one has to characterise organic compound in waste water. A peak at 280 nm indicates presence of azo group; a peak at 186 nm shows presence of carbonyl group; peaks at 240-280nm shows possibility of the presence of aromatic compounds like napthalene or styrene, respectively. Visible spectrophotometry has in fact made the greatest revolution. In air pollution analysis, SO_2 is determined with p-roseaniline (PRA) method or NO-NO_2 from air is determined by **Saltzman method**; H_2S is analysed spectrophotometrically by molybdenum-blue method; in water pollution analysis metal pollutants like iron (1-10 phenanthroline), Cr (sym diphenylcarbazide),

***Table** 2.* **Ultraviolet absorption of pollutant with chromophores.**

Chromophore	max nm λ	Molar absorptivity ε	Nature of transitions
Alkene	177	1.3×10^4	$\pi \longrightarrow \pi^*$
Carbonyl	186	1.0×10^{-3}	$\pi \longrightarrow$ or $\pi \longrightarrow \pi^*$
Amide	214	60	$n \longrightarrow \pi^*$
Azo	339	5	$n \longrightarrow \pi^*$
Nitro	280	22	$n \longrightarrow \pi^*$
Olefin	184	1.0×10^4	delocalise π^*
Ketone	280	27	$n \longrightarrow \pi^*$
Methanol	184	1.5×10	$n \longrightarrow \alpha^*$
Methyl chloride	173	2×10^2	$n \longrightarrow \alpha^*$
Benzene	204	7.9×10^3	$\pi \longrightarrow \pi^*$
Toluene	207	7.9×10^3	$\pi \longrightarrow \pi^*$
Phenol	211	$6{\cdot}2 \times 10^3$	$\pi \longrightarrow \pi^*$
Aniline	230	8.6×10^3	$\pi \longrightarrow \pi^*$
Naphthalene	286	93×10^3	$\pi \longrightarrow \pi^*$
Styrene	244	1.2×10^4	$\pi \longrightarrow \pi^*$

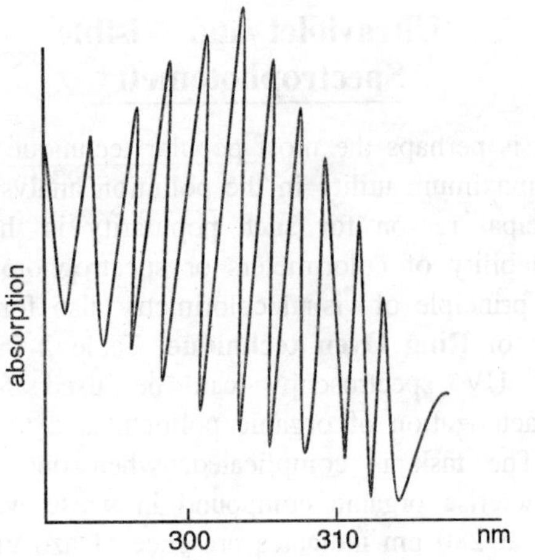

Fig. 1. UV spectra of SO_2

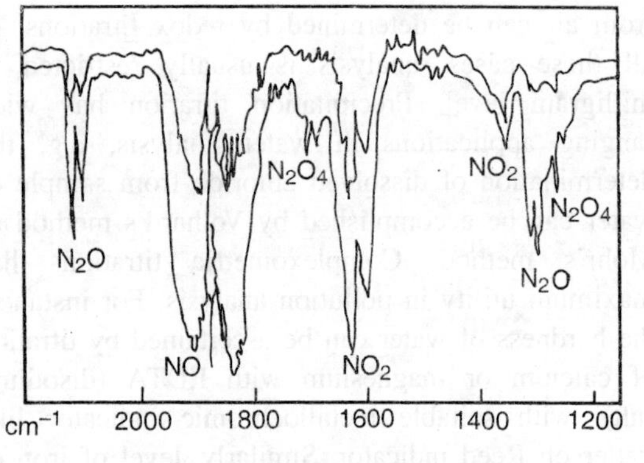

Fig. 2. IR spectra of NO–NO_x

Mn (formaldioxime); nickel (dimethylglyoxime); zinc (dithizone) methods are commonly used, where a chromogenic ligand is reacted with metal pollutant to form coloured complex. So long as the system adheres to Bear's law (viz $A = abc$, where A = absorbance, a = absorptivity, b = optical path, c = concentration), one can use this technique for analysis of majority of the metal pollutants in air and water.

Infrared and Raman Spectroscopy

While characterising the organic pollutant from air or water, only one technique may not furnish definite information. It is necessary to use more than two or three methods, to definitely ascertain the presence of certain pollutants. Infrared spectra originates on account of vibrational frequency of functional group in a molecule. As such every functional group has characteristic frequency. A typical group frequency can identify a molecule in aquatic environment or air. Table 3 lists such characteristic frequency of various functional groups, e.g. a peak at 1720-1740 cm^{-1} indicates the presence of > CO group. In fact this had formed the basis for analysis of carbon monoxide from air by nondispersive infrared spectroscopic technique (NDIR). We call this technique as non-dispersive, because we carry out measurement at fixed frequency or wave number, e.g. 1800 cm^{-1}. The presence of azide group would show maxima transmittance at 2120 cm^{-1}, the efflunet sample from dyestuff industry should show a maxima at 3500 cm^{-1} for amines and 1575 cm^{-1} for azo group present in sample of water. The Raman spectroscopy has come to the forefront only recently. It is more useful for the analysis of aqueous solution. Further, it is useful for remote sensing and detection of air pollutants.

Table 3. **Characterization of pollutants by IR spectroscopy.**

Group	Environment	Frequency (cm^{-1})	Group	Environment	Frequency (cm^{-1})
OH	Alcohols	3580-3650	> CO	Aldehyde	1720-1740
	Acid	2500-2700		Carboxylic acid	1700-1725
NH	Amines	3500		Ester	2000-2300
	Amides	3140-3320		Acyl halides	1795-1850
CH	Alkyne	3300	NOH	Oximes	1640-1690
	Aromatic	3030	-N=N-N	Azo	1575-1630
	Aldehydes	2700-2900	N-H	Amine	1575-1650
SH	Sulphur compounds	2500-2700	-$(CH_2)_n$	Any compound	722
			CN	Alkyl nitriles	2240-2260
N_3	Azides	2120-2160		Isocyanates	2240-2275

Light Scattering Techniques

Amongst these techniques we have turbidimetry and nephelometry. The former technique involves measurement of absorbance of turbid solutions like one containing $PbCrO_4$ or $HgCrO_4$, while the latter involves measurement of the intensity of scattered radiation by suspended particles. The classical method involving measurement of turbidity of water is done by Jackson's **candle technique**. The unit involved is JU. This method involves personal error during such measurement and hence is unreliable. Instead a nephelometry with NTU units is a more reliable method for such purpose. The best method for the analysis of SO_4^{2-} from water is by measurement of $BaSO_4$ by nephelometry.

Molecular Luminescence Methods

These methods are generally termed as chemiluminescence techniques. They have made a spectacular progress in the analysis of gaseous pollutants like SO_2 or NO-NOx from atmosphere. These are most reliable methods. The analysis of Be (morin, i.e. pentahydroxy-flavanol) Th (alizarin), Al (quinalzarine) by fluoroscence technique is well known. The analysis of organic compounds, e.g. riboflavin, thiamine hydrochloride, quinine from waste water-emanating from pharmaceutical industry, is best carried out by fluourescence spectroscopy. In comparison, the phosphorescence spectroscopy has not become popular in environmental analytical chemistry. With the rise in pollution in sugar industry, this technique will pick up in years to come. A relatively cheap set of fluorimeter or phosphorimeter in India will make this technique more popular in future.

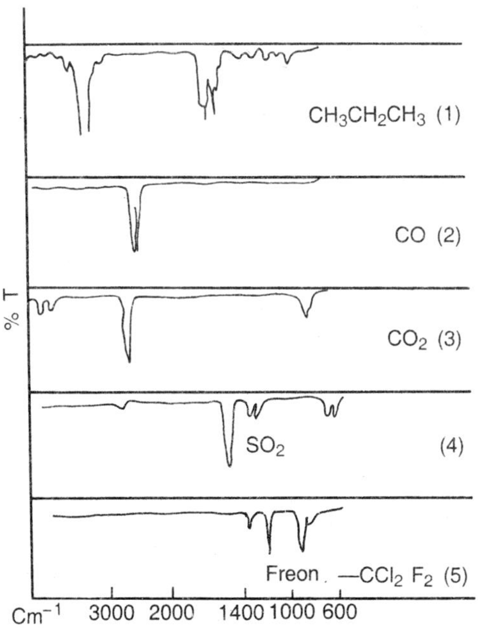

Fig. 3. IR spectra of gaseous pollutants.

Atomic Absorption Spectroscopy (AAS)

This technique has made a radical difference in quantitative chemical analysis. The main reason for popularity of this method is the possibility of analyzing large number of samples. This is useful for multi-element analysis. It is applicable for micro and nanogram concentration of the metal pollutant analysis. The notion that there is no need of a chemist if AAS is available is totally ill founded. Certain critical analysis of metals like As, Sb, Sn, Se, Te, Bi need hydride generator and one must know what kind of thermal stability the hydrides have. Table 4 lists prospective metal pollutants which can be determined by AAS. In spite of the discovery of cold vapour AAS technique for mercury, most of the state pollution control laboratories prefer Bindscheiderr's Green for spectrophtometric method of analysis. A look at sensitivity (Table 4) indicates certain metals like mercury and uranium have poor sensitivity.

Table 4. **Atomic absorption spectroscopic methods for metal pollutant analyses.**

Metal	Wavelength $(\lambda)_{max}$ nm	Sensitivity µg/ml	Type of flame used
Zn	213	0.009	AA
Pb	217	0.110	AA
As	197	0.600	AH
Be	234	0.016	NA
Cd	228	0.011	AA
Cr	357	0.550	AA
Hg	253	2.200	AA
Mn	279	0.210	AA
U	358	113	NA

Table 5. **Flame Emission Spectroscopic Analysis of Toxic Metal Pollutants.**

Element	Wave length (λ)nm	Sensitivity μg/ml	Source of pollution
Li	670	0.017	Glass, photocells
Na	589	0.003	Water, soap, alkali
K	766	0.009	Soap, photocells, pharmacy
Ca	422	0.013	Milk, plants, water, vegetation
Sr	460	0.041	Fission reaction, soil, leaf
Ba	554	0.200	Vegetables, glass, X-ray

Atomic Emission Spectroscopy

This technique includes Flame Emission Spectroscopy, Inductively Coupled Plasma-Atomic Emission spectroscopy (ICP-AES) and conventional spectrography. Of these methods, flame photometry is relatively cheap and dependable. Table 5 lists metal pollutants which can be analyzed by flame photometry. The greatest advantage of this equipment, is that, it is relatively a cheap instrument with appropriate filters available in the market All determinations can be carried out in visible region of the spectra. A greater accuracy can be sought by standard addition and the internal standard method. Only metals like Rb or Cs can be determined at near IR region, for which appropriate light filters are not easily available at present in India.

The ICP-AES technique is of recent origin. It is quite expensive but very rapid and reliable. It is useful for the multi-element determination of large number of samples containing metal pollutants. The accuracy obtained is quite satisfactory. An argon torch is used for the purpose of excitation with radio frequency generator. In developed countries, it is used as the hyphenated technique by coupling with HPLC or a similar suitable technique.

Conventional spectrography technique is useful for the nondestructive testing of sample. X-ray fluorescence will also provide the same result with greater advantage.

Radio Analytical Methods

Amongst nuclear methods of analysis, neutron activation analysis and isotope dilution methods are most useful. However, the greatest limitations of these methods in Indian context is nonavailability of radioactive isotope specially through private sector. The neutron source with high flux is available only with Atomic Research Centres, with restricted access to Government agencies. In more advanced countries like Canada and France, such facility is readily available through private enterprises.

In neutron activation analysis, a sample to be analyzed is irradiated with slow neutron source to form unstable isotope, with mass number greater by one unit. Such unstable isotope undergoes transmutation (n,γ) reaction to revert; to its original isotope, with emission of γ-radiation. These emitted gamma (γ)-radiation are proportional to the amount of metal irradiated. By comparing known weight and the activity, it is possible for us to ascertain weight of the unknown by measuring its activity on irradiation. Many metal pollutants like Fe, Mn, Cu, Sb, Bi, Cd, Zn, V can be easily determined at nanogram concentrations by neutron activation analysis technique (NAA).

The second largely used technique is the isotope dilution method (IDM). This method involves the dilution of active isotope within active material. Consequently, the reduction in activity is measured and from this indirectly the concentration of material is evaluated. It would take quite some time to popularize these methods in India, unless a cheap source of neutron for irradiation and easy availability of (γ)-ray counters are present. Till then we have to depend upon spectral or the electroanalytical techniques, which are described in the following section.

Electro Analytical Techniques

These techniques comprise of four major groups, viz. potentiometry, conductimetry, coulometry and polarography (Table 6). Potentiometry method involves measurement of the potential. The indirect application of this technique in pollution analysis is the measurement of pH of solution. The technique of chronopotentiometry can be used easily for the

Table 6. **Limits of analysis by electroanalytical methods.**

Method	Limit
Ac polarography	10^{-4} – 10^{-5}
Classical polarography	10^{-5} – 10^{-6}
Sq. wave polarography	10^{-6} – 10^{-7}
Pulse polarography	10^{-7} – 10^{-8}
Anodic stripping voltametry	10^{-7} – 10^{-9}

Table 7. **Polarographic characterisation of metals.**

Metal pollutant	Half-wave-potential ($E_{½}$)
Cd	–0.76 V
Co	–1.46 V
Cu	–0.47 V
Fe	–1.12 V
Pb	–0.76 V
Zn	–1.50 V

analysis of the metal pollutants. The potentiometric method can be used for indirect determination of the metal pollutant. The technique of conductimetry is used since ages, to ascertain quality of water. Apart from measuring purity of water, conductimetric technique is used for the continuous measurement of SO_2 from air. This technique is described in details in the chapter on air pollution. The electrical generation of bromine is compared with generation of bromine from KBr with SO_2 by reduction. This led to monitoring of SO_2 by coulometry. The anodic stripping voltametry (ASV) is an instance of the specialised category of the coulometric method. In recent years, ASV has become very popular. This involves two cells for reduction, while ion selective electrode (ISE) is an example of potentiometric technique. With the easy availability of specific ion electrodes, the analysis of anions from water is a matter of minutes. Even with advancement of solid state and enzyme electrode as well as electrodes fitted with liquid ion exchangers, or crown ethers the analysis of cationic species is reduced to single measurement.

Amongst electroanalytical techniques, polarography or voltametry has the greatest advantage over other methods. Table 7 summarises important metal pollutants with their half-wave potentials ($E_{½}$), which can be analyzed by polarography. The distinct advantage of such a technique is the possibility of identification of metal pollutant from the effluent sample. $E_{½}$ is the characteristic property of a metal under a set of supporting electrolyte, which helps one to identify a metal. The polarography has distinct advantage for analyzing the organic pollutants, e.g. the pesticide residues can be best analyzed by this technique with a suitable electrolyte like lithium hydroxide.

Ring-oven Technique

This technique was largely recommended by SCOPE for the analysis of metal pollutants. This is a relatively cheap method, easy to operate and dependable and useful for semiquantitative analysis. It is best suited for outdoor work, field analysis and *in situ* analysis, by comparison of rings with standard rings obtained by interaction of chromophoric group with the metal pollutant. It is quite possible to qualitatively analyse and get semiquantitative information of the metal to be analyzed. Tables 8 and 9 list typical results of analysis of metal pollutants from air and water by ring oven technique along with well-known quantitative methods.

Separation Methods

Before concluding this chapter, it is worthwhile to consider prominent separation methods utilized before quantitative analysis. Amongst separation methods, one thinks of chromatographic techniques. Within these methods HPLC and GLC have become most popular with advancement of instrumentation. However, it is worthwhile to consider them on the basis of physical properties, on which such techniques are classified.

Adsorption Chromatography

This largely consists of columnar method and gas-solid chromatography. These are based on the phenomenon of adsorption. Unfortunately, both techniques have limited applications in environmental separations.

Table 8. **Ring oven technique for analysis of air samples for metal pollutants in Mumbai.**

Metal ion present	Found by ring-oven ($\mu g/m^3$)	Found by comparison method ($\mu g/m^3$)
Pb	340	360
-	220	230
V	78	73
-	62	68
Se	26	27
-	24	28
Cd	13.5	14
	16	19

Table 9. **Ring-oven technique for metal analysis in water.**

Metal	Amount taken (μg/litre)	Amount found by ring-oven technique (μg/10 ml)					Amount found (μg/litre)
		A	B	C	D	Average	
Cd	100.0	0.90	1.00	1.10	0.90	0.975	95.5
	120.0	1.20	1.10	1.10	1.30	1.175	117.5
	130.0	1.30	1.20	1.20	-	1.233	123.3
	140.0	1.40	1.20	1.30	1.40	1.325	132.5
Cr(VI)	25.0	0.20	0.30	0.20	0.20	0.225	22.5
	50.0	0.50	0.40	0.50	0.40	0.45	45.0
	100.0	0.80	1.10	1.00	1.00	0.975	97.5
Hg	75.0	0.70	0.80	0.70	0.60	0.70	70.0
	100.0	1.00	1.10	1.00	1.10	1.05	105.0
	125.0	1.20	1.30	1.10	1.20	1.20	120.0
Pb	10.0	0.10	0.10	0.10	-	0.10	10.0
	50.0	0.50	0.60	0.50	0.50	0.525	52.5
	75.0	0.80	0.80	-	0.80	0.80	80.0
	100.0	1.00	0.90	0.90	1.10	0.975	95.5
	125.0	1.30	1.30	1.20	1.20	1.25	125.0
V	15.0	0.10	0.10	0.10	0.10	0.10	10.0
	50.0	0.40	0.40	0.50	0.40	0.425	42.5
	60.0	0.50	0.60	0.60	0.60	0.575	57.5
	75.0	0.80	0.80	0.80	0.80	0.80	80.0
	100.0	1.00	1.00	1.10	1.00	1.025	102.5

Partition Chromatography

This technique is based upon exploitation of difference in partition coefficients of solute for promoting differential migrations. The important methods under these class are paper chromatography, thin-layer chromatography, gas-liquid chromatography. Liquid-liquid partition (LLPC) and reversed phase extraction chromatography (RPEC). All these methods have extensive applications. Paper chromatography (both ascending and descending) is used for the separation of **inorganic as well as organic species,** e.g. **separation** of Hg, As, Pb with ethylacetate butanol mixture as stationary phase and hydrochloric acid as mobile phases.

TLC is used for characterisation and separation of pesticides residue. The GLC has extensive applications for organic pollutant analysis. GC-MS i.e. hyphenated gas chromatography mass spectrometry is very useful for the separation of volatile and thermally stable organic pollutants specially from air. All hydrocarbons, polymers, etc., from air can be characterized by GC with appropriate detectors like TCD, FID and ECD. Of these flame ionization detector finds extensive applications in the environmental pollution analysis. Mass spectrometer can have various kinds of analyzers like single channel, double channel, time of flight and quadrupole analysers. Of these, the last one is best for analysis.

Ion Exchange Chromatography

Both cation as well as anion exchange chromatography is very useful in environmental analysis. The well-known process of deionization of water is based upon the principle of ion exchange methods. Apart from this, any kinds of separations of ions can be done by anion exchange methods. All cationic impurities can be isolated by cation exchange chromatography. Liquid anion exchangers are more or less based on similar principles of anion exchange chromatography. In addition to separation of inorganic compounds, the organic compounds like protein, carbohydrates, aminoacids can best be separated by this technique.

Exclusion Chromatography

This technique is based upon the separation of molecules depending upon their geometry. Gel filtration is an example of this technique. Unfortunately, this technique has limited use in environmental analysis, excepting for the separation of biological products.

Electro Chromatography

Electrophoresis or electrochromatography has limited applications in environmental pollution analysis. It is used for separation of metals from effluents.

Ion Chromatography and HPLC

The ion chromatography has come to the forefront only recently. It has substantially helped in characterisation, identification and determination of anions from the samples of water. It is being used presently for the interesting work of chemical speciation of metal pollutants. The chemical speciation is having greater ramification, 'as the nature of species in the environment will throw light on the toxicity of such metals on human beings. As a matter of fact, nature of Hg, Cr or Fe in water was ascertained by ion chromatography. Usually sodium salts are used for the elution of ions taken up by ion exchange column. This eluent is subsequently passed on anion exchange column, which in turn generates corresponding acid to give rise in conductivity. Such change in conductivity is related to quantum of anions present in the solution.

HPLC or high performance liquid chromatography is a technique and not a class of chromatography. Any kind of chromatographic technique discussed above can be carried out with HPLC. What one needs is a good pump with pressure of 1000-3000 psi and a suitable detector like thermal, ultraviolet or refractive index. This technique has accelerated the pace of the work and facilitated quick separation of organic pollutants.

Solvent Extraction Separations

This is the most powerful tool for separation. It does not need sophisticated instruments, excepting a good separatory funnel. The separations are largely based upon exploiting the difference in distribution coefficient of solute in two solvents, which are immiscible with each other. Various kinds of solvents like ethers, ketones, aldehydes and alcohols have been used for the purpose. In many instances the macrocyclic polyethers like crown ethers and high molecular weight amines, i.e. liquid anion exchangers are used for separation of metal complexes. When the distribution ratio is exceedingly small, one resorts to extraction chromatographic technique, wherein hydrophobic extractant is coated on stationary support and interesting separations are carried out with mineral acids, as the mobile phase. The success of such a method depends upon the availability of large number of theoretical plates in the chromatography.

The important chelating extractants are β-diketone, oxine, oximes cupferron, dithizone, naphthol and azonaphthol, and xanthates and sodium diethyldithiocarbamates cupral. These extractant not only permit separation at microgram concentration, but also facilitates simultaneous extraction and spectrophotometric determination in one single step.

In conclusion, it can be seen that not all the methods available in analytical chemistry are always useful in the environmental pollution analysis. At the same time one can not all the time depend upon sophisticated instrumental methods, as on several occasions simple classical methods have furnished valuable data on the extent of pollution. What is more important is the level of analysis and background of analyte sample. We cannot all the time use instrumental methods specially in fields, we need a method suitable for the continuous measurements or monitoring. We will have to adopt radically different methodology while selecting a method for monitoring. In a developing country like India, another factor is the cost-benefit analysis. A method no doubt should be sensitive, but must also be economical. Such criteria shall be taken into account while selecting a method for the air and water pollution monitoring.

Important Questions

1. Enumerate different types of methods that can be applied in the quantitative analysis of various pollutants.
2. Give a detailed account of radio analytical and electro analytical technique used in the analysis of pollutants.
3. Write briefly on the following :
   (i) Ring oven technique, (ii) Infra red and Raman spectroscopy, (iii) Solvent extraction separations.

19 Air Pollution Analysis

Introduction

Basis of Air Pollution Measurement

The first step in air pollutant concentration is to define clearly the objectives of measuring concentrations of air pollutants, and to determine the target substances for measurement. The objectives that are usually intended are as follows. (i) To thoroughly understand the pollution levels and concentration fluctuations when the sources and pollutants are clearly known; (ii) When neither the source nor the pollutants are clearly known, to examine the causes of the pollution; (iii) When the source is identified, to thoroughly understand the levels of pollution and the types of pollutants emitted; (iv) When the pollutant has been identified, to specify the source and to determine the level of its contribution, (v) To easily undestand border area concentrations and exposure sites for voluntary periods of time; (vi) To thoroughly understand the board range pollution level and its fluctuations.

Measrements are taken using collection-analysis (manual analysis), concentration meters, continuous (automatic) analyzers, and other simple measuring equipment. Manual analysis is applicable to most of compounds that can be used with ordinary equipment such as spectrophotometers and gas chromatographs, because once has been collected at fields, it has to be carried back to the laboratory for analysis. The concentration meter obtains on-site values in a portable form for the target gas. The simple measuring equipment is inexpensive and easy to operate, and aims to be able to take measurements on-site. The continuous analyzer is used for fixed point observations, and records both the time course and the mean concentrations. In recent years, on-site analytical values have been obtained, and portable continuous analyzers have also been on the market, but the basic patterns of air pollution measurement are these four.

Of the above objectives, (ii) and (iii), require accurate analysis manually, while (i) and (vi) require continuous analysis, and (v) uses simple measuring equipment. For the (iv) objective, both manual and continuous analysis are used continuously. Even with expensive measring equipment, if the selection of the equipment and the operation employed are wrong, accurate environmental information will not be obtained, whereas even with inexpensive equipment, the above objectives can be attained, depending on the approach. If a specific measuring pattern is selected appropriately, rational measurements are entirely possible.

Measurement Methods Classification and Sampling

There are many different analysis and detection principles that can be used in the above four measuring patterns (1) (2). Fig. 1 shows them arranged in order. These selections are made while considering the sensitivity of the target substance, the selectivity (interference), accuracy, economic viability, ease of use, and so forth. Each measurement pattern is explained with reference to the next paragraph. In addition, there is laser remote sensing method, which can measure both airborne aerosols and gas across a wide area directly, without the need for sampling.

In environmental measuring, except for the aforementioned remote sensing, because only part of the air taken as sample, sampling is essential so that both spatial and temporal representative values might be obtained. In order to learn the pollution level for a given region, samples are taken at points so as to obtain mean concentrations and sites for which the highest concentrations can be expected: ground level of noxious substances emitted from specific chimneys and the side of major roads. On the other hand, because the concentration is governed by wind speed, climate, day of the week, and season, sampling is performed with reference to conditions that indicate both the highest and the lowest concentration in order to obtain an overview of the pollution level with only a small sample, or else measurements are taken continously throughout the year. Moreover, in order to determine the annual mean concentration, it is necessary to take samples twice a month, each sample being over a 24 hour period.

Manual Analysis Methods

This pattern is used for nearly all pollutants (Fig. 1), and the state in which they are introduced to the analyzing equipment is nearly always either liquid or gas. At this point, the concentrations of the samples in the air are determined by Eq. (1) (except for vessel collection), so that the quantitative concentration range is determined not only by the sensitivity of the analyzers, but also by the sample air volume.

$$C = \frac{M}{V} \qquad \text{... (1)}$$

Where, C: Concentration, M: Target substance amont (Detection amount x Collection quantity/ Injection quantity), V:Sample air volume (Aeration flow rate x Time)

Consequently, in order to measure lower concentrations with the same equipment, it is necessary to increase the sample air volume within a range that does not affect accuracy. Measurement accuracy [in addition to operational errors and analytical instrument accuracy] are governed by collection efficiency and the measurement accuracy of sample air flow rate. For this reason, a balance between them is important, and if reasonable collection conditions are unclear, it is necessary to verify the collection efficiency and then, correctly connect a integrated flow meter, and start the collection. The collection efficiency by both the concentration and the flow (or gas meter) rate. This can be verified by connecting up the two collector in series. It is important to be careful here, as the flow meter (including the rota meter and hot wire types) can be easily affected by contamination in the measuring line.

When analyzing air pollutants manually, both spectrometry (absorption spectrophotometry, atomic absorption spectrometry, and ICP emission method), which is widely used, and chromotography (gas chromatography and liquid chromatography) are given in detail as examples as follows.

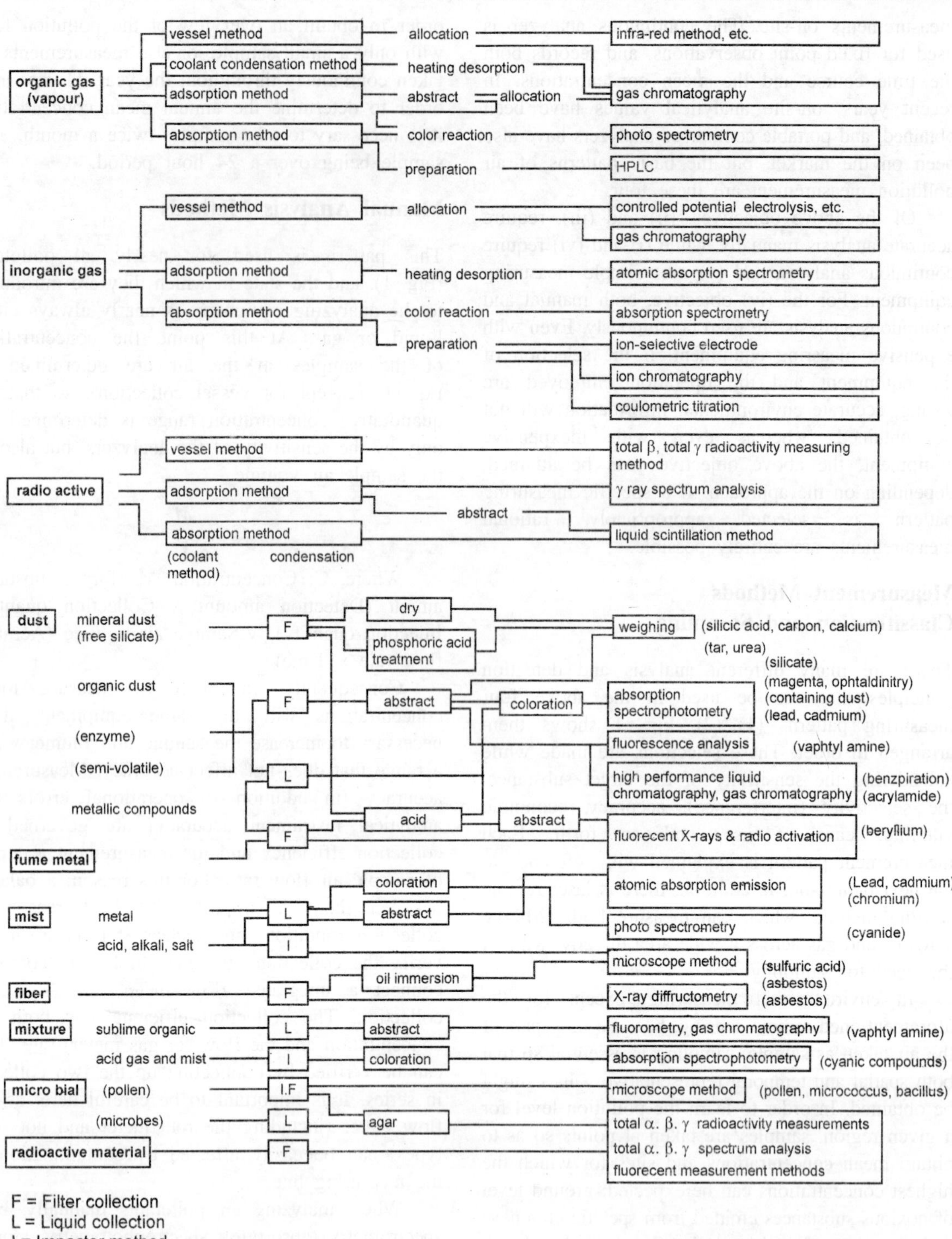

Fig. 1. Measuring pattern of various kinds of pollutants using manual methods.

Spectrometry

The responses (relative values of absorption and emission strength) for the sample solutions and the standard solutions are obtained using a spectrophotometer. The calibration curve is usually prepared for the determination. The responses are plotted as the Y-axis and concentrations of five types or more of the standard solution as X-axis. Which are prepared by diluting the proto standard solution (standard substances dissolved in solvents, and sometimes available on the market). Using the usually linear relationship, the amount of the target substance in the samples determined from the sample solution responses, parallel with which, the blank values (the smaller the better) are determined from responses to the unused absorption solution and the extract from the filter paper, the difference between them being the amount of the target substance. The causes of error of the process are thought to be (i) operating error (injection of the sample solution into the analyzer and transfer of the specimen of the collected target substance to the sample solution) and the analytical instrument and (ii) error due to the reproducibility of the equipment itself and (iii) interference from coexisting shstances. Against the (iii) causes of error, we are to use specific collecting solutions, to select the spectrometer conditions (wave length of the spectrometer and atomization atmosphere, emission temperature, etc.), and to pretreat the sample appropriately, but these are not perfect to avoid the interference. On the other hand, the standard addition method is effective in correcting the negative and systematic error.

Chromatography

Chromatography, representative differential analytical method, is to identify over a retention time of the chromatogram peak, and then determine over the peak area. Both gas chromatograph and liquid (ion) chromatograph analyzers are composed of a separating column, a detector and carrier introducer, and a thermostat. In order to use one, it is essential to set the temperature, the length of the column, internal diameter, packing, species of stational faces liquid, type of detector, flow rate and species of carrier gas, (composition of carrier solution), sample injection volume, and other analysis conditions. In particular, the column conditions govern the degree of separation, and the detector, the sensitivity and selectivity. The standard substance is injected under the set conditions, and the peak retention time is measured. Unknown samples of many kind of volatile organic compound should be identified in parallel with a mass spectrometer because the peak positions may well overlap. The atmospheric concentration is normally low, so that by collecting as shown in Fig. 1 and infusing either the whole sample collected or part thereof, the response of the volume of the control substance and the sample can be compared and calculated as per Eq. (2).

$$C = \frac{\left(\frac{v}{v_0}\right)\times\left(\frac{P_0}{P}\right)\times m}{V} \quad ....(2)$$

Where, C = Concentration; v = Sample volume, v_0=Injection volume, P = Response for standard substance, P_0 = Response for sample; m=Amount of standard substance, V = Volume of air sample.

The linearity of the calibration curve must be confirmed once in the concentration range used. Moreover, the blank values are measured in determination with the pretreatment, such as the concentration operation. The error factors, such as collection conditions, including the collection rate, and the injection operation, the reproducibility of the equipment and so forth, are the same as for the spectrometry.

Computer software with data loggar, or built-in computer data processors are usually used for chromatogram data processing, but manual calculation with a pen recorder is essentially the same. Rather, it is essential to monitor such analogue data as the peak shape and so forth, and never be remiss in checking and evaluating the analytical results.

The reproducibility of the peak position (retention time) is characteristic in the chromatography to effect on errors of the identification. Because the carrier flow rate and the temperature govern the peak position and area, they must be checked after setting a stable condition. Further, over long periods, the column suffers from deterioration due to the flow out of the stationary phase liquid (gas chromatograph) and the contamination (liquid chromatograph), so that the retention time gradually changes. The retention time and area of the standard must be checked once every few days dring continuous use, as well as when the equipment is first to be used each time. Moreover, the air sample collected in the vessel can be used to check the preservability, and the active gas should be collected to be changed into stable components.

Concentration Meter

Both gas concentration meters and total suspended dust concentration meters are used. Gas concentration meters introduce the air sample to the measuring equipment, and thereby measure the concentration of the target substance directly. For coexisting substances, there is a sufficient selectivity factor (response for the target gas/response for the coexisting gas), and if the detection limit is less than 1/10 of the environmental standard, the detection is very efficient. However, the concentration meter has limits to its selectivity and accuracy, therefore especially in measuring the approximate concentration level of the coexisting gases, which interfere positively with the measrement, so it is essential to check in advance the extent of the interference due to an accumulation in the concentration and reciprocal selection factors.

The meter is set to zero passing zero gas that does not contain the target component, and sets the sensitivity controlling tweezers so that the index value fits in that of standard gas. The frequency of adjustment depends on the principles involved. For example if the principle is photometric, regular checks by the manufacturer are few and far between, and if the principle is electrochemical, the checks must be carried out each time the equipment is used. The precision is expressed as the coefficient of variation and the zero drift per unit time. Dust concentration meters are also relative concentration meters, which introduce the standard dust flow to the concentration meter, and thereby adjust the sensitivity, and neither principle experiences much in the way of fluctuation in sensitivity during normal operation, so that regular checks by the manfacturer alone are sufficient to use it.

Continuous Analyzers

Continuous analyzers are automatic devices that continuously introduce the air sample, and record the output either continuously or with intervals. Such devices have standard gas generators built-in, and introduce the standard gas in place of the air sample on average once a day, check the sensitivity, and adjust it as necessary, so that the equipment involved usually tends to be rather large. The accuracy is expressed in the same way as for the concentration meters.

Measurement Accuracy

This section recounts detection limits and determination limits which depend upon measurement accuracy. Taking the detection limit (Cd in Fig. 2) to be the threefold value of the standard deviation (S_b) of the response (mean value R_{B1})of the blank sample is also recommended in a 1UPAC report (Fig. 2.) The R_b and S_b in Fig. 2 are determined by the blank tests of 10 to 20 times. Around the detection limit, the coefficient of variation is extremely huge. Fig. 2 also shows the relation between the "coefficient of variation" and the concentration of Zn in 1CP emission analysis). If the "minimum determination limit" (Ct in Fig. 2)

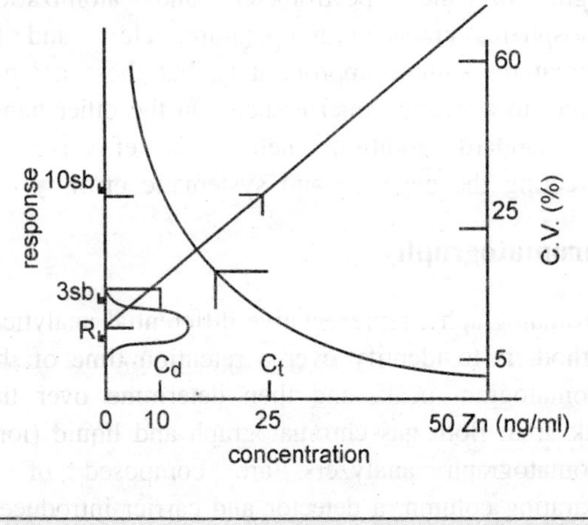

Fig. 2. Determination limits (Ct), detection limits (Cd) (Y-axis on the left) and standard deviation of blank (sb) in the calibration curve, and example of the relation between coefficient of variation (C.V.) and concentration of zinc in ICP emission spectrometry.

is taken as a concentration equivalent to R_b+10S_b, an accuracy of about 10% can be expected. On the other hand, generally, because accuracy is also reduced at high concentrations, is also important to review the fact that there is a maximum determination limit. When only measurement accuracy is researched from literature, the determination limit is viewed as being in the range of 10 to 100 times the measurement accuracy.

The base line (zero air) noise band (peak to peak for 100 noise units) can be corresponded to in the recorder charts and concentration meter responses and the detection limits and determination limits defined as previously.

Moreover, if the environmental concentration has no specific objectives, an effective figure for the mean value of two digits alone is sufficient.

Accuracy Guarantees and Management : Tracability

No matter which measurement of the three given above which needs collection of air pollutants requires a standard for guaranteeing the accuracy. With both the liquid and solid standard substances, it is essential to consider purity of the standard substance (minimum 99.9%, though 99% alone is sufficient upon occasion.) and the stability of the prepared stadard solution. On the other hand, with the concentration meters or the continuous analyzers, a standard gas cylinder is often used, and the manufacturer is requested to manage the accuracy of the cylinder concentration. Further, there are also concentration meters for which the regular inspection for the management is obligatory, and because for example, a part of the NO can chage to NO_2 while it is stored, or substances such as formaldehyde may be absorbed on the inside wall of the cylinder, these cylinders must be handled with care in the user's position.

Laboratory Management

When using a laboratory to analyze hazardous substances, it is important to consider both the environment and safety. Environment means hygiene in the work environment for the analysts, and countermeasures to contamination of air and water. Basically, it is best to choose processes that use as small amount of hazardous chemicals as possible. It is essential, for example, to use a dry process and to redce the amount of preparation of standard solutions used to the minimum.

The first and foremost problem in the work environment is exposure of analysts to toxic vapor and suspended particles. Local ventilation must be installed in the rooms and the rooms must be kept well ventilated. Secondly waste of analytical solution that has been used must be treated. Organic solvents can be burned, and metalicion waste solution is treated by both adsorption and sedimentation, and if even small amount of the waste is extremely toxic, it must be put in a safe container, and labeled as such, and stored appropriately.

For safety, it is important to manage flammable gas and solvents. Large amount of hydrogen gas may leak or organic solvents could be volatilize, which when mixed with the air in the room, even to concentration of only a few percent, once they meet a flammable source, detonation may start in the room. Care must be taken so that the storage shelves do not collapse, and that ventilation is good. Moreover, there is no danger in an ordinary room (not tightly closed) when the hydrogen leaks out of an FID gas chromatograph because it is diluted. Secondly is anoxia deficient room environment. This can be caused by major leaks of odorless nitrogen and argon. Thirdly, misoperation of the equipment should be prevented.

When setting out to analyze hazardous chemical substances such as dioxin, which has recently become a serious problem, it is needed to provide the hardware aspect such as buildings and other facilities, high quality analyzers. And so forth, analysis must be carried out in such facility as maintains rigorous safety management, such as control of waste substances, and security system for people coming and going, and the work state. Also essential are a Quality Assurance/quality Control (QA/QC) system, the introduction of recording systems, and a thorough comprehension of the history of a sample, from income of sample, up to the final treatment and disposal.

Because dioxin is 5,000 times more toxic than potassium cyanide, it must be kept in a room with reduced pressure to prevent its escape into the surrounding environment. In order to achieve sufficient pressure reduction, a special work box and compartment must be used. Dioxin emission gasses and waste water from the laboratory must be treated by means of activated carbon, preventing its escape to the outside. Further, laboratory waste materials such as wipe clothes and used activated carbon must be stored in perpetuity, so appropriate facilities are also required.

Dioxin normally has a determination limit of approximately 1pg (pico gram, or 10^{-12}g), so that solvents, reagents, and glass wears must be of the best quality so as to prevent contamination, and used only for dioxide analysis. Further, a blank test is combined, and the blank value from contamination during experiments is checked to be below the determination limit.

Sampling of Gaseous Pollutants

Sampling of gaseous pollutants is somewhat simpler, because of the fact that by and large they are homogeneous. Sometimes, the task becomes difficult, because of sudden variation in wind velocity, direction etc. For such considerations we will have to consider several meterological parameters. At the moment we would consider important methods for sampling of gaseous pollutants. The sampling methods for aerosols are classified as those involving storage or a grab sampling, condensation, adsorption and absorption.

Storage or Grab Sampling

A portion of ambient air is closed and stored in a container. Mere isolation without concentration is possible by this technique. Grab sampling is also another name for this method. The storage at atmospheric pressure is made in rigid containers. Glass or stainless steel is used as container material. In a few instances, mylar-a special kind of material is used, as it is elastic and nonodorant. The nature of container selected will be decided on the basis of quality and kind of the air pollutant to be collected.

Condensation

The low temperature condensation called cryo-sampling is an excellent method for air sampling at low temperature. Here the species condenses and gets concentrated. The cooling agent used consists of liquid hydrogen or even of liquid oxygen. This sampling technique provides an additional advantage of concentration.

Adsorption

In this method the gas is adsorbed on solid material at reduced temperature and then evacuated or flushed out with an inert gas like N_2 or Ar at elevated temperature. The material used for adsorption consists of porous material like silica, alumina, kieselguhr, diatomaceous earth or activated carbon. Large amount of gas can be easily sampled by this technique. Only limitation of this method is, polar substance cannot be easily desorbed from solid substrate. The process of adsorption is a surface phenomenon, which is used for purification of air for experimental purposes, like sample dilution.

Absorption

This is the most popular method for sampling of gaseous pollutants. The reactive pollutants are absorbed in aqueous solution, e.g. SO_2 is absorbed in water or H_2O_2; ozone is absorbed in a solution of potassium iodide; the absorption of NO_2 is done in NaOH, as its absorption in water is very slow; CO can be absorbed in a solution of ammonical cuprous chloride; O_2 is absorbed in the solution of alkaline pyrogallol; CO_2 is absorbed in the solution of alcoholic KOH. In fact this forms the basis of Orsat gas analyser. Thus by the process of absorption, a component of gas phase is transferred into a bulk of solid or liquid phase. The transfer process involves a chemical interaction and fixing of a particular species in the liquid phase. The ventilation, spraying, bubbling ensures intimate contact between gas and liquid or solid absorption; such sampling can also be classified as active and passive absorption sampling. The use of ion-exchange resin in packed bed can also be used as an excellent sampling medium. However, it is essential to maintain the sample in an extremely dry state so as to get successful, reliable and reproducible results of the final analysis.

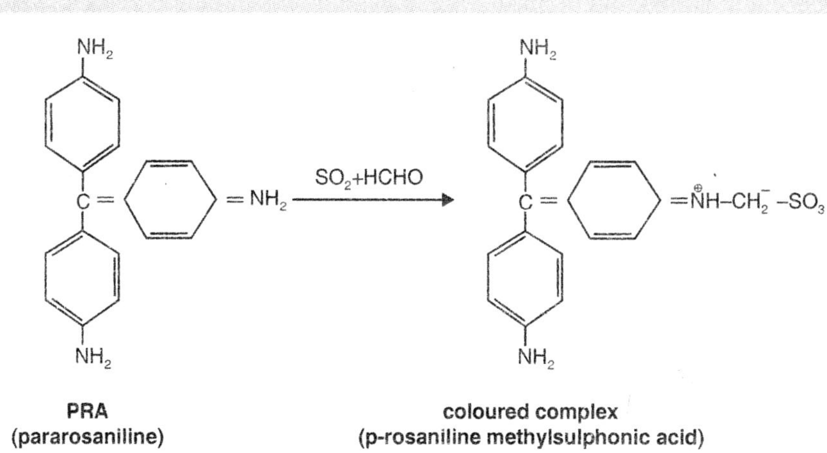

Fig. 3. Reaction mechanism of SO_2.

Analysis of Aerosols

The aerosols are analyzed to ascertain the composition of the entire sample in terms of its various constituents. This will enable us to obtain information of individual composition of the particles. The methods generally employed are bulk methods. Here in total content of atmosphere is expressed in terms of μ g/m^3 (or ppm) for large samples, which are collected by electrostatic precipitator (ESP) or by filtration. The sample is then dissolved and analyzed for its metal pollutant contents by AAS, ICP-AES, or spectrophotometry. Gravimetric or volumetric methods are useless for such purposes. Ring-oven technique is ideal for such a job. The single particle method is composed of three parts, viz. morphological examination, micrugy test and microspot investigation. In morphological examination, an attempt is made to recognize a chemical species by mere observation or sight. In micrugy test, the sample identification or characterization is done under light microscope with the use of precise micromanipulator. Finally in microspot investigation, a specific reagent is used for the identification of a material, e.g. nickel with dimethylglyoxime. The identification of radioactive material is done by radioactography.

Analysis of Gaseous Pollutants

The method for the characterization and determination of atmospheric trace gases are more or less individual rather than collective. The use of different sampling methods for gases depends upon the availability and diversity of analytical techniques used for determination. The non-selective or the general method involve condensation of samples and analysis by mass spectrometry. Most reactive gases cannot be analyzed by gas chromatography (GLC), as they are lost during collection. Non-selective methods are useful for less reactive gases, pollutants and closely related homologous series of hydrocarbons and aldehydes. GLC if used involves use of FID (flame ionization detector) or ECD (i.e. electron capture detector). In the specific analyzer, polar traces of gases are usually absorbed in solution. Frankly no method of analysis is perfect and every method is subject of controversy. We will however select such methods which have minimum objections. In years to come, it is hoped that newer methods will be invented.

In the following sections therefore, an endeavour is made to consider laboratory methods for the analysis of SO_2, H_2S, NH_3, NO-NO_x, CO, CO_2, O_3 and organic vapours. Such methods largely consist of spectrophotometric methods of analysis. In addition volumetric technique, conductometric analysis, infrared method, fluorescence measurement techniques are also used.

Sulphur dioxide Analysis

Acid Titration

The important properties are acidity, reducing character and precipitation method for gravimetry. There are also three spectrophotometric methods.

Table 1. **Determination of sulphur dioxide.**

(1) SO_2 in H_2O_2, barium chloroanilate ⟶ Red complex ⟶ λ_{max} = 530 nm
(2) $FeCl_3$, NH_4Cl, HCl, 1, 10-phenanhroline ⟶ coloured complex λ_{max} = 510 nm PRA method
Absorbing solution: NaCl, $HgCl_2$
Reagent: PRA (para rosaniline) and formaldehyde (leucobase)
λ_{max}: 560 nm; $\varepsilon = 3.0 \times 10^4$
Colour development 20 min
Working range : 1–10 μg

In the first method SO_2 is collected over H_2O_2 or H_2O and corresponding change in acidity is measured by titration or by measuring a change in conductivity, but the latter method is more reliable. Only drawback of this method is that, HF, HCl if present interfere but NO_2 does not interfere due to low solubility in water. NH_3 causes negative error.

Reduction Method

The second method involves use of reducing property of SO_2. Here SO_2 is allowed to react with KI and the liberated iodine is titrated against standard solution of $Na_2S_2O_3$. It is possible to collect SO_2 over NaOH and continue with redox titration. The reduction method suffers from positive interference from other redox reagents, e.g. H_2S. Organic matter do interfere in such a determination, O_3 also interferes but NO_2 does not.

Lead Candle Method

In this technique a candle made of PbO_2 is exposed to atmosphere of SO_2 to undergo the following reaction: $PbO_2 + SO_2 \longleftrightarrow PbSO_4$. The change in weight gives an idea about SO_2 in the air. The only limitation of this method is that dust and particulate matter get deposited on lead peroxide to give erroneous results.

Spectrophotometric Determination of SO_2

The best methods for laboratory analysis of sulphur dioxide are spectrophotometric methods. Such methods are summarized in Table 1.

There are three methods which are commonly used. The first method is used for direct analysis of SO_2 with absorption solution containing H_2O_2 and barium chloroanilate to give a red coloured complex with absorption maxima at 530 nm. This method is good for fine gas analysis, but lacks sensitivity required for ambient air analysis. Second method is based on absorption of SO_2 into a mixture of ferric chloride and ammonium chloride, $HClO_4$ and 1-10 phenanthroline. A colour formed is spectrophotometrically measured at 510 nm. The development of the colour is rapid, but the fading of colour is also equally fast. H_2S in addition shows strong interference. Third method is the most widely used one known as PRA method. In this method sodium chloride and mercury chloride are reacted with para rosaniline (leucobase) in formaldehyde, which gives intense red-violet colour of p-rosaniline methylsulphonic acid, showing strong absorbance at 560 nm – 575 nm. The sensitivity of the method is in the range 1-10 ppm and the colour is stable.

H_2S Analysis

In the absence of SO_2 it can be determined by reduction technique. SO_2 if present can be removed by glass fibre filter impregnated with K_2CO_3. H_2S forms coloured precipitate with second group (of qualitative analysis) metals, e.g. Pb acetate turns black. In iodometric titration H_2S solution reacts

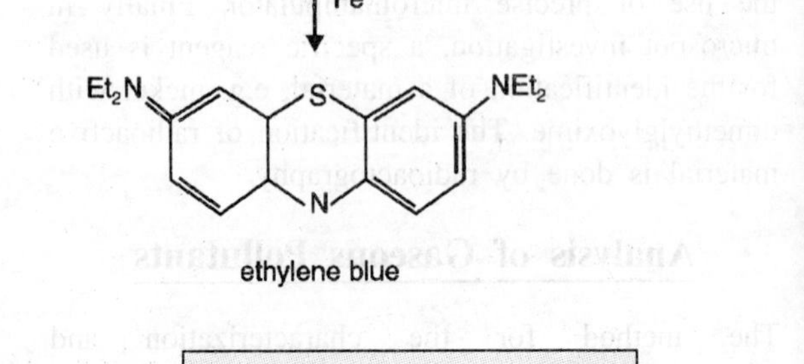

Fig. 4. Reaction mechanism of H_2S.

with KI and liberated iodine is titrated with standard solution of thiosulphate.

Spectrophotometric Determination of H_2S

There is only one reliable method called ethylene blue method. In this method the absorbing solution used, contains $CdSO_4$ and NaOH. The dye ethylene blue so formed by interaction of $FeCl_3$ and N-N'-diethylphenylene diamine is measured at 670 nm. The Beer's law limit is 1–10 μg/ml with molar absorptivity $\varepsilon = 3.5 \times 10^4$. The reaction mechanism is depicted in Fig. 2. Gases like SO_2, O_3, NH_3 do not interfere, but sulphites, thiosulphates show strong interference, which can be eliminated with $FeCl_3$. The method is more sensitive if the complex is extracted in chloroform. For colorimetry, Cd, Pb or As are most useful for formation of coloured sulphides.

NO-NO_x Analysis

All possible oxides of nitrogen exist in polluted atmosphere. NO-NO_x, are most prevalent. They can be determined by gas chromatography. NO converts to NO_2 to give rise to photochemical smog. The most useful method is Saltzman method, performed using a spectrophotometer.

Spectrophotometric Determination of NO-NO_x

There are several methods of analysis as shown in Table 3. In phenoldisulphonic acid method, reaction of nitrogen oxide in H_2O_2 and H_2SO_4 is used to develop colour measurable at 400 nm as :

e.g. $2NO + H_2O_2 \longrightarrow 2HNO_3$

$$2NO + 3H_2O_2 \longrightarrow 2HNO_3 + 2H_2O$$

$$HNO_3 + HO\ C_6H_3\ (SO_3H)_2 \longrightarrow HOC_6\ H_2\ (NO_2)\ (SO_3H)_2 + H_2O$$

Table 2. **Spectrophotometric determination of hydrogen sulphide.**

Ethylene blue method	
Absorbing solution :	015°4, NaOH, FeCI
N-N' diethyl p-phenylene diamine (8)	
	Reagents ethylene blue
Colour :	Instantaneous
λ_{max}	: 670 nm $\varepsilon = 3.5 \times 10^4$
Working Range 1 - 10 εg/ml	
Extractive spectrophotometry in $CHCl_3$-better sensitivity	

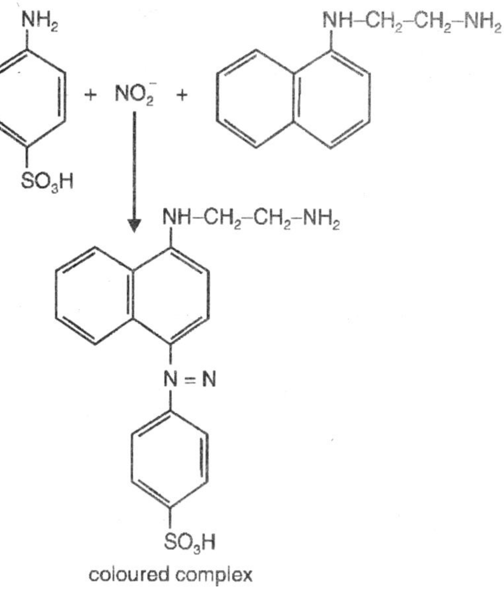

Fig. 5. Reaction mechanism of NO-NO_x

This method does not work beyond 25 ppm. Organic nitrogen shows strong interference. In xylenol method, nitrite ion react with $KMnO_4$ and propylene glycol with 2-4 xylenol to give a yellow complex with absorption maxima at 435 nm, limit of analysis is 2-5 μg/ml. All operations can be performed in single step. In the third method, sodium arsenite gas is absorbed on H_2O_2, in presence of sulphamide; H_2SO_4 and N-(napthyl) ethylene diamine hydrochloride (NEDA) a red coloured complex is measured at 550 nm. SO_2 does not interfere, the only limitation is that $NaAsO_3$ is toxic in nature. In triethnolamine method, the sample is absorbed in an aqueous solution of triethanolamine in butanol. Colour development is effected by diazotization reaction using NEDA to produce colour with maximum absorbance at 550 nm. The range of analysis is 0.005-0.5 ppm. In modified method, absorbing solution is NaOH treated with H_2O_2, sulphanilamide, H_3PO_4, NEDA to form a coloured complex with the limit of analysis as 0.04-1.5 ppm. However, Saltzman's method is an excellent method for the analysis of NO-NO_x. The principal reactions involved in such analysis are depicted in Fig. 3. In this method absorbing solution is NaOH, trienthanolamine sulphanilic acid, glacial CH_3COOH and NEDA.

Table 3. **Spectrophotometric determination of oxides of nitrogen.**

1. Phenoldisulphonic acid (A. = 400 nm) useful up to 25 μg, Organic nitrogen interfere
2. Xylenol, $KMnO_4$ Propylene glycol $\longrightarrow$ Yellow complex λ_{max} 435 nm Working range 2–500 $\mu g/ml$
3. $NaAsO_3$ (H_2O_2, sulphamide, H_3PO_4 NEDA) λ = 550 nm
4. Triethanolamine, n-butanol λ_{max} 550 nm
5. Saltzmann method
   Absorbing solution : Triethynolamine in NaOH
   Reagents : NEDA, Sulphanilic acid and CH_3COOH
   λ_{max} : 550 nm, ε = 4.0 × 104
   Colour development : 15 minutes (stability : 24 hours)
   Working range : 0.01 – 1.5 $\mu g/ml$

Colour is developed instantaneously due to process of dye formation. It can be measured at 550 nm. The (e) molar absorptivity is 4×10^4 with sensitivity of 0.01-1.5 $\mu g/ml$. The principal interferences are due to O_3 and high concentration of SO_2.

CO-CO_2 Analysis

The analysis of CO_2 is simple. It is bubbled through a solution of NaOH or KOH to form carbonates. The unreacted alkali is titrated against a standard solution of some acid. The measurement of CO_2 is the index of human and plant activity, as a significant portion of CO_2 in the air is anthropogenic. For CO analysis detection methods are many, e.g.

$$I_2O_5 + CO \longrightarrow I_2 + CO_2$$
(colorimetry)

$$HgO + CO \longrightarrow CO_2 + Hg$$
(by AAS-cold vapour Hg analysis)

$$PdCl_2 + CO \longrightarrow COCl_2 + Pd$$
(Pd by reflectance spectroscopy)

Since CO is odourless, colourless, and tasteless gas, such indicator tubes are very useful in mines and deep sea operations.

Spectrometric Method of Analysis

Indirect methods for analysis of CO are already summarised in Table 3. In direct method CO reduces yellow silico – molybdate to form molybdenum blue. The colour change from yellow-green to green and then to a permanent blue is gradual. Silica impregnated to ammonium molybdate in H_2SO_4 is reacted with CO to give blue solution with absorption maxima at 660 nm. The method is sensitive. Only organic compounds, H_2S, moisture can reduce molybdenum and give wrong results. This method is comparable with NDIR technique. But that method of non-dispersive infrared measurement is best suited by continuous measurements or monitoring.

Ozone Analysis

The volumetric method involving redox reaction is the most popular method of analysis. The reaction involved is $O_3 + 2KI + H_2O \longrightarrow O_2 + 2KOH + I_2$ (at > 0.5 ppm of O_3). In this reaction, interfering substance should be absent. 2% KI is buffered at pH 7. Final iodine concentration is measured volumetrically. It can also be determined spectrophotometrically at 352 nm. An alkaline solution of KI can also be used. The solution can be added to a mixture of H_3PO_4 and sulphuric acid. The method is useful for field analysis of O_3. Such titrations can be carried out by amperometry or coulometry. A fluorimetric method involves interaction of O_3 with fluorescent acridine to give fluorescence. The reliable techniques are spectral methods.

Spectrophotometric Determination of Ozone

Various methods for such analyses are summarized in Table 5. The phenolphthaleine method is based on the development of pink colour with reduced form of dye. It is oxidised by H_2O_2 with $CuSO_4$ as catalyst to give a pink colour with the maximum absorbance at 530 nm. SO_2 interferes in this method. The reaction of O_3 with 1-2-di-4 (-pyridyl)-ethylene in CH_3COOH glacial gives a yellow colored complex measurable at 442 nm. The aldehyde forms coloured compounds with 3-methyl-2-benzothiazolone hydrazine hydrochloride. The

Table 4. **Spectrophotometric determination of carbon monoxide.**

Indirect method :

(1) Mercuric oxide-Reflectance spectroscopy
($HgCl_2$, CO) of Hg, H_2O, Olefins, interfere (15)

(2) Palladium chloride-Reflectance spectroscopy (16)
($PbCl_2$, CO) metallic Pd

Direct method :

(3) SiO_2, $(NH_4)_2$ MnO_4, CO $\longrightarrow$ Molybdenum blue
(λ_{max} = 660)
Absorbing solution : Silica gel impregnated by Ammonium molybdate
λ_{max} : 660 nm
Colour development : Instantaneous
Working range : 1–10 μg
Interference : Organics, H_2S and Moisture

Table 5. **Spectrophotometric determination of ozone.**

1. Phenolphthalein, H_2O_2, $CuSO_4$ $\longrightarrow$ pink colour (λ_{max} : 530 nm)
2. 1, 2-Di (4-pyridyl) Ethylene $\longrightarrow$ (λ_{max} = 442 nm) Yellow colour
3. N-tetramethyl diaminophenyl methane $\longrightarrow$ Blue-violet colour λ_{max} 565 nm
4. Diphenyl amine sulphonate
Sodium diphenyl amine, $HClO_4$ $\longrightarrow$ max = 593 nm
Turquise red-violet colour
5. 4-4' dimethyl stilbene $\longrightarrow$ Blue (λ_{max} : 610 nm)
6. Iodide Method
Absorbing solution: Phosphate buffered KI solution Reaction : O_3 + 3KI + H_2O $\longrightarrow$ KI_3 + 2KOH + O_2
λ_{max} : 353 nm Interference : SO_2 NO_2, peroxy acetyle nitrate and H_2S

intense yellow coloured complex is measured at 442 nm. In N-tetramethyldiaminodiphenyl methane in dilute acetic acid gives a violet colour, measurable at 565 nm. When NO–NO_x are present, green colour turns to yellow (λ_{max} -565 nm). In diphenylamine sulphonate method, $HClO_4$, sodium diphenylamine gives turquise-red colour (λ_{max} = 593 nm). While in 4-4' dimethoxy stilbene method, blue colour (λ_{max} = 610 nm) is obtained. NO_2, SO_2 do not interfere. Finally, reaction of phosphate buffered KI solution can be used at A° = 352 nm. The interference is of SO_2, NO_2 and peroxyacetyl nitrate, H_2S.

NH_3-Analysis

The air sampling methods for determination of NH_3 involves the absorption of gas into dilute H_2SO_4. Various methods for analysis are summarised in Table 6. In indophenol method, $(NH_4)_2$ SO_4, phenol, sodium-nitroprusside and NaOCl are reacted to give a blue complex, measurable spectrophoto-metrically at 630 nm. Only formaldehyde interfere. Sensitivity is 0.025-1 ppm. The nitrite method is based on reaction of $(NH_4)_2$ SO_4 with HOCl and Br_2 gas to give coloured complex (λ_{max} = 550 nm). The direct determination of NH_3 in air can be achieved at 204 nm in a 100 mm quartz cell where $\varepsilon = 2.7 \times 10^3$ with sensitivity of 7 ppm. A direct one-step method for analysis of ammonia involves its absorption in dioxone containing o-(benzene sulphonamido) p-benzoquinone. It gives a coloured complex (λ_{max} = 480 nm).

Finally in the Nessler method which is the best method, the brown colour is measured at 450 nm. The important reaction is $2HgI_4^{2} + NH_3 + 3OH^- \longrightarrow NH_2Hg_2IO$ (brown) + $7I^-$ + $2H_2O$. This is a sensitive method; the method however shows interference of aliphatic amines and H_2S. The method is simple and as such suffers minimum interference.

Table 6. **Spectrophotometric determination of ammonia.**

1. Indophenol-$(NH_4)_2SO_4$ Phenol, Sodium nitropruside NaOCl
   Blue λ_{max} = 630 nm
   Formaldehyde interfere
2. $(NH_4)_2$ SO_4, HOCl, Br_2 $\longrightarrow$ NO_2 formed diazotization orange (λ_{max} = 550 nm)
3. NH_3 in quartz cell at λ = 204 nm and ε = 2 – 6 × 10,
4. I, 4-Dioxane, Benzene sulphimido-p-benzoquinone $\longrightarrow$ λ_{max} 480 nm
5. Nessler's Method
   Absorbing Solution: H_2SO_4
   Reagents H_gCl_2, KI in NaOH
   λ_{max} : 450nm
   Working range 10-100 μg/ml
   Interference: Ammonium salts, Aliphatic amines, H_2S

Organic Gases and Vapour Analysis

The best method is GLC. Lighter organics are determined by adsorption chromatography. CH_4 is determined at ppb level by GLC. 3-4 benzopyrene and polycylic compounds are determined by GLC. HCHO is a component of photochemical smog and is determined with chromotropic acid in H_2SO_4. Olefins and acroleins are also analyzed by gas chromatography. It is always not possible to get definite information by GLC, but hyphenated GC-MS offers useful information in characterization of organic pollutants.

It will be noted that for rapid analysis of gaseous pollutants in Indian environment, the best method is spectrophotometry. The methods are simple, inexpensive, with availability of a plethora of organic ligands.

Important Questions

1. Describe the method used to collect the air samples. How the gaseous pollutants can be analyzed? Discuss different methods used for the analysis of sulphur dioxide.
2. Describe the procedure used for the estimation of NO_x, H_2S, and Ozone.
3. Describe the methods used for sampling and analysis of sulphur dioxide.

Monitoring of Ambient Air Pollution

20

Since it is necessary to measure air pollution on a regular basis, we need to identify some physical property of the pollutants for such measurements. The component of instrument which measures such physical parameters is called a 'Transducer'. A specific property, characteristic of a particular pollutant such as light transmittance or absorbance, electrical conductivity; change in potential, generation of material by passage of electricity, nucleation of fog formation or radio-activity is usually measured. Such properties are summarized in Table 1. The examples of gaseous pollutants which can be measured are also described. The monitoring instrument is usually composed of three components, viz. air remover, transducer and recorder. The air remover component consists of a flow meter and a pressure gauge. They measure rate of flow of air passing and the pressure under which gas pollutants exist. Transducer in fact is the heart of the instrument which measures a physical property, while the recorder notes change in physical property of gaseous pollutant e.g. flow colorimeters or spectrophotometers are used to measure the concentration of the pollutant. The instrument should be checked for response time, specificity, sensitivity, noise level, maintenance and downtime and overall accuracy. Very few instruments are available for aerosol analysis in this country.

Air Pollution Monitoring Instruments

The common air pollution instruments for measurement are summarized in Tables 2 and 3. The limits of analysis are specified

Table 1. **Physical principles involved in various monitoring methods.**

	Physical principle of measurement	Example
1.	Molecular absorbance (UV/visible/IR)	SO_2, NO_2, H_2S, CO
2.	Atomic absorption (AAS)	SO_2, Hg
3.	Atomic emission (ICP-AES)	SO_2 metal pollutants
4.	Molecular luminenscence (Fluoroscence)	SO_2, NO_2
5.	Light scattering (Nephelometry and Turbidimetry)	Particulates
6.	Magnetic resonance/Electron spin resonance (NMR/ESR)	Organics
7.	Polarographic-amperometry	Pesticides
8.	Conductance, High frequency	SO_2
9.	Potential-pH measurement, ion selective electrodes	NO-NO_x
10.	Coulometry-anodic stripping voltametry (ASV)	SO_2
11.	Radioanalytical (NAA/IDM)	Radioactive pollutants
12.	Gas chromatography (GC)	Organics, HCl

in Table 2, while the technique of measurement is given in the last column of Table 3. There are a good deal of instruments for measurement of SO_2, CO, CO_2, NO-NO_x and H_2S. They are based upon measurement of various physical properties listed in Table 1, e.g. for SO_2 monitor one can use either conductance measurement or coluometric technique. On the contrary, for H_2S we have only one method involving flow colorimetry (Table 2). The other uncommon pollutants like oxygen, ozone, smoke and dust, organic pollutants as well as metal pollutants, can also be monitored on a continuing basis. In such a technique, apart from conventional methods one also uses measurement of light scattering phenomena (smoke), fluorescence quenching (organic pollutant), emission and absorption spectroscopy (metal pollutants) for quantitative analysis.

Table 2. **Air pollution monitoring instruments and limit.**

Instrument	Pollutant to be measured	Limit of analysis (ppm)
IR gas analyzer	CO, CH_4, and HC	10-1000
NDIR analyzer	CO, CO_2	Non-dispersive
Car exhaust meter	Auto-exhaust analysis	-
CO-monitor	Catalytic oxidation	0-50
SO_2 monitor	Conductivity	0-100
SO_2 monitor	Coulometric titration	0-40
SO_2 monitor	Chemiluminescence	0-01
NO-NO_x-monitor	Chemiluminescence	0.05
H_2S analyzer	Colorimetry	0.40

Meteorological Instruments

While measuring air pollution, it is absolutely necessary to consider meteorological and topographical effects of air movements in the atmosphere. The important parameters usually considered are climate, direction of wind, frequency of certain type of weather (like periodical cyclones in the ocean), lapse rate and humidity in air. The topographic considerations include regional surface, local surface and urban structure. Variation in air temperature decides dispersal of pollutant at ground level, but when temperature of surrounding air decreases with height, the pollutant does not accumulate. The rising parcel of pollutant air expands as it rises and cools also. When there is inversion of temperature with height at ground level, vertical movement either upward or downward is strongly arrested and consequently pollution remains stagnant near the level at which it had emitted. Since lapse rate is negative, it leads to 'inversion'. When ground is cool, specially at night, low level or noctural inversion occurs. Then mist or fog is formed. The inversion level extends up to 30 m above in early morning. A subsidence inversion involves high atmospheric pressure, when air in high pressure system descend, leading to stability and inversion phenomena to a height of 2-3 km. The elevated inversion consist of inversion layer sandwiched between two neutral layers at cold polar air slides. Sea breeze is an important meteorological factor of consideration, as after sunrise cold sea air forms a ground based layer of air, which is 300-400 mm thick and moves under warmer inland air at a speed of 15 km/hr. In summary, meteorological parameters form an important

Table 3. **Air monitoring instruments and technique.**

	Instruments	Pollutant measured	Technique of analysis
1.	Conductometric analyser	SO_2	Conductometric measurement
2.	Continuous SO_2 monitor	SO_2	Coulometric measurement
3.	Gas liquid chromatograph	CO,NO hydrocarbons	Gas chromatography with different detectors
4.	Nitric oxide monitor	NO_2	Fluorescence technique
5.	O_2 analyser	O_2 in atmosphere	Measurement emission spectrograph
6.	Ozone monitor	O_3	Chemiluminiscence technique
7.	Infrared gas analyser	CO, CH_4 and other hydrocarbons	Infrared absorption limit of 10-1000 ppm for CO, NDIR technique
8.	Fluorescence spectroscope	Organic pollutant	Fluorescence, phosphorescence spectroscopy
9.	Smoke meter	Smoke, smog	Light scattering technique
10.	Atomic absorption spectrophotometer	Trace metal analysis	Atomic absorption spectroscopy
11.	Spectrograph	Metal pollutants at tracer levels	UV/visible spectroscopy

Table 4. **Meteorological instruments.**

	Name of instrument	Property measured	Technique
1.	Temperature recorder	Temperature	Temperature sensor by diode
2.	Anemometer and wind meter	Wind velocity and wind direction	Velocity threshold
3.	Tide and wave meter	Wave and tide	Hydrostatic pressure
4.	Salinity meter	Salinity of system	Conductivity cell
5.	Telemeter	Measurement of depth	Hydrostatic sensing probe
6.	Temperature logger	Temperature recorder	Probe with thermistors
7.	Water speed measurement	Water flow meter	Signal conditioners and loggers
8.	Water level meter	Water level	Resistance variation
9.	Capacitance bridge	Height and level of water indicator	Capacitance sensors measurement of difference
10.	Telemetry design	Data transmitter	UHF radiolink used
11.	Rain gauge	Rainfalls	Rain gauge measurement
12.	Humidity indicator	Humidity measurement	Measurement with thermistor probes

segment of various monitoring systems (Table 4). The important instruments required for such purpose are temperature, humidity, rain, wind direction and wind velocity instruments. Fortunately, this is one of the fields where meteorological department, ISRO, etc., have made spectacular development and progress, with the result that all kinds of instruments listed in Table 4 are manufactured in India.

We have excellent temperature sensors, hydrostatic pressure and sensing probes, thermistors, etc. The evaluation of these parameters would help us to exactly measure gases, pollutants, in atmosphere and furnish reliable and reproducible results.

Monitoring of Sulphur Dioxide

Various methods used for the monitoring of SO_2 are summarized in Table 5. It will be seen that important methods are based upon measurement of colour or electrical conductance, or use of electrochemical transducer, by chemiluminescence technique, NDIR measurement or gas chromatography. In simple barium perchlorate titration technique, SO_2 is reacted with H_2O_2 or H_2O to form H_2SO_4, which in turn is reacted to form $BaSO_4$. This method is valid when high concentrations of SO_2 are encountered, but many metals like Pb show strong interference. Flow colorimetry is the best technique. One involves

Table 5. **Monitoring methods for SO_2.**

Method	Remarks
1. Ba $(ClO_4)_2$-titration	Valid till 500 ppm but many metals interfere
2. Flow colorimetry	Barium chloranilate used as the chromogenic ligand but NO-NO_x interference
3. PRA-colorimetry	Very sensitive
4. Conductometric method	Commonly used
5. Coulometric titrations	KBr reduction with the use of the three electrodes
6. Electrochemical transducer	Semipermeable membrane used
7. Pulse fluorescence spectroscopy	Very sensitive (0.1–100 ppm)
8. NDIR technique	*In situ* monitoring
9. GLC-flame photodetector	Specific for SO_2 (but not for H_2S)

interaction of Ba-chloroanilate with SO_2 to give coloured compound, while in another prosaniline (PRA) react with SO_2 to give coloured species, which can be measured spectrophotometrically at regular intervals. In widely used conductometric method, conductance of an absorbing solution is measured at regular intervals. The increase in the conductance is caused by the ions formed, as SO_2 combines with the absorbing solution. The increase in conductivity in general is proportional to the concentration of SO_2 in the air. In fact this principle forms the basis of SO_2 monitor developed indigenously (Table 6). The liquid absorber monoethanol amine, triethanol amine, H_2O_2 and formaldehyde are used to eliminate interference of other gaseous pollutants like CO, H_2S, NO-NO_x and NH_3.

The SO_2 monitor permits analysis in the range of 0.1-80 ppm, when usual levels of SO_2 in atmosphere is 4-40 ppm. Other working details are also provided in Table 7. In coulometric technique, in alkali halide solution like KBr, a constant halogen-to-halide ratio is maintained by electric current. It actually measures the current required to regenerate the halogen depleted by SO_2, this current being proportional to the quantity of SO_2 which has been converted from halogen to halide. The only limitation of this technique is the periodic replacement of the reagent and constant cleaning of electrodes. Thus a cell containing acidic potassium bromide with four electrodes is taken,

Table 6. **SO_2 monitor.**

1. Working principle	Conductance measurement
2. Methods of analysis	Photometry, coulometry, chemiluminescence
3. Reacting solution	Acid, water, H_2O_2
4. Absorbing liquids	Monoethanol amine, formaldehyde and triethanolamine and hydrogen peroxide
5. Solid absorber	Glassfibre filters
6. Interferences	NO_2, NH_3, H_2S, CO
7. Special features	High accuracy, minimum maintenance IC used, reading is automatic
8. Level of analysis	0.1 -80 ppm
9. Threshold limit (TLV)	5 ppm
10. Advantages	Low cost (Rs. 15,000 approximately)
11. Atmospheric SO_2 level	4-40 ppm present in air
12. Toxic effects	Asphyxiation, lung, renal and hepatic disorder
13. Source of SO_2 pollution	Foundry, oil refineries, furnace oil, coal gas, heavy chemical units, and fertiliser industries.

SO_2 is passed and free Br_2 liberated, which causes imbalance. The signal is amplified and current is passed-to generate enough free bromide coluometrically to restore balance in the circuit. The generating current which is indirectly proportional to SO_2 present is continuously measured. In electrochemical transducer, a sealed coulometric devise is used. SO_2 selectively diffuses through a semipermeable membrane and as a dissolved gas through thin-film electrode. Current generated by oxidation of SO_2 is a measure of its concentration. Selectivity is determined by the choice of the membrane electrolyte and electrode materials of construction. The most efficient technique is pulsed fluorescence method. Here a pulsed ultraviolet source excites the SO_2 molecules, which emit a characteristic fluoroscence with intensity proportional to the quantity of SO_2 present, e.g.

$$SO_2 + h\nu \longrightarrow S^*O_2; S^*O_2 \longrightarrow SO_2 + \text{fluorescence}$$

Such fluorescence is detected by a photomultiplier tube and after suitable signal processing given to the meter and recorder. The only limitation of this method is humidity, which can quench fluorescence intensity. In nondispersive

Table 7. **Monitoring methods of NO-NO$_x$.**

Method	Remarks
1. Colorimetric technique	Saltzman method, needs somewhat longer time for colour development
2. Chemiluminescence technique	O_3 used to convert NO_2 to NO
3. Ion selective electrodes	Nitrate in aqueous phase is measured
4. Electrochemical transducer	Slow response time
5. Non-dispersive infrared/ UV method	Interference from SO_2, H_2S, resonance fluorescence show good specificity

IR method, a broad spectral absorption is measured and sensitized for a particular gas by a detector. Limitations are H_2O, CO, aromatic compounds show strong interferences, in the same region of SO_2 absorption. We can use filters to eliminate such interference. Finally, in gas chromatography, flame detector technique is useful for specific measurement of SO_2 but not for H_2S. Unfortunately, no instrument cost less than Rs. 50,000. So there is a dire need to develop these instruments in India.

Monitoring of NO-NO$_x$

Various methods are recommended for monitoring of oxides of nitrogen, which are listed in Table 7. Of these the best method is colorimetry involving Saltzman reaction. In this method, air to be sampled is bubbled through a mixture containing sulfonic and NEDA, i.e. N-(1-napthyl) ethylene diamine acetic acid).

NO_x present in the sample reacts with the solution to form a dye. The absorbance of this dye is a measure of NO_x concentration. Only a minor limitation is that colour development is not instantaneous. The second best method is chemiluminescence method. Air containing NO reacts with ozone in a small cell and gives chemiluminescence, which is highly specific, e.g.

$$NO + O_3 \rightarrow NO_2 + O_2;\ NO_2 + hv = N^*\ O_2;\ N^*O_2 \rightarrow NO_2 + \text{Chemiluminescence}$$

Anion reacting with O_3 gives positive interference, provided such ion should overlap the spectral region of ($NO + O_3$) emission; fortunately no such molecule exists in the atmosphere. Ions showing quenching of chemiluminescence show negative error. Usually O_2 and N_2 can show quenching, but their concentration in the atmosphere is fixed and is constant. A thermal conversion of $NO_2 \rightarrow NO$ is commonly utilized. Gold, stainless steel, carbon impregnated metals are used for such conversion. In ion selective electrode method, nitrite formed is oxidized to nitrate and is measured with ion selective electrode. Electrochemical transducers are slow to work, as response time is very poor. In NDIR method, SO_2 and H_2S seriously interfere, one has to use resonance fluorescence method in such a situation. For *in situ* monitoring, gas cell correlation technique is favourable. In an interferometer one uses Raman scattering for detection of NO in *in situ* analysis. Finally in Jacob's Hocheiser method, NO-NO$_x$, are collected over NaOH as $NaNO_2$ measurements followed by colorimetric analysis. No measurement can show large variation if dye is not properly formed. Usually NO, SO_2, interference are present. This was the basis of NO-NO$_x$, meter developed in several laboratories (Table 8).

Table 8. **NO-NOx meter.**

1. Principle	Flow colorimetry
2. Transducer	Phototube sensor, transmittance
3. Level of analysis	0.02-600 ppm
4. Power supply	230V AC or 6V DC accumulator
5. Recorder	10mV recorder possible
6. Digital display	Can be adopted with 3.5 digit meter
7. Reading solution	NEDA (l-napthyl)-ethylenediamine-hydrochloride and anthranilic acid in NaOH
8. Interferences	No ion interferes
9. Weight of analyser	8 kg roughly
10. Recorder print out	10 mV can be coupled
11. Cost of model	Rs. 9,000 approximately
12. Special feature	High accuracy, less time for analysis, no maintenance, trouble free working, low cost
13. Toxic effects of NO-NO$_x$	Irritation of nose and throat, eyes and skin, dermatitis, lower respiratory track affected, vertigo, vomitting
14. Source of pollution	Atmosphere, burning of nitrogenous matter and fuel, lightening conductor conversion, auto-exhaust emission

Table 9. **Monitoring methods for CO, CO_2.**

Method	Remarks
1. Principle	H_2O vapour interferes, but it is the most reliable method used as reference method
2. NDIR spectrometry	Specific, sensitive, reliable technique
3. IR fluorescence method	Sensitive, no interference by water vapour
4. AAS (Reduction of HgO-Hg)	Need charcoal filter, however H_2O and hydrocarbons interfere
5. Electro catalytic method	Needs selective scrubbing of SO_2, NO_2 but H_2 interferes
6. Electrochemical transducer	Ethylene and acetylene interfere seriously, battery operated, simple, inexpensive
7. FID (after CH_4 formation)	Very sensitive method as compared to NDIR
8. Hopcalite based CO monitor	Temperature rise for converting to CO_2 is measured

Monitoring of CO, CO_2

Various methods for monitoring CO are given in Table 9. These are all valid for CO. We rarely need methods for monitoring of CO_2, as the conventional classical titration technique is superior to any instrumental method. In NDIR technique, the extent of absorption of infrared energy by a column of sample gas in a specified narrow wavelength region (v - 1800 cm^{-1}) is determined. IR pneumatic detector is used in conjunction with interference filters of about 0.1 mm.

Sample needs no preconditioning. However, dust and moisture must be scrupulously absent. Gas flow rate need not be controlled. In NDIR correlation, spectrometer specification and selectivity is satisfactory. The IR fluorescence method is very sensitive, but excess water vapour creates problems. AAS method measures Hg after reduction of HgO to Hg by cold vapour AAS. Hydrocarbons and H_2O vapour however show strong interference. In electrocatalytic method, one has to use scrubber, while in electrochemical transducer ethylene and acetylene show strong interference. The instrument can work on battery, the model is portable and also inexpensive; but shows excessive drift which is a serious problem. GLC with FID gives good results where CO is hydrogenated to CH_4,

Table 10. **Monitoring or hydrocarbons and ozone.**

Method	Remarks
1 TCD gas chromatography	Good for mobile source, light organics
2 AD detectors	Coupled in gas chromatography useful for reactive hydrocarbons
3 Chemiluminescence for (HC)	$CH_2 = CH_2$, measured, reactive HC
4 Nondispersive IR spectroscopy	Ideal for heavy duty vehicles
5 Iodometric method	Wet chemical technique
6 UV absorption technique	Change in beam on passage through O_3 is measured
7 Chemiluminescence for CO)	$CH_2 = CH_2 + O_3$ gives light which is measured
8 Thermistor catalyst	O_3 passed, heat generated measured by imbalance in bright circuit.

nonmethane hydrocarbon can also be measured by this method.

A novel method for CO monitor is Hopcalite based on CO monitor. Here the temperature rise is measured. Such rise is due to heat generated in the exothermic conversion of CO to CO_2 in the presence of hopcalite catalyst. Oxides of Mn or Cu serve the purpose of such a catalyst. Humidity will affect measurement. Hence it is necessary to maintain catalyst at a temperature of 100°C.

Monitoring of Hydrocarbons (HC) and Ozone

Different methods for monitoring of hydrocarbons, ozone and oxidants are summarised in Table 10. Gaseous hydrocarbon may be reactive, i.e. ethylene and also non-reactive like methane. Gas chromaiography is a commonly used technique of analysis with AD or TCD analyzers.

Hydrocarbon level is expressed as methane equivalence hydrocarbon. Preconcentration of hydrocarbon gives reliable results. Silica gel column is useful for lighter organics. The reactive hydrocarbon can be measured with chemiluminescence detector. Less than 0.1 ppm of ethylene can be detected by the chemiluminescent detector at ppb level on silica gel column. The polyaromatic hydrocarbons (PAH) are usually collected with glassfibre filters. Various instruments including mass spectrometer can be used for such analysis. PAH can be best extracted in benzene and then analyzed by GLC. TLC can also detect them, but HPLC offers best results. NDIR method is used for hydrocarbons emitted from heavy duty vehicles. The iodometric method involving wet chemical technique is used for the analysis of oxidant, but SO_2 and NO_2 show interference.

The chemiluminescence method can also be used with O_3 and Rhodamine B probe on silica gel and NO in gas phase. Photochemical reactions can measure level of ozone. Photolysis of NO_2 followed by chemiluminescence detection of NO helps to analyse ozone. Ozone is formed by photochemical decomposition of NO_2 by sunlight in the lower atmosphere. Ozone is monitored with wet chemical methods. In this method, total oxidant is bubbled through neutral buffered KI reagent and liberated iodine is titrated and measured as indicator of ozone concentration. In chemiluminescence technique, ozone is reacted with ethylene and light produced is measured. In UV absorption technique, proportional intensity changes of UV beam as it travels through ozone is measured. Finally ozone is passed on two thermistors, one being coated with a catalyst. The heat of decomposition of ozone is then measured on thermistor bridge circuit.

Table 11. **Monitoring methods for suspended particulate matter (SPM).**

Method	Remarks
1. Gravimetry	Gravimetry, p-gauge analyzer, dilution tunnel, Piezoelectric balance, Thimble sampling
2. β-gauge analyzer dilution tunnel	β-rays used to note loss in weight of tape
3. Piezoelectric balance	Sensitive method, change in weight noted
4. Thimble sampling	Change in weight of cellulose, borosilic or glass ceramics filter is measured
5. Nephelometer	0.1-1 μm diameter can be measured
6. Lidar method	Measures reflection of light with laser beam
7. Acoustical particle	*In situ* analysis (5 μm)
8. Transmissometer	Measures optical density; low cost, cannot detect mass
9. Electrostatic precipitator	Measures particle flow

Monitoring of Suspended Particulate Matter

Various methods for monitoring of SPM are summarised in Table 11. The most reliable method is high volume sampler with gravimetry. SPM is collected on filter paper, millipore glass fibres or nucleopore using air, such as pumps and., residue is weighed. Pump can work between 12 and 24 hours. Moisture must be removed. Calibration flow meter measure total volume of air sampled; β-absorption analysis is also a good method. Here air is sampled through filter tape, which passes through radio-active source detector like GM counter with PM-147 or C14 detector. Decrease in count rate is recorded and is related to level of SPM. In piezoelectric balance, two quartz crystals oscillating at some frequency are used. One crystal is encapsulated, while the other crystal is open, coated with selective chemical, which absorbs SPM. Rise in weight is measured. In Thimble sampling, change in weight on deposition of SPM on cellulose filter (150 dc), boroglass filter (300°C) or ceramics filter (>300°C) is accurately measured.

In nephelometric technique, beam of light is focused on spot and air is sampled through. Light is scattered, which is measured on photocell. Usually the scattering of right angles is utilized for measuring particle density. In Lidar method, laser beam is used as light source and is used for measurements. Other important methods include acoustical particle counter, which involves *in situ*

Table 12. **More methods for analysis of particulate matter.**

Name	Mode of operation	Technique
1. High volume	Filtration	Gravimetry
2. Paper taps	Filtration	Transmission densitometer
3. Durham	Impaction	Counting
Anderson	Impaction	Counting
Cascade	Impaction	Microscopic Examination
4. Midget impinger	Impingement	Gravimetry
5. Cyclone	Centrifugal separation	Gravimetry
6. Electrostatic and	Precipitation	Nonquantity
thermal precipitator	Precipitation	
Gravimetry		

measurement of individual particles above 5 μm. It needs sample conditioning. In transmissiometer, optical density of suspended particles is measured, which has a low cost of operation. Only limitation of this technique is, it cannot detect mass of the particles. In electrostatic precipitator, it measures particle flow rate, the system has low potential as mass monitor. To evaluate particle size, electronmicroscopy, light scattering, impaction, minicyclones, laser doppler velocity meter and charged particle drift spectrometry are usually used.

Table 12 summarises some more methods for analysis of particulate matter. They are based on the same principle as narrated in the earlier section. Only difference is, some of them have names of persons who have discovered the techniques.

Important Questions

1. Give a detailed account of different air pollution monitoring instruments. Discuss the procedure of ambient air monitoring of any two air pollutants.
2. Write briefly on the following:
(i) Ambient monitoring of hydrocarbons, (ii) Monitoring of suspended particulate matter, (iii) Monitoring of carbon dioxide.

21

Water Pollution Analysis

To ascertain suitability of water for consumption, it is necessary to undertake examination of quality of water. Such quality can be ascertained in three ways i.e.

(1) Physical examination of water.
(2) Chemical characterization of water.
(2) Biological investigation of water.

Physical Examination of Water

Much information on the quality of water can be ascertained by physical examination (Table 1). We consider then such examination, as study of colour, conductivity, temperature, odour, turbidity and hardness.

Colour

The classical method of measurement of colour consists comparison of colour with one prepared by dissolving known weight of dipotassiun hexachloroplatinate and cobalt chloride. This is called as the platinum-cobalt method of comparison. The unit of colour is one produced by 1 mg platinum /litre in the form of chloroplatinate ion. Thus 1.25 gm of K_2PtC_6 and 1 gm of $COCl_2$ $6H_2O$ are dissolved in 100 ml of concentrated hydrochloric acid and made up to one litre with distilled water. The resulting stock solution has colour of 500 units. This method of analysis involves personal error. However, the spectrophotometric method is the most reliable method, wherein the absorbance of water is measured between 400 and 700 nm. The

Table 1. **Physical characteristics of water (average value in brackets).**

Physical characteristics of water
1. Acidity-no definite data
2. Alkalinity-10-500 mg/litre as $CaCO_3$ (100) (total)
3. Colour—50 platinate units (10)
4. Hardness- 5-1000 mg/litre $CaCO_3$ (ISO)
5. pH 6.0-9.0 (7.5)
6. Specific conductance 30-1000 micro ohms (400)
7. Temperature 0-30°C (20°C)
8. Turbidity 0-1000
9. Odour-3 TON

tristimulus colorimetric method is also used for measurement of colour.

Conductivity

The equivalent conductance of various ions is listed in Table 2. The conductance is the measure of concentration of mineral constituents present in water. This gives a rapid method to get an idea about dissolved solids in water. The conductance is reciprocal of resistance, which is measured usually between two electrodes kept one cm apart, with area of cross-section as one cm^2. The value depends upon presence of total concentration of ionised substances. It also checks the reliability of mineral analysis or quality of distilled water. The average value should be less than 2 μ ohms. The self-contained conductivity instruments are available for such measurements. In conductivity cell, first it is necessary to evaluate cell constant. Usually conductivity is measured at a fixed temperature.

Temperature

It is measured immediately after collecting the water sample. The depth temperature is required for limnological studies, which may be measured with a reversing thermometer or thermophone or thermistor. The last device, viz. thermistor is the most reliable.

Odour

The volatile compounds produce odour. The dilution of sample at which odour is detectable is a measure of its intensity and thus odour can be quantitatively measured in the laboratory. The odour is qualitatively described as medicinal (phenolic) and fishy (due to algae), earthy (decaying matter) or chemical (chlorine).

Table 2. **Equivalent conductance of various ions.**

	Anion	Conductance μ moh/mg/litre	No.	Cation	Conductance μ moh/mg/litre
1.	Cl^-	2.14			
2.	SO_4^{2-}	1.54	6	Ca^{2+}	2.60
3.	CO_3^{2-}	2.82	7	Mg^{2+}	3.82
4.	HCO_3^{2-}	0.71	8	Na^+	2.16
5.	NO_3^-	1.15	9	K^+	2.00

Inspite of advancement of science and technology, no instrument has so far been developed for the measurement of odour. Such measurement largely depends upon contact of a stimulating substance with appropriate human receptor cell. Such stimuli are chemical in nature and hence termed as chemical senser. We are confining to odour of water in this chapter. It is measured in terms of TON i.e. threshold odour number, indicating the number of times the dilution one should carry out with odour free water, in order to get no perceptible odour, e.g. TON = 4.0 indicates if we dilute with water in the ratio of 1 : 4, no odour will persist. Obviously, smaller the value of TON, better is its quality. Accepted average value of TON = 3.

Turbidity

It is a measure of the light absorbing properties of the water sample. It can be measured either with nepheloturbidimeter or by conventional Jackson Candle Turbidimeter. Usually turbidity is caused by suspended matter. It is an expression of optical quality of water. The standard method for determination of turbidity has been based on Jackson Candle Turbidimeter, but lower turbidity values can be measured by nephelometer. In visual or Jackson turbidity measurement, a candle turbidimeter (similar to measuring cylinder with reverse graduations) is kept on ground glass. The candle is lighted and held below the turbidimeter. Water is then poured in turbidimeter and the flame is viewed from top. As soon as the flame disappears (if we continue to pour water) reading on the cylinder is noted. The units on cylinder indicates turbidity units of water. Alternatively, it is very easy

Table 3. **Classification of hardness.**

	Hardness $CaCO_3$ mg/litre	Remarks
1.	0-40	Soft
2.	40-100	Moderately hard
3.	100-300	Hard
4.	300-500	Very hard
5.	500-1000	Extremely hard

to measure turbidity of water by nephelometer in terms of NTU units. The instrument permits measurement from 1000 NTU, while Jackson model permits 25-1000 JU limits. Unfortunately, so far no direct corelationship has been established between units of Jackson candle turbidimeter and nephelometer, i.e. in terms of turbidity measurement units.

Hardness

As a matter of fact this should be classified as the chemical property of water. Hardness of water is caused due to presence of sulphates and chlorides of calcium and magnesium. Hardness sometimes is attributed due to sulphates or chlorides of iron, manganese and aluminium. This causes what is called the permanent hardness, while temporary hardness is caused due to the presence of bicarbonates of calcium and magnesium and can be eliminated by mere boiling. In order to ascertain the hardness of water, one has to use soap test. Water will form soft and beautiful lather with soap if water is soft. However, if water is hard then Ca and Mg will combine with stearates in soaps to form curd or insoluble lather of Ca-stearate or Mg-stearate. Alkali metal stearates are soluble. Usually hardness is expressed in terms of $CaCO_3$/litre. Table 3 lists hardness of water for practical purposes.

Thus a water with 25 mg/litre $CaCO_3$ is considered soft water, while water with 500 mg/litre of $CaCO_3$ is termed as hard water. The usual method for analysis of hardness is titration method, one involving $KMnO_4$ titration, while an other method is involving the use of EDTA for the purpose, which is more popular. The reactions involved in permanganate titrations are as follows :

$$CaCl_2 + H_2C_2O_4 \longrightarrow CaC_2O_4 + 2HCl \text{ (precipitate filtered)}$$

$$CaC_2O_4 + H_2SO_4 \longrightarrow CaSO_4 + H_2C_2O_4 \text{ (in solution)}$$

$$2MnO_4^- + 5H_2C_2O_4 + 6H^+ \longrightarrow 2Mn^{2+} + IOCO_2 + 8H_2O$$

The most commonly utilized method is EDTA titration

$$CaCl_2 + 2EDTA \longrightarrow Ca(EDTA)_2 + 2NaCl \text{ (with metallochromic indicator)}$$

Thus we use mureoxide as an indicator. During titration the pH value is maintained up to 4.5. If magnesium is present, then the reaction is

$$MgSO_4 + 2EDTA \longrightarrow Mg\ (EDTA)_2 + Na_2SO_4$$

The indicator used is Eriochrome black T, where pH is maintained at 10.0. Usually EDTA combines first with Ca from water; when magnesium can be first precipitated as $Mg(OH)_2$. So titration value gives the amount of calcium only. Solochrome dark-blue can also be used instead of mureoxide indicator, with equal efficiency for calcium. When EBT is used, one gets reading for both Ca and

Table 4. **Physical, chemical and biological examination of water.**

Chemical characteristics	Physical properties	Biological investigations
Ca^{2+}	Colour	Total coliform
Mg^{2+}	Conductivity	Faecal coliform
Na^+	Temperature	Faecal streptococii
K^+	Odour	Crenothrix
Cl^-	Turbidity	Plankton
SO_4^{2-}	Hardness	Algae
CO_3^{2-}		*Nitrosomonas*
HCO_3^{2-}		
Total dissolved solid		Diatomaceous algae
Al^{3+}		
Ba^{2+}		Protozoa
Boron		Rotifers
NO_2^-		*Escherichia coli*
NO_3^-		(i.e. *E. coli*)
PO_4^{3-}		
Fe^{3+}		
Mn^{2+}		

Table 5. **Major components or water and their concentrations (figures in parenthesis indicate mean level) in mg/litre).**

Component	Concentration	Component	Concentration
Ca	0–250 (150)	Mg	0–100 (15)
CO_3^{2-}	0–10 (<5)	Mn	0–0.2 (0.25)
HCO_3^{2-}	0–300 (100)	NO_3^-	0–5 (1)
Cl^-	0–500 (50)	K	0–25 (15)
Dissolved Solids	0.0–750 (300)	SiO_2	0–100 (25)
F^-	0.20 (0.5)	SO_4^{2-}	0–500 (100)
Fe	0-0.5 (0.25)		

Mg. Usually EBT is grounded with solid NaCl in the ratio of 1 : 1, and is used during titration. A new indicator called Patton Reeder indicator is best for determination of calcium in hard water. It permits simultaneous analysis of Ca and Mg.

Chemical Characterisation of Water

Most important part of water quality assessment is the chemical characterization of water. Table 4 lists important chemical constituents of water, which are generally analyzed to assess its quality. In addition to chemical parameters, this table also lists important physical properties of water, which we have already discussed in the preceding section. The biological factors which are generally investigated are also listed in the same table. The various components which are present in major concentrations in potable water are calcium, magnesium, sodium, potassium, chloride, sulphate, carbonates, bicarbonates and dissolved solids. The important minor constituents of potable water are aluminium, barium, boron, fluoride, bromide, iodide, nitrate, nitrite, phosphates, polyphosphates, iron, manganese and trace elements. In addition we do consider other important properties such as acidity/alkalinity, dissolved oxygen (DO), biochemical oxygen demand (BOD), chemical oxygen demand (COD) generally considered for waste water and finally nitrogen from ammonia, nitrite and nitrates.

Table 5 describes the major components of water and their concentrations. The values in bracket indicate mean level of the component present in sample of water. The metals constitute an important portion of drinking water. Table 6. describes WHO

Table 6. **Major elements present in drinking water (mg/litre).**

Element	PHS-limit	WHO-limit
As	0.05	0.20
Ba	1.0	None
Cd	0.01	Nil
Cr	0.05	0.05
Cu	1.0	1.5
Fe	0.03	1.0
Pb	0.05	0.10
Mn	0.05	0.50
Se	0.05	0.05
Ag	0.05	None
Zn	5.0	15.0

limit of metals, which is in agreement with that prescribed by public health services (PHS) in India. This gives guidelines for the environmental engineer to control purity of drinking water, by devising proper water treatment process. It is worthwhile at this stage to consider two important aspects of chemical constituents. First is their significance in determining quality of water and second is their analysis in the laboratory. We would consider both aspects simultaneously.

Calcium

This is a major component of natural water. It is dissolved from rocks and soils which causes hardness and forms scale which is generally deposited in conduit tubes and pipes. The concentrations up to 100 mg/litre of calcium is capable of forming scales in pipes and boilers. Fortunately, it has no adverse physiological manifestation on human system, and in fact a person consuming water containing certain amount of calcium is likely to have less chances of heart trouble or cardiac disorder, than a person drinking soft water without any calcium content. The usual method of analysis of calcium is by gravimetric estimation, if present in large concentration. This is weighed as CaO, e.g.

$$Ca^{2+} + H_2C_2O_4 \longrightarrow CaC_2O_4 + 2H^+;$$
$$CaC_2O_4 \longrightarrow CaCO_3 \longrightarrow CaO + CO_2$$

If the level is small, one can use $KMnO_4$ titration by dissolving the oxalate in sulphuric acid and carrying redox titration as described earlier. Similarly, the EDTA titration is the best method which is narrated in under hardness. In addition to mureoxide, one can use indicators like calcein purpurate, etc. Fe, Mn if present are masked at pH value of 10.0 with alkali cyanide. For conversion factor, we have 1 ml of 0.01 EDTA corresponding to 1 mg $CaCO_3$ or 0.4008 mg of $CaCO_3$.

Magnesium

In comparison to calcium, magnesium is present in a smaller concentration. It is usually determined by titration with EDTA with EBT (Eriochrom Black T in NaCl) at pH 10.0. If a large amount is present gravimetrically it is weighed as $Mg_2P_2O_7$ given by the equation :

$$MgCl_2 + (NH_4)_2\ HPO_4 \longrightarrow 2MgHPO_4 \longrightarrow Mg_2P_2O_7 + H_2O$$

In very few instances, it is determined by spectrophotometer, by making use of the brilliant yellow solution.

Sodium

It is a major component of potable water. The average level of sodium is > 100 mg/litre. If high amount of sodium is present, it will render boiler operations difficult. No doubt sodium has medicinal effect on health. However, high concentration in blood leads to hypertension. The best method for analysis is by flame emission spectroscopy at 590 nm. In this analysis, potassium does not interfere, as it has a maxima at 770 nm. One can also use standard addition and internal standard method during flame photometric analysis. One can estimate 5×10^{-3} ppm of sodium or potassium in the sample.

Potassium

It is not present in high concentration. As a rule ratio of sodium to potassium is 10 : 1 or 20 : 1. The method of analysis is flame photometry at 770 nm. If moderate levels are encountered, one can resort to colorimetry with sodium cobaltnitrate solution.

Chloride

The concentration of chloride varies from sample to sample. It has no adverse effect on health, but it imparts bad taste to drinking water. With this increase in level of chloride in water, its corrosiveness on metals also increases. Usual methods for the determination of chloride are Mohrs and Volhard's methods. In such methods important reactions involved are :

$$NaCl + AgNO_3 \longrightarrow AgCl + NaNO_3$$

(excess of $AgNO_3$ added for back titration)

$$AgNO_3 + NH_4SCN \longrightarrow AgSCN + NH_4NO_3$$

(Equivalance point)

$$3NH_4SCN + Fe^{3+} \longrightarrow \underset{\text{red}}{Fe(SCN)_3} + 3NH_4^+$$

(colour after end point

We add excess of $AgNO_3$ to water containing chloride, and titrate excess of unreacted $AgNO_3$ with KSCN or NH_4SCN. After end point, blood red colour appears due to iron thiocyanate. In Mohr's method, we use K_2CrO_4 as an indicator for indirect titration. The reactions are

$$NaCl + AgNO_3 \longrightarrow AgCl + NaNO_3$$

(till end point)

$$2AgNO_3 + K_2CrO_4 \longrightarrow Ag(CrO_4)_2 + 2KNO_3$$

(end point red

Both methods are excellent for analysis of dissolved chloride.

Sulphate

This is a major anion present in water. This is formed by biological oxidation of sulphur compounds present in water. Luckily it has no adverse effect upon health. If the amount is large, it can be gravimetrically estimated as $BaSO_4$. If the amount is moderate, it can be determined by the nephelometric method. It is also possible to estimate it colorimetrically using sodium rhodiazote as chromogenic ligand. Gravimetry is useful if SO_4^{2-} > 10 ppm. Titration method involves interaction with $BaCl_2$ with thorin as an indicator. The method is best if SO_4^{2-} 5-150 mg/litre. Formaldehyde is added if interfering ions are (like SO_3^{2-}) present.

Carbonates and Bicarbonates

Their presence in water renders it temporarily hard. 'They are formed due to dissolution of CO_2 in water at lower pH (bicarbonates) or at higher pH (carbonates). Their level is 40-400 mg/litre. They form a scale in pipes and boilers. The temporary hardness can be removed by the following process :

Table 7. **Comparison of standards for drinking water by different countries.**

	Parameter	WHO	EEC	USA	Canada	France	Acceptable value
1.	Dissolved solid	-	-	-	-	-	500
2.	Colour	-	5	3-15	15	5	5
3.	Turbidity	-	5	1-5	5	5	5
4.	pH	-	6.5-8.5	-	6.5-8.3	7-8.5	7.0-8.5
5.	Conductivity	-	400	-	-	2000	-
6.	Hardness	-	35	-	18	-	100
7.	Dissolved oxygen	-	5	-	-	1-1.5	-
8.	Sulphate	200-400	5	250	500	250	200
9.	Chloride	-	5	250	250	200-600	200
10.	Free chlorine	-	-	0.2-0.3	-	-	-
11.	Nitrate	45	-	45	10	5100	-
12.	Cyanide	0.05	0.05	1.01-0.2	0.01-0.2	0.05	0.05
13.	Fluoride	1.5	0.7-1.5	1.4-2.4	-	1.5	0.71.0
14.	Ammonia	-	0.05	-	0.5	0.05	-
15.	Boron	-	-	-	5	-	-
16.	Phosphorous	-	0.3	-	0.002	-	-
17.	Calcium	-	100	80-100	200	-	5
18.	Magnesium	-	30	8100	150	-	30
19.	Silver	-	0.01	0.05	0.05	-	-
20.	Arsenic	0.05	0.05	0.05	0.01-0.5	0.5	0.05
21.	Barium	-	0.1	1.0	1.0	-	-
22.	Cadmium	0.01	0.005	0.01	0.01	0.005	0.01
23.	Chromium	0.05	0.05	-	-	-	-
24.	Copper	-	0.05	0.2-1.0	1.0	0.05	0.05
25.	Iron	-	0.3	0.05-0.3	0.3	0.1	0.1
26.	Mercury	0.001	0.001	0.002	0.05	0.01	0.001
27.	Manganese	-	0.05	0.01-0.05	-	0.05	0.05
28.	Nickel	-	0.05	-	-	-	-
29.	Lead	0.1	0.05	0.05	0.05	0.05	0.1
30.	Antimony	-	0.01	-	-	-	-
31.	Selenium	0.01	0.01	0.001	0.01	0.01	0.01
32.	Zinc	1.5-5.0	0.1-0.2	5	2	-	5

$$Ca(HCO_3)_2 \longrightarrow CaCO_3 + H_2O + CO_2 \text{ (by heating)}$$

or $Ca(HCO_3)_2 + Ca(OH)_2 \longrightarrow 2CaCO_3 + 2H_2O$ (by addition of lime)

They are generally estimated by the usual acid-base titration.

Dissolved Solids

They are present in the range 10-20 mg/litre. Certain bad water will have as much as 1000 mg/litre. The excess level in drinking water can cause stomach upset, fever and impart salty taste to water. Total solids are determined by evaporating a known volume of water to dryness and then by weighing its percentage in water.

Alkalinity/Acidity or pH

This is a measure of the capacity of water to neutralise H^+ and is expressed in terms of equivalent amounts of $CaCO_3$. It inhibits corrosion. This is determined by titrating 50 ml of water with 0.02 N NaOH to pH 8.3 or 50 ml of H_2O with 0.02 N H_2SO_4 till a pH value of 4.5. Alkalinity is expressed as phenolphthalein and total alkalinity. During titration, CO_3^{2-} is converted to HCO_3^{2-} at pH 8.3. The end point of pH 8.3 is called phenolphthalein alkalinity. However, if same titration is continued further, HCO_3^{2-} reacts with acid to form H_2CO_3. The reaction is complete at pH 4.5.

The amount of acid required to react is termed as total alkalinity. The alkalinity is expressed in terms of $CaCO_3$. While other term acidity originates due to dissolution of CO_2 from atmosphere, CO_2 is produced in water also due to biological oxidation of organic matter. Mineral acidity is present in many industrial wastes. The salts of trivalent metals (e.g. Fe, Al) hydrolyse to release mineral acidity. The mineral acidity is measured by titration to pH 4.5. When methyl orange is used as an indicator, it is called methyl orange acidity. The titration of sample to phenolphthalein end point of pH 8.3 is called total acidity or phenolphthalein acidity. This is also expressed in terms of $CaCO_3$. As $CaCO_3$ has equivalent weight of 50, N/50 NaOH when used give 1 ml = 1 mg of acidity in $CaCO_3$.

In chemical characterization of water, certain parameters like dissolved oxygen, BOD, residual chlorine, pH, odour and bacteria are determined immediately, while some aspects like hardness, Na, K, Ca, Mg, F, Cl, SO_4, colour, turbidity, specific conductance, alkalinity, dissolved solids can be determined at leisure. Finally, a few like nitrogen ammonia, nitrate-nitrogen, suspended solids or heavy metals need addition of some preservative, before commencing analysis in laboratory. Accepted standard for potable water indicating maximum, minimum and average limit of different constituents for various countries is presented in Table 7. Such characterization is of extreme importance in deciding water treatment process.

Biological Investigation of Water

Apart from direct bacteriological examination, indirect proof for the presence of microorganism and biodegradable organic matter can be found out from the knowledge of dissolved oxygen (DO) and biochemical oxygen demand (BOD).

Dissolved Oxygen of Water

All living organisms are dependent on one another, in order to maintain the metabolic processes that produce energy for growth and reproduction. N_2 and O_2 dissolve poorly in water, but their solubility increases with temperature as per Henry's law. At saturation, dissolved gases in water has 38% oxygen. The solubility is 14.6 mg/litre at 0°C and it rises to 7 mg/litre at 35°C at one atmosphere pressure. Further, the rate of dissolution of O_2 in polluted water is much less than in pure water. Thus DO determines whether biological changes are brought out by aerobic or anaerobic organisms. Former uses free oxygen for oxidation to produce innocuous end products. DO is one single test to indicate how aquatic life is supported; as all aerobic process depend upon DO. Samples of water for DO analysis are collected from fields. The dissolved oxygen from water is determined by Winkler's method. The important reactions are :

$$MnSO_4 + 2KOH \longrightarrow Mn(OH)_2 + K_2SO_4$$
$$2Mn\ (OH)_2 + O_2 \longrightarrow 2MnO(OH)_2$$
$$MnO\ (OH)_2 + 2H_2SO_4 \longrightarrow Mn(SO_4)_2 + 3H_2O$$
$$Mn(SO_4)_2 + 2KI \longrightarrow MnSO_4 + K_2SO_4 + I_2$$
$$2Na_2S_2O_3 + I_2 \longrightarrow 2NaI + Na_2S_4O_6$$

Thus we use manganese hydroxide, which is oxidised to manganic hydroxide by dissolved oxygen. This manganic hydroxide is in turn converted to manganic sulphate which is reacted with KI to liberate free iodine, which in turn titrated against standard solution of thiosulphate. The amount of iodine consumed represents the dissolved oxygen in water used in oxidation. The oxidising agents in water will produce positive error, while the reducing agents produce negative error. Thus NO_2^-, Fe^{3+} can oxidise I_2° to and give high results; also reducing agents like Fe^{2+}, SO or S^{2-} give negative results, as they reduce I_2 to I^-. The Winklers reaction can be also given in ionic form as :

$$Mn^{2+} + 2OH^- \longrightarrow Mn(OH)^2 \text{ white ppt}$$
$$Mn^{2+} + 2(OH)_2 + \tfrac{1}{2}\ O_2 \longrightarrow MnO_2 + H_2O$$
(fixation of oxygen)
$$Mn\ (OH)_2 + \tfrac{1}{2}O_2 \longrightarrow MnO_2 + H_2O$$
$$MnO_2 + 2I^- + 4H^+ \longrightarrow Mn^{2+} + I_2 + 2H_2O$$
$$2Na_2S_2O_3 + I_2 \longrightarrow 2NaI + Na_2S_4O_6$$

In case excess of nitrite is present in water, we have to make modifications to Winkler's method called Azide modification. This involves addition of azide to destroy nitrite as :

$$2\,NO_2^- + 2I^- + 4H^+ \longrightarrow I_2 + N_2O_2 + 2H_2O$$
(Nitrite-wrong result)
$$N_2O_2 + \tfrac{1}{2}O_2 + H_2O \longrightarrow 2\,NO_2^- + 2H^+$$
(Excess iodine is consumed)

Such interference is eliminated by addition of NaN_3 as :

$$NaN_3 + H^+ \longrightarrow HN_3 + Na$$
$$HN_3 + NO_2^- + H^+ \longrightarrow N_2(g) + N_2O(g) + H_2O$$

Thus nitrite interference is eliminated. The Rideal-Stewart modification eliminates many interferences caused by reducing agents. $KMNO_4$ is used for pretreatment. Excess $KMnO_4$ is removed with $K_2C_2O_4$ e.g.

$$5\,NO_2^- + 2MnO_4^- + 6H^+ \longrightarrow 5\,NO_3^- + 2Mn^{2+} + 3H_2O$$
$$5Fe^{2+} + MnO + 8H^+ \longrightarrow 5Fe^{+3} + Mn^{2+} + 4H_2O$$
then $$5(COO^-)_2 + 2Mno_4^- + 16H^+ \longrightarrow 10CO_2 + 2Mn^{2+} + 8H_2O$$

After this treatment, regular Winkler's reaction is carried out. Apart from Winkler's method, modern trend is to use DO meter or ion analyzer with ion specific electrode for dissolved oxygen.

Biochemical Oxygen Demand

BOD is defined as the amount of oxygen required by bacteria while stabilizing decomposable organic matter under aerobic conditions. In other words, BOD represents quantity of dissolved oxygen in mg/litre required during oxidation of decomposable or biodegradable organic matter by aerobic biochemical action. The decomposable organic matter at a time serves as the food for bacteria and energy is obtained due to such oxidation. Thus BOD gives an idea about the extent of pollution. It serves as a test to evaluate the purifying capacity of receiving bodies of water. BOD test is a bioassay test devised to measure oxygen consumed by living organisms, while using organic matter present as waste in water. While evaluating this, samples are protected from sunlight, excessive agitation or shaking, and kept at a fixed temperature in an incubator. This also favours uniform bacterial growth. To complete such growth 20 hours are required. BOD test is a wet oxidation procedure. Usually a 5-day BOD test gives a reliable information on quality of water. Two 300 ml bottles are filled with water and dissolved oxygen of first bottle is determined immediately by Winkler's method. The second bottle is incubated under 20°C in the dark for 5 days (sometimes 3 days; we need to keep it for 20 days in order to get a complete

Table 8. **BOD of various samples of water.**

Type of sample	BOD (mg/litre)	Remarks
H_2O	1.0-3.0	Reasonable
River	5.0-20.0	Tolerable
Sewage	50.0-100	Very bad
Industrial waste	100-10,000	Extremely poor

picture) and dissolved oxygen is once more measured. The reduction in oxygen content is due to demand exerted by the microbiological population and is a measure of oxidisable organic matter in sample value of 5-day BOD. The DO varies from 9.2 to 1.0 mg/litre showing 8.2 mg/litre as BOD value. Typical BOD values of different samples of water is listed in Table 9.

Bacterological Examination of Water

The disease producing organism, i.e. pathogens should be removed from water. Those producing infectious disease are bacteria or viruses. The common indicator organism are from coliform group present due to sewage contamination. By special test, their number is determined. Faecal coliforms and faecal streptococcii are also isolated. They are generally determined by various methods. Their population is usually expressed in terms of MPN, i.e. most probable number. For example, for untreated water, coliform density should not exceed 5000/ml. Table 4 has already listed other kinds of bacteria which are likely to be present in water under special circumstances. The MPN or plate count throws light on the quality of water.

Biological Water Quality Assessment, Importance, Objectives and Scope

Environmental pollutants from anthropogenic sources affect the aquatic ecosystem in a synergistic manner, which cannot be detected comprehensively by determination of selected physico-chemical parameters alone. Whereas, biological system can integrate all environmental variables over a long period of time in terms of effects, which can be easily measured and quantified. The objective of biological water quality assessment is as follows :

- Physico-chemical and biological water quality assessment of surface water bodies in problem areas.

Table 9. **Biological Water Quality Criteria (BWQC).**

	Taxonomic groups	Range of saprobic score (BMWP)	Range of diversity score	Water quality characteristics	Water quality class	Indicator colour
1.	Ephemeroptera, Plecoptera, Trichoptera, Hemiptera, Diptera	7 and more	0.2 - 1	Clean	A	Blue
2.	Ephemeroptera, Plecoptera, Trichoptera, Hemiptera, Odonata, Diptera	6-7	0.5 - 1	Slight Pollution	B	Light blue
3.	Ephemeroptera, Plecoptera, Trichoptera, Hemiptera, Odonata, Crustacea, Mollusca, Polychaeta, Coleoptera, Diptera, Hirudinea, Oligochaeta	3-6	0.3 - 0.9	Moderate Pollution	C	Green
4.	Mollusca, Hemiptera, Coleoptera, Diptera, Oligochaeta	2-5	0.4 & less	Heavy pollution	D	Orange
5.	Diptera, Oligochaeta or no macro-invertebrates	0-2	0 - 0.2	Severe pollution	E	Red

- To assess the improvement in water quality over the years as a result of actions taken for pollution control in problem areas.
- Bio-monitoring of water bodies associated with problem areas and assessment of water quality through Primary Water Quality Criteria (PWQC) and Biological Water Quality Criteria (BWQC) in terms of designated best-use.

Central Pollution Control Board (CPCB) during the development and validation of bio-monitoring methodology, established the fact that among all the biological components of the aquatic ecosystem, benthic macro-invertebrates are best suitable for evaluation of water quality (Fig.1). Most of these macro-invertebrates particularly insect larvae, which are aquatic, share their biological life in fresh water, while their adults fly over for miles together in search of suitable fresh water environment for reproduction, breeding and laying eggs in suitable habitats and establish biological communities.

Two methods for biological water quality evaluation has been adopted :

- Sequential comparison for diversity score
- BMWP (Biological-Monitoring Working Party) for saprobic score.

Biological Water Quality Criteria (BWQC)

The biological water quality evaluation of water bodies has been undertaken using BWQC developed by Central Pollution Control Board (Table 10). The combination of range of saprobic score with diversity score indicates the ecological health and environmental conditions. The water quality classes obtained from biological water quality evaluation, may be interpreted in terms of designated best uses. The ranges prescribed for saprobic score and diversity score are based as guideline. Benthic macro invertebrates are shown in Fig 1.

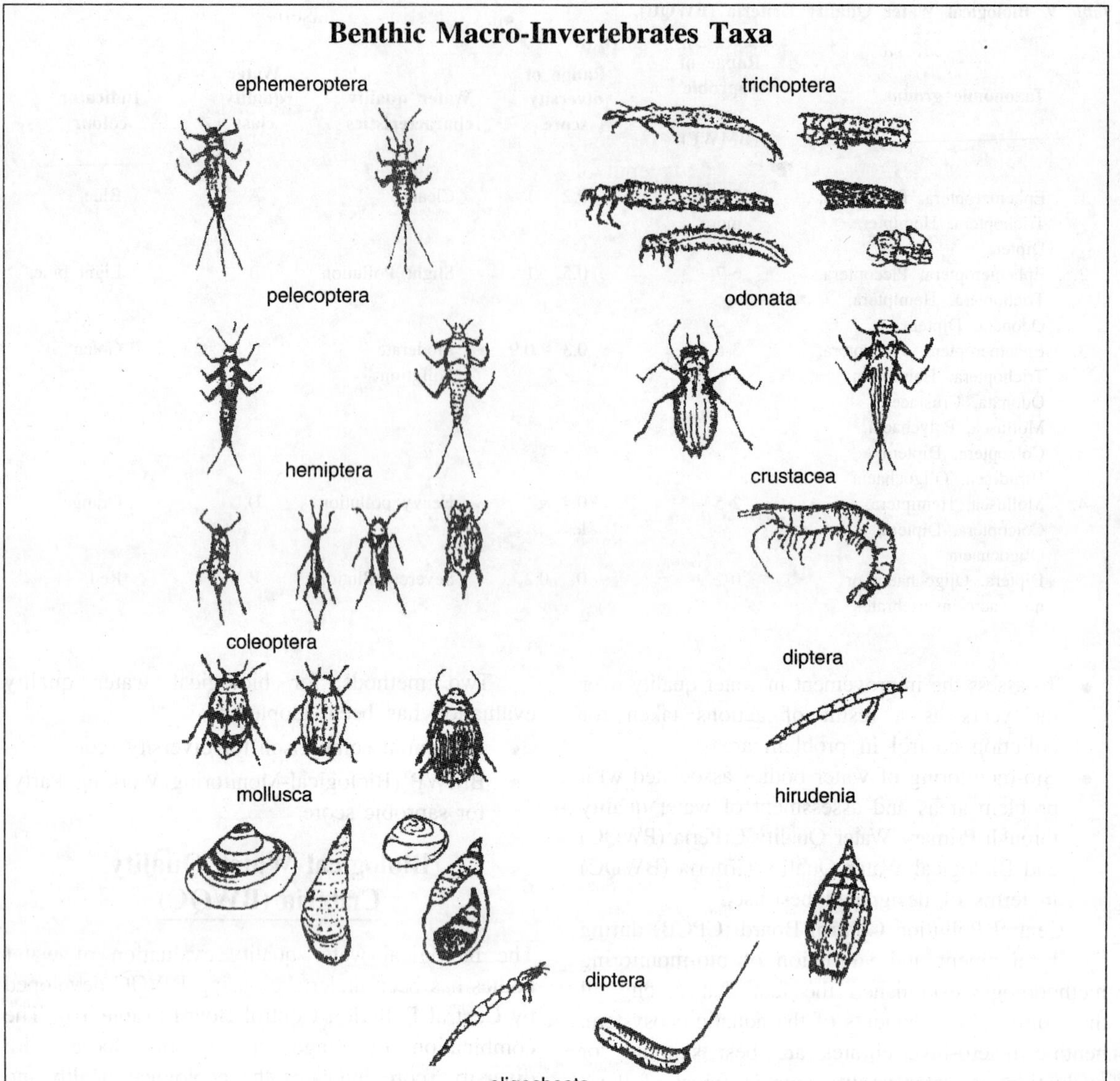

Fig. 1.

Steps Involved for Bio-Monitoring of Surface Water Bodies in Problem Areas in the Country

- Collection of detailed map of area, identifying the surface water bodies existing and marking all physical features including the location of point and non-point sources of pollution to the water bodies.
- Collection of preliminary information on ecological conditions and physico-chemical characteristics of water quality on MINARS sampling points if any located water bodies.
- Selection of the location for establishment of bio-monitoring stations based on ecological data derived from the survey.
- Identifying the reference station on water bodies for bio-monitoring.

- Selection of proper time at particular location for biological sampling, determining the flow variations in Rivers/Canals and Reservoirs/Lakes etc. for, water quality evaluation.
- Identifying the sampling devices to be used for various types of substratum and depth of water bodies.
- Collection of baseline information with regard to inventorisation of polluting sources, agricultural activities, human influences, confluences of water bodies and discharges on upstream and downstream of location.

Important Questions

1. Describe different methods used for the physical examination of water.
2. Discuss different methods used for chemical characterization of water.
3. Give an account of different methods used for the biological examination of water.
4. Write briefly on the following:
   (i) Turbidity, (ii) Biochemical oxygen demand, (iii) Biological water quality criteria (BWQR).

22 Soil Pollution and Pesticide Analysis

Agricultural activity directly influences the chemistry of environment in several ways; like disposal of animal, plant or food processing waste; the contamination from applications of pesticides and fertilizers; depletion of natural soil nutrients and finally salt and mineral accumulation from irrigation. Thus agricultural waste is more serious than the solid or liquid waste generated due to industrial activity. For instance, the waste from food and milk industry may pose a serious problem in future in India. The excessive growth of fruits like oranges (in Vidharbha) and apples (in Kashmir) may pose problem of disposal of solid waste. The food processing industry produces more than 60% of waste from fruit peels. No doubt it can be used for animal feed and as manure in soil. Cotton waste is useless as it contains a good amount of pesticide residue, which in the long run is harmful to animal or cattle. The mechanized meat processing industry will produce a liquid waste due to residual blood, flesh and bones which will be difficult to dispose. It will also add to the nuisance of flies and vultures.

There is substantial evidence to prove that fertilizers contribute in water pollution. However, it leads to excess release of nitrogen and phosphorus in soil. Nitrate is the worst enemy of high-yield farming. Nitrate is reduced to nitrite in the stomach and causes a disease called methemoglobinemia (blue babies). Phosphate is also a wide spread pollutant from agriculture. It travels much slower in the soil as compared to nitrate, but it promotes eutrophication of water with algal bloom. Nitrogen and phosphorus pollution illustrate far reaching chemical consequences of man's agricultural activity.

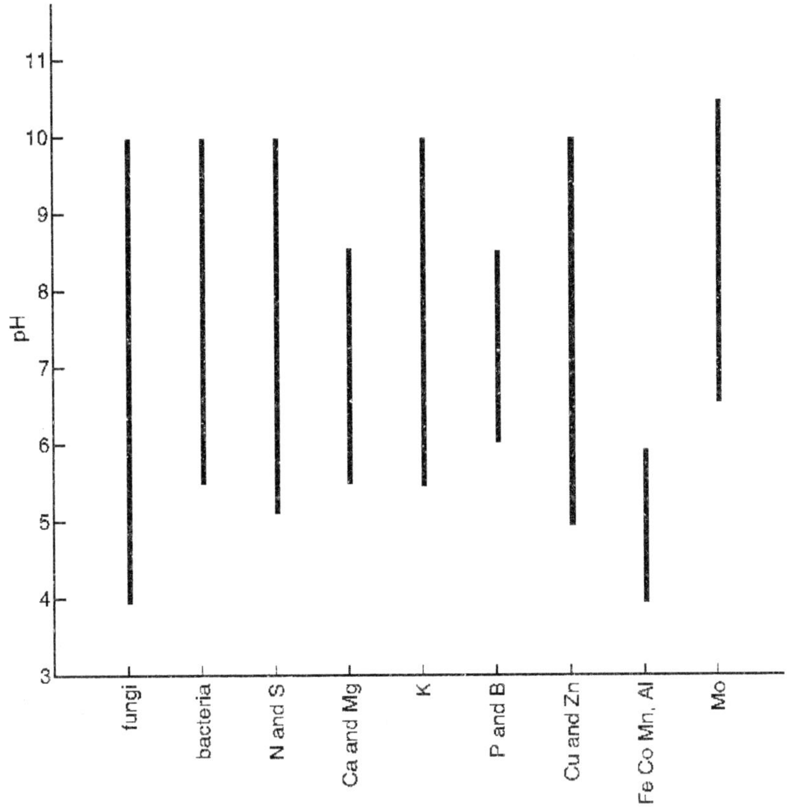

Fig. 1. Soil micronutrients as function of pH.

Table 1. **Micronutrients present in soil of sugarcane crop**

Iron total (%)	Copper total μg/gm	Zinc total (%)	Manganese total μg/gm	Molybdenum total μg/gm	Boron total (%)
7.95	380	0.90	1810	10.08	0.001
6.02	203	1.10	1187	9.08	0.069
3.51	161	0.51	653	15.10	0.032
6.90	283	0.65	450	4.80	0.071
8.10	150	0.70	750	12.10	0.011
9.20	190	0.90	820	15.10	0.012

Agricultural activity removes these materials from lithosphere and drops them into the sea, which is a permanent sink for chemicals. Thus agricultural pollution represents a permanent and irreversible depletion of the resources of the lithosphere.

Role of Micronutrients in Soil

Mineral contents of the soil get depleted due to rain, seepage, growth of plants and crops. The soil deficient in mineral contents is rendered unsuitable for further cultivation. As a matter of fact nitrogen, phosphorus and potassium are essential for growth of plants, but they are replenished through organonitrogen and organophosphorus compounds, which are dumped in soil as the sink by plant and vegetable kingdom. However, more important than these are elements like iron, manganese, zinc, copper, molybdenum, and boron, which are most essential for the healthy upkeep of soil. It is not true that each and every plant or crop needs all of these metals, but they thrive better on at least one of them. The plants have a tendency to extract one or more of these elements. Content of such an element is termed as 'available element' contents, while whatever is available in total soil is termed as the 'total amount of a particular element' in the soil. Figure 1 depicts the relationship of nutrient availability and pH of the soil.

It will be noted from this figure that there is good availability in soil of molybdenum, copper, zinc and to a lesser extent iron, mangnese, cobalt and alumnium. No doubt calcium, potassium, magnesium, nitrogen, sulphur and phosphorus are otherwise present in substantial concentrations in the soil. The figure also shows beyond pH 10 in alkaline media, at which value the micronutrients are not available to plants. Tables 1 to 3 indicate the role of micronutrients in proper growth of crop.

The results in Table 1 indicate high levels of manganese in soil, perhaps was conducive for growth of sugarcane (1810 μg/gm of soil). Table 2 indicates high levels of manganese as well as copper, indicating thereby that they were the best micronutrients for growth of paddy. Table 3 represents micronutrients contents of *jowar* field. The study showed high level of manganese, copper, zinc and iron, showing zinc was conducive for growth of *jowar.*

Analysis of Micronutrients in Soil

Tables 4 and 5 indicate available trace elements and total trace elements in soil. Before considering their analysis, it is worthwhile to consider the procedure for sampling of soil. Usually surface samples are collected from 10 cm horizon. The samples are ground to fine powder (100 mesh). In order to determine total element content, they are digested in a mixture of nitric-perchloric acid. The resulting residue is evaporated to dryness and then extracted with water and made to a known volume before analysis by AAS. For the analysis of available trace elements from soil, the samples are extracted with suitable buffers for various elements as follows :

(1) Iron with ammonium acetate buffer (pH 4.8)
(2) Zinc with ammonium acetate buffer, (pH 6.5)
(3) Manganese with ammonium acetate buffer (pH 7.0)
(4) Molybdenum with ammonium oxalate buffer (pH 3.3)
(5) Copper with ammonium citrate buffer (pH 8.5)

***Table** 2.* **Micronutrients present in the soil of *paddy* crop.**

Iron total (%)	Copper total μg/gm	Zinc total (%)	Manganese total μg/gm	Molybdenum total μg/gm	Boron total (%)
7.99	200	1.00	645	7.01	0.084
9.6	170	2.00	1120	5.00	0.062
9.6	140	0.90	1230	10.00	0.010
9.73	295	1.20	606	4.00	0.007
11.50	290	1.21	1050	18.21	0.095
12.01	310	0.980	950	19.00	0.090

***Table** 3.* **Micronutrients present in the soil of *Jowar* crop.**

Iron total (%)	Copper total μg/gm	Zinc total (%)	Manganese total μg/gm	Molybdenum total μg/gm	Boron total (%)
6.81	160	1.20	1:291	15.85	0.090
7.90	170	1.35	1083	16.10	0.091
8.01	150	0.90	1045	12.00	0.061
9.89	198	0.99	833	7.85	0.09
11.01	140	0.69	940	12.01	0.095
11.90	291	0.92	940	8.50	0.025

Table 4. **Available trace element contents of soil samples.**

Soil sample No	Concentration of trace elements in soil samples in μg				
	Mn	Fe	Cu	Zn	Mo
Reference	19.80	20.50	4.40	5.40	1.10
1	32.70	44.60	2.00	6.70	0.08
2	67.40	42.50	11.00	6.90	0.20
3	72.00	58.30	10.80	6.30	0.10
4	102.30	28.50	8.00	6.40	0.20
5	115.30	19.20	6.00	6.20	0.20
6	117.60	35.10	11.50	6.80	1.50
7	120.00	28.20	7.00	6.30	0.10

Table 5. **Total trace element contents of soil samples.**

Soil sample No	Concentration of trace elements in soil samples in μg				
	Mn	Fe	Cu	Zn	Mo
Reference	1260.00	28,400.00	102.00	70.00	16.00
1	1512.00	20,700.00	110.00	140.00	5.50
2	1718.00	20,150.00	110.00	98.00	13.80
3	2074.00	21,750.00	135.00	81.00	19.20
4	2010.00	19.900.00	130.00	50.00	7.30
5	2194.00	20,650.00	195.00	98.00	14.20
6	2521.00	20,700.00	140.00	92.00	9.20
7	2590.00	20,500.00	124.00	102.00	11.70

(6) Boron with sodium carbonate buffer (pH 6.0)

All these elements are extractable in appropriate buffers. The organic contents from extract can be destroyed by dry ashing with nitric perchloric acid treatment. The residue is laxivated with water and the available contents of element is analyzed by AAS. The difference in the available and total contents gives an idea of extractability by plants.

Trace Elements Analysis in Soil

Sometimes it is necessary to determine trace elements from soil. A Van Vee Grab sampler is used to collect samples of sediments. They are dried at 100°C. The dried samples are dissolved in nitric perchloric acid mixture to destroy organic matter. The residue is dissolved in dilute hydrochloric acid and trace elements are analyzed as usual. Thus tables 4 and 5 give information on available trace elements and total trace elements in soil.

The wavelength for analysis, detection limit and type of flame used in AAS for various micronutrients is listed in Table 6.

As regards analysis of boron, it was usually carried out by spectrophotometric technique using caramine red as the chromogenic ligand. The only limitation in such analysis was the need to avoid glassware. It is essential to use only polythene, teflon or platinum ware. This is because glass contains a substantial amount of boron and is bound to give erroneus results during determination of boron.

Boron is one of the micronutrients amongst nonmetals. It is conducive for the growth of citrus fruits, e.g. oranges, lemon grow in size, if the soil sample is fed with reasonable concentration of boron compounds like say boric acid. The amount of boron is 0.001-0.095% in western Maharashtra. On the contrary, soils in Vidharbha which is the courtyard or orchard of oranges, shows the level of boron in the range 0.095-0.10%.

Pesticides and Pollution

Similar to agricultural pollution, pesticides are the worst enemy of man on this planet. It not only contaminates lithosphere, but also pollutes the

Table 6. **AAS determination of micronutrients.**

	Element	AAS wavelength (nm) λmax	Detection (μg/ml)	Types of flame	Recommended spectrophotometric method
1	B	249.8	2.0	Nitrous-actylene	Caramine red
2	Cd	228.8	0.002	Air acetylene	Dithizone
3	Cu	324.8	0.004	Air acetylene	Cupferron
4	Fe	248.3	0.03	Air acetylene	1-10 phenanthroline
5	Mn	279.5	0.003	Air acetylene	Permanganate
6	Mo	313.3	0.03	Nitrous-acetylene	Thiocyanate
7	Zn	213.9	0.003	Air acetylene	Dithizone
8	Pb	283.6	0.02	Air acetylene	Dithizone

atmosphere. Pesticides include herbicides, insecticides, fungicides or rodenticides. These are persistent pollutants obtained during interaction of lithosphere and biosphere. They are cumulative poisons in the body, they usually accumulate in food chain and are hence hazardous. Few of them undergo metabolic formation and biodegradation. The pesticides residue so formed by degradation is more dangerous than the parent compound. Usually they break down in the environment, involving either of the following process, namely oxidation, dehydrogenation, reduction, conjugation like metal complex formation; hydrolytic reaction like cleavage, exchange reaction and sometimes isomerisation. The reaction in body involves interaction with iron porphyrins. Several residues are carcinogenic. The metabolic products are also dangerous. Some arsenic pesticides have made soil permanently infertile. They may sometimes increase instead of decreasing pest population, due to effect of immunization. A pesticide like DDT changes fertility of mammals. Pesticides thus pose an alarming problem for mankind. DDT kills mosquitoes which spread malaria. Inspite of this its use in developed countries has gone down due to its harmful effects. However, the production has remained same due to its consumption by developing countries. Its indiscriminate application poses a serious problem.

Highest production was in 1960-1965, with somewhat less production in 1975. Amongst pesticides, highest production is of insecticides, followed by herbicides and finally fungicides. Lithosphere and atmosphere act as sink for these pesticides, as chlorinated hydrocarbons are transported easily in air. DDT, the worst among pesticides is lost to the soil by volatilisation, removal by harvesting of organic compounds, water run-off, and chemical degradation. It is removed to atmosphere by rainfall, settling of aerosols, diffusion and chemical photodegradation.

Pesticide Analysis

Among agro-chemicals, pesticides comprise of one of the biggest and vitally important groups of compounds. Analytical methods are widely used for pesticide analysis involving study of pesticide residue, degradation products and new formulations. Largely chromatographic methods, polarographic technique and spectroscopic methods of analysis are used for their characterization. The important chromatographic techniques include thin-layer chromatography (TLC), gas-liquid chromatography (GLC), and high performance liquid chromatography (HPLC), while the spectral methods of analysis cover UV-IR spectrophotometry, NMR spectrometry and GC-MS technique. Since persistent use of pesticide (e.g. chloroorgano compounds), the pesticide residue and degradation products accumulate in biota, thus needing analysis. GLC detects nanogram and picogram of pesticides. NMR helps to identify metabolites and degradation products of pesticides. They are extracted by extraction or adsorption on column. TLC is a cheap method and is useful for qualitative as well as quantitative analysis. For example, carbamates are best analyzed by TLC in preference to GLC. In GLC, organochlorine pesticides are detected by electron capture detector. While organophosphorus pesticides are best analyzed with FID in GLC, pesticides containing oxidisable or reducible groups are determined by polarography. Pesticide residues are best analyzed by IR spectroscopy. NMR technique has low sensitivity, but is useful for elucidation of the structure of a pesticide. Isomers can be best analyzed by NMR methods. Mass spectrometry is useful for identification of new pesticides. A brief review shall be taken for analysis of typical pesticides by chromatography, spectroscopy and polarography.

Chromatographic Characterisation of Pesticides

The organochlorine pesticides are best detected by TLC, e.g. parathion or malathion with $AgNO_3$-bromophenol blue spraying reagent in TLC. Presence of 100-200 μg of pesticide can be easily detected. The carbamate pesticides like zectran, carbaryl (sevin) and organophosphorus pesticides like phorate, malathion, are best characterized by TLC technique. Gas chromatography is useful for the analysis of volatile pesticides. The residue analysis of chlorinated pesticide is carried out by GLC. Acetonitrile is used as the solvent. Hexane is also used as the solvent for organophosphorus pesticides. From, drinking water, chlorinated pesticide can be absorbed on a column packed with resin Amberlite XAD-2 and eluted and analyzed by GLC, e.g. lindane, DDT, DDE, aldrin can be thus analyzed. Polychlorinated biphenyl (PCB) is characterized by GC-MS with glass capillary column. The HPLC is a new invention for the analysis, it is mainly useful for analysis of new formulations. Here photometric, fluorometric detectors are generally used. So far HPLC is not routinely used for pesticide analysis.

Polarographic Analysis of Pesticides

Chlorine containing pesticides e.g. hexachloro cyclohexane, endrin, aldrin and dieldrin are analyzed on DME in LiCl in isopropyl alcohol. The half-wave potential ($E_{1/2}$) of nitrogroup containing pesticides is available in literature. The supporting electrolytes used are nitric acid (0.1 M), acetate buffer, sodium hydroxide (0.1 N) and ammonia-ammonium chloride buffer. Half wave potential (v), varies from - 0.32 V to -0.72 V for parathion, e.g. - 0.26 V in HNO_3, - 0.62V in acetate buffer and + 0.74 V in ammonia buffer. Voltametric methods can also be used. The sensitivity of the method is however not satisfactory. The chief advantage of polarography in the pesticide analysis is the advantage of identifying a particular pesticide from the knowledge of half--wave potential in a sample of industrial effluent. This is followed by a quantitative chemical analysis.

Spectroscopic Analysis of Pesticides

UV-spectrophotometry is used for formulation analysis. The standardised adsorbents are required for clean up before analysis. The direct reflectance spectrometry is very useful, e.g. analysis of triazine herbicides. IR methods are used for analysis of several isomers of heptachlor or BHC. IR is less sensitive than UV and not suitable for residue analysis; the only advantage is that IR does not need rigorous clean up and offers a choice of peaks. NMR methods are useful for identification and characterization of pesticide compounds. Proton NMR is best for such purposes; DDT and DDE are best analyzed by NMR. Mass spectrometry, is the most reliable and definite tool for the analysis of pesticides belonging to the class of carbamates, chlorinated hydrocarbons and metabolites. Chlorophenols can be studied by mass spectrometry. The metabolites of 2, 4 D were studied by mass spectrometry. GC-MS gives more reliable information. Lindane 2, 4, 7, 8, T and PCB were best analyzed by GCMS. The development of several ionization techniques will lead to further enhancement of sensitivity and reliability in elucidation of the structures of pesticides. In fact mass spectrometry is not in true sense a spectral method of analysis. Only due to similarity of spectrum lines with mass resolution line, it was termed as spectrometry. The hyphenated GC-MS or GC-HPLC is likely to indicate spectacular results in future.

Important Questions

1. How can different micro nutrients of the soil be analyzed ?
2. How can trace elements present in the soil be analyzed ? Discuss the method with a suitable example ?
3. How can pesticides present in the soil be analyzed ? Discuss a gas liquid chromatogmphic method in details ?

23 Noise Pollution Measurement

What is Noise ?

Sound is a form of energy and requires a medium for propagation. Sound can propagate through solids and liquids but not through vacuum. All vibrations are capable of producing sound. In loudspeaker, the diaphragm moves forward and backward to generate sound. On account of compression, gas molecules move back and forth progressively. These oscillating molecules with definite frequency are responsible for creation of sound pressure. If the pressure varies regularly and repeatedly, then time between successive high and low pressure is called the period. The frequency is the reciprocal of period. Sound is defined as the energy in the frequency range 0.02-20 kHz or 20-20,000 Hz Hertz (Hz) is the unit of frequency representing cycles per second; which is the typical range of hearing of human ears. The lowest frequency which is audiable is 20 Hz, while the highest audible frequency is 12,000 Hz. This region is called frequency band, which defines a range of frequencies between the specified or implied limits.

Intensity of sound can be determined with precision and is related to the amount of sound energy received per second from the source of sound. The intensity level is ten times the logarithm of intensity ratio. For instance if I_L represents intensity level, then $I_L = 10. \log (I/I_0)$, if I = measured intensity, I_0 = reference intensity. The reference intensity has magnitude of $1 \times 10^{12} W_m^{-2}$. Since $I_L = (P)^2 = 2 \times 10. \log (P/P_o) = 20 \log (P/P_o)$ = SPL. Thus there are practical difficulties in measuring the intensity, however, the variation in pressure can be

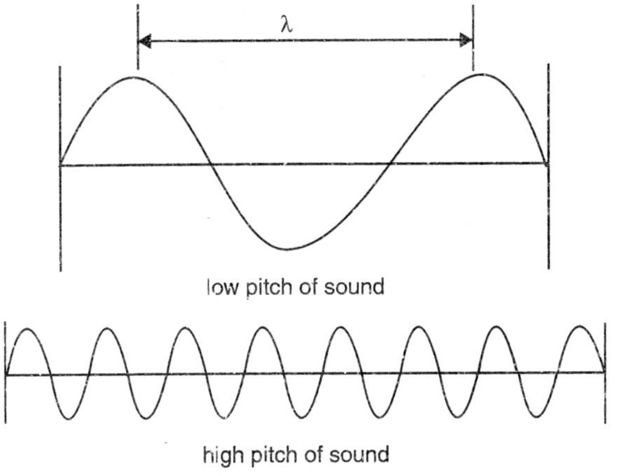

Fig. 1. Pitch of sound.

easily measured. As intensity is directly proportional to the square of the pressure, the sound pressure level (SPL) in dB is defined by SPL = 20 log (P/P_o) dB, while P_o (reference pressure) = 2×10^{-5} N_m^{-2} where P is the measured pressure in N_m^{-2}. This value is used since it is the nearest whole number corresponding to the reference intensity.

The sounds vary in pitch, which is defined as the relative highness or lowness of a sound. Pitch is determined by the frequency of sound wave-the rapidity with which it vibrates. A high pitched sound with its fast vibration is more penetrating than one with low pitch (Fig. 1). The intensity of sound is measured in decibels (dB). This scale was devised to measure the smallest difference in sound which is detectable by the human ears. Its gradations move up not in simple arithmetic progression, but in multiple progression based on logarithmic scale, i.e. each increase of one dB represents a large change of intensity of sound.

Noise Measurement

There are several devises to measure sound or noise. There are sound level metres (SLM), octave band analyzer, magnetic tape recorder, pen recorder, statistical analyzer, noise average meter and noise analyzers. The sound level metre (SLM) is used for evaluation of sound pressure on linear or weighted scale. The dynamic characteristics of metres is possibly of slow, fast and impulsive sound measurements. There are two grades of sound level metre, one with limited accuracy (IEC-123), while the other with (IEC-179) high degree of accuracy. Former are cheaper and robust while the latter are expensive but accurate.

Main objective of sound measurement is to reduce its level, so as to enjoy it as music; carry out scientific analysis to reduce it's annoying effect, to ascertain its capability to cause hearing damage and to serve as powerful diagnostic tool to reduce it. Sound travels at the rate of 750 miles per hour or 3 kilometer per second or 5 seconds per mile. Apart from dB, we can measure sound in pascal units, e.g. weakest sound is 20μPa, i.e. approximately 0 dB (Fig. 2). Pascal scale is not practical, e.g. 35 dB = 960μPa or 70 dB = 70,000 μPa, etc. Each time we multiply sound pressure in Pa by 10, we add 20 dB to the resulting level. For example, 2000μPa (2000 micropascal × 10) + 20 = 40 dB. As shown in Fig. 3 sound is measured on 'A' scale. If a sound is *of* short duration, i.e. less than one second, it is termed an impulsive sound (Fig. 4).

The octave band analyzer is used in conjunction with SLM to determine the average sound pressure of the standard octave bands. It gives an idea about frequency contents of noise to decide abatement technique. The magnetic tape recorder is used to record actual noise for storage and latter evaluation. If run at high speed, it gives a real picture of sound frequency. The pen recorder can be fed directly to SLM. A continuous record of SLM against time is used for storage. The statistical analyzer is mechanical or electronic. It is used in conjunction with a pen recorder. The noise average

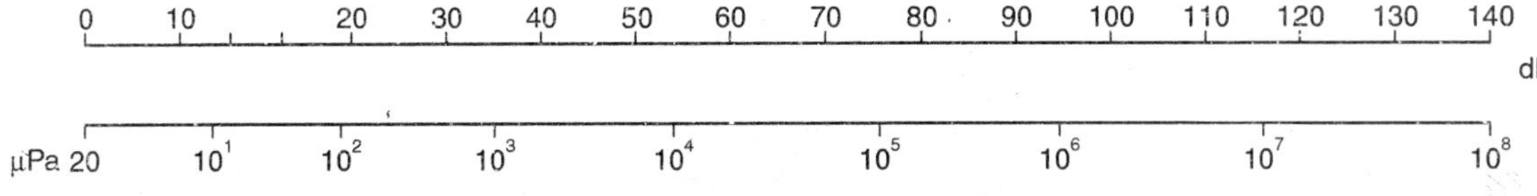

Fig. 2. Comparison of decibal and Pascal scale.

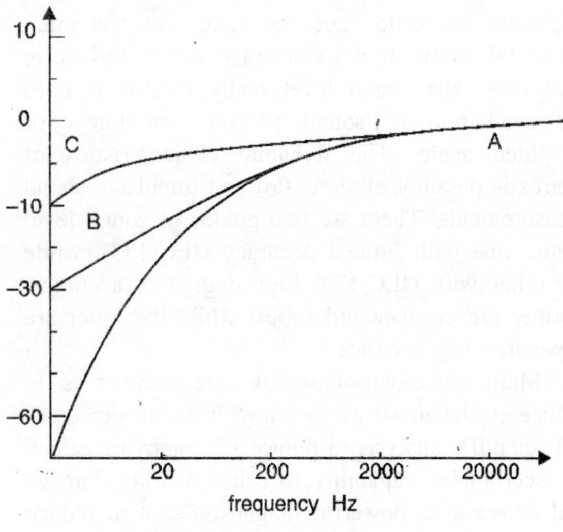

Fig. 3. Measurement of sound pressure.

metre is fed directly or form magnetic tape recording to give leg. Leg is equivalent to continuous sound pressure level or amounts of energy, with certain limitations, capable of causing the same effect. Finally noise analyzer is fed directly to SLM. The company called Bruel and Kajaer in Denmark manufactures excellent sound metres. Unfortunately, so far no attempt has been made to fabricate them in India. The sound signal is converted into electrical signal by high quality microphone. The signal is usually amplified. Such a signal drives the metre to measure sound in dB scale. The microphone has to be Om in directional sensitivity, i.e. sensitive in all directions.

Noise Mapping

In order to assess the impact of noise on human health. It is necessary to undertake a survey of noise levels in different parts of a locality. To do this sound maps are prepared. These are also called as topographs. The areas which are sound prone, like dwellings around industrial establishments, airports, railway stations, cinema houses or commercial plaza are selected for sound mapping.

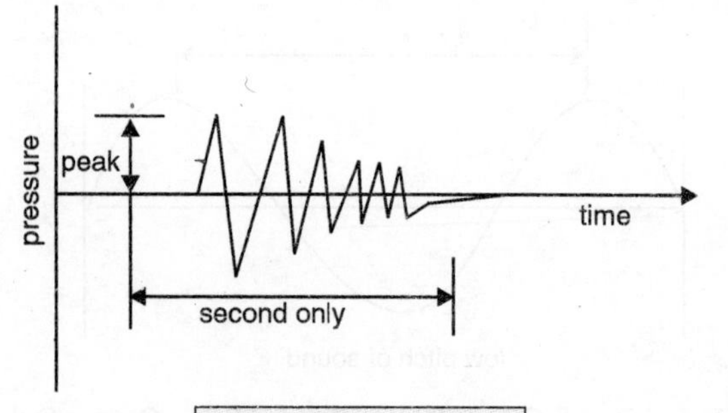

Fig. 4. Impulsive sound.

Noise-topograph is usually obtained by connecting lines drawn between the points of equal sound levels to exhibit sound distribution patterns. A topograph indicates zones of noise danger and is a first step to mitigate or abate sound nuisance. A topograph with red zone would indicate need of putting waxed ear plugs or ear muffets to prevent damage to hearing.

Anechoic Chamber

Further it is possible to contain such noise danger zone by constructing, anechoic chambers or sound absorbing rooms. After measuring sound in field free of reflecting objects, an anechoic chamber is constructed. The roof, sidewalls, ceiling, floor are covered by highly absorbing materials to eliminate reflection. The sound reflecting chambers are called reverberation chambers. These are opposite of anechoic chambers.

Environment and Noise Measurements

Wind blowing around noise metre would give wrong results hence a ball of porous polyurethane sponge should be used over a microphone. Humidity up to 90% does not affect sound level metre (SLM), but rain and snow does. SLM operates in -10° to 50°C range. A variation in pressure of about ± 10% will not affect measurement. Vibration should be avoided during sound measurements. Foam rubber pads dampen vibrations effectively. The magnetic field influences sound level measurements.

Important Questions

1. Define noise. What are the units to measure the noise?
2. Describe the method used to measure the noise with the help of a sound level meter (SLM).

Applications of Computer in Modern Biology

24

Biology by and large has been an observational rather than a deductive science. Until recently biological observations have been made with various degrees of precision depending upon the type of method or instrument used. However, use of computer in biological methods has made these observations more quantitative and precise. Several computer aided instruments viz : spectrophotometers, chromatographic systems, microscopes, & ELISA readers etc. are commercially available now. The biology has now been converted into deductive science. The quality and quantity of data thus generated encourage a biologist to broadly aim at the following goals :

- To understand the integrative aspect of the biology of organisms viewed as coherent complex systems.
- To understand the three dimensional structure of proteins, nucleic acids and protein nucleic acid complexes.
- To deduce events in evolutionary history.
- To support applications to medicine, agriculture and other scientific fields.

Computer science is a flourishing field with the goal of making most effective use of information technology. It is used to solve a number of biological problems now. A few of these applications are discussed below.

(1) Analysis of algorithms — An algorithm is a complete and precise specification of a method for solving a problem.

(2) Data structure and information retrieval — This system makes efficient responses to queries.

On – "Omics" — A Glossary

Bioinformatics :

The science of managing and analyzing biological data using advanced computing techniques, especially important in analyzing genomic research data.

Data mining :

The extraction of relevant parameters stored in a database.

Genomics :

The study of genes and their function. Genomics differs from genetics in that genetics looks at single genes, one at a time, whereas genomics looks at all gene, over time. to determine how they interact and influence biological pathways, neworks, and physiology.

Metabolimics :

The study of the total metabolite pool (the metabolome) through a wide spectrum of technologic methods including liquid chromatography-mass spectrometry, gas chromatography-mass spectrometry, and nuclear magnetic resonance.

Metabonomics :

The study of the total metabolite pool (the metabolome) specifically through nuclear magnetic resonance profiling.

Microarray :

Sets of miniaturized chemical reaction areas, they may also be used to test DNA fragments, antibodies, or proteins.

Pharmacogenomics :

The analysis of the effect of genomic – in particular, genetic, variation (polymorphisms) – on drug response.

Pharmacogenetics :

A subset of pharmacogenomics encompassing the study of genetic variation underlying differential response to drugs, particularly genes involved in drug metabolism. Often used to refer specifically to tests that predict drug response.

Proteomics :

The study of the full set of proteins (the proteome) encoded by a genome.

Single nucleotide polymorphism (SNP) :

A position in the genome where some individuals have one DNA base (e.g. A) and others have a different base (e.g., C) SNPs and point mutations are structurally identical, differing only in their frequency. Variations that occur in 1% or less of a population are considered point mutations, and those occurring in more than 1% are considered SNPs.

Toxicogenomics :

The study of how genomes respond to environmental stressors or toxicants. Combines genome-wide mRNA expression profiling with protein expression patterns. Using bioinformatics to understand the role of gene-environment interactions in diseases and dysfunction.

Transcriptomics :

The generation of messenger RNA expression profiles.

(3) Software engineering — It refers to computer languages such as C, C^{++}, PERL (practical extraction and report language) or FORTRAN. The choice of programme depends upon the nature of algorithm and associated data structure.

Computer applications, have helped in the development of several disciplines in biological sciences. This chapter describes a few of them viz : bioinformatics, genomics and proteomics.

Bioinformatics

Bioinformatics is an interdisciplinary science that involves biology, computer science, mathematics and statistics to analyze a biological sequence, data, genome content and genome arrangement to predict the structure and function of macromolecules. It employs following concepts.

Database is a computerized storehouse of data that provides a standardized way for locating, adding, removing and changing data.

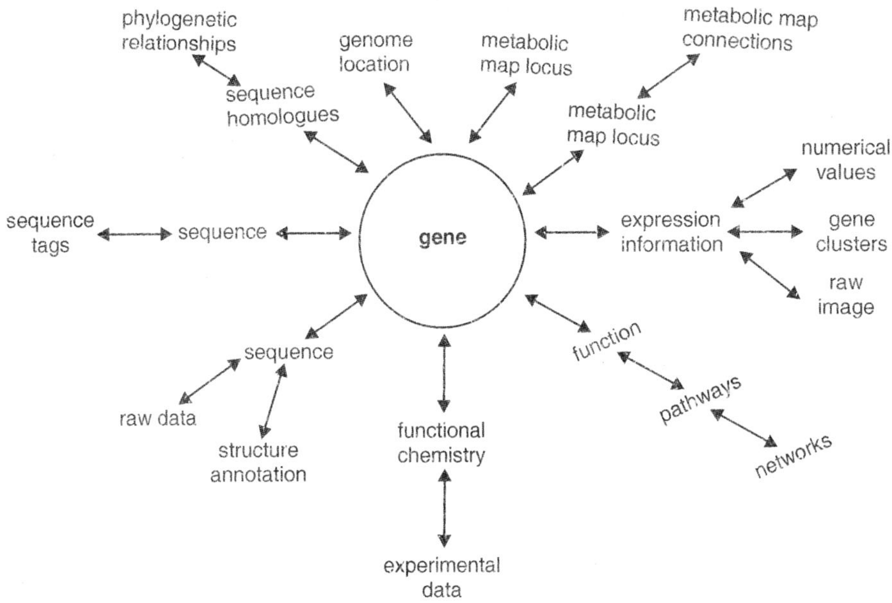

Fig. 1. Information (annotation) associated with a single gene. (Source : Env. Hlth.Persp.,111,2003)

A **databank** includes an archive of information a logical organization or structure of that information and tools to gain access to it. Databanks in molecular biology cover nucleic acid and protein sequences, macromolecular structures and function. They include

(1) Archival databanks of biological information
  (i) DNA and protein sequences including annotation
  (ii) nucleic acid and protein structures, including annotation
  (iii) databanks of protein expression patterns

(2) Derived databanks : These contain information collected from the archival databanks, and from the analysis of their contents. For instance :
  (i) sequence motifs (characteristic 'signature patterns' of families of proteins)
  (ii) mutations and variations in DNA and protein sequences
  (iii) classifications or relationships (connections and common features of entries in archives; for instance a databank of sets of protein sequence families, or a hierarchical classification of protein folding patterns)

(3) Bibliographic databanks

(4) Databanks of web sites
  (i) databanks of databanks containing biological information
  (ii) links between databanks

Internet has further allowed the explosion of knowledge in biological sciences. This is a worldwide system that links computers, local networks, research, commercial and governmental institutions and the World Wide Web (www). Consequently the new expanding and exciting areas in bioscience research are emerging. A few of them are described below :

Genomics

Genomics is the term for the study of the genome. The term genome has been used traditionally to define the haploid set of chromosomes in the nuclei of multicellular organisms e.g. fly genome, mouse genome, human genome. Genomes vary greatly in size as measured by their DNA content. Computer has enormously helped in the analysis of a genome sequence. The collective efforts of global genome organizations have completed the genome sequencing of 31 bacteria, the megabase (Mb) – sized nuclear

Table 1. Some major biological data and information resources for gene annotation.[a]

Subject	Source	Link
Biomedical literature	PubMed	http://www.ncbi.nlm.nih.gov/entrez/query.fcgl
Nucleic acid sequence	GenBank	http://www.ncbi.nlm.nih.gov:80/entrez/query.fcgi?db=nucleotide
(e.g., for the rat)	RGD	http://rgd.mcw.edu/ebEST; http://rgd.mcw.edu/EBEST/
Annotation (mouse)	MGI	http://www.informatis.jax.org/
Genome sequence	GenBank	http://www.ncbi.nlm.nih.gov:80/entrez/query.fcgi?db=genome
		http://www.ncbi.nih.gov/PMGifs/Genomes/euk_g.html
	TIGR	http://www.tigr.org/tdb/; http://www.tigr.org/tdb/tgi/
Protein sequence	GenBank	http://www.ncbi.nlm.nih.gov:80/entrez/query.fcgi?db=protein
	Swiss-Prot	http://www.expasy.ch/sprot/
Protein structure	Protein DB	http://www.rcsb.org/pdb/
	PIR	http://www.nbrf.georgetown.edu
Protein mass spectra	PROWL	http://prowl.rockefeller.edu
Posttranslational mods	RESID	http://nbrf.georgetown.edu/pirwww/search/textresid.html
Biochemical pathways	KEGG	http://www.genome.ad.jp/kegg//
	WIT	http://wit.mcs.anl.gov/WIT2/; http://emp.mcs.anl.gov
	Path DB	http://www.ncgr.org/software/pathdb/

Source : Enviror. Hlth. Perspect., 111, 2003

genomes of baker's yeast *Saccharomyces cerevisiae* (12 Mb), the nematode worm *Caenorhabditis elegans* (100 Mb), the fly *Drosophila melanogaster* (180 Mb). The genomes of humans *Homosapiens* (3300 Mb) and two plants, the wall cress (*Arabidopsis thaliana* 125 Mb) and rice (*Oryza sativa,* 430 Mb), have also been completed.

To address the bioinformatics and interpretive challenges basic gene annotation has largely been automated; annotation resources are routinely consulted to provide a complete range of updated gene/protein information. The process of gene annotation is illustrated in Figure 1, and some major biological data and information resources for gene annotation are shown in Table 1.

Comparative Genomics

The availability of whole genome sequence information in the human is important in its own right, but the full power of this knowledge requires the additional availability of whole genome sequence information from model organisms, especially *Drosophila melanogaster* (common fruit flies) and mice. *Drosophila* has been at the forefront of genetics research for nearly 80 years. This species is an important model for combining genetics, electrophysiology, and molecular biology. A brief listing of some medically important fruit fly genes is shown in Table 2. Many gene families, ranging literally from A to Z (aldolases to zinc finger transcription factors), suggest that a single invertebrate gene corresponds to a handful of equally related vertebrate genes on different chromosomes. Thus, gene duplication is the engine that drove vertebrate evolution.

In the case of vertebrate organisms, not only does homology to human genes exist, there is also something more meaningful called **synteny**. This means there are related genes arrayed on chromosomes with an evolutionary history common to human counterparts, in a comparable order in terms of exons and gene regulatory elements. Thus, a mouse chromosomal region with such a common evolutionary history and genetic arrangement is said to be syntenic and the relevant mouse and human genes are said to be orthologs. Synteny and the capacity to overlay complete human and mammalian genome sequences (especially mouse) will affect gene discovery and our understanding of gene structure and function in ways without precedent. We expect the completion of other genomes with importance to pharmacology and toxicology, e.g. rat and canine genomes, not too far behind those of humans and mice. These advances will allow an integration of information from transgenic animals and gene knockout models in far-reaching ways and

Table 2. **Model organism, gene names, and human disease.**

Fruit flies[a]	Mice	Humans
Congenital heart defects Tinman	Csx/NKx2.5	Csx/NKx2.5
Huntington's polyglutamine repeats cause neural degeneration	Polyglutamine repeats	Polyglutamine repeats
Alzheimer's APPL	APP	APP
Amyotrophic lateral sclerosis SOD	SOD1	SOD1
Cancer Cdx(2) caudal	cdx2	cdx2
Diabetes insulin receptor	Insulin receptor (knockout mice)	Insulin receptor
Retinitis pigmentosa rhodopsin	Rhodopsin	Rhodopsin
NF MERLIN	NF2	NF2
Ataxia telangiectasia mei-41	ATM	ATM

[a]Human disease, APP, amyloid precursor protein; SOD, superoxide dimutase, NF, neurofibromatosis.

will stimulate novel strategies for currently intractable therapeutic problems.

The implications of these advances can perhaps be illustrated with a few examples. The **homeobox genes** are an interesting case. An excellent website by Gaunt can be consulted (http://www.bi.bbsrc.ac.uk/world/sci4Alll/gaunt/dud/gaunt.htm). We can examine homeobox *(Hox)* genes (113), a family of genes that are conserved in evolution in detail. These genes direct the development of the body plan and body parts of many morphologically distinct species. The homeobox is a highly conserved 180-bp nucleotide sequence shared by this family of transcription factors. The homeobox in turn encodes the DNA binding region, called the homeodomain, a DNA binding motif.

Genome Mapping

One of the earliest applications of restriction enzymes, in the early 1970s was in the generation of physical maps of DNA molecules. An aim of molecular biology is to determine the size and location of each gene in the genome of an organism. Until about 1970 all mapping involved determination of genetic linkage between markers, as assessed by measurements of recombination freqtency. The first attempts to correlate genetic map position with physical location on a chromosome involved rather cumber some electron microscopic techniques.

Restriction fragmentation is a far easier way to generate a physical map-in this case a map of cleavage sites for a type II restriction nuclease. Referring to Figure 25.6, you can see that cleavage of λ DNA with one enzyme, such as *EeaRI,* gives the lengths of all six fragments in the digest but gives no information about the order of these fragments in the intact phage genome. Comparable information comes from analysis of the *BamHI* sites. However, if DNA is digested with both *EeaRI* and *BamHI,* this double-digest pattern gives much more information about the placement of sites for both enzymes. From analysis of three fragmentation patterns, a researcher can often obtain maps for two restriction sites, as you can see if you work Problems 9 and 11 of Chapter 25. If-the data are difficult to interpret-for example, because a digest contains two or more different fragments that have the same sizxe-the needed information can be obtained from I a partial digest, that is, by running the restriction cleavage reactions only partly to completion. Another way to simplify the interpretation of mapping data is to label the 5 ends with γ-[^{32}p] ATP and polynucleotide kinase and then carry out partial digestion, followed by electrophoresis and radioautography of the labeled fragments (Figure 25A.1). The radioautogram gives a ladder of fragments, comparable to that seen in a Maxam-Gilbert sequencing gel (page 1025), which allows ordering of sites from the 5 end.

By methods such as these, the restriction maps of many small DNAs-from viruses, organelles, and plasmids-were generated in the late 1970s and early 1980s. Genomes up to about 200 kbp, or kilo base pairs (2×10^5 nucleotide pairs) could be mapped. However, the smallest cellular genomes are about 20 times that size, and the difficulty of mapping a genome increases disproportionately to increases in the size of the genome, because of the gigantic number of restriction fragments that must be analyzed. Clearly, new technologies were needed to handle the enormous amounts of data generated by the mapping effort.

In 1987 two laboratories described physical maps of the *E. coli* genome, which contains 4.7 million base pairs; this effort was essential to the complete sequence determination of the genome, completed a decade later. One laboratory cloned and separately mapped 3400 restriction fragments resulting from cleavage of *E. coli* DNA by restriction nucleases that recognize six-base cutting sites. The other laboratory used a restriction nuclease, NotI, which recognizes an eight-base cutting sequence and, hence, generates fewer (but larger) fragments. These fragments were separated by pulsed field gel electrophoresis, a technique that involves periodic changes in the orientation of the electrical field. This technique allows resolution of DNA fragments the size of whole chromosomes-up to 3000 kbp in length.

Now consider the effort that must be expended in mapping the human genome-a genome containing 2.9 billion base pairs of DNA in the haploid state, several hundred times larger and more complex than the E. *coli* genome. That effort, the Human Genome Project, is now well under way. Several techniques are being used to clone and analyze large DNA fragments, particularly the use of yeast artificial chromosomes (YACs). YACs are constructed by recombinant DNA techniques from a yeast centromere, two telomere sequences (chromosome ends), selectable markers, and cloned DNA in the megabase range (1000 kbp). Most of the gene mapping data from the Human Genome Project actually result from large-scale direct DNA sequence analysis.

Much of the mapping effort in the Human Genome Project has led to isolation of genes whose defective function is responsiole for specific diseases (see Tools of Biochemistry 25D). At the smaller-scale level of genome mapping, much has been learned from analysis of human mitochondrial DNA. Mitochondrial genes are maternally inherited, because few mitochondria from the sperm cell enter the fertilized egg. By comparing mitochondrial DNA restriction maps of 147 individuals of varying origins, Allan Wd. son concluded that all mitochondrial lineages are derived from one woman, who lived in Africa about 200,000 years ago. That conclusion has generated intense controversy, which has continued past the untimely death of Wilson. Regardless of the outcome of this controversy, the fact that relatively simple data can lead to any generalizations about human origins indicates the power of restriction mapping techniques.

Gene Cloning

In classical biology a clone is a population of organisms that are genetically homogeneous because they were derived from a single ancestor. For example, all of the bacterial cells in one colony represent a clone, because they were derived from a single cell that was deposited at that location on a Petri plate. In 1973 Herbert Boyer and Stanley Cohen realized that they could use restriction enzymes to "clone" a gene in comparable fashion. They constructed in vitro a novel DNA molecule consisting of a restriction fragment containing a gene of interest, linked to another DNA molecule, such as a plasmid, capable of directing its/own replication. This molecule could then be propagated biologically by introduction into a bacterial cell. As the bacterium grows, this recombinant DNA molecule, so called because it is formed by end-to-end joining of two different DNAs, replicates along with its host cell. In an early application of the technique, a recombinant plasmid containing the gene for tryptophan synthase was introduced into bacteria lacking this enzyme, whereupon the transformed bacteria acquired the ability to grow in the absence of tryptophan.

Boyer and Cohen realized that, because of the symmetry in type II restriction sites, enzymes giving staggered or offset cuts generated cohesive ends that could be joined covalently by DNA ligase, just as occurs in A phage DNA replication (see Chapter 24). DNA molecules from any sources are capable of being joined, so long as they have the same cohesive ends (Figure 25B.1).After the DNA ligase reaction in vitro, the mixture of DNAs is introduced into bacteria that have been rendered permeable either by treatment with calcium chloride followed by heat shock or by a pulse of electric current. About 0.01 % of the bacteria can undergo genetic transformation-the uptake of DNA and its replication in the recipient cell. This process is illustrated in Figure 25B.2.

Successful cloning of a gene requires several elements. First, one needs a DNA fragment thought to contain the gene of interest. Usually this is a restriction fragment, but PCR is often used to create a fragment containing the gene. Cohesive ends can also be generated by synthesis. An enzyme called terminal deoxynucleotidyl transferase adds nucleotides to 3' DNA termini, without a need for a template. Thus, one can put a poly(dC) "tail" on one DNA and a poly(dG) "tail" on the other, and these tails are complementary to each other, just like the cohesive ends created by restriction nucleases. Also, techniques are now available for the end-to-end j9Jining of blunt-ended DNA fragments and also for cloning PCR products, which often have single-strand ends just one nucleotide long. DNA copies (cDNA), created by reverse transcriptase action on messenger RNA, are often used as substrates for gene cloning.

Second, one needs a vector, or DNA molecule into which the target gene will be inserted. A vector can be any DNA that contains an origin of replication and can replicate after its entry into a suitable cell (usually a bacterium, although genes are also cloned into eukaryotic cells). Plasmids and bacteriophage chromosomes are most often used as vectors, because they can replicate independently of the host cell into which they are introduced. This allows one to amplify the recombinant DNA; that is, one can cDNA hybridized with DNA from a particular colony makes that colony radioactive replicate it to a much higher copy number than that of the chromosomal DNA.

Third, because ligation and transformation both occur with low efficiency, one needs a suitable screening technique-a method to identify bacteria that contain the cloned gene, in the presence of a huge excess of cells that do not. If one expects that the cloned gene will be expressed, one can select conditions in which the cloned gene confers a selectable phenotype on the recipient bacterium, such as resistance to a particular drug or loss of a nutritional requirement. Reaction with an antibody against the product of the cloned gene is another way to screen for desired clones among a large number of transformants. However, if one doesn't know whether the cloned gene will be expressed, one can search for the desired *DNA sequences* instead of the product of the cloned gene. In a technique called colony hybridization, one uses a labeled nucleic acid probe homologous to the desired sequence to search among individual bacterial colonies for the presence of I that DNA sequence (Figure 25B.3). The hybridization probe can be either a restriction fragment of natural DNA or a chemically synthesized oligonucleotide known to contain a sequence represented in the desired clone. Alternatively, if the DNA has been cloned into a phage vector instead of a plasmid, one can carry out plaque hybridization, in which individual phage plaques are screened in much the same way.

Screening for desired recombinants is aided greatly by the design of vectors with suitable restriction sites and selectable markers. pBR322 is a popular plasmid vector that is itself a recombinant DNA molecule produced in vitro (Figure 25B.4). pBR322 is a circular DNA molecule containing a replication origin from a naturally occurring plasmid, CoIEl, plus genes conferring resistance to the antibiotics ampicillin *(amp^R)* and tetracycline (*tet^R*). Some restriction sites lie within either the *amp^R* or the *tef*genes, the genes conferring resistance to ampicillin and tetracycline, respectively. A researcher may "clone into» the HindIII site, for example, by opening pBR322 with *HindIII* and ligating DNA to the resulting DNA ends, thereby creating a recombinant in which the cloned gene forms an insert that splits, and hence inactivates, the *tet^R* gene. This technique aids greatly in screening for clones. All bacteria that are transformed, whether with the original vector or with a recombinant DNA, become ampicillin-resistant. However, only the bacteria that contain a recombinant Irlasmid are also tetracycline-sensitive. Transformation with the unaltered plasmid confers resistance to both antibiotics. Therefore, individual transformant colonies can be picked from ampilillin plates and replaced in the presence of tetracycline. Cells not growing on these plates probably contain recombinant plasmids.

Since the introduction of pBR322, hundreds of different cloning vectors have been described.

Particularly useful are expression vectors, in which control regions affecting transcription and translation have been introduced, to allow high-level expression of cloned genes, for production of the gene products. We shall see numerous examples of the utility of gene cloning as a research tool. However, the excitement generated by recombinant DNA technology derived in large part from its potential for attacking practical problems. The earliest such example was the cloning and expression in *E. coli* of a gene encoding human insulin. This was accomplished in 1977, and by 1982 the purified recombinant product was available for use in treating diabetes. Other recombinant products include blood clotting factors, clot dissolving enzymes used to treat heart attack victims, other polypeptide hormones (including pituitary growth hormone), and interferons.

A useful adjunct to expression-vector cloning is the addition of "tags" to recombinant proteins, to facilitate their purification after expression. A popular application of this technique is the "histidine tag." An oligonucleotide containing six histidine codons is spliced adjacent to the insert in an expression vector, such that the expressed recombinant protein has a sequence of six histidine residues, linked at either the C- or N-terminus. The imidazole ring in histidine causes the hexahistidine sequence to bind tightly to an affinity column containing nickel ion coordinated with a çovalently bound chelator, nitriloacetate (as shown in the following figure). Thus, when a crude extract containing the Histagged recombinant protein is applied to such a column, the recombinant protein binds tightly and specifically and can later be eluted **from** the column with an imidazole buffer. Often this allows complete purification of a recombinant protein with just this single fractionation step. The tag can be removed afterward, if desired, by designing the oligonucleotide to contain both the **six** His codons and a cleavage site **for** a specific protease.

Much interest is focused on genetic engineering of plants to endow them with desirable properties, such as resistance to cold, to dehydration, to viruses, or to insect pests. Nature has provided an excellent vehicle **for** introducing novel genes into plants. *Agrobacterium tumefaciens* is a pathogenic bacterium that causes a disease called crown gall, through transfer of some of its own DNA into infected plants. The disease-causing genes are carried on a plasmid called the **Ti plasmid**. Foreign genes can be introduced into the plasmid by recombinant DNA methodology, and infection of plants by the resultant modified *Agrobacterium* can transfer these novel genes into plants. Current efforts *focus* on controlling the expression of these genes after infection and directing their integration into the cellular genome, so that the desirable characteristics become permanently incorporated into the genome.

Comparable gene transfer techniques exist **for** animals as well. In 1982, Ralph Brinster and Richard Palmiter introduced, by microinjection, a cloned gene **for** rat growth hormone into the male pronucleus of fertilized mouse eggs. The gene was cloned downstream **from** an inducible promoter to increase its chances of being expressed. After insertion of the microinjected eggs into the uterus of a **foster** mother mouse, a significant number of offspring expressed the gene, produced high levels of rat growth hormone, and grew to about twice the size of normal mice.Although the early success of this experiment with transgenic animals was perhaps fortuitous, more recent developments have greatly increased our ability to achieve homologous recombination of DNA after transfer into mammalian cells. In fact, these techniques are currently being tested **for** treatment of a small number of human genetic diseases, including the immunodeficiency associated with a lack of adenosine deaminase (see pages 805-806).

Gene Sequencing with Dideoxynucleotides

In Chapter 4, we mentioned the pioneering Maxam-Gilbert DNA sequencing technique, which involves base-specific cleavages of a 5' end-labeled DNA molecule to give a series of fragments of varying lengths, which can be analyzed by gel electrophoresis. In 1976 Fred Sanger introduced an alternative sequencing methodology, which is now in almost universal use because it can be applied to longer fragments and is more rapid and amenable to automation.

Sanger sequencing is similar in principle to Maxam-Gilbert sequencing in that it generates a set of fragments with a common 5' origin and base-specific 3' termini. However, those 3' termini are created not by base-specific cleavage starting from a full-length molecule but by base-specific **interruption** of enzymatic synthesis of the molecule in vitro, by incorporation of nucleotide analogs that serve as chain terminators. The principle of the method is shown in Figure 25C.1. First, one usually clones the fragment to be sequenced into a vector that allows it to be isolated as singlestrand DNA (although similar methods work for double-strand DNAs). Bacteriophage M13 is most commonly used as a vector. One can isolate the double-strand replicative form of this virus and clone the target sequence into it, just as one clones into a plasmid such as pBR322. After introduction of the double-strand DNA into a bacterium, the cell produces virus particles, which contain single-strand DNA. The M13 genome has been genetically engineered for this type of cloning-first, to contain suitable restriction sites for cloning and, second, to allow fast identification of plaques containing phage that have acquired a DNA insert in the cloning process.

Isolated single-strand circular DNA from phage containing the desired insert becomes the template for four DNA polymerasecatalyzed reactions. The primer is an oligonucleotide that is complementary to an M 13 sequence lying just 3' to the insert. Extension of this primer by DNA polymerase will copy the insert. These polymerase reactions are run in the presence of deoxyribonucleoside triphosphate analogs, the 2', 3'-dideoxyribonucleoside triphosphates, which serve as terminators of chain extension because they lack 3' hydroxyl termini. The dideoxy analog (ddATP) of adenosine triphosphate is shown here.

To generate a series of A-terminated fragments, one runs the DNA polymerase reaction in the presence of equivalent concentrations of dATP, dCTP, dGTP, and dTTP, plus one-tenth equivalent of ddATP. When T is in the template strand, DNA polymerase occasionally inserts ddAMP instead of dAMP. When that happens, chain elongation stops and the fragment is released from the enzyme. Thus, a series of fragments of varying lengths accumulates, with each fragment identifying a T in the nucleotide sequence of the insert. Similarly, one identifies sites terminated by C, G, or T simply by running comparable polymerase reactions with the other three dideoxy analogs. Inclusion of a radioactive label in the polymerization mixture and gel electrophoresis followed by radioautography generate four sequencing ladders, with each ladder absolutely base specific.

More recently introduced technology allows automated sequence determination by the Sanger method. The sequencing primer is derivatized at its 5' end with a fluorescent dye that is red, blue, green, or yellow. Each of the four sequencing reactions is run with a differently colored primer, which imparts a characteristic fluorescence to all fragments terminated by A, T, G, or C, respectively. This allows both for sequence determination without radioisotopes and for computer-assisted reading of the sequence gel and processing of the data. Other recently introduced methods allow direct sequence determination with double-strand DNAs, without the necessity for cloning them into a single. I strand DNA vector such as M13.

Application of these and other high-throughput sequencing modifications had led, by the late 1990s, to complete sequence determination of several bacterial genomes. The genome sequence of the yeast *Saccharomyces cerevisiae* has also been reported, and the complete genome sequence of a multicellular organism, the nematode *Caenorhabditis elegans,* was reported in late 1998. Scientists predict that the entire human genome will have been sequenced within the first two or three years of the twenty-first century. Already, the gene mapping and sequencing effort involved in the Human Genome Project has identified many so called disease genes-human genes in which defined mutations are responsible for specific disease states. These mapping techniques involve nucleic acid hybridization analysis, which is described in Tools of Biochemistry 25D.

Proteomics

Global studies that aim to achieve a comprehensive view of all the proteins expressed in a cell are known as proteomics. The term proteome was coined in 1994 by Marc Wilkins We can learn from a proteome the following :

(1) Cellular adaptation to environmental signals
(2) Mechanism of cellular differentiation and organismal development

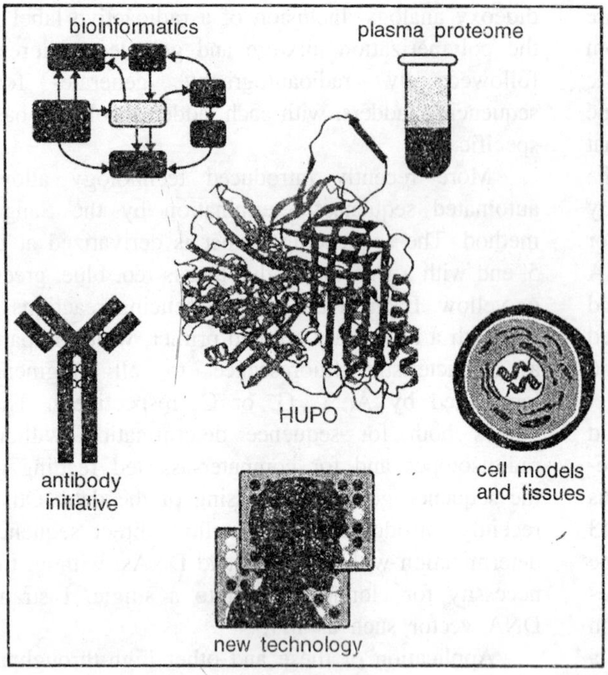

Fig. 2. Steps involved in the human protome organization (HUPO).

(3) Cellular aspects of disease processes
(4) Cellular response to ageing
(5) Difference between individuals within species i.e. the molecular basis of individuality in physiology, disease susceptibility and response to therapeutics and environmental exposures.

Analysis of Proteome

No technology is yet available that can identify the entire proteome of a cell. However, recent developments in technology allow a large sampling of proteins to be viewed at once. O'Farrel (1975) introduced two-dimensional polyacrylamide gel electrophoresis (2D PAGE). Since then these techniques have been a workhorse of proteomics laboratory. 2D PAGE separate proteins from cell extracts in the first dimension according to their charge and in the second dimension according to their molecular weight. Staining of these gels can reveal as many as several thousand spots, each corresponding to a single protein species. The available techniques such as determining amino acid composition, masses of peptide fragments, or partial N-terminal sequencing were both time consuming and characterized by low throughput.

Recently computer programmes have been developed to search the sequence databases for candidate proteins that matched one of these criteria. Mass spectroscopy technology has provided a quantum leap in sensitivity. Mass spectrometers measure the mass of chemical fragments with exquisite resolution, sometimes down to less than a single Dalton. Two types of MS approaches have revolutionized protein identification. In the matrix-assisted laser desorption/ionization (MALDI) approach a 'peptide mass' fingerprint for a protein is obtained by determining the masses of peptide generated by a protease. Computer algorithms are able to compare the fingerprint against the predicted peptide masses of all the protein. A second option, tandem electrospray ionization (ESI) mass spectroscopy, employs an initial mass spectroscopy step whereby an unseparated mixture of peptide fragments is fed into a mass spectrometer by ESI. Individual separated peptides are selected, fragmented further, and fed into a second tandem mass spectrometer for determination of partial amino acid sequence of the peptides. These partial sequences permit more specific identification than is possible by MALDI MS alone. Despite these advances, there are still limitations inherent in 2D gel technology. Although resolution is excellent, there are serious problems with consistency and reproducibility with a technology that is difficult to automate. Many important classes of proteins, glycoproteins and membrane proteins in particular may be insoluble or may not enter the gel. Separation difficulties exist because a single spot can represent multiple comigrating proteins, and a single protein can migrate as multiple spots. But the most daunting difficulty is the 10 million-fold range in concentration among proteins within a cell, from tens or hundreds of copies for low-abundance proteins to many millions of copies for high-abundance proteins. Low-abundance proteins are neither visible on 2D gels nor detectable by current MS technology, and increasing sample quantity is not an option since 2D- gel resolution is severely distorted by protein overloading.

Future improvements in 2D-gel technology, such as robotic automation of gel preparation and processing, more powerful database searching and analysis, and advances in mass spectroscopy technology are likely to circumvent some of these limitations. Additional strategies are to specifically enrich or limit the diversity in the protein sample before loading onto the gel. Apart from 2D gels, two alternative approaches for proteome analysis are under development. 'Multidimension chromatography' separates proteins on a column (or a number of columns in series) which can be automatically linked to a mass spectrometer to process samples with high throughput. A second alternative is to use protein chips similar to DNA chips used for mRNA expression analysis. This strategy entails using some sort of 'bait,' be it other proteins, antibodies, peptides, or small molecules, which is immobilized on a two-dimensional array. A crude protein sample is applied, and those proteins in the sample that bind to the bait are detected by one of several possible methods.

Gene Microarrays

Gene microarrays allow the rapid parallel analysis of the expression of thousands of genes against hundreds of tissues, cell types, and conditions whether using oligonucleotide arrays or arrays of gene fragments. Because of the compatibility of glass with fluorescently labelled probes, the most effective gene microarrays are those constructed on glass surfaces, as opposed to arrays on nylon membranes. Because fluorescent probes exhibit little-to-no signal dispersion, very dense array spacing is possible, and deposition of DNA samples at densities of thousands of discrete DNA spots per 1.0 cm have been attained. Another advantage of dense arrays on small glass surfaces is that the volumes required for hybridization are very small, thereby allowing the use of probes from small amounts of tissues.

The number and variety of microarray applications is virtually unlimited. Gene microarrays are being used extensively to generate broad and in-depth data on gene expression patterns in normal and diseased tissues, both in human and in animal systems. Although many effective drugs have been developed against targets that are widely expressed in the body (e.g. the angiotensin convening enzyme), highly selective tissue expression of a drug target, such as that seen for cathepsin K, is attractive, as the potential for unwanted side effects may be more restricted. Perhaps the most promising application of microarrays is the study of differential expression in disease. The up- or down-regulation of a gene can be the cause of the disease or its result. In addition, microarrays are a powerful tool to help dissect the mechanism of action of drugs and drug candidates. They also increasingly contribute to the analysis of metabolic pathways for drugs, understanding and prediction of toxic or adverse events *in vitro* and *in vivo*, as well as the potential identification of surrogate markers to follow the dose efficacy of a drug in the clinical setting.

Microarray-based assays yield several hundred data points for thousands of genes, and this in turn demands the development of fully automated and standardized **software systems** for the collection, quality scoring, and tracking of data points. The rush to apply this new technology should not ignore quality assurance because low-quality data will only generate poor biological conclusions. It will therefore be critical that strict and broadly accepted quality standards be developed, so that data from different laboratories can be compared and combined.

Microarrays are not the panacea for gene expression analysis. They have number of limitations that must be addressed by complementary technologies. First, the sensitivity of detection is about 1 in 100,000. More sensitive but lower throughput methods such as quantitative polymerase chain reaction, e.g. recently automated **Taqman technology** must be utilized for the analysis of genes that are expressed in low abundance. Second, the labor-intensive *in situ* hybridization and immunocytochemistry methods will continue to make important contributions because they provide a critical link to histology and cytology that the best microdissection of cells from tissues is unlikely to provide. Third, mRNA levels may not be paralleled at the protein level. To address this, high-throughput methods for the analysis of differential expression at the protein level are being developed to characterize translational and post-translation regulation. This emerging technology is referred as proteomics.

Gene Therapy

Gene therapy is a therapeutic technique that offers the possibility of introducing a functioning gene into somatic cells of a patient to correct a defective gene and thereby restore biological function. The major interest of the pharmaceutical industry in gene therapy will undoubtedly be centered around *in vivo* treatment protocols, although more invasive *ex vivo* methods (whereby cells are removed from the patient, transfected with the gene of interest, and then placed back into the patient) may be acceptable for certain serious diseases (e.g. cancer). Currently, genetic information can be transferred into cells by a number of protocols, including the use of DNA plasmids, DNA liposomes, or a variety of viruses. The most effective transforming agents are viral vectors, such as adenovirus, adeno-associated viruses, and retroviruses. Although retroviruses require cell division to incorporate the new information into the genome, adenovirus and adeno-associated viruses will transfer their information into nonreplicating cells. Despite considerable efforts that have gone into vector design during the past decade, delivery of genes still represents one of the major problems associated with the gene therapeutic approach. Encouragingly, recent work has demonstrated the ability of certain viral vectors to stably incorporate genetic material *in vivo*, resulting expression of the resultant proteins, which can be maintained for periods of several months.

Food and Drug Administration has approved approximately 90 clinical studies involving gene therapy, which represents one of the fastest growing areas in biomedical research. Safety is, and will continue for some time to be, an issue with this approach, and many of the clinical trials involving gene therapy are directed toward patients with life-threatening diseases (e.g. cancer patient's already receiving conventional therapy). Most reports to date have been phase I clinical studies confirming gene transfection and demonstrating safety, but evidence of efficacy has been anecdotal. Properly controlled phase II and phase III clinical trials involving-gene therapy are yet to be done and will tax the current development capacity within the pharmaceutical industry.

Some published examples of clinical studies of gene therapy in the cardiovascular arena have appeared. For example, the intra-arterial gene transfer of a plasmid that encodes for vascular endothelial growth factor has been tested for its ability to increase coronary and peripheral angiogenesis. The initial results from these early clinical trials suggest that vascular endothelial growth factor gene transfer produces angiogenesis and reduces ischemic symptoms. However, as mentioned above, these studies are inadequately controlled and the results can only be considered anecdotal.

Gene therapy has received much attention for the treatment of inherited metabolic diseases. One such disease in which preclinical data suggest promise targets familial hypercholesterolemia. Replacement of the low-density-lipoprotein receptor gene by adenovirus transfection into mice in which the gene for this receptor had been knocked out resulted in correction of the dyslipidemia.

Important Questions

1. Explain the following terms :
   (i) Bioinformatics, (ii) Genomics, (iii) Comparative genomics, (iv) Proteonomics, (v) Gene microarrays, (vi) Gene therapy.
2. Give a brief account of different applications of computer in biological analysis.

Perfusion, Organ Ablations/ Surgical Techniques

25

The best way to preserve tissues is by perfusion, which is usually effected by infusion in the left ventricle of the heart and by opening the sinus venosus to provide for proper circulation. Perfusion of isolated organs (liver, kidneys) is another possibility. Before perfusion, the animals are anaesthetized with barbiturate, administered in combination with nitrate and heparin to ensure vasodilation and prevent clotting. A solution consisting of 77·5 ml sodium nitrite (1·25%) in water, 10 ml heparin (5000 IU/ml) and 12 ml pentobarbital (60 mg/ml), of which 10 ml is administered per kg body weight, is satisfactory. Then the blood is removed with an isotonic saline solution using slight overpressure. When all the blood has left the body via the sinus venosus or right atrium, the body may be perfused with the fixative.

Perfusion is sometimes not possible especially in experiments where the recording of organ weights is important (i.e. in sub chronic toxicity studies). This difficulty can be solved by increasing the number of experimental animals, though this may lead to a considerable increase in costs. Perfusion of large numbers of animals is possible using simple facilities at low cost (Fig. 1).

Perfusion Techniques

Perfusion of the isolated liver .was used for metabolic studies by **Luchsinger** in 1875 and **Von Frey** and **Gruber** in 1885. By the turn of the century hepatic perfusion techniques were in vogue, and interest in these procedures continued until they were superseded by the simpler liver slice incubation technique introduced by **Arburg** and

Fig. 1. Setup for serial perfusion experiment.

Minami in 1923. The need for adequate oxygenation was stressed in these early perfusion studies (**Grube**, 1903), and the necessity for rapidly reestablishing the circulation after the necessary dissection was emphasized (**Brodie**, 1903).

Previously described methods for perfusion of the isolated liver with whole heparinized or defibrinated blood have met with many difficulties. Glucose concentrations in the perfusate increase beyond physiologic ranges (600-1000 mg. %).

Potassium, sodium, and water shifts similar to those that occur in the liver slice were observed: the perfused liver takes up salt and water. **Bauer** *et. al.* (1932) noted that during the course of relatively short-term perfusions, the flow rate steadily declined and the liver became edematous. As the flow rate diminished during the perfusion, swelling and edema of the organ increased progressively (**Chakravarti** and **Tripod**, 1940). Swelling and engorgement of the liver vascular bed remind one of the state of the liver in histamine shock or in hemorrhagic shock.

There have been a number of attempts to obviate these problems. By using a dilute, low-viscosity perfusing solution instead of whole, heparinized blood a greater flow rate is possible. Increasing the inflowing perfusing pressure or lowering the outflow pressure also increases flow. Perfusing "backward," i.e., through the hepatic veins and collecting the efflux via the portal system was suggested as a means of obviating the influence of the outlet sinusoidal sphincters on the hepatic vascular bed. Addition of glucose (1000 mg. %) has been used as a means of avoiding glycogenolysis; potassium has also been used as an additive. Although in the past, rat liver has been most frequently used for perfusions, the canine liver has been investigated in this laboratory because its size allows frequent biopsies and because measurements of the rates of hepatic metabolic reactions observed in the perfused liver may be, compared with those measured in the unanesthetized dog.

Method of Hepatic Perfusion *in vivo*

A method was developed for perfusing the *in vivo, in situ* canine liver with heparinized, whole blood, and preliminary data on concentration changes of several selected constituents of the perfusing blood or plasma were presented (**Shoemaker** *et al.*, 1961a). The porta hepatis is denervated in order to minimize or eliminate neural influences on the hepatic vascular resistance. A catheter is introduced into the splenic vein and threaded up until the tip is floating free within the lumen of the portal vein. A second catheter is introduced into the vena cava via the femoral vein in a similar manner. These catheters do not obstruct the blood flow in the portal vein or cava. Ligatures or nooses are placed around the portal vein and vena cava; the diaphragm is opened and a ligature is loosely placed around the thoracic vena cava. When these three ligatures are simultaneously drawn up and tied, the catheters become, in effect, cannulae, and the hepatic circulation is instantaneously and completely divorced from the remaining systemic circulation; at no time is there interruption of normal pressure and flow of oxygenated blood to the liver. After the perfusion is safely underway the hepatic artery is temporarily ligated and a system of catheters is placed which conducts blood from the portal and femoral veins (distal to the points of the nooses or snares) back into the systemic circulation via the jugular vein. After completion of the perfusion, the normal vascular relationships may be reestablished. On occasion, long-term survival of the animal after perfusion has been obtained.

Although the term "in *vivo* perfusion" has been previously applied to acute preparations, it may be used with reference to this preparation to indicate that viability has been preserved as demonstrated by survival after the perfusion. This is not taken to indicate that entirely "normal" chemical equilibria conditions between the hepatic cell and perfusate have been met. The introduced technique, however, has as its primary objective the perfusion of the canine liver with whole, heparinized blood at near normal hemodynamic and metabolic relationships.

Denervation of the hepatic vasculature is carried out immediately on opening the abdomen. This should be done first, since even minimal manipulation of the liver incident to the operative technique may initiate hepatic swelling which then becomes progressively worse and limits the duration of satisfactory perfusion.

Secondly, instead of cannulae, catheters are placed in each of the vessels to be used prior to the perfusion. The catheters are of sufficient size to carry the proper flow at near normal pressures, yet without obstructing blood flow in their respective vessels. When one wishes to start the actual perfusion, all the loosely placed ligatures or nooses may be drawn up simultaneously so that there is instantaneous changeover without interruption of normal pressure and flow relationships of either the inflowing and outflowing hepatic circulation.

Both the portal vein blood and hepatic arterial blood normally empty into the hepatic sinusoid in the canine liver. In this perfusion system, therefore, partially oxygenated (70-85%) blood is introduced into the inflow catheter, although it is realized that there may be certain advantages in providing separate reservoirs, oxygenators, and pumps for perfusion through both portal vein and hepatic artery.

Perfusion in the Unanesthetized State

A variation of this system can be used when "semi chronic" conditions are desired. All catheters are placed in their respective sites, and specially devised nooses or snares are loosely placed about the vessels and their respective catheters. The ends of these snares and the catheters are exteriorized through individual stab incisions in the flanks; dilute heparin is instilled into the catheters, and the abdominal wound is closed. After the animal has recovered from the effects of the anesthesia, perfusion may be carried out as above by starting the extracorporeal pump oxygenator and simultaneously pulling up all snares.

Biopsies of the liver during this type of preparation are possible using an exposed hepatic lobe similar to that described below. The number and size of the biopsies are limited, however; this type of perfusion is usually reserved for chemical studies on the perfusion blood.

Perfusion for Prolonged Metabolic or Endocrine Studies

The perfused canine liver is most frequently used for metabolic studies where multiple large biopsies are required, and where relatively normal flow rates at near normal inflow and outflow pressures are desired for periods of several hours. Although multiple biopsies affect pressure and flow relationships and definitely limit the time of satisfactory perfusion, it is possible to maintain near normal conditions for periods of 4-6 hours.

Endocrine or metabolic studies involving multiple biopsies over prolonged periods preclude long-term, postperfusion survival of the animal. When such studies are desired, the perfusion system is modified in the following manner — (i) Shunts for bypassing portal vein and caval occlusions are omitted; instead (ii) the aorta is damped immediately before or after the hepatic perfusion system has been established; and (iii) the outflow catheter is inserted directly into the inferior vena cava above the renal veins instead of through one of the femoral veins.

Hepatic hemodynamics and metabolism may be measured in an experimental preparation which allows rapid and frequent sampling of blood entering and leaving the liver under chronic unanesthetized conditions (**Shoemaker** *et al.*, 1959a). Catheterization of the left common hepatic vein, portal vein, and splenic artery may be accomplished in the dog in a one-stage procedure through an abdominal approach. This allows sampling and measurement of various blood constituents in all three limbs of the hepatic vascular system without the necessity of anesthetic agents. The animal carries the catheters free of encumbrance or discomfort for several weeks, and may be studied at intervals under rigidly controlled experimental conditions.

Following the catheterization studies of the right heart by **Forssmann** (1929), **Cournand** and **Ranges** (1941), and **Cournand** *et al.* (1945), the hepatic vein was catheterized in a retrograde manner by **Warren** and **Brannon** (1944). **Bradley** and his associates (1945) measured the hepatic plasma clearance of bromosulfalein (BSP) as an estimation of hepatic plasma flow in dog and man, using the retrograde hepatic vein catheter and an arterial needle. **London** (1935) described a two-stage procedure in which free fascial grafts were placed over the hepatic veins; later, in the second stage, a metal cannula was placed between the fascial grafts and the surface of the abdominal wall. After the animal had recovered from the operation, sampling of the vein was accomplished by the introduction of a needle through the cannula.

The hepatic venous drainage is of special interest in relation to the technique to be described. There are a variable number of hepatic veins; usually between 7 and 10 of these are 2 mm in diameter or more. In addition we have found between 7 and 26 (mean 18) hepatic veins less than 2 mm in diameter. The largest hepatic vein in width and length is the left common hepatic vein. This vein drains the left lateral and left central lobes; at or just before its junction with the cava it receives the vein draining the left posterior lobe and the caudate lobe. There are no other major venous outflow channels from the left side of the liver. By contrast the hepatic lobes on the right side have 1 to 4 large (2 mm or more) veins and from 2 to 12 or more smaller hepatic veins.

Process of Catheterization

Fasted mongrel dogs weighing over 15 kg. are anesthetized with pentobarbital (thiopental). The approach is through an upper abdominal incision; the incision should be extended up to the base of the ensiform cartilage. The area between the left central and left lateral hepatic lobes is exposed; the branches of the biliary system and portal vein supplying these two lobes are identified. The left common hepatic vein (Fig. 2) may be further exposed by incising the hepatic capsule. A purse string suture of 0000 arterial silk is placed in the vein wall. A small incision is made in the center of the purse string, and a polyethylene tube (Clay-Adams, size PE 240) is inserted. A ligature is placed about the tube 1 cm. from its end prior to insertion, so that the precise position of the tip of the catheter may be ascertained. The purse-string suture is drawn up and tied when the ligature around the catheter is just visible. Alternatively, a trocar large enough to admit the plastic tubing may be used to insert the hepatic vein catheter.

A second catheter is placed as a cannula in the splenic artery in a routine manner. The third catheter is inserted into the splenic vein. The latter catheter is guided upward into the portal vein so that the tip of the catheter projects several centimeters into this vein. Splenectomy may then be carried out. A fourth catheter may be used to cannulate the common bile duct when indicated.

The vascular catheters should be flushed early with saline to prevent clotting. At the end of the operation they are brought out through a stab incision in the left below the 13th rib posteriorly, sutured to the skin with number 30 steel wire, and then filled with heparin 5-10 mg. per catheter. Thereafter, 1-2 ml. heparin solution, 10 mg/ml are instilled into each catheter at 8-12-hour intervals. When clots appear to block the catheter, additional amounts of heparin may be required. A jacket which encloses the chest and upper abdomen is used to prevent the dog from gaining access to the catheters.

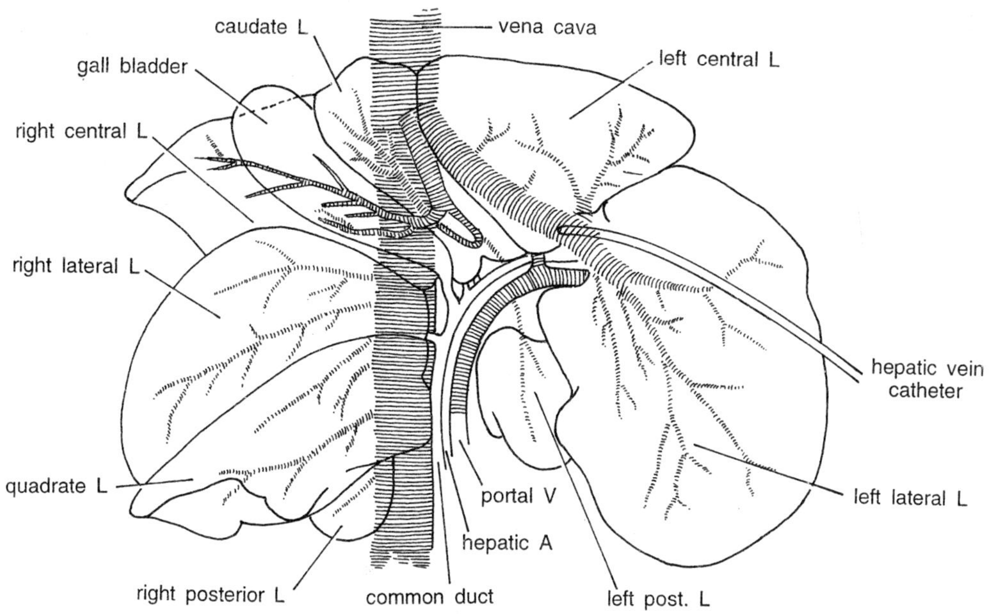

Fig. 2. Diagrammatic view of the canine liver and the hepatic venous system showing the position of the catheter in the left common hepatic vein. The left central, caudate, and right central lobes have been reflected upward to expose the hilus of the liver, the portal vein, the hepatic artery and the biliary tree. The distal aspect of the left common hepatic vein is seen in the fissure between the left central and left lateral lobes. The hepatic capsule has been removed in this area to expose the bifurcation of this vein.

Overiectomy in Rodent

The animal is placed in a large jar and anesthesia is induced with ether. When the animal has ceased to move or struggle, it is removed and placed on an operating board; anesthesia is continued with an ether cone. The hair may then be clipped from the back, although it is not essential to do so. The area is cleansed with 1:1000 Zephiran, *and an incision from 1·0 to 1·5 cm long is made in the skin midway between the last rib and the knee about 1 cm lateral to the spinal muscles (Fig. 3 A).

A second incision is made through the muscle layer and into the peritoneal cavity. If the incision is correctly placed, the ovary will be seen immediately underneath, embedded in a mass of fat (Fig. 3 B). The fat is withdrawn, and the ovary is separated and tied off with a silk ligature (Fig. 3 C, D). It may then be cut away and the uterus returned to the peritoneal cavity. The incision through the muscle is then closed with one or more sutures and the skin with two or more stitches. The ovary on the opposite side may then be removed through a separate incision.

In cases where mice or young rats are used, it may not be necessary to tie off the ovary as hemorrhage is insignificant. It is only necessary to pinch the fallopian tube and vessels present at the point where the cut will be made. This can be done with a mosquito hemostat or fine forceps of the watchmaker type. One may also simply sew the skin and disregard the incision through the muscle, if the latter is not too long.

Orchidectomy in Rodent

Castration in the male is a rather simple operation, especially in animals with external testes. In such animals, the testes are usually removed through a small incision made in the scrotum. Orchidectomy results in changes in protein and fat metabolism of the organism as well as in atrophy of the accessory organs and modification of the secondary sexual characteristics and sex behavior patterns.

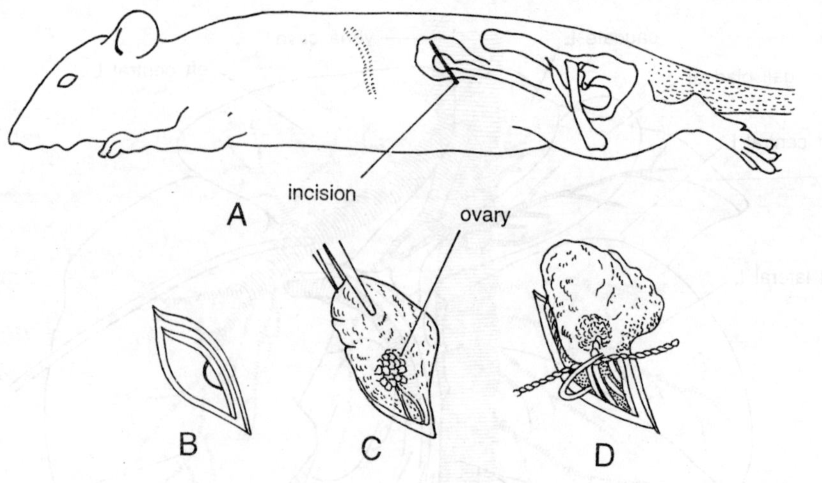

Fig. 3. Ovariectomy of the rat.

After anesthesia has been induced with ether, place the animal on an operating board, on its back. The hind legs then may be tied down and, if desired, the hair overlying the scrotal area clipped. Cleanse the skin with zephiran. An incision is made through the skin of the scrotum, and the testis on one side is separated from the surrounding tissue by blunt dissection. A second incision is then made through the transparent tunica vaginalis. This enables the tunica to be retracted and the testis to be exposed. A ligature is made around the tunica vaginalis and spermatic cord, thus interrupting the blood supply and leaving the entire testis exposed. The gland is removed by a cut close to the ligature. The second testis is then removed in the same manner and the skin incision is closed with two or three sutures. Care must be taken not to interfere with the function of the rectum and anus.

Adrenalectomy in Rodent

In order to study the symptoms and effects of adrenalectomy, complete removal of the gland is essential. Any adrenal rests or any cortical tissue that remain following surgery may regenerate into a functioning adrenal cortex. Studies on the regeneration of the enucleated adrenal gland reveal that, like adrenalectomy, removal of the gland from its capsule is followed by a rapid disappearance of corticoids from the blood and a rise in pituitary ACTH. The high levels of ACTH are maintained until the cortex regenerates and begins to secrete the various corticoids again.

Complete removal of the adrenal glands induces profound physiological changes in the animal which include a susceptibility to shock. Ether must be administered carefully and the animal watched closely, especially after one adrenal has been removed, in order to prevent death. At the conclusion of any experiment based on adrenalectomy, the animals should be examined

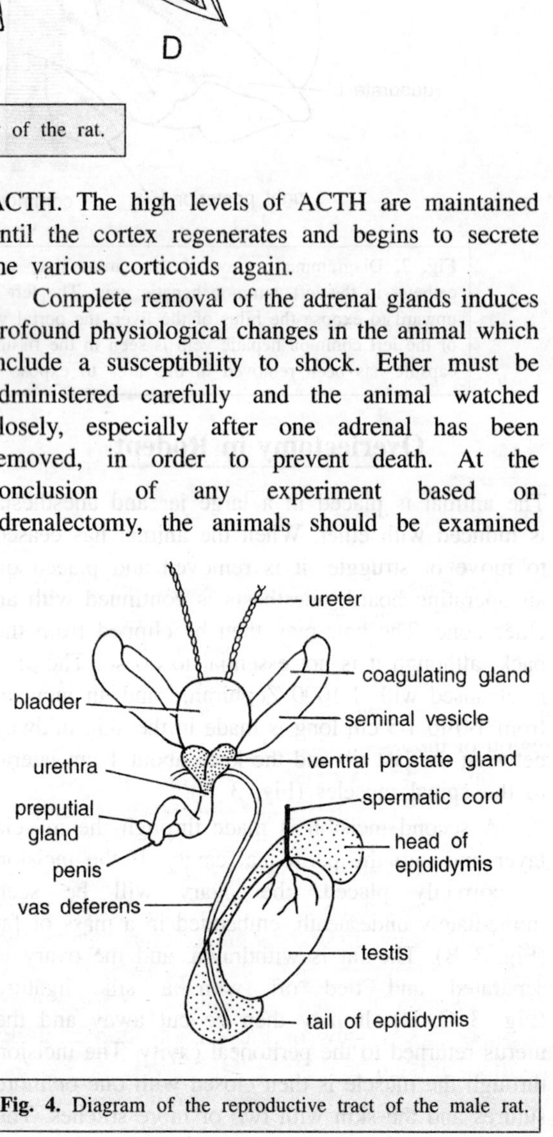

Fig. 4. Diagram of the reproductive tract of the male rat.

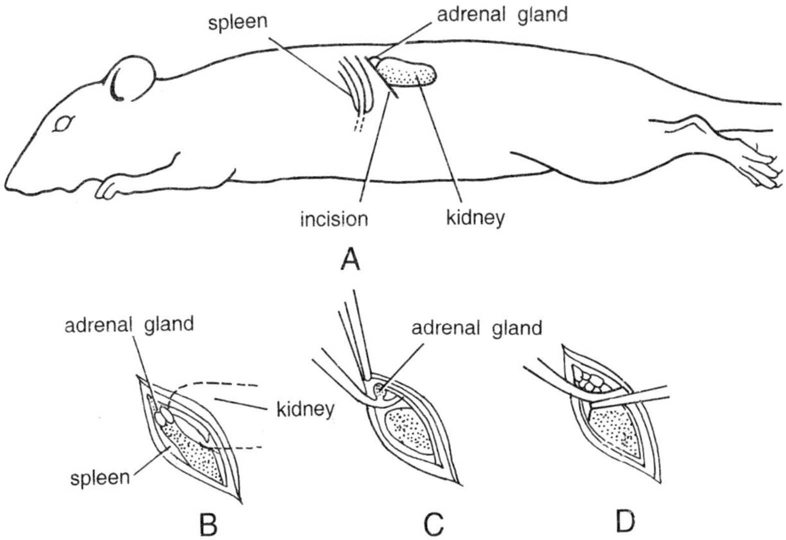

Fig. 5. Surgical adrenalectomy in the rat.

Note: At this point be sure to observe the response of the animal to the anesthetic, as it may be quite sensitive to ether.

carefully to validate the absence of adrenal tissue. While the surgical procedure is relatively simple in most experimental animals, adrenalectomy in the bird is difficult, for the glands lie close to the vena cava. Some investigators have been successful in destroying the glands by electrocautery, but even with this method the blood vessels may be damaged.

Procedure

Anesthetize a rat or mouse with ether and place the animal on an operating board, ventral side down with its nostrils exposed to an ether cone. Clip the hair from the area on both sides of the back in the region of the last rib and swab the site with zephiran solution.

Make an incision high on the right side at an angle between the last rib and vertebral column. See Fig. 5 which illustrates the incision for adrenalectomy. Take care to avoid cutting the muscles around the vertebral column. Once the incision through the skin is complete, a small cut is made through the muscle layer with iridectomy scissors, and the tips of the scissors are carefully inserted through the cut and spread to widen the opening. The kidney is readily seen and the adrenal gland will be found at the anterior pole of the kidney. The perirenal fat may be grasped with forceps and carefully pulled through the opening. Grasp the fat below the adrenal gland with curved forceps and separate it from the kidney with a second pair of forceps used to tear the fat between the forceps beneath the gland and the kidney. Extreme care must be exercised to avoid grasping the adrenal gland itself since it is a fragile structure and will tear easily, leading to an incomplete adrenalectomy. The excised gland should be placed on a moistened paper towel and inspected to be sure that the entire gland has been removed. Once the gland has been removed, the incision is closed with separate sutures applied to the muscle layer and skin. The skin incision may be closed with skin clips.

Proceed to remove the left adrenal gland in a similar manner. However, in making the incision for the removal of the left gland, make the opening slightly more posterior and central. The spleen may have to be moved anteriorly to expose the adrenal gland. It is also possible to remove the adrenals with a single skin incision across the back, which can then be pulled to the right or the left side for the placing of the incisions through the muscle.

Postoperative care and experimental. Adrenalectomized animals should be housed individually if possible, and maintained at an even temperature, slightly higher than that normally used (80-82ºF is optimal). Satisfactory maintenance requires a constant food supply, preferably a high-carbohydrate diet, and a 1% NaCl drinking solution.

Thyroidectomy in Rat

Studies on the function of thyroid gland frequently require complete ablation of thyroid in order to illustrate the physiological effect of thyroxine insufficiency. Thyroidal tissue can be destroyed by radioiodine or the synthesis of thyroxine prevented with goitrogens, but surgical removal of the gland is a relatively simple procedure. In the rodent, and other animals, surgical thyroidectomy is accompanied by a partial or complete removal of parathyroid tissue. The resulting parathormone insufficiency should be relieved by including in diet the calcium salts in the postoperative care of the animal. Surgical removal of thyroid gland must be carried out with care to avoid severing the carotid arteries or recurrent laryngeal nerves, which are lateral to the trachea.

Procedure

The animal is anesthetized with ether in a jar and placed on an operating board; anesthesia is continued with an ether cone. Make a midventral incision along the neck and retract the skin, fascia, and submaxillary glands to expose the sternomastoid and sternohyoid muscles (Fig. 6). Carefully separate the muscles along the midventral line to expose the trachea and thyroid gland. If retractors are not available, bent paper clips or piano wire attached to rubber bands may be used. If possible, use a dissecting microscope to visualize the gland and the related vascular and neural network. Use fine forceps (watchmaker's forceps) to dissect carefully one lateral edge of thyroid gland. Lift this edge and hold iridectomy scissors in a horizontal plane to clip the tissue between thyroid gland and the trachea. Proceed to work under the gland, across the surface of trachea. A delicate approach will result the removal of both lobes of gland and the connecting isthmus intact. When the gland has been removed, inspect the tissue and surface of trachea for completeness of thyroidectomy. Allow the muscles to return to normal position and close the incision on the skin with sutures. During the operation, cotton pellets may be used as sponges to reduce hemorrhage, but such pellets must be removed before the wound is closed.

Experimental. These animals may now be used to study the effects of thyroidectomy on oxygen consumption, growth and other functions.

Parathyroidectomy in Pigeon

For many years parathyroidectomy was performed by removal of thyroid gland, and hence the parathyroids also, since latter are usually embedded in the former. This operation is, in reality, called a thyroparathyroidectomy and is surgically adequate but requires that the animal be maintained on thyroxine so that the results of parathyroid deficiency

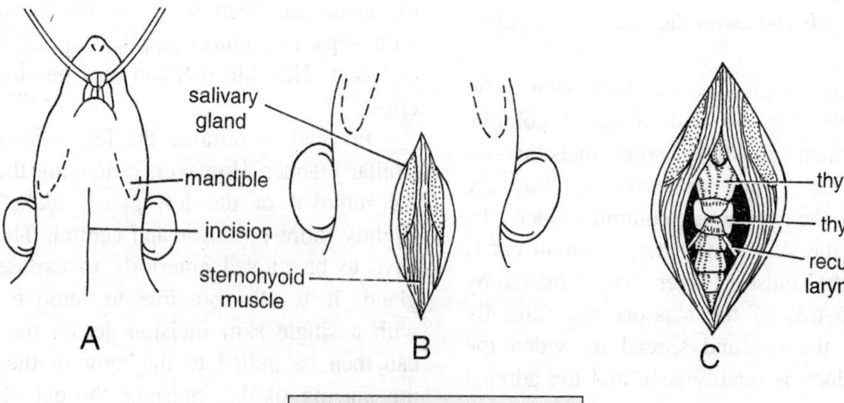

Fig. 6. Thyroidectomy in rat.

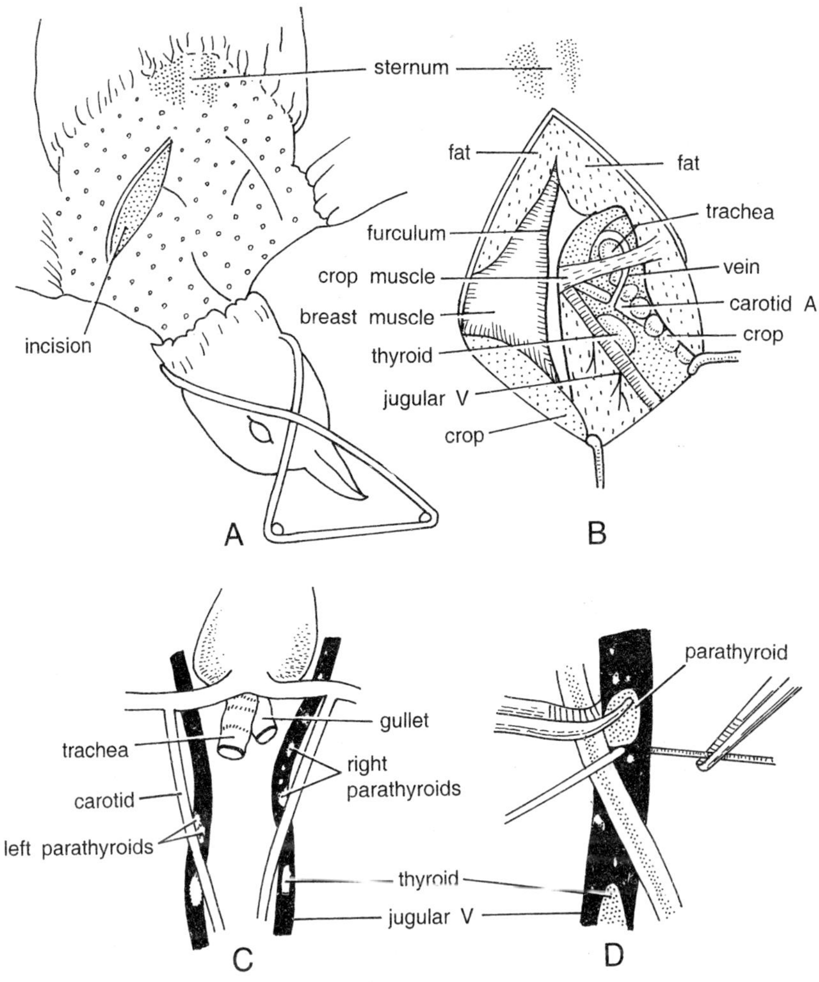

Fig. 7. Parathyroidectomy in pigeon.

are not complicated by lack of thyroid hormone. By careful dissection, it is possible to remove surgically the single pair of parathyroid glands in rat. Recently, however, another excellent method has been employed successfully that of using electrocautery as a means of destroying the tissue.

Procedure

1. Surgical procedure in rat.

(1) Place the rat under barbiturate anesthesia (Nembutal).

(2) After it has lost consciousness, place the rat on a board and secure it firmly as if for thyroidectomy.

(3) Swab the neck region with zephiran and expose the thyroid gland. Use retractors to keep the area clearly exposed.

(4) Using a dissecting microscope (15 X), carefully dissect free the lateral edges of the thyroid gland to expose the single pair of parathyroid glands: whitish bodies on the lateral edges of the anterior poles of the thyroid gland.

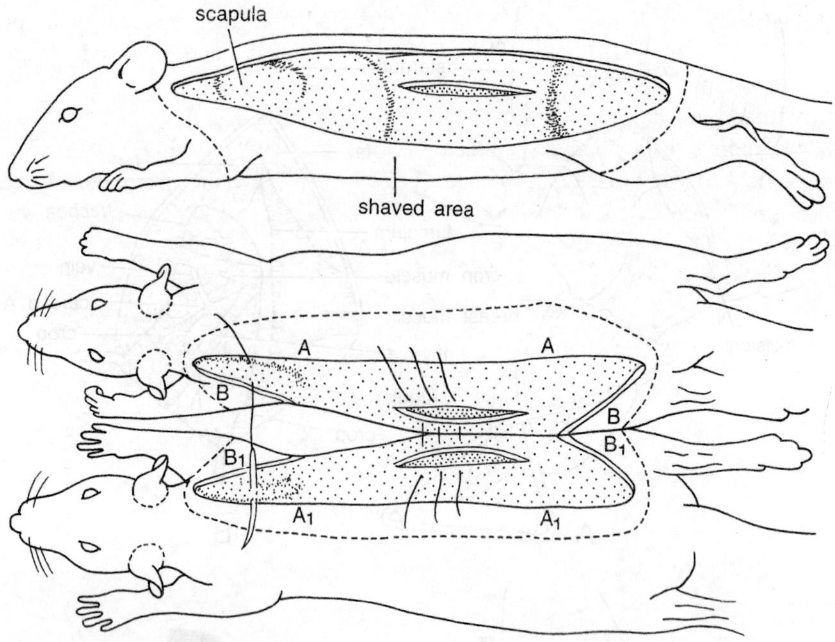

Fig. 8. Parabiosis in rat. A-A, dorsal edges clipped, b-b, ventral edges clipped.

(5) Carefully destroy each gland by electrocautery.
(6) Remove retractors and close the skin with several sutures.

2. Surgical procedure in pigeon.

(1) Anesthetize the pigeon with nembutal (25 mg per kilogram body weight) via the radial vein.
(2) Place the bird on the operating board and restrain it with rubber straps in such a position that its head is nearest the operator.
(3) Pluck the feathers over the neck and crop sac areas and make an incision 6 cm long through the skin on the left side from shoulder to sternum.
(4) Separate the crop sac from the furculum and push gently to the midline.
(5) Puncture and tear open the air sac. Fasten the bird's head securely to the board. Strangulation is not a problem since the bird can breathe through the, open air sac.
(6) Pull the trachea to the midline with retractors.
(7) Retract the crop sac and skin out of the area.
(8) Clear the region posterior to the thyroid and expose the carotid artery and jugular vein.
(9) The parathyroids are usually seen together. They may lie on the jugular vein and under the carotid artery at a point where the two vessels cross.
(10) The gland can be partly freed, ligated, and lifted out after careful separation. Care must be taken not to tear the jugular vein.
(11) The operation is completed by closing the skin with sutures and swabbing out the animal's mouth to remove mucus.
(12) The right parathyroids are removed in a similar fashion, except that the gullet is retracted and the bird's head is strapped down on the right side of the board.

It is suggested that the operation be carried out in two stages 1 week apart to reduce operative trauma and make it easier to control the resulting tetany.

Parabiosis in Rat

Parabiotic union has proved a useful method in investigation of pituitary-gonadal relationships. In unions in which one animal is hypophysectomized and the other ovariectomized, the effects of increased pituitary secretions can be observed in the gonads and reproductive tract of the hypophysectomized mate. Because the steroid hormones are rapidly inactivated by liver and other tissues, the feedback mechanism does not operate effectively since effective amounts of steroid hormones are not available to the ovariectomized partner.

The following method of parabiosis is relatively successful if young littermates of similar weight are used. The sex of the parabionts will of course depend upon which parameters are of interest. Males may be united with females.

Procedure

Two animals, preferably littermates of similar weights, between 30 and 60 days of age usually give the best results in terms of compatibility and survival. The hair is clipped from the opposite side of each animal, so that a bare section of skin extending longitudinally from behind the ear to the tail, and ventrally from the spinal cord around to the mid ventral line, is exposed. The hair on the lateral surfaces of the upper fore- and hind limbs is also removed. Wash the exposed area with 1: 1000 benzalkonium chloride (zephiran).

One animal is placed under ether anesthesia, and a single incision is made from a point about 1·0 cm behind the ear in a posterior direction (1·0 cm lateral to the middorsal line) to a point on the lateral surface of the hind leg at the level of the posterior margin of the ischium. The incision is now continued in an anterior direction over the anterior portion of the upper hind limb, along the ventrolateral margin of the abdomen and thorax, and finally toward the ear to meet and complete an elipse of excised skin. The skin section is carefully reflected (leaving as much fat as possible adhering to the animal.) and removed. A sterile gauze pad, moistened with physiological saline, is used to cover the exposed wound while the opposite side of the second animal is similarly prepared. Care must be taken to ensure an approximately equal size of the exposed areas of both animals. (This section of skin is removed so that a tighter joining can be effected, thus limiting the twisting of animals and stretching of skin which may ensue postoperatively.)

When both animals have been suitably prepared, a longitudinal incision on the lateral surface of the abdominal cavity is made (Fig. 8 A), and interrupted sutures are taken simultaneously through all four flaps of muscle, thus joining the animals. Although some experiments may necessitate leaving the abdominal cavities of both animals open to each other, it is usually more practical to suture the muscle flaps so that no herniation of intestine can occur from one animal into the next (Fig. 8B).

Medial edges of the adjoining scapulae should be anchored to each other by two or three sutures. These sutures will loosen after-several days, but need not be retaken since their main purpose is to facilitate healing of the areas by limiting movement of the animals.

Wound clips (11 mm) are laid out on a paper towel to facilitate handling. One suture is taken behind the ear to oppose the dorsal edges of each skin flap evenly. Wound clips are fastened into the skin edges along the dorsal surface about 1 inch apart, taking care that the incision is clipped evenly with the undersurfaces in opposition along its length. Turn the animals over on their backs and proceed in a similar fashion on the ventral surface. Fit in with wound clips so that they are spaced about 8 mm apart. Care should be taken that the anterior and posterior ends of the incision are well closed. Reinforcement of these areas with sutures is recommended. One or two sutures should be taken to join the adjacent ears of the animals to each other. This operation aids in limiting movement during the postoperative period. Clips may be removed after 10-14 days.

The critical period for the parabiont is during the first 2 weeks postoperatively. During this time, parabiosis intoxication can occur, killing both animals. Use of young llittermates and maintenance of semisterile technique during the operation tends to minimize this reaction. Successful parabionts can maintain life for periods as long as the life span of single animals.

Experimental

(1) Determine the vaginal cycles of each of a pair of parabionts. Do they coincide?

(2) Stimulate the cervix of one partner and observe any changes in cycle length in both partners. What happens?

(3) Inject into one of a pair of parabionts 1·0 μg estradiol for 7 days. What is the effect of the estrogen on the vaginal smears of both animals? Autopsy; weigh ovaries and uteri of both animals.

(4) Inject into one of a pair of parabionts 50 IU PMS. Observe vaginal smears. Autopsy both animals 3 days later and weigh ovaries and uteri. Compare with noninjected controls and with animals treated with estrogen.

(5) Establish several parabiotic unions between normal and castrated littermates. Inject varying doses of estrogen or androgen for I week into the castrated parabiont of each pair. Weight the gonads and reproductive tract of the normal parabiont.

Important Questions

1. Define perfusion. Discuss the perfusion technique with a suitable example.
2. How will you perform the following surgical processes in a rat/rabbit?
   (i) Ovariectomy, (ii) Orchidectomy, (iii) Adrenalectomy, (iv) Thyroidectomy, (v) Parathyroidectomy.
   (vi) Parabiosis

Management of Laboratory Animals

26

Good Laboratory Practices (GLP) for animal facilities are required to assure quality maintenance and safety of animals used in laboratory studies while conducting biochemical and behavioral research and testing of drugs and chemicals.

The goal of this chapter is to promote the care of animals used in biomedical and behavioral research and testing with the basic objective of providing education that will enhance animal well-being, and quality in the pursuit of advancement of biological knowledge relevant to man and animals.

Laboratory Animal

Adequate veterinary care must be provided that is the responsibility of a veterinarian or a person who has training or experience in laboratory animal sciences and medicine.

Daily observation of animals can be accomplished by someone other than a veterinarian; however, a mechanism of direct and frequent communication should be adopted so that timely and accurate information on problems in animal health, behaviour, and well-being is conveyed to the attending veterinarian.

The veterinarian can also contribute to the establishment of appropriate policies and procedures for ancillary aspects of veterinary care, such as reviewing protocols and proposals, animal husbandry and animal welfare; monitoring occupational health hazards containment, zoonosis control programmes; and supervising animal nutrition and sanitation. Institutional requirements will determine the need for full-time or part-time or consultative veterinary services.

Animal Procurement

All animals must be acquired lawfully as per the CPCSEA guidelines applicable in India. A health surveillance programme for screening incoming animals should be carried out to assess animal quality. Methods of transportation should also be taken into account.

Each consignment of animals should be inspected for compliance with procurement specifications, and the animals should be quarantined and stabilized according to procedures appropriate for the species and circumstances.

Quarantine, Stabilization and Separation

Quarantine is the separation of newly received animals from those already in the facility, until the health and possibly the microbial status of the newly received animals have been determined. An effective quarantine minimizes the chance for introduction of pathogens into an established colony. A minimum duration of quarantine for small lab animals is one week and larger animals is 8 weeks (cat, dog, monkey, etc.)

Effective quarantine procedures should be used for non-human primates to help limit exposure of humans to zoonotic infections.

Regardless of the duration of quarantine, newly received animals should be given a period for physiologic, psychologic and nutritional stabilization before their use. The length of stabilization time will depend on the duration of animal transportation, the species involved and the intended use of the animals.

Physical separation of animals by species is recommended to prevent interspecies disease transmission and to eliminate anxiety and possible physiological and behavioral changes due to interspecies conflict.

Such separation is usually accomplished by housing different species in separate rooms; however, cubicles, laminar-flow units, cages that have filtered air or separate ventilation, and isolators shall be suitable alternatives.

In some instances, it shall be acceptable to house two species in the same room, if they have a similar pathogen status and are behaviorally compatible.

Surveillance, Diagnosis, Treatment and Control of Disease

All animals should be observed for signs of illness, injury, or abnormal behavior by animal house staff. As a rule, this should occur daily, but more-frequent observations might be warranted, such as during postoperative recovery or when animals are in or have a physical deficit. It is imperative that appropriate methods be used for disease surveillance and diagnosis.

Unexpected deaths and signs of illness, distress, or other deviations from normal health condition in animals should be reported promptly to ensure appropriate and timely delivery of veterinary medical care. Animals that show signs of a contagious disease should be isolated from healthy animals in the colony. If an entire room of animals is known or believed to be exposed to an infectious agent (e.g. *Mycobacterium tuberculosis* in non-human primates), the group should be kept intact and isolated during the process of diagnosis, treatment, and control. Diagnostic clinical laboratory may be made available.

Animal Care and Technical Personnel

Animal care programmes require technical and husbandry support. Institutions should employ people trained in laboratory animal science or provide for both formal and on the job training to ensure effective implementation of the programme.

Personal Hygiene

It is essential that the animal care staff maintain a high standard of personal cleanliness. Facilities and supplies for meeting this obligation should be provided e.g. showers, change of uniforms, footwear's etc.

Clothing suitable for use in the animal facility should be supplied and laundered by the institution.

A commercial laundering service is acceptable in many situations; however, institutional facilities should be used to decontaminate clothing exposed to potentially hazardous microbial agents or toxic substances. In some circumstances, it is acceptable to use disposable gear such as gloves, masks, head covers, coats, coveralls and shoe covers. Personal should change clothing as often as is necessary to maintain personal hygiene. Outer garments worn in the animal rooms should not be worn outside the animal facility. Washing and showering facilities appropriate to the programme should be available. Personnel should not be permitted to eat, drink, smoke or apply cosmetics in animal rooms. A separate area or room should be made available for these purposes.

Animal Experimentation Involving Hazardous Agents

Institutions should have policies governing experimentation with hazardous agents. Institutional Biosafety Committee whose members are knowledgeable about hazardous agents, possess higher level education, research experience in many pharmaceutical industries for safety issues. This committee shall also examine the proposal on animal experiments involving hazardous agents in addition to its existing functions.

Since the use of animals in such studies requires special consideration, the procedures and the facilities to be used must be reviewed by both the Institutional Biosafety Committee and Institutional Animal Ethics Committee (IAEC).

No animal should be used for experimentation for more than 3 years unless adequate justification is provided.

Duration of Experiments

Brief physical restraint of animals for examination, collection of samples, and a variety of other clinical and experimental manipulations can be accomplished manually or with devices be suitable in size and design for the animal being held and operated properly to minimize stress and avoid injury to the animal.

Prolonged restraint of any animal, including the chairing of non-human primates, should be avoided unless essential to research objectives. Less restrictive systems, such as the tether system or the pole and collar system should be used when compatible with research objectives.

Important Guidelines for the Use of Restraint Equipments

(1) Restraint devices cannot be used simply as a convenience in handling or managing animals.
(2) The period of restraint should be the minimum required to accomplish the research objectives.
(3) Animals to be placed in restraint devices should be given training to adapt to the equipment.
(4) Provision should be made for observation of the animal at appropriate intervals.
(5) Veterinary care should be provided if lesions or illness associated with restraint are observed. The presence of lesions, illness, or severe behavioral change should be dealt with by the temporary or permanent removal of the animal from restraint.

Physical Plan

The physical condition and design of animal facility determine, to a great extent, the efficiency and economy of their operation. The design and size of an animal facility depend on the scope of institutional research activities, animals to be housed, physical relationship to the rest of the institution, and geographic location. A well-planned, properly maintained facility is an important element in good animal care.

Physical Relationship of Animal Facilities to Laboratories

Good animal husbandry and human comfort and health protection require separation of animal facilities from personnel areas such as offices, conference rooms, and most laboratories.

Laboratory animals are very sensitive to their living conditions. It is important that they should be housed in an isolated building located as far away from human habitations as possible and not exposed to dust, smoke, noise, wild rodents, insects and birds. The building, cages and environment of animal rooms are the major factors, which effect the quality of animals.

This separation can be accomplished by having the animal quarters in a separate building, wing, floor, or room. Careful planning should make it possible to place animal housing areas adjacent to or near laboratories, but separated from them by barriers such as entry locks, corridors, or floors.

In planning an animal facility the space should be well divided for various activities. The animal rooms should occupy about 50-60% of the total constructed area and the remaining area should be utilized for services such as stores, washing, office and staff, machine rooms, quarantine and corridors. The environment of animal room (macro-environment) and animal cage (micro-environment) are factors on which the production and experimental efficiency of the animal depends. Since animals are vary sensitive to environmental changes, sharp fluctuations in temperature, humidity, light, sound and ventilation should be avoided. The recommended space requirements for animal rooms, for different species are given below.

Functional Areas

The size and nature of a facility will determine whether areas for separate service functions are possible or necessary. Sufficient animal area required to :

- ensure separation of species or isolation of individual projects when necessary;
- receive, quarantine, and isolate animals; and
- provide for animal housing.
- in facilities that are small, maintain few animals or maintain animals under special conditions (e.g., facilities exclusively used for housing germfree colonies or animals in runs and pens), some functional areas listed below could be unnecessary or included in a multipurpose area. Professional judgment must be exercised when developing a practical system for animal care.
- specialized laboratories or
- individual areas continuous with or near animal housing areas for such activities as surgery, intensive care, necropsy, radiography, preparation of special diets, experimental manipulation, treatment, and diagnostic laboratory procedures containment facilities or equipment, if hazardous biological, physical, or chemical agents are to be used :
- receiving and storage areas for food, bedding
- pharmaceuticals and biologics, and supplies
- space for administration, supervision, and direction of the facility
- showers, sinks, lockers and toilets for personnel
- an area for washing and sterilization equipment and supplies,
- an autoclave for equipment
- food, and bedding; and separate areas
- for holding soiled and cleaned equipment
- an area for repairing cages and equipment
- an area to store wastes prior to incineration or removal

Physical Facilities

1. Building materials. Building material should be selected to facilitate efficient and hygienic operation of animal facilities. Durable, moisture-proof, fire-resistant, seamless materials are most desirable for interior surfaces including vermin and pest resistance.

2. Corridor (s). Corridors should be wide enough to facilitate the movement of personnel as well as equipments and should be kept clean.

3. Utilities. Utilities such as water lines, drain pipes, and electrical connections should preferably be accessible through service panels or shafts in corridors outside the animal rooms.

4. Animal room doors. Doors should be rust, vermin and dust proof. They should fit properly within their frames and provided with an observation window. Door closures may also be provided. Rodent barriers can be provided in the doors of the small animal facilities.

5. Exterior windows. Windows are not recommended for small animal facilities. However, where power failures are frequent and backup power is not available, they may be necessary to provide alternate source of light and ventilation. In primate rooms, windows can be provided.

6. Floors. Floors should be smooth, moisture proof, nonabsorbent, skid-proof, resistant to wear, acid, solvents, adverse effects of detergents and disinfectants. They should be capable of supporting racks, equipment, and stored items without becoming gouged, cracked, or pitted, with minimum number of joints.

A continuous moisture-proof membrane might be needed. If sinks are installed at the entrance to a room, they should be designed to allow for convenient passage of equipment.

7. Drain. Floor drains are not essential in all rooms used exclusively for housing rodents. Floor in such rooms can be maintained satisfactorily by wet vacuuming or mopping with appropriate disinfectants or cleaning compounds. Where floor drains are used, the floors should be sloped and drain taps kept filled with water or corrosion free mesh. To prevent high humidity, drainage must be adequate to allow rapid removal of water and drying of surfaces.

8. Walls and ceilings. Walls should be free of cracks, unsealed utility penetrations, or imperfect junctions with doors, ceilings, floors and corners. Surface materials should be capable of withstanding scrubbing with detergents and disinfectants and the impact of water under high pressure.

9. Storage areas. Separate storage areas should be designed for feed, bedding, cages and materials not in use.

Refrigerated storage, separated from other cold storage, is essential for storage of dead animals and animal tissue waste.

10. Facilities for sanitizing equipment and supplies. An area for sanitizing cages and ancillary equipment is essential with adequate water supply.

11. Experimental area. All experimental procedures in small animals should be carried out in a separate area away from the place where animals are housed. For larger animal functional areas for aseptic surgery should include a separate surgical support area, a preparation area, the operating room or rooms, and an area for intensive care and supportive treatment of animals.

Environment

1. Temperature and humidity control. Air conditioning is an effective means of regulating these environmental parameters for laboratory animals. Temperature and humidity control prevents variations due to changing climatic conditions or differences in the number and kind of room occupants.

Ideally, capability should be provided to allow variations within the range of approximately 18 to 29°C (64·4 to 84·2°F) which includes the temperature ranges usually recommended for common laboratory animals.

Relative humidity should be controllable within the range of 30% to 70% throughout the year. For larger animals a comfortable zone (18 to 37°C) should be maintained during extreme summer by appropriate methods for cooling.

2. Ventilation. In renovating existing or in building new animal facilities, consideration should be given to the ventilation of the animals primary enclosures.

Heating, ventilating, and air-conditioning systems should be designed so that operation can be continued with a standby system. The animal facility and human occupancy areas should be ventilated separately.

3. Power and lighting. The electrical system should be safe and provide appropriate lighting and a sufficient number of power outlets. It is suggested that a lighting system be installed that provides adequate illumination while people are working in the animal rooms and a lowered intensity of light for the animals.

Fluorescent lights are efficient and available in a variety of acceptable fixtures. A time-controlled lighting system should be used to ensure a regular diurnal lighting cycle wherever required. Emergency power should be available in the event of power failure.

4. Noise control. The facility should be provided with noise free environment. Noise control is an important consideration in designing an animal facility. Concrete walls are more effective than metal or plaster walls containing noise because their density reduces sound transmission.

Animal Husbandry

[I] Caging or Housing System

The caging or housing system is one of the most important elements in the physical and social environment of research animals. It should be designed carefully to facilitate animal well being, meet research requirements, and minimize experimental variables (Fig. 1-4).

The housing system should —

- provide space that is adequate, permit freedom of movement and normal postural adjustments, and have a resting place appropriate to the species;
- provide a comfortable environment
- provide an escape proof enclosure that confines animal safety
- provide easy access to food and water;
- provide adequate ventilation
- meet the biological needs of the animals, e.g., maintenance of body temperature, urination, defecation, and reproduction;
- keep the animals dry and clean, consistent with species requirements;
- facilitate research while maintaining good health of the animals.

They should be constructed of sturdy, durable materials and designed to minimize cross infection between adjoining units. Polypropylene,

Fig. 1. Polypropylene rat cage.

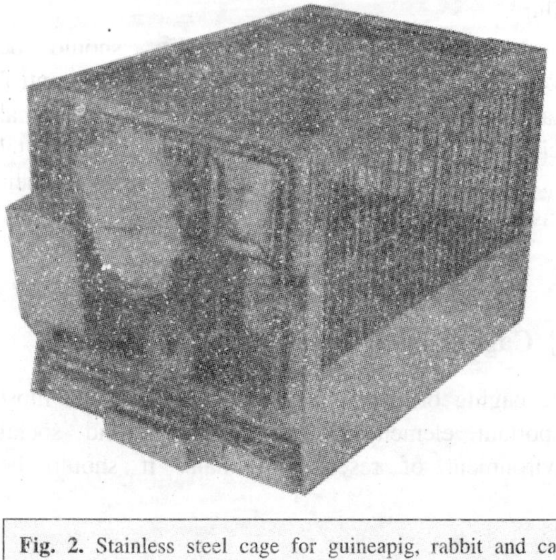

Fig. 2. Stainless steel cage for guineapig, rabbit and cat.

Fig. 3. Stainless steel cage for rabbit with partition.

Fig. 4. Metabolic cage to collect urine and excreta.

polycarbonate and stainless steel cages should be used to house small lab animals. Monkeys should be housed in cages made of steel or painted mild steel. To simplify servicing and sanitation, cages should have smooth, impervious surfaces that neither attract nor retain dirt and a minimum number of ledges, angles, and comers in which dirt or water can accumulate.

The design should allow inspection of cage occupants without disturbing them. Feeding and watering devices should be easily accessible for filling, changing, cleaning and servicing.

Cages, runs and pans must be kept in good condition to prevent injuries to animals, promote physical comfort, and facilitate sanitation and servicing. Particular attention must be given to eliminate sharp edges and broken wires, keeping cage floors in good condition.

[II] Sheltered or Outdoor Housing

When animals are maintained in outdoor runs, pans, or other large enclosures, there must be protection from extremes in temperature or other harsh weather conditions and adequate protective and escape mechanism for submissive animals, as in case of monkeys by way of an indoor portion of a run, should be provided.

Shelter should be accessible to all animals, have sufficient ventilation, and be designed to prevent build up of waste materials and excessive moisture.

Houses, dens, boxes, shelves, perches, and other furnishings should be constructed in a manner and made of materials that allow cleaning or replacement in accordance with generally accepted husbandry practices when the furnishings are soiled or wornout.

Ground-level surfaces of outdoor housing facilities can be covered with absorbent bedding, sand, gravel, grass, or similar material that can be removed or replaced when that is needed to ensure appropriate sanitation.

Buildup of animal waste and stagnant water should be avoided by, for example, using contoured or drained surface. Other surfaces should be able to withstand the elements and be easily maintained.

[III] Social Environment

The social environment includes all interactions among individuals of a group or among those able to communicate. The effects of social environment on caged animals vary with the species and experience of the animals.

In selecting a suitable social environment, attention should be given to whether the animals are naturally territorial or communal and whether they will be housed singly or in groups.

When appropriate, group housing should be considered for communal animals. In grouping animals. It is important to take into account population density and ability to disperse; initial familiarity among animals; and age, sex and social rank.

Population density can affect reproduction, metabolism, immune responses, and behavior. Group composition should be held as stable as possible, particularly for canine, non-human primates, and other highly social mammals, because mixing of groups or introducing new members can alter behavioral and physiological functions.

Non-human primates should have a run for free ranging activities —

1. Activity. Provision should be made for animals with specialized locomotor pattern to express these patterns, especially when the animals are held for long periods. For example, ropes, bars, and perches are appropriate for branching non-human primates.

Cages are often used for short-term (up to 3 months) housing of dogs and may be necessary for postsurgical care, isolation of sick dogs, and metabolic studies.

Pans, runs, or other out-of-cage space provide more opportunity, for exercise, and their use is encouraged when holding dogs for long periods.

2. Food. Animals should be fed palatable, non-contaminated, and nutritionally adequate food daily unless the experimental protocol requires otherwise.

Feeders should allow easy access to food, while avoiding contamination by urine and faeces.

Food should be available in amounts sufficient to ensure normal growth in immature animals and maintenance of normal body weight, reproduction, and lactation in adults.

Food should contain adequate nutrition, including formulation and preparation; freedom from chemical and microbial contaminants; bio-availability of nutrients should be at par with the nutritional requirement of the animal.

Laboratory animal diets should not be manufactured or stored in facilities used for farm feeds or any products containing additives such as rodenticides, insecticides, hormones, antibiotics, fumigants, or other potential toxicants.

Areas in which diets are processed or stored should be kept clean and enclosed to prevent entry of insects or other animals.

Precautions should be taken if perishable items such as meats, fruits, and vegetables are fed, because these are potential sources of biological and chemical contamination and can also lead to variation in the amount of nutrients consumed.

Diet should be free from heavy metals (e.g., lead, arsenic, cadmium, nickel, mercury), naturally occurring toxins and other contaminants.

Exposure to extremes in relative humidity, unsanitary conditions, light, oxygen, and insects hasten the deterioration of food.

Meats, fruits, vegetables, and other perishable items should be refrigerated if required to be stored. Unused, open food should be stored in vermin - proof condition to minimize contamination and to avoid potential spread of disease agents.

Food hoppers should not be transferred from room to room unless cleaned and sanitized. The animal feed should contain moisture, crude fibre, crude protein, essential vitamins, minerals crude fat and carbohydrate for providing appropriate nutrition.

3. Bedding. Bedding should be absorbent, free of toxic chemicals or other substances that could injure animals or personnel, and of a type not readily eaten by animals. Bedding should be used in amounts sufficient to keep animals dry between cage changes without coming into contact with watering tubes.

Bedding should be removed and replaced with fresh materials as often as necessary to keep the animals clean and dry. The frequency is a matter of professional judgement of the animal care personnel in consultation with the investigation depending on the number of animals and size of cages. However, it is ideal to change the bedding twice a week.

Desirable criteria for rodent bedding is sterillizable, deleterious products not formed as a result of sterilization, easily stored, non – desiccating to the animal, uncontaminated, unlikely to be chewed or mouthed, non - toxic, non -malodorous, nestable, disposable by incineration, readily available, remains chemically stable during use, manifests batch uniformity, optimizes normal animal behaviour, non -deleterious to cage - washers, non - injurious and non - hazardous to personnel, non-nutritious and non - palatable.

Nesting materials for newly delivered pups wherever can be provided (e.g. paper, tissue paper, cotton etc.).

4. Water. Ordinarily animals should have continuous access to fresh, potable, uncontaminated drinking water, according to their particular requirements. Periodic monitoring of microbial contamination in water is necessary.

Watering devices, such as drinking tubes and automatic waterers if used should be examined routinely to ensure their proper operation. Sometimes it is necessary to train animals to use automatic watering devices.

It is better to replace water bottles than to refill them, however, if bottles are refilled, care should be taken that each bottle is replaced on the cage from which it was removed.

5. Sanitation and cleanliness. Sanitation is essential in an animal facility. Animal rooms, corridors, storage spaces, and other areas should be cleaned with appropriate detergents and disinfectants as often as necessary to keep them free of dirt, debris and harmful contamination.

Cleaning utensils, such as mops, pails, and brooms, should not be transported between animal rooms.

Where animal waste is removed by hosting or flushing, this should be done at least twice a day. Animals should be kept dry during such procedures. For larger animals, such as dogs, cats, and non - human primates, soiled litter material should be removed twice daily.

Cages should be sanitized before animals are placed in them. Animal cages, racks, and accessory equipments, such as feeders and watering devices, should be washed and sanitized frequently to keep them clean and contamination free. Ordinarily this can be achieved by washing solid bottom rodent cages and accessories once or twice a week and cages, racks at least monthly.

Wire - bottom rodent cages for all other animals should be washed at least every 2 weeks, it is good practice to have extra cages available at all times so that a systematic cage-washing schedule can be maintained. Cages can be disinfected by rinsing at a temperature of 82·2°C (180°F) or higher for a period long enough to ensure the destruction of vegetative pathogenic organisms.

Disinfection can also be accomplished with appropriate chemicals; equipments should be rinsed free of chemicals prior to use. Periodic microbiologic monitoring is useful to determine the efficacy of disinfection or sterilization procedures.

Rabbits and some rodents, such as guinea pigs and hamsters, produce urine with high concentration of proteins and minerals. Minerals and organic compounds in the urine from these animals often adhere to cage surfaces and necessitate treatment with acid solutions before washing.

Water bottles, sipper tubes, stoppers, and other watering equipment should be washed and then sanitized by rinsing with water of at least 82·2°C (180°F) or appropriated chemical agents (e.g. hyperchlorite) to destroy pathogenic organisms, if bottles are washed by hand, powered rotating brushes at the washing sink are useful, and provision should be made for dipping or soaking the water bottles in detergents and disinfectant solutions. A two - compartment sink or tub is adequate for this purpose.

Some means for sterilizing equipments and supplies, such as an autoclave or gas sterilizer, is essential when pathogenic organisms are present. Routine sterilization of cages, food and bedding is not considered essential if care is taken to use clean materials from reliable sources. Where hazardous biological, chemical, or physical agents are used, a system of equipment monitoring might be appropriate.

Deodorizers or chemical agents other than germicidal should not be used to mask animal odors. Such products are not a substitute for good sanitation.

6. Assessing the effectiveness of sanitation. Monitoring of sanitation practices should be appropriate to the process and materials being cleaned; it can include visual inspection of the materials, monitoring of water temperatures, or microbiologic monitoring.

Intensity of animal odors, particularly that of ammonia, should not be used as the sole means of assessing the effectiveness of the sanitation program.

A decision to alter the frequency of cage - bedding changes or cage - washing should be based on such factors as the concentration of ammonia, the appearance of the cage, the condition of the bedding and the number and size of animals housed in the cage.

7. Waste disposal. Wastes should be removed regularly and frequently. A waste should be collected and disposed of in a safe and sanitary manner. The most preferred method of waste disposal is incineration. Incinerators should be in compliance with all central, state, and local regulations.

Waste cans containing animal tissues, carcasses, and hazardous wastes should be lined with leak - proof, disposable liners. If wastes must be stored before removal, the waste storage area should be separated from other storage facilities and free of flies, cockroaches, rodents, and other vermin. Cold storage might be necessary to prevent decomposition of biological wastes. Hazardous wastes should be rendered safe by sterilization, contamination, or other appropriate means before they are removed from an animal facility for disposal.

8. Pest control. Programmes designed to prevent, control, or eliminate the presence of or infestations by pests are essential in an animal environment.

10. Emergency, weekend and holiday care. Animals should be cared for by qualified personnel every day, including weekends and holidays, to safeguard their well-being including emergency veterinary care. In the event of an emergency, institutional security personnel and fire or police officials should be able to reach people responsible for the animals. It can be organised by prominently posting emergency procedures, names, or telephone numbers in "animal facilities" or by placing them in the security department or telephone center. A disaster, plan that takes into account both personnel and animals should be prepared as part of the overall safety plan for the animal facility.

11. Record keeping. The animal house should maintain following records :

- Animal house plans, which includes typical floor plan, all fixtures etc.
- Animal house staff record - both technical and non - technical
- Health record of staff - animals
- All SOPs relevant to the animals
- Breeding, stock, purchase and sales records
- Minutes of institute animals ethics committee meetings
- Records of experiments conducted with the number of animals used (copy of Form D)
- Death record
- Clinical record of sick animals
- Training record of staff involved in animal activities
- Water analysis report

12. Standard operating procedures (SOPs) guidelines. The institute shall maintain SOPs describing procedures/methods adapted with regard to animal husbandry, maintenance, breeding, animal house microbial analysis and experimentation records. A SOP should contain the following items :

- Name of the Author
- Title of the SOP
- Date of preparation
- Reference of previous SOP on the same subject and date (issue no and date)
- Location and distribution of SOPs with sign of each recipient
- Objectives
- Detailed information of the instruments used in relation with animals with methodology (model no., serial no., date of commissioning, etc.)
- The name of the manufacturer of the reagents and the methodology of the analysis pertaining to animals
- Normal value of all parameters
- Hazard identification and risk assessment

Personnal and Training

Selection of animal facility staff, particularly the staff working in animal rooms or involved in transportation, is a critical component in the management of an animal facility.

The staff must be provided with all required protective clothing (masks, aprons, gloves, gumboots, other footwears etc,) while working in animal rooms, facilities should be provided for change over with lockers, wash basin, toilets and bathrooms to maintain personal hygiene. It is also important that medical check-up is arranged for the workers to ensure that they have not picked up any zoonotic infection and also that they are not acting as a source of transmission of infection to the animals. The animal house in-charge should ensure that persons working in animal house don't eat, drink, smoke in animal room and have all required vaccination, particularly against tetanus and other zoonotic diseases.

Initially in-house training of staff at all levels is essential. A few weeks must be spent on the training of the newly recruited staff, teaching them the animal handling techniques, cleaning of cages and importance of hygiene, disinfection and sterilization. They should also be made familiar with the activities of normal healthy and sick animals so that they are able to spot the sick animal during their daily routine check up for cages.

Transport of Laboratory Animals

The transport of animals from one place to another is very important and must be undertaken with care. The main considerations for transport of animals are, the mode of transport, the containers, the animal density in cages, food and water during transit, protection from transit infections, injuries and stress.

The mode of transport of animals depends on the distance, seasonal and climatic conditions and the species of animals. Animals can be transported by road, rail or air taking into consideration of above factors. In any case the transport stress should be avoided and the containers should be of an appropriate size so as to enable these animals to have a comfortable, free movement and protection from possible injuries. The food and water should be provided in suitable containers or in suitable form so as to ensure that they get adequate food and more particularly water during transit. The transport containers (cages or crates) should be of appropriate size and only a permissible number of animals should only be accommodated in each container to avoid overcrowding and infighting.

Anaesthesia and Euthanasia

The scientists should ensure that the procedures, which are considered painful, are conducted under appropriate anaesthesia as recommended for each species of animals. It must also be ensured that the anaesthesia is given for the full duration of experiment and at no stage the animal is conscious to perceive pain during the experiment. If at any stage during the experiment the investigator feels that he has to abandon the experiment or he has inflicted irrepairable injury, the animal should be sacrificed. Neuromuscular blocking agents must not be used without adequate general anaesthesia.

In the event of a decision to sacrifice an animal on termination of an experiment or otherwise an approved method of euthanasia should be adopted and the investigator must ensure that the animal is clinically dead before it is sent for disposal. The data about large animals, which have been euthanised, should be maintained.

Anaesthesia

Unless contrary to the achievement of the results of study, sedatives, analgesics and anaesthetics should be used to control pain or distress under experiment. Anaesthetic agents generally affect cardiovascular, respiratory and thermo-regulatory mechanism in addition to central nervous system.

Before using actual anaesthetics the animal is prepared for anaesthesia by over night fasting and using pre-anaesthetics, which block parasympathetic stimulation of cardio-pulmonary system and reduce salivary secretion. Atropine is most commonly used anti-cholinergic agent. Local or general anaesthesia may be used, depending on the type of surgical procedure.

Local anaesthetics are used to block the nerve supply to a limited area and are used only for minor and rapid procedures. This should be carried out under expert supervision for regional infiltration of surgical site, nerve blocks and for regional and spinal anaesthesia. A number of general anaesthetic agents are used in the form of inhalants. General anaesthetics are also used in the form of intravenous or intra-muscular injections such as barbiturates. Species characteristics and variation must be kept in mind while using an anaesthetic. Side-effects such as excessive salivation, convulsions, excitement and disorientation should be suitably prevented and controlled. The animal should remain under veterinary care till it completely recovers from anaesthesia and postoperative stress.

Euthanasia

Euthanasia is resorted to events where an animal is required to be sacrificed on termination of an experiment or otherwise for ethical reasons. The procedure should be carried out quickly and painlessly in an atmosphere free from fear or anxiety. For accepting an euthanasia method as human it should have an initial depressive action on the central nervous system for immediate insensitivity to pain. The choice of a method will depend on the nature of study, the species of animal to be killed. The method should in all cases meet the following requirements :

(1) Death, without causing anxiety, pain or distress with minimum time lag phase.
(2) Minimum physiological and psychological disturbances.
(3) Compatibility with the purpose of study and minimum emotional effect on the operator.
(4) Location should be separate from animal rooms and free from environmental contaminants.

Tranquilizers have to be administered to larger species such as monkeys, dogs and cats before an euthanasia procedure.

Laboratory Animal Ethics

All scientists working with laboratory animals must have a deep ethical consideration for the animals they are dealing with. From the ethical point of view it is important that such considerations are taken care at the individual level, at institutional level and finally at the national level.

Transgenic Animals

Transgenic animals are those animals, into whose germ line foreign gene(s) have been engineered, whereas knockout animals are those whose specific gene(s) have been disrupted leading to loss of function. These animals can be bred to establish transgenic animal strains. Transgenic animals are used to study the biological functions of specific genes, to develop animal models for diseases of humans or animals, to produce therapeutic products, vaccines and for biological screening, etc. These can be either developed in the laboratory or produced for R&D purpose from registered. scientific/academic institutions or commercial firms, and generally from abroad with approval from appropriate authorities.

Maintenance

Housing, feeding, ventilation, lighting, sanitation and routine management practices for such animals are similar to those for the other animals of the species as given in guidelines. However, special care has to be taken with transgenic/gene knockout animals where the animals can become susceptible to diseases where special conditions of maintenance are required due to the altered metabolic activities. The transgenic and knockout animals carry additional genes or lack genes compared to the wild population. To avoid the spread of the genes in wild population, care should be taken to ensure that these are not inadvertently released in the wild to prevent cross breeding with other animals. The transgenic and knockout animals should be maintained in clean room environment or in animal isolators.

Disposal

The transgenic and knockout animals should be first euhanized and then disposed off as described elsewhere in the chapter. A record of disposal and the manner of disposal should be kept as a matter of routine.

Breeding and Genetics

For initiating a colony, the breeding stock must be procured from CPCSEA (Committee for the purpose of control and supervision of experiments on animals) registered breeders or suppliers ensuring that genetic makeup and health status of animal is known. In case of an inbred strain, the characters of the strain with their gene distribution and the number of inbred generation must be known for further propagation. The health status should indicate their origin, e.g. conventional, specific pathogen free or transgenic, xenotobiotic or knockout stock.

Important Questions

1. What are good laboratory practices? Describe them with special reference to animal procurement, quarantine, control of disease and personal hygiene.
2. Describe the method used in animal experiments involving hazardous agents.
3. Write an essay on animal husbandry.
4. Describe briefly the laboratory animal ethics.
5. Write short notes on the following:
   (i) Indoor and outdoor housing of laboratory animals, (ii) Transport of laboratory animals, (iii) Anesthesia and euthenasia.

27
Biostatistics

Broadly speaking, statistics is a branch of scientific methodology which deals with collection, compilation, analysis and interpretation of observational data for drawing reasonable and valid conclusions.

The application of statistical methods to biological problems is called Biostatistics. In all areas of biology and specially in the fields of genetics and plant breeding, data regarding quantitative and qualitative characters are an essential components of experimental work, which need statistical analysis and interpretations. For example, when we deal with population of total number of organisms to measure the size of any organism or its organ(s) we need to analyze the data in order to reach at some conclusions. There are two types of statistics more commonly used in biological studies. These are sample statistics and test statistics.

1. Sample statistics. It is utilized to calculate population parameters, such as mean, standard deviation, etc. It explains the nature of distribution of data. The data in this case are immediately calculated in order to provide biologists the first hand results. It also gives the knowledge of statistically significant or non significant results.

2. Test statistics. It is used to test hypotheses about one or more sample data. In statistical test, one has to choose more data for analysis, obtained by conducting an experimental design. It includes the study of chi-square and t-test, etc.

Sampling and Sampling Methods

A biologist needs to have data and that data originates from samples. The methodology of collecting samples is known as sampling. It is simply the process of bearing about the population on the basis of sample drawn from it.
The sampling methods are based on certain facts given below—
(1) Research objectives.
(2) Experimental designs.
(3) Practical considerations.

To determine them, a sample is required and the process of collecting samples is known as sampling. In biological sets of experiments, it becomes very difficult to consider about the whole populations. The best and scientific methodology is to select samples. The selected samples must have relationship with population.

Population. Total number of organisms from which all possible data pertaining to a particular experiment can be drawn.

Sample. A part of population, which is selected with the objective of investigation. The number in a sample is basieally known as the sample size.

Sampling techniques. It is very difficult to deal about sampling methods in a condense form. But it is equally important aspect in some of the disciplines such as genetics, ecology, physiology, plant-breeding, etc.

If a character of living population is to be studied, it is not possible to measure the variations found in all the individuals, however, it can be done by simply studying the representative samples drawn from each population. If sampling technique is correct the conclusion drawn from the data will be truly representative. The most important thing which one should bear in mind, at the time of collecting data, is that the sample must be of proper size in relation to the population.

The samples may be drawn at random or at a regular intervals. In random sampling every individual of population has equal chances for its representation. In case of sampling by design, samples at regular intervals are taken, i.e., in a row of plants, every plant may be taken as a sample. If a population is heterogeneous in nature different kinds of plants or every type must be represented in the sample.

The sample must be such that if conclusion is drawn from different sets of sample, it must lead to close relation to all respect of any character. If they differ widely, it may be due to wrong techniques in sampling. It is important that sampling techniques must be correct and samples must be large enough to give reliable data about a population.

Sampling and Sampling Designs

Different sampling designs can be grouped under two broad categories – Random sampling and non-random sampling.

Random sampling is referred to as probability sampling because sampling process is random and the law of probability can be applied.

Advantages of random sampling. The following are the basic advantages of random sampling :

(1) It does not depend upon the existence of detailed information.
(2) Random sampling provides estimates which are essentially unbiased and has measurable precision.
(3) When the probability sampling is used, it is possible to evaluate the relative efficiency of various sample designs.

Limitations. Despite great advantages of probability sampling technique, it has certain limitations, too. These are as follows :

(1) It requires a high level of skill and experience for its use.
(2) The costs involved in sampling are large.
(3) It requires a lot of time to plan and execute the probability sampling.

Non-random sampling is the process of sample selection without the use of randomization. The selection is done on the basis of consequences or expert judgement.

The most important difference between random and non-random sampling is that in case of random sampling, the pattern of sampling can be ascertained while in case of non-random sampling, there is no way of knowing the pattern of variability of the process.

Simple random sampling refers to the sampling techniques in which each and every item of the population has an equal and independent chance of being included in the sample.

Random samples are characterized by the way in which they are selected. Random is not used here in the sense of 'haphazard' or 'hit' or 'miss'.

To ensure randomness of selection, one may adopt either the lottery system or consult the Table of random numbers.

Lottery method. This is very popular method of taking random sample. Under this method, all items of the population are numbered or named on a separate slip of paper of identical size and shape. These slips of paper are then folded and mixed up in a container or drum. A blindfold selection is then made. With the help of an example, this method would be quite clear. For example, if we want to take a sample of 10 persons out of a population of 100 persons, the procedure is to write the names of all the 100 persons on a separate slips of the paper, fold these slips, mix them thoroughly and then select at random any 10 slips.

Table of random numbers. Several standard tables of random numbers are available, among which the following may be specially mentioned, as they have been tested extensively for randomness.

(1) **Tippett's** (1927)
(2) **Fisher** and **Yates's** (1938)
(3) **Rao, Mitra and Matthai's** (1966)

Non-random sampling: It includes three types:

(1) Judgement sampling
(2) Convenience sampling
(3) Quota sampling.

1. Judgement sampling. The choice of sample items basically depends on the discretion of the investigator. For example, if a sample of ten students is to be selected from the class of sixty for analysis of the spending habit of students, the investigator would select 10 students who, in his own opinion, are representative of the class.

This method is often utilized in solving business and economic problems. This method has several limitations.

(1) Though this method is simple, but it is not a scientific method.
(2) It involves the risk of wrong conclusions.
(3) Since an element of subjectiveness is possible, this method cannot be recommended for general use.

2. Convenience sampling. In this method, a fraction of the population being investigated which is selected neither by probability nor by judgement, but by convenience. Convenience sample is done in case of interview. The results obtained by following convenience method can hardly be representative of the populations. They are generally biased and unsatisfactory.

3. Quota sampling. Quota sampling is a type of judgement sampling. In quota sample, quota are set up according to some specified characteristics, such as so many in each age, so many in each of several income groups, etc.

Quota sample is often used in public opinion studies. It provides fruitful and satisfactory results, if the interviewers are fully-trained and follow the instructions carefully.

Selection of Samples

Samples may be of two types in the broad sense:

(1) Qualitative sample
(2) Quantitative sample.

1. Qualitative sample. Qualitative samples are representing the quality of the populations or when we compare the two samples or objects. For example, plants are taller in one area than in another, colour of fruit; smaller or bigger size of cells etc. These are qualitative samples.

2. Quantitative sample. When a sample is representing the quantity, the number is involved such as height of plant, total number of fruits per plant, size of fruit, etc. In this sample, numerical measurements are playing its important role in drawing useful conclusions.

Selection of Appropriate Method of Sampling

After discussing the different methods of sampling; the objective is which method is to be adopted in a particular situation? It is observed that the selected single method will prove to be the best under all situations.

Sample size. Sample size is an important matter to be taken while adopting a sample technique. Some experts are of the opinion that sample size should be 5% of the size of the population while others believe that sample size should be at least 10%. The following two considerations may be kept in mind in determining the appropriate size of the sample.

(1) The size of the sample should increase as variation in the individual items increases.
(2) The greater the degree of accuracy desired, the larger should be the sample size.

Merits of sampling. The sampling technique has the following merits:

(1) Less time
(2) Less cost
(3) More reliable results
(4) More detailed information

Limitations of sampling. Despite the various advantages of sampling, it does have certain limitations. Some of the difficulties involved are given below :

(1) Sample survey must be carefully planned and executed, otherwise the results obtained may be inaccurate.
(2) Sampling generally requires the services of an expert.

Sampling and non-sampling errors. The error arising, due to drawing inference(s) about the populations on the basis of few observations (sampling) is termed as sampling error. However, the error chiefly arising due to ascertainment is termed as non-sampling error.

Sometimes, care has not been taken in selecting sample. The result of sample study may not be accurate to true value. Hence, sampling gives rise to certain errors known as sampling error (or sampling fluctuations).

Sampling errors are of two types :

(1) Biased errors
(2) Unbiased errors.

Biased errors arise from any bias in selection elimination, etc. while unbiased errors arise due to chance of differences between the members of a population included in the sample and those not included in the population,

Biased error may arise due to :

(1) Faulty process of selection
(2) Faulty work during the collection of information and
(3) Faulty methods of analysis.

Non-sampling errors. When a complete enumeration of units in an area is prepared as data from errors, errors arising in this way are termed as non-sampling errors. They are due to factors other than the inductive process of inferring about the population from sample.

Non-sampling errors can occur at every stage of planning. Such errors can arise due to a number of causes such as defective method of collecting the data and its tabulations, incomplete coverage of sample, etc. The non-sampling errors may arise from one or more of the following factors :

(1) Inaccurate methods of interview or observation of measurement.
(2) Lack of trained and experienced investigators.
(3) Lack of adequate supervision of primary staff.
(4) Errors due to non-response, i.e., incomplete coverage with respect to units.
(5) Errors in data processing operations such as coding, branching, verification, tabulation, etc.
(6) Errors committed during presentation and printing of tabulated results.

These sources are not exhaustive but are able to point out the possible source(s) of error.

Control of non-sampling errors. In some situations, the non-sampling errors may be large and deserve greater attention than the sampling errors. Sampling errors decrease with increase in sample size, non-sampling errors tend to increase with the sample size. Non-sampling errors require to be controlled and reduced to a level at which their presence does not spoil the use of final results.

Measures of Central Tendency

In statistical work, it is quite essential to compare two frequency distributions. Measure of central tendency means the measurement to locate the calculated value, which describes this characteristic of a frequency distribution. The commonly used measures of central tendency are the averages. The central tendency refers to some central value in a data. It is the numerical average of collection of numbers. Besides the sample averages, some other types of measurements of central tendency are as follows :

(1) Arithmetic mean
(2) Median
(3) Mode

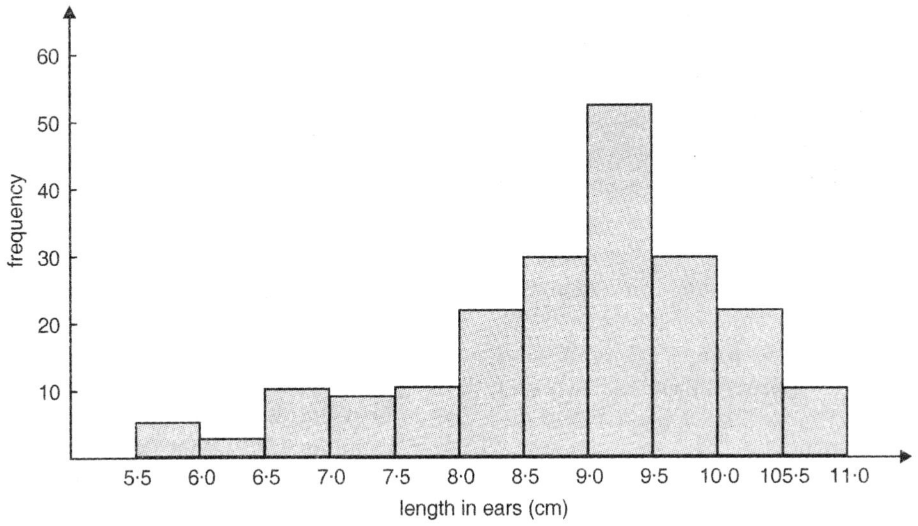

Fig. 1. A typical histogram.

Arithmetic Mean

The functional role of arithmetic mean is the condensation of data. The mean is a measurement of unit most frequently used to describe a frequency distribution of the same types of average.

Arithmetic mean or average is calculated by totalling all the observations and then dividing their sum (total) by the number of observations taken. If the total observations is S or Σ the total number of observations taken is n, and each individual observation is $x_1, x_2, x_3, ...,x_n$. Now $\bar{x}$ (arithmetic mean) can easily be calculated by dividing S by n.

$$\bar{x} = \frac{S}{n}$$

or $$\bar{x} = \frac{x_1+x_2+x_3+........+x_n}{n}$$

or $$\bar{x} = \frac{\Sigma x}{n}$$

where summation x,

$$\Sigma x = x_1 + x_2 + x_3 + ...+ x_n$$

n = total number of observations.

Example. The total length of 10 frogs is 15, 21, 17, 21, 19, 14, 16, 17, 13 and 15 cm. Calculate the arithmetic mean of the length of the frogs.

Ans. Tabulate the data as follows :

Observations	Length in cm
1.	15 (x_1)
2.	21 (x_2)
3.	17 (x_3)
4.	21 (x_4)
5.	19 (x_5)
6.	14 (x_6)
7.	16 (x_7)
8.	17 (x_8)
9.	13 (x_9)
10.	15 (x_{10})
Total n = 10	Σx =168

$$\bar{x} = \frac{\Sigma x}{n} = \frac{168}{10} = 16{\cdot}8 \text{ cm.}$$ **Ans.**

Mean can also be calculated by preparing a frequency distribution Table. It is used in case of large numbers of observations, i.e., more than 10.

Median

It is the middle value, if we arrange the whole data in an increasing order.

If there are odd numbers of observations in a series, the median is the middle value. If the data is in even numbers, median is the average of two middle values.

The methods of calculating the median are comparatively simple. The value of the median is not affected by change in extreme values.

Example. Find out the median value of the following data :

3, 9, 2, 8, 7, 1, 1, 4, 5, 6, 6, 2, 9, 7, 8 and 4.

Ans. Arrange the data in an ascending order.

1, 1, 2, 2, 3, 4, 4, 5, 6, 6, 7, 7, 8, 8, 9, 9 = (16) (even number) Because there are two mid values or positions.

$$M = \frac{5+6}{2} = \frac{11 \cdot 0}{2} = 5 \cdot 5 \textbf{ Ans.}$$

Median for Group Data

From the group data, the median falls in the class in which the middle position. i.e., the *N/2* item lies. Therefore, to locate this class viz. the median class, the median can now be obtained by using formula given below :

$$\text{Median} = l + \frac{(N/2-c)}{f} \times i$$

where

l = lowest limit of median class or the frequency obtained by adding the frequency to either ascending or descending order

c = cumulative frequency of the class preceding the median class

f = frequency of median class

i = width of median class.

Example. The weight (kg) of 55 students of a class are given below :

42, 74, 40, 60, 82, 115, 41, 61, 75, 83, 63, 53, 76, 84, 50, 67, 65, 78, 77, 56, 95, 68, 69, 104, 80, 79, 54, 73, 59, 81, 100, 66, 44, 77, 90, 84, 76, 42, 54, 70, 80, 72, 50, 79, 52, 103, 96, 51, 86, 78, 94, 71, 20, 70, 79.

Calculate the median and mode.

Ans. Frequency distribution

Class interval	Mid value x_i	Tally mark	Frequency f	C.F.	$f_i \times x_i$	f_i / x_i
40 – 50	45	~~IIII~~	05	05	225	0·11
50 – 60	55	~~IIII~~ IIII	09	14	495	0·16
60 – 70	65	~~IIII~~ IIII	09	23	585	0·14
10 – 80	75	~~IIII~~ ~~IIII~~ ~~IIII~~	15	38	1125	0·20
80 – 90	85	~~IIII~~ III	08	46	680	0·09
90 – 110	95	IIII	04	50	380	0·04
100 – 110	105	III	03	53	315	0.03
110 – 120	115	II	02	55	230	0.02
		$\Sigma f_1 = 55/2 = 27.5$			$\Sigma f_1 \times x_1 = 4035$	$\Sigma f_1 / x_1 = 0.77$

To find out median class, we use the formula

$$\text{Median} = \frac{N}{2} = \frac{55}{2} = 27 \cdot 5 \textbf{ Ans.}$$

Now, we see that 27·5 lies in the C.F. of the class interval 70–80.

So median class is 70 – 80

i = upper limit - lower limit

i = 80 – 70 = 10

Now, use the formula :

$$M = l + \frac{(N/2 - C.F.)}{f} \times i$$

$$M = 70 + \frac{27 \cdot 5 - 23}{15} \times 10$$

$$= 70 + \frac{4 \cdot 5}{15} \times 10 = 70 + 3$$

M = 73. **Ans.**

Merits

(1) It is calculated easily and can be exactly located.
(2) It does not get affected by abnormally large or small values.
(3) Its size cannot be changed much by adding a few more items.
(4) Median can be used in quantitative measurements.

Demerits

(1) The median of two or more series cannot be calculated by using the median of the component series.
(2) It may not be represented in the actual data.
(3) It can also not be used where weightage is given to some items.

Mode

Mode is another unit of measurement frequently used to obtain quick estimates of central tendency. It is defined as the most fashionable value which shows the repeated occurrence of a particular value in a set of observations.

Out of all the numbers, there is a particular figure which comes maximum number of times or number which is coming again and again is called mode.

Example. From the following number of birds, find out the mode size :

2, 4, 1, 2, 7, 7, 6, 6, 6, 5, 4, 2, 6, 6, 6, 3, 3

Ans. Mode = 6.

For group data, the mode can be calculated by identifying the class with the highest frequency as follows :

$$M = L_1 + \frac{f_m - f_1}{2f_m - f_1 - f_2} \times i$$

where L_1 = lower limit of mode class
f_m = frequency of mode class
f_1 = frequency of preceding mode class
f_2 = frequency of, succeeding mode class
i = width of the class interval.

Merits

(1) Mode is based on all the values and can be subjected to further algebraic treatments.
(2) It represents the group as well as extreme items and is not affected unless they are in the modal classes.

Demerits

It requires intricate calculations and cannot be used for future calculations and interpretations.

Measures of Dispersion or Spread

Presentation of data in the various ways such as Tables graphs and histograms gives an idea about the kind of variation available in the frequency distribution. Similarly, the measures of central tendency put forward the idea about the nature of clustering. It does not show the relationship between closeness with clustering of data around the central value, i.e., (mean, median, or mode). In other words numerical measures are very essentially required that will describe the variation of dispersion or spread of the data around the central values.

There are some measures of dispersion or measures of spread available :

(1) Range
(2) Mean deviation
(3) Standard deviation
(4) Variance
(5) Standard error of mean
(6) Coefficient of variation.

Range

The range of distribution is the difference between the largest and smallest of observations. It provides certain amount of variability.

For the data 1, 2, 3, 4. 5
Range = 1 to 5, i.e., (5 - 1) = 4.

Merits and Demerits

(1) Range is not based on complete set of data, but sample represents the two extremes of observations. So it cannot be considered as a reliable measure of variability.
(2) It is extremely influenced by the variation in sampling.
(3) Range is very much sensitive for the size of the sample/population.

Mean Deviation

Another way to provide or represent the measure of dispersion is by means of mean deviation. It can be calculated by adding the deviation of individual observations from their arithmetic mean without any consideration to the sign and dividing the sum by the total number of observations. The formula used for calculating mean deviation is given below :

$$\text{Mean deviation} = \frac{\Sigma fd}{n}$$

where f = class frequency

d = deviation from mid-value

n = total, number of observations.

The mean deviation is only simple measure of variation and does not help much for statistical analysis.

Example. Calculate the mean deviation of data for maize plants as given in the following Table:

Class value (x)	Frequency (f)	Frequency class value (f. x)	Deviation from mean (d)	f.d
(1)	(2)	(3)	(4)	(5)
58	5	290	+5.25	26.25
54	52	2808	+1.25	65.00
50	32	1600	+2.75	88.00
48	8	384	+4.75	38.00
56	28	1568	+3.25	91.00
52	75	3900	+0.75	56.25
	n = 200	Σ $f.x$ = 10,500		Σ $f.d$ =364.50

(1) $\bar{x} = \dfrac{10550}{200} = 52{\cdot}75$ cm.

(2) Mean deviation $= \dfrac{364{\cdot}50}{200} = 1{\cdot}82$ cm.

Standard Deviation

It is the measure of variability of dispersion which is the positive square root of mean of the deviation of the individual observations from their arithmetic mean or in other words the square of the standard deviation is equal to the mean of the squares of the deviation of individual observations from their arithmetic mean.

Let us suppose that total of n observations (x_1, x_2, x_3, x_4,.....,x_n) have been made. The total sum of the values of all the observations is S.

The arithmetic mean $\bar{x} = \dfrac{S}{N}$

Now square of standard deviation

$$(SD)^2 = \frac{(x_1-\bar{x})^2+(x_2-\bar{x})^2+(x_3-\bar{x})^2+\ldots\ldots+(x_n-\bar{x})^2}{n}$$

$$SD = \sqrt{\frac{(x_1-\bar{x})^2+(x_2-\bar{x})^2+(x_3-\bar{x})^2+\ldots\ldots+(x_n-\bar{x})^2}{n}}$$

where x_1, x_2, x_3, ..., x_n = individual observations

$\bar{x}$ = arithmetic mean

n = total number of observations.

Example. Find out the standard deviation of the following data :

1, 2, 3, 5, 7, 9, 11, 13, 14 and 15

Ans. 1, 2, 3, 5, 7, 9, 11, 13, 14, 15 $= \dfrac{80}{10} = 8$

After the determination of arithmetic mean ($\bar{x}$) it can be calculated in the following way :

S. No.	Observations	Mean ($\bar{x}$)	Deviation from the mean ($x-\bar{x}$)	Square of the deviation from the mean $(d)^2$
1.	1	8	-7*	49
2.	2	8	-6*	36
3.	3	8	-5*	25
4.	5	8	-3*	09
5.	7	8	-1*	01
6.	9	8	1	01
7.	11	8	2	04
8.	13	8	5	25
9.	14	8	6	36
10.	15	8	7	49
n= 10	S = 80			240

* No importance is given to the sign.

Thus

$$(SD)^2 = \frac{240}{10}$$

SD = 4.899. **Ans.**

Variance

It refers to arithmetic mean of square of deviation obtained from the mean. It can be calculated by the following formula :

$$S^2 = \frac{\Sigma(x-\bar{x})^2}{n}$$

$$S^2 = \frac{\Sigma(x-\bar{x})^2}{n-1}$$

$n - 1$ is used in order to avoid errors which can occur due to biased conditions. It is very useful measure of dispersion employed for population data. Just by knowing the expectations and variance of a random sample the good idea about the shape of its distribution can be obtained.

Standard Error of the Mean (SEM)

The standard deviation computed for sample mean is called by the name standard error of mean. This is calculated by the following formula :

$$S.\ E. = \frac{S.D.}{\sqrt{n}}$$

where $S.\ D.$ = standard deviation of individual observations

n = total number of observations.

Example. In a sample of herbs from I square metre plot, the height of 100 plants was measured. The standard deviation was calculated as 5.4. What is the standard error of the sample?

Ans. Since

$$S.\ E. = \frac{S.D.}{\sqrt{n}}$$

$$S.\ E. = \frac{5{\cdot}4}{\sqrt{100}} = \frac{5{\cdot}4}{10} = 0{\cdot}54$$

Coefficient of Variation

It measures the relative magnitude of variations present in observations and is related to the magnitude of their arithmetic mean. It is defined as the ratio of standard deviation to arithmetic mean and is expressed in percentage.

Or when the standard deviation is compared to the mean in terms of percentage we get coefficient of variation. It expresses the relative variability of each observation.

The coefficient of variation (CV) can be calculated with the help of following formula :

$$CV\ (\%) = \frac{S.D.}{\sqrt{\bar{x}}} \times 100$$

where SD = standard deviation of sample

$\bar{x}$ = arithmetic mean.

Example 11. Compare the relative variability of two samples for the following data :

Sample 'A' : Mean = 20; Standard deviation = 1·5,

Sample 'B' : Mean = 30; Standard deviation = 2·5,

(i) C.V. of sample A = $\frac{1 \cdot 5 \times 100}{20}$ = 75% **Ans.**

(ii) C.V. of sample B = $\frac{2 \cdot 5 \times 100}{30}$ = 8·3% **Ans.**

Tests of Significance

Tests of Hypotheses

Hypothesis testing determines the validity of the assumption (technically described as null hypothesis) with a view to choose between two conflicting hypotheses about the value of a population parameter. It helps in deciding, on the basis of sample data, whether a hypothesis about the population is likely to be true or false. Statisticians have developed several tests of hypotheses (also called tests of significance) for this purpose which are : Parametric tests (assume certain properties of parent population from which we draw samples), e.g. Z-test, *t*-test, χ^2-test. *F*-test, etc.

Following symbols are used to test a hypothesis :

H_a = alternative hypothesis
H_b = null hypothesis

Levels of Significance

There are two commonly used levels of significance for statistical calculations/interpretations, i.e., 1% and 5%. In short, if any calculated value exceeds the tabulated value at 1% or 5% level of significance, the observed result is said to be statistically significant. The null hypothesis is rejected in such cases. If the former value is less than the tabulated value the difference is not significant. It applies to various tests namely t-lest, *F*-test, χ^2-test etc.

Z-test

It is based on the normal probability distribution and is used for judging the significance of several measures, particularly the mean. The relevant test statistics is worked out and compared with its probable value (to be read from table showing area under the normal curve) at a specific level of significance for judging the significance of measure concerned. It is generally used to compare the mean of a sample to some hypothetical mean for population in case of large sample.

$$Z = \frac{\bar{x} - \mu_0}{\sigma / \sqrt{n}}$$

where $\bar{x}$ = sample mean
μ_0 = hypothetical mean
σ = standard deviation of the population
n = total number of observations.

t-test

It is one of the simplest tests and is often used for small samples. It was worked out by student (pen name of W.S. Gosset). It refers to a quantity of representing differences between the mean of samples mean and mean/population mean (expressed in terms of standard error). The *t*-value is calculated from the following formula :

$$t = \frac{(\bar{x} - \mu)}{S\bar{x}}$$

where $\bar{x}$ = sample mean
μ = population mean (it is a hypothetical value usually regarded as 0)
$S\bar{x}$ = standard error of the sample mean.

To compare two samples of small size, *t*-value can be determined as :

$$Z = \frac{\text{difference between sample means}}{\text{standar error of difference between means}}$$

$$OR \quad = \frac{\bar{x}A - \bar{x}B}{Sd}$$

where $\bar{x}A$ = mean of *A* sample
$\bar{x}B$ = mean of *B* sample
S_d = standard error of difference in means.

After calculating *t*-value from above said formula, this value is compared with the tabulated value of *t* as given in the Fisher & Yates's Table. To find out the number of degrees of freedom, formula *nA* + *nB* – 2 can be used. For **Example**, 15 readings for each A and B samples were used to collect data, then the number of degrees of freedom is 15 + 15 – 2 = 28. This degree of freedom is considered while finding tabulated *t*-value for probability. Generally 5% or 1% level of significance is considered to find difference. If calculated *t*-value exceeds the tabulated value then the observed difference is considered statistically significant.

Example. There are two varieties of wheat variety *A* and variety *B*. They were collected from 4 different localities which showed difference in yield per acre as given in the table below. Find out the superiority of the variety by *t*-test.

Table

Locality	Wheat yield in kg/acre		Differences	Square of differences
	Variety A	Variety B		
1.	800	810	10	100
2.	825	855	30	900
3.	750	770	20	400
4.	780	800	20	400
		Sum	80	1800

Ans. Mean differences $= \dfrac{80}{4} = 20$

Standard error of differences

$$= \frac{\sqrt{1800 - \dfrac{(80)^2}{4}}}{(4-1)\times 4}$$

$$= \frac{\sqrt{1800 - \dfrac{6400}{4}}}{12}$$

$$= \frac{\sqrt{200}}{12} = \sqrt{16 \cdot 66} = \pm\, 4 \cdot 07$$

(In making the statement on some measurement, the average should be mentioned as ± standard error)

Therefore, $t = \dfrac{20 \cdot 00}{4 \cdot 07} = \pm\, 4 \cdot 91$

Degree of freedom = $nA + nB - = 4 + 4 - 2 = 6$.

From the *t*-table, it can be found that calculated (–value is higher than the tabulated value, hence the difference is statistically significant.

Goodness of Fit

When an observed sample data is consistent with the probability model, it is called goodness of fit, or any observed data can be compared with the expected data to find out how closely it fits with latter.

CHI-Square Test

It is often used to determine the goodness of fit. This test is commonly used in genetics and breeding programmes. In short, it is a statistical comparison between observed and expected phenotypic ratios.

Generally a 'good fit' has the calculated χ^2 value smaller than the tabulated value at 5% level of significance.

χ^2 value is calculated by the following formula :

$$\chi^2 = \Sigma \frac{(\text{observed value} - \text{expected value})}{\text{expected value}}$$

$$\chi^2 = \Sigma \frac{(O-E)^2}{E} + \frac{(O-E)^2}{E}$$

$$\text{OR} = \Sigma \frac{(d)^2}{E} + \frac{(d)^2}{E}$$

where χ^2 = Greek letter (chi)

Σ = sum of all observations (summation)

O = observed value

E = expected value

d = difference or deviation between O & E value.

Each χ^2 distribution is characterized by numbers called degrees of freedom (df). It can be deduced from the formula of No. of classes/phenotypes – 1, e.g., in F_2 generation of a typical monohybrid cross, there are 2 phenotypes so df = 1.

After calculating χ^2 value, probability is found from Table against particular degree of freedom. If it exceeds the tabulated value at 1 % level (or 0·01) the observed result is statistically significant at that level, the null hypothesis (H_o) is rejected.

However, this test has limitations against its use, as it cannot be used in all cases of genetics/breeding, where frequency in any class is less than five.

Example. From a cross between tall and dwarf plants, Mendel observed 787 as tall and 277 as dwarf plants in F_2 generation. By using chi-square test, find out the goodness of fit.

Ans.

$$\chi^2 = \Sigma \frac{[\text{observed no. (tall – expected no. (tall)}]}{\text{expected no. (tall)}}$$

$$= + \frac{\text{observed no. (dwarf) Œ expected no. (dwarf)}^2}{\text{expected no. dwarf}}$$

$$= \Sigma \frac{(O-E)^2}{E} + \frac{(O-E)^2}{E}$$

$$= \frac{(787-798)^2}{798} + \frac{(277+266)^2}{266}$$

$$= \frac{(121)^2}{798} + \frac{(121)^2}{266}$$

$\chi^2 = 0.61$

d.f. $(n) = 2 - 1 = 1$

$p > 50$ NS (not significant) or between p. 50 & p 30. Hence the null hypothesis is accepted.

Important Questions

1. Describe different methods used in collecting the biological samples and their analysis.
2. Write short notes on the following
   (i) Arithmetic mean, (ii) Median, (iii) Mode, (iv) Range, (v) Mean deviation, (vi) Standard deviation, (vii) Standard error, (vii) Test of significance.

Preparation of Reagents, Stains and Buffers

28

Molar Solution

A molar solution (1 M or M) of a substance is a solution containing its gram molecular weight in 1000 ml. Thus, 0·5 M or 0·25 M solution etc. will contain ½ gram mol. wet. and ¼th gram mol. wet. of the substance respectively in 1000 ml.

Example : To prepare 0·25 M NaOH solution.

The molecular weight of Na OH is 40 and 0·25 M solution will contain40 ÷ 0·25 (40/4) : 10 gm. of NaOH in 1000 ml. distilled water.

Normal Solution

A normal solution (IN or N) of a substance is a solution containing its gram equivalent weight in 1000 ml. Thus 0.5 N, 0·25 N solution will contain ½ g. equivalent weight and ¼ gm equivalent wt in 1000 ml. From known equivalent weights, solutions of any normality can be prepared. Liquids, as acids, sometimes present some problems both for preparation of molar or normal solution.

Example : Preparation of N-hydrochloric acid.

HCl has a molecular weight 36. Thus the strength is 36% by weight. Itmeans 100 gm of given acid contains 36 gm of pure HCl. Now according to information 36 gm of pure HCl will have to be made upto 1000 ml. withwater. The problem is to get 36 g. of pure HCl.

The volume of 100 g of given acid can be calculated from the specific gravity. Specific gravity for HCl is 83·3. Thus 83·3 ml. of the given acid (containing 36 g of pure HCl) will have to be diluted to 1000 ml to prepare IN or NHCl.

Chemical Fixatives

Formalin-Acetic Acid-Alcohol (FAA)

It is a very satisfactory preservative for museum specimens. Two formulae are in common use :

Alcohol 50%	90 ml.
Formalin (commercial)	5 ml.
Glacial acetic acid	5 ml.

Other variation of this formula is :

Alcohol, 90%	85 ml.
Formalin (commercial)	10 ml.
Glacial acetic acid	5 ml.

Transean's Algal Preservative

Water	6 parts
Alcohol	3 parts
Formalin (commercial)	1 part

The addition of glycerin equaling about 5% of the total volume will serve an excellent fixative for most blue green algae.

10% Formalin

Commercial formalin	10 ml.
Water	90 ml.

To prepare a neutral formalin solution, saturate the solution with calcium carbonate or magnesium carbonate.

Cornoy's Fluid

Ethyl alcohol	60 ml.
Chloroform	30 ml.
Acetic acid glacial	10 ml.

Stains

Hematoxylin (Aqueous)

Heat 100 ml. of distilled water to boiling. Remove from flame and add 200 mg. of hematoxylin when boiling stops. It is ready for use as soon as the solution cools.

Delafield's Hematoxylin

Saturate 100 ml of distilled water with ammonia alum (aluminium ammonium sulphate) and filter. Dissolve 1 gm of hematoxylin crystals in 5 ml of absolute alcohol. Add the hematoxylin solution drop by drop to the ammonia alum solution and keep it in light for fifteen days. Then add 25 ml of methyl alcohol and the same amount of glycerin. The solution should have a dark bluish purple colour. It is ready for use after filtering. If not contaminated, this dye will remain in good condition for a year or more.

Aceto-Carmine

Mix 45 ml of glacial acetic acid with 55 ml. of distilled water. Heat this solution to boiling and add 0·5 gm – 1 gm of carmine. Shake well and filter. Use after cooling.

Aceto-Orcein

The standard solution is 1·0% in 45% acetic acid. Because of deterioration in dilute acid, the stain is best kept as 2·2% stock solution in glacial acetic acid which can be further diluted to 45% as required.

Safranine

Safranine Y crystals	1 gm.
Alcohol 50%	100 ml.

Leishman Stain For Blood

Dissolve 0.15 gms of Leishman powder in 100 ml of methyl alcohol. The stain is ready & works well for blood films.

Mayer's Haemalum

In 1000 ml (1 litre) of distilled water, dissolve

Haematoxylin	1 gm.
Sodium iodate	0.2 gm.
Potassium alum	50 gm.

Shake frequently till solution is blue-violet (few hours) now add

Chloral hydrate	50 ml.
Citric acid crystals	1 gm.

Solution will turn red-violet, store in a hard glass bottle.

Mayer's Carmalum

In 200 cc of distilled water dissolve

Potassium alum	10 gm.
Carminic acid	1 gm.

Heat gently, cool and filter and then add

Salicylic acid	0.2 gm
or	
Formalin	0.1 ml.

Mann's Methyl Blue Eosin

(A) 1% aqueous methyl blue	35 ml
1% aqueous eosin	45 ml
Distilled water	100 ml

Add a few drops of formalin as preservative.

(B) 70% alcohol with one drop of saturated solution of orange G (Dobell's differentiater).

Stain in solution A overnight, rinse in distilled water, differentiate in solution B, dehydrate and mount.

Mallory's Triple Stain

This is an excellent histological stain comprising of three steps. First of all sections are stained with solution A for thirty seconds and washed in distilled water. Then they are stained in solution B for 1-5 minutes and again washed in distilled water. Now the sections are kept is solution C for 30 seconds and are washed again in distilled water, dehydrated, cleared and mounted.

Solution A.	1. Acid fuchsin	1.0 gm.
	2. Distilled water	100 ml.
Solution B.	1. Aniline blue	0.5 ml.
	2. Orange G	2.0 gm.
	3. Phosphomolybdic acid	2.0 gm.
	4. Distilled water	100 ml.
Solution C.	1. Phosphomolybdic acid	1.0 gm.
	2. Distilled water	100 ml.

Eosin

Two types of eosin are in common practice. One is aqueous eosin and the other is alcoholic eosin.

Aqueous Eosin

Eosin powder	1.0 gm.
Distilled water	100 gm.

Alcoholic Eosin

Eosin powder	1.0 gm.
Alcohol (70% or 90%)	100 ml.

Light Green

Light green & fast green solutions are good cytoplasmic dyes. Generally they are used as counter-stains. 1% or 2% solution in distilled water or 90% alcohol can be prepared as desired.

Borax-Carmine

This is a widely used stain for whole mounts. The solution of borax and carmine stain prepared as given below are boiled for about half an hour so that it changes its colour. Now add equal volume of 70% alcohol, allow it to stand for few hours and filter. The solution ripens in 2-3 days and it is ready for use.

Borax	4 gm.
Carmine	2 gm.
Distilled water	100 ml.

Schiff's Reagent for DNA

Dissolve 1·0 gm of basic fuchsin in 200 ml of boiling distilled water. Shake for 5 minutes and cool to exactly 50°C. Filter and add to the filtrate 20 ml of N-HCl. Cool to 25°C and add 1.0 gm of sodium (or potassium) metabisulphite ($Na_2S_2O_5$). Stand this solution in dark for 14-24 hours. Add 2 gm of activated charcoal and shake for 1 minute. Filter the solution thus prepared. It should be colourless or straw yellow. Store the reagent in refrigerator and allow it to reach at room temperature before use.

Aniline-Acid Fuchsin for Mitochondria

This is a saturated solution of acid fuchsin in 5% aniline. For this method to work well, it is important to have the maximum amount of acid fuchsin in solution. A 15% solution is satisfactory. Acid fuchsin is added slowly over a period of twenty four hours. The solution is filtered before use.

Other Useful Reagents

Acid Cleaner

Sulfuric acid (commercial)	400 ml.

Potassium or sodium dichromate enough to make a saturated solution.

This reagent may be used over several times for cleaning glassware. When a greenish colour develops, it has lost its cleaning properties.

Mayer's Egg Albumen

Egg albumen	25 ml.
Glycerine	25 ml.
Phenol (carbolic acid) crystals	0.5 ml.

Filter through linen cloth, it is ready for use.

Acid Alcohol

Conc. HCl	1 ml.
70% alcohol	99 ml.

N-Hydrochloric Acid

Conc. HCl	8·25 ml.
Distilled water	91·75 ml.

Iodine for Starch Test

Iodine	0·3 gm.
Potassium iodide	1·5 gm.
Distilled water	100 ml.

Rousselet's Solution

It is a recommended narcotic for rotifers.

2% cocaine HCl	3 ml.
90% alcohol	1 ml.
Distilled water	6 ml.

In place of cocaine, eucaine may also be used.

Navashin's Fluid

Solution A.	Chromic anhydride	1·5 ml.
	Glacial acetic acid	10 ml.
	Distilled water	90 ml.
Solution B.	40% Formalin	40 ml.
	Distilled water	60 ml.

These two solutions are mixed together in equal proportions immediately before use. Optimum fixation time is 24 hours.

Ringer's Solution

Sodium chloride	0·6 gm.
Potassium chloride	0·0075 gm.
Sodium bicarbonate	0·01 gm.
Calcium chloride	0·01 gm.
Distilled water	100 ml.

Arsenic-Alum Mixture

Take white arsenic and powdered alum in equal parts and mix them. This powder is applied to the moist skin, protecting hands with gloves.

Millon's Reagent

Digest 1 part by weight of mercury with 2 parts by weight of conc. HNO_3. Dilute this digest with two volumes of water.

Fehling's Solution

(1) Dissolve 34.65 g of $CuSO_4.5H_2O$ in water and make up 500 ml.

(2) Dissolve 125 g of KOH and 173 g of Rechelle salt in water and make upto 500 ml.

Mix equal volumes of (a) and (b) immediately before use.

Benedict's Solution

(1) 1% $CuSO_4$ solution

(2) 40% sodium hydroxide solution

Sudan III Solution

Dissolve 0.1 gm. of Sudan III in 50 ml of 95% alcohol. Now add 50 ml of glycerine by stirring. It is ready for use.

Phenol 80%

Melt phenol by keeping the bottle in an oven at 60°C for few minutes. Pour 80 ml of phenol in a 100 ml. graduated cylinder, add 20 ml of distilled water and mix. Care should be taken that the phenol is whitish or slightly pinkish. Oxidized red phenol should not be used.

Ninhydrin 0·1%

Dissolve 100 mg. ninhydrin in N-Butanol and make upto 100 ml with N-butanol. The reagent should be kept in a brown bottle and should not be used after one week.

Ammonium Molybdate Reagent

Dissolve 25 g of pure ammonium molyboate in about 200 ml of distilled water. In a one litre flask place 300 ml of sodium sulphate. Add the molybdate solution to it and dilute with distilled water making a total volume of 1000 ml.

Ammonical Silver Nitrate Solution

Dissolve 26 g silver nitrate in about 500 ml of distilled water, add enough ammonium hydroxide to redissolve the precipitate which forms upon the first addition of ammonium hydroxide, and make the volume of the mixture to 1000 ml with distilled water.

Decalcifying Reagents

A decalcifying fluid is required to soften the material normally so hard that it can not be sectioned. The removal of calcium has for many years been achieved principally with acids in which calcium carbonate and phosphate are soluble. A simple 10% solution of conc nitric acid is suitable for fixed bone or teeth. Several other formulae are also employed, important are given below.

Carleton and Leach Method

Nitric acid	10 ml.
40% formalin	10 ml.
Distilled water	80 ml.

Fixed or unfixed bones are kept in this solution till soft. Then they are washed in 5% sodium sulphate and sectioned as usual.

Jenkin's Fluid

Hydrochloric acid	80 ml.
Acetic acid	200 ml.
95% Alcohol	1460 ml.
Water	200 ml.

Well fixed blocks are treated with this fluid for 16-48 hours, as necessary, and post fix for 48 hours in 10% neutral formalin.

De-Castro's Fluid

Chloral hydrate	50 g.
Absolute alcohol	300 ml.
Water	670 ml.
Nitric acid (conc.)	30 ml.

The material may be processed as for Jenkin's fluid.

Hillemann and Lee Method

Neutral formalin fixed tissues are kept is 5.5% versene in 10% formalin, renewing the solution every week till suitable. The material is then dehydrated, cleared and embedded in paraffin wax.

Mounting Media

Following histological staining of cells or tissue, the tissue must be mounted in a mounting medium that preserves the staining pattern and the integrity of the tissue, and allows thin cover slipping to assist in viewing the tissue morphology and antigen distribution. In addition to the recipes listed below, there are several aqueous and nonaqueous (organic) mounting media that are commercially available as a Ix solution. If nonaqueous media are used (such as Permount), the tissue must first be dehydrated through graded alcohols and xylene. If aqueous media are used (such as Aquapolymount), this is not necessary. If using aqueous mounting media, it is necessary to first check that the color product obtained is insoluble in water. Many of these recipes came from *Drosophila:* **A Laboratory Manual** (where specific citations and instructions for use can be found), although they can be applied to other sources of material.

Caution: See Appendix 1 for appropriate handling of materials marked with.

Aqueous Mountants

Apathy's mountant, "Refractive index 1.41"

Gum Arabic crystals	50 gm.
Cane sugar	50 gm.

Distilled water 100 cc.
Thymol 100 mg.
Dissolve with moderate heating.

Glycerine jelly "Refractive index 1.47"

Gelatine 10 gm.
Distilled water 60 cc.
Glycerol 70 cc.
Phenol 0.25 gm.

Dissolve the gelatin in distilled water in incubator or water bath before adding the remaining ingredients. This medium sets solid and requires melting before use.

Phosphate buffered glycerine jelly "Refractive index 1.47"

0.2 M phosphate buffer pH 100 ml.
Glycerol 100 ml.
Gelatin 15 g.

Slowly dissolve gelatin in phosphate buffer with moderate heat; when dissolved add glycerol and mix well. Filter through glass wool when hot.

Resinons Mountants

Canada balsam "Refractive index 1.54"

Solid Canada balsam 60 gm.
Xylene 100 ml.

DPX "Refractive index 1.52"

Distrene 80 10 gm.
Dibutylphtha-late 5 ml.
Xylene 35 ml.

Polystyrene mountant "Refractive index 1.52"

Polystyrene granules 25 gm.
Dibutyl phthalate 5 ml.
Xylene 70 ml.

Preparation of Buffers

1. Acetate Buffer

Stock solutions

A : 0.2M solution of acetic acid (11·55ml in 1000 ml) **B** : 0.2M solution of sodium acetate (16·4g of C_2H_2Na or 27·18 of $C_2H_3O_2Na.\ 3H_2O$ in 1000 ml). xml of *A*, yml of B, diluted to a total of 100 ml with distilled water.

x	y	pH
46·3	3·7	3·6
44·0	6·0	3·8
41·0	9·0	4·0
36·8	13·2	4·2
30·5	19·5	4·4
25·5	24·5	4·6
20·0	30·0	4·8
14·8	35·2	5·0
10·5	39·5	5·2
8·8	41·2	5·4
4·8	54·2	5·6

2. Boric Acid-Borax Buffer

Stock solutions

A : 0·2M solution of boric acid (12·4g in 1000 ml)
B : 0·05M solution of borax (19·05g in 1000 ml; 0·2M in terms of sodium borate) 50 ml of A, xml of *B*, diluted to a total of 200 ml. with distiled water.

x	pH
2·0	7·6
3·1	7·8
4·9	8·0
7·3	8·2
11·5	8·4
17·5	8·6
22·5	8·7
30·0	8·8
42·5	8·9
59·0	9·0
83·0	9·1
115·0	9·2

3. Carbonate-Bicarbonate Buffer

Stock solutions

A : 0.2M solution of anhydrous sodium carbonate (21.2g in 1000ml)
B : 0.2M solution of sodium bicarbonate (16.8g in 1000ml) xml of *A*, yml of *B*, diluted to a total of 200ml. with distilled water.

x	y	pH
4·0	46·0	9·2
7·5	42·5	9·3
9·5	40·5	9·4
13·0	37·0	9·5
16·0	34·0	9·6
19·5	30·5	9·7
22·0	28·0	9·8
25·0	25·0	9·9
27·5	22·5	10·0
30·0	20·0	10·1
33·0	17·0	10·2
35·5	14·5	10·3
38·5	11·5	10·4
40·5	9·5	10·5
42·5	7·5	10·6
45·0	5·0	10·7

4. Citrate Buffer

Stock solutions

A: 0·1M solution of citric acid (21·01g in 1000 ml)

B: 0·1M solution of sodium citrate (29·41g $C_6H_5O_7Na_3$ $2H_2O$ in 1000 ml) xml of *A*, yml of *B*, diluted to a total of 100 ml. with distilled water.

x	*y*	pH	*x*	*y*	pH	*x*	*y*	pH
465	35	3·0	33·0	17·0	4·0	18·0	32·0	5·2
43·7	6·3	3·2	315	18·5	4·2	16·0	34·0	5·4
40·0	10·0	3·4	28·0	22·0	44	13·7	36·3	5·6
37·0	13·0	3·6	25·5	245	4·6	11·8	38·2	5·8
35·0	15·0	3·8	23·0	27·0	4·8	9·5	415	6·0
			20·5	295	5·0	7·2	42·8	6·2

5. Glycine-HCl Buffer

Stock solutions

A: 0·2M glycine (15·01g in 1000 ml)

B: 0·2N HCl

25 ml of *A*, xml of *B* diluted to a total of 100 ml.

x	pH	*x*	pH
22·0	2·2	5·7	3·0
16·2	2·4	4·1	3·2
12·1	2·6	3·2	3·4
8·4	2·8	2·5	3·6

6. Phosphate Buffer

Stock solutions

A: 0·2M solution of monobasic sodium phosphate (27·8g in 1000 ml)

B: 0·2M solution of dibasic sodium phosphate (53·65g of $Na_2HPO_4.7H_2O$ or 71·7g of $Na_2HPO_4.12H_2O$ in 1000ml)

xml of *A*, yml of *B*, diluted to a total of 200 ml.

x	*y*	pH	*x*	*y*	pH
93·5	6·5	5·7	45·0	55·0	6·9
92·0	8·0	5·8	39·0	61·0	7·0
90·0	10·0	5·9	33·0	67·0	7·1
87·7	12·3	6·0	28·0	72·0	7·2
85·0	15·0	6·1	23·0	77·0	7·3
81·5	18·5	6·2	19·0	81·0	7·4
77·5	22·5	6·3	16·0	84·0	7·5
73·5	26·5	6·4	13·0	87·0	7·6
68·5	31·5	6·5	10·5	89·5	7·7
62·5	37·5	6·6	8·5	91·5	7·8
56·5	43·5	6·7	7·0	93·0	7·9
51·0	49·0	6·8	5·3	94·7	8·0

7. Tris (hydroxymethyl) Aminomethane (Tris. HCl) Buffer

Stock solutions

A: 0·2M solution of Tris (hydroxymethyl) aminomethane (24·2g in 1000 ml)

B: 0·2N HCl

50ml of *A*, xml of *B*, diluted to a total of 200 ml.

x	pH	*x*	pH
5·0	9·0	26·8	8·0
8·1	8·8	325	7·8
12·2	8·6	38·4	7·6
165	8·4	41·4	7·4
21·9	8·2	44·2	7·2

8. Glycine-NaOH Buffer

Stock solutions

A: 0·2M solution of glycine (15·01g in IL)

B: 0·2M NaOH

50 ml of *A* + xml of *B*, diluted to a total of 200 ml.

x	pH	*x*	pH
4·0	8·6	22·4	9·6
6·0	8·8	27·2	9·8
8·8	9·0	32·0	10·0
12·0	9·2	38·6	10·4
16·8	9·4	45·5	10·6

Andre's Mounting Medium

To 50 ml of H_2O, add 20 ml of glycerol, 30 g of gum arabic, and 200 g of chloral hydrate.

Note: This is similar to the older Faure's mounting medium but has a higher chloral hydrate content to increase its refractive index.

Gary's Magic Mountant

Dissolve 1.5-2 g of Canada balsam in 1 ml of methylsalicylate (oil of wintergreen). Stir, without heat, in a metal container for about 2 days to dissolve Canada balsam. Gary's Magic Mountant never sets hard and can be dissolved in methylsalicylate for remounting.

Gelatin/Glycerol Mountant

Allow 7 g of gelatin to swell in 42 ml of H_2O for several minutes and then dissolve by placing beaker in a boiling-water bath. Add 50 ml of glycerol and a crystal of phenol V as a bactericide. Keep at 4°C when not in use; warm to 45°C for use.

Mayer's Albumin

Mayer's albumin can be used to provide an adhesive coating to slides, e.g., for tissue sections. Prepare by mixing egg white and glycerol in equal volumes. Filter through coarse filter paper and add a preservative (e.g., thymol crystals). To coat slides, place a small drop on a cleaned slide and spread as thinly as possible.

Methacrylate

Methacrylate vapors are toxic; avoid inhalation. Methacrylate is a soluble plastic used for embedding tissue prior to sectioning. Two forms are supplied, n-butylmethacrylate and methylmethacrylate (as monomers), and mixed to provide a plastic the hardness of which depends on their ratio. The greater the proportion of methylmethacrylate, the harder the plastic is. After the plastic is mixed, 2% benzoyl peroxide is used to catalyze polymerization.

Methacrylate kits are available from Polysciences but have an inhibitor added, so as to prevent polymerization during storage. To remove, shake about 150 ml of the n-butylmethacrylate/methylmethacrylate mixture in a separatory funnel with an equal volume of 1 N NaOH. Remove the lower, aqueous phase and discard; repeat the procedure until this phase is no longer brown. To remove trace H2O (which would result in poor sections), freeze the methacrylate solution overnight at -20°C and remove the ice crystals by vacuum filtration, using a Buchner funnel and Whatman IPS phase-separating paper. Store the methacrylate over a molecular sieve (8 x 12-mesh beads of sodium alumina silicate, pore diameter 4 A, with indicator beads), protected from the light, but not for more than 6 months.

When methacrylate is used to prepare sections for RNA in situ, polymerization is normally done at high temperature. It is suggested that UV polymerization is preferable if integrity of tissue RNA is not important: Catalyze with 0.1% benzoin *iso-propyl* ether 3 inches above a UV lamp overnight. Apparently, enough UV penetrates the plastic capsules to ensure polymerization.

Mollenhauer's Mixture No.2

This is a plastic embedding mixture for histology.

A. Epon 812 — 62 ml
Araldite 506 — 81 ml
dibutyl phthalate — 7 ml

B. dodecenyl succinic anhydride

For hard blocks (i.e., 7- to 20-llm sections), mix 3.0 ml of A and 2.0 ml of B and add 9-10 drops of DMP-30. For softer blocks (i.e., 25- to 40-llm sections), mix 3.0 ml of A and 1.6 ml of Band 9.-10 drops ofDMP-30. (DMP-30 is 2,4,6-tri-(dimethylaminomethyl)phenol)

For either type of block, mix A and B and shake well (e.g., in a disposable plastic scintillation vial), place in an oven at 60°C for 5 minutes, and then add DMP-30 to warm mixture and shake well. Aliquot excess resin and freeze for future use.

Take precautions when handling these plastics-always wear gloves and work in a well-ventilated hood. Polymerize any excess resin before disposal.

Mountants, Nonaqueous

Nonaqueous mountants are either resin-based or synthetic. The solvents are usually xylene or toluene, and material to be mounted must first be dehydrated in an ethanol series and then in xylene. Euparal is an exception, and material can be transferred from absolute ethanol into this mountant. Canada balsam is usually purchased as a solution (-60-65% [w/v]) in xylene.

Mountant	Class	n	Transfer from
Canada balsam	resin	1.5447	xylene
Euparal	Semisynthetic resin (gum sandarac)	1.5174	ethanol
Per mount	-pinene	1.5286	xylene
DPX	polystyrene	1.517	xylene
Epon 812	epoxy		propylene oxide

Refractive indices are of the solid. A solvent for Euparal is sold by BDH as Euparal Essence.

p-Phenylenediamine / Glycerol Mountant

Dissolve 100 mg of p-phenylenediamine in 10 ml of phosphate buffer (10 mM at pH 7.4) and 150 mM NaCl, and add 90 ml of glycerol; adjust to pH 8.0 with 500 mM bicarbonate buffer (pH 9.0). Aliquot and store at -20°e.

n-Propyl Gallate Mountant

To mix in 80% glycerol, pulverize 4% n-propyl gallate V with a mortar and pestle to help solubilization. Dissolve in 20 mM Na carbonate buffer at pH 9.5 (20%) and glycerol (80%).

This mountant is a buffered glycerol for mounting chromosomes. Mix 9 ml of glycerol and 1 ml of 1 M Tris-HCI buffer (pH 8).

29 Hazardous Laboratory Materials/Chemicals

Acetic acid (concentrated) must be handled with great care. It may be harmful by inhalation, ingestion, or skin absorption. Wear appropriate gloves and goggles and use in a chemical fume hood.

Acrylamide (unpolymerized) is a potent neurotoxin and is absorbed through the skin (the effects are cumulative). Avoid breathing the dust. Wear appropriate gloves and a face mask when weighing powdered acrylamide and methylene-bisacrylamide. Use in a chemical fume hood. Polyacrylamide is considered to be nontoxic, but it should be handled with care because it might contain small quantities of unpolymerized acrylamide.

Actinomycin D is a teratogen and a carcinogen. It is highly toxic and may be fatal if inhaled, ingested, or absorbed through the skin. It may also cause irritation. Avoid breathing the dust. Wear appropriate gloves and safety glasses, and always use in a chemical fume hood. Solutions of actinomycin D are light sensitive.

Ammonium acetate ($H_3CCOONH_4$) may be harmful by inhalation, ingestion, or skin absorption. Wear appropriate gloves and safety glasses. Use in a chemical fume hood.

Ammonium chloride (NH_4Cl) may be harmful by inhalation, ingestion, or skin absorption. Wear appropriate gloves and safety glasses. Use in a chemical fume hood.

Ammonium hydroxide (NH_4OH) is a solution of ammonia in water. It is caustic and should be handled with great care. As ammonia vapors escape from the solution, they are corrosive, toxic, and can be explosive. Use only with mechanical exhaust. Wear appropriate gloves and use only in a chemical fume hood. Bottle should be cooled before opening.

Ammonium persulfate ($(NH_4)_2S_2OS_8$) is extremely destructive to tissue of the mucous membranes and upper respiratory tract, eyes, and skin. Inhalation may be fatal. Wear appropriate gloves, safety glasses, and protective clothing. Use only in a chemical fume hood. Wash thoroughly after handling.

Antifade, *see* Phenylenediamine

Aprotinin may be harmful by inhalation, ingestion, or skin absorption. It may also cause allergic reactions. Exposure may cause gastrointestinal effects, muscle pain, blood pressure changes, or bronchospasm. Wear appropriate gloves and safety glasses. Do not breathe the dust. Use only in a chemical fume hood.

Bacterial strains (shipping of): The Department of Health, Education, and Welfare (HEW) has classified various bacteria into different categories with regard to shipping requirements (see Sanderson and Zeigler, **Methods Enzymol. 204**: 248-264 [1991]). Nonpathogenic strains of *E. coli* (such as K12) and *B. subtilis* are in Class 1 and are considered to present no or minimal hazard under normal shipping conditions. However, *Salmonella, Haemophilus,* and certain strains of *Streptomyces* and *Pseudomonas* are in Class 2. Class 2 bacteria are "Agents of ordinary potential hazard: agents which produce disease of varying degrees of severity...but which are contained by ordinary laboratory techniques." For detailed regulations regarding the packaging and shipping of Class 2 strains, see Sanderson and Ziegler (**Methods Enzymol. 204:** 248-264 [1991]) or the instruction brochure by Alexander and Brandon (**Packaging and Shipping of Biological Materials at ATCC [1986]**) available from the American Type Culture Collection (ATCC), Rockville, Maryland.

BCIG, *see* S-Bromo-4-chloro-3-indolyl-j3-D-galactopyranoside BCIP, *see* S-Bromo-4-chloro-3-indolyl-phosphate

Benzoic acid is an irritant and may be harmful by inhalation, ingestion, or skin absorption. Wear appropriate gloves and safety glasses. Do not breathe the dust.

Benzyl alcohol is an irritant and may be harmful by inhalation, ingestion, or skin absorption. Wear appropriate gloves and safety glasses. Keep away from heat, sparks, and open flame.

Benzyl benzoate is an irritant and may be harmful by inhalation, ingestion, or skin absorption. Avoid contact with the eyes. Wear appropriate gloves and safety glasses.

Bisacrylamide is a potent neurotoxin and is absorbed through the skin (the effects are cumulative). Avoid breathing the dust. Wear appropriate gloves and a face mask when weighing powdered acrylamide and methylene-bisacrylamide.

Blood (human) and blood products and Epstein-Barr virus. Human blood, blood products, and tissues may contain occult infectious materials such as hepatitis B virus and HIV that may result in laboratory-acquired infections. Investigators working with EBV-transformed lymphoblast cell lines are also at risk of EBV infection. Any human blood, blood products, or tissues should be considered a biohazard and should be handled accordingly. Wear disposable appropriate gloves, use mechanical pipetting devices, work in a biological safety cabinet, protect against the possibility of aerosol generation, and disinfect all waste materials before disposal. Autoclave contaminated plasticware before disposal; autoclave contaminated liquids or treat with bleach (10% [v/v] final concentration) for at least 30 minutes before disposal. Consult the local institutional safety officer for specific handling and disposal procedures.

BLOTTO (Bovine Lacto Transfer Technique Optimizer) contains sodium azide. *See* Sodium azide.

Boric acid, H_3BO_3, may be harmful by inhalation, ingestion, or skin absorption. Wear appropriate gloves and goggles.

BrdU, *see* 5-Bromo-2' -deoxyuridine

5-Bromo-4-chloro-3-indolyl-β-D-galactopyranoside (BCIG; X-gal) is toxic to the eyes and skin and may be harmful by inhalation, ingestion, or skin absorption. Wear appropriate gloves and safety goggles.

5-Bromo-4-chloro-3-indolyl-phosphate (BCIP) is toxic and may be harmful by inhalation, ingestion, or skin absorption. Wear appropriate gloves and safety glasses. Do not breathe the dust.

5-Bromo-2'-deoxyuridine (BrdU) is a mutagen. It may be harmful by inhalation, ingestion, or skin absorption. It may cause irritation. Avoid breathing the dust. Wear appropriate gloves and safety glasses and always use in a chemical fume hood.

Bromophenol blue may be harmful by inhalation, ingestion, or skin absorption. Wear appropriate gloves and safety glasses. Use in a chemical fume hood.

Calcium chloride ($CaCl_2$) may be harmful by inhalation, ingestion, or skin absorption. Wear appropriate gloves and safety glasses. Use in a chemical fume hood.

Chloral hydrate is extremely destructive to tissues of the mucous membranes and upper respiratory tract. It may be harmful by inhalation, ingestion, or skin absorption. Wear appropriate gloves and safety glasses. Use in a chemical fume hood.

Chloramphenicol may be harmful by inhalation, ingestion, or skin absorption, and is a carcinogen. Wear appropriate gloves and safety glasses. Use in a chemical fume hood.

Chloroform (**$CHCl_3$**) is irritating to the skin, eyes, mucous membranes, and respiratory tract. It is a carcinogen and may damage the liver and kidneys. It is also volatile. Avoid breathing the vapors. Wear appropriate gloves and safety glasses and always use in a chemical fume hood.

Citric acid is an irritant and may be harmful by inhalation, ingestion, or skin absorption. It poses a risk of serious damage to the eyes. Wear appropriate gloves and safety goggles. Do not breathe the dust.

Colchicine is highly toxic, may be fatal, and may cause cancer and heritable genetic damage. It may be harmful by inhalation, ingestion, or skin absorption. Wear appropriate gloves and safety glasses and use only in a chemical fume hood. Do not breathe the dust.

Coomassie brilliant blue may be harmful by inhalation, ingestion, or skin absorption. Wear appropriate gloves and safety glasses.

Copper sulfate ($CuSO_4$) may be harmful by inhalation or ingestion. Wear appropriate gloves and safety glasses.

Cycloheximide may be fatal if inhaled, ingested, or absorbed through the skin. Wear appropriaJe gloves and safety glasses. Use in a chemical fume hood.

DAB, *see* 3,3' -Diaminobenzidine tetrahydrochloride

DAPI, *see* 4',6-Diamidine-2'-phenylindole dihydrochloride DEPC, *see* Diethyl pyrocarbonate

(BC–43)

4',6-Diamidine-2'phenylindole dihydrochloride (**DAPI**) is a possible carcinogen. It may be harmful by inhalation, ingestion, or skin absorption. It may also cause irritation. Avoid breathing the dust and vapors. Wear appropriate gloves and safety glasses and use in a chemical fume hood.

3,3' -Diaminobenzidine tetrahydrochloride (**DAB**) is a carcinogen. Handle with extreme care. Avoid breathing vapors. Wear appropriate gloves and safety glasses and use in a chemical fume hood.

Dibutyl phthalate may be harmful by inhalation, ingestion, or skin absorption. Wear appropriate gloves and safety glasses. Do not breathe the vapors.

Diethyl pyrocarbonate (**DEPC**) is a potent protein denaturant and is a suspected carcinogen. Aim bottle away from you when opening it; internal pressure can lead to splattering. Wear appropriate gloves and lab coat. Use in a chemical fume hood.

N,N-Dimethylformamide (**DMF**), **HCON** (**$CH_3)_2$**, is irritating to the eyes, skin, and mucous membranes. It can exert its toxic effects through inhalation, ingestion, or skin absorption. Chronic inhalation can cause liver and kidney damage. Wear appropriate gloves and safety glasses. Use in a chemical fume hood.

Dimethyl pimelimidate (**DMP**) is irritating to the eyes, skin, mucous membranes, and upper respiratory tract. It can exert harmful effects by inhalation, ingestion, or skin absorption. Avoid breathing the vapors. Wear appropriate gloves, face mask, and safety glasses.

Dimethyl sulfoxide (**DMSO**) may be harmful by inhalation or skin absorption. Wear appropriate gloves and safety glasses. Use in a chemical fume hood. DMSO is also combustible. Store in a tightly dosed container. Keep away from heat, sparks, and open flame.

Dithiothreitol (**DTT**) is a strong reducing agent that emits a foul odor. It may be harmful by inhalation, ingestion, or skin absorption. When working with the solid form or highly concentrated stocks, wear appropriate gloves and safety glasses and use in a chemical fume hood.

DMF, *see* N,N-Dimethylformamide

DMp, *see* Dimethyl pimelimidate DMSO, *see* Dimethyl sulfoxide

DTT, *see* Dithiothreitol

EMS, *see* Ethyl methane sulfonate

ENU, *see* N-Nitroso-N-ethylurea (ENU)

Ethanol, CH_3CH_2OH, may be harmful by inhalation, ingestion, or skin absorption. Wear appropriate gloves and safety glasses.

Ethanolamine, $HOCH_2CH_2NH_2$, is toxic and harmful by inhalation, ingestion, or skin absorption. Handle with care and avoid any contact with the skin. Wear appropriate gloves and goggles and use in a chemical fume hood. Ethanolamine is highly corrosive and reacts violently with acids.

Ethidium bromide is a powerful mutagen and is toxic. Consult the local institutional safety officer for specific handling and disposal procedures. Avoid breathing the dust. Wear appropriate gloves when working with solutions that contain this dye.

Ethyl methane sulfonate (**EMS**) is a volatile organic solvent that is a mutagen and carcinogen. It is harmful if inhaled, ingested, or absorbed through the skin. Discard supernatants and washes containing EMS in a beaker containing 50% sodium thiosulfate. Decontaminate all material that has come in contact with EMS by treatment in a large volume of 10% (w/v) sodium thiosulfate. Use extreme caution when handling. When using undiluted EMS, wear protective appropriate gloves and use in a chemical fume hood. Store EMS in the cold. DO NOT mouth-pipette EMS. Pipettes used with undiluted EMS should not be too warm; chill them in the refrigerator before use to minimize the volatility of EMS. All glassware coming in contact with EMS should be immersed in a large beaker of 1 N NaOH or laboratory bleach before recycling or disposal.

Ethylnitrosourea (**ENU**), *see* N-Nitroso-N-ethylurea $FeCl_3$, *see* Ferric chloride

Ferric chloride, $FeCl_3$, may be harmful by inhalation, ingestion, or skin absorption. Wear appropriate gloves and safety glasses. Use only in a chemical fume hood.

Formaldehyde (**HCHO**) is highly toxic and volatile. It is also a carcinogen. It is readily absorbed through the skin and is irritating or destructive to the skin, eyes, mucous membranes, and upper respiratory tract. Avoid breathing the vapors. Wear appropriate gloves and safety glasses. Always use in a chemical fume hood. Keep away from heat, sparks, and open flame.

Formamide is teratogenic. The vapor is irritating to the eyes, skin, mucous membranes, and upper respiratory tract. It may be harmful by inhalation, ingestion, or skin absorption. Wear appropriate gloves and safety glasses. Always use a chemical fume hood when working with concentrated solutions of formamide. Keep working solutions covered as much as possible.

Formic acid, **HCOOH**, is highly toxic and extremely destructive to tissue of the mucous membranes, upper respiratory tract, eyes, and skin. It may be harmful by inhalation, ingestion, or skin absorption. Wear appropriate gloves and safety glasses (or face shield) and use in a chemical fume hood.

β-Galactosidase is an irritant and may cause allergic reactions. It may be harmful by inhalation, ingestion, or skin absorption. Wear appropriate gloves and safety glasses.

Glassware, pressurized, must be used with extreme caution. Autoclave and cool sealed bottles in metal containers, pressurize bottles behind Plexiglas shields, and encase 20-liter bottles in wire mesh. Handle glassware under vacuum, such as desiccators, vacuum traps, drying equipment, or a reactor for working under argon atmosphere, with appropriate caution. Always wear safety glasses.

Glutaraldehyde is toxic. It is readily absorbed through the skin and is irritating or destructive to the skin, eyes, mucous membranes, and upper respiratory tract. Wear appropriate gloves and safety glasses. Always use in a chemical fume hood.

Glycine may be harmful by inhalation, ingestion, or skin absorption. Wear gloves and safety glasses. Avoid breathing the dust.

Guanidine hydrochloride is irritating to the mucous membranes, upper respiratory tract, skin, and eyes. It may be harmful by inhalation, ingestion, or skin absorption. Wear appropriate gloves and safety glasses. Avoid breathing the dust.

Guanidine thiocyanate may be harmful by inhalation, ingestion, or skin absorption. Wear appropriate gloves and safety glasses.

Guanidinium hydrochloride, *see* Guanidine hydrochloride

Guanidinium isothiocyanate, *see* Guanidine thiocyanate

Guanidinium thiocyanate, *see* Guanidine thiocyanate H3B03, *see* Boric acid

Hydrochloric acid (HCl) is volatile and may be fatal if inhaled, ingested, or absorbed through the skin. It is extremely destructive to mucous membranes, upper respiratory tract, eyes, and skin. Wear appropriate gloves and safety glasses and use with great care in a chemical fume hood. Wear goggles when handling large quantities.

Hydrogen peroxide (H_2O_2) is corrosive, toxic, and extremely damaging to the skin. It may be harmful by inhalation, ingestion, and skin absorption. Wear appropriate gloves and safety glasses and use only in a chemical fume hood.

Hydroxylamine (H_2NOH) is corrosive and toxic. It may be harmful by inhalation, ingestion, or skin absorption. Wear appropriate gloves and safety glasses and use only in a chemical fume hood.

Iodoacetamide (C_2H_4INO) can alkylate amino groups in proteins and can therefore cause problems if the antigen is being purified for amino acid sequencing. It is toxic and harmful by inhalation, ingestion, or skin absorption. Wear appropriate gloves and safety glasses and use only in a chemical fume hood. Do not breathe the dust.

IPTG, *see* Isopropyl-β -D-thiogalactopyranoside

Isopropyl-β -D-thiogalactopyranoside (IPTG) may be harmful by inhalation, ingestion, or skin absorption. Wear appropriate gloves and safety glasses.

Isotope ^{125}I accumulates in the thyroid and is a potential health hazard. Consult the local radiation safety office for further guidance in the appropriate use and disposal of radioactive materials. Wear appropriate gloves when handling radioactive substances. The $^{125}I_2$ formed during oxidation of $Na^{125}I$ is volatile. Work in an approved chemical fume hood with a charcoal filter when exposing the $Na^{125}I$ to oxidizing reagents such as chloramine- T, IODO-GEN, or acids. Because the oxidation proceeds very rapidly and releases large amounts of volatile $^{125}I_2$ when chloramine- T is used, it is important to be well prepared for each step of the reaction, so that the danger of contamination from volatile radiation can be minimized. Shield all forms of the isotope with lead. When handling the isotope, wear one or two pairs of appropriate gloves, depending on the amount of isotope being used and the difficulty of the manipulation required.

KCl, *see* Potassium chloride K4Fe(CN)6o3H2O, *see* Potassium ferrocyanide

$KH_2PO/K_2HPO/K_3PO_4$, *see* Potassium phosphate KOH, *see* Potassium hydroxide

Leupeptin (or its hemisulfate) may be harmful by inhalation, ingestion, or skin absorption. Wear appropriate gloves and safety glasses. Use in a chemical fume hood.

Lithium chloride (LiCl) is an irritant to the eyes, skin, mucous membranes, and upper respiratory tract. It may be harmful by inhalation, ingestion, or skin absorption. Wear appropriate gloves, safety goggles, and use in a chemical fume hood. Do not breathe the dust.

Lysozyme is caustic to mucous membranes. Wear appropriate gloves and safety glasses.

Magnesium acetate tetrahydrate may be harmful by inhalation, ingestion, or skin absorption. Wear appropriate gloves and safety glasses.

Magnesium chloride ($MgCl_2$) may be harmful by inhalation, ingestion, or skin absorption. Wear appropriate gloves and safety glasses and use in a chemical fume hood.

Magnesium sulfate ($MgSO_4$) may be harmful by inhalation, ingestion, or skin absorption. Wear appropriate gloves and safety glasses, and use in a chemical fume hood.

Manganese chloride ($MnCl_2$) may be harmful by inhalation, ingestion, or skin absorption. Wear appropriate gloves and safety glasses. Use in a chemical fume hood.

β-Mercaptoethanol (2-Mercaptoethanol) ($HOCH_2CH_2SH$) may be fatal if inhaled or absorbed through the skin and is harmful if ingested. High concentrations are extremely destructive to the mucous membranes, upper respiratory tract, skin, and eyes. _-Mercaptoethanol has a very foul odor. Wear appropriate gloves and safety glasses. Always use in a chemical fume hood.

Methacrylate is toxic and may be harmful by inhalation, ingestion, or skin absorption. Wear appropriate gloves and safety glasses. Do not breathe the vapors.

Methanol, H_3COH, is poisonous and can cause blindness. It may be harmful by inhalation, ingestion, or skin absorption. Adequate ventilation is necessary to limit exposure to vapors. Avoid inhaling these vapors. Wear appropriate gloves and goggles. Use only in a chemical fume hood.

Methotrexate (**MTX**) is a carcinogen and a teratogen. It may be harmful by inhalation, ingestion, or skin absorption. Exposure may cause gastrointestinal effects, bone marrow suppression, liver or kidney damage. It may also cause irritation. Avoid breathing the vapors. Wear appropriate gloves and safety glasses and always use in a chemical fume hood.

N,N' **-Methylenebisacrylamide** is a poison and may effect the central nervous system. It may be harmful by inhalation, ingestion, or skin absorption. Wear appropriate gloves and safety glasses. Do not breathe the dust.

3-(N-Morpholino)-propanesulfonic acid (**MOPS**) may be harmful by inhalation, ingestion, or skin absorption. It is irritating to mucous membranes and the upper respiratory tract. Wear appropriate gloves and safety glasses and use in a chemical fume hood.

Nitric acid (**HNO_3**) is volatile and must be handled with great care. It is toxic by inhalation, ingestion, and skin absorption. Wear appropriate gloves and safety goggles and use in a chemical fume hood. Do not breathe the vapors. Keep away from heat, sparks, and open flame.

4-Nitro blue tetrazoliumchloride (**NBT**) is hazardous. Handle with care.

N-Nitroso-N-ethylurea (**END**) may be carcinogenic and is a potent mutagen. It may be harmful by inhalation, ingestion, or skin absorption. Wear appropriate gloves and safety glasses and use in a chemical fume hood. Do not breathe the dust. Decontaminate all material that has been in contact with END in 1 N NaOH.

Paraformaldehyde is highly toxic. It is readily absorbed through the skin and is extremely destructive to the skin, eyes, mucous membranes, and upper respiratory tract. Avoid breathing the dust. Wear appropriate gloves and safety glasses, and use in a chemical fume hood. Paraformaldehyde is the undissolved form of formaldehyde.

PEG, *see* Polyethyleneglycol

Pepstatin A may be harmful by inhalation, ingestion, or skin absorption. Wear appropriate gloves and safety glasses. Use in a chemical fume hood.

Phenol is extremely toxic, highly corrosive, and can cause severe burns. It may be harmful by inhalation, ingestion, or skin absorption. Wear appropriate gloves, goggles, and protective clothing. Always use in a chemical fume hood. Rinse any areas of skin that come in contact with phenol with a large volume of water and wash with soap and water; do not use ethanol.

Phenylenediamine may be harmful by inhalation, ingestion, or skin absorption. Wear appropriate gloves and safety glasses. Use in a chemical fume hood.

Phenylmethylsulfonyl fluoride (**PMSF**), **$C_7H_7FO_2S$ or $C_6H_6CH_2SO_2F$**, is a highly toxic cholinesterase inhibitor. It is extremely destructive to the mucous membranes of the respiratory tract, eyes, and skin. It may be fatal by inhalation, ingestion, or skin absorption. Wear appropriate gloves and safety glasses and always use in a chemical fume hood. In case of contact, immediately flush eyes or skin with copious amounts of water, and discard contaminated clothing.

Phosphoric acid (**H_3PO_4**) is highly corrosive and may be harmful by inhalation, ingestion, or skin absorption. Wear appropriate gloves and safety glasses.

PMSF, *see* Phenylmethylsulfonyl fluoride

Polyacrylamide is considered to be nontoxic, but it should be treated with care because it may contain small quantities of unpolymerized material (*see* Acrylamide).

Polyethyleneglycol (**PEG**) may be harmful by inhalation, ingestion, or skin absorption. Avoid inhalation of powder. Wear appropriate gloves and safety' glasses.

Potassium chloride, **KCl**, may be harmful by inhalation, ingestion, or skin absorption. Wear appropriate gloves and safety glasses.

Potassium ferrocyanide (**$K_4Fe(CN)_6.3H_2O$**) may be fatal by inhalation, ingestion, or skin absorption. Wear appropriate gloves and safety glasses and always use with extreme care in a chemical fume hood. Keep away from strong acids.

Potassium hydroxide (**KOH**) can be highly toxic. It may be harmful by inhalation, ingestion, or skin absorption. Solutions are caustic and should be handled with great care. Wear appropriate gloves.

Potassium phosphate (**$KH_2PO_4/K_2HPO_4/K_3PO_4$**) may be harmful by inhalation, ingestion, or skin absorption. Wear appropriate gloves and safety glasses. Do not breathe the dust. K_2HPO_4?$3H_2O$ is dibasic and $KHzPO_4$ is monobasic.

Propidium iodide may be harmful by inhalation, ingestion, or skin absorption. It is irritating to the eyes, skin, mucous membranes, and upper respiratory tract. It is mutagenic and possibly carcinogenic. Wear appropriate gloves, safety glasses, and protective clothing, and always use with extreme care in a chemical fume hood.

n-Propyl gallate (**NPG**), *see* Benzoic acid

Proteinase K is an irritant and may be harmful by inhalation, ingestion, or skin absorption. Wear appropriate gloves and safety glasses.

Radioactive substances: When planning an experiment that involves the use of radioactivity, include the. physico-chemical properties of the isotope (halflife, emission type and energy), the chemical form of the radioactivity, its radioactive concentration (specific activity), total amount, and its chemical concentration. Order and use only as much as is really needed. Always wear appropriate gloves, lab coat, and safety goggles when handling radioactive material. X-rays and gamma rays are electromagnetic waves of very short wavelengths either generated by technical devices or emitted by radioactive materials. They may be emitted isotopically from the source or may be focused into a beam. Their potential dangers depend on the time period of exposure, the intensity experienced, and the wavelengths used. Be aware that appropriate shielding is usually of lead or other similar material. The thickness of the shielding is determined by the energy(s) of the X-rays or gamma rays. Consult the local safety office for further guidance in the appropriate use and disposal of radioactive materials. Always monitor thoroughly after using radioisotopes. A convenient calculator to perform routine radioactivity calculations can be found at: http://www.graphpad.com/calculators/radcalc.cfm

SOS, *see* Sodium dodecyl sulfate

Silver nitrate, **$AgNO_3$** is a strong oxidizing agent and should be handled with care. It may be harmful by inhalation, ingestion, or skin absorption. Avoid contact with skin. Wear appropriate gloves and safety glasses. It can cause explosions upon contact with other materials.

Sodium azide (**NaN_3**) is highly poisonous. It blocks the cytochrome electron transport system. Solutions containing sodium azide should be dearly marked. It may be harmful by inhalation, ingestion, or skin absorption. Wear appropriate gloves and safety goggles and handle with great care. Sodium azide is an oxidizing agent and should not be stored near flammable chemicals.

Sodium cacodylate may be carcinogenic and contains arsenic. It is highly toxic and may be fatal by inhalation, ingestion, or skin absorption. It also may cause harm to the unborn child. Effects of contact or inhalation may be delayed. Do not breathe the dust. Wear appropriate gloves and safety goggles and use only in a chemical fume hood.

Sodium carbonate (**Na_2CO_3**) may be harmful by inhalation, ingestion, or skin absorption. Wear appropriate gloves and safety glasses. Use in a chemical fume hood.

Sodium citrate, *see* Citric acid

Sodium deoxycholate is irritating to mucous membranes and the respiratory tract and may be harmful by inhalation, ingestion, or skin absorption. Wear appropriate gloves and safety g\asses when handling the powder. Do not breathe the dust.

Sodium dihydrogen phosphate (**NaH_2PO_4**) (sodium phosphate, monobasic), may be harmful by inhalation, ingestion, or skin absorption. Wear appropriate gloves and safety glasses. Use in a chemical fume hood.

Sodium dodecyl sulfate (**SDS**) is toxic, an irritant, and poses a risk of severe damage to the eyes. It may be harmful by inhalation, ingestion, or skin absorption. Wear appropriate gloves and safety goggles. Do not breathe the dust.

Sodium hydrogen phosphate, Na_2HPO_4 (**sodium phosphate, dibasic**), may be harmful by inhalation, ingestion, or skin absorption. Wear appropriate gloves and safety glasses and use in a chemical fume hood.

Sodium hydroxide, NaOH, and solutions containing NaOH are highly toxic and caustic and should be handled with great care. Wear appropriate gloves and a face mask. All other concentrated bases should be handled in a similar manner.

Sodium N-Iauroylsarcosinate may be harmful by inhalation, ingestion, or skin absorption. Wear appropriate gloves and safety glasses. Do not breathe the dust.

Sodium phosphate (**$NaH_2PO_4/Na_2HPO_4/Na_3PO_4$**) is an irritant to the eyes and skin. It may be harmful by inhalation, ingestion, or skin absorption. Wear appropriate gloves and safety goggles. Do not breathe the dust.

Sodium pyrophosphate is an irritant and may be harmful by inhalation, ingestion, or skin absorption. Wear appropriate gloves and safety glasses. Do not breathe the dust.

Solvents should be handled with great care. Wear appropriate gloves and a face protector, and use in a chemical fume hood.

Spermidine may be corrosive and harmful by inhalation, ingestion, or skin absorption. Wear appropriate gloves and safety glasses, and use in a chemical fume hood.

Streptomycin is toxic and a suspected carcinogen and mutagen. It may cause allergic reactions. It may be harmful by inhalation, ingestion, or skin absorption. Wear appropriate gloves and safety glasses.

Sulfosalicylic acid (dihydrate) is extremely destructive to the mucous membranes and respiratory system. Do not breathe the dust. Wear appropriate gloves and safety glasses and use only in a chemical fume hood.

Sulfuric acid (H_2SO_4) is highly toxic and extremely destructive to tissue of the mucous membranes and upper respiratory tract, eyes, and skin. It causes burns, and contact with other materials (e.g., paper) may cause fire. Wear appropriate gloves, safety glasses, and lab coat and use in a chemical fume hood.

TCA, *see* Trichloroacetic acid

TEMED, *see N,N,N ',N* , - Tetramethylethylene-diamine

Tetracycline may be harmful by inhalation, ingestion, or skin absorption.

Wear appropriate gloves and safety glasses and use in a chemical fume hood.

N,N,N',N' - Tetramethylethylenediamine (TEMED) is extremely destructive to tissues of the mucous membranes and upper respiratory tract, eyes, and skin. Inhalation may be fatal. Prolonged contact can cause severe irritation or burns. Wear appropriate gloves, safety glasses, and other protective clothing and use only in a chemical fume hood. Wash thoroughly after handling. *Flammable:* Vapor may travel a considerable distance to source of ignition and flash back. Keep away from heat, sparks, and open flame.

Trichloroacetic acid (TCA) is highly caustic. Wear appropriate gloves and safety goggles.

Triethanolamine may be harmful by inhalation, ingestion, or skin absorption. Wear appropriate gloves and safety glasses and use only in a chemical fume hood.

Triethylene is highly toxic and flammable. It is extremely corrosive to the mucous membranes, upper respiratory tract, eyes, and skin. It may be harmful by inhalation, ingestion, or skin absorption. Wear appropriate gloves and safety glasses and use in a chemical fume hood. Keep away from heat, sparks, and open flame.

Tris may be harmful by inhalation, ingestion, or skin absorption. Wear appropriate gloves and safety glasses.

Uranyl acetate is toxic if inhaled, ingested, or absorbed through the skin. Wear appropriate gloves and safety glasses and use in a chemical fume hood.

X-gal may be toxic to the eyes and skin. Observe general cautions when handling the powder. Note that stock solutions of X-gal are prepared in DMF, an organic solvent. For details, *see* N,N-dimethylformamide (DMF). *See also* 5Bromo-4-chloro-3-indolyl-/3-M-galactopyranoside (BCI G).

Xylene is flammable and may be narcotic at high concentrations. It may be harmful by inhalation, ingestion, or skin absorption. Wear appropriate gloves and safety glasses and use only in a chemical fume hood. Keep away from heat, sparks, and open flame.

Xylene cyanol, *see* Xylene

Zinc chloride, $ZnCl_2$, is corrosive and poses possible risk to the unborn child. It may be harmful by inhalation, ingestion, or skin absorption. Wear appropriate gloves and safety glasses. Do not breathe the dust.

Pictograms are based on widely acepted standards

Suggested Further Readings

Chapter : 1 (Assay)

Beynon, R.J. (1993). Postgraduate Study in the Biological Sciences : A Researchers Companion. Portland Press Ltd, London.

Garner, W.Y; Barge, M.S. and Ussuary, J.P. (eds.) (1992). Good Laboratory Practice Standards : Applications for Field and Laboratory Studies, ACS Professional Handbook. American Chemical Society, Washington, DC.

Harris, D. C. (1995). Quantitative Chemical Analysis, 4th ed. W. H. Freeman & Co. New York.

Samuels, M.L. (1991). Statistics for the Life Sciences. Dellen Publishing Co./Collier Macmillan Inc., San Francisco.

Chapter : 2 (Cell and Tissue Culture)

Gartlar, S.M. (1967). 2nd Bicennial Review Conf. Cell, Tissue and Organ Culture, NaCl Monographs, pp. 167-195.

Barile, M.F. (1977). in R.T. Acton, J.D. Lynn, eds., Cell Culture and its applications, Academic Press, New York.

Freshney, R.I. (1994). Culture of Animal Cells, a Manual of Basic Technique, Wiley-Liss, New York.

Chapter : 3 (Basic Requirements in a Biological Laboratory)

Ewing, G.W. Instrumental methods of chemical analysis. McGraw-Hill Book Co., New York.

Robinson, J.W. (1976). Undergraduate instrumental analysis. Marcel Dekker, New York, USA.

Oser, B.L. Hawk Physiological Chemistry, McGraw-Hill Inc. Book Co., New York.

Chapter : 4 (Fixation)

Baker, J.R. (1969). Cytological technique. Methuen and Co. Ltd. and Science Paper Backs, London.

Lillie, R.D. (1954). Histopathologic Technic and Practical Histochemistry. Blakiston Co. Inc., Philadelphia.

Walker, F.J. (1964). Formaldehyde, 3rd ed. Reinhold, New York.

Pearse, A.G.E. (1968). Histochemistry Theoretical and Applied, Volume I, Third Edition J. & A. Churchill Ltd. London.

Fugger, E.F; Bustillo, M; Dorfmann, A.D. and Schulman, J.D. (1991). Human preimplantation embryo cryopreservation : Selected aspects. *Hum. Reprod.* 6, 131-135.

Kahn, J.A; von During, V; Sunde, A; Sordal, T. and Molne, K. (1993). The efficacy and efficiency of an *in vitro* fertilization programme including embryo cryopreservation : A cohort study. *Hum. Reprod.* 8, 247-252.

Queenan, J.T; Veeck, L.L. and Muasher, S.J. (1995). Clinical and laboratory aspects of cryopreservation. *Sem. Reprod. Endocrionol.* 13, 69-71.

Trounson, A.O. (1990). Cryopreservation. *Br. Med. Bull.* 46, 695-708.

Chapter : 5 (Histological Techniques)

Cohrs, P; Jaffe, R. and Meesen, H. (1958). Pathology of laboratory animals. Springer-Verlag, Berlin, Vol. 2 (in German).

Cotchin, E. & Roe, F.J.C. (1967). Pathology of laboratory rats and mice. Blackwell, Oxford, Edinburgh.

Pearse, A.G.E. (1968, 1972). Histochemistry, theoretical and applied. 3rd ed. Churchill Livingstone, Vol. I & II. Edinburgh.

Bancroft, J.D. and Gamble, M. 2002. They avel Practice of Histological Techniques. Churchill Livingstone London.

Chapter : 6 (Microscopy)

Carr, K.E. (1971). Applications of Scanning Electron Microscopy in Biology. Int. Rev. Cytology, 30:183.

Cuello, A.C. (1983). Immunohistochemistry. IBRO Publishers Oxford.

Everhart, T.E. and Hayes, T.L. (1972). The Scanning Electron Microscope. Scientific American, January, p. 54.

Gabe, M. (1976). Histological Techniques. Springer-Ver-lag, Berlin.

Haggis, G.H. (1966). The Electron Microscope in Molecular Biology. John Wiley & Sons, New York.

Koehler, J.K. (1973). Advanced Techniques in Biological Electron Microscopy. Springer-Verlag, Berlin.

Pearse, A.G.E. (1980). Histochemistry : Theoretical & Applied. Vol. 1. 4th Ed. Churchill, London.

Sternberger, L.A. (1979). Immunocytochemistry. 2nd ed. John Wiley & Sons, New York.

Chapter : 7 (Centrifugation)

Birnie, G.D. and Rickwood, D. (1979). Centrifugal separations in molecular and cell biology. Butterworth, London.

Ford, T.C. and Graham, J.M. (1991). An introduction to centrifugation. Bios Scientific, Oxford.

Bickwood, D. (ed.) (1984). Centrifugation, 2nd edn. Published in the Practical Approaches to Biochemistry Series, IRL Press, Oxford/Washington DC.

Van Holde, K.E; Johnson, W. C. and HO, P. S. (1998). Principles of Physical Biochemistry. Prantice Hall, Upper Saddle River NJ.

Chapter : 8 (Spectrophotometry)

Brown, S.B. (1980). An introduction to spectroscopy for biochemists. Academic Press, London.

Beluca, M.A. (ed.) (1978). Methods in Enzymology, vol. 57. Bioluminescence and Chemiluminescence. Academic Press, London.

Haster, R.E. and Girling, R.B. (eds.) (1991). Spectroscopy of Biological Molecules. Royal Society of Chemistry Special Publication, Cambridge.

Lakowicz, J.R. (1983). Principles of fluorescence spectroscopy. Plenum Press, New York.

Chapter : 9 (Mass Spectrophotometry)

A.E. Ashcroft 1997. Ionization Methods in organic Mass Spectrometry.

J.R. Barker 1998. Mass Spectrometery. 2nd Edition.

J.R. Chapman 1993 Practrical Organic Mass Spectrometry, 2nd Edition.

Chapter : 10 (Electron Spin Resonance Spectroscopy and Nuclear Magnetic Resonance Spectroscopy)

Berliner, L.J. and Renben, J. (ed.) 1993. EMR of paramagnetic molecules. In "Biological Magnetic Resonance", Vol. 13, Plenum Press, New York.

Chapter : 11 (X-ray Diffraction)

Van Holde, K.E; Johnson, W.C. and Ho, P.-S. (1998) *Principles of Physical Biochemistry,* Prentice Hall, Upper Saddle River, N.J.

Chapter : 12 (Chromatography)

Jinno, K. (ed.) (1996). Chromatographic separations based on molecular recognition. Wiley VCH, New York.

Bobards, K; Haddad, P.R. and Jackson, P.E. (1994). Principles and Practice of modern chromatographic methods. Academic Press. London.

Snyder, L.R; Kirkland, J.J. and Glajch, J.L. (1997). Practical HPLC method development, 2nd edn. Wiley Interscience, New York.

Chapter : 13 (Electrophoresis)

Andrews, A.T. (1986). Electrophoresis : Theory, techniques and biochemical and clinical applications. Oxford University Press, Oxford.

Dunn, M.J. (1993). Gel electrophoresis : Proteins. Bios Scientific, Oxford.

Hawcroft, D.M. (1996). Electrophoresis : The basics. IRL Press, Oxford.

Chapter : 14 (PCR)

Mullis, K; Ferre, F. and Gibbs, R. A. eds. (1994). The Polymerase Chain Reaction, Birkhauser, Boston.

White, B. A. ed. (1997). PCR Cloning Protocols, from Molecular Cloning to Genetic Engineering. Methods in} Molecular Biology, Vol. 67, Humana Press, Clifton, NJ.

Bagastra, O. and Hansen, J. (1997). *In Situ* PCR Techniques. Wiley, New York.

Rapley, R. ed. (1996). PCR Sequencing Protocols : Methods in Molecular Biology. Vol. 65, Humana Press, Clifton, NJ.

Chapter : 15 (Immunodiagnostic Methods)

Engvall, L. and Hay, F.C. (1976). *Practical Immunology*, Blackwell Scientific Publishers, London.

Meyer, R.J. and Walker, J.H. (1987). Immunochemical methods in Cell and Molecular Biology, Academic Press, London.

Paul, W.E. (ed.) (1984). Fundamental Immunology, Raven Press, USA.

Weir, D.M; Blackwell, C.C. and Herzenberg, L.A. (eds.) (1986). Handbook of Experimental Immunology, 4 volumes, Blackwell Scientific, Oxford, England.

Chapter : 16 (Radio-isotopes Techniques)

Chapman, J.M. and Avery, G. (1981). The use of radioisotopes in the life sciences. George Unwin, London.

Slater, R.J. (2000). Radioisotopes in biology. A practical approach, 2nd ed.

Chapter : 17 (Electrochemical Methods)

Class, A. E. G. (ed.) (1990). Biosensors : A practical approach. IRL Press, Oxford.

Hall, E.A.H. (1990). Biosensors. Open University Press, Milton Keynes.

Riley, T. and Tomlinson, C. (1987). Principles of electroanalytical methods. Wiley, Chichester.

Chapter : 18 (Methods of Environmental Analysis)

De, A.K.; Khopkar, S.M. and Chalmers, R.A. (1970). Solvent extraction of metals. Van Nostrand Reinhold.

Dean, J.A. (1970). Chemical separation methods. Van Nostrand Reinhold, London.

Khopkar, S.M. (1985). Basic concepts of Analytical Chemistry. Wiley Eastem Ltd.

Chapter : 19 (Air Pollution Analysis)

'Environmental pollutants : Selected Analytical methods SCOPE'. 6 (1975). Butterworths, London.

APHA (1972). Method for air sampling and analysis. American Public Health Association.

Chapter : 20 (Monitoring of Ambient Air Pollution)

Seinfele, J.H. (1975). Air Pollution : Physical and chemical fundamental. McGraw Hill Book Company, New York.

Watson, A.K; Bates, R.R. and Kennedy, D. (1988). Air pollution, automobile and public health. National Academy Press, Washington.

Ganguly, A.K. (1976). Report of the panel on Environmental monitoring instruments. Electronics Commission, Government of India, New Delhi.

Harvey, T.E. (1978). Notes on Environmental pollution monitoring and control. Tottenham College of Technology, London.

Chapter : 21 (Water Pollution Analysis)

Grasshoff, G. (1975). Methods of sea water analysis. Verlag-Chemie, Weinhem (1975).

Burrell, D.C. (1974). Atomic spectrometric analysis of heavy metal pollutants in water. Ann Arbor Science Publishers, Ann Arbor.

APHA. (1981). Standard methods for the examination of water and waste water. 15th ed.

Samant, H.S. (1973). Methods for chemical analysis of water and waste water. Surveillance report EPSS. AR. 73-12. Canada.

Marr, I.L. and Cresser, M.S. (1983). Environmental chemical analysis. International Textbook Co.,

Chapter : 22 (Soil Pollution and Pesticide Analysis)

Hesse, P.R. (1971). A textbook of soil chemical analysis. John Murray, London.

Black, O.A. (1965). Methods of soil analysis Part 2. American Society of Agronomy, USA.

Volborth, A. (1969). Elemental analysis in geochemistry. Elsevier, New York.

Das, K.G. (1981). Pesticide analysis. Marcel Dekker, New York.

Krueger, R.F. and Seiber, J.N. (1984). Treatment and disposal of pesticide waste. American Chemical Society, Washington.

Chapter : 23 (Noise Pollution Measurement)

Faulkner, L.L. (1976). Handbook of industrial noise control. Industrial Press, New York.

Harvey, T. editor (1977). Notes on Environmental pollution, Monitoring and Control. Tollenham College of Technology, London.

Miller, R.K. (1976). Handbook of industrial noise management. The Paramount Press Inc. Atlanta, Georgia.

Chapter : 24 (Application of Computer in Biological Sciences)

Brown, T.A. (1999). Genomes, John Wiley and Sons, New York, NY. p. 472.

Lewin, B. (2000). Genes VII, Oxford University Press, Oxford, UK. p. 990.

Mount, D.W. (2001). Bioinformatics : Sequence and Genome Analysis, Cold Spring Harbor Laboratory Press, Cold Spring Harbor, NY.

Russell, P.J. (2001). Genetics, Benjamin Cummings, San Francisco, CA.

Weaver, R.F. (1999). Molecular Biology, WCB/McGraw-Hill, Boston, MA. p. 788.

Chapter : 25 (Organ Ablations / Surgical Techniques)

WHO (1978). Principles and methods for evaluating the toxicity of chemicals. Part I. Environ. Health Criteria 6.

Cotchin, E. and Roe, F.J.C. (1967). Pathology of laboratory rats and mice. Oxford, Edinburgh, Blackwell.

Zarrow, M.X. et. al. 1964. Experimental Endocrinology. Academic Press. New York and London.

Chapter : 26 (Management of Laboratory Animals)

Williams, C.S.F. (1976). Practical guide to laboratory animals. C.V. Mosby, St. Louis.

Evans, I.E. and Maltby, C.J. (1989). Technical laboratory animal management. MTM Associates, Manassas, VA.

Guide for the care and use of laboratory animals, U.S. Department of health and human services, Public health service, National Institute of Health, NIH Publication No. 86-23. Revised 1996.

Chapter : 27 (Biostatistics)

Brownlee, K.A. (1965). Statistical theory and methodology in science and engineering, 2nd ed. New York : John Wiley & Sons, Inc.

Hicks, C.R. (1973). Fundamental concepts in the design of experiments. 2nd ed. New York : Holt, Rinehart and Winston.

Li, C.C. (1964). Introduction to experimental statistics. New York : McGraw-Hill Book Company.

Walpole, R.E. (1982). Introduction to statistics. 3rd ed. New York : Macmillan Publishing Company.

Chapter : 29 Hazardous Material and Chemicals

Roskams J. and Rodgers L. 2004. Lab Ref. i.k. International Pvt. Ltd., New Delhi.

(BC–43/JMD/03012)